An Age of Controversy

Discussion Problems in
Twentieth Century European History
ALTERNATE EDITION

An Age of Controversy

Discussion Problems in
Twentieth Century European History

ALTERNATE EDITION

edited by
GORDON WRIGHT
STANFORD UNIVERSITY

and
ARTHUR MEJIA, JR.
CALIFORNIA STATE UNIVERSITY, SAN FRANCISCO

DODD, MEAD & Company

New York   Toronto   1973

Preface

As Adam and Eve were departing from the Garden of Eden, Eve allegedly turned to her companion and remarked: "Adam, we live in an age of transition." That overworked label can be applied to almost any historical epoch; and so, no doubt, can the phrase "an age of controversy." Transition and controversy are woven into the very texture of human affairs; they are certainly not unique to the twentieth century.

Still, who could deny the appropriateness of the label "an age of controversy" as a description of our time? Since 1900, Europe (like the rest of the world) has been in a state of almost constant turmoil. Both its institutions and ideas have undergone revolutionary changes—greater and more rapid changes, perhaps, than ever before in human history. To judge their causes and consequences is not easy, so soon after the event (or, better, from our position within the maelstrom, for the process of transformation does not seem to have ended). It is not surprising that twentieth-century developments are the subject of intense controversy among observers of the process, and even among historians, who are supposed to possess a kind of inhuman objectivity, an ability to cut through complexity to some sort of inner truth.

This book of readings is based on the assumption that if complexity and controversy are not always virtues, they are facts of life, and must be reckoned with by students of history as well as by professional historians. It is easier, and perhaps more pleasant, to rely on a survey textbook whose author will have predigested the monographic literature and can thus present a smooth, coherent account of events. The risk is that truth comes to be regarded as "what the book says." Historical truth, unfortunately, is not so simply arrived at. Different historians, confronted with exactly the same documentary sources of information, may arrive at sharply different conclusions. Ideological factors, national biases, temperamental traits all come into play. Historical writing thus turns out to be not a collection of congealed "facts" but a set of subjective judgments about the past. And for the recent past, this subjectivity and lack of consensus is probably more obvious than for any other period.

Such a view of the "science" or "art" of history is frustrating to many beginning students, as it is also to mathematicians and others who are charmed by the beauty of precision and certainty. Some of them will conclude that since the experts do not agree, and since historians admit their subjectivity, one man's version is as good as another's. The editors believe, however, that total relativity in history can be avoided. One can learn to analyze and judge the motives and methods of different historians, just as one learns to judge the credibility and the perceptiveness of witnesses in a court of law, or of acquaintances in daily life, or of politicians in an election campaign (they, too, have been known to use and misuse history for a variety of purposes). We hope that student discussion of these historical problems may help to develop some standards of judgment, some tests by which any historian's work (and any politician's claims) can be examined with greater penetration and a more critical sense. The instructor's function, as we see it, is to furnish some wise and informed guidance in this enterprise.

Ten years have gone by since we prepared the original edition of this volume. Our purpose has not changed; but our perspective has shifted somewhat. Men view recent and contemporary history as from the observation platform of a moving train: parts of the terrain recede into the distance, other parts stand out more clearly than before, while new horizons loom up ahead. We have thought it time, therefore, to reexamine the problems and selections chosen in 1962, and to adapt them to the concerns of 1973.

Experience, too, suggests the need for some changes. Both of us have found in our own courses that certain chapters struck fire more effectively than others. Teachers and students who have used the book elsewhere (and it has been used—somewhat to our surprise—in more than 400 colleges and universities) have sent us thoughtful suggestions. In addition, we have felt that a volume like this, designed to be a supplementary rather than a basic text, ought to be shortened. In consequence, the number of problems has been cut back from fifteen to twelve (plus a "Prologue"), and the number of selections from ninety-six to sixty-four. Only seventeen of the selections in the original edition have been retained in this one; thus the book is three-fourths new. Several of the old problems have been jettisoned in favor of fresh ones; those that survive have been partially or totally rejuvenated through the use of new selections.

Some users of the book may find the change too drastic, and may prefer the more familiar landscape of the original edition. That edition will, therefore, remain in print—hence the label "alternate edition" to describe this one. We hope that teachers and students may find merit in them both.

We are grateful to those authors and publishers who have authorized us to reprint the selections contained herein. Our thanks are due also to Mr. William Oman and Mrs. Genia Graves of Dodd, Mead & Company; they have both borne cheerfully with the idiosyncracies of the editors, and Mrs. Graves has once again seen the book through the press. David S. Wright served most effectively as research assistant.

G. W. and A. M., Jr.

Contents

PROLOGUE

Transition to the Twentieth Century

Few contrasts in modern history are more striking than that between the Europe of the nineteenth century and the Europe of the twentieth. The nineteenth century, viewed in retrospect, now appears to us as an unparalleled period of peace, progress, and hope. From 1815 to 1914, Europe experienced an unprecedented ninety-nine years without a general war. In almost every realm there was steady advance—in material production, technology, ease and comfort of living, literacy, the practice of constitutional government. The world, under unchallenged European leadership, seemed to be moving toward a kind of automatic, self-balancing economic system, with few barriers to the flow of goods, capital, or people. Psychologically, it was an age of optimism and confidence, of faith in an unlimited destiny for man.

No one born into the mid-twentieth century needs to be provided with a catalog of the differences between that age and his own. Since 1914 (which is often regarded as the true breaking point between the nineteenth and twentieth centuries) Europeans have almost constantly been fighting a war, or recovering from a war, or preparing themselves for a new war. Indeed, the French critic Raymond Aron calls our time an age of chain wars, in which each conflict creates more issues than it settles, and thus serves as catalyst or trigger for its bigger and better successor. Since 1914, the old quasi-automatic world economic system has given way to chronic instability and inflation. And in the psychological realm, the dominant mood has come to be marked by doubt, pessimism, even despair. Someone has observed that if one compares the outlook of late nineteenth-century western man with that of his mid-twentieth-century successor, one finds evidence of the most rapid mental revolution in human history.

It is tempting to suppose that the disastrous war of 1914–18—still "the Great War" to many Europeans—was responsible for destroying the comfortable and optimistic nineteenth-century world. Some scholars have advanced this thesis, and have described August 1914 as "the axial date in modern Western history," or as "the beginning of the end of the bourgeois civilization of Europe." [1] Such a thesis, in its simplest and most extreme form, would suggest that a healthy and stable western world was shaken down by a war which might have been avoided, and which left a heritage of chronic instability and violence.

There is another point of view that finds the roots of twentieth-century disorder

1. William Barrett, *Irrational Man* (New York: Doubleday, 1958), pp. 32–33.

1

in the more distant past—either in the rise of secularism from the Renaissance on-ward (as some Catholic moralists have argued), or in the Enlightenment with its allegedly overrationalistic view of man (as some conservatives contend), or in that very nineteenth century which seems in retrospect to have been so progressive and confident. No doubt we have been too much inclined to stress the differences between the nineteenth and twentieth centuries, and thus to overlook the traits that they may have in common or the impact of the one upon the other. "During certain periods of history," observes Gerhard Masur, "the stabilizing forces prevail over the dynamic forces; during others the process is thrown into reverse. The nineteenth century saw the static energies give way to revolutionary tidal waves which are still surging up in our time." [2] Certainly the nineteenth century's change and flux went deep enough to undermine most of Europe's old institutions and to prepare the way for upheaval as a possible alternative to ordered progress.

"Sometime around 1890," writes the historian H. Stuart Hughes, "the intellec-tual revolution of our time apparently began." [3] That revolution, whose nature and significance appear more clearly to us than they did to contemporaries, seems to have originated out of two parallel challenges to the dominant world-view of the age. One challenge was external: it represented an attack on scientistic ration-alism by men who stood outside that dominant current of ideas and who disliked everything about it. The second challenge was internal: it amounted to a process of questioning and re-examining, conducted by men who stood within the scien-tistic-rationalistic tradition itself.

The external challenge, mainly esthetic in nature, had been anticipated even before 1890 by such sensitive thinkers as the Russian novelist Fedor Dostoevsky and the German philosopher-essayist Friedrich Nietzsche. Theirs was a kind of emotional revulsion against what they regarded as the crass materialism, the sti-flingly narrow rationalism, the worship of science, the faith in progress that had become the orthodoxy of the age. It was carried forward by schools of artists and writers of neoromantic temper, who raised the banner of art for art's sake and reasserted the role of the emotions as the proper guide to truth and beauty. Many of them became declared disciples of Nietzsche; in most central and western Eu-ropean countries, a dedicated coterie of Nietzscheans was active by 1914.

Far more important than this external attack was the parallel challenge that originated within the scientistic-rationalistic mood itself. Even before 1890, the dominant faith in inevitable progress through science and reason (so well ex-pressed by its quasi-official spokesman Herbert Spencer) was being confronted by an attitude of pessimistic determinism that viewed man as caught in the grip of powerful elemental forces, as a helpless product of heredity and environment, rather than as master of his own fate through enlightened rational action. Such a viewpoint, shaped in part by a kind of corrupted Darwinism, emerged most clearly in fictional form—notably in the grim, oppressive novels of Emile Zola.

This new current of thought disturbed some reflective scholars who clung to the faith that man ought to be able to shape his own destiny through science and reason. Products themselves of the scientistic-rationalistic age, trained in its meth-ods, they set out to use those methods in an effort to deepen their understanding of man and society, and thus to reassert the validity of the orthodox world-view. Some of them—like Sigmund Freud and Ivan Pavlov—were psychologists, con-cerned primarily with problems of individual behavior. Others—like Gustave Le Bon, Gaetano Mosca, Vilfredo Pareto, Robert Michels, Max Weber—were sociolo-

2. Gerhard Masur, *Prophets of Yesterday* (New York: Macmillan, 1961), p. 38.
3. H. Stuart Hughes, *An Essay for our Times* (New York: Knopf, 1949), p. 15.

gists, concerned with the activities of men in groups. Whatever their purposes, their discoveries tended to have a common impact: they cast a blinding new light on man's nonrational side, on the subconscious motivation of much of human behavior, on the tendency of small elites to dominate every sort of social or political group, on the frequent contrast between appearance and reality in human affairs. The net effect was to shake the foundations of some of the nineteenth century's most cherished beliefs.

It is true that these new conceptions, essentially antirationalistic and antiequalitarian in nature, had not seriously weakened the hold of scientistic-rationalistic orthodoxy by 1914. Most Europeans remained confident, hopeful, convinced that science and reason could ensure progress. Perhaps the new thought would never have affected more than a limited avant-garde had it not been for the disintegrative impact of the Great War. Or perhaps the orthodox nineteenth-century view would have been swept away in any case, since scientific investigation had now proved it to be based on shaky foundations, on a set of half-truths about the nature of man and society. Or perhaps, if Europeans had been spared the shattering effect of the war and its aftermath, the valid parts of the nineteenth-century world-view might have been blended with the new insights of the innovators of 1890–1914.

The reading selections in this Prologue, unlike those in the body of the book, have not been chosen to represent contrasting points of view in a historical debate. Rather, they embody three thoughtful interpretive judgments about the quarter-century from 1890 to 1914, viewed as a transitional epoch linking the nineteenth to the twentieth century. The period has been described as "the intellectual seedbed of our times." If that description is valid, we need to understand what happened then, how attitudes and values changed, in order to get some perspective on our own historical epoch.

I. *Henry Steele Commager:*
1900-1950: From Victorian to Atomic Age

The mid-century mark—January 1, 1950—brought forth a rash of articles in which historians and journalists sought to assess the character and significance of that half-century. One of the most lucid essays of the sort was written by Henry Steele Commager, professor of history at Amherst College and prolific author and lecturer in the field of United States history. Commager sharply contrasts our time with the optimistic, complacent Victorian Era, and explains the reasons for the repudiation of the Victorian synthesis just after 1900.

T he twentieth century opened with Queen Victoria still on her throne. Already she had given her name to an era, and already men were beginning to pronounce that era the best, the most prosperous, and the most enlightened in history, forgetting or ignoring the poverty and misery, the

From Henry Steele Commager, "1900–1950: From Victorian to Atomic Age," in *The New York Times Magazine*, December 25, 1949, pp. 3–7. Reprinted by permission of Professor Commager and *The New York Times*.

cruelty, oppression and wars, that had stained its history. "Whatever may be thought of the nineteenth century," wrote the editor of the new World's Work, "when it can be seen in the perspective of universal history, it seems the best time to live that has so far come." It was the age of peace, plenty and contentment; it was the age of confidence; it was the age of progress.

And as men looked back over the years since the defeat of Napoleon at Waterloo they had some reason for pride in the past, and for confidence in the future. The nineteenth century had seen the abolition of slavery throughout the English-speaking world, and the end of serfdom in Russia. It had seen the emergence of the backward peoples of the world, the development of a more benevolent imperialism, the growth of justice and the acknowledgment of international law. Science had at last come into its own, and science promised the conquest of disease and of want and the creation of a world incomparably richer than any that men had known in the past.

The standard of living had been raised everywhere, and there were no material wants that science and technology could not supply. Popular education had spread throughout the Western world, and universal education was about to be realized. The ravages of the industrial revolution, it was felt, were being overcome, and industry tamed; everywhere reformers were busy christianizing the social order, and among the "dark Satanic mills" men were building a new Jerusalem.

Not only had the Victorian Era created what appeared to be general prosperity, it had created a new international order and brought about an era of peace. It was a bit awkward to insist upon the dawn of peace, to be sure, what with the Chinese-Japanese war, the Spanish-American war, the Boer War, and half a dozen minor wars in Africa, all in the decade of the Nineties, but men could argue, at least, that there had been no general war since Napoleon, and that wars seemed, now, to be banished to the fringes of western civilization. And throughout the western world there was free movement of men, money and goods—an achievement the full significance of which only a later generation would appreciate.

The nineteenth century had been a century of mounting nationalism, and of imperialism, but both, now, it seemed, were tempered and tamed. A balance of power had been achieved, and nations no longer needed to struggle for their places in the sun, while great new powers like the United States and Japan could advance without necessarily infringing on other nations.

The naked imperialism of the bad old days was giving way to an enlightened imperialism. The imperialism of the white man's burden had its philosophers in Benjamin Kidd and Josiah Strong, and its poet laureate in Rudyard Kipling, and, what was more, it seemed to be justifying itself by its good works in the backward areas of the earth. The British Empire stood as a vindication of imperialism. It was the empire on which the sun never set; of it men could repeat the proud boast of Horace Walpole after the great triumphs of 1763: "Burn your Greek and Roman books, histories of little people." And Britain had learned her lesson; the empire was gradually being transformed into a commonwealth of nations, bound together by common ideals and loyalties, stronger by far than when it was held together by force.

The nineteenth century had seen, too, enormous strides toward democracy. It was not merely that suffrage was extended more widely—even to women in some more enlightened countries—but that the principle of popular government was acknowledged everywhere in the western world, and the machinery for making democracy effective was rapidly being perfected. The United States had led the way, and the triumph of the North in the Civil War had gone far to vindicate democracy in the Old World. In the last quarter of the century democracy had come on with a rush in many European countries—notably Germany, which was inaugurating experiments in social reform, in Scandinavia and Britain and France, and in the British dominions. As the nineteenth century melted into the twentieth, liberals could congratulate themselves that the long struggle for democracy was all but won and could look forward confidently to the spread of democratic rule everywhere on the globe.

And along with democracy went humanitarianism and reform. There was little doubt in the minds of contemporaries that the forces of righteousness were triumphing over the forces of evil. The enlightened social conscience was at work in every field and in every country, improving the lot of the laborer, championing the welfare of women and children, eliminating poverty and slums, eradicating disease, spreading education, lifting up the backward peoples, caring for the dangerous and the perishing classes, realizing the teachings of Christianity.

Not only had the nineteenth century achieved such progress as men could scarcely imagine, it had vindicated the philosophy of progress. That philosophy had been formulated in the eighteenth century, but its formulation was on the basis of philosophy now discarded. The nineteenth century had furnished a new and sounder scientific foundation for the doctrine of progress and, what was more, it had found a scientist-philosopher who proved that progress was a scientific fact. This was Herbert Spencer, who —so it was asserted by his rapt contemporaries—boasted the most capacious intellect of all time, and whose genius surpassed that of Aristotle and Newton, as the telegraph surpassed the carrier pigeon. Spencer succeeded in bringing all human phenomena within the framework of scientific laws and of proving that evolution implacably imposed progress on man. "Progress," he wrote, "is not an accident but a necessity. . . . Always toward perfection is the mighty movement—toward a more complete development and a more unmixed good."

Then, gradually, a haze drew over the bright Victorian skies. One by one the buoyant hopes of the Victorians were doomed to disappointment. Within less than half a century prosperity gave way to ruin, universal peace to universal war, certainty to fear, security to insecurity, the ideal of progress to the doubt of survival. Never before in history had such bright hopes been so ruthlessly shattered; never had the philosophical temper undergone so profound a change. "My generation," wrote the philosopher James H. Tufts, "has seen the passing of systems of thought which had reigned since Augustus. The conception of the world as a kingdom ruled by God subject to His laws and their penalties . . . has dissolved. The sanctions of our inherited morality have gone. Principles and standards which had stood for nearly two thousand years are questioned."

They were not only questioned; they were repudiated. Philosophically the Spencerian faith in evolutionary progress was already giving way to scientific determinism. The new world of physics, chemistry and biology that science was unveiling was illimitable, impersonal and amoral. Matter, which had once seemed unimpeachable, lost its solidity and became but a complex of electrical reactions, "a wave of probability undulating into nothingness." Mind, which had once seemed to distinguish man from all other creatures here below, was seen as indistinguishable from matter. God, Providence, Design, First Causes and Final Ends, all evaporated.

As the telescope and mathematics disclosed a universe so vast that it defied computation except in thousands of millions of light years and reduced the earth to a grain of pollen floating in illimitable space; as the microscope discovered a universe surging about each atom; as biology found the source of life in a series of apparently fortuitous chemical reactions; as the psychologists reduced the most profound thoughts of man, his highest flights of genius, to merely chemical impulses and uncontrollable reactions —the cosmic system familiar to the Victorians in which man possessed a soul, found meaning in life, and was sure of progress and of destiny, slipped quietly away.

Henry Adams, the most profound of all American interpreters of the new day, tells us that after 1900

he found himself in a land where no one had ever penetrated before; where order was an accidental relation obnoxious to nature; artificial compulsion imposed on motion; against which every free energy of the universe revolted; and which . . . resolved itself back into anarchy at last. He could not deny that the law of the new multiverse explained much that had been most obscure, especially the persistently fiendish treatment of man by man; the perpetual effort of society to establish law and the perpetual revolt of society against the law it had established; the perpetual building up of authority by force and the perpetual appeal to force to overthrow it; the perpetual symbolism of a higher law, and the perpetual relapse to a lower one; the perpetual victory of the principles of freedom, and their perpetual conversion into principles of power.

He himself came to the conclusion that mankind was like a clock that was running down, and that history would exhaust itself in another generation or two.

More important—certainly more consequential in conduct—was the teaching of the new psychology, especially that associated with Freud. The new psychology broke down the boundaries between the normal and the abnormal, revealing the unconscious origins of most impulses. Over these impulses man had no control. To Plato the doctrine "that there was no knowing and no use in seeking to know" was but idle fancy, but the new psychological school embraced idle fancy enthusiastically. The new psychology gave a powerful impulse toward irresponsibility and irrationality, and the twentieth century may yet be remembered not as the age of reason but as the age of unreason. Reason, normality, and morality were rejected not so much because they were wrong as because the concepts themselves had been drained of meaning.

It is the misfortune of every philosophy and every science to be vulgarized, and it was not, perhaps, the fault of the new physicists or the new psychologists, that their versions of the nature of man and the relation of man to the universe struck almost mortal blows at authority of all kinds—the authority of law, of morality and of reason. Yet the convulsions that overtook the world in the generation after 1914 and especially in the years after 1930—the rejection of law, the abandonment of morals, the ruthless destruction of life—were not unconnected with these new philosophical and scientific ideas.

Other developments in science, technology, philosophy and even in economy, accelerated the flight from reason and from responsibility. Of these the most obvious was the growing secularization of life, the decline of the influence and authority of the church and of religion. Secularism was no new phenomenon, but it may be doubted whether at any time for three hundred years religion had meant so little to Western man as it meant in the first half of the twentieth century. The decline of faith weakened the sanctions of moral conduct, and it was no accident that the two great powers that specifically repudiated religion, Germany and Russia, were those guilty of the most diabolical affronts to the dignity of man.

The decline of religious faith was, to be sure, as much a symptom as a cause. It was part of the general decline of authority, of the passing of the absolute in fields of thought. It was reflected in literature, art, music, in the social sciences, as in politics and morals. Where in such countries as Britain and the United States, however, this breakdown of authority led to self-expression, experimentation and liberation, in countries without strong traditions of individualism and freedom of thought, such as Germany, Italy and Russia, it led to a frantic search for new authority—even the authority of force.

Science, technology, urbanization and corporate growth all made their contributions to irresponsibility. Science came to seem too much for men, and for the first time since the emergence of modern science, men felt themselves unable to control what they had discovered. As Adams said, with the new science he had "entered a universe where all the old roads ran about in every direction, overrunning, dividing, subdividing, stopping abruptly, vanishing slowly, with sidepaths that led nowhere and sequences that could not be proved." Technology was often dehumanizing, transferring the center of gravity from the individual to the machine. The corporate device was, by its nature, artificial; it concentrated power but dissipated authority: natural man could never wholly escape moral considerations, but a purely artificial man could. The shift from country to city meant, among other things, a removal from the long discipline of nature—of the farm and of animals, of small communities—to the impersonal atmosphere of city and factory.

Soon it was a truism that science had outrun social science, and it was notable that Comte and Spencer had no successors. That science saved millions of lives, enabled millions of others to live who could not otherwise have been supported, released energies, provided leisure, enhanced man's enjoyment of life, could not for a moment be doubted. That it would be put to evil as well as to beneficent uses was no new idea. What was new was the fear that Adams expressed, that "science is to wreck us, and that we are like monkeys monkeying around with a loaded shell." The generation that lived in the shadow of atomic and bacteriological warfare was not one that could take the beneficence of science for granted.

2. *H. Stuart Hughes: Consciousness and Society*

Only in the last generation have intellectual historians begun to make a serious attempt to comprehend and explain the contemporary era in western culture. H. Stuart Hughes's *Consciousness and Society,* which examines the era from 1890 to 1930, is a pioneering work that has already achieved rank as the classic in the field. Hughes, who is professor of history at Harvard, is concerned with what he calls "the reorientation of European social thought" in the twentieth century; he attempts to portray the emergence and development, in the period 1890–1930, of the ideas that would come to inspire the "governing elites" of the western world in the era after 1930. The selections that follow provide a brilliant analysis of the first generation of positivist rebels against positivism (during the 1890's), and of their immediate successors, whom Hughes describes as "the generation of 1905."

There are certain periods in history in which a number of advanced thinkers, usually working independently one of another, have proposed views on human conduct so different from those commonly accepted at the time—and yet so manifestly interrelated—that together they seem to constitute an intellectual revolution. The decade of the 1890's was one of such periods. In this decade and the one immediately succeeding it, the basic assumptions of eighteenth- and nineteenth-century social thought underwent a critical review from which there emerged the new assumptions characteristic of our own time. "A revolution of such magnitude in the prevailing empirical interpretations of human society is hardly to be found occurring within the short space of a generation, unless one goes back to about the sixteenth century. What is to account for it?" [1]

Nearly all students of the last years of the nineteenth century have sensed in some form or other a profound psychological change. Yet they have differed markedly in the way in which they have expressed their un-

From H. Stuart Hughes, *Consciousness and Society: The Reorientation of European Social Thought* (New York: Alfred A. Knopf, 1958), pp. 33–37, 63–66, 336–44. Copyright 1958 by H. Stuart Hughes. Reprinted by permission of Alfred A. Knopf, Inc.

1. Talcott Parsons, *The Structure of Social Action,* second edition (Glencoe, Ill., 1949), p. 5.

derstanding of it. In the older, more aesthetically oriented interpretations (we may think of Henry Adams), the 1890's figured as the *fin de siècle:* it was a period of overripeness, of perverse and mannered decadence—the end of an era. We need not stop to ask ourselves how much of this was simply an artistic and literary pose. For our present purposes, it is irrelevant: the *fin de siècle* is a backdrop, nothing more.

Somewhere between an aesthetic and a more intellectual interpretation, we might be tempted to characterize the new attitude as neo-romanticism or neo-mysticism. This formulation has considerable plausibility. Unquestionably the turn toward the subjective that we find in so much of the imaginative and speculative writing of the quarter-century between 1890 and the First World War recalls the aspirations of the original Romanticists. It is not difficult to think of writers who in the 1890's or early 1900's felt that they were reaching back over a half-century gap to restore to honor those values of the imagination that their immediate predecessors had scorned and neglected. It was writers such as these who established the cult of Dostoyevsky and Nietzsche as the literary heralds of the new era. There is a pathetic paradox in the fact that the year of Nietzsche's madness—1889—coincides with the time at which his work, after two decades of public neglect, first began to find wide acceptance. Again and again in the course of the present study we shall find one or another social thinker elaborating more rigorously and systematically the suggestions with regard to unconscious strivings and heroic minorities which Nietzsche had thrown out in fragmentary form.

Yet to call Nietzsche a neo-romantic is surely misleading. Any such characterization does less than justice to the critical and Socratic elements in his thought. And when it is applied to the social thinkers of the early twentieth century, it fits only a very few—and these are minor figures like Péguy and Jung. The truly great either were hostile to what they took to be neo-romantic tendencies or, like Freud and Weber, sought to curb the romanticism they discovered within themselves. Durkheim was perhaps the most categorical of his contemporaries in protesting against what he called a "renascent mysticism," but he was not an isolated case.[2] It was rather the "mystic" Bergson (whom Durkheim may have been aiming at) who was less typical. Indeed, of the major new doctrines of the period, the Bergsonian metaphysics was unique in having frankly mystical aspects—and even this doctrine was couched so far as possible in acceptable philosophic terminology. It was on the "lower" levels of thought, rather—on the level of semipopular agitation—that the neo-romantic tendencies were to have their greatest effect. And it was here that their application to politics eventually produced that "betrayal of the intellectuals" which Julien Benda assailed with such telling effect three decades later.

If not "romanticism," will "irrationalism" serve as a general description? It is neat, it is frequently used, and it at least begins to suggest the real

2. Preface to the first edition of Emile Durkheim: *Les Règles de la méthode sociologique* (Paris, 1895), translated from the eighth French edition by Sarah A. Solovay and John H. Mueller as *The Rules of Sociological Method* (Chicago, 1938), p. xl.

concerns of early twentieth-century social thought. Unquestionably the major intellectual innovators of the 1890's were profoundly interested in the problem of irrational motivation in human conduct. They were obsessed, almost intoxicated, with a rediscovery of the nonlogical, the uncivilized, the inexplicable. But to call them "irrationalists" is to fall into a dangerous ambiguity. It suggests a tolerance or even a preference for the realms of the unconscious. The reverse was actually the case. The social thinkers of the 1890's were concerned with the irrational only to exorcise it. By probing into it, they sought ways to tame it, to canalize it for constructive human purposes. Even Sorel, who has often been held up as the supreme irrationalist, had as his life's goal the enunciation of a political formula that would fit the new world of industrial logic and the machine.

Sorel, Pareto, Durkheim, Freud—all thought of themselves as engineers or technicians, men of science or medicine. It is obviously absurd to call them irrationalists in any but the most restricted sense. As a substitute, the formula "anti-intellectualist" has sometimes been employed.[3] This characterization is both flexible and comprehensive. It suggests the revulsion from ideology and the *a priori*, from the abstract thought of the century and a half preceding, which served to unite writers otherwise so far apart as Durkheim and Sorel. It recalls the influence and prestige of William James—an influence at the same time comparable, opposed, and complementary to that of Nietzsche. "Anti-intellectualism," then, is virtually equivalent to Jamesian pragmatism. It offers a satisfactory common denominator for grouping a large proportion of the intellectual innovations of the 1890's.

Yet it is at the same time too broad and too narrow. It fails to take account of the unrepentant abstraction and intellectualism in the thought of Benedetto Croce—or, to take quite a different example, the later elaboration by Max Weber of social theory in terms of "ideal types." It suggests, moreover, that the turn from the principles of the Enlightenment was more complete and decisive than was actually the case. The main attack against the intellectual heritage of the past was in fact on a narrower front. It was directed primarily against what the writers of 1890's chose to call "positivism." By this they did not mean simply the rather quaint doctrines associated with the name of Auguste Comte, who had originally coined the term. Nor did they mean the social philosophy of Herbert Spencer, which was the guise in which positivist thinking was most apparent in their own time. They used the word in a looser sense to characterize the whole tendency to discuss human behavior in terms of analogies drawn from natural science. In reacting against it, the innovators of the 1890's felt that they were rejecting the most pervasive intellectual tenet of their time. They believed that they were casting off a spiritual yoke that the preceding quarter-century had laid upon them.

As a preliminary characterization, to speak of the innovations of the 1890's as a revolt against positivism comes closest to what the writers in question actually thought that they were about. Yet even this last formula

3. For example, by Richard Humphrey in his *Georges Sorel: Prophet without Honor: a Study in anti-Intellectualism* (Cambridge, Mass., 1951).

has its pitfalls. We must be on guard against the tendency of someone like Croce to use positivism as a philosophic catch-all, to embrace under this epithet every doctrine for which he had a dislike. We must not forget the number of influential thinkers of the period—men like Durkheim and Mosca—who remained essentially in the positivist tradition. And, finally, we must take proper account of the others, like Freud, who continued to use mechanistic language drawn from the natural sciences long after their discoveries had burst the framework of their inherited vocabulary. . . .

. . . We may outline in preliminary and schematic form the major ideas that were initially stated in the 1890's, preparatory to their fuller elaboration in the first decade of the twentieth century.

1. Most basic, perhaps, and the key to all the others was the new interest in the problem of consciousness and the role of the unconscious. It was the problem implicit in the title of Bergson's first book, the *Essay on the Immediate Data of Consciousness.* In it he had tried to distinguish between a "superficial psychic life" to which the scientific logic of space and number could properly be applied, and a life in the "depths of consciousness" in which "the deep-seated self" followed a logic of its own: he had come to the conclusion that the world of dreams might offer a clue to this secret and unexplored realm. "In order to recover this fundamental self," he had added, "a vigorous effort of analysis is necessary." [4] A decade later, and proceeding from a philosophic and professional preparation almost totally in contrast to that of Bergson, Freud began to carry out the program that the former had outlined. Freud's first major work, *The Interpretation of Dreams,* built on his own "vigorous effort" of self-analysis a theory of unconscious motivation to which the life of dreams offered the key.

2. Closely related to the problem of consciousness was the question of the meaning of time and duration in psychology, philosophy, literature, and history. It was the problem to which Bergson was to return again and again in an effort to define the nature of subjective existence as opposed to the schematic order that the natural sciences had imposed on the external world. It represented one aspect of the task that Croce had set himself in trying to establish the qualitative and methodological differences between the realm of history and the realm of science. In somewhat different form it was the problem with which the natural scientists were themselves contending in postulating a universe that no longer strictly conformed to the laws of Newtonian physics. Finally it was the dilemma that obsessed the novelists of the first two decades of the new century—Alain-Fournier, Proust, Thomas Mann—the tormenting question of how to recapture the immediacy of past experience in language that in ordinary usage could reproduce no more than the fragmentized reality of an existence that the logical memory had already stored away in neat compartments.

3. Beyond and embracing the questions of consciousness and time, there loomed the further problem of the nature of knowledge in what Wilhelm

---

4. *Essai sur les données immédiates de la conscience* (Paris, 1889), authorized translation by F. L. Pogson as *Time and Free Will: An Essay on the Immediate Data of Consciousness* (London and New York, 1910), pp. 125–7, 129.

Dilthey had called the "sciences of the mind." In the early 1880's Dilthey had attempted to establish rules that would separate the areas in which the human mind strove for some kind of internal comprehension from the realm of external and purely conventional symbols devised by natural science. A decade later Croce had resumed the task, with his first important essay, "*La storia ridotta sotto il concetto generale dell'arte.*" Croce soon abandoned the simple solution of including history among the arts. But his conviction of the radical subjectivity of historical knowledge remained. By 1900 it was apparent to the more imaginative of Croce's contemporaries that the nineteenth-century program of building an edifice of historical and sociological knowledge by patient accumulation and painstaking verification no longer sufficed. By such means it would prove forever impossible to penetrate beneath the surface of human experience. One had, rather, a choice between the exercise of the sympathetic intuition postulated in Croce's neo-idealistic theory of history, and the creation of useful fictions, as Max Weber was later to elaborate them, as models for critical understanding.

4. If the knowledge of human affairs, then, rested on such tentative foundations, the whole basis of political discussion had been radically altered. No longer could one remain content with the easy assurances of the rationalistic ideologies inherited from the century and a half preceding—liberal, democratic, or socialist as the case might be. The task was rather to penetrate behind the fictions of political action, behind what Sorel called the "myths," Pareto the "derivations," and Mosca the "political formulas" of the time. Behind these convenient façades, one could postulate the existence of the actual wielders of power, the creative minorities, the political elites. The discussion of politics, then, had been pushed back from the front of the stage to the wings—from the rhetoric of public discussion to the manipulation of half-conscious sentiments.

Such, indeed, is the most general characterization we may give to the new intellectual concerns of the 1890's. They had displaced the axis of social thought from the apparent and objectively verifiable to the only partially conscious area of unexplained motivation. In this sense the new doctrines were manifestly subjective. Psychological process had replaced external reality as the most pressing topic for investigation. It was no longer what actually existed that seemed most important: it was what men thought existed. And what they felt on the unconscious level had become rather more interesting than what they had consciously rationalized. Or— to formulate the change in still more radical terms—since it had apparently been proved impossible to arrive at any sure knowledge of human behavior—if one must rely on flashes of subjective intuition or on the creation of convenient fictions—then the mind had indeed been freed from the bonds of positivist method: it was at liberty to speculate, to imagine, to create. At one stroke, the realm of human understanding had been drastically reduced and immensely broadened. The possibilities of social thought stretched out to infinity. It was perhaps this that Freud had in mind when in 1896 he spoke of "metapsychology"—the definition of the origin and nature of humanity—as his "ideal and problem child," his most challenging task for the future [5]. . . .

In the retrospect of the [First World War], the year 1905 most clearly offered the watershed. It marked the first time for a quarter-century that all Europe seemed astir. The revolution in Russia had come as the first major social disturbance since the Paris Commune of 1871—and for a moment the Socialist parties of France and Germany, Austria and Italy, had faced the embarrassing prospect that they might be obliged to give reality to the Marxist professions that had gradually been transformed into little more than a litany for the faithful. The revolutionary danger soon passed. But the effects of the other decisive event of the year—the First Moroccan Crisis—were not to be eradicated so quickly. From 1905 on, one diplomatic crisis followed on another in regular succession. The shock of Tangiers—as Péguy put it—"within the space of . . . two hours" introduced a new epoch in his own life, as it did in the history of his country and of the world.[6] For the next decade the youth of Europe lived and breathed in an atmosphere of impending war.

It was this prospect of war service which most sharply marked off the new generation from those who had reached intellectual maturity in the 1890's. By 1905, men like Freud and Weber, Durkheim and Bergson, Mosca and Croce, were already getting too old for front-line duty. Of them, Weber alone put on a uniform during the war, and even he was not permitted to engage in actual combat. The war, when it came, was not *their* war: it was their sons' war. For them the decisive experience had been the intellectual renewal of the 1890's—or perhaps, in the case of the French, the defense of Captain Dreyfus. For the generation of their sons the great event was obviously the war itself. Here we find a dramatic instance of the contrasting experiences that serve to demarcate one age group from another in intellectual history.

Living as it did in a state of nearly constant war alert, the new generation was more impatient than that of its fathers. It respected its elders: in this it differed from the conventional image of a younger generation. But it was looking for something more arresting and dogmatic than its seniors had provided. It admired the discoveries they had made—but it understood these discoveries in cruder fashion. Where the writers of the 1890's had restricted themselves to a questioning of the potentialities of reason, the young men of 1905 became frank irrationalists or even anti-rationalists. This crucial distinction, which so often remains blurred in the history of ideas in our century, was largely a matter of contrasting age groups. The younger men were no longer satisfied with the urbane detachment of their elders. Everywhere they were in search of an ideal and a faith.

Thus in Germany they began to apply the teachings of Nietzsche in the sense of direct action, and thought of themselves as that "first generation of

5. Jones: *Freud*, I: *The Formative Years and the Great Discoveries 1856–1900* (New York, 1953), p. 294.

6. *Notre Patrie* (originally published in the *Cahiers de la Quinzaine*, October 22, 1905) (Paris, 1915), p. 120.

fighters and dragon-slayers" whom he had called on to establish the "Reich of Youth." One of Nietzsche's self-styled disciples—Stefan George—became their poet; from George they learned to regard themselves as a new spiritual aristocracy, with a lofty if ill-defined mission. The newly formed youth groups gave them an organizational outlet and an intoxicating sense of physical and spiritual liberation. Ten months before the outbreak of the war, in October 1913, representatives of the Free German Youth assembled on the Hohen Meissner hill in central Germany and drew up a melodramatic pledge to "take united action . . . under any and all circumstances . . . for the sake of . . . inner freedom." It was young people of this sort that Weber encountered four years later, when, at a gathering at Burg Lauenstein in Thuringia, he declined to serve as the prophet for whom they longed.[7]

In Italy the years between the turn of the century and the First World War brought into prominence new writers, new reviews, and new political organizations. The reaction from positivism that in Croce's case had expressed itself in rational and measured form, with the younger generation became a kind of spiritual explosion. Nationalism in politics, dynamism and "Futurism" in literature, above all the example—both artistic and personal—of the flamboyant word-magician Gabriele D'Annunzio, marked the changed temper of Italian youth. . . .

It was in France, however, that the cleavage between generations was most self-consciously delineated, and it is from here that we shall chiefly draw the literary evidences of a changed temper. In France after the turn of the century, as in Germany a decade earlier, the young people began to declare themselves Nietzscheans. André Gide's *The Immoralist,* published in 1902, is an early example. Subsequently, still younger writers like Alain-Fournier were to recognize the influence, either explicit or unconscious, of Nietzsche on their own thought.[8] But in France the Nietzscheans were only a minority. It was Bergson, rather, who ranked as the tutelary deity of the new generation. After 1905 the educated youth of France became militantly "Bergsonian."

The young people seized hold of Bergson with avidity and interpreted him according to their own tastes. They read into his teaching the notion of direct-action politics—usually of the Right—which was distinctly in contrast with his own convictions, and of dogmatic religion, on which his personal position still remained obscure. As so often has happened in the history of ideas, the originator of the doctrine lost control of his own creation: his disciples escaped from his tutelary guidance. For the half-decade before the First World War, "Bergsonism" was living a life of its own, almost independent of its founder.

7. Klemens von Klemperer, *Germany's New Conservatism: Its History and Dilemma in the Twentieth Century* (Princeton, N.J., 1957), pp. 43–6; Marianne Weber, *Max Weber: Ein Lebensbild,* new edition (Heidelberg, 1950), pp. 642–7.

8. Geneviève Bianquis, *Nietzsche en France* (Paris, 1929), pp. 62–7. Compare the more deprecating statements about Nietzsche in the entry for November 4, 1927, in Gide's *Journal 1889–1939* (Paris, 1948), translated and edited by Justin O'Brien as *The Journals of André Gide* (New York, 1947–9), II, 419–20.

It was a curious phenomenon, this new generation in which the sons were more conservative than the fathers. The latter had done battle for the innocence of Dreyfus and fought the power of the "reactionaries" and the clergy. Their children were as likely as not to embrace the neo-royalism of Charles Maurras and the *Action Française,* or the milder version of conservative nationalism preached by the novelist Maurice Barrès. At the Ecole Normale Supérieure the influence of Lucien Herr, the librarian, and of Jean Jaurès, the great Socialist alumnus, began to wane; Léon Blum—who three decades later was to be prime minister of France, but who at this period still ranked only as a brilliant lawyer and a rather precious *littérateur* —was one of the last of their great converts. And, to the more critical of the younger minds, Blum seemed rather superficial; he still took Jaurès's rolling periods seriously [9]. . . .

In 1900, in intellectual circles, it had been bad form to be a practicing Catholic. By 1910, while the majority still consisted of unbelievers— philosophical positivists for the most part—a growing minority of the sensitive and discriminating spirits were returning to the faith in which they had been baptized. A few great conversions had served as examples—the poet Paul Claudel from the elders, the philosopher Jacques Maritain in the younger generation. It was the latter who was to appeal in vain with the anti-clerical wife of Péguy to ease her husband's torments of conscience by letting her children be baptized.

In 1905 only three or four students at Normale openly professed their religious faith. By 1912 there were perhaps forty—a third of the student body. The great institution that had so long ranked as "a citadel of bantering agnosticism" was gradually being penetrated by the new spirit.[10] And the same thing was going on in other educational centers and other intellectual circles. This changed attitude toward things religious has been admirably documented by André Gide's younger friend and literary associate, Roger Martin du Gard. In his novel *Jean Barois,* published in 1913, Martin du Gard traced the spiritual pilgrimage of his own generation. With an acute sense for the nuances of religious scruple, he depicted the slow transformation of a child's tender, naive piety into a "Modernist" interpretation of dogma in a symbolic sense. But in the case of the fictitious Jean Barois, as with so many of his actual contemporaries, Catholic "Modernism" could be only an uneasy compromise: the Pope himself was to condemn it. Beyond it lay an aggressive irreligion of a materialist and positivist type, and beyond that in turn a final reconciliation with the Church. In this intellectual progression, Martin du Gard's protagonist seemed typical of the new century. But for religiously minded readers the book had a disconcerting backtwist: Jean Barois's return to Catholicism was denied the character of conscious and responsible choice—it was the despairing product of sickness, personal misery, and fear of death.

Thus Jean Barois is still a transition figure, hovering in unhappy self-di-

9. Entry for April 27, 1906, *Ibid.,* I, 181.
10. Jacques Chastenet, *Une Epoque pathétique: la France de M. Fallières* (Paris, 1949), p. 218.

vision between the skepticism of the older liberal faiths and the dogma-
tisms of the future. When as a middle-aged man he is faced with two
university students come to enlighten him on the new tendencies among
French youth, he finds that they are speaking an unfamiliar and rather
frightening language. He is repelled by their denigration of science and
their cult of force. To him they represent a mere "reaction": in their own
eyes they are the bearers of spiritual renewal.

With this contrast, we touch the central ambiguity in the generation of
1905. In France—and the same was true in Germany—during the years
just before the outbreak of the war there reigned among the youth a spirit
that combined respect for authority with the cult of spontaneous creation.
Depending on where they have chosen to lay their emphasis, historians of
the epoch have judged it very differently. On the one hand, they have
found in it a threatening proto-fascist atmosphere, on the other hand a renaissance of culture and of living brutally cut off at its start. This was the
generation of French and Germans of whom the best were to perish in
battle—or so, at least, their contemporaries saw it. And the tragic irony of
the matter was that they greeted the outbreak of the slaughter with enthusiasm. The more bellicose felt at last within their grasp the life of action
for which they had longed. The more reflective welcomed it as a deliver-
ance from unfruitful anticipation: "Better that war should come," they repeated, "than to go on with this perpetual waiting. . . ." [11]

3. *Geoffrey Barraclough: Introduction to Contemporary History*

Historians deal with the past, and feel most comfortable when they can view
their subject in long perspective. The passage of time clarifies matters, sorts
things out, permits historians to impose some shape on the buzzing confusion
of human affairs and to pin descriptive labels on each age. Observers of history are by nature hesitant to judge the present and the immediate past;
"who follows truth too closely at the heels may have his brains kicked out."
Occasionally, however, a professional historian takes the risk. Geoffrey Barraclough, Chichele Professor of Modern History at Oxford, has written extensively on both medieval and contemporary history. In a recent book, he
argues that the world since about 1960 has entered upon a new epoch, still
unnamed, but as fundamentally different from the modern age as this latter
period was from medieval times. The years from 1890 to 1960, he contends,
constitute a transitional period during which the old was giving way to the
new.

11. Pierre Andreu, *Notre Maître, M. Sorel* (Paris, 1953), p. 89, quoting Drieu La Rochelle; Chastenet, *La France de M. Fallières*, pp. 11–12, 353.

From Geoffrey Barraclough, *An Introduction to Contemporary History* (New York:
Basic Books, 1964), pp. 2, 4, 16–18, 21–22, 229–34. Footnotes omitted. © 1964 Geoffrey Barraclough. Reprinted by permission of the publisher.

Looking back from the vantage-point of the present, we can see that the years between 1890, when Bismarck withdrew from the political scene, and 1961, when Kennedy took up office as President of the United States, were a watershed between two ages. On one side lies the contemporary era, which is still at its beginning, on the other there stretches back the long vista of "modern" history with its three familiar peaks, the Renaissance, the Enlightenment and the French Revolution. It is with this great divide between two ages in the history of mankind that this book will chiefly be concerned; for it was then that the forces took shape which have moulded the contemporary world. . . .

There is . . . little difficulty in identifying moments when humanity swings out of its old paths on to a new plane, when it leaves the marked-out route and turns off in a new direction. One such time was the great social and intellectual upheaval at the turn of the eleventh and twelfth centuries . . . ; another, it is usually agreed, was the period of the Renaissance and Reformation. The first half of the twentieth century has all the marks of a similar period of revolutionary change and crisis. . . . If we view the fifty or sixty years beginning around 1890 from this standpoint, it is difficult to avoid certain important corollaries. The first is that the twentieth century cannot be regarded simply as a continuation of the nineteenth century, that "recent" or "contemporary" history is not merely the latter end of what we call "modern history". . . . In short, contemporary history should be considered as a distinct period of time, with characteristics of its own which mark it off from the preceding period, in much the same way as what we call "medieval history" is marked off—at any rate, for most historians—from modern history. . . .

It is true that no sharp line divides the period we call "contemporary" from the period we call "modern." In this we can agree with the upholders of the doctrine of historical continuity. The new world grew to maturity in the shadow of the old. When we first become aware of it, towards the close of the nineteenth century, it is little more than an intermittent stirring in the womb of the old world; after 1918 it acquires a separate identity and an existence of its own; it advances towards maturity with unexpected speed after 1945; but it is only in the very recent past, beginning around 1955, that it has thrown off the old world's tutelage and asserted the inalienable right to decide its own destiny. . . .

When we seek to isolate those strands in the history of the period which lead forward to the future, it soon becomes evident . . . that they converge with surprising regularity at the same approximate date. It is in the years immediately preceding and succeeding 1890 that most of the developments distinguishing "contemporary" from "modern" history first begin to be visible. . . . Before the nineteenth century had closed, new forces were bringing about fundamental changes at practically every level of living and in practically every quarter of the inhabited globe, and it is remarkable, if we examine the literature of the period, how many people were aware of the way things were moving. . . . Their perception, often dim but sometimes acute, that the world was moving into a new epoch was not simply an illusion.

When we seek to identify the forces which set the new trends in motion, the factors which stand out are the industrial and social revolution in the later years of the nineteenth century and the "new imperialism" which was so closely associated with it. . . . None of the changes we shall have to consider . . . —neither the transition from a European to a global pattern of international politics, nor the rise of "mass democracy," nor the challenge to liberal values—was decisive in itself; none alone was sufficient to bring about the shift from one period to another. What was decisive was their interaction. Only when the constellation of political forces, which was still confined to Europe in the days of Bismarck's ascendancy, became involved with other constellations of political forces in other parts of the world; only when the conflict between peoples and governments interlocked with the conflict of classes, which was still not the case in 1914; only when social and ideological movements cut across frontiers in a way (or at least to an extent) that was unknown in the period of national states: only then did it become clear beyond all dispute that a new period in the history of mankind had arrived. . . .

By the end of 1960 it may fairly be said that the long period of transition was over; the new world was in orbit. Even so, we must not think in terms of a clear-cut break. When the decisive changes began towards the close of the nineteenth century, they had done so in a world which, for all its expansiveness and in spite of symptoms of *fin de siècle* malaise, was securely anchored to two fixed points: the sovereign national state and a firmly established social order stabilized by a prosperous property-owning middle class. Both characteristics proved remarkably tenacious. They weathered the storms of two world wars, and are still factors to be reckoned with in the world of today. Concepts such as sovereignty, the national state, and a property-owning democracy, middle-class in structure though expanded by the absorption of large segments of the working class, have been carried over as components of a society essentially different from that of 1914. . . . It is possible that these are dying elements, mere survivals which will disappear in the course of a few generations . . . ; it is possible that they will remain—transformed, no doubt, and adapted to new conditions, but powerful and active—as constituent elements of the new society. We do not know and it would be pointless to speculate. All we can say with certainty is that they exist as counterbalancing factors in the contemporary situation, as elements of continuity which offset the elements of discontinuity and change. They indicate—what any historian with experience of similar changes in the past would expect—that the world which has emerged is neither sharply cut off from the world out of which it emerged nor simply a continuation of it; it is a new world with roots in the old. . . .

If the contemporary period marks the onset of a new epoch in the history of mankind, it would be reasonable to expect to see this change mirrored not only in the social environment and in the political structure, but also in human attitudes. . . . In following the process of change as it affects human attitudes, we can fairly easily distinguish three main phases or periods. The first, which extends from about 1880 to the First World War, was marked above all by reaction against the tradition of the past four hundred years; the second, roughly equivalent to the inter-war years, but extending back to the decade before 1914, was a period of great experimentation in new modes of expression; in the third, which followed the Second World War, much of the experimentation of the inter-war period was left behind, but it was still not easy to perceive the crystallization of a new outlook on the world. . . .

For the historian it is easier to trace the disintegration of old attitudes and patterns than the formation of new ones. The central fact marking a break between two periods was the collapse—except in formal education, which was thereby increasingly cut off from the mainstream of social development—of the humanist tradition which had dominated European thought since the Renaissance. The attack on humanism took many forms and came from many directions; but at its heart was disillusion with humanism itself, and it was the discrepancy between its professions—namely, respect for the dignity and value of the individual—and its practice— namely, the dehumanization and depersonalization of the working classes —that initiated the revolt. What brought it to a head, after a period of growing disquiet, was the sharp deterioration of conditions in town and factory resulting from the new industrialism, and it was fostered by the new preoccupation with the maladies of poverty, unemployment and distress which marked the generation from Henry George's *Progress and Poverty* (1879) to William Beveridge's *Unemployment* (1909). It found its most eloquent expression in the best of Zola's writing, notably in his greatest novel *Germinal* (1885), with its insistent hammering on the themes of hardship, endurance, darkness, mass action and mass suffering. Something of the same quality infused Gerhart Hauptmann's greatest drama, *The Weavers* (1892).

Works such as *Germinal* exposed the hollowness of humanist professions, the implicit contradiction at the heart of liberal philosophy between human dignity and equality in theory and economic inequality and indignity in fact. At the same time Nietzsche—the mature Nietzsche of *Also sprach Zarathustra* (1883–5) and *Beyond Good and Evil* (1885–6)—was savagely attacking its moral pretensions, tearing away the ideological veil erected to conceal the power structure on which the social order was based, and hammering home the brutal truism of the will to power. "Seek ye a name for this world? A solution for all its puzzles? . . . This world is the will to power—and nothing else." With a directness without parallel before him Nietzsche penetrated through the optimism of his day, the facile belief in progress automatically assured by natural selection and the survival of the fittest, the assumption that man, the individual, is an infinite reservoir of possibilities and that all that is necessary is to rearrange society for these possibilities to prevail. Morality was "itself a form of immorality"; philosophy from Plato to Hegel had falsified reality and degraded life. "Nothing has been bought more dearly," Nietzsche proclaimed, "than that little bit of human reason and sense of freedom which is now the basis of our pride." It was this frontal attack on the values and assumptions on which all western culture was based that made him, after 1890, the inspired prophet of the new generation in Europe.

Nietzsche's disruptive influence on the nineteenth century's picture of intellectual man, the purposive master of his own fate, was reinforced by the work of the French philosopher, Henri Bergson, with his assertion of the superiority of intuition over intelligence. It was reinforced also by new trends in the physical sciences and by the impact of new psychological insights. Both contributed, with increasing force as time passed, to the decline of the certitudes which had sustained the commonly accepted picture of man and the universe. Science, in the first place, dissolved the old concepts both of nature and of man's place in nature. The French mathematician, Henri Poincaré, denied that science could ever know anything of reality; all it could do, he asserted, was to determine the relationship between things. In England a similar view of the world as a structure of emergent relationships was put forward in F. H. Bradley's *Appearance and Reality* (1893) and developed by Whitehead and the relativists. "Nature by itself," Bradley maintained, "has no reality"; the idea that nature was "made up of solid matter interspaced with an absolute void," which had been inherited from Greek metaphysics, was untenable and must be discarded. Space, Bradley asserted, was only "a relation between terms which can never be found." Thus nature, which from the time of Giordano Bruno had been a fixed point of reference—the totality of things and events which man encountered around and about him—began to retreat into inaccessibility; it became an intricate network of relations and functions which was beyond common experience and could only be conceptualized abstractly, until finally it dissolved into a "lost world of symbols."

The trend of modern science was to suggest that the universe is unintelligible, senseless and accidental, and that man, in Eddington's phrase, is "no more than a fortuitous concourse of atoms." Such views, as they passed into wider circulation, could not but have a dissolving effect, and the same was true of the new psychology of Pavlov and Freud. Freud, whose *Interpretation of Dreams* appeared in 1899, must be ranked with Lenin as the herald of a new age. Although his main influence was not felt until after 1917, he was a figure of formidable stature and influence, with whom, in the scientific field, only Einstein could compare. The Freudian theory of the subconscious had an immeasurable impact, above all by destroying the image of man as a co-ordinated individual responding intelligently and predictably to events. Freud's discovery that man's actions could be motivated by forces of which he knew nothing exploded the individual's illusion of autonomy, and sociology which, in Dewey's phrase, conceived "individual mind as a function of social life," worked in the same direction. If science left man groping after an elusive external reality, Freud left him seeking in vain for the reality of his inner self.

I

The Origins of the First World War

The seemingly endless disputes concerning the responsibility for the outbreak of the first world war provide a valuable source of enlightenment for the student of history. Not only have great efforts been made to trace most of the ills of the twentieth century back to the blows which western society received from the coming of war in 1914, but these disputes are an excellent illustration of the principal theme of this book, that though the facts of any issue are the *sine qua non,* they do not speak for themselves; one's conclusion depends upon one's interpretation, and the slightest variation in interpretation can deflect the entire line of argument and the entire range of conclusions.

In the allied countries the earliest interpretations of the causes for the outbreak of the war were little but propaganda. One of the best examples is Henry Morgenthau's *Secrets of the Bosphorus.* Lurid and dramatic, it recounts how the "greatest of human tragedies was hatched by the Kaiser and his imperial crew" at the Potsdam conference of July 5, 1914, and how this momentous secret was revealed to Morgenthau by an important German diplomat, who seemed "rather proud of the whole performance; proud that Germany had gone about the matter in so methodical and far-seeing a way." [1] A strong reaction, however, came very quickly, a number of factors being responsible. Feelings of guilt over the alleged unfairness of the Versailles treaty in general, and of the war-guilt clause in particular, played a part; cynicism and war-weariness—in part a revulsion against the extreme Germanophobia cultivated during the war and in part a revulsion against the horror of war itself—were also significant; moreover, the publication of prewar diplomatic documents showed how incomplete and "doctored" much of the allied wartime propaganda had been. Especially significant in this latter regard was Germany's publication, beginning in 1922, of extensive selections from its diplomatic documents. Other countries responded with selections from their own archives, and the final result was an unusually large body of original material from which historians could draw. Some of the historians went to what now seems the other extreme, and insisted that the French and the Russian governments desired

1. Henry Morgenthau, *Secrets of the Bosphorus* (London: Hutchinson, 1918), p. 55. It is interesting to compare Sidney B. Fay's account of the Potsdam conference with Morgenthau's: see *The Origins of the World War* (New York: Macmillan, 1929), II, Chapter IV. See also, for a more recent interpretation which is less favorable to Germany than Fay's, Luigi Albertini, *The Origins of the War of 1914,* translated from the Italian by Isabella M. Massey (London: Oxford University Press, 1953), II, 178–80.

the war; [2] others tried hard to balance the responsibilities and thus to achieve a degree of "objectivity"; [3] still others refused to revise their original conceptions at all, and, like R. C. K. Ensor,[4] held firmly to the theory that Germany plotted for war in 1914.

Since the second world war, one may see some reversion on the part of historians to the stress on German responsibility. Much emphasis is now being placed on the role of the military in Wilhelmine Germany. Scholars like the German Gerhart Ritter [5] and the American Gordon A. Craig [6] point out that the military, with its entrée to the Kaiser's court, with the sway it held over much of the German upper and middle classes, and with its rigid strategy and lack of political sense, contributed greatly to the coming of war, and was even eager for war; by overriding and dominating the diplomats and the civilian ministers, it made negotiations and restraint exceedingly difficult in 1914. This line of interpretation was further developed by Fritz Fischer in his exhaustive study, *Germany's Aims in the First World War*, originally published in 1961.[7] Fischer's study, in fact, revitalized the whole controversy, especially since it was written by an outstanding German historian, and placed the burden of responsibility, to a great extent, on Germany's lust for power. The German drive toward world power, according to Fischer, was calculated, and by no means limited to military circles; the Foreign Office, and the Imperial Chancellor himself, risked war as part of a policy carefully designed to further Germany's grandiose ambitions. These ambitions, furthermore, were later demonstrated by Germany's plans for the reorganization of Europe after the war: "The July crisis must not be regarded in isolation. It appears in its true light only when seen as a link between Germany's 'world policy,' as followed since the mid-1890s, and her war aims policy after August, 1914." [8]

The questions which arise in any discussion of the responsibilities for the outbreak of the first world war are obviously numerous and intriguing. For example, there is the issue of Serbian complicity. To what degree was the government in Belgrade aware of the plot to assassinate the Archduke? If it was aware of the plot, did it encourage the assassins, directly or indirectly? Other questions concern the mobilizations and their timing. In 1914 did mobilization mean war? Did the Russian mobilization set in motion a reaction which inevitably terminated in war, or would the subsequent mobilizations have come about independently of the Russian action? One might also consider if there was ever a chance of localizing the war, and if the attempts to do so were sincere; perhaps Europe was so closely meshed—economically, technically, and diplomatically—that there was no chance of localizing the conflict, and all the apparent attempts to do so were merely propagandistic in intent.

2. E. g., Harry Elmer Barnes, *The Genesis of the World War* (New York: Alfred A. Knopf, 1926).

3. In addition to Fay and Albertini, cited above, see Bernadotte Schmitt, *The Coming of the War, 1914* (New York, Scribner's, 1930).

4. See his *England, 1870–1914* (Oxford: Clarendon Press, 1936), pp. 469–71, 481–83.

5. In his *The Sword and the Scepter: The Problem of Militarism in Germany*, Volume II, *The European Powers and the Wilhelminian Empire, 1890–1914*, trans. by Heinz Norden (Coral Gables: University of Miami Press, 1970). Originally published in Germany in 1960.

6. In his *The Politics of the Prussian Army, 1640–1945* (Oxford: Clarendon Press, 1955).

7. The English translation was published in 1967 (London: Chatto and Windus). See particularly pp. 3–92.

8. *Ibid.*, p. 92.

Especially interesting are the problems of Austrian responsibility and of the role of the "balance of power." Austrian statesmen sincerely believed, and were possibly correct in believing, that nationalism, especially among the Slavs, would soon prove fatal to the Empire. To what lengths can a nation justifiably go to protect its existence? Was Austria entitled to run the risk of involving all Europe in a war to save itself? As to the balance of power, was it, as so many have asserted, responsible for the war? Were all the great powers so tied to their allies that in a crisis they felt obliged to offer them unqualified support, regardless of the result? Was Germany afraid of alienating Austria, by urging moderation over an issue which involved Austria's survival; was France afraid of alienating Russia, by urging moderation over an issue which involved Russia's status as a great power? Or did the balance of power fail because some nations violated its rules: would peace have been preserved had England offered unqualified support to France and Russia, and had therefore maintained the balance; or was England's potential role already discounted in German military strategy? All this raises the basic question: at what point is war most apt to come in a balance of power situation? And from this basic question others arise. Is peace in greatest danger when the power blocs are approximately equal in strength, or when one bloc has a convincing superiority over the other? Or is war most apt to come when the balance is in flux, the various nations being unsure of their relative strengths? What was the state of the balance of power in 1914?

It has often been asserted that history has few if any lessons to teach, and that the most one can hope for is a vague type of understanding. Today, in the age of nuclear weapons and worldwide ideological conflict, it is strongly maintained by many people that history cannot offer even this vague understanding. Yet, in the immediate origins of the first world war, perhaps some lessons for today can be found; for it may be that in mid-1914 the failure to keep the peace resulted from the inability of the governmental, and especially the diplomatic, machinery to function effectively in a moment of crisis. Professor Craig has written that "In the fateful summer of 1914 there was . . . none of that co-ordination of political and military strategy which is desirable when a nation goes to war. The technicians were too naïve to understand the necessity of such co-ordination." [9] It is important for the student to think about the naïveté of those technicians. Is there always a point in the development of a crisis when the "escalation" has gone so far that there can be no turning back, either because of pride or because of technology? If everyone does not know exactly where that point is, is there danger that it can be passed by accident?

Finally, it is profitable to speculate about the types of material that are most appropriate in a chapter such as this. Is purely diplomatic history—the record of "what one clerk said to another clerk," [10] as G. M. Young once described it—of any particular significance? Do accounts based mainly on diplomatic documents really reflect anything of value; are they even partially accurate reflections of what was being thought and decided in the highest places? Should not one always be concerned with the "deep and underlying" factors, ranging from the level of education and the circulation of newspapers to the dominant movements and "isms," all of which are the real determinants of events? And even if one is inclined to look for answers by means of diplomatic history, should not the concentration be on the long-range—on shifting power balances and on social, eco-

9. Craig, *op. cit.*, pp. 294–95.
10. Quoted in A. J. P. Taylor, *The Struggle for Mastery in Europe* (Oxford: Clarendon Press, 1954), p. 574.

nomic, and technological irritants to international concord—rather than on the details of the final and hurried slide into disaster? Or, on the other hand, will a detailed study of the documents of one sad segment of diplomatic endeavor reveal something, which would otherwise be lost to view, of the mechanics and the mentality which went to make up that uniquely European creation, a diplomacy "polite, discreet, pacific, and on the whole sincere," in which "words counted, and even whispers," and which was designed to keep the nations and the empires of the day "lapped in the accumulated treasures of the long peace" and "glittering and clanking in their panoply," while securely "fitted and fastened . . . into an immense cantilever"? Certainly, "the old world in its sunset was fair to see." [11]

I. *Sidney B. Fay: The Origins of the World War*

Sidney B. Fay's *The Origins of the World War* has become the most durable of the "revisionist" accounts. Fay was a specialist in seventeenth- and eighteenth-century Prussian history, and he has been accused of allowing a pro-German bias to creep into his work. Is such an accusation just? Fay's account will be easier to read if the characters are identified in advance: Pashitch was the Serbian Prime Minister; Berchtold, the Austro-Hungarian Minister for Foreign Affairs; Bethmann, the German Chancellor; Sir Edward Grey, the British Foreign Secretary; and Poincaré, the President of France.

One may. . . . sum up very briefly the most salient facts in regard to each country.

Serbia felt a natural and justifiable impulse to do what so many other countries had done in the nineteenth century—to bring under one national Government all the discontented Serb people. She had liberated those under Turkish rule; the next step was to liberate those under Hapsburg rule. She looked to Russia for assistance, and had been encouraged to expect that she would receive it. After the assassination, Mr. Pashitch took no steps to discover and bring to justice Serbians in Belgrade who had been implicated in the plot. One of them, Ciganovitch, was even assisted to disappear. Mr. Pashitch waited to see what evidence the Austrian authorities could find. When Austria demanded cooperation of Austrian officials in discovering, though not in trying, implicated Serbians, the Serbian Government made a very conciliatory but negative reply. They expected that the reply would not be regarded as satisfactory, and, even before it was given, ordered the mobilization of the Serbian army. Serbia did not want war, but believed it would be forced upon her. That Mr. Pashitch was aware of the plot three weeks before it was executed, failed to take effective steps to

11. Winston S. Churchill, *The World Crisis, 1911–1914* (New York: Scribner's, 1924), p. 199.

From Sidney B. Fay, *The Origins of the World War* (New York: Macmillan, 1929), II, 550–58. Copyright 1928, 1930 by The Macmillan Company, renewed 1956, 1958 by Sidney Bradshaw Fay. Reprinted by permission of the publisher.

prevent the assassins from crossing over from Serbia to Bosnia, and then failed to give Austria any warning or information which might have averted the fatal crime, were facts unknown to Austria in July, 1914; they cannot therefore be regarded as in any way justifying Austria's conduct; but they are part of Serbia's responsibility, and a very serious part.

Austria was more responsible for the immediate origin of the war than any other Power. Yet from her own point of view she was acting in self-defence—not against an immediate military attack, but against the corroding Greater Serbia and Jugoslav agitation which her leaders believed threatened her very existence. No State can be expected to sit with folded arms and await dismemberment at the hands of its neighbors. Russia was believed to be intriguing with Serbia and Rumania against the Dual Monarchy. The assassination of the heir to the throne, as a result of a plot prepared in Belgrade, demanded severe retribution; otherwise Austria would be regarded as incapable of action, "worm-eaten" as the Serbian press expressed it, would sink in prestige, and hasten her own downfall. To avert this Berchtold determined to crush Serbia with war. He deliberately framed the ultimatum with the expectation and hope that it would be rejected. He hurriedly declared war against Serbia in order to forestall all efforts at mediation. He refused even to answer his own ally's urgent requests to come to an understanding with Russia, on the basis of a military occupation of Belgrade as a pledge that Serbia would carry out the promises in her reply to the ultimatum. Berchtold gambled on a "local" war with Serbia only, believing that he could rattle the German sword; but rather than abandon his war with Serbia he was ready to drag the rest of Europe into war.

It is very questionable whether Berchtold's obstinate determination to diminish Serbia and destroy her as a Balkan factor was, after all, the right method, even if he had succeeded in keeping the war "localized" and in temporarily strengthening the Dual Monarchy. Supposing that Russia in 1914, because of military unpreparedness or lack of support, had been ready to tolerate the execution of Berchtold's designs, it is quite certain that she would have aimed within the next two or three years at wiping out this second humiliation, which was so much more damaging to her prestige than that of 1908–09. In two or three years, when her great program of military reform was finally completed, Russia would certainly have found a pretext to reverse the balance in the Balkans in her own favor again. A further consequence of Berchtold's policy, even if successful, would have been the still closer consolidation of the Triple Entente, with the possible addition of Italy. And, finally, a partially dismembered Serbia would have become a still greater source of unrest and danger to the peace of Europe than heretofore. Serbian nationalism, like Polish nationalism, would have been intensified by partition. Austrian power and prestige would not have been so greatly increased as to be able to meet these new dangers. Berchtold's plan was a mere temporary improvement, but could not be a final solution of the Austro-Serbian antagonism. Franz Ferdinand and many others recognized this, and so long as he lived, no step in this fatal direction had been taken. It was the tragic fate of Austria that the only man who might have had the power and ability to develop Austria along sound lines became the innocent victim of the crime which was the occasion of the World War and so of her ultimate disruption.

Germany did not plot a European War, did not want one, and made genuine, though too belated efforts, to avert one. She was the victim of her alliance with Austria and of her own folly. Austria was her only dependable ally, Italy and Rumania having become nothing but allies in name. She could not throw her over, as otherwise she would stand isolated between Russia, where Panslavism and armaments were growing stronger every year, and France, where Alsace-Lorraine, Delcassé's fall, and Agadir were not forgotten. Therefore, Bethmann felt bound to accede to Berchtold's request for support and gave him a free hand to deal with Serbia; he also hoped and expected to "localize" the Austro-Serbian conflict. Germany then gave grounds to the Entente for suspecting the sincerity of her peaceful intentions by her denial of any foreknowledge of the ultimatum, by her support and justification of it when it was published, and by her refusal of Sir Edward Grey's conference proposal. However, Germany by no means had Austria so completely under her thumb as the Entente Powers and many writers have assumed. It is true that Berchtold would hardly have embarked on his gambler's policy unless he had been assured that Germany would fulfil the obligations of the alliance, and to this extent Germany must share the great responsibility of Austria. But when Bethmann realized that Russia was likely to intervene, that England might not remain neutral, and that there was danger of a world war of which Germany and Austria would appear to be the instigators, he tried to call a halt on Austria, but it was too late. He pressed mediation proposals on Vienna, but Berchtold was insensible to the pressure, and the Entente Powers did not believe in the sincerity of his pressure, especially as they produced no results.

Germany's geographical position between France and Russia, and her inferiority in number of troops, had made necessary the plan of crushing the French army quickly at first and then turning against Russia. This was only possible, in the opinion of her strategists, by marching through Belgium, as it was generally anticipated by military men, that she would do in case of a European War. On July 29, after Austria had declared war on Serbia, and after the Tsar had assented to general mobilization in Russia (though this was not known in Berlin and was later postponed for a day owing to the Kaiser's telegram to the Tsar), Bethmann took the precaution of sending to the German Minister in Brussels a sealed envelope. The Minister was not to open it except on further instructions. It contained the later demand for the passage of the German army through Belgium. This does not mean, however, that Germany had decided for war. In fact, Bethmann was one of the last of the statesmen to abandon hope of peace and to consent to the mobilization of his country's army. General mobilization of the continental armies took place in the following order: Serbia, Russia, Austria, France, and Germany. General mobilization by a Great Power was commonly interpreted by military men in every country, though perhaps not by Sir Edward Grey, the Tsar, and some civilian officials, as meaning that the country was on the point of making war—that the military machine had begun to move and would not be stopped. Hence, when Germany learned of the Russian general mobilization, she sent ultimatums to St. Petersburg and Paris, warning that German mobilization would follow unless Russia suspended hers within twelve hours, and asking what would be the attitude of France. The answers being unsatisfactory, Germany then mobilized and declared war. It was the hasty Russian general mobilization, assented to on July 29 and ordered on July 30, while Germany was still trying to bring Austria to accept mediation proposals, which finally rendered the European war inevitable.

Russia was partly responsible for the Austro-Serbian conflict because of the frequent encouragement which she had given at Belgrade—that Serbian national unity would be ultimately achieved with Russian assistance at Austrian expense. This had led the Belgrade Cabinet to hope for Russian support in case of a war with Austria, and the hope did not prove vain in July, 1914. Before this, to be sure, in the Bosnian Crisis and during the Balkan Wars, Russia had put restraint upon Serbia, because Russia, exhausted by the efforts of the Russo-Japanese War, was not yet ready for a European struggle with the Teutonic Powers. But in 1914 her armaments, though not yet completed, had made such progress that the militarists were confident of success, if they had French and British support. In the spring of 1914, the Minister of War, Sukhomlinov, had published an article in a Russian newspaper, though without signing his name, to the effect, "Russia is ready, France must be ready also." Austria was convinced that Russia would ultimately aid Serbia, unless the Serbian danger were dealt with energetically after the Archduke's murder; she knew that Russia was growing stronger every year; but she doubted whether the Tsar's armaments had yet reached the point at which Russia would dare to intervene; she would therefore run less risk of Russian intervention and a European War if she used the Archduke's assassination as an excuse for weakening Serbia, than if she should postpone action until the future.

Russia's responsibility lay also in the secret preparatory military measures which she was making at the same time that she was carrying on diplomatic negotiations. These alarmed Germany and Austria. But it was primarily Russia's general mobilization, made when Germany was trying to bring Austria to a settlement, which precipitated the final catastrophe, causing Germany to mobilize and declare war.

The part of France is less clear than that of the other Great Powers, because she has not yet made a full publication of her documents. To be sure, M. Poincaré, in the fourth volume of his memoirs, had made a skilful and elaborate plea, to prove "*La France innocente.*" But he is not convincing. It is quite clear that on his visit to Russia he assured the Tsar's Government that France would support her as an ally in preventing Austria from humiliating or crushing Serbia. Paléologue renewed these assurances in a way to encourage Russia to take a strong hand. He did not attempt to restrain Russia from military measures which he knew would call forth German counter-measures and cause war. Nor did he keep his Government promptly and fully informed of the military steps which were being taken at St. Petersburg. President Poincaré, upon his return to France, made efforts for peace, but his great preoccupation was to minimize French and Russian preparatory measures and emphasize those of Germany, in order to secure the certainty of British support in a struggle which he now regarded as inevitable.

Sir Edward Grey made many sincere proposals for preserving peace; they all failed owing partly, but not exclusively, to Germany's attitude. Sir Edward could probably have prevented war if he had done either of two things. If, early in the crisis, he had acceded to the urging of France and Russia and given a strong warning to Germany that, in a European War, England would take the side of the Franco-Russian Alliance, this would probably have led Bethmann to exert an earlier and more effective pressure on Austria; and it would perhaps thereby have prevented the Austrian declaration of war on Serbia, and brought to a successful issue the "direct conversations" between Vienna and St. Petersburg. Or, if Sir Edward Grey had listened to German urging, and warned France and Russia early in the crisis, that if they became involved in war, England would remain neutral, probably Russia would have hesitated with her mobilizations, and France would probably have exerted a restraining influence at St. Petersburg. But Sir Edward Grey could not say that England would take the side of France and Russia, because he had a Cabinet nearly evenly divided, and he was not sure, early in the crisis, that public opinion in England would back him up in war against Germany. He could resign, and he says in his memoirs that he would have resigned, but that would have been no comfort or aid to France, who had come confidently to count upon British support. He was determined to say and do nothing which might encourage her with a hope which he could not fulfil. Therefore, in spite of the pleadings of the French, he refused to give them definite assurances until the probable German determination to go through Belgium made it clear that the Cabinet, and Parliament, and British public opinion would follow his lead in war on Germany. On the other hand, he was unwilling to heed the German pleadings that he exercise restraint at Paris and St. Petersburg, because he did not wish to endanger the Anglo-Russian Entente and the solidarity of the Triple Entente, because he felt a moral obligation to France, growing out of the Anglo-French military and naval conversations of the past years, and because he suspected that Germany was backing Austria up in an unjustifiable course and that Prussian militarists had taken the direction of affairs at Berlin out of the hands of Herr von Bethmann-Hollweg and the civilian authorities.

Italy exerted relatively little influence on the crisis in either direction.

Belgium had done nothing in any way to justify the demand which Germany made upon her. With commendable prudence, at the very first news of the ominous Austrian ultimatum, she had foreseen the danger to which she might be exposed. She had accordingly instructed her representatives abroad as to the statements which they were to make in case Belgium should decide very suddenly to mobilize to protect her neutrality. On July 29, she placed her army upon "a strengthened war footing," but did not order complete mobilization until two days later, when Austria, Russia, and Germany had already done so, and war appeared inevitable. Even after being confronted with the terrible German ultimatum, at 7 p.m. on August 2, she did not at once invite the assistance of English and French troops to aid her in the defense of her soil and her neutrality against a certain German assault; it was not until German troops had actually violated her territory, on August 4, that she appealed for the assistance of the Powers which had guaranteed her neutrality. Belgium was the innocent victim of German strategic necessity. Though the German violation of Belgium was of enormous influence in forming public opinion as to the responsibility for the War after hostilities began, it was not a cause of the War, except in so far as it made it easier for Sir Edward Grey to bring England into it.

In the forty years following the Franco-Prussian War, . . . there developed a system of alliances which divided Europe into two hostile groups. This hostility was accentuated by the increase of armaments, economic rivalry, nationalist ambitions and antagonisms, and newspaper incitement. But it is very doubtful whether all these dangerous tendencies would have actually led to war had it not been for the assassination of Franz Ferdinand. That was the factor which consolidated the elements of hostility and started the rapid and complicated succession of events which culminated in a World War, and for that factor Serbian nationalism was primarily responsible.

But the verdict of the Versailles Treaty that Germany and her allies were responsible for the War, in view of the evidence now available, is historically unsound. It should therefore be revised. However, because of the popular feeling widespread in some of the Entente countries, it is doubtful whether a formal and legal revision is as yet practicable. There must first come a further revision by historical scholars, and through them of public opinion.

2. *Imanuel Geiss: The Outbreak of the First World War and German War Aims*

The revival of interest in the origins of the war was clearly demonstrated when, in 1966, *The Journal of Contemporary History* devoted an entire issue to the subject. The controversy inspired by Fritz Fischer's *Germany's Aims in the First World War* permeated most of the articles, and the German historian Imanuel Geiss carried the burden of defending Fischer's point of view.

From Imanuel Geiss, "The Outbreak of the First World War and German War Aims," *The Journal of Contemporary History*, I, No. 3 (1966), 82–91. Footnotes omitted. Reprinted with permission of George Weidenfeld & Nicolson Ltd.

Geiss's article, like Fay's, will be more intelligible if one knows in advance to whom or to what Geiss is alluding. The Auswärtiges Amt is the German Foreign Office, which was located on the Wilhelmstrasse. Kurt Riezler, whose diaries are now a prime source of information on Bethmann's attitude during the crisis, was Bethmann's protégé; Hohenfinow was Bethmann's country house. Moltke was the German chief of staff; Conrad von Hötzendorf his Austrian opposite number. Falkenhayn was the Prussian Minister of War, and Jagow the German Foreign Minister. Count Hoyos was the secretary for Balkan affairs in the Austro-Hungarian Foreign Ministry, and Tisza was the Hungarian premier. Jules Cambon was the French ambassador in Berlin, and Lichnowsky the German ambassador in London.

After Sarajevo Germany could not at once make up her mind which course to follow. The Auswärtiges Amt clearly saw the danger involved in Russia's trying to protect Serbia if Austria made war, namely, that a world war might result. This is why the Auswärtiges Amt from the first counselled moderation both to Austria and to Serbia. The German General Staff, on the other hand, was ready to welcome Sarajevo as the golden opportunity for risking a preventive war. In this situation it was the Kaiser's word that proved decisive. Wilhelm II was incensed at the murder, perhaps most because it attacked his cherished monarchist principle. When he received the report of Tschirschky, the German ambassador to Vienna, of 30 June, telling of his moderating counsels to the Austrians, the Kaiser commented in his usual wild manner and provided the specious slogan "Now or never"! which turned out to be the guiding star of German diplomacy in the crisis of July 1914.

On 5 July, Count Hoyos came to Berlin, bringing with him two documents on Austrian policy towards the Balkans. The Austrian ambassador, Szogyeny, handed them to the Kaiser at a special audience at the Potsdam Palace, in which he apparently used fairly warlike language, although the documents of his own government spoke of war, if at all, only by implication. After initial hesitation, Wilhelm II promised German support to the Dual Monarchy, whatever Austria did. His promise soon came to be called the German *carte blanche* to Austria. But the Kaiser was not satisfied with giving his ally a free hand against Serbia. He urged Vienna, which apparently had not made up its mind, to make war on Serbia, and that as soon as possible. Bethmann Hollweg and the Emperor's other civilian and military advisers duly endorsed these imperial decisions.

When Bethmann returned to Hohenfinow, he told Riezler what had happened at Potsdam. From what Riezler recorded in his by now famous diary, it appears that the Chancellor was not only fully aware of the possible consequences when taking his "leap into the dark"—war with Britain, i.e. world war—but that already at that stage his first objective seems to have been war with Russia and France; a diplomatic victory—France dropping Russia, Russia dropping Serbia—would have been accepted only as a second best.

Impressed by the German stand, Berchtold swung round in favour of

Conrad's line. His colleagues in the Cabinet followed suit, last of all Tisza, and so did Emperor Francis Joseph. Preparations were made in Vienna and Berlin for the *coup* against Serbia: it was decided to confront Serbia with an ultimatum which would be designed to be unacceptable as soon as the French president Poincaré and his prime minister Viviani had finished their state visit to Russia. That was to be on 23 July.

Meanwhile, the Austrian and German governments did everything to create a peaceful impression. The two emperors enjoyed their usual summer holidays, as did the leading generals of the Central Powers. But they returned to their respective capitals before or just after the ultimatum was handed over at Belgrade. Austria kept the German government informed of her intentions through the normal diplomatic channels, while the German government pressed Austria to start the action against Serbia as soon as possible. Privately the Germans aired serious misgivings at the lack of energy Austria displayed, and the Auswärtiges Amt suspected her of being unhappy about Germany's urgency. These suspicions were not unfounded: the Austrians had waited to make a decision until the German declaration of 5 July, but even then they moved slowly. According to Austrian plans, mobilization would begin after the rupture of diplomatic relations with Serbia, but it was originally intended to delay the actual declaration of war and the opening of hostilities until mobilization was completed, i.e., until approximately 12 August. The Wilhemstrasse, however, deemed such delay absolutely intolerable. It was quick to see that the powers might intervene diplomatically during the interval to save Serbia from humiliation. As the German government was bent on preventing any mediation, it spurred Vienna on, as soon as it learned of the Austrian time-table, to declare war on Serbia immediately after the rupture with Belgrade and to open hostilities at once. On 25 July, Jagow told Szogyeny that the German government

takes it for granted that upon eventual negative reply from Serbia, our declaration of war will follow immediately, joined to military operations. Any delay in beginning warlike preparations is regarded here as a great danger in respect of intervention of other powers. We are urgently advised to go ahead at once and confront the world with a *fait accompli.*

On the other hand, Jagow justified his refusal to pass on British proposals of mediation to Vienna by the alleged fear that Vienna might react by rushing things and confronting the world with a *fait accompli.* Yet when Austria, giving way to German pressure, did declare war immediately, the German Secretary of State told the British Ambassador, Sir Edward Goschen, that now the very thing had happened he had always warned against: namely, Austria rushing things as an answer to proposals of mediation.

German pressure on Vienna to declare war on Serbia without delay had an immediate and telling effect: on 26 July, Berchtold, who had been wavering and who tended to be timid rather than aggressive, adopted the German idea, and in this he was vigorously supported by Tschirschky. Conrad, however, was far from happy. Although usually thought of as the most warlike on the side of the Central Powers, he would have preferred to stick to the original timetable, but he gave in, and the Austrian government decided on an early declaration of war. On 27 July the final decision was taken to declare war the following day.

Now the German government had accomplished one of its short-term aims: Austria had confronted the world with a *fait accompli* in the form of an early declaration of war against Serbia, which was bound to undermine all attempts at mediation between Austria and Serbia. The following day, 29 July, the Austrians rushed things even more, again following German advice, when they started the bombardment of Belgrade. The immediate effect was catastrophic: the Russians took the bombardment of Belgrade as the beginning of military operations against Serbia, as it was meant to be. They had, on 28 July, already ordered partial mobilization against Austria in order to deter her from actual warfare against Serbia. Now the Russian generals, thinking war with Austria and Germany imminent, successfully pressed for immediate general mobilization, since Russian mobilization was known to be far slower than Austrian or German. The Tsar ordered a halt to general mobilization and a return to partial mobilization after the receipt of a telegram from Wilhelm II late in the evening of 29 July, but the next afternoon the generals and the foreign minister Sazonov renewed their pressure on him. Nicholas gave way and Russian general mobilization was ordered for a second time on 30 July, at 6 p.m.

The German government rushed things also in two more respects: on 27 July Jagow had assured Jules Cambon and Sir Horace Rumbold, the British chargé d'affaires in Berlin, that Germany would not mobilize so long as Russia mobilized only in the south, against Austria. Two days later, however, the Auswärtiges Amt received a lengthy memorandum from General Moltke, whose arguments boiled down to an insistence on German general mobilization. Again the Auswärtiges Amt followed the lead of the generals. After 30 July, Berlin demanded the cancellation of Russian mobilization not only against Germany, but also against Austria, and that demand was expressly included both in the German ultimatum to Russia on 31 July and in the declaration of war of 1 August. When the French ambassador reminded Jagow of his words only a few days earlier, Jagow apparently shrugged his shoulders and replied that the generals wanted to have it that way, and that his words had, after all, not been a binding statement.

The second point was at least as serious: while the Entente powers tried desperately to prevent a local war, in order to avert a continental and world war, by making a whole series of proposals of mediation, the German government not only flatly rejected them or passed them on to Vienna without giving them support, but also stifled the only initiative from the German side which might have saved the general peace. This time, the initiative had come from the Kaiser. Wilhelm had returned from his sailing holiday in Norway after learning of the Austrian suspension of diplomatic relations with Serbia on 25 July. He arrived at Potsdam on the 27th. Early the following morning he read the Serbian answer to Austria's ultimatum. Like nearly everybody else in Europe outside Germany and Austria, the Kaiser was impressed by Serbia's answer, which had conceded practically everything except one point, and made only a few reservations. Suddenly all his warlike sentiments vanished and he minuted:

a brilliant achievement in a time-limit of only 48 hours! It is more than one could have expected! A great moral success for Vienna; but with it all reason for war is gone and Giesl ought to have quietly stayed on in Belgrade! After that I should never have ordered mobilization.

He immediately ordered the Auswärtiges Amt to draft a note for Vienna, telling the Austrians that they should accept the Serbian answer. To satisfy the army, and at the same time as a guarantee for what the Serbians had conceded, the Kaiser suggested that Austria should content herself with occupying Belgrade only and negotiate with the Serbians about the remaining reservations.

Apparently the Auswärtiges Amt took fright at their sovereign's weakness. The moment that had come during both Moroccan crises threatened to come again: that the Kaiser would lose his nerve and beat the retreat. This time, however, Bethmann Hollweg and the Auswärtiges Amt did not listen to their sovereign as they had done on 5 July. The Chancellor despatched the instructions to Tschirschky on the evening of 28 July, i.e., after he had learned that Austria had declared war on Serbia. Furthermore, he distorted the Kaiser's argument by omitting the crucial sentence that war was now no longer necessary. The occupation of Belgrade was not meant to be, in Bethmann's words, a safeguard for the implementation of Serbian concessions, but a means to enforce Serbia's total acceptance of the Austrian ultimatum. Finally, the Chancellor added a comment which was sure to defeat any conciliatory effect of his démarche, if any chance of this had remained.

In these circumstances, the démarche, when executed by Tschirschky, had no effect whatsoever, nor did a later British proposal along similar lines.

When developments had gone so far, Bethmann Hollweg undertook his most important move, the bid for British neutrality. On 29 July he had despatched the ultimatum to Belgium to the German minister in Brussels. The violation of Belgian neutrality made it vital for Germany that at least British acquiescence be secured. During the evening of 29 July, Bethmann, returning from talks with the Kaiser and his military advisers at Potsdam, summoned the British ambassador. The Chancellor asked for England's neutrality in return for the promise that Germany would not annex French or Belgian territory. The reaction of the Foreign Office was scathing, as is borne out by Crowe's comment.

A British answer to the German demand was no longer needed, for, just after Goschen left the Chancellor, a telegram from London arrived: Lichnowsky reported Grey's warning that Britain would not remain neutral if France were involved in a continental war. Now Grey—at last—had spoken in such a way that even the German Chancellor had to abandon his cherished hope of British neutrality, which would have meant certain victory for Germany in the imminent continental war. Bethmann Hollweg was dumbfounded, for he saw clearly the consequences of Grey's warning—a world war which Germany could hardly win. In his panic, he tried to salvage what seemed possible. He now pressed the Austrians in all sincerity to modify their stand, but did not go so far as to advise the Austrians to drop the whole idea of war against Serbia. He only pleaded with them to accept the British version of the "halt-in-Belgrade" proposal and to open conversations with the Russians. In such conversations the Austrians were to repeat their promise not to annex Serbian territory, a pledge which, as the Chancellor knew quite well, was regarded by Russia as insufficient. Bethmann made his proposals in the vague hope that by shifting the blame to Russia the British might stay out after all. At the same time he wanted to persuade the German public, especially the social-democrats, to follow his policy by demonstrating his peaceful intentions. The Chancellor did not want to put an end to the local war, which had just seen its second day; what he wanted was to improve Germany's position in a major conflict.

Bethmann Hollweg failed in his first objective; he succeeded in his second only too well. The social-democrats supported the German war effort, and the Russians are still blamed in Germany today for having started the war. For this same reason—to shift the blame to Russia—Bethmann also resisted the pressure of the General Staff who pleaded for immediate German mobilization. The Chancellor urged that Russia be allowed to mobilize first against Germany, since, as he put it, he could not pursue military and political actions at the same time. In other words, he could not simultaneously put the blame on Russia and order German mobilization before Russian general mobilization.

On 29 July, the German generals still appreciated Bethmann Hollweg's policy. But during the 30th they became impatient. In the evening, about two hours after Russian general mobilization had been definitely ordered, they told the Chancellor that he had to make up his mind about German mobilization immediately. The Chancellor won a delay until noon next day, but there was little doubt which way the decision was meant to go. Bethmann Hollweg agreed, in the hope that the Russians might order general mobilization beforehand. During the morning of 31 July the Germans waited for the news of Russian general mobilization as their cue to rush into military action themselves. Luckily enough for Bethmann Hollweg and generations of German historians, Sazonov lost his nerve and had, in fact, already ordered Russian general mobilization.

At 11 a.m. Bethmann, Moltke, and Falkenhayn met again, anxiously waiting for news from Russia with only one hour left before the deadline they had set themselves. At five minutes to twelve a telegram from Pourtalès, the German ambassador to St. Petersburg, was handed to them. It confirmed the rumours that Russian general mobilization had been ordered. Now they could order German mobilization with what they thought a clear conscience. Immediately after the receipt of the telegram the state of threatening war, the phase of military operations which immediately preceded general mobilization, was declared in Germany. The same afternoon, two ultimata went off—one to Russia demanding that she stop all military preparations not only against Germany but also against Austria, the other to France, asking about the stand France would take in a war between Germany and Russia. At the same time the Auswärtiges Amt prepared the declarations of war on both countries. Thus war had become inevitable, even more so since German general mobilization, according to the famous Schlieffen plan, meant opening hostilities against neutral Belgium a few days after mobilization had actually started.

After noon on 31 July, therefore, the catastrophe could no longer be averted. On 1 August, Germany ordered general mobilization, at the same hour as France. In the evening of that day, Germany declared war on Russia. An hour before a curious and revealing incident had occurred. A telegram from Lichnowsky arrived suggesting that Britain might remain neutral if Germany were not to attack France. The Kaiser and his military, naval, and political advisers were happy, since their tough line during the July crisis seemed to be paying off after all. Only Moltke demurred. He was shocked by the idea of having to change his plan, and even feared that Russia might drop out as well. Late in the evening another telegram from London arrived, making the true position clear.

The French answer was evasive in form but firm in content: France would not forsake her ally. At the same time, France tried desperately to secure British support. The Russians, the French, and Crowe in the Foreign Office, urged Grey to make Britain's stand quite clear, that she would not remain neutral in a continental war. Grey had warned Germany before, but his language had not been straightforward enough to destroy German illusions. When Grey made the British policy unmistakably clear, even to the German Chancellor, it was too late.

How much Germany up to the last hour still hoped for British neutrality can be seen by the invention of a whole series of alleged border incidents, some of which were so crudely presented that outside Germany nobody believed them. They were part of the German manoeuvre to put the blame this time on France and to impress Britain. The German invasion of Belgium, however, removed the last hesitations: Britain sent an ultimatum to Germany demanding the immediate withdrawal of German troops from Belgium. When Germany refused, Britain entered the war automatically after the time-limit of the ultimatum had expired, i.e., at 11 p.m. Greenwich time on 4 August.

In trying to assess the shares of responsibility for the war two basic distinctions have to be made: on the one hand between the three stages of war connected with its outbreak: local war (Austria v. Serbia), continental war (Austria and Germany v. Russia and France), and world war (Britain joining the continental war). On the other hand, one has to distinguish between the will to start any of those three stages of war and the fact of merely causing them.

Since the world war developed out of a local war, then of continental war, the major share for causing it lies with that power which willed the local and/or continental war. That power was clearly Germany. She did not will the world war, as is borne out by her hopes of keeping out Britain, but she did urge Austria to make war on Serbia. Even if Austria had started the local war completely on her own—which, of course, she had not—Germany's share would still be bigger than Austria's, since a German veto could have effectively prevented it. Germany, furthermore, was the only power which had no objection to the continental war. So long as Britain kept out, she was confident of winning a war against Russia and France. Germany did nothing to prevent continental war, even at the risk of a world war, a risk which her government had seen from the beginning.

Austria, of course, wanted the local war, after—with German prodding —she had made up her mind, but feared a continental war. In fact, she hoped that Germany, by supporting her diplomatically, might frighten Russia into inaction.

Russia, France, and Britain tried to avert continental war. Their main argument for mediation between Serbia and Austria was precisely that to prevent the local war would be the best means of averting continental war. On the other hand, they contributed to the outbreak, each in her own way: Russia by committing the technical blunder of providing the cue for German mobilization, instead of waiting until Germany had mobilized. The French attitude was almost entirely correct; her only fault was that she could not hold back her Russian ally from precipitate general mobilization. Britain might have made her stand clear beyond any doubt much earlier, since this might have been a way of restraining Germany, although it is doubtful whether this would have altered the course of events to any appreciable degree. The share of the Entente powers is much smaller than Germany's, for it consisted mainly in reacting—not always in the best manner—to German action.

Looking back on the events from the mid-sixties, the outbreak of the first world war looks like the original example of faulty brinkmanship, of rapid escalation in a period of history when the mechanisms of alliances and mobilization schedules could still work unchecked by fear of the absolute weapon and the absolute destruction its use would bring in what would now be the third world war.

3. *History of the Communist Party of the Soviet Union*

Marxists are among the few people who harbor no doubts about the origins of the war. Economic factors are seen as decisive at all times. The following passage is taken from the official history of the Communist party, and is a clear

From *History of the Communist Party of the Soviet Union*, second, revised edition (Moscow: Foreign Languages Publishing House, 1963), pp. 181–86.

and concise statement of the communist view. As usual, no opportunity is lost to denounce those socialists who failed to follow Lenin, or to argue that capitalists carefully prepared for war by misleading the working class with "patriotic" propaganda. Is any evidence used by the Communists to buttress their case, or is their approach an attempt to make history serve ideology? Whatever one thinks, it is important to remember that the ideas expressed below illustrate how a large part of Europe, and the world, learns its history.

The imperialist world war broke out on August 1. . . . 1914. It was the cumulative result of sharp imperialist contradictions.

The distinctive feature of imperialism, the highest and last stage of capitalism, is the domination of monopolies—syndicates, trusts and similar organisations of a handful of millionaires controlling vast amounts of capital. Not content with the home market, the capitalists made their way into the colonies and economically underdeveloped countries in search of profit. By the beginning of the century the whole world had already been divided among a small group of leading capitalist powers.

But under capitalism, an even course of development is impossible. Individual enterprises, industries and, indeed, countries overtake and outstrip others, which have to give way to their more successful competitors; or the latter themselves yield place. Imperialism, with its domination of giant monopolies, accentuates this unevenness, both in the economic and political fields. The development of capitalism becomes spasmodic, and this uneven development constantly upsets the international equilibrium, changing the relative economic and military strength of the powers. And the greater their strength, the more insistent becomes their demand for more markets and for new colonies, because in a society based on private ownership of the means of production, division of spoils is always in accordance with strength or capital. With the world already divided up among the biggest capitalist states, its redivision could only take place at the expense of one or another of these states, that is, through war.

Lenin pointed out that the emergence of powerful capitalist monopoly associations and their struggle for an economic redivision of the world which was already divided territorially was bound to lead to imperialist wars.

The imperialists had, in fact, long been preparing for a war to redivide the world. The most bellicose in this respect were the German militarists, who considered that they had been cheated out of their share of colonies. By the close of the last century, Germany had overtaken Britain in industrial development and was ousting her from her traditional markets. Germany's aim was a radical redivision of the world in her favour. This contradiction between British and German imperialism was in fact the root cause of the war. However, a big part was also played by the imperialist contradictions between Germany and France, Russia and Germany, etc. Long before the war, in 1879–82, Germany had formed an alliance with Austria-Hungary and Italy against Russia and France. The latter retaliated by forming an alliance of their own, and the British imperialists, fearing

Germany's advance to world domination, concluded an agreement (Entente) with France to combat Germany by joint effort. In 1907 Russia concluded a treaty with Britain, as a result of which Russia joined the Entente. The two mutually opposed imperialist blocs in Europe thus took final shape.

Economically dependent, mainly on French and British capital, Russia was drawn into the war on the side of the Entente. But the tsarist government had its own reasons for taking part in the imperialist war. The Russian capitalists strongly resented German competition in the domestic market. The dominant classes of Russia wanted new markets in which there would be no competition. The Russian imperialists were out to gain possession of Constantinople and the straits leading from the Black Sea to the Mediterranean; they wanted to seize Turkish Armenia and thereby bring the whole of Armenia under Russian rule. This clashed with German imperialist plans in the Middle East: Germany was penetrating into Turkey and Iran and had secured a concession for a railway from Berlin to Baghdad. Russo-German contradictions in the Middle East became especially keen in the twentieth century.

Another major cause of the war was the imperialists' desire to suppress the revolutionary movement, which in the past ten years had grown to powerful dimensions. The Russian revolution of 1905–07 had greatly stimulated the working-class struggle in Europe and America and set off a national liberation movement in the East. The governments of the leading powers—and the tsarist government first and foremost—feared a further spread of the revolution, and believed that war would sidetrack the masses from revolutionary struggle. The imperialists hoped that by instigating the workers of different countries against each other they could split the international proletarian movement, poison it with the venom of chauvinism, physically annihilate a big section of the advanced workers and in this way crush, or at any rate weaken, the revolutionary pressure of the masses. . . .

The bourgeois parties of every country urged the people to support the war. In Germany, the people were told that Russian tsarism would destroy all their democratic gains. In France, the argument was that Prussian militarism would trample down French democracy. In Russia, the people were told the Germans had attacked their country with the object of enslaving it. In short, the bourgeois parties tried to condition the people to the belief that the war was being fought for national salvation and that everyone had to take up arms in defence of the bourgeois fatherland. There was the propaganda figment that this was to be the last war. The petty-bourgeois parties also supported the capitalists and sought to justify the war.

Following in the wake of the bourgeois parties, nearly all the parties of the Second International, which considered themselves to be the representatives of the proletariat, disregarded the class interests of the workers and came out in support of the war. The German Socialists, for many years regarded as the foremost party of the Second International, voted in parliament for war credits. The French Socialists, and their colleagues in Britain and Belgium, went a step further and joined the reactionary capitalist governments in order to facilitate prosecution of the war.

In Russia, the Menshevik Duma members at first voted against war credits, so strong were anti-war sentiments among the workers. But their move turned out to be merely a manoeuvre motivated by fear of losing whatever influence they still enjoyed within the working class. Thereafter the Mensheviks accepted the bourgeois slogan of defence of the fatherland. The Socialist-Revolutionaries were divided on the war issue. The bulk of them supported the tsarist government; the Left wing at first came out against the war and even shared in international Socialist anti-war conferences, but flatly refused to break with defencists in their party.

The Second International collapsed and fell to pieces: the Socialists of the Entente countries (including the Russian Mensheviks and Socialist-Revolutionaries) held a conference in London in 1915, while the Socialists of the German bloc met in Vienna. Both conferences voted for defence of their bourgeois fatherlands.

This was open betrayal of the interests of the working class and outright treachery to the socialist cause. Up to that time the Social-Democratic leaders had time and again adopted resolutions against war and had given a pledge to the workers of their countries, and to the international labour movement generally, to oppose an imperialist war. Moreover, the Stuttgart (1907) and Basle (1912) congresses of the Second International had solemnly, in the name of all the Socialist parties, appealed to the workers not only to fight against the outbreak of war and for its cessation if it did break out, but also to take advantage of the crisis created by the war in order to hasten the overthrow of the bourgeoisie. Now, by betraying the proletariat and supporting their own bourgeoisie, the parties of the Second International were assuming political responsibility for the long and devastating war into which the imperialists had plunged mankind.

How did it come about that the Socialist parties went back on their own Basle manifesto and betrayed socialism?

Colonial rapine enabled the imperialists to share part of their profits with other sections of the population. In a number of developed capitalist countries, over several decades, there emerged a labour aristocracy, a legal trade union officialdom, Social-Democrat parliamentarians and a staff of assistants. Thus a petty-bourgeois opportunist trend came into being in the Second International. Through it the bourgeoisie spread its influence among the workers. Lenin described the opportunists as agents of the bourgeoisie in the working-class movement. They advocated class collaboration and repudiated the class struggle; they renounced revolutionary methods and helped the bourgeoisie and the government of their particular country. . . .

In the whole of the Second International *only one party* had worked out a consistently revolutionary Marxist policy on war and peace and was heroically fighting for its application. That party was the *Bolshevik Party*. . . Led by Lenin, the Party called for a struggle against the imperialist war and for converting it into a civil war; it called on the peoples to fight against their own governments, against their own bourgeoisie and land-lords. Above the strident chorus of imperialist toadies, who were glorify-ing war, rose the courageous voice of the fighters for socialism and for the people's interests. Amidst the flood of opportunism which, it seemed, had drowned the whole international working-class movement for a long time to come, Lenin and the Bolshevik Party raised aloft the banner of Marx-ism, of internationalism, and set an example of devotion to the cause of in-ternational proletarian solidarity.

4. *Pierre Renouvin: Histoire des relations internationales*

Pierre Renouvin, one of France's most distinguished historians, is emeritus professor at the University of Paris. He is an authority on diplomatic history, and among his many works is an antirevisionist study of the events of July 1914, *The Immediate Origins of the World War*, written in the 1920's. In the fol-lowing selection from a more recent book he presents an interpretation which is notable for its breadth and balance and for its refusal to denounce and accuse. It presents a particularly vivid contrast to the simplicity of the Marxist argu-ment. Renouvin's analysis ought to inspire reflection on the role of economic factors in diplomacy, on the importance of individual statesmanship, and on the question of the "inevitability" of the conflict.

In an over-all view of these years that mark the apogee of Europe and the first signs of its decline, diplomatic conflicts take on their proper signifi-cance only within the framework of economic and social change. Vast scope and accelerated speed of industrial development; rapid development of finance capitalism; tensions between social classes; broad movement of transatlantic emigration; spread of primary education; power of the daily press, and also—let us not forget—increase in military obligations and costs: all these aspects of a transformed world lend a new appearance to international relations. We must try to evaluate, therefore, the respective influence of these underlying causes and of diplomatic initiatives. . . .

The role of individual initiatives, always important in diplomatic action, appears quite different when one compares the "Bismarckian period" with the period that followed it.

Before 1890, how can one study this aspect of history without focusing on the deeds or the designs of that statesman on whom all the others—Disraeli and Gladstone, Jules Ferry, Gorchakov—kept their eyes steadily fixed? In the diplomatic correspondence, nothing is more striking than this constant presence of the German chancellor or of his shadow: what will

From Pierre Renouvin, *Histoire des relations internationales* (Paris: Hachette, 1955), VI, 377–84. Translated by the editors. Reprinted by permission of Librairie Hachette.

Bismarck think, and what is he planning to do? No doubt this master of diplomacy had his blind spots: he had little comprehension of economic questions; he took a dim view of colonial expansion; he failed to recognize, in Posen and Alsace, the strength of nationalist protest. But he retained his gift of seeing through his adversary, his faculty of long-range political foresight, and his incomparable virtuosity. The uneasiness that he inspired among his partners as well as among his opponents spread outward into public opinion as well. "Bismarckianism" was a reality of collective psychology and, in consequence, constitutes an indispensable element in the study of that epoch.

After the fall of the Chancellor, the scene changes completely. William II, for want of finding "his Bismarck"—but if he had found one, would William have tolerated him for long?—was forced to fall back on "supporting actors," or at most on brilliant diplomats. Were the other European governments any better off? The epoch was poor in statesmen. In some cases, a disturbing instability of character—that of an Izvolsky or a Berchtold—or a mediocrity that even contemporaries could detect; in other instances, the routine honesty of a high-ranking bureaucrat who adequately managed day-to-day affairs without looking beyond them; or again, a man too clearly marked by parliamentary life, one who pursued "diplomatic victories" even when those victories were useless or dangerous. No doubt some men of conspicuous qualities emerge from this greyness: Salisbury's finesse and Raymond Poincaré's firmness of spirit stand out, for example. Yet even those leaders whose achievements were most important and whose programs went beyond the usual horizon—Joseph Chamberlain, Delcassé, Aehrenthal—demonstrated strength of will and audacity rather than long-range foresight.

Along with these ministers, what sort of men collaborated in the shaping of foreign policy?

In all of the major states, the ranks of career diplomacy contained many men whose professional conscience, whose shrewdness in gathering political information, whose dexterity as negotiators were excellent, and whose opinions got a hearing. But only in the case of France were the principal ambassadors, during the first years of the twentieth century, men of sufficient character and personal authority to become, at moments of serious tension, advisers to their government and even, at times, what one might describe as "mentors." In no country did diplomatic agents exceed their instructions with more tranquil assurance than in autocratic Russia. An examination of this diplomatic world remains indispensable for an understanding of political action; certainly it allows one to comprehend the outlook of a closed social milieu which, in many cases, tended to neglect deeper trends and to believe that the intentions or the maneuvers of chancelleries were the center of interest in international relations. An awareness of this fact is a necessary element in explaining history.

The high military and naval personnel of the period deserve no less attention, if one reflects on the need for harmonizing the orientation of foreign policy with the quality of the armed forces. It is certainly not useless

to observe that in democratic and parliamentary countries each government, between 1900 and 1914, unceasingly supervised the plans of its general staff, perhaps for the simple reason that it secretly distrusted the military leaders—while, on the other hand, the German general staff was freer
in its action, freer also to succumb to the temptation of profiting by its superiority in armaments.

The fact remains, nevertheless, that in the development of international
"tensions" during the early years of the twentieth century, individual actions had far less importance than in the period 1850–1870. . . . In the
"Old Continent," the actions of statesmen seem to have been dominated by
conditions that they may not have perceived clearly, and that they certainly felt themselves unable to control. Even in the final crisis, although
certain "choices" made by the various governments appear to have been
decisive, how can one study these choices without taking account of the
deeper forces?

The action of economic and financial factors was unceasingly demonstrated: it was guided especially by the influence of private interests and
by the quest for profits; but it also took into account the nation's interests
insofar as the citizens of a given state, despite the social conflicts that divided them, were conscious of their solidarity in confronting other nations.
These factors were a powerful motive force in Europe's expansion into
other continents and, therefore, in the jealousies and rivalries that resulted:
competition among the great powers of Europe for the conquest of new
markets or reserves of raw materials, and for the "control" of land or sea
routes of communication, weighed almost constantly upon political relationships. These same factors played an essential role in Europe itself, in
the development of war potential and in determining the relative level of
armed forces, while at the same time they created suspicion and hostility
between certain great states—Germany and England particularly. Germany, when it demanded its "place in the sun," was responding to imperi-
ous economic necessity. "In seeking to plug up every outlet of a boiler,"
noted Jules Cambon in 1913, "doesn't one risk an explosion, and shouldn't
one avoid constant antagonism to an inevitable expansion?" This rise in
economic power also exerted its influence on national psychology or on the
psychology of social classes. In that mood of superiority which marked the
German people from the Bismarckian era, and which began to affect the
United States at the end of the nineteenth century, industrial achievements
played an important part. Finally, the attitude of a social group toward
questions of foreign policy is sometimes shaped by its economic and its
class interests.

All this confirms the value of the "economic explanation." But should one
neglect the factors that correct or limit it?

Rivalries among the various colonial imperialisms often reached the critical point where the adversaries seemed to have said their "final word";
and yet conflicts did not always follow threats: the question of Afghanistan
was settled in 1885 by an Anglo-Russian compromise; the English cabinet,
despite the importance of Far Eastern markets for the British economy,

abandoned Port Arthur to Russia in 1898; and the French government, however eager to reopen the "Egyptian question," retreated at the moment of Fashoda rather than face an armed conflict. At bottom, governments and peoples were conscious that these clashes of material interests were not worth a war, at least a "great war."

Competition between national economies seems to have been no more decisive. In the tension between France and Germany, and in the Russo-German difficulties, economic interests undoubtedly played a role, but a secondary role, so far as one can judge on the basis of research to date. And in the "typical example"—the Anglo-German trade rivalry—what do we see? Did English business circles, even those that were most directly affected by German competition, think of destroying this competition by force of arms? There is no sign that this was the case; and the mood of the financiers of the City hostile in July 1914 to a policy of armed intervention on the continent, suggests a negative response. Did the German heavy industrialists, in order to avert possible but future dangers, have any interest in making war on Russia, their best European source of supply, and on Great Britain, their best customer? Did they need to resort to force in order to open new foreign markets, when the prosperity of their enterprises in 1914 was in no way threatened in the immediate future, and when they had an opportunity to broaden their outlets in Asia Minor and Africa by agreements made with Great Britain? It must be said that the proofs are lacking.

No doubt competition between material interests helped shape the collective consciousness, intensify the atmosphere of mutual distrust and reinforce the "desire for power"; therefore it increased the risks of general war, but it does not seem to have been the direct cause of its outbreak. . . .

Historical explanation can be no simpler than the behavior of human groups. When it isolates one aspect of this behavior, it denatures that behavior, for between the drives of material interests and the impulsion of nationalism, there is a reciprocal influence. In 1914, the character of the relationships among states or peoples would surely have been much different if the world's economic life had not undergone profound changes during the preceding half-century. But was the European war the necessary result of this clash of material interests? In fact, the conflict broke out only at the moment when there was a violent clash of political aims: concerns for security, or desires for power. No doubt economic interests may have had a place within these aims; governments and peoples were not unaware of the material advantages that would result from such successes. But it was not this calculation that determined their acceptance or their choice. The decisive impulse was provided by national sentiment and bursts of passion.

5. *Herman Kahn: On Thermonuclear War*

Many Americans stoutly maintain that history is nothing but a "cultural" subject, something for the dilettante, and something for the student who is not sure what he wants to make of his life. It may be that history's "cultural" value alone is great enough to justify its retention in college curricula, but on the more "practical" level some people insist on pushing ahead with attempts to find useful lessons. Herman Kahn, a physicist by training, is an expert on the relationship between weapons and strategy; he has been a consultant to the Atomic Energy Commission and to the Office of Civil Defense Mobilization. In his book *On Thermonuclear War,* Kahn has arrived at conclusions which some readers consider exceedingly valuable and realistic, and which others regard as cynical, dangerous, and inaccurate. Whether one agrees with his broader conclusions or not, it is interesting to note that he has supported them by a study of the origins of the first world war, and has found many parallels between our own time and July 1914.

The most interesting thing about World War I in addition to its technology and tactics is the prewar situation, the manner in which the war got started. The last really big European war had ended in 1815 with the defeat of Napoleon. The last moderately large war in Europe, the Franco-Prussian, had terminated in 1871. The next forty-three years, until 1914, were for the European continent years of almost complete peace, marred only by small wars between relatively unimportant Balkan nations and a relatively innocuous war between the Russians and the Turks in 1877. That is, Europe had had about a century of relative peace and almost half a century of almost complete peace. The thought of war had grown unreal to the governments involved. They got used to making threats to go to war, either directly or by implication, and they even got used to getting their way when they made these threats strong enough. There were a number of crises which made newspaper headlines and scared both governments and people, but after a while even these became unreal and the armies were thought of more as pieces in a game played by diplomats (called "let's find a formula") than as tools to be used. Even though the two sides snarled ferociously at each other, one side was always expected to give way graciously, or ungraciously, before it came to a trial of arms. Both consciously and unconsciously, all the top decision makers were afraid of being involved in a large war. In spite of the optimistic calculations of some of the military, there was a feeling in all the governments that the war would be big and that it was too risky an activity to engage in unless the odds were overwhelmingly in one's favor, and none of the nations felt the odds were sufficiently high in 1914. Therefore, *just because neither side really wanted war, one side or the other would presumably withdraw before things got out of hand.*

As far as I know, just about all modern historians agree on this thesis—that none of the top statesmen or the rulers and very few, if any, of the soldiers wanted a world war in 1914 (though some wanted a war somewhat later, after certain preparations had been made), and only the Serbs and the Austrians wanted even a small war. And yet war came. How did it happen?

The British historian A. J. P. Taylor described the prewar situation in an article in *The Observer.* . . .

The statesmen of Europe with one accord accepted the theory of "the deterrent": the more strongly and firmly they threatened, the more likely they were both to preserve the peace of Europe and get their way. . . .

. . . The German rulers were firmly wedded to the theory of the deterrent. A resolve to go to war, loudly proclaimed; and the other side would give way. In Jagow's words: "The more boldness Austria displays, the more strongly we support her, the more likely Russia is to keep quiet." Those who condemn the German policy should reflect that Sir Edward Grey did the opposite from the Germans: he failed to make his position clear in advance. And for this he has often been saddled with responsibility for the war. . . .

The amateur strategist, devising actions without inquiring whether they were technically possible, was a recurring theme in July 1914. . . . It was no doubt the penalty for forty years of peace, years in which armies and campaigns had been weapons of diplomacy, not of war.

The most striking feature of the July crisis was the total lack of contact in every country between the political and military leaders. Military plans were at their most rigid in the railway age; yet no statesman had the slightest idea what the timetables involved. Their sensations, when diplomacy collapsed, were those of a train passenger who sees the express thundering through the station at which he intended to alight.

As Taylor says, World War I was a railroad war. It was a war for which the general staffs of the four great continental powers had spent decades planning meticulous timetables. The war plans were literally cast in concrete in the sense that governments built railroads according to the requirements of the war plan. One could look at a nation's railroads and get a very accurate idea of what its war plans were. All nations except Britain had very large numbers of trained reserves available that were quite different from the kind of manpower we refer to as reserves today; the 1914 conscripts were prepared to be mobilized into fighting armies. As soon as they were called to the colors, most of them could march into battle on an equal footing with the best professional troops available. This ability to increase one's force by a large factor and in a very short period of time gave a disastrous instability to the situation, because it promised to give the nation that mobilized first a crucial advantage.

As General Boisdeffre, the assistant chief of the French General Staff explained to Tsar Nicholas:

The mobilization is the declaration of war. To mobilize is to oblige one's neighbor to do the same. . . . Otherwise, to leave a million men on one's frontier, without doing the same simultaneously, is to deprive oneself of all possibility of moving later; it is placing oneself in a situation of an individual who, with a pistol in his pocket, should let his neighbor put a weapon to his forehead without drawing his own.

While the Tsar answered that that was his understanding also, his general staff in 1912 decided that the belief that "the proclamation of mobilization is equivalent to the declaration of war," had serious disadvantages for the Russians, since it took them so long to mobilize. Therefore, they formally annulled the rule and instructed the Foreign Office, "It will be advantageous to complete concentration without beginning hostilities, in order not to deprive the enemy irrevocably of the hope that war can still be avoided. Our measures for this must be masked by clever diplomatic negotiations, in order to lull to sleep as much as possible the enemy's fears."

While the above is a perfectly reasonable "military requirement," since it is very valuable to be able to steal a march on the enemy, it is not a reasonable diplomatic requirement. The Foreign Office felt that the enemy was just not going to be fooled by soothing words while the Russians prepared to draw (rather noisily) their pistols. As a matter of fact the Russian Foreign Office was wrong; they did succeed, in the crisis of July 1914, in holding off a German mobilization for about a week while the Russians went through preparatory moves. They did this not by being superlatively clever, but by not knowing themselves what they really intended to do and managing to transmit this confusion to the Germans. The Germans had not prepared any temporizing measures; unlike the other nations they had no plans to mobilize and then hold, but only plans to mobilize and attack. From the precrisis viewpoint of the German General Staff this was not a serious disadvantage, since they felt that it would be a military disaster to hold off and let the Russians complete their mobilization; but in the event itself, the government could not make the decision for war. As long as the situation was ambiguous, it was not willing to make an irrevocable step, and no temporizing measures had been prepared, so the German government did nothing while its enemies stole a march on it. As we know, when war finally came the Germans were not able to meet their schedule, but it is possible that if they had not allowed the Russians to steal this march, they might have met the original timetable and won World War I according to plan. The trouble was that the Russians attacked East Prussia in the second week of the war in such strength that Von Moltke got frightened and detached two army corps from the crucial right wing of the German offensive against the French and sent them East to reinforce the German army in Prussia. It is widely believed that if he had not done this the Germans might have won the battle of the Marne and defeated France, though it is clear that troop fatigue, logistic problems, and possibly some poor tactical decisions played an important role. The final irony occurred when the Germans succeeded in defeating the Russian attack before the two army corps reached the Eastern front. . . .

Thus it turned out that the German plan for protecting themselves by quick countermeasures failed. There were many reasons for this failure. We have mentioned the first and most important, the Germans' failure to react quickly. This is, of course, the standard problem in dealing with any situation in which there might be false alarms and in which the reaction to a false alarm is costly. One may be unwilling to react. Countries are usually reluctant to go to war except at a time and manner of their own choosing, and as long as there is any chance of peace they usually feel obligated to discount the signals they are getting; because they do not want to be premature, they accept the risk of giving the enemy precious time until the threat becomes unambiguous.

A second reason that the timing of the German plan was thrown off was that the Russians turned out to be somewhat better at mobilizing than expected. In addition to mobilizing faster than the experts thought they could, the Russians attacked before being fully prepared. Either out of enlightened self-interest or possibly from loyalty to their alliance they were determined to create a diversion that would help the French, even if it meant attacking prematurely and risking a disaster (which it did). This, too, is a standard problem. Whenever a plan depends on a very precise estimate of either the enemy's capability or his willingness to run risks, it is automatically unreliable.

Like the Germans, the Russians had a rather rigid war plan. All their thinking had been devoted to the problem of how to attack Germany and Austria together, and they had not considered any other kind of large war. In particular, they had made no plans for attacking just Austria-Hungary. The Russian government found, to its surprise and consternation, that it could not even carry out a partial mobilization for the purpose of threatening Austria without threatening the Germans by troop movements on their frontier and at the same time leaving themselves helpless before a German mobilization or attack, because they could not reverse their movements. The rigidities and pressures toward pre-emptive action contained in the Russian and German war plans proved disastrous in the events that followed. In much the same way, careless and rigid plans today by either the Russians or the Americans to use certain kinds of quick reaction as a defense might be disastrous.

Many people realized then that the basic situation was unstable and that a chain of events could erupt into a conflagration, but I think relatively few people took the possibility seriously; that is, few of the decision makers "cared" until events had gone too far. The possibility of war by miscalculation was too hypothetical; the civilians tended to leave such matters to the military and the military tended to take a narrow professional view of the risks. The fact that the hypothetical situation could be predicted made it seem even more impossible that it would happen. People do not deliberately walk off cliffs; they believe that only hidden cliffs are dangerous. Only it did not prove to be really like that. . . .

The more historians examine World War I, the more it seems to be clear that this was a war none of the responsible governments wanted, a war set in motion by relatively trivial circumstances, a motion which, given the state of the world, could not be stopped. It is quite possible that if there had been a really great statesman in a responsible position the war could have been averted. But there was no such statesman, and so the automatic machinery that had been set in motion ground on to its inevitable conclusion.

6. *Herbert Lüthy: The Folly and the Crime: Thoughts on 1914*

The Swiss historian Herbert Lüthy emphasizes the strange, senseless quality of the circumstances that brought war in 1914. Nobody seemed to want anything specific, so there was nothing to fight for; war aims were devised after the war broke out. There may have been a desire for war in many circles, but the desire had a kind of generalized nature. All of this heightens the tragedy, for Europe plunged into four and a half years of horror which destroyed much of what had been built up over centuries—and for reasons which statesmen of previous generations would not have accepted as reasons at all. If he must be classified at all, Lüthy is an antirevisionist, arguing that it was Berlin "that built the main span of the bridge leading from a local incident to a world war"; yet the main interest of his article is its broader thesis of a war which made up in hate what it lacked in sense.

It would all have been quite simple had there been some solid reason for the war, had Austria bluntly demanded a Protectorate in Serbia, or Germany claimed some concrete prerogative, some strong-point or slice of territory either in Europe or abroad. (As France did, as soon as war broke out, with her demand for the return of Alsace-Lorraine; as Russia did with her claim to the Straits.) Such demands would have been a matter of dispute but also and therefore a matter for discussion. The discussion might have failed initially, and war have broken out, but it could always have been resumed once it was established whether or not the demands could be satisfied by military action. But there was absolutely no definable area of disagreement and therefore no problems to be solved, the solution of which would mean peace. It was this that turned the First World War into an insane orgy of destruction. With the lack of any rational declaration of intentions, the formulation of the whole conflict was left to the apocalyptic imagination. Blind hatred reached the level of delirium, because there was nothing, no handhold, to which articulate thought might cling. When in 1916 President Wilson attempted to discover the intentions and wishes of the belligerents in order then to undertake the task of mediating between them, he was acting from the sensible premise that somewhere behind the

From Herbert Lüthy, "The Folly and the Crime," *Encounter,* March 1965, pp. 17–20, 23–24. Reprinted by permission of *Encounter.*

witches' sabbath there must lie tangible causes. So materialistic an attitude was, however, totally out of tune with the spirit of the age, and only caused the combatants to tap their foreheads sadly. Thinkers, poets, leading journalists everywhere—with the Germanists far ahead of all—had long ago retreated to the age of Attila and Totila. Diplomacy and statecraft might be all very well for dealing with international disputes; but when it came to "the final struggle between Teutons, Slavs, and Gauls" not even Machiavelli himself could have invented a solution. Versailles could not solve it, nor Locarno, nor Munich, and what began in 1914 ended only in 1945.

The attempts to establish war guilt or war innocence that took place during the breathing space between 1919 and 1939 produced the picture of an apparently senseless panic that had plunged Europe into war. All those involved whose word could be trusted were unanimous in their protestations that they "had not wanted it to happen." And what emerged from all the research was the image of a tragedy of fate. Alfred von Wegerer, in his monumental work, *The Outbreak of the War of 1914* (the publication of which coincided with the outbreak of the war of 1939), concludes with this pathetic sentence: "So the outbreak of the World War was an act not of will but of fate!" And no one is ever responsible for *Schicksal*.

Yet the running amuck of 1914 is not to be explained merely in terms of all that had gone before, the conflicts of interests, the rearmament, the intrigues and alliances that had happened since 1815 or 1871 or 1900, nor is it correct to deduce that the final explosion was the inevitable outcome of all these tensions, for this state of affairs had been the diplomats' daily bread for a century *without* such an explosion. Neither is it an adequate explanation to say that war was "in the air," not only in Germany, that cheering mobs and delirious intellectual élites hailed its outbreak with joy, in the belief that "the great experience" would provide an escape from the grey materialism of everyday life. For it was not the cheering mobs who fell upon one another, but admirably disciplined armies who would only march when ordered to and who would never march if that order were withheld. Fate is never quite as anonymous as all this.

The outbreak of the war was due in the first place, and quite simply, to the fact that war was declared, and it was declared in due conformity to all the long-established formalities and after detailed consultation of the relevant works on international law, from Grotius to Bluntschli and Heffter; and, secondly, by the fact that in the preceding weeks every diplomatic alternative to war—the quite routine attempt to solve the crisis by international discussion—had been icily forbidden.

I shall not take part. . . . In questions where honour or vital interests are involved one does not seek the opinions of others.

So spoke the Kaiser on July 26th, in reply to a British proposal that the uninvolved powers, Germany, Britain, France, and Italy, should mediate in the Austro-Serbian conflict. And his highly individualistic concept of diplomacy is to be seen in a top-secret document which he sent to the Ministry of the Navy and to the Admiral Staff, with copies to the War Ministry and the General Staff, on July 31st. In this he said that he had, through Prince Heinrich, approached the King of England "who is apparently not at all clear as to what his role and his responsibility in the crisis are." What Prince Heinrich was to say to King George V was this:

> Instead of proposals for conferences, etc., H. M. the King ought to *order* the Russians and the Gauls, point-blank . . . to desist from mobilising at once and await Austria's proposals. . . . The full responsibility for the most fearful holocaust the world will have ever seen rests fairly and squarely on his shoulders, and he will be judged accordingly by the world and by history.

Early on the morning of July 30th the German Chancellor, in an apparent moment of aberration, did telegraph to Vienna the surprising demand that the Austrians should consider international mediation subject to the condition, already accepted in principle by the Powers, that Belgrade "or other places" should be occupied. This was, however, a futile gesture. Before Vienna, in no hurry either to go to war or to return to peace, had even sent a reply, a further telegram from the German Chancellor, despatched at midday on the 31st, cancelled his earlier one: "We await from Austria immediate, active participation in the war against Russia." All the reading and re-reading of the July 1914 documents, all the weighing and re-weighing of the evidence, permit only one possible interpretation of the German attitude: Germany thought she spoke from such a position of strength that all other European discussion must fall silent, and if the mere existence of such overwhelming German strength were not enough to bring this about, then "the guns must speak."

It is true that the common man likes to read of positive action in his newspaper, has never had a high opinion of conferences or negotiations, and tends to despise the polite chatter of cookie-pushing diplomats. True, too, that in this respect Wilhelm II was an all too common man. Recent European conferences had been no occasions for garnering glory; without presuming to any great perspectives of world history or wide views of the world's problems, they had, by tedious market-place haggling, sought and found, for better or for worse, compromise solutions. Like all compromises these satisfied none of the parties directly concerned, neither Germany nor France in Morocco, neither Austria, Russia, nor Serbia in the liquidation of the Balkan crises. And for a quarter of a century no German Chancellor had nourished the ambition of being the arbiter of Europe, as Bismarck had been at the time of the Berlin Congresses of 1878–85, a period which had set the final seal of triumph on his whole career: indeed since 1890 the German Empire no longer had a statesman at its helm. Conferences and negotiations at which papers were passed back and forth and the bureaucrats of politics, the chancellor and the diplomats did the work and talking, held no appeal for the martial young Emperor. Since Bülow's attempt to side-track him as a diplomatic dilettante, he had grown thoroughly disgusted with all such goings-on. If this were normal procedure, then of what real use were his invincible army and his magnificent, expensive, new navy? Only when the sabre was rattled did he, the German Kaiser, stand beneath the spotlights, a warning and a threatening figure in the very centre of the stage which, by the Grace of God, was his rightful place. "Pride goeth before a fall."

Maybe the whole secret of July 1914 is really as banal as that platitude which the Kaiser scribbled in the margin of a report describing the atmosphere at the Tsar's court. And the historical background to the "tragedy of fate" may be found in a single passage of Prince Bernard von Bülow's *Deutsche Politik*. Writing of Bismarck's acts of genius which created the Second Reich, he said:

> By an unsurpassed act of statesmanlike creativeness and audacity, the completion of the task of unifying Germany has been entrusted, not to the political talents of the Germans, which are by heredity their weakest side, but to their innate military virtues, which are their strongest.

Thus when the time came to search for a political issue out of a self-created diplomatic maze, all that the German *Reich* had on hand was the Schlieffen Plan—and nothing more.

Of course there is no proof that a European Conference of Powers would have succeeded, nor that the next crisis would not have been the explosive one. History's might-have-beens are never subject to proof. But with hindsight, and taking into account all the conflicting factors involved, it is hard to see why, despite all the difficulties that might have been expected to arise at such a conference and despite the nature of the demands that Austria might there have made upon Serbia, Count Berchtold and Bethmann-Hollweg should have believed that they could not expect to reach agreement with the other Powers. Whatever Kaiser Wilhelm may have felt about European congresses, conferences, and mediation, the European order which vanished in 1914 knew no alternative other than these to brute force; and throughout a century of crises about far more important subjects of controversy than the Sarajevo assassination, Europe had been conspicuously successful in choosing that alternative. To reject it meant war. And this choice was an act "not of fate, but of will."

During the 19th century the European Balance of Power had become a very firmly established institution. Upon its permanence all developments in international law, both in the public and the private sectors, were based. How firm it was materially is proved even by the First World War and the fearful fact that once it had started there was no way out. Despite the most reckless use of the most extreme violence, the balance could only be broken when the entire European political system lay at last in ruins. Scores of political scientists and authorities on international affairs have described the procedure which constitutes the intrinsic law of the Balance of Power: any one power that attempted to dominate the continent must infallibly call into existence a hostile coalition of all the other powers. And that is what happened, nor could it have happened otherwise.

Only Wilhelmian Germany could have created the coalition that confronted the *Reich* in August 1914, and only a German declaration of war could have brought that coalition into the field against her. It was fashionable at one time to detect a sinister fatality in the defensive alliances and military conventions of the age, and to make them responsible for the World War. But the fact that they were defensive, and were quite incapable of being used offensively, was proved by events as soon as that war began. The Triple Alliance, only recently renewed, was shattered on the day that Germany declared war while only then did the shadowy, unformulated Triple Entente assume reality. The German system of alliances, which yoked Austria to her "historic enemy" Italy, was certainly both fragile and "unnatural," but the opposing group was no less so. Of all the European systems of alliances perhaps the only "natural" one had been the *Dreikaiserbund,* the old Austro-Russo-German alliance cemented by the partition of Poland; and it was precisely these three powers who finally clawed each other over the edge of the abyss in the First World War. But the Dual Alliance, which the Autocrat of All the Russias signed with a French Republic, was regarded as immoral, and the subsequent linking of these two powers with a Britain that was the "historic enemy" of them both and that was generally regarded as being "naturally" favourable to the cause of the German grouping, was automatically put into force by Germany's double declaration of war.

True, the British General Staff had held most secret conversations with their French counterparts concerning a common action in the event of a German attack in the west; but Britain's only formal alliance was the one concluded with Japan against Russia. Without the invasion of Belgium and Bethmann-Hollweg's "scrap of paper" the minority within the British cabinet that was not prepared to accept a German continental domination imposed by force (and therefore always referred to in German literature as the British "war party") would have been unable to impose their views on their cabinet colleagues even in August 1914.

The balance between the European powers, reinforced by the balance of armaments and alliances, had become so intricate that it could not be upset. This was the state of things from which most students of European affairs drew the optimistic conclusion: European war had become an absurdity. They were quite right, and this was overwhelmingly confirmed by four years of immense battles neither won nor lost. They were wrong only in the further conclusion they drew: that because something is absurd, it will not happen.

Thus in a Europe that had become almost inextricably intertwined, in an almost ordered world that had Europe for its centre, German political theory nourished on heroic legends and twilights of the gods set about destroying the infra-structure upon which it all relied. And there was nothing to stop them. The European Balance of Power, as the political scientists had rightly seen, was simply a confederation which had never created the political institutions essential to its own survival. Yet without such institutions it contained within itself a permanent danger of war. The collective diplomacy of the Concert of Europe had only come into play as, from crisis to crisis, the need for it arose, and through common agreement of all the great powers; as soon as one of them refused to play the game, the Concert itself had ceased to exist.

"When honour or vital interests are involved, one does not seek the opinions of others." When Kaiser Wilhelm II scribbled this in the margin of the British proposal that a conference be called, a century of collaboration between the nations received its death blow. Yet according to the statutes of the Hague Court he was fully entitled to behave in this way. The declarations of war followed, each one meticulously phrased according to the formulae of international law. And it was the uncontested right of any sovereign State to declare war whenever it wished.

The "power of facts" was thus pulverised by the facts of power. The functional integration of Europe, which had seemed as solid as bronze, burst like a soap bubble. World economy and world communications ceased on the day that war broke out, the frontiers were sealed, and enemy property sequestrated. The fundamental unity of European laws irrespective of frontiers vanished the day when the enemy was outlawed and "necessity knew no law" any more. The international technical organisations were put in cold storage, or were used to forward the letters written by prisoners of war. The international sea-ways became traps for enemy ships and hunting grounds for blockading navies and counter-blockading U-boats. And the great European railways were now mere branch lines along which troops were shunted to the front. It was the peace, not (as Norman Angell had written in 1910) the war, that turned out to be "the great illusion."

After four years not only were Europe's reserves exhausted, not only had the eastern half of the continent relapsed from war into civil war and tribal war, but all those preconditions upon which the European order and the Europacentric world had once rested were destroyed, forever. The period between the wars was one hopeless attempt to recreate a peaceful European order upon the narrow western fringe of Europe that was still more or less intact. But neither did this attempt lead to an order which could be recognised as rightful, nor could it be firmly established by force, and in its economic set-up it was living only from hand to mouth on American loans. Finally a quite ordinary crash on the New York stock exchange brought the rickety edifice of war debts, reparations, and credits crashing to the ground. The Great Slump marked the end of the post-war, and the beginning of the new pre-war period.

A chain reaction of violence began in 1914 which has meant that for us, now, the period before that date is as remote and indeed unimaginable as almost any other period in history. For what ended in 1914 was an epoch in which the ordinary citizen had no need to remember that it is political order or disorder, not economic integration or international technology, that will decide his fate. But always to know this only in retrospect is at best cold comfort.

II

Revolution and
Nonrevolution: 1917-1919

When the Great War broke out in August 1914, an obscure Austrian exile named Adolf Hitler fell on his knees and "thanked Heaven from an overflowing heart for granting me the good fortune of being permitted to live at this time." [1] A second exile, the Russian who called himself N. Lenin, responded to the news with similar enthusiasm (though for somewhat different reasons); he believed that wars are the locomotives of revolution. Both men felt in their bones something that we can see quite clearly in retrospect: that the strains and stresses of protracted war can lead to profound social upheaval.

The first cycle of twentieth-century social revolution coincided with the disintegration of the old autocratic empires at the end of the Great War. The Russian tsarist regime was the first victim in March 1917; a democratic republic, controlled by bourgeois liberals and moderate socialists, attempted for a few months to deal with the growing chaos but was swept away in November by Lenin's Bolshevik movement. As some historians see it, the Bolshevik victory was "nothing but a fluke," since a Marxist party really had no business taking power in "the most backward of the great nations." [2] Marx's teachings, after all, had seemed to suggest that the proletariat would triumph where it was strongest—namely, in the most industrialized nations. The "fluke" was the vacuum produced in Petrograd by the incapacity of the tsarist regime (and its democratic successor) to deal with the pressures of protracted war. Certain historians carry the argument even farther by insisting that the war interrupted a profound socioeconomic transformation that was under way in Russia before 1914. "Pre-revolutionary Russia was a backward but highly dynamic society . . . , well on the way towards entering the family of nations enjoying the advantages of modern civilization. . . . Think the war away, and you can very easily see Russia peacefully advancing according to her historical lines." [3]

Fluke or no fluke, Lenin's victory was clearly connected with wartime political and social disintegration. One would think that similar conditions in central Europe just a year later might have led to similar results. In Germany and Austria-

1. Adolf Hitler, *Mein Kampf*, trans. by Ralph Manheim (Cambridge, Mass.: Houghton Mifflin, 1962), p. 164.
2. Joseph A. Schumpeter, *Capitalism, Socialism, and Democracy*, third edition (New York: Harper, 1950), p. 359.
3. Nicholas S. Timasheff, *The Great Retreat* (New York: E. P. Dutton, 1946), pp. 39–40, 58.

Hungary, the terrible strain of four years of war was compounded by the bitter taste of defeat—a defeat for which few Germans were prepared in any psychological sense, and which was therefore doubly shattering. Dynasties fell in both Berlin and Vienna; the Hapsburg Empire came apart at the seams, and there were even some signs that Bismarck's Reich might do the same. Demobilized soldiers flooded back from the front; hundreds of thousands of unemployed milled aimlessly about in the cities; food was scarce, hunger intense. And to the east, Lenin's Bolshevik regime loomed up as a symbol of what revolutionary leaders might aspire to achieve at such a moment.

Social revolution, then, might seem to have been the natural outcome of disintegration and mass resentment in central Europe. Yet except for some brief successes—a week in Berlin, a month in Munich, four months in Budapest—the exponents of social revolution were frustrated; the Leninist model in the end was confined to Russia. Why revolution failed in such apparently propitious circumstances, after having succeeded in Petrograd, is the subject of this chapter's readings.

I. *Theodore H. Von Laue: Why Lenin? Why Stalin?*

Not all historians share the view that prewar Russia was on the highroad to modernity, or that the stresses of war provided Lenin with his opportunity. Theodore Von Laue, Hiatt Professor of History at Clark University, contends that it was not the war but the experience of freedom in 1917 that opened the way to Bolshevik rule. In a society like that of Russia, freedom meant anarchy; in central Europe, the "invisible resources of unity and social discipline" made possible a different result.

Russian politics from May, 1917, to the spring of 1921, when the riot of spontaneity died out in utter exhaustion, cannot be understood by the concepts of western democratic practice. They must be viewed primitively, in terms of Hobbesian social mechanics, in terms of crude violence among masses uprooted by war and revolution. . . .

[By November, 1917,] liberal democracy in Russia—using the term broadly—had proved unequal to the task. Since March it had given the country every opportunity to speak its will, and the result had been division, violence, and a breakdown of government. Spontaneity, leaving the population to its own devices, had produced anarchy. The invisible resources of unity and social discipline, which in the western democracies restrained liberty from degenerating into license and made possible not only effective government in peace but also unprecedented voluntary sacrifices in war, were found wanting in Russia. A few years later they were equally found wanting in Italy, Spain, Poland, or Germany (to mention but a few parallel cases). None of these countries had had a chance in the past of knitting the tight habit of subconscious unity before they copied western democracy. Russia was merely the first case in a long series of similar breakdowns, the one that occurred under the most exceptional circumstances.

Viewing the events of the summer of 1917 in this perspective, we must conclude that the failure of democracy in Russia was inevitable, if not in 1917 then surely in the years following (assuming that a Russian state still survived). Only decades, if not centuries, of relative immunity to the pressures of power politics and an active internal melting pot might have helped the discordant elements to grow together. Now there was no time. In the extreme moments of the twentieth century, a country either possessed that cohesion or had to create it artificially, if it did not want to fall apart. . . .

The elemental revolt aiming at the smashing of the old state machinery was a phenomenon possible only in Russia (or underdeveloped countries like China). Only there did the run of the population still live in relative self-sufficiency, with hardly a stake in the government. "Soviet Russia" had little to lose from the overthrow of the government, neither protection of property or status, nor social security, nor extensive public education, nor any other boon of government. In urban-industrial Europe, on the other hand, the majority of the population had long since acquired such a stake. State, society, and the economy were interwoven a thousandfold; all citizens were patently interdependent for their very livelihood. Thus nearly everyone had a vested interest in order and security, regardless of his political views. Threaten him, in time of crisis and internal disunity, with the overthrow of the government and he would rush headlong into the arms of a Mussolini or Hitler. And if he longed for a change of regime, he would still insist that the transition be accomplished "legally," without disturbing the continuity of the public services. There would never be a chance, in other words, of a Bolshevik revolution in the West. . . .

The war, on which the Bolshevik victory is so often blamed, had rather little to do with that extremist turn of events. It may have contributed to the savagery of the revolt, but it destroyed neither liberal democracy nor Russian "capitalism." Freedom, the heady freedom of the new [Kerensky] regime, did that. Given its own ideals, liberal democracy in Russia could never have been more than a brief transition phase. It would always have led to "soviet democracy," the freedom of the "black people," which signified, under existing conditions, spontaneity carried to the point of anarchy.

By the same logic, however, freedom was bound to destroy itself. If Russia was to survive as a Great Power, with the same universal appeal as the others—these were the harsh terms of the competition—it needed the discipline of cooperation under both government and an industrial economy. . . .

The Russian civil war was the center of the universal cyclone which shook all of Europe—a Europe wanly emerging from the war—and jolted the world as well, as Lenin had predicted. What a dismal spectacle the chief regions of Europe presented at the end of the war, and what an opportunity for revolutionary agitation! In eastern Europe a great landslide was underway. The three empires which had given order and stability to the marches of Europe had collapsed (not to mention the Ottoman Empire, whose final dismemberment spread the cataclysm into the Near and Middle East). As a result, not only Russia . . . but the broad stretch of liberated lands from the Baltic to the Black Sea and Mediterranean found itself in a profound state of flux, traversed by two revolutions.

The first was the revolution of national self-determination, which created a series of new sovereign states. . . . The other revolution, compounding the first, was a social one. In the lands carved from the old Russia, Austria-Hungary, and Germany, the monarchical order of life was overthrown and western democracy introduced, yet not without some competition from the Soviet model. . . . The vanquished peoples of central Europe were likewise shaken by social revolution. The defeat of their country and of their political ambitions in Europe and the world had come as a terrible shock to most Germans. It had set off not only a widespread revulsion against the Bismarckian system of government . . . but also a clash of extremist groups on the right and left. The Bolsheviks had many allies among Spartacists, Shop Stewards, and Independent Socialists, but also fanatical opponents. At the outset the radical left took the offensive, staging many uprisings in the winter and spring of 1919. In April, a Soviet-type government ruled over Munich. Who in these months could have been sure that the German republic would not go the way of the Kerensky regime? And who, furthermore, could foretell whether the workers of Vienna would remain loyal to their moderate socialist leaders? In Hungary, indeed, democracy took the Soviet turn under the dictatorship of Bela Kun, one of the prisoners of war whom the Russian Communists had converted. Not even the victorious Allies in western Europe were immune to the revolutionary fever. For a week in January, 1919, the red flag flew from the municipal flagpole in Glasgow, and at least one British radical ventured the hope that it would also be hoisted over Buckingham Palace. . . .

Yet in the end, the revolutionary potential proved far less effective than Lenin had anticipated. In its periphery, the cyclone merely produced a mild disturbance. No red flag flew from Buckingham Palace or the Champs Elysées, no socialist revolution took place in central Europe where the chances had seemed so propitious. Nationalism rather than socialism and communism attracted the uprooted intellectuals. The bulk of the German proletariat was committed to the continuity of the state organizations which rescued employment, social security, and all the other benefits of order from the defeat; it turned a cold shoulder to Lenin's overtures and, under Social Democratic leadership, became one of the pillars of the Weimar republic. In Austria, the moderate socialists, likewise, retained the leadership of the workers and played a prominent part in the early years of the new republic. In Hungary, Bela Kun's regime, unpopular even with the workers, was suppressed without much trouble. . . . Throughout eastern Europe, nationalism proved an effective rampart against communism. The

Communists, to be sure, succeeded in gradually transforming the extreme groups among the European socialists into pliant and dependable Communist parties; but in the end they could not prevent a new era of "capitalist consolidation."

2. *Winston S. Churchill: The Aftermath*

One of the earliest attempts to contrast the Russian revolution with the German nonrevolution was made by Winston Churchill. When his political ambitions were frustrated (as was the case through much of his life), he turned to the writing of history; in the late 1920's he produced a multivolume study of the Great War and its aftermath. Churchill had been an active and influential political figure during the years 1917–1919; he had urged allied intervention in Russia to nip the Bolshevik menace in the bud. Ten years later he still regretted the failure of the West to act, and warmly praised the man who, in his judgment, had headed off Bolshevism in Berlin. Readers may differ over whether the following selection is good history; they can hardly deny that it is a classic example of Churchill's rolling rhetoric.

From the circle of panoplied and triumphant states soon to gather from all over the world to the Peace Conference in Paris there was one absentee. . . . Russia. . . . Just when the worst was over, when victory was in sight, when the fruits of measureless sacrifice were at hand, the old Russia had been dragged down, and in her place there ruled "the nameless beast" so long foretold in Russian legend. Thus the Russian people were deprived of Victory, Honour, Freedom, Peace and Bread. Thus there was to be no Russia in the Councils of the Allies—only an abyss which still continues in human affairs.

A retrospect is necessary to explain how this disaster had come upon the world, and to enable the reader to understand its consequences.

The Czar had abdicated on March 15, 1917. The Provisional Government of Liberal and Radical statesmen was almost immediately recognised by the principal Allied Powers. The Czar was placed under arrest; the independence of Poland was acknowledged; and a proclamation issued to the Allies in favour of the self-determination of peoples and a durable peace. The discipline of the fleets and armies was destroyed by the notorious Order which abolished alike the saluting of officers and the death penalty for military offences. The Council of Soldiers and Workmen's deputies at Petrograd so prominent in the revolution, the parent and exemplar of all the soviets which were sprouting throughout Russia, maintained a separate existence and policy. It appealed to the world in favour of peace without annexations or indemnities; it developed its own strength and connections and debated and harangued on first principles almost continuously. From the outset a divergence of aim was apparent between this body and the Provisional Government. The object of the Petrograd Council was to undermine all authority and discipline; the object of the Provisional Government was to preserve both in new and agreeable forms. On a deadlock being reached between the rivals, Kerensky, a moderate member of the Council, sided with the Provisional Government and became Minister of Justice. Meanwhile the extremists lay in the midst of the Petrograd Council, but did not at first dominate it. All this was in accordance with the regular and conventional Communist plan of fostering all disruptive movements, especially of the Left and of pushing them continually further until the moment for the forcible supersession of the new government is ripe.

The Provisional Ministers strutted about the Offices and Palaces and discharged in an atmosphere of flowery sentiments their administrative duties. These were serious. All authority had been shaken from its foundation; the armies melted rapidly to the rear; the railway carriages were crowded to the roofs and upon the roofs with mutinous soldiers seeking fresh centres of revolt and with deserters trying to get home. The soldiers' and sailors' Councils argued interminably over every order. The whole vast country was in confusion and agitation. The processes of supply, whether for the armies or for the cities, were increasingly disjointed. Nothing functioned effectively and everything, whether munitions or food, was either lacking or scarce. Meanwhile the Germans, and farther south the Austrians and the Turks, were battering upon the creaking and quivering fronts by every known resource of scientific war. The statesmen of the Allied nations affected to believe that all was for the best and that the Russian revolution constituted a notable advantage for the common cause.

In the middle of April the Germans took a sombre decision. Ludendorff refers to it with bated breath. Full allowance must be made for the desperate stakes to which the German war leaders were already committed. They were in the mood which had opened unlimited submarine warfare with the certainty of bringing the United States into the war against them. Upon the Western front they had from the beginning used the most terrible means of offence at their disposal. They had employed poison gas on the largest scale and had invented the "Flammenwerfer." Nevertheless it was with a sense of awe that they turned upon Russia the most grisly of all weapons. They transported Lenin in a sealed truck like a plague bacillus from Switzerland into Russia. Lenin arrived at Petrograd on April 16. Who was this being in whom there resided these dire potentialities? Lenin was to Karl Marx what Omar was to Mahomet. He translated faith into acts. He devised the practical methods by which the Marxian theories could be applied in his own time. He invented the Communist plan of campaign. He issued the orders, he prescribed the watchwords, he gave the signal and he led the attack.

Lenin was also Vengeance. Child of the bureaucracy, by birth a petty noble, reared by a locally much respected Government School Inspector, his early ideas turned by not unusual contradictions through pity to revolt extinguishing pity. Lenin had an unimpeachable father and a rebellious elder brother. This dearly loved companion meddled in assassination. He was hanged in 1894. Lenin was then sixteen. He was at the age to feel. His mind was a remarkable instrument. When its light shone it revealed the whole world, its history, its sorrows, its stupidities, its shams, and above all, its wrongs. It revealed all facts in its focus—the most unwelcome, the most inspiring—with an equal ray. The intellect was capacious and in some phases superb. It was capable of universal comprehension in a degree rarely reached among men. The execution of the elder brother deflected this broad white light through a prism: and the prism was red.

But the mind of Lenin was used and driven by a will not less exceptional. The body tough, square and vigorous in spite of disease was well fitted to harbour till middle age these incandescent agencies. Before they burnt it out his work was done, and a thousand years will not forget it. Men's thoughts and systems in these ages are moving forward. The solutions which Lenin adopted for their troubles are already falling behind the requirements and information of our day. Science irresistible leaps off at irrelevant and henceforth dominating tangents. Social life flows through broadening and multiplying channels. The tomb of the most audacious experimentalist might already bear the placard "Out of date." An easier generation lightly turns the pages which record the Russian Terror. Youth momentarily interested asks whether it was before or after the Great War; and turns ardent to a thousand new possibilities. The educated nations are absorbed in practical affairs. Socialists and Populists are fast trooping back from the blind alleys of thought and scrambling out of the pits of action into which the Russians have blundered. But Lenin has left his mark. He has won his place. And in the cutting off of the lives of men and women no Asiatic conqueror, not Tamerlane, not Jenghiz Khan, can match his fame.

Implacable vengeance, rising from a frozen pity in a tranquil, sensible, matter-of-fact, good-humoured integument! His weapon logic; his mood opportunist. His sympathies cold and wide as the Arctic Ocean; his hatreds tight as the hangman's noose. His purpose to save the world: his method to blow it up. Absolute principles, but readiness to change them. Apt at once to kill or learn: dooms and afterthoughts: ruffianism and philanthropy: but a good husband; a gentle guest; happy, his biographers assure us, to wash up the dishes or dandle the baby; as mildly amused to stalk a capercailzie [wood-grouse] as to butcher an Emperor. The quality of Lenin's revenge was impersonal. Confronted with the need of killing any particular person he showed reluctance—even distress. But to blot out a million, to proscribe entire classes, to light the flames of intestine war in every land with the inevitable destruction of the well-being of whole nations—these were sublime abstractions. . . .

With Lenin had come Zinoviev. Trotsky joined them a month later. It appears that it was actually at the request of the Provisional Government that he was allowed to leave Halifax, Nova Scotia, where he had been shrewdly intercepted by the Canadian authorities. Under the impulsion of these three the differences between the Soviet and the Provisional Government were soon brought to a head. During May and June the two powers faced each other in armed and brawling antagonism. But the Provisional Government had to maintain the daily life of the nation, to keep order and to produce military victory over the Germans, while the sole immediate aim of the Bolsheviks was a general smash. The eminent Liberal statesmen, Guchkov and Milyukov, well-meaning and unwitting decoy-ducks, soon passed from the scene. They had played their part in the astounding pageant of dissolution now in progress. With the best of motives they had helped to shake old Russia from its foundations; by their example they had encouraged many intelligent and patriotic Russians to put their shoulders to the work. They now found themselves destitute of influence or control. Venerable and in their own way valiant figures they slipped from the stage, a prey to tormenting afterthoughts. Said Guchkov, "It is now to be proved whether we are a nation of free men or a gang of mutinous slaves." But words had ceased to count in the universal chatter.

However, the agony of Russia did not find her without some last defenders. Among these with all his vanities and self-delusions Kerensky has his place. He was the most extreme of all the immature and amateur politicians included in the Provisional Government. He was one of those dangerous guides in revolutionary times, who are always trying to outvie the extremists in order to control them, and always assuring the loyal and moderate elements that they alone know the way to hold the wolf by the ears. Successively he forced changes of policy which moved his colleagues week by week further to the Left. There was a point beyond which Kerensky did not mean to go. Once that point was reached he was ready to resist. But when at last he turned to fight, he found he had deprived himself of every weapon and of every friend.

Kerensky succeeded Guchkov as Minister of War in the middle of May. He became Prime Minister on August 6. The tide of events which had carried him during a summer from a revolutionary to a repressive temper had been strengthened by two personalities. One was the General Kornilov, a patriotic soldier, resolute, popular, democratic; ready to accept the revolution; ready to serve the new Russian régime with the loyalty he would more gladly have given to the Czar. Trusted by the troops; not obnoxious to the politicians of the hour—he seemed to possess many of the qualities, or at any rate many of the assets, which a revolutionary government wishing to wage war and to maintain order required in a commander.

But a more dynamic figure had arisen in the background—Boris Savinkov, the ex-Nihilist, the direct organizer of the pre-war assassinations of M. de Plehve and the Grand Duke Serge, had been recalled from exile in the early days of the revolution. Sent as military commissar to the Fourth Russian Army, he had grappled with mutiny and dissolution with a quality of energy which amid these boorish Russian tumults recalls the tenser spirit of the French Revolution. In so far as comparisons are possible he seems in some respects to resemble in fiction Victor Hugo's Cimourdain, and to some extent in real life St. Just; but with this difference, that while second to none in the ruthlessness of his methods or the intrepidity of his conduct, his composed intellect pursued moderate and even prosaic aims. He was the essence of practicality and good sense expressed in terms of nitroglycerine. Above and beyond the whirling confusion and chaos of the Russian tragedy he sought a free Russia, victorious in the German war, hand in hand with the Liberal nations of the West, a Russia where the peasants owned the land they tilled, where civic rights were defended by the laws, and where parliamentary institutions flourished even in harmony perhaps with a limited monarchy. This man of extreme action and sober opinions had risen in two months to a position of central dominance in Russian military affairs. Assistant Minister for War to Kerensky, and in control of the Petrograd garrison, Savinkov had his hand on the vital levers. He knew all the forces at work; he had the root of the matter in him and he shrank from nothing. Would he be allowed to pull the levers, or would they be wrested from his grasp? Would they act or would they break?

Savinkov reached out for Kornilov, he pressed him upon Kerensky as the one indispensable sword. As the result of a prolonged internal struggle at the end of July, even the Petrograd Soviet agreed by a majority to the use of unlimited authority to restore discipline in the army. On August 1, Kornilov became Commander-in-chief; on September 8, the death penalty for breaches of discipline was restored. But meanwhile the German sledgehammers were still beating in the front. The Russian summer offensive, Kerensky's supreme effort, had been repulsed with a woeful slaughter of the truest and best. In the middle of July the German counter-offensive had rolled forward, and the towns of Stanislau and Tarnopol were retaken by the Austro-German forces on July 24. The hostile advance continued. On September 1 the German Fleet in concert with their armies entered the Gulf of Riga. Riga fell on the 3rd. The forlorn nation had to bear simultaneously all that could be done by Ludendorff, and all that could be done by Lenin. At the culminating crisis the electric currents fused all the wires, physical and psychological alike. Kornilov revolted against Kerensky; Kerensky arrested Kornilov; Savinkov striving to keep the two together and to fortify the executive power was thrust aside. There was a fleeting interlude of Babel, of courageous hardwon Duma Resolutions, and of Russian Democratic Congress appeals for stability. The Duma, the Parliament of Russia, presented a large anti-Bolshevik majority. The Provisional Government issued manifestoes in favour of a liberal policy and loyalty to the Allies. So far as words and votes would serve, nothing was left undone. Meanwhile the German hammer broke down the front and Lenin blew up the rear.

Who shall judge these harassed champions of Russian freedom and democracy? Were they not set tasks beyond the compass of mortal men? Could any men or any measures have made head at once against the double assault? Politicians and writers in successful nations should not too readily assume their superiority to beings subjected to such pressures. Caesar, Cromwell, Napoleon, might have been smothered here like Captain Webb in the rapids of Niagara. All broke, all collapsed, all liquefied in universal babble and approaching cannonade, and out of the anarchy emerged the one coherent, frightful entity and fact—the Bolshevik punch. . . .

The Supreme Committee, sub-human or superhuman—which you will—crocodiles with master minds, entered upon their responsibilities upon November 8. They had definite ideas upon immediate policy—"Down with the War," "Down with Private Property," and "Death to all internal Opposition." Immediate peace was to be sought with the foreign enemy and inexpiable war was to be waged against landlords, capitalists and reactionaries. These terms were given the widest interpretation. Quite poor people with only a handful of savings, or a little house, found themselves denounced as "Bourjuis." Advanced Socialists found themselves proscribed as reactionaries. Pending more detailed arrangements, Lenin issued a general invitation to the masses to "Loot the looters." The peasants were encouraged to kill the landlords and seize their estates; and massacre and pillage, collective and individual, reigned sporadically over immense areas.

The domestic programme was thus initiated with remarkable promptitude. The foreign situation was more intractable. Lenin and his confederates began their task in the belief that they could appeal by wireless telegraphy to the peoples of every warring state over the heads of their governments. They did not therefore contemplate at the outset a separate peace. They hoped to procure under the head of Russia and under the impact of the Russian desertion a general cessation of hostilities, and to confront every government, Allied and enemy alike, with revolt in their cities and mutiny in their armies. Many tears and guttural purrings were employed in inditing the decree of peace. An elevated humanitarianism, a horror of violence, a weariness of carnage breathed in their appeal—for instance the following:—". . . Labouring peoples of all countries, we are stretching out in brotherly fashion our hands to you over the mountains of corpses of our brothers. Across rivers of innocent blood and tears, over the smoking ruins of cities and villages, over the wreckage of treasures of culture, we appeal to you for the re-establishment and strengthening of international unity." But the Petrograd wireless stirred the ether in vain. The Crocodiles listened attentively for the response; but there was only silence. Meanwhile the new régime was sapiently employed in securing intimate and effectual control of the Czarist police and secret police.

By the end of a fortnight the Bolsheviks abandoned the plan of "peace over the heads of the government with the nations revolting against them." On November 20, the Russian High Command was ordered to "propose to the enemy military authorities immediately to cease hostilities and enter into negotiations for peace," and on November 22 Trotsky served the Allied Ambassadors in Petrograd with a note proposing an "immediate armistice on all fronts and the immediate opening of peace negotiations." Neither the Ambassadors nor their governments attempted any reply. The Russian Commander-in-Chief, the aged General Dukhonin, refused to enter into communication with the enemy. He was instantly superseded at the head of the Russian armies by a subaltern officer, Ensign Krilenko, who delivered the arrested general to be torn to pieces by a mutinous mob. The request for an armistice was then made to the Central Powers. These Powers also remained for a time plunged in silence. The promise of "an immediate peace" had however to be made good at all costs by the Bolshevik Government, and orders were issued to the army at the front for "compulsory fraternisation and peace with the Germans by squads and companies." All military resistance to the conqueror thenceforward became impossible. On November 28 the Central Powers announced that they were ready to consider armistice proposals. On December 2 firing ceased on the long Russian fronts and the vast effort of the Russian peoples sank at last into silence and shame. . . .

Meanwhile Germany had been travelling fast. German writers are prone to dwell upon the humiliations their people endured at the hands of the conquerors in this period. But their own country was all the while the scene of events most important and helpful to them and to civilisation. Some brief account has been given in these pages of the Russian revolution. The German revolution was the paroxysm of an incomparably stronger and more highly nerved organisation. It passed across our anxious, satiated, jaded consciousness with no more attention than surviving troops just withdrawn into rest quarters after battle would pay to a distant cannonade. The story requires a book to tell. The interest is enhanced by comparison with what happened in Russia. So many of the conditions and episodes and their sequence are exactly reproduced. The nation is beaten in war, the Fleet and Army mutiny and dissolve, the Emperor is deposed, and Authority bankrupt is repudiated by all. Workmen's and soldier's councils are set up, a Socialist Government is hustled into office; upon the famine-stricken homeland return millions of soldiers quivering from long-drawn torment, aching with defeat. The Police have disappeared; industry is at a standstill; the mob are hungry; it is winter. All the agencies which destroyed Russia are ready. They are organised; each individual knows his task; the whole procedure of Communist revolution is understood and scheduled. The Russian experiment stands as a model. In Karl Liebknecht, in Rosa Luxemburg, in Dittmann, in Kautsky and a score of others are the would-be Lenins and Trotskys of the Teutonic agony. Everything is tried and everything happens; but it does not happen the same way.

The Communists seize the greater part of the capital; but the seat of government is defended. The would-be constitutional assembly is attacked; but the assailants are repulsed. A handful of loyal officers—loyal to Germany—disguised as privates, but well armed with grenades and machine-guns, guard with their lives the frail nucleus of civic government. They are only a handful; but they win. A naval division infected with Bolshevism seizes the Palace; they are expelled, after bloody fighting, by faithful troops. In the mutinies which overturned authority in almost every regiment, the officers were deprived of their epaulettes and swords; but not one was murdered.

In the midst of all we discern a rugged, simple figure. A Socialist workman and Trade Unionist—Noske by name. Appointed Minister of National Defence by the Social-Democratic Government, furnished by them with dictatorial powers, he does not fail the German people. A foreign opinion of German heroes is necessarily very detached and can only be expressed with diffidence; but in the long line of kings, statesmen and warriors which stretches from Frederick to Hindenburg it may be that Noske has his place —a son of the people, amid universal confusion acting without fear in the public cause.

The fibre and intellect of "all the German tribes" enabled the Provisional Government to hold elections. Always the reader will see in these pages the same tactics by the same forces: their one object—to prevent the people from choosing a Parliament. In Russia they have succeeded: in Germany they fail.

3. *R. Palme Dutt:* Balance Sheet of Two Decades

A striking contrast to the Churchillian view is provided by the following selection from the writings of another Englishman, R. Palme Dutt. Dutt's biographical sketch in the British *Who's Who* states proudly that he was "expelled from Oxford for propaganda of Marxism 1917." Born in 1896, he entered the British Communist party when it was founded, and served from 1922 to 1965 on its Executive Committee. A prolific journalist and historian, he edited the *Labour Monthly* for almost a half-century, and has been awarded an honorary doctorate in history by the University of Moscow. The excerpt that follows, written in the mid-1930's, forcefully presents the communist view of why revolution failed in central Europe in 1918–1919.

A well-known writer once said that the most important happening in nineteenth-century England was the revolution that did not happen. In a more far-reaching sense it may be said that the most important fact of post-war Central and Western Europe and beyond is the socialist revolution that did not happen, or rather, the high revolutionary struggles that for the time ended in defeat. This issue lies behind all the subsequent crucifixion of Versailles, of the world economic crisis, of mass unemployment and suffering, of declining standards of life and rising armaments, of the madhouse of Fascism. . . .

From the outset the dominant concentration of all the leading statesmen of imperialism after the war was directed to the defeating of the revolution. This issue overshadowed the Paris Peace Conference. The clearest and most conscious expression of this outlook was given by Lloyd George in his Memorandum to the Peace Conference in March 1919. He stated:

"The whole of Europe is filled with the spirit of revolution. There is a deep sense not only of discontent, but of anger and revolt, amongst the workmen against pre-war conditions. The whole existing order in its political, social and economic aspects is questioned by the masses of the population from one end of

From R. Palme Dutt, *World Politics 1918–1936*, pp. 45–52. Copyright 1936 and renewed 1964 by R. Palme Dutt. Reprinted by permission of Random House, Inc.

Europe to the other. . . . There is a danger that we may throw the masses of the population throughout Europe into the arms of the extremists. . . .

"The greatest danger that I see in the present situation is that Germany may throw in her lot with Bolshevism and place her resources, her brains, her vast organising power at the disposal of the revolutionary fanatics whose dream it is to conquer the world for Bolshevism by force of arms [sic]. This danger is no mere chimera. The present Government in Germany is weak; it has no prestige; its authority is challenged; it lingers merely because there is no alternative but the Spartacists, and Germany is not ready for sparticism, as yet. But the argument which the Spartacists are using with great effect at this very time is that they alone can save Germany from the intolerable conditions which have been bequeathed her by the war. They offer to free the German people from indebtedness to the Allies and indebtedness to their own richer classes. They offer them complete control of their own affairs and the prospect of a new heaven and earth. It is true that the price will be heavy. There will be two or three years of anarchy, perhaps of bloodshed, but at the end the land will remain, the people will remain, the greater part of the houses and the factories will remain, and the railways and the roads will remain, and Germany, having thrown off her burdens, will be able to make a fresh start.

"If Germany goes over to the Spartacists it is inevitable that she should throw in her lot with the Russian Bolshevists. Once that happens all Eastern Europe will be swept into the orbit of the Bolshevik revolution. . . .

"Bolshevik imperialism [sic] does not merely menace the States on Russia's borders. It threatens the whole of Asia and is as near to America as it is to France. It is idle to think that the Peace Conference can separate, however sound a peace it may have arranged with Germany, if it leaves Russia as it is to-day."

(Memorandum of LLOYD GEORGE to the Peace Conference, March 25th, 1919, published in 1922, Cmd. 1614)

A similar consciousness of the fight against Bolshevism as the decisive task of the Peace Conference was expressed by President Wilson during his journey to France on board the *George Washington*, according to the report of his secretary, Stannard Baker:

The poison of Bolshevism was accepted because it is a protest against the way in which the world has worked. It was to be our business at the Peace Conference to fight for a new order.

(R. STANNARD BAKER, *Wilson and World Settlement*, 1923)

In the same way, Hoover, in charge of American relief in Europe, expressed concisely the aim in a letter in 1921:

The whole of American policy during the liquidation of the Armistice was to contribute everything it could to prevent Europe from going Bolshevik or being overrun by their armies.

(HERBERT HOOVER, letter to O. Garrison Villard, August 17th, 1921, quoted in Louis Fischer, *The Soviets in World Affairs*, Vol. 1, p. 174)

The efforts of the imperialist counter-revolution were directed to overthrow Bolshevism in Russia and prevent its spread in other countries. For this purpose the chain of newly created States in Eastern Europe, together with the enlarged Rumanian State, were given the task to form a "cordon sanitaire" against Bolshevism from the Baltic to the Black Sea. Every type of counter-revolutionary army of the old white reactionary elements was subsidised, armed and equipped by Western imperialism to raise the banner of civil war against the Soviet régime. British, French, American and Japanese armed forces invaded Soviet territory on every side. Terrorism, assassination, sabotage and forgery were organised from the highest quarters in London and Paris. Poland was egged on, with French military instructors and British munitions, to invade Russia, although its aggression turned out unfavorably for itself when the Red Army reached the gates of Warsaw. A war on twenty-three fronts with all the resources of imperialism was let loose against the new Soviet State.

Nevertheless, all these efforts of imperialism to overthrow the Soviet régime by every means in its power ended in complete failure. The history of the Paris Commune was not repeated. The overwhelming material superiority of the imperialist and counter-revolutionary forces did not result in victory. Why? First, because of the unbreakable resistance of the Russian workers and peasants, who knew for what they fought, who had complete confidence in their leadership, who were fighting for the possession of their own land, to be masters of their lives, against the exploiters, landlords, reactionary officers and imperialist invaders, and therefore fought with a superhuman energy, tenacity and resource unequalled even in the records of revolutionary war. Second, because all the forces of the international revolution, of the international working class were united with them in the common struggle. Revolt after revolt in the invading armies as well as in the forces at home, strikes and unrest in the imperialist countries, refusals of the dockers and transport workers to handle munitions and supplies for the counter-revolutionary armies, paralysed the action of imperialism. The British Chief of Staff, Sir Henry Wilson, had to report to the Cabinet in January 1919 that "even now we dare not give an unpopular order to the troops, and discipline was a thing of the past" (quoted Fischer, *op. cit.*, p. 163), and again, that the only policy was to "get our troops out of Europe and Russia, and concentrate all our strength in *our* coming storm centres, England, Ireland, Egypt, India" (*ibid.*, p. 180). The plans of Foch, Ludendorff and Churchill for the large-scale combined invasion of Russia broke down, not because of lack of will of the Governments, but because they had not the forces to carry them out. The revolutionary wave in the other countries was not high enough to overthrow imperialism, but it was high enough to prevent the success of the interventionist armies against the nucleus of the world revolution. The victory of Soviet Russia against the superior forces of imperialism was in every sense a victory of the international revolution, of decisive significance for the whole future.

On the other hand, in the other countries imperialism was finally successful in crushing the revolutionary uprisings. In Finland the Whites, unable to overthrow the workers' rule by their own strength, had already in the earlier part of 1918 called in the invading German armies to overthrow the workers' rule and set up the White Terror under Mannerheim; and here, as in the Baltic States, the Entente took over after the Armistice from their German class-allies the task of maintaining the counter-revolution. Against the Soviet régime in Hungary, which maintained power for three months and carried out far-reaching reforms in that period, the Entente not only employed the weapon of economic blockade, but sent the invading Rumanian armies to overthrow it, to pillage and destroy, and finally hand over to the White dictatorship of Horthy. Against Germany during the critical period of the revolution the Entente continued the weapon of the blockade, causing three-quarters of a million deaths by starvation after the Armistice. The power of the workers' and soldiers' councils, which had carried through the revolution, was undermined by the Social-Democratic leadership, who armed the monarchist officers and reactionary officers against them; these shot the revolutionary leaders Liebknecht and Rosa Luxemburg . . . , and drowned the revolution in blood. On this basis was established the Weimar Republic of nominal "democracy," with a wide show of concessions of social reforms to the workers in the early stages, but actually representing only the façade behind which was being built up the armed power of the reactionary forces against the workers; until these reactionary forces in the fulness of time finally overthrew the democratic forms and the Social-Democratic puppets and established open Fascism. In Austria the same history was gone through stage by stage; the power of the workers and soldiers, who had made the revolution, was undermined from within by the Social-Democratic leadership, through the stages of bourgeois democracy and social reform, to the final outcome in Fascism. In Britain, France and the United States the method of social and economic concessions to the workers was employed, while the Labour leadership sought by every means to hold in the revolutionary forces during the critical period 1919–1921; the concessions then rapidly gave place to the capitalist economic offensive.

What underlay the defeat of the revolution in Central and Western Europe after the war? The rulers of Western imperialism were convinced that their economic weapon in the conditions of post-war chaos, the power of withholding or granting food supplies and necessaries of life according to the character of the régime in each country, was the decisive weapon. Thus the British Director of Relief in Central Europe, Sir William Goode, wrote on "European Reconstruction" in 1925, quoting from his official report of 1920:

Food was practically the only basis on which the Governments of the hastily created States could be maintained in power. Half of Europe had hovered on the brink of Bolshevism. If it had not been for the £137 million in relief credits granted to Central and Eastern Europe between 1919 and 1921, it would have been impossible to provide food and coal and the sea and land transport for them. Without food and coal and transport, Austria and probably several other countries would have gone the way of Russia. . . . Two and a half years after the Armistice the back of Bolshevism in Central Europe had been broken, largely by relief credits. . . . The expenditure of £137 million was probably one of the best international investments from a financial and political point of view ever recorded in history.

(SIR WILLIAM GOODE, *The Times*, October 14th, 1925)

The economic weapon, however, was not alone the decisive weapon, nor yet the military weapon, as instanced in the Rumanian army invasion of Soviet Hungary. A revolutionary union of Central and Eastern Europe with Soviet Russia could have withstood these weapons; and indeed, as the memorandum of Lloyd George already quoted illustrates, this was the menace which the Western rulers most feared. The decisive weakness was an inner weakness. The Labour and Socialist movements in Europe west of Russia had grown up in the conditions of highly developed imperialism, and in their upper strata had become permeated with the influence of imperialism, which was able to offer, on the basis of the super-profits of colonial exploitation, privileged conditions to the upper sections of the working class, and especially to the Labour bureaucracy, separating them off from the mass of the workers and from the rest of the world proletariat. Hence arose the split in the working class in Western Europe and America, and the permeation of the apparatus of the Labour movement by opportunism, which was already evident before the war. The year 1914 brought this to a head with the open passing over of the main rival imperialist masters and the collapse of the Second International. In consequence, when the process of the war brought the working masses and soldiers into revolutionary movement, the main body of the apparatus of the Labour and Socialist movements, who held control of the organisations and were looked to by the main body of the workers as their leadership against capitalism, in fact operated as a counter-revolutionary force in the interests of capitalism, doing everything in their power to suppress the revolutionary movement and to assist the restoration of capitalist order. For this purpose they were ready, where necessary, as in Germany, to use the most violent means, including the arming of the most reactionary forces to shoot down the militant worker—thus in fact preparing the conditions for their own ultimate downfall. This was the rôle of the Social-Democratic leadership, in varying forms according to the conditions in each country, of Ebert, Scheidemann or Noske in Germany, of Renner or Bauer in Austria, of Renaudel or Albert Thomas in France, of MacDonald, Henderson or J. H. Thomas in England. This rôle was the decisive rôle in the defeating of the revolution in Central and Western Europe.

4. *W. E. Mosse: The February Regime— Prerequisites of Success*

Historians are inclined to shy away from explicit comparisons—perhaps because they fear to be mistaken for sociologists, perhaps because they are excruciatingly aware of the uniqueness of each chain of events in the past. Occasionally, however, a historian does venture onto this thin ice, and escapes

W. E. Mosse, "The February Regime—Prerequisites of Success," *Soviet Studies*, XIX (1967), 100–08. Footnotes omitted. Reprinted by permission of Basil Blackwell, Publisher.

without a ducking. W. E. Mosse, professor of history at the University of East Anglia, squarely confronts the problem posed in this chapter: revolution in Russia, nonrevolution in Germany. His comparison avoids the common trap of oversimplification; it is rich in detail, and restrained in judgment. Its content impels one to reflect on a number of questions. If the crisis of 1917–19 ended differently in Russia and Germany, can that outcome be traced to differences in the conduct and outlook of the revolutionary leaders in the two countries? to differences in the conduct and outlook of the "Establishment" leaders? to differences in the national heritage, or even in what some might venture to call "national character"? Finally, one might speculate on an outrageously "iffy" question: might it have been better for Europe and the world if an advanced industrial country like Germany had embraced communism in 1918? Might communism have taken a different and less baleful form than it did in an underdeveloped country like Russia? Would a communist Germany have been less menacing than the kind of Germany that did in fact emerge (with a fifteen-year delay) from the defeat of 1918?

The Social Democrats were psychologically unprepared for power. The sudden collapse of the imperial regime took them unawares. It left a void which they alone were able to fill. They assumed the burden of office with understandable misgivings. They had no time for deliberation, no time to chart their course with the care which the situation demanded. The horrible mess bequeathed by the old ruling classes had to be cleaned up without delay. Problems of every description clamoured for solution. The danger of civil war was always present. Defeat, starvation and economic dislocation cast their shadow everywhere. It was under these disheartening circumstances that the work of national reconstruction had to be undertaken.

Russia on the morrow of the February revolution? No, this was written of Germany following her own "February," the November revolution of 1918. Clearly the two situations had a good deal in common. Yet if the starting points of the two attempts at reconstruction showed similarities, the outcomes differed widely. Little over eight months after the overthrow of tsarism, Alexander Kerensky was himself a fugitive. Friedrich Ebert, within four months of first assuming power, had become president of a democratic German Republic. The infant republic, after weathering many storms, was in process of consolidation. Thus, however striking the similarities in the two situations, the differences were, in the end, to prove the more important. A comparison of the two helps to explain the reasons for the failure of the February regime.

Both the Russian and German imperial regimes collapsed discredited with defeat staring them in the face. Both disappeared virtually overnight without a blow being struck in their defence. In each case a mutiny in the armed forces—the Petrograd garrison and the High Seas Fleet at Kiel respectively—marked the decisive shift in the balance of forces that destroyed the old order. Both revolutions reflected a widespread spirit of war-weariness.

If the circumstances of the two revolutions were similar, so was the political complexion of the reluctant beneficiaries. In each case, the potentially strongest grouping in the new government was that of the moderate socialists. SR's and Mensheviks in Russia, like the Social Democrats (SPD) in Germany, had been unwilling revolutionaries. Caught unawares by events, they had been reluctant to assume power. They showed a willingness to compromise with representatives of the old regime but were prevented from doing so. Thereafter, they agreed to coalitions with bourgeois elements. The latter, too, bore a family resemblance. The "Progressive Bloc," oppositional since at least 1915, was the child of Russia's "sham-constitutionalism." Its German counterpart, the bourgeois and intellectual Progressives . . . and the mainly bourgeois confessional Catholic Centre Party similarly were the products of the German brand of imperial parliamentarism.

Both coalitions were faced with extremist opponents of both the left and the right. The Bolsheviks and internationalist splinter groups in Russia were paralleled by the Spartakus League, the radical Shop Stewards and the left wing of the Independent Socialists in Germany. In Russia, as in Germany, the division between Majority Socialists and extreme left sprang from different attitudes to the war, different views of revolution and a different approach to coalition with bourgeois groups. At the opposite end of the political spectrum, irreconcilable right-wing and monarchist groups in each case opposed the revolution "root and branch."

Moreover, starting with the same basic ingredients, the two situations evolved in a roughly similar direction. The burden of government, in each case, was assumed by a coalition of moderate Socialists and bourgeois groups. Both coalitions were, of necessity, uneasy ones. There were differences over foreign policy (in Russia over war aims, in Germany over the armistice and the treaty of Versailles), over social policy and over attitudes towards the extreme left.

Both coalitions were confronted with similar enemies. Whilst maximalists of the left clamoured for integral proletarian revolution, those of the right openly expressed their hankering after a "restoration of order." Both in Russia and in Germany the extremists were determined to overthrow by force the precarious and not over-popular coalitions. The Petrograd "July Days" were reproduced in Berlin in December 1918 and January 1919. Kapp's attempt in 1920 echoed the abortive Kornilov *putsch* (both defeated, essentially, by the working class through a general strike). In Russia the "second wave" from the left, in October 1917, engulfed Petrograd and spread rapidly over large parts of the empire. The corresponding coup in Munich resulting in the setting up of the Bavarian Soviet Republic was, on the other hand, defeated by loyalist forces. It was from this point onwards that developments in the two countries finally diverged.

In fact, notwithstanding the seeming similarities of the two revolutionary governments, there were important differences in the legacies bequeathed to them by their predecessors. Thus Germany, at the moment of revolution, could look back on several generations of relatively free political life. Universal suffrage—something Russia had never known—had been introduced already in the days of Bismarck. Furthermore, following persecutions in the seventies and eighties, political parties had secured the right to unimpeded organization and propaganda. Among the beneficiaries of this relative political freedom (though without either power or responsibility) the Social Democrats had been prominent. Following early clashes with Bismarck, they had moved from strength to strength. Supported by millions of voters, the SPD had ended by becoming the strongest party in the imperial *Reichstag*. In spite of the breakaway, during the war, of a minority of internationally-minded dissidents, it had entered the revolutionary crisis as a compact, massive, well-organized and effectively disciplined body.

No comparable opportunities had been available to moderate Socialists in tsarist Russia. Such organizations as they had been able to maintain had been rudimentary. Their leaders had lived as political émigrés abroad, as exiles in Siberia or, occasionally, underground. A handful of deputies in the later Dumas (heavily infiltrated by the tsarist police) could not play a major role. The organization of local branches—quite unlike that of the SPD in Germany—was elementary. Russian conditions, in fact, had ruled out the possibility of organizing a mass following. Moreover, unlike the "monolithic" SPD, Russia's moderate Socialists were divided into different factions. The Socialist Revolutionaries, potentially a mass party, appealed primarily to the peasants, notoriously hard to organize. The Mensheviks, on the other hand, sought support from a proletariat which had but recently emerged from the ranks of the peasantry and which was both numerically weak and deficient in education and discipline. Russia's moderate Socialists, in fact, reflected in important respects Russia's social and political backwardness.

In other respects also, the different political traditions of the two empires had left their mark. Thus Lenin and the Bolshevik party bore indelibly the imprint of the conditions in which the struggle against tsarist autocracy had had to be waged: conspiratorial activity, centralization, the small revolutionary élite grouped around a single-minded leader of unchallenged authority. Nothing comparable had come—or indeed could come—into existence in Germany with her relatively open political life. Neither conspiracy nor the technique of revolution had figured prominently in the thinking of even the extreme left. In outlook and political philosophy Liebknecht and Luxemburg had little in common with Lenin.

Again, in Germany large sections of the working class as well as the great majority of its political spokesmen had, over the decades, become thoroughly "parliamentarized." Social Democracy had come to derive much of its political influence from its representation in the democratically elected *Reichstag*. In the *Reichstag*, moreover, Social Democratic parliamentarians had learnt to work with representatives of oppositional bourgeois groups, notably the Progressives and spokesmen of the Catholic Centre Party. Both socialist and bourgeois leaders had, as a result, come to share in a common political tradition and to owe a common allegiance to political democracy. There would, in consequence, be common ground in the search for a new democratic order. No comparable development had occurred in tsarist Russia. Here, following the revolution of 1905, proletariat and bourgeoisie had developed separate political traditions. The Stolypin Dumas, with their restricted franchise, had offered something of a parliamentary forum mainly for bourgeois liberals (apart, of course, from the supporters of the government). The working-class political tradition in the Russian capital had, on the other hand, centred on the institution of the soviet. The area of possible "overlap" between the two, represented by a handful of left-wingers in the later Dumas, was minimal. (It explains, however, among other factors, the political importance of Kerensky.) In consequence, the February revolution had led, naturally and spontaneously, to the "Dual Power." The absence of a common political tradition in Russia would make it harder than in Germany to set up a stable new regime.

A further consequence of the difference in political traditions, scarcely less far-reaching in its consequences, was the different pace in setting up the new order. In Germany, with its parliamentary tradition, agreement existed between the partners in the coalition about the need for a speedy return to legality. Ebert, the new leader, was eager to divest himself as rapidly as possible of revolutionary power. The bourgeois elements in the coalition equally favoured wholeheartedly the early convocation of a constituent assembly. In these circumstances the new Electoral Law was promulgated—with amazing speed—only three weeks after the revolution (on 29 November). Within less than two months—on 19 January 1919—elections to the National Assembly were held. It was formally opened on 6 February. In Russia, on the other hand, eight crucial months were allowed to elapse between the revolution and the opening of the Constituent Assembly. Indeed, the organization of elections was finally overtaken by the October revolution.

Among the reasons for the difference in pace, the greater degree of disorganization in Russia and the lack of the necessary machinery for democratic elections suggest themselves. Scarcely less important, however, was the difference in the attitudes of the bourgeois constitutionalist groups. The German Democrats and members of the Centre Party made every effort to bring about a speedy return to legality. Hugo Preuss, the Democrats' leading authority on public law, became the father of the new democratic constitution—enacted with remarkable despatch (on 11 February 1919). In Russia, on the other hand, the Kadets spared no pains to delay the convocation of the assembly—preferably until the end of the war. Their "Preuss," Fedor Kokoshkin (chairman of the Special Council on the Constituent Assembly) successfully employed delaying tactics to stave off the convocation of an assembly which seemed certain to legalize social revolution, particularly in the countryside. Indeed, neither partner in the Russian coalition wholeheartedly supported parliamentary democracy. The Kadets would have preferred—ideally—an assembly elected on a limited franchise (something like the moribund imperial Dumas which retained the Kadets' secret allegiance). The Socialists, on the other hand, owed allegiance to the soviets from which they derived their support and which many preferred to a constituent assembly. In Russia, unlike Germany, therefore, whatever lip-service might be paid to such an assembly, there were widespread reservations about its utility. There was, consequently, an absence of basic agreement about the most desirable form of future political organization. The lack of urgency about a return to legality may have been not unconnected with these doubts.

Behind these differences of approach it is possible to detect a still more profound distinction. It would probably be true to say, at least as a generalization, that the German revolution, born of a near-parliamentary regime with mass participation in politics, was essentially political in character. Its major aim was the introduction of fuller political democracy and responsible government. Social reform—and this was widely desired—would follow later by democratic methods as part of the broad process of "democratization." This was a platform on which moderate Socialists could unite with at least the left wing of the bourgeoisie. In spite of friction over details of social policy there was, in the German coalition, no basic ideological cleavage. The Russian crisis, on the other hand, contained from the start major elements of social revolution. The masses—and many of the left-wing leaders representing them—were concerned less with political reformation than with the solution of pressing social problems in field and factory. Not only, in consequence of Russian social development under the tsars, were social questions more immediately urgent than in Germany. The absence in Russia of a solid political tradition of the German type made political issues—as well as political methods—a matter of secondary importance. The new revolutionary power was expected—both by the masses and by the left wing of the coalition—to settle issues by revolutionary, not parliamentary means. The bourgeois partner in the Russian coalition was, correspondingly, preoccupied with social issues. Whereas the German bourgeoisie was politically divided . . . with only the left wing included in the coalition, in Russia the bulk of the class rallied behind the Kadets. Commercial and industrial interests thus secured a strong footing in the very heart of the coalition. In consequence, on all social issues the Russian coalition, to a far greater extent than the German, was fundamentally divided.

The picture was the same with regard to foreign policy. Here also, whilst both coalitions were troubled by major disagreements, the Russian problems were the more intractable. In the first place, the two imperial regimes had left behind different legacies. The German coalition took over from its predecessor an official request for the termination of hostilities (formally transmitted on 3–4 October). Among its first acts (in the small hours of 11 November) was the signing of an armistice agreement. The Russian Provisional Government, on the other hand, took over a hopelessly lost and widely unpopular war which the attitude of the right-wing partner in the coalition as well as the intransigence of the enemy prevented it from liquidating. Furthermore, the German government on 23 June 1919 accepted under protest the peace treaty of Versailles. The February regime throughout its brief career was saddled with the conduct of a hated war and reaped in full measure the odium resulting from its failure to bring it to an end. However unacceptable the treaty of Versailles (and it was greeted with indignation by the bulk of the German population), an unpopular peace seemed preferable (at least in the short and medium term) to the continuation of a hopeless war.

The differences in the two situations were reinforced by internal factors. In Germany the bourgeois elements in the government (above all the Centre led by Mathias Erzberger) readily accepted the pacific foreign policy pursued by the moderate Socialists (though the Democrats, to a lesser extent the Centre, and even some Social Democrats, baulked at swallowing the terms of Versailles). Former nationalists (among them Gustav Stresemann) had been carefully excluded from the new Democratic Party (and hence from the coalition). In Russia the bourgeois elements in the original coalition, represented particularly by Milyukov, the Foreign Minister, continued to pursue wholeheartedly (as far as circumstances permitted) the foreign policy of the fallen regime. Guchkov and following him Kerensky supported, as War Ministers, the continuation of the war. This made foreign policy a major divisive issue in the Russian coalition. The continuance of the war, moreover, lent greater urgency (also for the man in the street) to issues of foreign policy.

As a result of these factors the German coalition, whatever its internal frictions, worked more smoothly than the Russian, which was all but paralyzed by its internal divisions and contradictions. The basic prerequisites for firm political decisions were thus present in the German situation but were completely lacking in Russia.

This difference was reinforced by the different characters of the leading personalities. The German Social Democrats (Ebert, Noske, Scheidemann), senior party functionaries of petty bourgeois extraction, were prepared by training and experience to take important decisions. Though originally divided on the issue, they proclaimed a republic in the early days of the revolution (in reply to popular clamour). It took Russia's moderate Socialists many months to do this. The German Social Democrats, in spite once again of divisions and at the cost of severe domestic crises, accepted first a harsh armistice and later a draconian peace. Only Lenin, in the face of bitter opposition, dared do the same in Russia. Above all, German ministers were prepared to assert their authority. Noske, in particular, was ready to assume a heavy responsibility (in January 1919, Germany's "July Days," the number of killed ran into four figures). His counterpart Tsereteli allowed himself to be restrained after the July Days from crushing the beaten opposition. There was no attempt to create in Russia the equivalent of Noske's "Volunteer Force."

Indeed in the willingness and ability to use force in defence of the new order lies perhaps the most significant difference between German and Russian developments. Neither the German coalition nor its Russian counterpart disposed of armed forces of its own with which to defend itself against opponents from left and right. The armed forces of the old order,

where they had not totally disintegrated, remained under the control, however imperfect, of members of the old officer corps. Such embryonic forces
of the left as had come into being—and their military value was more than
doubtful—were, as a rule, controlled by extremist opponents of the regime.
They were, in any case, a very one-sided weapon. Sufficient—especially in
conjunction with the effective strike weapon—to defeat the attempts of
right-wing *putschists,* they were, almost by definition, useless to defend
moderate regimes against attack from the extreme left. If, therefore, the coalitions were to defend themselves successfully against left-wing radicalism, they had to look for support elsewhere. This was a fact apparent to
the moderate German Socialists. Indeed almost immediately after the successful revolution they had turned to the General Staff (represented by
Field Marshal von Hindenburg and First Quartermaster General Gröner).
As early as 10 November 1918, Ebert and Gröner (with the tacit support
of Hindenburg) had agreed to cooperate against the soviets being set up
all over Germany. In return for confirmation of its control over the armed
forces, the Supreme Command undertook to support the moderate Socialists against their opponents, particularly of the left. (As regards opponents
from the right, its attitude would, more likely, be one of neutrality, perhaps
benevolent.) By this agreement the coalition had created for itself a power
base from which to fight attempted coups from the left. "Backed by the
regular army, the Social Democrats were now in a position to suppress the
radicals. The doom of German Bolshevism was apparently sealed."

Events had taken a very different turn in Russia. In the early days of the
revolution, and throughout the months which followed, the soviet majority
(constituting the backbone of the coalition) decisively assumed a position
of "no enemies to the left." It treated the General Staff, and indeed the entire officer corps, with a mixture of suspicion and contempt. There was no
question of possible cooperation. Matters, however, changed somewhat in
the course of the "July Days." Pressed by extremists of the left, the Provisional Government called for military support, and loyalist troops, rushed
to Petrograd, saved the hardpressed ministers. In these circumstances, co-
operation between the government and the generals became a possibility.
The outcome of the situation was the ambiguous understanding between
Kerensky and Kornilov, the equivalent of that reached later in Germany
between Ebert and Hindenburg. However, unlike the more prudent Germans, the Russian generals then attempted a direct intervention in politics.
Kerensky, at the last moment, drew back in alarm, denouncing Kornilov
and the generals. In doing so, he destroyed the basis of his military support. Henceforth, he was all but defenceless in the face of attacks from the
left. Such, indeed, was his unpopularity with the soldiers now that many
preferred even a Bolshevik victory to a continuance of his regime. . . .

The difference in the relations of moderate socialists and professional
soldiers in Germany and Russia is connected with another difference of
considerable importance in the two situations. Neither the generals nor
Kerensky, during his spell of authority, knew what was to happen in October and after. The Germans, on the other hand, generals and Social Demo-

cratic leaders alike, knew only too well the fate which had befallen the Russian Provisional Government. Indeed, during the most critical years in the history of the Weimar Republic, the Russian experience was never far from people's minds. Some wished to emulate the Russian example. Many more shrank from it in horror. Whatever their reaction, Germans were "drawing lessons" from what had happened in Russia. It may be that these "lessons" had not a little to do with the different outcomes of basically similar situations.

The differences, then, were more important than the similarities. They stemmed, in the main, from differences in the political evolution of the two empires. German Social Democracy, with its virtues as well as its faults, was the child of Wilhelminian Germany, its *Reichstag* and democratic elections, trade unions, educational system and national discipline. Thanks to these Germany—if barely—possessed the prerequisites necessary for a democratic republic. Russia, however, did not. Neither her masses nor their leaders had received, under the "Stolypin constitution," even the most elementary "training for democracy." Russia had had no free political opposition, no free trade unions, no free Socialist press. Every major prerequisite for democratic socialism was lacking. Furthermore, the social problems left behind by a relatively well-integrated society like imperial Germany bore no comparison with those tsarist Russia had failed to solve. Last but not least, the imperial German government, as a last "service" to its successor, had taken the painful first step designed to take the country out of the war. The last Romanov, loyal to his allies to the end, had rendered no comparable service. The future of the new regime, therefore, was heavily mortgaged from the start.

The German Social Democrats, better situated than their Russian counterparts, were able to set up their democratic republic. Russia's moderate Socialists, denied similar advantages, had little hope of success. The differences in their circumstances point to the reasons for the failure of the February regime. These are to be sought less in the men and events of 1917 than in the previous course of Russian historical development.

III

The Search for a New Balance of Power

Few things strike one as more tragic than the fact that the end of the Great War in 1918 did not bring peace. For three or four years international and domestic strife continued to prevail over much of Europe: in Russia, and soon in Turkey, revolution and a struggle against foreign intervention raged simultaneously. In Germany, Hungary, and Italy insurrections and civil disorder made stability a mere dream. Open warfare raged in Poland and the Baltic states; even England, it seemed, was not to be a home fit for heroes—by 1920 a postwar depression set in, unemployment became a fixture, and a general strike threatened. Nevertheless, statesmen searched for a solution: could a new balance of power be created in Europe, or a new set of rules for international relations be devised, that would insure the peace of the world? The selections in this chapter present, from various points of view, the story of that search.

The search soon was viewed with great cynicism, as many people became convinced that the Paris conference had been a monstrous fraud. John Maynard Keynes published *The Economic Consequences of the Peace* in December 1919 and it immediately became a best seller. It left in the minds of many people the firm conviction that Germany had been ill-treated, and that the Versailles treaty was an example of inexcusable stupidity. As one later critic of Keynes described the book:

"Paris," wrote Mr. Keynes, "was a nightmare, and everyone there was morbid. . . ." Its atmosphere was "hot and poisoned," its halls "treacherous" . . . Paris was a "morass." The European statesmen of the Conference were "subtle and dangerous spellbinders . . . ," the "subtlest sophisters and most hypocritical draftsmen"; what inspired them was "debauchery of thought and speech . . . ," "greed, sentiment, prejudice and deception. . . ." Their labours were "empty and arid intrigue," "the dreams of designing diplomats," "the unveracities of politicians," "endless controversy and intrigue," "contorted, miserable, utterly unsatisfactory to all parties." President Wilson was "a blind and deaf Don Quixote"; he was "playing blind man's buff" in the party; he ended in "collapse" and "extraordinary betrayal." The Treaty was clothed with "insincerity," with "an apparatus of self-deception," with "a web of Jesuitical exegesis," which were to distinguish it "from all its historical predecessors." Its provisions were "dishonourable," "ridiculous and injurious," "abhorrent and detestable"; they revealed "imbecile greed," "senseless greed overreaching itself," "oppression and rapine." For the Treaty "reduced Germany to servitude." It refused Germany "even a modicum of prosperity, at least for a generation to come"; it "perpetuated its economic ruin"; year by year, if it were enforced, "Germany must be kept impoverished and her children starved and crippled." Thus the Peace, that would "sow the decay of the whole civilized life of Europe," was "one of the most outrageous acts of a cruel victor in civilized history." [1]

This critic even went so far as to argue that no book since Burke's *Reflections on the Revolution in France* "may be said to have wielded over the destinies of Europe such a widespread and immediate influence." [2]

Whether or not Keynes was correct in his dire predictions, others agreed with him that what happened in Paris represented, as Charles Péguy would have put it, a rapid descent from *mystique* to *politique*. A sensible and intelligent observer like Harold Nicolson did not deny, as he reconstructed from his diaries the atmosphere of the time, "the ghastly hypocrisy of the Paris Treaties"; he only contended "that this hypocrisy was not, in every case, conscious or deliberate; that it was not, in every case, humanly avoidable; and that similar hypocrisy may not, in every case, be humanly avoidable in the future." [3] At any rate, it is clear that a reaction set in very soon, and the struggle to find stability in Europe in the years after the war was badly compromised by feelings of cynicism and guilt on the part of the English, and by insecurity and frustration on the part of the French, who had failed to gain either a frontier on the Rhine, or an Anglo-American guarantee of their security against future German attack. [4] All of this, combined with Germany's—and Italy's—rage at the peace treaties created the worst possible environment for constructive statesmanship.

The selections in this chapter also emphasize other problems that the statesmen of the time had to face: for example, the power vacuum in central Europe, and the withdrawal of the United States and the Soviet Union from active participation in European affairs. Was it possible to construct a viable system of international relations in Europe under these conditions? Did the League of Nations offer any hope whatsoever for the stability of Europe? Were the leaders of Europe seeking a settlement in a realistic manner, or were they simply attempting to restore the prewar world—something which was beyond the power of human endeavor? Did the utopian theories of international relations that grew up during the war help or hinder in the search for a permanent peace? Another problem concerned the rapid decline after the war of the influence of the professional diplomat. What was the longterm impact of that development? Was it an inevitable consequence of modern communications and the democratization of politics? [5]

1. From Etienne Mantoux, *The Carthaginian Peace, or The Economic Consequences of Mr. Keynes* (New York: Scribner's, 1952), p. 5. M. Mantoux's book, published originally in 1946, is the principal attack on Keynes; Keynes is defended by his biographer, Roy Harrod, in *The Life of John Maynard Keynes* (London: Macmillan, 1951), pp. 275 ff. The latest exhaustive study of the peace treaty, and the general state of Europe after the war, is Arno Mayer, *Politics and Diplomacy of Peacemaking* (New York: Alfred A. Knopf, 1967).

2. Mantoux, *op. cit.*, p. 6.

3. Harold Nicolson, *Peacemaking, 1919* (London: Constable, 1933), p. 189.

4. See, in this regard, Arnold Wolfers, *Britain and France Between Two Wars* (New York: Norton, 1966), Part I. Published originally in 1940.

5. For good discussions of this problem see Harold Nicolson, *Diplomacy* (London: Oxford, 1939), and Gordon Craig, "The British Foreign Office," in Gordon Craig and Felix Gilbert, editors, *The Diplomats, 1919–1939* (Princeton: Princeton University Press, 1953), pp. 15–48.

In considering the problems of their time, one must keep in mind that the war itself, although it did not undermine the old elites in western and central Europe to the extent that is sometimes maintained, had, at least after 1917, been turned into a type of modern religious struggle, which allegedly pitted good against evil. This view of the war brought back to the forefront of world politics the idea of guilt, and the need for the punishment of the guilty. Was the development of this view an outgrowth of the nature of the war itself, with its all-embracing horror? Did the "war guilt" clause of the Versailles treaty point the way to the Nuremberg Trials, and poison many attempts at goodwill? One might also consider carefully the background and nature of the Locarno "settlement," which supposedly ushered in, several years after the armistice, an era of true peace. What were the motives of the various powers at Locarno? Was Locarno a vain attempt at appeasement, foreshadowing Munich and compromising the security of eastern Europe? Was it, from the English and French point of view, an attempt to divert German ambitions to the East? Was the Locarno pact intended by the Germans to lull the West into a false sense of security while they plotted to escape from the terms of the Versailles "diktat"? Or did the pact provide the one great opportunity to establish the Weimar Republic more firmly—an opportunity perhaps lost because the western powers failed, especially in regard to the reparations problem, to be more generous with the Germans? It may be, in fact, that the failure to construct the foundation of a lasting peace in Europe in the 1920's indicated that the era of the nation-state was gone forever, as surely as the era of the city-state had disappeared centuries before. Was the age of the continental superpower about to dawn, while the statesmen of Europe tried to perpetuate the outdated practices of the nineteenth century?

One historian has written of the search for stability after the war: "The events and distribution of power in the years 1919–1925 posed more questions than were answered. Only if the states of Europe redefined their foreign policies and national interest in the light of events and the facts of power would it be possible to know whether a balance of power had emerged." [6] One should ask what attempts were made at redefinition, and why they ultimately failed.

1. Gordon A. Craig: The Revolution in War and Diplomacy

The effort to remake Europe after the first world war appears, in retrospect, to have been a nearly hopeless project. Gordon Craig, Sterling Professor of Humanities at Stanford University, and an authority on military and diplomatic history, clearly discusses in this selection two of the principal problems faced by the statesmen of the time: the popular passions unleashed by the war itself, and the revolution in diplomacy. When reading Craig, and the subsequent selections in this chapter, one must wonder if the leaders of the

6. William J. Newman, *The Balance of Power in the Interwar Years, 1919–1939* (New York: Random House, 1968), p. 63.

From Gordon A. Craig, "The Revolution in War and Diplomacy," in Gordon A. Craig, Carl J. Friedrich, Hans Kohn, and Charles Hirschfeld, editors, *World War I: A Turning Point in Modern History* (New York: Alfred A. Knopf, 1967), pp. 9–22. Copyright © 1967 by Roosevelt University. Reprinted by permission of Alfred A. Knopf, Inc.

European powers had any realization that the rules of the game had been fundamentally changed; if they did not, did they have any chance whatsoever to establish lasting peace in a world of instant communication and mass democracy?

Before it was over, the war had wrought changes in almost every aspect of Western society—its structure, its institutions, its values—and it is possible that, if we look at those changes with the benefit of fifty years of hindsight, we may succeed in throwing a little light upon some of our present perplexities. These pages will attempt to deal with the effects of the 1914 conflict on two of the most important institutions of the Western world—war itself and diplomacy. . . .

When we talk of the revolution that has taken place in warfare in our time, we think first of the frightening ways in which science and technology have enhanced its potential for destruction. This process, which culminated (or perhaps merely reached its penultimate stage of dreadfulness) in the Second World War, began during the first, and did so with a suddenness that startled the soldiers themselves. After one of the first British attacks in Flanders, a young subaltern said to Lieutenant General Sir Douglas Haig, "Sorry, sir. We didn't know it would be like that. We'll do better next time." The remark was prompted by the ghastly experience of learning for the first time what the combination of well-placed machine guns and barbed wire could do to massed attacks across an open field. Similar excuses must have been made on other occasions by regular officers of the armed forces—by Austrian commanders on the Drina and Galician fronts in 1914, for example, or by Russian officers on the Gorlice-Tarnow line in 1915—for those who had made a career of soldiering before 1914 always seemed to be more surprised than the non-professionals by the forms their vocation took during the First World War. Conventional assumptions about strategy and tactics were repeatedly shattered by the appearance of new weapons, or combinations of weapons, or techniques of combat. Neither the machine gun nor the use of wire was new in 1914, but their combination in articulated defensive systems and scientifically devised patterns of fire was new enough to have escaped the attention of those who made war plans, and this had a decisive effect upon the tactics of the war. Nor was this combination the only innovation. Others were the Big Bertha gun, the use of the submarine on a massive scale, the employment of smoke and poison gas to screen infantry attacks, the use of manned aircraft for reconnaissance, for anti-troop and anti-air combat, and for the bombing of installations, and the introduction of the tank. And this list is not exhaustive. . . .

Important as this change in the nature of warfare was, it was less revolutionary than another: the extent to which war now absorbed the full energies of the societies that engaged in it. The war of 1914 was the first total war in history, in the sense that very few people living in the belligerent countries were permitted to remain unaffected by it during its course. This had not been true in the past. Even during the great wars against Napoleon many people could go on living as if the world were at peace. All of Jane Austen's characters did so; none of them ever mentions the campaigns on the continent at all. It is said that on the evening of the allied disaster at Austerlitz there was great excitement in London, caused not by the military defeat, but rather by a boxing match between two well-known champions. This kind of detachment, which was true also of the wars in Central Europe in the 1860s, was wholly impossible during World War I. This was, for one thing, the first war in which the distinction between soldier and civilian broke down, a development that was partly due to the expansion of warfare made possible by those technological innovations already mentioned. When dirigibles began to drop bombs over London and submarines began to sink merchant ships, war had invaded the civilian sphere and the battle line was everywhere. . . .

Moreover—and here we come to the most fateful aspect of these changes —precisely because war became so total and was so prolonged, it also became ideological, taking on a religious cast that had not characterized warfare in the West since the Thirty Years' War. Frontline soldiers could feel sympathy for fighting men on the other side who had to put up with the same dangers and miseries that they bore themselves; and, on holidays, they could even declare private armistices with them and exchange presents. Aviators, with a chivalry that belonged to older forms of war, were known to drop wreaths on the graves of enemy fliers or—as in the case of the German ace Richthofen, who was shot down behind French lines—to give them elaborate funerals. The civilian was not given to this kind of behavior. He could not look the enemy in the face and recognize him as another man; he knew only that it was "the enemy," an impersonal, generalized concept, that was depriving him of the pleasures of peace. As his own discomfort grew, his irritation hardened into a hatred that was often encouraged by government propagandists who believed that this was the best way of maintaining civilian morale. Before long, therefore, the enemy was considered to be capable of any enormity and, since this was true, any idea of compromise with him became intolerable. The foe must be beaten to his knees, no matter what this might cost in effort and blood; he must be made to surrender unconditionally; he must be punished with peace terms that would keep him in permanent subjection.

The result of this was. . . . that rational calculation of risk versus gain, of compromise through negotiation versus *guerre à outrance,* became virtually impossible for the belligerent governments. There were soldiers and statesmen during the First World War who understood the truth later expressed by Professor Herbert Butterfield, when he wrote, after the second world conflict:

If you possess an international order, or if it is your desire to assert the existence or the authority of such an order, you are the party which must refrain from conceiving the ends of war as though you were fighting barbarian hordes entirely outside the system. . . . So long as an international order exists, or so long as we may desire one to exist, wars must come short of the last degree of irreconcilability and must retain some of the characteristics of a conflict between potential allies, some trace of the fact that they are quarrels between friends.[1]

Unfortunately, those who felt this way were few and ineffective. As the war expanded in scope and violence, the masses who had to bear its rigors closed their minds to reason and called for a war of extermination. . . .

The changes wrought by the war in diplomacy were equally profound and were rooted in the tendency of warfare to assume its absolute and most unrestrained forms by 1917 and 1918.

In the first place, as has already been indicated, the very context within which diplomats had operated in the past was altered out of recognition by the prolongation of the war. The nineteenth-century diplomatic system—Europe-centered and dominated by five self-confident and, for the most part, monarchical powers—dissolved in a holocaust unparalleled in history. The Habsburgs, the Hohenzollerns, and the Romanovs now left the stage of history, and out of their empires the peace-makers in Paris fashioned new states that entered the diplomatic community without either tradition or experience to guide them. The war also loosened the ties of empire, inspiring the British dominions to demand a stronger voice in the determination of imperial policy and arousing a desire for full sovereignty and independence in foreign affairs among the dependencies and protectorates of all colonial powers. Even during the course of the war, it had become apparent—with the intervention of Japan and the United States—that Mazzini's description of Europe as the lever that moved the world was no longer a true one, and that the course of world affairs could no longer be determined by congresses or ambassadorial conferences like those of Berlin and Algeciras. With the sharp increase in the number of geographically diverse states participating in world affairs—a tendency accelerated by the Second World War—new forms of diplomatic organization had to be found; the League of Nations was only the first of the attempts made since 1919 to cope with this problem.

The expansion of the diplomatic community was not the only change. Equally disturbing in its effects was the breakdown of intellectual homogeneity of the diplomatic system. Before 1914, the states which were active in international affairs were in general agreement about basic things. As Charles Burton Marshall has written:

> Their regimes drew on a generally common fund of history. The frame of discourse among them was unified to a degree permitting any government participating significantly in world affairs to be confident of having its utterances understood by others in the sense intended. None was a revolutionary power. Ideologies were "a minor theme" through most of the period. . . . The basis of general order was not at issue. A common notion of legitimacy prevailed.[2]

After 1918, all that was changed. The nations no longer accepted the same norms of international behavior, and it was often true that their representa-

---

1. Herbert Butterfield, *Christianity, Diplomacy and War* (New York, n.d.), pp. 96–97.
2. Charles Burton Marshall, "The Golden Age in Perspective," *Journal of International Affairs*, XVII, 1 (1963), 11.

tives used the same words in ways quite different from their colleagues from other lands.

The fact that the war ended, on one hand, in revolution and, on the other, with a punitive peace settlement made this almost inevitable. In the first flush of their victory, the new regime in Russia, for example, made their rejection of all of the principles of the old diplomacy explicit, and Lenin and Trotsky earnestly attempted to abolish what they considered a wicked bourgeois institution that was wholly inappropriate for a proletarian state. When this attempt failed and they were forced in self-defense to cultivate contacts with other powers through traditional channels, and even to seek admittance to organizations like the League of Nations, they practiced diplomacy in what they considered to be the true bourgeois spirit—with as much disingenuousness, duplicity, and cynicism as they could get away with. Secretary of State Bainbridge Colby wrote indignantly in 1920 that the government of the United States had become convinced, against its will, that "the existing regime in Russia is based upon the negation of every principle of honor and good faith, and every usage and convention, underlying the whole structure of international law; the negation, in short, of every principle upon which it is possible to base harmonious and trustful relations, whether of nations or of individuals." How could there be any common ground, he asked, upon which the Western powers could stand with a government whose conceptions of international relations were so entirely alien to their own?[3] This was a question that must often have been in the minds of diplomats whose governments could not, like the United States government, simply ignore the Soviet Union and who, therefore, had to go on trying to adjust their traditional concepts of diplomatic practice to Soviet wrecking tactics.

Nor did they have to concern themselves only with Lenin and his successors. Governments that resented the treatment they had received at Paris were not disinclined to follow the Soviet example, and some of them found leaders whose virtuosity matched that of the men sent forth from the Kremlin. Mussolini built a career upon his discovery that a flagrant breach of custom sometimes elicited more consternation than effective resistance; and Hitler won his early successes by means of outrageous falsehoods that were accepted by Western statesmen schooled in the tradition that diplomats were gentlemen and gentlemen did not lie to each other. In a sense, the whole period between the two world wars was a *dialogue des sourds* between those governments attempting to construct a genuine comity of nations on the ruins left by the war and seeking new rules that would be accepted by all its members, and those revolutionary powers that preferred to recognize no rules at all or desired to retain the freedom to determine when they would obey rules and when they would break them.

The degeneration of accepted standards of international intercourse and the confusion of the intellectual atmosphere in which diplomacy had to be conducted was further increased by the fact that the newly created or re-

3. U.S. Department of State, *Foreign Relations of the United States* (Washington, D.C., 1920), Vol. III, 460 ff.

cently liberated nations were also likely to show a disinclination to accept traditional restraints. Their late arrival on the scene and their relative lack of status was often in itself a goad to defiance of the restrictions that a genuine community of nations requires; and in some cases resentments inherited from a colonial past inspired a rejection of legal arrangements, diplomatic principles, or methods of procedure simply because they were Western in origin or character. The behavior of the new nations—regarded from the standpoint of self-interest—was often illogical and self-defeating; but their leaders ignored this in their gratification over the confusion they proved capable of creating, and contributed powerfully to the complexities and the failures of communication of the new diplomacy.

Finally, it should be noted that in those countries having the greatest interest in maintaining public law and creating an effective international system after 1919, the ability of professional diplomats to cope with the problems caused by the war was seriously diminished by the loss of their former prestige and public support. In Great Britain and the United States in particular, it was widely believed that the diplomats had caused the war, because they had been the authors of what Woodrow Wilson called that "concatenation of alliances and treaties, [that] complicated network of intrigue and espionage which unerringly caught the entire family in its meshes." [4] As if intent on sharing Lenin's prejudices, politicians in both countries demanded that foreign policy be removed from the hands of the professionals and turned over to the people and were roundly applauded for doing so. There was little objection (except among officials of the Foreign Office and the State Department) when heads of state began to use persons with no special qualification in foreign affairs as their diplomatic advisers, or to send politicians and businessmen abroad as envoys extraordinary in time of crisis, or even to go to foreign capitals themselves and to supersede their own ambassadors in negotiations.

George F. Kennan has written that summit diplomacy, a method of negotiation that has brought much imprecision and many unreasonable expectations into international intercourse since 1945, had its start during the Paris Peace Conference of 1919, where the Council of Four was a permanent summit conference in which heads of state, often without the assistance of professional diplomatic aides, sought to plaster loose formulae over intractable problems. Despite indifferent success at Paris, the experiment was carried further by the statesmen of the interwar period, the British being particularly prone to what came to be called "open diplomacy." Lloyd George, Ramsay MacDonald, and Neville Chamberlain all found it impossible to delegate the execution of policy and the delicate tasks of negotiation to professionals, of whom, indeed, they had an opinion bordering on contempt, and whose methods—the time-tested procedures of negotiation on the basis of written documents—they considered ill-suited to the conditions of the new age.

These tendencies, which had unfortunate results in British practice, were

4. Wilson on October 16, 1916, quoted in Bernadotte Schmitt, *Triple Alliance and Triple Entente* (New York, 1931), p. 1.

not confined to Britain. In France, when Briand and Laval were prime ministers, the Foreign Office was less than perfectly informed of the nature of their conversations with, and the extent of their commitments to, foreign statesmen like Stresemann and Mussolini. Nor would anyone deny that the distrust of professional diplomacy inspired by the First World War caused dislocation, imprecision, and confusion in the administration of foreign affairs in the United States. Wilson was not alone in his distrust of the techniques of the old diplomacy. The history of the London Economic Conference of 1933 and the elaborate methods employed subsequently by Franklin Roosevelt to by-pass the State Department (methods commented upon most recently in the memoirs of Robert Murphy) were in full accord with the kind of pattern set by the Council of Four in 1919 and Lloyd George's personal diplomacy in the years that followed.

2. *Hajo Holborn: The Political Collapse of Europe*

The late Hajo Holborn was a professor at Yale and one of the world's most respected authorities on German history. His brief book, *The Political Collapse of Europe*, from which this selection is taken, is an impressive work of compression and analysis. Does Holborn leave one with the impression that the foundations of the European state system were so shaky, and the nations of Europe so basically suspicious of one another, that all the efforts that were made in the 1920's to achieve a permanent peace amounted to little more than a patchwork job?

The Paris peace treaties were considered to constitute a world settlement; but they never did. The peace conference could do little about the problems of the Far Eastern Pacific except distribute the German colonies located in that area. But of even greater consequence was its failure to deal with Bolshevist Russia. This is not to suggest that a solution of the Russian problem would have been simple or even possible in 1919. The French were stubbornly opposed to any diplomatic contacts with the Bolshevists, whom they judged to be tools of the Germans and traitors of Russian political and financial commitments to the West. Opposed, also, was Winston Churchill, then the British secretary for war. But the West was unable to intervene in the Russian civil war except by giving arms and other implements of war to the White Russian groups fighting in various parts of Russia against the Bolshevists entrenched in Moscow and St. Petersburg. Few Allied soldiers were willing to be sent to Russia, since after the German armistice everybody was convinced that the fighting was over and that Allied war aims had been achieved.

Winston Churchill, in his Boston speech of March 31, 1949, character-

From Hajo Holborn, *The Political Collapse of Europe* (New York: Alfred A. Knopf, 1951), pp. 111–121, 125–137. Copyright 1951 by Hajo Holborn. Reprinted by permission of Alfred A. Knopf, Inc.

ized the "failure to strangle Bolshevism at its birth and to bring Russia . . . by one means or another into the general democratic system" as one of the great mistakes of Allied statesmen in 1919.[1] This statement seems historically correct, and Churchill deserves credit for having seen in 1919 the loss and danger to Europe involved in the isolation of a hostile Russia. It still remains doubtful however, whether the policies in support of the White Russian counterrevolutionaries could ever have been successful, even if they had been conducted by the western European Governments with full unanimity and determination. Churchill himself in retrospect expressed some concern whether the White Russians could ever have won out against the Bolshevists.[2] Their leaders like Denikin and Kolchak were certainly not inspired by any democratic sentiment, but were outright Czarist reactionaries. Their victory would have threatened the seizure of the land by the peasants, which had taken place during the Bolshevist Revolution. Moreover, they were active collaborators with the Western powers and could, therefore, be identified as partners in the despoilment of the Russian empire, which, with the blessings of the Western powers, was deprived of all her European provinces conquered by the German army during the war. . . .

The policy of half-hearted intervention was followed by the lukewarm policy of the *cordon sanitaire*. This policy represented the open admission of the inability of the Western powers to influence the course of Russian internal affairs except by increasing the difficulties first of the stabilization and then of the forced expansion of the Russian economy. It must be added, however, that the policy of the *cordon sanitaire* contributed to the defeat of early Soviet attempts to turn the Russian Revolution into a world revolution, although events like the German recovery in the mid-twenties and the anti-Communist turn of the revolution in China were undoubtedly more important.

The failure to integrate Russia in some fashion into a European system created serious uncertainties about the future of the Continent. To be sure, for about a decade or more after the revolution, Russia was too weak to exercise any strong direct influence on Europe beyond the ideological impact of the Third International. But the existence of an independent Communist Russian state that controlled an international political movement made the whole European settlement unsafe. The Communist movement intensified everywhere the social unrest that followed in the wake of the peace settlement of Paris, and the Russian state encouraged every nation willing to resist the peace treaties of 1919. . . .

That the Paris settlement did not become a world settlement was also owing to the withdrawal of the United States from Woodrow Wilson's great design. This withdrawal was not caused by popular dissatisfaction with the treatment meted out by the Paris peace treaties to the vanquished enemies. In so far as the Senate's opposition was more than a display of

1. The *New York Times*, April 1, 1949.
2. W. S. Churchill: *The Aftermath, The World Crisis, 1918–28* (New York: 1929), p. 264.

partisan spirit, it centered around the fear of seeing the United States sucked into an international system whose obligations—if they were clearly understood at all—were dreaded by many Americans. In retrospect it may be asked whether Wilson's adamant insistence on the American ratification of the full Covenant showed good political judgment. Probably even an amended and watered down Covenant acceptable to the United States Senate would have been preferable to a Covenant rejected by it, since the United States could then have been kept in contact with the unfolding European situation.

But even the rejection of the Covenant by the United States might not have been a major catastrophe if America had backed the Mutual Assistance Pact for the Rhine settlement. Theodore Roosevelt and Senators Lodge and Knox felt that it would be better to build any future American participation in world affairs around the practical experience already gained. In their opinion the wartime alliance with the Allied nations ought to be the nucleus of any future American co-operation in international affairs.[3] Thus they were ready to subscribe to the Rhine pact rather than to the League of Nations Covenant. From both an American and a universal point of view, it would have been desirable to have the United States join in the establishment of a world organization for the maintenance of peace; but an American guarantee of the crucial western European frontiers could have been equally decisive. In the fierce party struggle between the President and the Senate both possibilities were lost, and the subsequent neglect of international affairs makes one wonder whether or not the American people would in any case have given their support to international commitments for any length of time. . . .

Europe after 1920 was left alone to cope with her political problems. It appeared at once doubtful that she would be able to do so. Quite apart from the great financial and economic questions, which could have been solved only by world-wide arrangements, the whole European scene as envisaged by the peacemakers while they still acted in concert was drastically changed by America's withdrawal. France was immediately affected. She had foregone her demands for a separation of the Rhineland in exchange for an Anglo-American guarantee of the demilitarization of the left bank of the Rhine. The great French concessions at the Peace Conference now seemed to have been made in vain.

France was particularly alarmed by the British refusal to sign the mutual guarantee pact. It was true that the Anglo-French treaty as drafted in Paris depended on the willingness of the United States to subscribe to a parallel treaty. The British decision to drop the treaty was no breach of promise, but it was a grave error of judgment. The Rhine was the natural defense line of Britain as much as of France, as World War I had abundantly shown. If Britain declined to co-operate without reservation in the defense of the Rhine, the French had reasons to distrust the good intentions or the good judgment of British policy. Were the British, once they had achieved

---

3. W. Lippmann: *U.S. War Aims* (Boston: 1944), pp. 160 ff.

the full realization of their war aims—the destruction of Germany as a naval and colonial power—determined to leave the Continent unprotected? France therefore proceeded to build up a system of alliances with the eastern European states.

It was dubious from the beginning whether the new eastern states would be able to live between the Soviet Union and Germany if neither were integrated in some fashion into a European system. Actually, many people forgot Russia altogether. To them Poland seemed to have taken the place that Russia had occupied in Europe before 1914, while Czechoslovakia, Yugoslavia, and Rumania, which formed in 1920–1 alliances chiefly directed against a restoration of Habsburg rule in Hungary, were considered to constitute a substitute for the Habsburg empire. But neither this group of states, called the Little Entente, nor Poland could compare to the former Habsburg or Romanov empires. . . .

Actually, France was not in a position to uphold the treaties by her own strength, but in the years immediately following the War she seemed stronger than she really was. The postwar depression, which affected the United States and Britain very severely, hardly touched France, owing to the reconstruction work going on in the war-devastated French provinces. Moreover, although at the end of 1918 the British army and airforce were probably stronger than the French services, British armed strength was dissolved with amazing speed. In 1920, needing military strength in India, in the Middle East, and in Ireland, the British army of around 300,000 men could spare only 13,000 men for occupation duty in the Rhineland and nothing but a few battalions to help in the policing of the plebiscite areas in Upper Silesia and East Prussia, though British diplomacy had been responsible for having these plebiscites instituted. By contrast the French army seemed powerful.

The inequality in mobilized military strength added to the air of unreality that surrounded Franco-British relations in the early years after the war. The two powers even indulged in unfriendly squabbles in the Near East. But the French were chiefly worried by the thought that with the return to a small professional army the British would be incapable of assisting them in gaining security—for them the real prize of the war. France wished to see any future war fought east of the French borders and brought to a quick decision there. If Germany could invade France again or if a war should last long enough to enable Germany to mobilize her superior manpower and industrial potential, France would be destroyed again. A simple promise by Britain, as finally offered by Lord Curzon in 1922, that she would consider any German violation of the demilitarization of the Rhineland an act of aggression seemed to Frenchmen an inadequate insurance as long as Britain did not provide military forces ready to act instantaneously with the French army in the case of any threat.

Poincaré between 1922 and 1924 attempted to employ the preponderant might of France for the achievement of a European position in which France would no longer have to rely on British support. The occupation of the Ruhr in January, 1923, was undertaken to make Germany pay reparations or, in the case of German opposition, to secure the productive resources that would recompense France. In spite of German "passive resistance" French policy was successful in finally forcing Germany to come to terms; but France, as a result of her exertions, was financially exhausted and could not impose her own conditions. American and British intervention instituted the Dawes Plan, which for a period of five years removed reparations from the agenda of European diplomacy. More important, France recognized that she could not conduct an independent European policy, but would have to act in close co-operation with Britain, even at the sacrifice of some French advantages and hopes.

It is doubtful that Britain after World War I had a clear conception of the future of Europe. In less than a year after the signing of the Treaty of Versailles she developed, if not a new European policy, at least a new attitude toward European problems. Britain had been severely jolted by her inability, in conjunction with her European allies, to bring the war against the Central Powers to a victorious conclusion. America's intervention had been necessary to decide the war, and the United States proposed to maintain thereafter a navy of a size equal to the British navy. The withdrawal of the United States from European affairs was profoundly alarming to Britain, and the new world situation seemed to make it unwise to assume international obligations as far-reaching as those she had accepted prior to 1914. . . .

Frenchmen did not share the British belief in disarmament as a step to security. The League of Geneva was almost exclusively an Anglo-American brainchild. The French plan, defeated at the Paris Conference and dubbed by Woodrow Wilson "international militarism," [4] aimed at assembling preponderant military power against any nation that would challenge the European order established by the Paris peace treaties. After America's refusal to join, France was even more determined to turn the League into an armed organization for the defense of the *status quo*.

The Covenant, particularly as it was interpreted by most of its members, proposed to deal with threats to the peace or actual breaches of the peace primarily through obligatory conference; for the British felt that the war of 1914 could have been avoided if the European powers had agreed to confer on the Austro-Serbian conflict. The League was supposed to place all international disputes under the review of an international conference. It could then proceed to impose sanctions or even go to war against the recalcitrant member or nonmember, provided the League Council unanimously agreed; but in the absence of unanimity the individual members regained their freedom of action, which included the right to go to war. To fill this gap and to make League action against aggression automatic and of irresistible force, France, supported by her allies, pressed for supplementary arrangements.

The first result was the Draft Treaty of Mutual Assistance of 1923, which

4. D. H. Miller: *The Drafting of the Covenant* (New York: 1928), Vol. II, p. 294, quoted in W. M. Jordan: *Great Britain, France, and the German Problem* (London: 1943), p. 206.

tried to solve the problem of what constituted aggression and to array an international military force against it. The treaty, which incidentally had a great influence on the United Nations Charter, was emphatically rejected by the British Labor Government as being a militaristic document.[5] Instead, with the consent of the British and French Governments, the Geneva Protocol which placed the emphasis upon compulsory arbitration, was drafted in 1924. The member states of the League were to bond themselves to submit their disputes to arbitration, and refusal to accept the arbitration award was to be considered an act of aggression. The Geneva Protocol appealed to the rigid French sense of law. It seemed to contain a clear-cut definition of aggression, though from a French point of view it still left much to be desired with regard to the scope and automatic immediacy of sanctions. In the eyes of its British supporters the Geneva Protocol established arbitration as the supreme instrument of peaceful settlement, and they believed it to be so effective as to make the actual application of sanctions highly unlikely. (The Labor party remained, at least to 1934, pacifist and in favor of drastic disarmament as the chief means of general pacification.)

However, the ratification of the Geneva Protocol was refused by the new British Conservative Government, which superseded the MacDonald cabinet and in which Sir Austen Chamberlain served as foreign secretary. In his opinion the protocol committed British power to an extent that might prove unbearable. There was only one aspect of the protocol that found favor also with the British Conservatives: it was directed against any aggressor, and not against a specific nation. This feature, though confined to the strategic area of northwestern Europe, also recommended the Locarno Treaty of Mutual Guarantee of 1925 to the new British Government.

Before appraising the work of Locarno it is necessary to discuss both the German and the British attitude toward eastern Europe. Germany could not hope for more than co-operation with the western European powers, which, at least for economic and financial reasons, was highly desirable; but she could hope for more power in the east. Her strongest resentment against the Versailles Treaty, indeed, arose from its eastern provisions, especially those concerning the Polish corridor and Danzig, but also those affecting Austria. For eastern Europe seemed to offer opportunities for making political gains at not too distant a date. The new states were weak without exception, and in their rear there loomed the Russian colossus; since this colossus was not yet firmly on its feet, Germany could assume leadership in Russo-German co-operation, which had begun with the Rapallo Treaty of 1922.

British policy towards eastern Europe was never certain after World War I. At the time of the Paris Conference Lloyd George had already seen to it that Poland was kept within bounds defined by the principle of national self-determination; the plebiscites in the German-Polish borderlands were the most important concessions the German Government achieved in

---

5. Jordan: *Great Britain, France, and the German Problem*, p. 205.

Paris. In the drafting of the statute for the Free City of Danzig, British diplomacy again greatly favored German claims. In the Polish-Russian conflict British policy had aimed at an eastern Polish boundary also grounded as much as possible on the principle of nationality. But Poland, once she was saved from the Red army by the good counsel of General Weygand and the mistakes of the Russian armies (which were probably to some extent the errors of the young Stalin), claimed territories far to the east of the Curzon line. In a conversation with Aristide Briand at Downing Street in December, 1921, Lloyd George said that "the British people were not very much interested in what happened on the eastern frontier of Germany; they would not be ready to be involved in quarrels which might arise regarding Poland or Danzig or Upper Silesia. On the contrary, there was a general reluctance to get mixed up in these questions in any way." And then, in language closely akin to the tenor of Neville Chamberlain's statement of 1938 on Czechoslovakia as "that faraway country," he added: "The British people felt that the populations in that quarter of Europe were unstable and excitable; they might start fighting at any time, and the rights and wrongs of the dispute might be very hard to disentangle. He did not think, therefore, that his country would be disposed to give any guarantees which might involve them in military operations in any eventuality in that part of the world. . . .

The historical adviser to the British Foreign Office, Sir James Headlam-Morley, . . . argued that Great Britain could be defended only on the European Continent, irrespective of the fact that she formed at the same time the center·of a world-wide empire. England had always been a part of the European political system, and most certainly so in her great days. . . . The British historian was also right in calling it the supreme achievement of statesmanship in the first half of the nineteenth century that France was brought back to the councils of the great European powers without being allowed to upset the order of Europe established by the Congress of Vienna. He recommended analogous concessions to Germany, particularly by a revision of reparations, but warned the British statesmen not to give Germany the chance to wreck the basic arrangements of the Paris settlement. Such sabotage would be possible, he correctly predicted, if the new eastern European states were left without general protection and if Germany were permitted to co-operate with Russia against them.

But British diplomacy, in line with prevailing public opinion in England, chose a different course. Sir Austen Chamberlain, in spite of his strong personal sympathies for France and his suspicions of Germany, was swayed by the general sentiment that Britain could and should avoid continental entanglements except for limited commitments made for the security of the English Channel. By confining British guarantees at Locarno to western Europe, Britain gave the impression that she was willing to tolerate changes in eastern Europe, in contrast to the declared French policy.

The idea of concluding a Franco-Belgian-German pact reaffirming the Rhine settlement of Versailles and placing this pact under an Anglo-Italian guarantee originated largely in Germany. Germany was anxious to forestall any future repetition of a French invasion of the Ruhr and also to create the basis for the withdrawal of the Allied occupation forces from the Rhineland. It was obvious, however, that the Germany of 1925 could not hope to achieve revisions of the sections of the Peace Treaty of Versailles applying to the Rhine except with regard to the occupation terms, and the German foreign minister Gustav Stresemann found a majority in support of his Locarno policy among the Germans largely because it was hoped that the treaty would open the gates for a revision of the Versailles Treaty in the East.[6] To be sure, Germany had to sign arbitration treaties with Poland and Czechoslovakia, and France strengthened her own political ties with the two states by concluding alliances with them simultaneously with the signing of the Locarno Treaty of Mutual Guarantee. But the eastern security settlement was not reinforced by a British guarantee. Moreover, Germany, in a special protocol, was assured by the other Locarno powers that her co-operation in the defense of the League Covenant against a Russian infraction would take into account her "military situation" as well as "geographical situation." [7] Germany was thus deliberately given great latitude to determine her relations with Russia without much reference to her League obligations. When in April, 1926, Germany concluded the Treaty of Berlin with the U.S.S.R., providing for neutrality in case of an unprovoked attack by other powers against either signatory, Stresemann could tell the Soviet Government that the question of whether or not the U.S.S.R. would be judged an aggressor by the League of Nations in the event of a conflict with a third state "could only be determined with binding force for Germany with her own consent." [8]

The Locarno treaties and Germany's entrance into the League have often been described as the apogee of the international system of 1919. In reality Locarno did not create a secure foundation of a European peace. It covered up certain deep cracks that had appeared in the building, but failed to repair the structural weaknesses. It would have been desirable, and in any case unobjectionable, to make concessions to Germany between 1924 and 1930 in such matters as the occupation of the Rhineland and reparations. Probably much more should have been done to enable the young German democracy to develop under favorable conditions. But it was absolutely essential for Britain and France to keep control of any changes in Germany's position in Europe. Any revision of the Versailles Treaty should have been sought by procedures of international law and multilateral agreement and by the determined refusal of unilateral *faits accomplis*. It was a tragic fallacy to believe that eastern Europe could be neglected po-

6. Stresemann's close political friend and successor, Julius Curtius, wrote with reference to the Hague Conference of 1929: "In the liquidation of the War the differentiation between West and East that we had already successfully struggled for at Locarno had to be maintained." J. Curtius: *Sechs Jahre Minister der Deutschen Republik* (Heidelberg: 1948), p. 100.

7. A. B. Keith (ed.): *Speeches and Documents on International Affairs, 1918–37* (London: 1938), Vol. 1, p. 124. The various Locarno treaties are conveniently printed together in this volume.

8. Note by the German Foreign Minister Stresemann to the Soviet Ambassador Krestinski, April 24, 1926, ibid., pp. 128 ff.

litically and economically without courting the gravest dangers. Even worse was the unfounded belief that international conflicts would dissolve if the states scuttled their armaments.

. . . The new eastern European states did not possess sufficient unity among themselves. Nor was this lack of unity among them surprising, since they had developed in different directions as borderlands of the historic European community. For a time the Habsburg monarchy had bound the nationalities of the Danube basin together, and thus Austria had been a major force in the maintenance of a European order. But once the Turkish pressure subsided and democratic national movements raised their heads, the Habsburg empire was doomed. No doubt, the establishment of some sort of Danubian federation after 1919 would have been desirable for many reasons, but it alone would not have solved the decisive problems of security of the new eastern states. They could have found a solution only within a closely integrated European system, which the League of Nations and the European diplomacy of the interwar period failed to provide.

The fragile nature of the political conditions of Europe was further endangered by the pious hope that international disarmament by itself constituted a means for the creation of greater security. Large sections of the British people entertained this expectation with an almost religious fervor, and America gave their aspirations strong moral support. But in spite of the idealism of these sentiments, which deserved respect, they were utterly incapable of improving the actual political conditions of Europe. There disarmament could only mean the disarmament of the victors and new strength for Germany. In the absence of ready and fully equipped armed forces elsewhere, the superior industrial and manpower resources of Germany were bound to become even higher trumps than they were before. It would even have been preferable to raise the level of German armaments by international agreement, rather than demand the curtailment of the French army.

In most cases disarmament was claimed to be the cure of Europe's political ills by the very people who wanted all nations to accept the rule of international law. But they did not admit what is a truism in national life, that unenforceable law becomes a mockery of justice. Who was to protect the eastern states against Germany or against a revived Russia? Who was to defend western Europe, including the Lowlands and Great Britain, against the onrush of a remilitarized Germany, possibly abetted by Russia? Only one lonely European statesman warned the world that the French army was the single stabilizing factor in Europe and that "the sudden weakening of that factor of stability . . . might open floodgates of measureless consequences in Europe at the present time, might break the dyke and 'Let the boundless deep/Down upon far off cities while they dance—/or dream.'" [9]

But the British people were not inclined to listen to Winston Churchill in those years. From 1926 to 1934, first on the Preparatory Commission for

9. *House of Commons Debates,* June 29, 1931, col. 936, quoted in Jordan: *Great Britain, France, and the German Problem,* p. 162.

the Disarmament Conference, then at the Disarmament Conference itself, which started its sessions in Geneva in 1932, steady pressure was brought on France to decrease her armaments. Even after Hitler's accession to power, Ramsay MacDonald pushed a disarmament plan that would have equalized French and German armed strength. France in British eyes appeared petulant in her insistence upon a system of general security or at least upon international arms inspection as preconditions of a further reduction of armaments. The result of all the disarmament discussions in the interwar period was the further discredit of the peace settlement of 1919 and the psychological preparation of a large segment of world opinion for German rearmament.

Locarno did not lay a safe foundation of a lasting European peace, though it created, at least for a while, closer co-operation between Germany and the two western European powers. The personal relationship established between Sir Austen Chamberlain, Aristide Briand, and Gustav Stresemann gave Europe a kind of unofficial council that tended to stabilize the European scene in spite of continuous German desire for change. Besides, for the time being Germany was in no position to press her claims for revision at the expense of eastern countries. Nevertheless, Great Britain, though she had refused to guarantee the eastern states, feared eastern conflicts. Consequently, British diplomacy chose the easy course and backed the strongest power, France.[10] As late as 1931 British policy supported the French opposition to the Austro-German customs union. Once Germany had become stronger than France the eastern policies of Britain were to be reversed.

By hindsight it is easy to say that the years between 1925 and 1930 were the years in which Europe could have been reconstituted, not as an entirely self-contained political system, but as a strong powerblock in world politics if the beginnings of co-operation between Britain, France, and Germany had been carried to a full understanding on all the major issues of Europe. Such a firm understanding among the three powers could also have led to a common program for the strengthening of the eastern European states. Britain, however, was not willing to consider additional commitments in Europe. Perhaps Germany and France could have acted alone, disregarding the British sensitiveness to separate Franco-German co-operation;[11] but Germany felt that France would never voluntarily make those concessions that Germany considered her due and that France was aiming exclusively at bolstering the *status quo*. Briand's proposal for the formation of a European Federal Union, first broached in 1929, was too vague and did not contain special concessions that might have won over Germany. Britain poured cold water on the plan, while Germany at first took a reserved attitude. Later, in March, 1931, the German Government used the idea of a European federation as a cloak for the Austro-German customs union, judged by France to be a unilateral revision of the Paris

10. Cf. A. Wolfers: *Britain and France between Two Wars* (New York: 1940), pp. 265 ff.

11. Jordan: *Great Britain, France, and the German Problem*, p. 199.

settlement rather than a step in the direction of a European federation. By then the chance for real understanding was gone.

The five years after 1925 gave Europe a last Indian summer before the blizzard of the world economic crisis struck in 1931. Nobody foresaw that Europe, politically and economically, lived on borrowed time. Once confidence had been restored, Europe showed her vigor. By 1925 most nations of Europe had achieved their prewar production levels, and in the subsequent five years the expansion of European production proceeded at a faster rate than that of American production during the boom period. Most startling was Germany's progress. In 1919 her industrial production was only one third of what it had been in 1913. By 1922 a considerable recovery had taken place in spite of the instability of the German currency, which was not the result of German reparation payments, as is so often asserted, but of the inability of the German Republic to put its finances in order. The decision to meet the French invasion of the Ruhr by passive resistance and to cover the bill by the printing of money led to the German hyper-inflation that was stopped only at the end of 1923,[12] and in that year German industrial production fell again to 40 per cent of the 1913 figure. But in 1924 Germany doubled her output, and by 1927 she had reached her prewar position and resumed her place as the chief industrial country of Europe.

Another aspect of these five years was the ease with which Europe as a whole rebuilt her trading position, even though, while Europe had been at war, the overseas countries, primarily the United States but also other nations such as Japan, had greatly expanded their productive capacity. Higher world production seemed to find a greater world market. It was not recognized that the market conditions were largely the result of the credit expansion caused by American capital looking for profitable investment. The foreign capital issues publicly offered in the United States between 1920 and 1931 amounted to 11.6 billion dollars, of which Europe received 40 per cent, Canada almost 29, and Latin America 22 per cent.[13] In Europe, American capital was augmented by British, Swiss, and Dutch funds. Germany in the six years between 1924 and 1929 received from all these countries more than 4 billion dollars, about half of these funds coming from the United States and constituting a greater grant of foreign funds than the rest of the world received in those years.

The economic expansion of credit thus made it possible to postpone the adjustment to the structural changes of the world economy produced by the war. For the same reason a realistic financial settlement of the World War could be delayed for many years. The Dawes Plan of 1924 had set up a payment schedule of German reparations without, however, revising the original total sum demanded by the Allies in 1921. The stillborn Young Plan of 1929, announced as the final reparation settlement on the eve of the big crash, once again evaded the most fundamental political problems. Germany, beginning in 1926, paid 10,333 million German marks as repara-

12. Cf. C. Bresciani-Turroni: *The Economics of Inflation* (London: 1937), p. 93.
13. J. B. Condliffe: *The Commerce of Nations* (New York: 1950), p. 447.

tions, which was a little less than two and a half billion dollars. But the transfer of German funds could not have been made if private American loans had not gone to Germany at the same time. The Allies in turn used these sums to service their American loans or war debts. Winston Churchill called this system "insane." [14]

Once the bubble burst and it dawned upon the world that there had been general overproduction and overinvestment, the American Government preferred virtually to stop all intergovernmental debts, reparations, and inter-Allied obligations in order to save the American private loans that more directly affected the American banking situation. President Hoover proposed in 1931 a holiday of reparation and inter-Allied debt payments. In 1932 at the Conference of Lausanne reparations were actually buried.[15] But at that time Germany was already determined not only to demand a radical revision of the Paris settlement in her favor but to force a full reversal of the historic decisions of World War I.

3. *A. J. P. Taylor: The Origins of the Second World War*

A. J. P. Taylor is a historian whose output of scholarly works is extraordinary. He also finds the time to appear on the BBC, to give newspaper interviews, and to write popular articles and book reviews for the mass circulation press. One of his most widely discussed books is *The Origins of the Second World War*, which caused considerable controversy because of its discussion of Adolf Hitler's planning—or lack of planning—for war. In the passages quoted below, however, Taylor deals with an earlier phase of the "German problem." Does his interpretation differ significantly from Holborn's? Is he more optimistic about the chances that existed for the establishment of a permanent peace? Does Taylor play favorites among the statesmen of the time?

The history of Europe between the wars revolved round "the German problem." If this were settled, everything would be settled; if it remained unsolved, Europe would not know peace. All other problems lost their sting or were trivial in comparison. The Bolshevik peril, for example —never as acute as people thought—ended abruptly when the Red armies were thrown back from Warsaw in August 1920; from that moment there was not the slightest prospect, during the next twenty years, that Communism would triumph anywhere in Europe beyond the Russian frontiers.

14. W. S. Churchill: *The Second World War: The Gathering Storm*, Vol. I (Boston: 1948), p. 9.

15. Cf. J. W. Wheeler-Bennett: *The Wreck of Reparations* (New York: 1933); also C. R. S. Harris: *Germany's Foreign Indebtedness* (London: 1935).

From A. J. P. Taylor, *The Origins of the Second World War* (New York: Atheneum, 1961), pp. 40–58. Footnotes omitted. Copyright © 1961 by A. J. P. Taylor. Reprinted by permission of Atheneum Publishers and Hamish Hamilton, Ltd.

Again, Hungarian "revisionism" made much noise during the nineteen-twenties—more noise indeed than German revisionism from a territorial point of view. It did not raise more than a shadow even of local war, never a shadow of general upheaval. Italy, too, bickered with Yugoslavia over Adriatic questions; and later claimed to be an unsatisfied "have-not" nation. The most Italy could do was to hit the headlines, not raise an alarm. The German problem stood alone. This was new. The problem of German strength had existed before 1914, although not fully recognised; but there had been other problems—Russia's desire for Constantinople; French desire for Alsace-Lorraine; Italian irredentism; the South Slav problem within Austria-Hungary; the endless troubles in the Balkans. Now there was nothing of any moment except the position of Germany.

There was a second difference of great significance. Before 1914 the relations of the Great European Powers had often been shaped by questions outside Europe—Persia, Egypt, Morocco, tropical Africa, Turkey-in-Asia, and the Far East. Some good judges believed, though wrongly, that European questions had lost their vitality. H. N. Brailsford, an intelligent and well-informed observer, wrote early in 1914: "The dangers which forced our ancestors into European coalitions and Continental wars have gone never to return. . . . It is certain as anything in politics can be, that the frontiers of our modern national states are finally drawn." The exact opposite proved to be the case. Europe was turned upside down and then continued to harass statesmen. Not a single one of the problems outside Europe which had raised difficulties before 1914 caused a serious crisis among the European powers between the wars. No one could really suppose, for example, that Great Britain and France would go to war over Syria, as they might once have done over Egypt. The only exception was the Abyssinian affair of 1935, but this concerned European politics in the shape of the League of Nations; it was not a conflict over Africa. There was another apparent exception: the Far East. This caused grave difficulties in international affairs, but Great Britain was the only European power on whom it had practical impact.

This, too, was new. Great Britain was now the only world power in Europe. Before 1914, too, she had been a world power of the first rank. But Russia, Germany, and France also counted for much in "the age of imperialism." Now Russia was outside Europe and in alliance with the anti-European revolt of the colonial peoples. Germany had lost her colonies and had relinquished her Imperial ambitions at any rate for the time being. France, though still a colonial power, was obsessed with European difficulties and let her Empire take second place in disputes with others, including of course the British. The Far East showed how things had changed. Before 1914 there had been a balance there, quite as complicated as the balance in Europe. Japan had had to reckon with Russia, Germany, and France as well as with Great Britain; and the British could safely go sometimes with Japan, sometimes against her. The United States had an active policy in the Far East for a few years after the war, but it was short indeed. By the time of the Manchurian crisis of 1931, Great Britain faced Japan in the Far

East virtually alone. It is easy to understand why the British felt distinct from the Powers of Europe and why they often wanted to withdraw from European politics. . . .

By 1921 much of the peace-treaty was being enforced. It was reasonable to assume that it would gradually lose its contentious character. Men cannot go on wrangling over a settled question year after year, however embittered they may feel at first. The French forgot Waterloo; they even tended to forget Alsace and Lorraine, despite repeated resolves not to do so. The Germans, too, might have been expected to forget, or at any rate to acquiesce, after a time. The problem of German power would remain; but it would not be aggravated by an acute determination to destroy the settlement of 1919 at the first opportunity. The reverse happened: resentment against the treaty increased with every year. For one part of the treaty remained unsettled; and the disputes over this put the rest of the treaty in constant question. The unsettled issue was the payment of reparations—a striking example of good intentions, or to be correct, good ingenuity, gone wrong. In 1919 the French wished to lay down uncompromisingly the principle that Germany must pay the full bill for war damage—an indeterminate liability that would swell in the future with every step of German economic recovery. The Americans, more sensibly, proposed to state a fixed sum. Lloyd George appreciated that, in the heated atmosphere of 1919, this sum, too, would be far beyond German capacity. He hoped that in time men (himself included) would come to their senses: the Allies would make a reasonable demand, the Germans would make a reasonable offer, and the two figures would more or less coincide. He therefore swung round behind the French, though for exactly the opposite reason: they wanted to make the bill fantastically large, he wanted to scale it down. The Americans gave way. The peace treaty merely stated the principle of reparations; their amount was to be settled at some time in the future.

Lloyd George had meant to make reconciliation with Germany easier; he made it almost impossible. For the divergence between British and French views which had been covered over in 1919 rose again to the surface as soon as they tried to fix a figure: the French still trying to push it up, the British impatiently scaling it down. Nor did the Germans show any willingness to co-operate. Far from attempting to estimate their capacity to pay, they deliberately kept their economic affairs in confusion, well knowing that, if they once got things straight, the bill for reparations would follow. In 1920 there were angry meetings between the Allies, and then conference with the Germans; more conferences in 1921; still more in 1922. In 1923 the French tried to enforce payment by occupying the Ruhr. The Germans first answered with passive resistance; then surrendered at discretion, under the catastrophe of inflation. The French, almost as exhausted as the Germans, agreed to a compromise: the Dawes plan, drafted—largely at British prompting—under an American chairman. Though this temporary settlement was resented by both French and Germans, reparations were in fact paid for the next five years. Then there was another conference—more wrangling, more accusations, more demands, and more evasions. . . .

No doubt the Germans could have paid reparations, if they had regarded them as an obligation of honour, honestly incurred. In actual fact, as everyone now knows, Germany was a net gainer by the financial transactions of the nineteen-twenties: she borrowed far more from private American investors (and failed to pay back) than she paid in reparations. This was of course little consolation to the German taxpayer, who was not at all the same person as the German borrower. For that matter, reparations gave little consolation to the taxpayers of allied countries, who immediately saw the proceeds transferred to the United States in repayment of war debts. Setting one thing against another, the only economic effect of reparations was to give employment to a large number of bookkeepers. But the economic facts about reparations were of little importance. Reparations counted as a symbol. They created resentment, suspicion, and international hostility. More than anything else, they cleared the way for the second World war. . . .

Reparations had also a critical influence on the relations between France and Great Britain. In the last days of the war, the British—both politicians and public—had shared the French enthusiasm for reparations. It was a British statesman of high competence, not a Frenchman, who proposed to squeeze the German orange till the pips squeaked; and even Lloyd George had been more clamorous for reparations than he subsequently liked to imagine. Soon however the British changed round. They began to denounce the folly of reparations once they had themselves carried off the German merchant navy. Perhaps they were influenced by the writings of Keynes. Their more practical motive was to restore the economic life of Europe so as to promote the recovery of their own export industries. They listened readily to the German stories of the endless woes which would follow the payment of reparations; and, once they had condemned reparations, they soon condemned other clauses of the peace treaty. Reparations were wicked. Therefore the disarmament of Germany was wicked; the frontier with Poland was wicked; the new national states were wicked. And not only wicked: they were a justified German grievance, and the Germans would be neither content nor prosperous until they were undone. The British grew indignant at French logic, at French anxiety about German recovery, and particularly indignant to French insistence that treaties should be honoured once they had been signed. French claims to reparations were pernicious and dangerous nonsense; therefore their claim for security was pernicious and dangerous nonsense also. The British had some plausible ground for complaint. In 1931 they were forced off the gold-standard. The French, who had claimed to be ruined by the war, had a stable currency and the largest gold-reserve in Europe. It was a bad beginning for the years of danger. The disagreements over reparations in the years after the first World war made it almost impossible for the British and French to agree over security in the years before the second.

The most catastrophic effect of reparations was on the Germans themselves. Of course they would have been aggrieved in any case. They had not only lost the war. They had lost territory; they had been compelled to disarm; they had been saddled with a war-guilt which they did not feel.

But these were intellectual grievances: things to grumble over in the evenings, not the cause of sufferings in everyday life. Reparations hit every German, or seemed to, at each moment of his existence. . . .

Once men reject a treaty, they cannot be expected to remember precisely which clause they rejected. The Germans began with the more or less rational belief that they were being ruined by reparations. They soon proceeded to the less rational belief that they were being ruined by the peace treaty as a whole. Finally, retracing their steps, they concluded that they were being ruined by clauses of the treaty which had nothing to do with reparations. German disarmament, for instance, may have been humiliating; it may have exposed Germany to invasion by Poland or France. But economically it was to the good so far as it had any effect at all. This is not what the ordinary German felt. He assumed that, since reparations made him poor, disarmament did also. It was the same with the territorial clauses of the treaty. There were defects, of course, in the settlement. The eastern frontier put too many Germans in Poland—though it also put too many Poles in Germany. It could have been improved by some redrawing and by an exchange of populations—an expedient not contemplated in those civilised days. But an impartial judge, if such existed, would have found little fault with the territorial settlement once the principle of national states was accepted. The so-called Polish corridor was inhabited predominantly by Poles; and the arrangements for free railway-communication with East Prussia were adequate. Danzig would actually have been better off economically if it had been included in Poland. As to the former German colonies—also a fertile cause of grievance—they had always been an expense, not a source of profit.

All this was lost sight of, thanks to the link between reparations and the rest of the treaty. The German believed that he was ill-dressed, hungry, or out-of-work, because Danzig was a Free City; because the corridor cut off East Prussia from the Reich; or because Germany had no colonies. Even the highly intelligent banker Schacht attributed Germany's financial difficulties to the loss of her colonies—a view which he continued to hold, sincerely no doubt, even after the second World war. The Germans were not being self-centered or uniquely stupid in holding such views. This outlook was shared by enlightened liberal Englishmen such as Keynes; by nearly all the leaders of the British Labour party; and by all Americans who thought about European affairs. Yet it is difficult to see why the loss of colonies and land in Europe should have crippled Germany economically. After the second World war Germany had much greater territorial losses, yet became more prosperous than at any time in her history. There could be no clearer demonstration that the economic difficulties of Germany between the wars were due to defects in her domestic policy, not to unjust frontiers. The demonstration has been in vain; every textbook continues to attribute Germany's difficulties to the treaty of Versailles. The myth went further, and still does. First, the economic problems of Germany were blamed on the treaty. Then it was observed that these problems continued. From this it was held to follow that nothing was done to conciliate Germany or to modify the system set up in 1919. "Appeasement" was supposed to have been attempted only in 1938; and by then it was too late.

This is far from the truth. Even reparations were constantly revised, and always downwards; though no doubt the revision dragged out tiresomely long. In other ways appeasement was attempted sooner, and with success. Lloyd George made the first attempt. Emerging with difficulty from the morass of reparations, he resolved to summon a new, and more genuine, peace conference, which should be attended by everyone, by the United States, by Germany, by Soviet Russia, as well as by the Allies. A fresh start should be made on creating a better world. Lloyd George's initiative was seconded by Briand, then French premier—another political wizard, who could conjure problems out of existence. The partnership had an abrupt end. In January 1922 Briand was defeated in the French Chamber— ostensibly for having taken a lesson in golf from Lloyd George, actually because he was "weakening" over the peace treaty. Poincaré, his succes- sor, was unmoved by a British offer to guarantee France's eastern fron- tier; and a French representative attended the conference, which met at Genoa in April 1922, only to insist on the payment of reparations. The Americans refused to attend.

The Russians and Germans attended, but with the not unjustified suspi- cion that they were to be played off one against the other. The Germans were to be invited to join in exploiting Russia; the Russians were to be urged to claim reparations from Germany. Instead the representatives of the two countries met secretly at Rapallo and agreed not to work against each other. The treaty of Rapallo wrecked the Genoa conference, and ac- quired great notoriety in the world. At the time, the Bolsheviks were re- garded as outcasts, and it was therefore counted great wickedness in the Germans to conclude a treaty with them. Later on, when the Germans be- came the cause of offence, the moral obliquity of Rapallo was chalked up against the Russians.

In fact the treaty of Rapallo was a modest, negative affair. It is true that it prevented a European coalition for a new war of intervention against Russia; it is also true that it prevented any revival of the old Triple En- tente. Neither of these was a practical proposition in any case; and the treaty did no more than record the fact. But there was equally little chance of active co-operation between the two signatories. Neither was in a posi- tion to challenge the peace-settlement; both asked no more than to be left alone. The Germans thereafter provided Soviet Russia with a certain amount of economic assistance, though—absurdly enough—the Americans, who did not recognise Soviet Russia at all, provided more. The Russians enabled the Germans to evade the restrictions of the treaty of Versailles (to which after all the Russians were not a party) by setting up gas schools and flying schools on Soviet territory. These were trivialities. There was no sincerity in German-Soviet friendship; and both sides knew it. The Ger- man generals and conservatives, who promoted the friendship, despised the Bolsheviks; and they in their turn were friendly with Germany only ac- cording to the Leninist maxim of taking a man by the hand, preparatory to taking him by the throat. Rapallo gave a warning that it was easy for Russia and Germany to be friendly on negative terms, whereas the Allies would have to pay a high price for the friendship of either. But it was a warning which took effect in a comparatively distant future.

The conference of Genoa was Lloyd George's last creative effort. His position as the sporadically enlightened leader of an obscurantist coalition made it impossible for him to achieve any striking result. In the autumn of 1922 he fell from power. The Conservative government under Bonar Law which succeeded him was impatiently sceptical of European affairs. The way was clear for Poincaré, then French premier, to attempt the enforcement of reparations by occupying the Ruhr. This was the one break in the record of appeasement; and it was a break of a limited kind. Whatever secret hopes some Frenchmen might have that Germany would disintegrate, the sole purpose of the occupation was to get an offer of reparations from the Germans; and it had to be ended as soon as an offer was made. The occupation had a terrible effect on the French franc. Poincaré may have thought at the outset that France could act independently. By the end of 1923 he was as convinced as Clemenceau had been that the prime necessity for France was to be on close terms with England and America. The French voter passed his own verdict on the affair in 1924 by returning a Left coalition hostile to Poincaré. The occupation of the Ruhr provided, in the long run, the strongest argument in favour of appeasement. For how did it end? In fresh negotiations with Germany. It gave a renewed, and more powerful, demonstration that the treaty of Versailles could be carried out only with the co-operation of the German government; in that case more was to be gained by conciliation than by threats. The argument was not only effective in the present; it went on being effective in the future. When Germany began to disregard the conditions of the treaty on a more massive scale, men—particularly Frenchmen—looked back to the occupation of the Ruhr, and asked: what would be gained by the use of force? Only new German promises to fulfil the promises which they are now breaking. The cost would be ruinous; the result negligible. Security could be regained only by winning the Germans over, not by threatening them.

It would be wrong to suggest that the occupation of the Ruhr was without effect on Germany. Though it taught the French the folly of coercion, it also taught the Germans the folly of resistance. The occupation ended with a surrender by Germany, not by France. Stresemann came to power with the avowed policy of fulfilling the treaty. Of course this did not mean that he accepted the French interpretation of the treaty or that he would acquiesce in the French demands. It meant only that he would defend German interests by negotiations, not by resistance. Stresemann was as determined as the most extreme nationalist to get rid of the whole treaty lock, stock, and barrel: reparations, German disarmament, the occupation of the Rhineland, and the frontier with Poland. But he intended to do this by the persistent pressure of events, not by threats, still less by war. Where other Germans insisted that revision of the treaty was necessary for the revival of German power, Stresemann believed that the revival of German power would inevitably lead to revision of the treaty. There was a great outcry in allied countries against Stresemann after his death when the publication of his papers revealed clearly his intention to destroy the existing treaty-settlement. The outcry was grotesquely unjustified. Given a great Germany—and the Allies had themselves given it by their actions at the end of the war—it was inconceivable that any German could accept the treaty of Versailles as a permanent settlement. The only question was whether the settlement would be revised, and Germany become again the greatest Power in Europe, peacefully or by war. Stresemann wanted to do it peacefully. He thought this the safer, the more certain, and the more lasting way to German predominance. He had been a bellicose nationalist during the war; and even now was no more inclined to peace from moral principle than Bismarck had been. But, like Bismarck, he believed that peace was in Germany's interest; and this belief entitles him to rank with Bismarck as a great German, even as a great European, statesman. Maybe even as a greater. His task was certainly more difficult. For Bismarck had only to maintain an existing settlement; Stresemann had to work towards a new one. It is the measure of his success that, while he lived, Europe moved towards peace and treaty revision at the same time.

This achievement was not due to Stresemann alone. Allied statesmen also contributed their part, foremost among them Ramsay MacDonald, who came to power in 1924; and thereafter, whether in or out of office, set his mark on British foreign policy for the next fifteen years. The MacDonald policy seemed to end in catastrophic failure with the outbreak of the second World war in 1939. His name is now despised; his very existence ignored. Yet MacDonald should be the patron-saint of every contemporary Western politician who favours co-operation with Germany. More than any other British statesman, MacDonald faced "the German problem" and attempted to solve it. Coercion was futile, as the occupation of the Ruhr had just shown. The alternative of bringing Russia back into Europe as a Great Power was ruled out on both sides during the nineteen-twenties, for good or ill. Only conciliation of Germany remained; and if conciliation were to be practised at all, it should be practised wholeheartedly. MacDonald did not ignore French anxieties. He met them more generously than any other British statesman had done or was to do. He assured Herriot in July 1924 that violation of the Treaty "would lead to the collapse of the permanent foundations on which rests the peace so painfully achieved"; and he promoted at the League of Nations the abortive Geneva Protocol, by which Great Britain, along with the other members of the League, guaranteed every frontier in Europe. But he was thus generous with the French because he thought that their anxieties had no real foundation. Even in August 1914 he had not believed that Germany was a dangerous and aggressive power, bent on the domination of Europe. He certainly did not believe it in 1924. Therefore the promises of the Protocol, which looked "Black . . . and big on paper," were in fact "a harmless drug to soothe nerves." Every problem could be solved by "the strenuous action of good-will." The important thing was to launch negotiations. If the

French could be lured into negotiating only by promises of security, then the promises should be given, much as a small child is lured into the sea by assurances that the water is warm. The child discovers that the assurances are false; but he gets used to the cold, and soon learns to swim. So it would be in international affairs. Once the French began to conciliate Germany, they would find the process less alarming than they imagined. British policy should urge the French to concede much, and the Germans to ask little. As MacDonald put it some years later: "Let them especially put their demands in such a way that Great Britain could say that she supported both sides."

MacDonald came just at the right time. The French were ready to disentangle themselves from the Ruhr by moderating their demand for reparations; the Germans were ready to make a serious offer on the other side. The temporary settlement of reparations by the Dawes plan, and the wider relaxation of temper between France and Germany which accompanied it, were essentially MacDonald's doing. The general election of November 1924 ended the Labour government; but, though MacDonald ceased to direct British foreign policy, he continued to shape it indirectly. The path of conciliation was, from the British point of view, too attractive to be abandoned by any British government. Austen Chamberlain, MacDonald's Conservative successor, specialised in loyalty (if only to atone for his father's activities in the other direction); and in his puzzled way would have liked to renew the offer of a direct alliance with France. British opinion —not Labour only, but Conservative also—was now resolutely against this. Stresemann suggested a way out: a pact of peace between France and Germany, guaranteed by Great Britain and Italy. This was wonderfully attractive to the British. A guarantee against an unnamed "aggressor" offered exactly the even-handed justice to which Grey had aspired before the war and which MacDonald preached now; yet the friends of France like Austen Chamberlain could console themselves that the only conceivable aggressor would be Germany—hence the Anglo-French alliance would be smuggled in unperceived. The proposal was also wonderfully attractive to the Italians who had been treated as poor relations ever since the war and now found themselves elevated to the British level as arbiters between France and Germany. The idea was less attractive to the French. Even though the Rhineland was to remain demilitarised, it would cease to provide France with an open door through which to threaten Germany, once it was placed under an Anglo-Italian guarantee.

But the French too had found the right statesman for the moment. In 1925 Briand returned as French foreign minister. He was a match for Stresemann in diplomatic skill, the equal of MacDonald in high-minded aspiration, and master of all in romantic utterance. Other French statesmen talked "hard" without meaning it. Briand talked "soft," and did not mean that either. The outcome of the Ruhr occupation had shown the futility of the hard way. Briand now had another chance to find security for France in a cloud of words. He deflated Stresemann's moral lead by proposing that Germany should promise to respect all her frontiers, east as well as west.

This was an impossible condition for the German government. Most Germans had acquiesced in the loss of Alsace and Lorraine; few of them even raised the question until after the defeat of France in 1940. The frontier with Poland was felt as a grievance by all Germans. It might be tolerated; it could not be confirmed. Stresemann stretched conciliation a long way, in German eyes, when he agreed to conclude treaties of arbitration with Poland and Czechoslovakia. Even so, he added that Germany intended to "revise" her frontiers with these two countries at some time in the future, though of course she would do it peacefully—a favourite phrase of statesmen who are not yet ready to go to war though perhaps, in Stresemann's case, sincere.

Here was a gaping hole in the system of security—an open repudiation by Stresemann of Germany's eastern frontiers. The British would not fill the gap. Austen Chamberlain spoke complacently of the Polish corridor "for which no British Government ever will or ever can risk the bones of a British grenadier." Briand provided an alternative solution. France reaffirmed her existing alliances with Czechoslovakia and Poland; and the signatories of Locarno agreed that French action under these alliances would not constitute aggression against Germany. In theory France thus remained free to go to the assistance of her Eastern allies across the demilitarised Rhineland without forfeiting British friendship. Her two contradictory systems of diplomacy were reconciled, at any rate on paper. Locarno enshrined the Western alliance with Great Britain, yet preserved the Eastern alliance with the two satellite-states at the same time.

Such was the treaty of Locarno, signed on 1 December 1925. It was the turning-point of the years between the wars. Its signature ended the first World war; its repudiation eleven years later marked the prelude to the second. If the object of an international agreement be to satisfy everyone, Locarno was a very good treaty indeed. It satisfied the two guarantor Powers. They had reconciled France and Germany and brought peace to Europe without incurring, as they supposed, anything beyond a moral obligation, a mere form of words. Neither Great Britain nor Italy ever made any preparations to fulfil their guarantee. How could they when the "aggressor" would not be known until the moment for decision arrived? The practical result of the treaty, odd and unforeseen, was to prevent any military co-operation between Great Britain and France so long as it remained in force. Yet Locarno also satisfied the French. Germany accepted the loss of Alsace and Lorraine; she agreed to keep the Rhineland demilitarised; Great Britain and Italy underwrote the German promise. Any French statesman of 1914 would have been bewildered with delight at such an achievement. At the same time the French were still free to operate their eastern alliances and to play a great part in Europe if they wished to do so. The Germans could be satisfied too. They were firmly protected against a new occupation of the Ruhr; they were treated as equals, not as the defeated enemy; and they kept the door open for a revision of their eastern frontier. A German statesman of 1919, or even of 1923, would have found no cause for complaint. Locarno was the greatest triumph of "appeasement." Lord Balfour called it rightly "the symbol and the cause of a great amelioration in the public feeling of Europe."

Locarno gave to Europe a period of peace and hope. Germany was admitted to the League of Nations, though after more delay than had been expected. Stresemann, Chamberlain, and Briand appeared regularly at the League Council. Geneva seemed to be the centre of a revived Europe: the Concert really in tune at last, and international affairs regulated by discussion instead of by the jangling of arms. No one in these years lamented the absence of Russia and the United States—affairs ran more smoothly without them. On the other hand, no one seriously proposed to turn the Europe of Geneva into either an anti-American or an anti-Soviet *bloc*. Far from wishing to be independent of the United States, the European countries were all busy borrowing American money. A few wild projectors talked of a European crusade against Communism; but there was nothing in it. Europeans had no desire to go on a crusade against anyone. Apart from this, the Germans wanted to keep friendship with Russia as a card in reserve, a form of reinsurance treaty which might some day be used against France's eastern alliances. Immediately after signing the treaty of Locarno, Stresemann renewed with the Russians the agreement made at Rapallo in 1922; and when Germany joined the League, Stresemann declared that she could not, in her disarmed state, participate in sanctions—a veiled assertion of neutrality towards Soviet Russia.

A graver flaw in the Locarno-Geneva system than the absence of the United States and Soviet Russia was the presence of Italy. She had been brought into the Locarno arrangement solely in order to reinforce the British appearance of impartiality. No one supposed at this time that Italy could really hold the balance between Germany and France. This did not matter while Locarno, like the League, rested on calculation and goodwill, not on direct force. Later, when circumstances grew harsher, the memory of Locarno helped to foster the delusion that Italy had real weight to throw into the scales; the Italian leaders themselves were the victims of this delusion. In the Locarno era Italy had a worse defect than lack of strength: she lacked moral standing. The Locarno Powers claimed to represent the great principles for which the war had been fought; and the League claimed to be an association of free peoples. No doubt there was something fraudulent in these claims. No country is ever as free or as high-principled as it makes out to be. But there was something genuine in the claims as well. The Great Britain of Baldwin and MacDonald; the Weimar republic in Germany; the Third republic in France were truly democratic countries, with freedom of expression, the rule of law, and good intentions towards others. They were entitled to claim that, grouped in the League, they offered the best hope for mankind; and that, broadly speaking, they offered a superior political and social order to that offered by Soviet Russia.

All this became a tawdry pretence when it was extended to the Italy of Mussolini. Fascism never possessed the ruthless drive, let alone the material strength, of National Socialism. Morally it was just as corrupting—or perhaps more so from its very dishonesty. Everything about Fascism was a fraud. The social peril from which it saved Italy was a fraud; the revolution by which it seized power was a fraud; the ability and policy of Mussolini were fraudulent. Fascist rule was corrupt, incompetent, empty; Mussolini himself a vain, blundering boaster without either ideas or aims. Fascist Italy lived in a state of illegality; and Fascist foreign policy repudiated from the outset the principles of Geneva. Yet Ramsay MacDonald wrote cordial letters to Mussolini—at the very moment of Matteoti's murder; Austen Chamberlain and Mussolini exchanged photographs; Winston Churchill extolled Mussolini as the savior of his country and a great European statesman. How could anyone believe in the sincerity of Western leaders when they flattered Mussolini in this way and accepted him as one of themselves? It is not surprising that the Russian Communists regarded the League and all its works as a capitalist conspiracy—though also not surprising that Soviet Russia and Fascist Italy early established and always maintained cordial international relations. Of course there is always some gap between theory and practice. It is disastrous for both rulers and ruled when the gap becomes too wide. The presence of Fascist Italy at Geneva, the actual presence of Mussolini at Locarno, were the extreme symbols of unreality in the democratic Europe of the League of Nations. The statesmen no longer believed their own phrases; and the peoples followed their example.

Though Stresemann and Briand were both in their different ways sincere, they did not carry their peoples with them; and each justified Locarno in his own country by contradictory arguments which were bound to end in disillusionment. Briand told the French that Locarno was a final settlement, barring the way against further concessions. Stresemann assured the Germans that the purpose of Locarno was to bring further concessions at an ever faster rate. Briand, the great rhetorician, hoped that a cloud of benevolent phrases would make the Germans forget their grievances. Stresemann, in his patient way, believed that the habit of concession would grow on the French with practice. Both men were disappointed; both were in sight of failure by the time they died. Further concessions were made, but always with ill-will. The Control Commission on German disarmament was withdrawn in 1927. Reparations were revised downwards by the Young plan in 1929, and external control of German finances was abandoned; the occupying forces left the Rhineland in 1930—five years ahead of time. Appeasement was not achieved. On the contrary German resentment was greater at the end than at the beginning. In 1924 German Nationalists sat in the Cabinet and helped to carry the Dawes plan; in 1929 the Young plan was carried only against fierce Nationalist opposition. Stresemann, who had put Germany back among the Great Powers, was harried into the grave.

The German resentment was partly a matter of calculation: the obvious way to obtain more concessions was to condemn each gain as not enough. The Germans had a plausible case. Locarno treated them as equals, freely negotiating an agreed treaty. What justification then could there be for preserving reparations or one-sided German disarmament? The French could think of no logical answer to this argument, yet knew that, if they accepted it, German predominance in Europe must follow. Most contemporaries blamed the French. Englishmen, particularly, agreed more and more with MacDonald that appeasement, once started, should be continued fast and whole-heartedly. Later on, men blamed the Germans for not accepting the defeat of 1918 as final. It is futile to suppose that more concessions, or fewer, would have made much difference. The conflict between France and Germany was bound to go on as long as the illusion persisted that Europe was still the centre of the world. France would seek to preserve the artificial securities of 1919; Germany would strive to restore the natural order of things. Rival states can be frightened into friendship only by the shadow of some greater danger; neither Soviet Russia nor the United States cast this shadow over the Europe of Stresemann and Briand.

4. *E. H. Carr: The Twenty Years' Crisis*

After the war a considerable amount of optimistic and utopian idealism was to be found in Europe; it may be that such idealism was necessary after so many years of horror. But collapsing idealism can also be very dangerous, and this is a central theme of E. H. Carr in the following selection. Carr, who is best known for his multivolume history of Bolshevik Russia, also provides in the selection a sensitive and perceptive account of the mood of Europe in the early 1920's, as well as a discussion of the ability of the nation-state to survive in a new environment. There is little doubt that "the collapse of the spacious conditions of nineteenth-century civilisation" left Europe with problems that are only partially solved today.

Periods of crisis have been common in history. The characteristic feature of the crisis of the twenty years between 1919 and 1939 was the abrupt descent from the visionary hopes of the first decade to the grim despair of the second, from a utopia which took little account of reality to a reality from which every element of utopia was rigourously excluded. The mirage of the nineteen-twenties was, as we now know, the belated reflexion of a century past beyond recall—the golden age of continuously expanding territories and markets, of a world policed by the self-assured and not too onerous British hegemony, of a coherent "Western" civilisation whose conflicts could be harmonised by a progressive extension of the area of common development and exploitation, of the easy assumptions that what was good for one was good for all and that what was economically right could not be morally wrong. The reality which had once given content to this

From E. H. Carr, *The Twenty Years' Crisis: An Introduction to the Study of International Relations* (New York: St. Martin's Press, 1958), pp. 224–32. Originally published in 1939. Reprinted by permission of St. Martin's Press and The Macmillan Company of Canada, Ltd.

utopia was already in decay before the nineteenth century had reached its end. The utopia of 1919 was hollow and without substance. It was without influence on the future because it no longer had any roots in the present.

The first and most obvious tragedy of this utopia was its ignominious collapse, and the despair which this collapse brought with it. "The European masses realised for the first time," said a writer before the second world war, "that existence in this society is governed not by rational and sensible, but by blind, irrational and demonic forces." It was no longer possible to rationalise international relations by pretending that what was good for Great Britain was also good for Yugoslavia and what was good for Germany was also good for Poland, so that international conflicts were merely the transient products of avoidable misunderstanding or curable ill-will. For more than a hundred years, the reality of conflict had been spirited out of sight by the political thinkers of Western civilisation. The men of the nineteen-thirties returned shocked and bewildered to the world of nature. The brutalities which, in the eighteenth and nineteenth centuries, were confined to dealings between civilised and uncivilised peoples were turned by civilised peoples against one another. The relation of totalitarianism to the crisis was clearly one not of cause, but of effect. Totalitarianism was not the disease, but one of the symptoms. Wherever the crisis raged, traces of this symptom could be found.

The second tragedy of the collapse of utopia, which proceeded from the first and further intensified it, was of a subtler kind. In the latter half of the nineteenth century, when the harmony of interests was already threatened by conflicts of increasing gravity, the rationality of the world was saved by a good stiff dose of Darwinism. The reality of conflict was admitted. But since conflict ended in the victory of the stronger, and the victory of the stronger was a condition of progress, honour was saved at the expense of the unfit. After 1919 only Fascists and Nazis clung openly to this outmoded device for rationalising and moralising international relations. But the Western countries resorted to an equally dubious and disastrous expedient. Smitten by the bankruptcy of the harmony of interests, and shocked by its Darwinian deviation, they attempted to build up a new international morality on the foundation, not of the right of the stronger, but of the right of those in possession. Like all utopias which are institutionalised, this utopia became the tool of vested interests and was perverted into a bulwark of the *status quo*. It is a moot point whether the politicians and publicists of the satisfied Powers, who attempted to identify international morality with security, law and order and other time-honoured slogans of privileged groups, do not bear their share of responsibility for the disaster as well as the politicians and publicists of the dissatisfied Powers, who brutally denied the validity of an international morality so constituted. Both these attempts to moralise international relations necessarily failed. We can accept neither the Darwinian doctrine, which identifies the good of the whole with the good of the fittest and contemplates without repugnance the elimination of the unfit, nor the doctrine of a natural harmony of interests which has lost such foundation in reality as it once had, and which inevitably becomes a cloak for the vested interests of the privileged. Both these doctrines have become untenable as the basis of international morality. Their breakdown has left us with no ready solution of the problem of re-conciling the good of the nation with the good of the world community; and international morality is in the melting-pot. . . .

The French Revolution, which inaugurated the period of history now drawing to its close, raised the issue of the rights of man. Its demand for equality was a demand for equality between individuals. In the nineteenth century, this demand was transformed into a demand for equality between social groups. Marx was right in perceiving that the individual in isolation could not be the effective unit in the struggle for human rights and human equality. But he was wrong in supposing that the ultimate unit was the so-cial class, and in discounting the cohesive and comprehensive qualities of the national unit. The great European figures of the later nineteenth cen-tury were Disraeli and Bismarck, who strove to weld together the "two na-tions" into one through the agencies of the social service state, popular ed-ucation and imperialism, refuted the taunt that "the worker has no country," and paved the way for "national labour," "national socialism" and even "national communism." Before 1914 the demand for equality was already beginning in Western Europe to pass over from the issue of equal-ity between classes to that of equality between nations. Italian writers had described Italy as a "proletarian" nation, using the term in the sense of "under-privileged." Germany demanded equality in the form of her place in the sun, which must, as Bernhardi said, be "fought for and won against a superior force of hostile interests and powers." In France, socialist and ex-socialist ministers appealed for industrial peace in the interests of na-tional unity. Imperceptibly the struggle between classes was coming to seem, even to the workers themselves, less important than the struggle be-tween nations. And the struggle for equality became, in accordance with the ordinary laws of political power, indistinguishable from the struggle for predominance.

This then is the basic reason for the overwhelming importance of inter-national politics after 1919. The conflict between privileged and unprivi-leged, between the champions of an existing order and the revolutionaries, which was fought out in the nineteenth century within the national com-munities of Western Europe, was transferred by the twentieth century to the international community. The nation became, more than ever before, the supreme unit round which centre human demands for equality and human ambitions for predominance. Everywhere in Europe, national gov-ernments and one-party states made their appearance; and where party is-sues survived, they were thought of as something outmoded and deplorable —a blot on national unity which cried out to be erased. The inequality which threatened a world upheaval was not inequality between individu-als, nor inequality between classes, but inequality between nations. "Just as inequality of wealth and opportunity between the classes often led to revo-lutions," said Mussolini, "so similar inequality between the nations is calcu-lated, if not peaceably adjusted, to lead to explosions of a much graver

character." The new harmony which was required was not (as the philosophers of *laissez-faire* assumed) a harmony between individuals, and not (as
Marx assumed when he denied the possibility of its realisation) a harmony
between classes, but a harmony between nations. To-day we need not
make the mistake, which Marx made about the social class, of treating the
nation as the ultimate group unit of human society. We need not pause to
argue whether it is the best or the worst kind of unit to serve as the focus
of political power. But we are bound to ask ourselves whether, and if so by
what, it is likely to be superseded. Speculation on this subject falls naturally into two questions:

(*a*) Are the largest and most comprehensive units of political power in the
world necessarily of a territorial character?
(*b*) If so, will they continue to take approximately the form of the contemporary nation-state?

The question whether the largest and most comprehensive power units
must necessarily be territorial cannot receive a dogmatic answer applicable
to all periods of history. At present, such units have a distinctively territorial form. It is easy to read past history as a gradual development leading up, with occasional relapses, to this consummation; and political power
is probably never, even in the most primitive societies, entirely divorced
from the possession of territory. Yet in many periods of history, of which
the mediaeval is the most recent, power has been based ostensibly—and in
part, really—on grounds other than those of territorial sovereignty. It was
acceptance of the principle *cuius regio eius religio* which substituted the
unit based on domicile for the unit based on religious allegiance, and
thereby laid the foundation of the modern nation-state. In no previous period of modern history have frontiers been so rigidly demarcated, or their
character as barriers so ruthlessly enforced, as to-day; and in no period, as
we have already seen, has it been apparently so impossible to organise and
maintain any international form of power. Modern technique, military and
economic, seems to have indissolubly welded together power and territory.
It is difficult for contemporary man even to imagine a world in which political power would be organised on a basis not of territory, but of race,
creed or class. Yet the enduring appeal of ideologies which transcend the
limits of existing political units cannot be ignored. Few things are permanent in history; and it would be rash to assume that the territorial unit of
power is one of them. Its abandonment in favour of some other form of organised group power would, however, be so revolutionary that little that
holds true of international politics in the present period would apply to the
new dispensation. International relations would be supplanted by a new
set of group relationships.

The question whether the territorial units of the future are likely to retain approximately their present form is one of more immediate practical
importance. The problem of the optimum size of units—whether units of
industrial or agricultural production or units of political and economic
power—is one of the most puzzling and important of the present time; and

the near future may well see striking developments. In the field of political power, two contrary tendencies may be observed.

In one direction, there is a clearly marked trend towards integration and the formation of ever larger political and economic units. This trend set in in the latter part of the nineteenth century, and appears to have been closely connected with the growth of large-scale capitalism and industrialism, as well as with the improvement of means of communication and of the technical instruments of power. The first world war threw this development into conspicuous relief.

Sovereignty, that is freedom to make decisions of wide historical importance [wrote Naumann in his famous book published in 1915], is now concentrated at a very few places on the globe. The day is still distant when there shall be "one fold, one shepherd," but the days are past when shepherds without number, lesser or greater, drove their flocks unrestrained over the pastures of Europe. The spirit of large-scale industry and of super-national organisation has seized politics. . . . This is in conformity with centralised military technique.

The interlude of 1918, when nationalism momentarily resumed its disintegrating role, proved—at any rate in Europe—a dangerous fiasco. The multiplication of economic units added disastrously to the problems of the post-war period. Naumann with his *Mittel-Europa* proved a surer prophet than Woodrow Wilson with his principle of self-determination. The victors of 1918 "lost the peace" in Central Europe because they continued to pursue a principle of political and economic disintegration in an age which called for larger and larger units. The process of concentration still continued. The more autarky is regarded as the goal, the larger the units must become. The United States strengthened their hold over the American Continents. Great Britain created a "sterling *bloc*" and laid the foundations of a closed economic system. Germany reconstituted *Mittel-Europa* and pressed forward into the Balkans. Soviet Russia developed its vast territories into a compact unit of industrial and agricultural production. Japan attempted the creation of a new unit of "Eastern Asia" under Japanese domination. Such was the trend towards the concentration of political and economic power in the hands of six or seven highly organised units, round which lesser satellite units revolved without any appreciable independent motion of their own. On the other hand there is some evidence that, while technical, industrial and economic development within the last hundred years has dictated a progressive increase in the size of the effective political unit, there may be a size which cannot be exceeded without provoking a recrudescence of disintegrating tendencies. If any such law is at work, it is impossible to formulate it with any precision; and prolonged investigation would be necessary to throw any light on the conditions which govern the size of political and economic units. The issue is, however, perhaps likely to be more decisive than any other for the course of world history in the next few generations.

One prediction may be made with some confidence. The concept of sovereignty is likely to become in the future even more blurred and indistinct

than it is at present. The term was invented after the break-up of the mediaeval system to describe the independent character of the authority
claimed and exercised by states which no longer recognised even the formal overlordship of the Empire. It was never more than a convenient
label; and when distinctions began to be made between political, legal and
economic sovereignty or between internal and external sovereignty, it was
clear that the label had ceased to perform its proper function as a distinguishing mark for a single category of phenomena. . . . It is unlikely that
the future units of power will take much account of formal sovereignty.
There is no reason why each unit should not consist of groups of several
formally sovereign states so long as the effective (but not necessarily the
nominal) authority is exercised from a single centre. The effective group
unit of the future will in all probability not be the unit formally recognised
as such by international law. Any project of an international order which
takes these formal units as its basis seems likely to prove unreal.

It may be well to add at this point that group units in some form will
certainly survive as repositories of political power, whatever form these
units may take. Nationalism was one of the forces by which the seemingly
irreconcilable clash of interest between classes within the national community was reconciled. There is no corresponding force which can be invoked
to reconcile the now seemingly irreconcilable clash of interest between nations. It is profitless to imagine a hypothetical world in which men no
longer organise themselves in groups for purposes of conflict; and the conflict cannot once more be transferred to a wider and more comprehensive
field. As has often been observed, the international community cannot be organised against Mars. This is merely another aspect of the dilemma with
which the collapse of the spacious conditions of nineteenth-century civilisation has confronted us. It seems no longer possible to create an apparent
harmony of interests at the expense of somebody else. The conflict can no
longer be spirited away.

IV

The Great Depression: Its Impact on Europe

Periods of intense and long-sustained crisis—wars, plagues, and the like—leave a lasting scar on the generations that experience them. Some social scientists have even suggested that just as an individual may suffer severe traumatic effects from some shattering personal experience, so a whole society may reveal a kind of generalized trauma or mass psychosis in consequence of a severe social upheaval of long duration. "Psychohistory" has already begun to attract a few venturesome historians, eager to work on the frontiers of knowledge.

If there is any validity at all in the theory of mass psychosis (and so far it is largely speculative), perhaps the great depression of the 1930's ought to be subjected to the scrutiny of the psychohistorians. In the depth and breadth of its impact on political life, on social structures, on ideas and attitudes, it may rate alongside any of our great wars or revolutions.

One of the curious things about the great depression is the meagerness of the retrospective literature about it. On both world wars we have books by the thousand; on the depression, a mere handful. True, economists of the depression era did expend a good deal of time and energy in examining the causes of the crisis; according to one story (no doubt apocryphal), a compiler was able to list some four hundred different theories, ranging from faulty currency policies to the influence of sunspots. But there have been few attempts to study the episode in perspective, to weigh the rival theories about its origins, to isolate and then synthesize its short- and long-term consequences. Perhaps that is because economists, who are technically equipped to handle such subjects, prefer to deal with present rather than past problems, while historians, who ought to be interested, usually lack the requisite technical expertise.

In very recent years, however, the depression has begun to draw some expert scholarly attention. J. K. Galbraith led the way with his *The Great Crash, 1929* (1955), which focused on the American scene; a few British and continental scholars have followed. Even so, it remains difficult, if not impossible, to provide in a book of readings like this one an adequate sampling of views about the causes of the depression; the subject is too complex and too technical to be popularized easily, or to be grasped by students of history unless they possess a fairly sophisticated grounding in economic theory. Ideally, one would like to confront some of the big controversial issues: for example, was the depression the outgrowth of a misguided attempt by European and American statesmen of the 1920's to restore the nineteenth-century world? Or was that attempt a quite sensible one, a real possibility that failed through the technical errors of politicians and businessmen of the postwar decade? Was the economic breakdown in large part a delayed consequence of the disruptions produced by the Great War and an unwise peace settlement? Were the Europeans merely the hapless victims of American short-sightedness and speculative frenzy, culminating in the Wall Street crash of 1929?

Fortunately, the problems associated with the depression's impact on European politics and society are somewhat more manageable. Technical expertise in economics, while useful here, is not a *sine qua non;* individuals and groups respond to economic crisis even when they are not quite sure what has hit them, and students of history can examine those responses, whether they are rational or irrational. In the readings that follow, then, the emphasis will be on consequences— on different national responses to the crisis, and on long-term effects on western society.

1. *Goronwy Rees: The Great Slump*

By far the most thoughtful and readable survey of the great depression is that of the Welsh scholar and essayist Goronwy Rees. Educated at Oxford, Rees has had a varied career as university teacher, editor, and businessman. In the selection that follows, he re-creates the mood of Europe just before and during the slump, describes some of the various responses to the crisis, and attempts to assess the historical significance of the episode. Rees sees it as a unique phenomenon: "nothing quite like it ever happened before; nothing quite like it has ever happened since." And he suggests that the depression ought perhaps to be viewed as one phase of a longer, more complex crisis from which we have not yet escaped.

In the summer of 1929, while the Great Bull Market was making its last convulsive advances, there were already some indications that the long period of economic prosperity which had originally inspired it was beginning to come to an end. In Europe, moreover, there were signs that the period of political stability, which had been the condition of her economic recovery, was also drawing to a close; even so, there were few observers at the time who foresaw the terrible consequences which were to follow. In spite of the shadows which were already apparent, the summer of 1929 was the last time in which the capitalist world as a whole might reasonably look forward to the future without forebodings of war, revolution or economic collapse; it was the last time, perhaps, in which men and women in the western world could still hold to that belief in the inevitability of progress, and the rationality of the social and political order, to which most of them had subscribed since the eighteenth century.

In this sense, the summer of 1929 may be regarded as marking the end of an era, in a way in which even the summer of 1914 had not. The war in-

From Goronwy Rees, *The Great Slump: Capitalism in Crisis 1929–1933,* pp. 38–39, 190–93, 280–89. Copyright © 1970 by Goronwy Rees. Reprinted by permission of Harper & Row, Publishers, Inc.

deed had dealt a disastrous, perhaps an irreparable, blow to the fabric of western civilization and had released uncontrollable forces of violence and destruction. But when it was over it was still possible for people to believe that, with goodwill and mutual understanding, between nations and individuals, the damage could be repaired. One of the most widely read books of 1929 was Robert Graves's autobiography, *Goodbye to All That*. It was a marvellously vivid and lucid account of how one man had survived the appalling holocaust of 1914–18. It could be read without pain, and with a measure of hope, because it seemed, as its title indicated, a record of events which were already far off and long ago; it was still possible to believe that the experiences which Graves described were wholly exceptional, and that the world might still return, and to a large extent already had, to the condition for which President Harding had invented the word "normalcy," that is to say a state of affairs such as had obtained before the war ever happened. . . .

The fall of the pound [1931] might be taken as the turning point in the crisis of capitalism provoked by the depression, and it was perhaps appropriate that it should have had its origin in Britain, the country which had done most to promote and develop the capitalist system as it had existed up to that date. The essence of the system had been the international exchange of goods and services on the freest possible basis, and Britain had played the primary role in promoting this system because of her need for cheap food to feed her industrial population and for the raw materials required by her industries. The system had developed certain characteristic features which were all of British creation and these had acquired an almost religious significance for those who operated it; they were the *lares* and *penates* of the capitalist world, exercising as powerful an influence on the mind of the capitalist as on his pocket. Free trade was not only an economic but a moral principle, because it was ultimately dependent on the maintenance of peace and goodwill among nations. The Royal Navy was not merely an instrument of British foreign policy, as, for instance, the German Navy was the instrument of German foreign policy; it was also, or until recently had been, a guarantee that, whatever happened on land, the seas should be free to the ships of all nations. The pound sterling was not only a national currency, but an international currency, indeed *the* international currency which provided the means of exchange for a large proportion of the world's trade, and the operations of millions of individual traders throughout the world were dependent on its stability and reliability as a standard of value.

The Great War of 1914–18, and the growth of nationalism of which it was both an effect and a cause, had given a fatal shock to this system, and indeed Britain's own involvement in it was a contradiction of what had hitherto been her traditional policies. It left behind a Britain which had lost her industrial, naval and financial supremacy and could no longer afford, out of her own resources, to act as the guarantor of the system as a whole. Moreover, the war had raised political and commercial barriers between nations which dislocated the working of the system and had left behind a burden of inter-governmental debts too heavy for its financial structure to carry. The gold standard had been painfully restored, at great cost to some countries, including Britain; but its rules were more often broken than observed, in particular by the two countries, the United States and France, in whose vaults the larger part of the world's monetary gold was effectively sterilized.

Many efforts had been made to find alternatives which would compensate for the dominating part which Britain had previously played in the working of the system: in the League of Nations, in an elaborate network of treaties by which nations mutually guaranteed each other against the instincts of aggression which all of them shared, in naval limitation and attempts to reduce the burden of armaments, in central bank cooperation to apply an international credit policy, in the creation of a special institution, the Bank of International Settlements, to ease the problem of inter-governmental debts. Britain herself had tried to reassume her former role as an international lender by drawing on the unused resources of other countries, particularly France and the United States; indeed, the weakness of sterling was largely a reflection of her efforts to finance Germany and Central Europe through the depression.

All these efforts failed in their underlying purpose of trying to restore confidence and faith in the system as a "going concern" and of providing centres of resistance to the forces which were pulling it apart. For some years, during the boom of 1924 to 1928, it appeared that they might succeed but the depression itself was the best proof of their failure. No calamity of such intensity and duration had ever struck the system before; it was still possible to believe, like Brüning or Hoover, that one day it would stop of its own accord if only they could survive so long, but at the end of 1931 there was still little or no evidence that the end was yet in sight. The prudent view was that things would get worse before they got better, and in the meantime the only safe course was to find what shelter one could from the storm.

The prudent view was, in this case, the right one, though its consequences were something very different from that restoration of confidence for which statesmen had hoped. The kind of shelters in which men sought refuge from the storm were the best evidence of how far the system had lost its international character. Though nations might still pay lip service to, or even sincerely believe in, the ideal of free trade, in practice what they put their trust in henceforward were the restrictions and constraints of economic nationalism: in tariffs, exchange control, quotas, import prohibitions, trade agreements, anything indeed which might help to protect their own share of a steadily diminishing total of world trade or promote their own self-sufficiency. Such arrangements had existed even in the most flourishing periods of the system and indeed classical economic theory allowed for cases in which they might be justified. But they had been regarded as transitional and exceptional; now they became the rule and in doing so profoundly changed the nature of the capitalist system as a whole.

If internationalism had been its characteristic feature in its earlier phase of development, economic nationalism became its distinguishing mark in the period which followed Britain's abandonment of the gold standard, and nothing illustrated the change more strikingly than the adoption of protective tariff by Britain herself, for whom free trade had for a century been the essential condition of her prosperity. The change was all the more significant because economics embodied only one of the aspects in which the growing force of nationalism revealed itself; in the new phase of capitalist development economics became subordinated to politics to a degree which had never been known and in some cases became the instrument of nakedly aggressive forces.

For those to whom the virtues of capitalism had outbalanced its vices, the change which took place after 1931 seemed wholly deplorable and they continued to hope, against the evidence, for some relaxation of political and economic tensions which would allow it to recover its international character. To others, for whom the depression was sufficient proof that the classical model of capitalism had broken down, the nationalist economics of the thirties were welcome because they allowed nations a greater degree of control over their own economic development, insulated them against the impersonal forces of a free economic market, and gave the opportunity for increased direction and planning of their domestic economies. Planning indeed became a keyword of the new era, largely because men saw in it the means both of finding a way out of the depression and of preventing its recurrence.

Both views embodied their own kind of hope that the depression could be overcome and that capitalism could be made viable. Neither foresaw that the forces of nationalism, in which political and economic motives reinforced each other, had acquired a ferocity and violence which could no longer be contained within the existing system. In the summer of 1931, while the attention of the western world was absorbed by the financial crisis, an incident in the Far East, hardly noticed at the time, gave warning of even graver developments. On 17 August the Japanese War Office announced that a Japanese staff officer, Captain Nakamura, with three companions, had been arrested and murdered by local Chinese forces in Manchuria and that the Japanese Foreign Office had demanded an apology, an indemnity and the punishment of those responsible. The incident seemed of little importance compared with the events which were shaking the financial structure of the world. Yet in fact it had even more sinister implications. It was an announcement that in Asia also the effects of the depression had become intolerable and that Japan, its leading industrial nation, had forsaken the attempt to solve her economic problems by peaceful means and had chosen instead the path of territorial conquest. In a different, yet equally significant way from Britain's abandonment of the gold standard, this decision also foreshadowed the end of the post-war attempt to restore the capitalist system in its pre-war image. . . .

With Franklin Roosevelt in the White House in Washington and Adolf Hitler in the Reichschancery in Berlin, the acute phase of great economic depression was over. Not that historical events ever have quite so neatly and dramatically defined endings, or beginnings; yet the period from the Wall Street Crash in November 1929 to the triumph of National Socialism in Germany, and of the New Deal in the United States, at the beginning of 1933, has a character sufficiently its own, and sufficiently unlike what went before and came after, as to be regarded as a distinct, even a unique, historical phenomenon. Nothing quite like it ever happened before; nothing quite like it has ever happened since. It fixed a gulf between what went before and what came after, and in the ways in which western society observed and judged its own development; in some strange way, which we certainly cannot wholly explain or understand, like some seismological disturbance it shifted the ground on which men stood. And perhaps it is pardonable to take the date of Roosevelt's inauguration, even though it occurred in the middle of one of the most acute financial crises which America has ever experienced, as the end of the Great Slump. That particular emergency was quickly over, and within thirteen days the American banking system was functioning normally again; of far greater significance in the era which was about to open was America's abandonment of the gold standard. But just as the Wall Street crash can, with qualifications, be taken as the beginning of the depression, so, with similar qualifications, Roosevelt's inauguration can be taken as its close. For in a sense the depression, though world-wide in its effects, was a peculiarly American phenomenon, to which what happened elsewhere was subsidiary. The economic defeat which America suffered during the depression was as much a proof of its crucial importance in the development of western society as a whole as the political and industrial predominance which it established in the years that followed.

The effects of the depression, of course, continued to operate long after March 1933; so great a crisis could not be surmounted in a few days, or months, or even years. In some senses, indeed, one can say that even by 1939 it had not been wholly overcome, and unemployment in particular continued to be a heavy burden on the capitalist economy as a whole. But what can be said is that by March 1933 the upward movement of that economy had begun and has continued ever since without any break which can be compared with the depression of 1929–33. But what also can be said is that economic recovery was not associated, as many hoped and expected, with an improvement in political conditions. Rather, it went along with a progressive political deterioration, and increased political tension, and indeed the immense increase in armaments which it provoked, especially in Germany, made a large contribution to economic recovery. Indeed, since the depression economic prosperity has come to depend, to an increasing extent, upon the growth of a military-industrial nexus which is one of the dominating features of the modern world. Thus those who, during the depression, believed that a stabilization of political conditions and the revival of confidence which would ensue were an essential ingredient of recovery, were twice confounded; recovery took place in spite of increased political tension and political tension was a positive contribution to recovery.

Indeed, the association of economic recovery with political deterioration during the thirties makes it tempting to believe that the crisis which the western world experienced during the depression was not so much surmounted as translated into another, political, form; and that, in this respect, the depression itself was only one incident in, and an aspect of, a continuous process of which we have not yet seen the conclusion.

It would be equally tempting, therefore, to regard the great depression exclusively from an economic point of view, in abstraction from its social and political context: on the ground that, between 1929 and 1933, the capitalist crisis revealed itself, for the time being, primarily in economic terms, to which other aspects of it were merely subsidiary. Yet it would be difficult to do so without falsifying the complicated interaction between political, economic, social and psychological factors: most of all perhaps without ignoring the extent to which purely personal factors determined the course of events. There can be little doubt, for instance, that the pressure of unemployment was a determining, probably the determining cause of the collapse of the Weimar Republic and the triumph of National Socialism; whether it would have led to such a result in the absence of so extraordinary a political evil genius as Hitler is, to say the least of it, highly problematical. On the other hand, it seems certain that the depression would not have taken the course it did in the United States if there had existed there a leader with the same gift of crystallizing and giving a revolutionary direction to the enormous body of mass discontent, desperation and frustration which the depression had engendered.

The depression was not only a crisis which profoundly affected and changed the lives of ordinary men and women throughout the world, condemning millions of them to destitution, misery and despair; it was also a crisis of ideas which even today continues to affect men's attitudes to economic, social and political problems. To take only one, if the most significant, example: no government today would, or could, contemplate permitting mass unemployment on the scale on which it existed during the depression, and ever since the social and political policies of all governments have been largely dominated by the objective of preventing its repetition; to such an extent indeed that other objectives have come to be regarded as subsidiary, and in consequence to assume proportions which make them equally difficult to solve.

No doubt such an attitude largely derives from growing humanitarian awareness of the waste of human lives involved in mass unemployment on such a scale, of the measureless humiliation and degradation it imposes, and from a common consciousness that it represents an intolerable affront to human dignity and to even minimum standards of civilized life. Such feelings are themselves a legacy of the depression, which left an entire generation—both of those who suffered directly by it, and of those who witnessed and sympathized with their suffering—with a conviction that such a state of affairs is intolerable. They were intensified by the vast literature inspired by the depression during the thirties, which by depicting and analysing the evils of mass unemployment impressed them upon the imagination even of those who were never likely to share them.

The left-wing writers of the thirties, indeed, however confused and often plainly misled in their political objectives, performed in a different field the same kind of task as the anti-militarist writers of an earlier generation; that is to say, they tried to depict the realities of mass unemployment truthfully and imaginatively as others had tried to paint the disasters of war. They were so far successful as to stimulate a general reaction of *Never Again!* and this effect has endured, even unconsciously, when many of their works have lost much of their original literary and artistic value.

But if there were powerful humanitarian, emotional and imaginative factors at work in the widespread revulsion from the evils of mass unemployment, there was also in it an equally strong element of rational calculation. The depression did not only bring the conviction that unemployment was morally offensive; it also involved, in economic terms, a loss of effective demand, a factor of widespread under-consumption, which threatened to bring the whole process of production to a halt, and had, for a short time, threatened the death of society in the western world. In Germany, if society had not been destroyed, certainly civilization had been; over large areas of the United States it had seemed at moments to sober and objective observers that capitalism could not endure much longer unless it had more to offer to the poor and deprived; France, the strongest country in Europe, had, though belatedly, been reduced to a condition of endemic civil war that continued up to and beyond the Second World War; Japan had been driven to a course of aggression that had set the whole of the Far East ablaze and destroyed the entire post-war structure of collective security. An elementary sense of self-preservation warned even conservative defenders of the established order that it had come very near to the end of its tether during the depression.

But if the depression had given a warning of disaster, it had also placed in the hands of governments the weapons by which it could be averted, and the freedom to use them; only they were double-edged weapons which in warding off one form of danger could also provoke another. The depression had administered an almost fatal shock to the foundations of western society, already gravely weakened by the First World War. It had brought into contempt and derision an entire class which had been used to preside over its most secret and esoteric economic and financial rituals, and in so doing it had largely discredited the system of accepted ideas which gave them an intellectual and rational basis. Among those ideas were the classical economic doctrines, largely inherited from the nineteenth century, which exercised a profoundly inhibiting effect upon governments in any effort to control their economic destinies. They rested on a conception, which even at its most valid had only been an abstraction from the real world, of an international world order, largely self-governing and self-regulating, in which peaceful exchanges between nations was guaranteed by free trade; the stability of currencies and the exchanges between them by the gold standard; the continuous growth of the system as a whole by a continually increasing division of labour between nations; and the economic relationship between the poor and the advanced countries by foreign lending on a scale sufficient to keep their accounts in balance.

By 1929 these classical conditions of an efficient and smoothly operating economic order were as much honoured in the breach as in the observance; by 1933 they had lost almost all relevance to the world as it actually was. Yet throughout the depression they still represented the ideal to which it was generally accepted that the economic order should approximate as closely as possible; and post-war history up to 1929 had been very largely a record of a patient, arduous, and, as it seemed for a time, remarkably successful effort to restore these conditions or, where that was plainly impossible, to create as close a substitute for them as was attainable in a highly imperfect world.

The first and most important of these objectives was the restoration of the international gold standard, and the conditions under which it could operate successfully. Formally, great progress was made towards this end; the shattered economies of the defeated central powers were very largely restored, currencies stabilized, foreign lending resumed, normal political relationships established. But the essential condition of the pre-war international gold standard, the willingness to allow internal credit conditions, interest rates, price levels, to fluctuate with the movements of gold was never restored; in particular, after 1927, nearly two-thirds of the world's stock of monetary gold was sterilized in Fort Knox and the vaults of the Banque de France.[1]

This was to maintain the fiction of the gold standard while refusing to accept its reality; instead of an effectively operating system, it became a hallmark of monetary respectability. The depression put an end to this curious combination of fact and fiction, of myth and reality, which the international gold standard had become, and intensified all the forces of economic nationalism which were already inhibiting its efficient operation. Under its relentless pressure nations were forced to abandon the attempt to restore the pre-war system and to seek their own salvation by creating national economies which were only kept in relation with one another by an increasingly elaborate and artificial structure of currency regulations, exchange controls, tariffs, quotas, import controls and trading agreements. Even relapse into primitive conditions of barter was not excluded.

The new system, if it could be so called, which emerged during and out of the depression had many disadvantages compared with its predecessor, and totally lacked the classical simplicity and coherence of its theoretical superstructure; it was more like a Gothic cathedral than a Greek temple. But it gave governments a new freedom to plan and control their own economies; planning indeed became the central concept in economic policy in the years that followed. This was possible because the depression, by *force majeure* in most cases, released men from certain categories of economic thought which had begun to conflict increasingly with reality. This

1. Both the United States and France refused to permit the expansion of credit which would have been justified by the strength of their gold reserves.

was not achieved as a result of abstract theoretical analysis; it came rather out of desperation, and to attempt to construct some kind of working system out of the ruins left behind by the depression. But in most cases the attempt was only made when events had made no other alternative possible.

In observing the events of the depression one is often tempted to wonder at the kind of grim courage, or obstinacy, of a man like Brüning, in his effort to revive the German economy by repeated doses of deflation so savage that the patient nearly died of the cure; certainly the cure induced in him a kind of delirium in which anything, even a reversion to barbarism, seemed preferable to a continuation of the treatment. It is also tempting to wonder, as one might at someone in the grip of a delusional obsession, at President Hoover's continuing conviction that America's only way out of the depression was by the maintenance, or restoration, of the international gold standard, which had ceased to work in practice, and the rules of which the United States herself had long ceased to observe. With even greater astonishment one observes the total intellectual confusion of Ramsay MacDonald and the majority of his socialist colleagues when called upon to meet the financial crisis in Britain and their despairing acceptance of remedies for it which were in total contradiction with their sincerely held socialist convictions.

It is difficult today to remember that for those in authority, and with the responsibility for taking action, during the depression there was in the field of economics or finance no clear intellectual frame of reference by which to guide their policies than the one offered by the accepted doctrines of classical economic theory. Socialism indeed professed to offer an alternative; but it was one which implied the destruction of the capitalist system, and up to 1933 provided little practical guidance on how to preserve it. Certainly it offered little help to practical men faced with the kind of crises and emergencies repeatedly thrust upon them by the depression.

The Soviet Union indeed offered an example, revered by communists and radicals the world over, of what could be achieved by the total destruction of the capitalist system, and the substitution for it of one based on ruthlessly centralized planning. On some radicals, alienated intellectuals, and certain sections, which however never even approached a majority, of the working class, it exercised a powerful attraction, which led some individuals to a total commitment which sometimes had tragic results; it was during the depression that the seeds were sown of that total rejection of capitalism and all its works which led some intellectuals into the labyrinth of the communist underground from which they did not emerge, to the astonishment of the world, until nearly twenty years later. Yet in fact, during the depression the Soviet Union itself was passing through, for the most part unknown to its admirers, an acute economic and political crisis of its own, of a particularly gruesome kind, with consequences that were even worse than in the west; and in the Marxist-Leninist scheme of things there was embedded a principle of authoritarianism which made it, and continued to make it, unacceptable to western society as a whole as a solution to its own troubles, however acute. Indeed, one of the most striking features of the depression was the failure, or the refusal, of communism to derive any advantage out of the crisis which had shaken the capitalist world to its foundations.

It is true, of course, that within the capitalist system economic thought also developed its own critique of accepted doctrines and its own alternative proposals for an amelioration, or reconstruction, of an evidently defective economic system. Such criticisms and alternatives came both from academic economists, some of whom, as in the United States, had a direct and powerful influence on governmental policy, and, especially in the field of monetary theory, from a wide and varied range of cranks and eccentrics. In the last winter of the depression in the United States the ideas of a group at Columbia University called Technocracy, directed by Howard Scott, an engineer who had been a friend of Thorstein Veblen, suddenly commanded wide public attention, enjoyed a brief and spectacular vogue, and were as suddenly forgotten; and this was only one of the many unorthodox ideologies to which the depression gave rise. The great revolution in economic thought inaugurated by Maynard Keynes was yet to come; the *Treatise on Money* was published, though scarcely understood, in 1930, but the *General Theory of Employment, Interest and Money* did not appear till 1936 and what Professor Lekachman has called *The Age of Keynes*, in which his ideas had imposed a new orthodoxy, did not dawn until after the Second World War. During the depression itself there was no alternative school of economic thought which could in any way effectively challenge the authority of classical economic theory, and in obeying its precepts statesmen, financiers, administrators, were merely acting in accordance with what had come to be regarded as self-evident truths. To have acted otherwise, indeed, would have been to forfeit the confidence of those to whom society had entrusted control of the economic and financial system.

Indeed, even after the depression, and the lessons it had taught, the domination of men's minds by classical economic theory did not cease; and even today its assumptions still form an essential ingredient in the attitude of most ordinary men to economic problems. An example of how powerful they remained in the thirties is to be found in Lord Robbins's classical work, *The Great Depression*, in which the author formulated four essential conditions of recovery. They were:

1. A return of business confidence, which could only be secured by the stabilization of currencies and the foreign exchanges.
2. The restoration of the international gold standard.
3. The removal of barriers and impediments to international trade.
4. The elimination of all forms of inflexibility in the economic structure, including the inflexibility of wage rates maintained at an artificially high level by the trade unions.

In general there was also required "a more or less complete reversal of contemporary tendencies to governmental regulation of business enterprise."

It is probably sufficient to say that in fact recovery was achieved although none of these conditions were realized; and indeed there was no reversal of, but rather a progressive increase in, "contemporary tendencies to governmental regulation of enterprise," which has continued to the present time. Yet Lord Robbins's view would have recommended itself to the overwhelming majority of those in commanding positions in government, finance and industry during the depression.

It is difficult therefore to condemn them. Their fault, if it was a fault, was that they acted in accordance with the world's accepted wisdom, and as a result nearly all of them met with political defeat, or the loss of a prestige and reputation which once seemed unassailable. The consequences of their actions were tragic; but for the most part they seem today like men who, in the bewildering sequence of events which overtook them, fought an unidentifiable enemy with defective weapons, in a fog which was an emanation from their own minds. Most of all, in their inability to understand what was happening to themselves or to their fellow men, they impress upon us, in Oxenstierna's words, "the littleness of the wisdom with which the world is governed"; but since in this respect the world has not changed much since then, it is not for us to pass harsh judgment on them.

If one wished to, one might perhaps look to R. G. Hawtrey's view in *The Art of Central Banking:*

In 1930 and 1931 producers all over the world found demand dwindling relentlessly. In desperate efforts to keep going they cut prices deeper and deeper. Their frantic competition for such demand as remained may be compared with the desperate struggles of the prisoners in the Black Hole of Calcutta to save themselves from suffocation by getting near the two small windows which were the only means of ventilation.

It is said that it was only by inadvertence that Surajah Dowlah shut 146 prisoners in a cell 18 feet by 15 feet. He merely followed precedent in committing prisoners to the guard room. In their agonies the victims sought to bribe the guard to carry an appeal for mercy to Surajah Dowlah. But he was asleep and the guards dared not awake him. He was very like a central banker.

2. *Dieter Petzina: Germany and the Great Depression*

Nowhere in Europe was the impact of the depression more profound or more dramatic than in Germany. The boom years of the late 1920s had brought Germany an unprecedented prosperity, but it rested on precarious foundations. When foreign loans and foreign markets dried up, the impact was immediate. By 1932, one German worker out of three was unemployed. Chancellor Heinrich Brüning (1930–1932) fell back on classic remedies for the crisis; but belt-tightening proved more painful than effective. That German

Dieter Petzina, "Germany and the Great Depression," *Journal of Contemporary History,* IV (1969), 59–64, 71–74. Footnotes omitted. Reprinted by permission of George Weidenfeld & Nicolson Ltd.

voters turned in desperation to a self-proclaimed savior, a "terrible simplifier" (in Burckhardt's phrase) is hardly surprising. The German experience is analyzed by a young economic historian, Dieter Petzina, a staff member of the Institut für Zeitgeschichte in Munich.

The world-wide economic crisis of 1929–33 marked the decisive turning point of the inter-war period. More than any other event during the years between 1919 and 1939 it affected people's lives, shattered prevailing social structures and the stability of the European and North American industrial societies, and became the starting point for fundamental political and social upheavals. The crisis lay not only chronologically between the wars; there was also a causal relationship between it and the end of the first and the beginning of the second world war. These causal relationships are clearer to us today—after an interval of forty years—than they were then. But even at that time there already existed an awareness of the epoch-making character of this crisis. . . .

Outwardly the picture of the crisis in Germany varied little from that in comparable countries. There were, however, important differences in the conditions leading up to the crisis which, together with other particular factors, explain the different reactions of German society compared with those of other countries. Let us first of all look at some statistics: with the end of inflation the German economy experienced a relatively steady growth, which allowed the national income to rise by 25 per cent between 1925 and 1928. But already in 1929 the national income had stagnated at 71 billion RM, and by 1932 it had sunk by no less than 43 per cent to 41 billion.

The decline in the gross national product was slightly less because of the relatively stable yield from indirect taxation (a result of Brüning's fiscal measures), but nevertheless spectacular enough at 37 per cent. The figures for individual economic fields only confirm to a greater or lesser degree the development of the total national yield. The production index for industry had sunk in 1932–3 to half of what it was in 1927–8, and in the particularly sensitive sector of capital goods, to a third. Whatever sector we examine, we see the picture of a crisis without parallel in the history of industrial capitalism. Its most extreme expression, the counterpart of falling production, was the sharp increase in unemployment: at the peak of the crisis, in 1932, the official German statistics showed 6 million unemployed. The actual figure was considerably higher because many people who were without jobs after years of unemployment no longer received support and were no longer included in statistical records. We shall not go far wrong if we assume that in 1932 one in every three of the working population had no job. And even those who still retained their jobs were under constant threat of dismissal because everyone was replaceable; there were vast numbers of competitors ready to take their place, and thus their whole existence was threatened.

These facts indicate that Germany, together with the United States, was the hardest hit by the crisis, which in both countries became particularly acute through the combination of various mutually intensifying causes, after both had experienced an economic boom lasting several years which had suppressed awareness of the crisis-prone character of the economic system. After the first world war structural changes in the system of the private economy reinforced the effects of the trade cycle which—conditioned by the cyclical movements of stocks, the rate of investment, and consumer demand—had been a characteristic feature of the capitalist economy. These changes gave a crisis which had been regarded as "normal" and "inherently self-corrective," a direction which observant contemporaries could see would end in the breakdown of the whole system. Among other factors, the system's loss of flexibility should be mentioned, due to monopolization of production and distribution, the increasing rigidity of prices and wages, the gradual destruction of the liberal world system of commerce and currency through the establishment of tariffs and trade restrictions, changes within the inner structure of firms, expressed above all in the wave of rationalization during the twenties. The result formed the decisive economic denominator of the crisis: a structural deficit in demand, something which, according to the liberal economic philosophy, was just not possible. It was the formal expression of the fact of surpluses in production over demand and purchasing power which tipped the balance to millions of unemployed. . . .

A fateful reciprocal action arose between the credit crisis and the general economic crisis, which further accelerated the collapse of the economy. If we bear in mind that almost half of all the deposits in the big German banks came from abroad, we can grasp the serious nature of this bank crisis, which reveals in exemplary fashion the connection between inflation, reparations policy, loans, and the world economic crisis, a connection that was one of the most outstanding characteristics of the state of affairs in Germany in 1930-2. . . .

The world economic crisis in its particular German manifestation had an increasingly powerful effect between 1929 and 1933 on the political scene, on power relationships within society, on the behaviour of individual citizens as well as on government policies. The internal political situation was characterized on the one hand by the rapid growth of the right-wing anti-democratic forces whose breakthrough into a mass movement was made possible by the impoverishment of millions, and on the other by the decline and deformation of the parliamentary system and the transition to the politics of presidential cabinets and emergency laws. But these could do nothing to halt the growing crisis. Economic helplessness gradually produced and merged with the helplessness of the democratic system, establishing a cause and effect relationship between the crisis and the fall of the Weimar Republic. . . .

The effects of the crisis were visible mainly in the economic and political fields where they can be measured and described. But this reflects only part of the reality, revealing no more than the rough social outline formed from the indications offered by statistics, political data, and social institutions. The impact on the lives of individuals and on the smaller social groups, as well as on the intellectual climate in German society, is far more difficult to evaluate. The difficulties lie partly in the untried methods of evaluation, although there is no lack of historical evidence. The following remarks are intended merely to trace some contours, not to give a rounded picture of the social-psychological state of affairs in Germany in 1930–2.

The material effects of the crisis were very similar for the workers and for the lower middle class: millions of workers lost their jobs for years on end; traders and artisans—directly dependent on mass purchasing power —saw their turnover decline from month to month, and farmers could hardly be sure of supporting themselves as prices continued to fall. Their political reactions, however, were dissimilar: the workers, at least the skilled workers who were members of trade unions, felt themselves confirmed in the political view of the world which they had acquired from the left-wing parties and their own unions, according to which capitalism was coming to an end and the time was ripe for taking new paths which would lead to socialism. On the other hand most of them, retaining their confidence in social democracy, supported the Republican regime, unlike the communists for whom the Republic was a reactionary and bourgeois obstacle to the realization of "true socialism." Common to both was the firm belief in a view of the world that helped them to understand the crisis, and, despite all the present misery, kept open the prospect of a better future.

Totally different was the political behaviour of the farmers, shopkeepers, artisans and tradesmen, the white-collar workers, public employees and the professional classes. It was in this section of the population, which as a heterogeneous residue in between the upper and lower social strata had not yet developed a sense of identity, that awareness of the crisis was most strongly reflected. Before 1914 they had regarded themselves as that section of the population which was the staunchest supporters of the regime, firmly ensconced in the authoritarian structure of the Wilhelmine state which, although according them little political influence, made possible a flourishing economy and gave them a consciousness of identity with the power and glory of imperial Germany. When, after 1918, Germany lost its position as a great power, and reparations and inflation destroyed the economic foundations of these middle classes, their earlier loyalty to the state turned into a rejection of the new state. The new Republic was blamed for what had been caused by the bankruptcy of the old order: the loss of greatness abroad, of the brilliant external image and of economic prosperity. Inflation and world economic crisis seemed to be merely part of a deeper German crisis in which earlier values had lost their validity. Fear of the chaos that they equated with communism, fear of the consequences of industrial rationalization—which often turned into a romantically distorted hostility towards industrial society as such—the very real fear of social degradation through the economic crisis, of sinking down into "the grey proletarian mass"—these were some of the reasons for the political disintegration of the middle classes. The Hitler movement promised new authority, which would enable them to identify once more, and seemed to break through the paralyzing hopelessness of the crisis years with activist élan.

The noisy activism, the radical rhetoric against the "system" onto which all the evils of the crisis were projected, the portrayal of a new, more colourful picture of the future, gave Hitler a decisive advantage over the dry doctrines of the communists and the plain-spoken sobriety of the bourgeois parties and the social democrats. After several years of crisis, many were neither willing nor able to examine the rational foundations of the demagogy of a Hitler or a Goebbels. Tired of the incapacity of the "parties of the system" to solve the crisis, people took refuge, in resignation or desperate hope, in the collective daydream of fascist propaganda.

Many phenomena which bore witness to the disintegration of traditional social behaviour have been rightly ascribed to the crisis. The change within family relationships, the questioning of moral standards, the rapid increase in crime, the coarsening and poisoning of human relationships, the spread of corruption, the neglect of externals, the sharpening of class hatred, violence and the general extension of the zone between legality and illegality—all these were symptoms and visible expressions of the crisis in the sphere of personal life. We should not however forget that in many respects the crisis only accelerated the operation of causes which had been at work for a long time as society was reshaped into the modern urban industrial pattern, or were a consequence of the war which had brought into question the ethical standards and traditional values of bourgeois society.

A particularly severe social problem was the lack of prospects for young people. Between 1929 and 1933 many left school without the faintest hope of ever being able to acquire skills or enter a profession, for the number of places for apprenticeship had sunk even more sharply than the number of jobs. Those leaving university had poor chances of finding employment, and formed an academic proletariat which flocked into the *Wehrverbände* of the national socialists. Hitler's movement attracted the young by skilfully playing off its activism, oriented towards the future, against the prevailing conditions which were so obviously without a future. The existing state of affairs stood in the eyes of many young people for philistinism and "rotten compromise"; by contrast, national socialism fascinated them by its refusal to be bound, its militarist ideology, its discipline. Its ideals seemed to be those of youth, revolutionary, seething, innovating, heroic. Its shrewd self-portrayal conveyed a dynamic and revolutionary impression, and was successful in directing the anti-capitalist longings of the masses into the channels of counter-revolution which, between 1930 and 1932, joined forces with the ruling classes in society.

It is hard to find a common denominator for the contradictions of these years. And yet there is a dialectical connection of apathy and excitement, hopelessness and activism, present misery and a visionary future, anarchic dissolution of society and the flight into disciplined *Kampfverbände*: linking them all was the feeling that the existing state of affairs could not last, a theme with manifold versions varying from the anti-technology complaints of the cultural critics to visions of the future—nationalist, anti-western, or socialist. It was Germany's particular tragedy that a correct insight into the necessary changes found a false answer: not that of a future to be formed rationally in the interests of the majority, but the intoxicated irrationality of counter-revolutionary fascism, whose method of overcoming the crisis ended in gross exploitation and the second world war.

3. *Derek H. Aldcroft: Development of the Managed Economy Before 1939*

By 1933, it was clear that traditional deflationary remedies were inadequate to cope with so great a crisis. Yet economic theorists had not yet managed to come up with either an adequate explanation or a workable solution; the *General Theory* of John Maynard Keynes did not appear until 1936. Since efforts at international cooperation had broken down, national governments were left to grope and stumble toward recovery. Derek Aldcroft, Senior Lecturer in Economic History at Leicester University (England) explains how most governments moved haltingly toward a planned and managed system; he gives particular attention to the antidepression techniques used in Sweden and in Nazi Germany.

The nature and causes of the severe economic crisis of 1929–32 need not concern us here. From our point of view the important thing is to determine its impact on government policy. It was almost inevitable, given the severity of the conditions, that governments would take action. The early thirties were characterized by a wave of currency devaluations as countries abandoned the gold standard, to be followed by the imposition of severe restrictions on trade, payments, and capital movements. These were primarily defensive measures designed to insulate domestic economies from adverse external influences. With the external side protected it was then possible for countries to adopt national policies designed, at least in part, to stimulate recovery from depression. "The 'planning' of foreign trade came to be more and more widely accepted as a normal function of the State, and the weapons which had been forged as an emergency defence of prices, production or currency were not discarded, but tended to be pressed into service as permanent elements of trade regulation, dovetailed into programmes of national economic development."

Generally the policies adopted in the 1930s have been regarded as reactionary and restrictive. In many respects they were, especially those relating to trade and payments, since they were implemented with little regard to their effects on other countries. As restrictions increased, trade was diverted more and more into bilateral channels and hence the scope for ex-

Derek H. Aldcroft, "Development of the Managed Economy Before 1939," *Journal of Contemporary History*, IV (1969), 122–24, 128–37. Footnotes omitted. Reprinted by permission of George Weidenfeld & Nicolson Ltd.

pansion became limited. Ultimately these policies were self-defeating, since the gains initially derived from devaluation and import controls soon disappeared as other countries followed similar courses of action. On the other hand it is easy, with the advantage of hindsight, to be critical about the restrictive nature of government policy in this decade. Admittedly external policy measures were restrictive and paved the way for the adoption of nationalistic domestic policies, but given the conditions of the time it is difficult to see how countries could have pursued effective internal recovery measures without some form of safeguard on the international side. What can be criticized is the reluctance of governments to relax these restrictions once recovery got under way and the somewhat limited and half-hearted efforts made to stimulate recovery in the first place. On the whole domestic recovery measures were reactionary and inadequate. Governments tended to concentrate their attention on bolstering up and protecting established producers instead of adopting expansionary fiscal policies which would have imparted a stimulus to the economy and revived business confidence. On the other hand there are signs that governments were beginning to realize, if somewhat late in the day, that policies could be constructive and that variations in the volume of state expenditure could help to control fluctuations in the level of economic activity. This is particularly true of Sweden and America for example. Moreover, several experiments were made in planning during the 1930s, notably in eastern Europe and Germany, with some degree of success.

Of course the techniques used were often primitive and the results achieved by no means spectacular. What is important is that in the 1930s the first real attempts at economic management began. Until that time government intervention had been markedly specific in nature, since the canons of sound finance and the implicit faith placed in classical economics had inhibited governments from assuming a managerial role. It was generally accepted that economic adjustment was best left to the free market and that excessive interference would simply complicate matters or make them worse. These ideas were of course still very prevalent in the thirties and it was on the theoretical side that the most revolutionary advances were made. On the other hand, the depression of the 1930s certainly forced governments to interpret their economic responsibilities more widely, though whether their policies were necessarily the most appropriate is another matter. . . .

Most governments did in fact eventually adopt public works programmes and other measures of relief, though few developed proper countercyclical management policies. There were of course exceptions. The Swedish government in particular deserves mention, not only because it attempted to phase public expenditure to offset fluctuations in business activity but also because it managed to avoid adopting many of the restrictive policies so common in other countries. In some respects Sweden was fortunate in that she was not affected by the depression until quite late, so that the adoption of expansionary policies tended to coincide fairly closely with the downswing of the cycle. Although initially certain deflationary measures were enforced, for example wage cuts, public expenditure continued to rise throughout the depression years and by the winter of 1932–3 nearly one quarter of the unemployed were being given relief work. Meanwhile the deflationary tendencies were being reversed. In 1931–2 the krona was devalued and a cheap money policy adopted. By the end of 1932 the need for more direct action was generally recognized. Budgetary policy was to be made an important instrument of recovery. The finance minister's speech of January 1933 was notable not only for its open declaration of an unorthodox budgetary policy but also because it formally acknowledged the state's responsibility for promoting recovery: "the budget is based on the assumption . . . that in Sweden there will be no spontaneous tendency towards recovery, except to the extent that the policy of the State will help to bring it about . . . In seeking to achieve this object, the State's financial policy must obviously play an important part." Accordingly a large programme of public works was implemented and the resulting budgetary deficit financed by loans which were to be amortized over a period of seven years. Thus whereas in the four financial years 1928–9 to 1931–2 a little over one twentieth of the total budgetary expenditure was met by borrowing, this proportion was raised to no less than one quarter in the two years 1933–4 and 1934–5, when public works absorbed between 15 to 20 per cent of the total budget. After 1935, when recovery was well under way, expenditure on public works was reduced sharply and the loans previously incurred were amortized.

One should not, however, overstate the importance of government policy in stimulating recovery. Certainly cheap money, currency devaluation, and deficit financing of public works were helpful, but it is doubtful whether policy was a decisive factor in setting revival in motion or in checking the inflationary pressures of 1936–7. Unfortunately, information about the Swedish economy in this period is still far from complete and it is difficult to reach a firm judgment. Certainly government policy was not the only relevant factor, since there were strong natural forces making for recovery, in particular the sharp revival in the export trade and a rapid growth of housing and the output of consumer durables from 1934 onwards. Moreover, although Sweden experienced fairly rapid growth in the thirties, recovery was by no means complete; unemployment was still high at the end of the decade. Yet however limited the role of policy in the recovery process may have been, the more praiseworthy and enlightened aspects of Swedish policy should be accorded recognition. Sweden did not impose restrictions and rigid economy measures to the same extent as other countries did in the early stages of depression. Indeed, government expenditure rose continuously, albeit slowly at first, during the years of depression. The ready acceptance and fairly rapid implementation of deficit-financed public works, even if somewhat belated, is particularly commendable. Furthermore, the Swedish plan for amortizing the loan debt from budget surpluses in years of active trade suggests that the government was aware of the need for a countercyclical policy. In fact in the later 1930s preparations

were made to continue the policy in any future slump and a report was issued in 1937 analysing the projected capital expenditure of public authorities for the subsequent decade. Following this a supplementary budget of
257 million krona was introduced for 1938–9 which could be used by the
government on construction works if and when a new slump developed. . . .

So far we have discussed the economic role of the state in those countries where the degree of state interference and regulation, though increasing, was still fairly limited. The policy measures taken to promote recovery
did not lead to extensive control of private business activity, since reliance
was placed on policies of an indirect type. Although most governments
were forced into taking more comprehensive action than hitherto to control
economic forces, management techniques were still limited and partial in
scope. Only in a few cases were tentative moves made towards adopting
countercyclical management policies, whilst long-term planning was discussed but rarely implemented. In most cases government policy had only
a marginal effect on the course of recovery, partly because the policies
themselves were often inappropriate and partly because they were pursued halfheartedly.

By contrast, economic control and management by the state was much
more extensive in many central and east European countries. This was in
part a response to the effects of the depression, but it was also conditioned
by the fact that these countries had experienced only limited industrial development before the 1930s. It is impossible to discuss the policies of these
countries in detail here, but it is necessary to say something about the German economy since it was in many respects unique. The German economic
system as it developed in the later 1930s was a prototype of rigid control;
the degree of state control was much more extensive than in any other
country barring Russia. But unlike Russia the means of production in Germany were never publicly owned and extensive state control of the economy was made compatible with private capitalism. Indeed, the nazi system
of production, distribution, and consumption defies classification in any of
the usual categories of economic systems:

It was not capitalism in the traditional sense: the autonomous market mechanism
so characteristic of capitalism during the last two centuries had all but disappeared. It was not State capitalism: the Government disclaimed any desire to own
the means of production, and in fact took steps to denationalize them. It was not
socialism or communism: private property and private profit existed. The Nazi
system was, rather, a combination of some of the characteristics of capitalism and
a highly planned economy. Without in any way destroying its class structure a
comprehensive planning mechanism was imposed on an economy in which private property was not expropriated, in which the distribution of national income
remained fundamentally unchanged, and in which private entrepreneurs retained
some of the prerogatives and responsibilities in traditional capitalism.

Whatever the precise features of the system, there is no denying that it
achieved spectacular results in terms of recovery. Moreover, by its extensive control of trade and payments the German economy exercised consid-

erable influence over the economies of central and south-eastern Europe.

Initially, nazi economic policy was geared to providing relief for the unemployed. By 1932, 6 to 7 million people or some 30 per cent of the labour force were without jobs. The deflationary policies of the Brüning and Papen governments had done little to alleviate the crisis, though in the middle of 1932 a moderate programme of public works was established. The main feature of nazi relief policy was a large-scale programme of public works entailing an outlay of some 6 billion RM. The employment-creating effects of this expenditure soon set recovery in motion, though before the sum had been spent the basis of economic policy had shifted dramatically. From November 1934 onwards priority was given to rearmament and preparation of the economy for war. This entailed a large increase in government expenditure, selective economic planning, and extensive regulation of many sectors of the economy, including in particular measures to stabilize wages and prices, extensive control of foreign trade and exchange, selective depreciation of the mark when it was used to pay foreign creditors, regulation of the money and capital markets, a high level of taxation, and measures designed to shift resources from consumer to producer goods industries.

To discuss in any detail the impact of these controls on every sector of the economy is not possible here, but a few comments and figures will convey some idea of the effects on the economy as a whole. Since policy was directly geared to rearmament it is not surprizing that this sector increased sharply in importance. Between 1933 and 1939 the government spent roughly 90 billion RM in preparing for war, a sum equivalent to twice the German national income in 1932 and to a little over one year's income on the standard of 1938. Military expenditure as a percentage of national income rose from 11·1 in 1934–6 to 22·4 in 1937–9, and by the latter date accounted for over one third of government spending. The state sector was however somewhat larger than this, for these figures refer only to direct military expenditure. By 1938 57 per cent of gross investment was made by the public sector as against 35·2 per cent in 1929, whilst total state expenditure as a percentage of national income increased from around 11 in 1929 to over one half by the end of the 1930s. In effect the government had become the largest investor and consumer in the German economy.

The vast expansion of the military sector would not have been possible without fairly extensive controls over consumption and a shift of resources away from this sector. To do this, tight control was maintained over private investment, especially in consumer goods industries, and new issues of capital were virtually prohibited; the consumer goods industries share of gross investment in manufacturing fell from 45 to 18 per cent between 1933 and 1939 whilst their output rose by only 38 per cent as against 200 per cent for producer durables (1932–8). Effective demand for consumer goods was kept down by controls over wages and prices and increased levels of taxation. Money wages remained stable from 1933 at a level somewhat below that of 1929, and the moderate rise in prices towards the end of the period meant a slight fall in real terms. Thus the general consumer failed to benefit from the increase in national income in the 1930s; per capita consumption in 1938 was probably no greater than in 1929, whilst private consumption as a proportion of national income fell from 73 to 52 per cent over the period.

In other words the bulk of the increase in national income was earmarked for government use, primarily for war purposes. The ratio of public revenues to national income rose from 31·6 per cent in 1933–4 to 39·1 per cent in 1938–9. The greater part of government expenditure was financed out of higher taxation and the increased yield from taxes as a result of the growth in national income, but taxation was insufficient to finance the whole programme and increasing recourse was had to borrowing and the creation of additional cash credits. Deficit financing, however, never became as important as in America; in fact borrowing rarely constituted more than 25 per cent of total government receipts, whereas something like one half the New Deal expenditure programme was deficit financed. Moreover, although the national debt increased it was a smaller proportion of national income than that of many other countries, whilst Germany's foreign debt was actually diminished by repudiation and default.

The network of controls was completed by extensive regulations imposed on trade, payments, and exchange, in order to restrict imports of inessential goods and boost exports, and to secure the benefits of the favourable terms of trade. The results in terms of exports were disappointing; as regards imports the policy was more successful. Increasingly, trade was directed to those countries with whom Germany had concluded bilateral clearing agreements, thus avoiding the necessity of releasing free exchange currency for the payment of imports. By 1938 about 40 clearing agreements had been negotiated covering 80 per cent of Germany's imports. These measures led to a significant change in the composition of imports—essential raw materials accounted for 37·2 per cent of the total import bill in 1936 as against 27·3 per cent in 1932—and to a striking shift in the direction of Germany's trade from western Europe to overseas and southeastern Europe, though with an inevitable rise in the net cost of imports.

This brief sketch hardly does justice to the complexity and ingenuity of the German economic system, but it is obvious that state control and management was far more extensive than in most other countries. Whatever the social costs of the system there can be no doubt that it was extremely successful in terms of recovery from the depression. Germany was the only country in which unemployment was eliminated. Within two years (January 1933 to December 1934) the number of insured workers unemployed fell from 6·0 to 2·6 million, and by the end of the decade unemployment was negligible. National income and industrial production roughly doubled between 1932 and 1938 and even on the basis of pre-depression levels of output the performance was fairly creditable.

Recovery would no doubt have taken place without government intervention but it is unlikely that the same results would have been achieved had it not been for the rapid growth of the public sector. On the other hand, government intervention in the 1930s was not determined primarily

by the dictates of modern business cycle theory and cannot therefore be regarded as a Keynesian pump-priming effort. By the time the first large
injection of government expenditure materialized with the relief programmes of 1933–4, recovery had already begun though there can be no
doubt that the process was markedly speeded up as a result of this policy.
After 1934 the government component increased sharply and was dominated almost entirely by rearmament policy and not by business cycle
theory, which would have dictated a phasing out of state expenditure. That
the latter continued to increase without producing severe inflationary conditions was due to the fact that such pressures were contained by extensive
economic controls. These controls moreover were essentially expedients for
securing short-run objectives, that is to adjust the economy to the exigen-
cies of war, and were not used as weapons for the propagation of long-term
planning, though tentative long-term plans were drawn up. Yet though
Government control was determined largely by political rather than economic considerations, the German experience suggests at least one thing:
that to achieve a rapid and complete recovery from a severe business cycle
recession the pump-priming effort may well have to be large and sustained,
though to achieve this there is no reason why the degree of control need
necessarily be as extreme as it was in Germany.

The economic crisis of the early 1930s was an important factor making
for increased government intervention in economic affairs. Given the severity of the conditions then prevailing, few governments could afford to
stand aloof. Initially, however, the policies adopted to counteract the recession only served to aggravate the crisis; they were the product of men
steeped in the traditions of orthodox finance who hankered after the past
rather than looked to the future. "Ministers, officials, economists and businessmen alike continued to think about the broad issues of commercial policy in the light of the economic and political conditions obtaining in the
pre-war era and desired the general re-adoption of long-run policies appropriate to these conditions." Only when it was realized that these policies
could not stimulate recovery did some governments move towards more expansionary programmes. Yet apart from Germany, whose economic system
was dominated by political considerations, government policies, even in
their more enlightened phase, had no more than a marginal effect on recovery. Only a few countries, notably Sweden and America, developed
what might be called countercyclical management policies, and these were
generally too limited in scope to be really successful. For the most part reliance was placed on orthodox weapons such as monetary policy, trade and
payments restrictions, and industrial reconstruction schemes. Though government interference increased in the 1930s one can hardly say that any
notable progress was made in the direction of *successful* management and
planning of economies. Managed economies there were, but the management was partial in scope and too weak and timid to be really effective.
Nevertheless the experience of this decade left a lasting impression and it
undoubtedly influenced government policies in the post-war period.

But the increasing economic responsibility of the state in the twentieth century cannot be attributed solely to the Great Depression. In fact in some cases, notably Britain, the crisis had little noticeable impact on the quantitative importance of the government's economic activity. This is not to say that the crisis did not have a profound influence upon attitudes towards state intervention and responsibility, but merely that any such influence was not reflected in any permanent shift in the pattern of government spending. On the other hand, war and its aftermath produced a marked "displacement" effect on government expenditure; as a percentage of GNP it was twice as high in the 1920s in Britain as before 1914, and undoubtedly the war was responsible for a good deal of this increase. Not only did it enable governments to impose higher levels of taxation which would have been unacceptable in peace-time; it also gave rise to, *inter alia,* an increasing public awareness of the need for governments to provide for the underprivileged members of society. Thus the extension of social security programmes in the 1920s can be regarded as a response to the change in attitudes brought about by the war.

Yet whilst not denying the important influence of both war and depression in stimulating ideas and policies regarding the economic role and obligations of the state, it would be wrong to attribute everything to these two factors. There is reason to believe that government intervention and expenditure would have increased independently of these factors though perhaps not quite so rapidly. Peacock and Wiseman in their study of British public expenditure suggest that the climate of opinion became increasingly favourable to the extension of public and social welfare services in the twentieth century. Although this trend was no doubt influenced strongly by exogenous factors such as war and depression, it was also conditioned by the growth of an increasingly informed mass electorate. Even before 1914 there was growing agreement about the desirability of increased public spending, especially on welfare services, and some European governments introduced social insurance schemes in this period. In the early twentieth century the Liberal government in Britain followed suit and as a result government spending rose sharply in the years before 1914. Had war and depression not intervened this trend would have continued though it is unlikely that progress would have been so rapid as it actually was. But what is important is that by the early twentieth century the collective responsibility of the state in economic matters was already becoming apparent and it was only a matter of time before the citadel of *laissez-faire* was demolished.

4. *H. W. Richardson: The Economic Significance of the Depression in Britain*

Perhaps we are somewhat inclined to overdramatize the great depression—to think in terms of masses of despairing unemployed, or rampant demagoguery and radicalism, of fundamental changes in public policy and private value-systems. In the following selection, an eminent British scholar argues a more unorthodox case: that Britain at least was only mildly affected by the slump, and that the effect on public policy was realitively meager. H. W. Richardson is Director of the Centre for Research in the Social Sciences at the University of Kent.

The depression in Britain between 1929 and 1932 was not an economic watershed. The main economic trends of the UK economy in the 1930s did not move in a direction different from the previous decade, though in some respects the pace of readjustment quickened. Some of the economic policies adopted after the depression were dissimilar to those followed in the 1920s, but these changes were not the direct consequence of the depression. In the United States, in Germany, and in certain primary producing countries, the onset of the world depression had a shattering impact, and its consequences may have governed the course of events throughout the 1930s. Britain did not escape unaffected, but the downswing was moderate and its effects soon obliterated.

The argument that the British depression was of limited economic significance will be conducted on three main lines. First, the depression started abroad and was imported into the UK through the balance of payments. Components of the balance of payments showed signs of stress, but the depression was relatively mild in domestic indicators, especially when compared with international experience. Moreover, the ground lost in the depression was soon made up in the strong recovery which followed. Second, the net effect of the depression on the forces of structural readjustment in the British economy was marginal, neither an obstacle nor a major stimulus. The rise in unemployment and the fall in investment were severe enough to slow down, and in many cases halt, the shift of resources towards rapidly expanding sectors. On the other hand, the effects of export collapse on the old-established basic industries were such as to make it clear to contemporaries that these industries could not offer a long-run solution to the problems of the economy. Third, although there was considerable public and private discussion on economic policy in the years after 1929, the measures adopted in the 1930s owed little to the direct effects of the depression. A few new ideas were circulated but they were not trans-

H. W. Richardson, "The Economic Significance of the Depression in Britain," *Journal of Contemporary History,* IV (1969), 3–4, 6–7, 13–14, 18–19. Footnotes omitted. Reprinted by permission of George Weidenfeld & Nicolson Ltd.

formed into official policy. In general, the government's handling of economic affairs remained orthodox. Where economic policy altered course from the previous decade, the changes were primarily dictated by short-run economic conditions or political considerations rather than by conscious acts to cure the slump. The depression in Britain failed, in contrast with experience overseas, to result in a radical reassessment of economic policy. . . .

Against the background of economic experience throughout the world, the most striking feature of the depression in Britain was its comparative mildness. . . . It is clear that the term "slump" needs drastic qualification, and that to emphasize the heavy rise in unemployment conveys a completely misleading impression. National income scarcely declined at all, consumers' expenditure increased year by year (apart from stability between 1931 and 1932), while real wages rose at an annual average rate of over 3 per cent up to 1933. The level of employment fell by little more than 5 per cent. Production, prices, investment, and profits fell rather more steeply, but their contraction was much milder than in the other major industrial economies. Moreover, their potential effects on welfare are not so serious as those of national income, consumption, and wages. . . .

Why was the depression in the United Kingdom so moderate? There are a number of obvious reasons. The weakness of the upswing in the late 1920s meant that there had been no serious overbuilding of capacity. The improvement in the terms of trade for an economy so involved in international trade helped to maintain real incomes and consumption, and this placed a high floor on the extent to which income could fall. Britain was spared the collapse of financial institutions and the dislocation of the banking system and the stock market which accompanied the slump in the United States and in parts of continental Europe. Private sector house-building expanded continuously between 1928 and 1934, and helped to maintain a relatively high rate of building activity through the depression. . . . The effects of the export slump were concentrated on the old industrial regions, and though these suffered severely, creating a colossal social problem, Southern England escaped almost unscathed. Employment fell by a mere 2–3 per cent in London and the South West, while numbers employed in South East England (excluding London) continued to expand throughout the depression. Since the centres of business decision-making outside the staple industries were disproportionately concentrated in these areas, business expectations remained relatively bright. Although the fall in profits and share values could hardly be passed off as negligible, it was not catastrophic enough to make businessmen and investors very pessimistic. These moderating forces helped to create the conditions for revival in the sense that recovery stimuli are much more likely to be effective when depression impulses are weak. . . .

British economic policy after the depression appeared very different from what it had been in the 1920s. High interest rates and a restrictive monetary policy had given way to a cheap money policy, measures to maintain the parity of sterling were abandoned in favour of devaluation, a predominantly free trade commercial policy was replaced by a general tariff, quota restrictions on food imports, increased imperial and colonial preferences, and an embargo on many types of overseas lending. Moreover, apparently new policies had been developed, such as intervention in industrial reorganization programmes and financial assistance to depressed regions. The *prima facie* case that the changes and extension in policy were the direct consequence of the depression seems a strong one, but it is, upon further examination, unconvincing. The changes in direction of policy can be exaggerated. Where new measures were applied, some of these had been urged by political parties before the depression, while others were introduced rapidly and without much foresight in response to short-run emergencies and crises which were linked only indirectly with the slump. The depression sometimes provided the excuse for implementing a policy that might have been inhibited in the previous decade by fear that it might be electorally disastrous. In the late 1920s and during the depression new remedies were suggested to raise the level of employment, but they were ignored because of the persistence of the old orthodoxies and the continued belief that the economy was self-regulating and that slumps cured themselves. There is no single example of the depression giving rise to a recasting of ideas on policy and to a subsequent adoption of measures expressly to induce revival.

These generalizations are confirmed when individual spheres of policy are considered. Fiscal policies were least responsive to the depression. In the world as a whole, the main innovation in economic policy was the use of deficit financing to induce recovery through higher government capital expenditure programmes. This weapon was employed with varying degrees of success in the United States, Sweden, Germany, and Japan. In Britain, however, no concessions were made in this respect. The theoretical justification for government fiscal action to stabilize income at, rather than below, the full employment level was not worked out until after the depression was over. The crude policy implication, that unemployment could be reduced by a huge public works programme financed out of borrowing, had already been suggested by the Liberal party in 1928 and 1929 before the depression began. These suggestions were taken up most seriously during the depression by Oswald Mosley in 1930, but his influence with policymakers was negligible. He was only a junior minister, and when his views were rejected in May 1930 he resigned. Keynes himself advocated a tariff more strongly than deficit financing, on the grounds that the latter would have had harmful effects on already depressed business confidence. The nearest the government came to having a fiscal policy in the early 1930s was its stress on a balanced budget, not for stabilization purposes but to restore business confidence at home and abroad. . . .

The argument urged here, that the new approaches to economic policy and increased government intervention were not a direct response to the slump, should not be overstressed. There is obviously a certain degree of interdependence between the cyclical behaviour of the economy and the character of economic policies adopted. But it is necessary to challenge the superficially attractive hypothesis that the main changes in economic policy in the 1930s were the direct consequence of the depression, and that the depression was a watershed in the development of control of the economy. This contrasts with the situation in, say, the United States and Germany, where the New Deal and Nazi employment and foreign economic policies respectively were designed specifically as recovery instruments. In Britain new policies were implemented either on grounds of expediency or because short-run considerations forced them on a reluctant government. The measures were not applied with the direct aim of inducing revival, and if they benefited recovery this was, in most cases, an incidental by-product.

The world slump after 1929 was a cataclysmic event which had tremendous economic repercussions across five continents. The dislocation of international trade, the fall in world commodity prices, and the collapse of the international investment and payments system had a retarding impact on long-term growth. In several countries, such as the United States and France, economic revival even in the late 1930s was so weak that the pre-depression levels of activity were scarcely exceeded. But some economies escaped the worst of the slump. For example, in Sweden and Japan a high trend rate of growth coupled with effective policy measures (deficit financing in the former case, currency depreciation and cheap money in the latter) led to strong upswings. It is therefore dangerous to particularize from the world depression as a major world event to the importance of the slump in a particular country. In the United Kingdom the depression had surprisingly little significance considering how much the economy was involved in overseas investment and trade. In most respects the downswing was mild, and the economy revived quickly and smoothly. The economic policies employed in the 1930s were not the direct result of the depression, and in any event were not as crucial as natural forces in securing recovery. Of course, the world slump had some impact on the composition and rate of economic activity. For example the fall in world trade necessitated a temporary switch in emphasis towards domestic sources of expansion and away from exports. Indeed, it might be argued that the main economic consequence of the depression was the realization that exports could not *automatically* lead the economy out of slumps.

To regard the post-1929 depression as a key turning point in the development of the British economy is in keeping with the historian's innate preference for sudden and dramatic changes. But drama and economic significance are not identical. The depression was almost irrelevant to the crucial economic problems of the interwar economy, and did little either to aid or impede their solution. These problems arose from the struggle of the oldest mature industrial nation to regain its vigour and dynamism in an increasingly competitive and industrializing world. The transformation process was neither sudden nor dramatic, but a slow and difficult path of readjustment, beginning before 1914 and continuing after 1945. Beside this perennial problem, the difficulties of the depression appear transient and trivial.

5. *E. H. Carr: The New Society*

In the end, the historian's goal is not only to explain what happened, but to try to assess its meaning in long-term perspective. Did the great depression really work a profound transformation in the European system? The noted British scholar Edward Hallett Carr insists that it did. Carr, who is a fellow of Trinity College, Cambridge, has been a career diplomat (1916–1936) and a journalist (assistant editor of *The Times*, 1941–1946). He has written extensively on diplomatic history, radical movements, and Soviet affairs.

Historically speaking . . . , it was neither the need to mitigate the struggle between capital and labour nor the need to protect the consumer which drove the last nail into the coffin of *laissez-faire* capitalism and provoked massive state intervention in every function of the economy. This was brought about by the problem of mass unemployment. The final blow was struck by the series of economic crises culminating in the great depression of the early 1930's. In orthodox capitalist theory, crisis was the catalyst which purged unsound and unhealthy elements from the system, the regulator which readjusted the delicate balance of supply and demand, the court of appeal which rewarded the industrious and the provident and condemned the foolhardy and the negligent to perdition. It was part of the normal procedure of punishing and expelling the inefficient, and operated as such in the nineteenth century with comparatively moderate results in economic dislocation and human suffering—results which were accepted as the proper and inevitable cost of a working economic system. But in the twentieth century both the practice and the theory of periodic economic crises were rejected as intolerable—partly because humanitarian people refused any longer to believe that men who had so brilliantly mastered the secrets of material production were unable to devise some less wasteful and preposterous method of organizing distribution, but mainly because the great organized forces of capital and labour now both revolted more and more sharply against each successive crisis and turned more and more impatiently to the state to rescue them from its impact. If the cry for help came even more strongly from the side of capital than from that of labour, this was probably because the capitalists had closer affiliations to the ruling class and more direct and impressive means of access to its ear. The Federation of British Industries and the National Union of Farmers were more effective forces than the trade unions in determining the course of British economic policy in the great depression; and, when the blizzard

From E. H. Carr, *The New Society* (Boston: Beacon Press, 1957), pp. 27–30. Reprinted by permission of St. Martin's Press and The Macmillan Company of Canada.

struck the United States, it was the bankers, the farmers and the industrialists who turned most desperately and most eagerly to Washington with the
plea to come over and help them.

It was thus the capitalists—the industrialists, farmers and financiers—
who, unwilling to see the capitalist theory of the elimination of the unfit
through periodic crises applied to themselves, begged the state to save
them by laying the foundations of an ordered national economy. They
were fully justified in so doing. The structure of industry and finance in the
twentieth century had been so firmly integrated and concentrated that its
main sectors were no longer separable either from one another or from the
national economy as a whole. It was unthinkable that a great bank or a
great railway, a major unit in the steel or chemical industries, should be
wound up for failing to meet its obligations. Far from watching the economic struggle from heights of Olympian aloofness, the state had to step
into the ring in the national interest to save the potential loser from being
knocked out. No doubt, the bankers and industrialists who in the hour of
distress invoked state support did not fully realize the implications of their
action; no doubt, they hoped that the state, having saved them from destruction in bad times, would allow them in good times to resume their unimpeded progress in earning profits under the flag of private enterprise.
But this was to overlook realities. What had once been done could not be
wholly undone: still less could it be expunged from the records or its lessons unlearned. For what had been clearly demonstrated in the moment of
crisis was that the national economy was one and indivisible. The concentration and enlargement of economic units had gone so far that there was
now no logical stopping point short of the nation as a whole—and perhaps
not even there. The conception of a national economy had taken root; and
by the same token some kind of planning authority had become inevitable,
whatever its name and purposes, however its functions were defined, and
through whatever agencies or methods it operated.

The same broad developments occurred in all the leading industrial
countries though with many variations and, above all, differences in tempo
due to different economic conditions. They would today be accepted as almost uncontroversial but for the practice and precept of the United States.
American capitalism was an exceedingly active and powerful growth
which reached maturity considerably later than European capitalism, and
reaped advantage from the time-lag in the form of higher mechanical efficiency. The first world war, which laid waste the economies of Europe,
gave an immense stimulus to American industry. After that war the United
States became beyond dispute the leading economic power, and the protagonist in an attempt to restore all over the world the shattered foundations of the capitalist order. The attempt, bolstered by a large-scale revival
of international lending under the sponsorship of American banks,
foundered in the great depression of the early 1930's. Though the great depression was in its origin an American crisis spreading across the Atlantic
over Europe, its lessons were more fully taken to heart, and more readily
accepted as conclusive, in shattered Europe than in the still relatively in-

tact economy of the United States. In the European countries, as well as in Great Britain, it became an axiom that another capitalist crisis could never be allowed to occur and that it was a primary duty of the state to prevent it from occurring. Acceptance of this axiom marked the final rejection of the *laissez-faire* philosophy; and, in so far as historical endings and beginnings can be precisely dated, the unplanned and uncontrolled capitalist system of the nineteenth century everywhere outside the United States was dead in 1933.

V

Fascism

Everybody knows about fascism, but very few people indeed have given much thought to what it actually is. Fascism seems to have a particularly elusive character, to be more of a mood than a carefully designed creed. This elusive quality may well be the reason why so many scholars are now being attracted to it as a fruitful area of study. The appeal of fascism was so wide, and its bases of support so obviously went beyond conventional political, social, or economic issues, that one can only suspect that fascism was more than a response to the ordinary tensions of modern society; it clearly provided something for which there was a deep craving.

The following selections do not provide direct confrontations of opinion about fascism so much as they represent the considered opinions of scholars about the fascist phenomenon. The time has passed for bitter controversy, and calm analysis is far more appropriate; it can only be misleading to use "fascism" as an epithet applicable to virtually anything one may dislike at the moment. This chapter is designed, therefore, to help the student put fascism in its proper historical context, and to understand its nature, insofar as possible.

This is an extraordinarily difficult task, for, as Eugen Weber has pointed out, there are many varieties of fascism.[1] If Christianity and Marxism have split into so many species, it is no surprise that fascism, which owes allegiance to no single body of doctrine, tends to take on differing colorations in a most confusing manner. Contradictions and anomalies appear at every turn, yet it is these very contradictions and anomalies that provide the key to understanding. Between the wars fascism was able to be all things to all men. Its anti-intellectualism, its nihilism, its cult of the leader, its craving for violence and action, its glorification of youth and regeneration, its tendency to reduce all issues to slogans, touched responsive chords in millions of people throughout Europe. Representing the ultimate in what Fritz Stern has called "the politics of cultural despair," [2] it raised irrationalism to a pedestal it has seldom occupied.

It is therefore difficult to put fascism into any category such as "left" or "right," "conservative" or "liberal." Mussolini and Hitler were as unlike Edmund Burke, with his belief in tradition, vested interests, and historical liberties, as they were unlike John Stuart Mill, with his belief in individualism, free speech, and parlia-

1. See his *Varieties of Fascism* (New York: Van Nostrand, 1964).
2. See his remarkable study of some forerunners of Nazism, *The Politics of Cultural Despair* (Berkeley and Los Angeles: University of California Press, 1961).

mentary democracy. They also seem far removed from men like Franco and Salazar, who came to power to protect the old elites for whom fascism had such contempt. Yet, if fascism was clearly a doctrine of revolution, it did not hesitate to
appeal to or cooperate with conservative interests when that suited its purpose. If
it was, in the 1920's and the 1930's, the incarnation of anti-Marxism, it is also
true that it shared many traits with communism.[3] Adolf Hitler himself admitted
that "There is more that binds us to Bolshevism than separates us from it. . . .
There is, above all, revolutionary feeling." [4] This is why so many ex-Communists
were drawn into Nazi organizations like the SS. They were known as beefsteak
Nazis—brown on the outside and red on the inside.[5] But was this feeling for revolution genuine, or just rhetoric? Was the anticapitalist raving of men like the
Belgian fascist, Léon Degrelle,[6] something to be taken seriously, or was it just
window dressing? How can one reconcile Mussolini's stated desire to merge Italian capitalism into the totality of his fascist state, with the reality of his cooperation with Italian big business? Would there have been an eventual showdown?
Or was there any plan at all in Mussolini's head, other than the cultivation of a
youthful and dynamic image? These questions can be multiplied a thousand-fold,
but little would be demonstrated other than what has already been emphasized:
fascism thrived on its contradictions. Perhaps the best summary of the fascist outlook was provided by Ernst von Salomon, the free corps leader who, after the first
world war, exemplified much of what was later to become Nazism: "What we
wanted, we did not know. And what we knew, we did not want!" [7] And the difficulty of placing fascism into a niche in conventional political terms might be
found in a slogan of Ramos Ledesma, one of the founders of Spanish fascism:

> Long live the new world of the twentieth century!
> Long live Fascist Italy!
> Long live Soviet Russia!
> Long live Hitler Germany!
> Long live the Spain we will make!
> Down with the bourgeois parliamentary democracies! [8]

Fascism is, therefore, a difficult concept for those students who wish to classify
various phenomena neatly. A social psychologist like Zevedei Barbu may be justified in arguing that the core of the Nazi party "was formed by socially nonde-
script people, frustrated in their efforts to achieve a certain status in society"; [9]
but then how does one explain the attraction of fascism for some conservative
businessmen, churchmen, and aristocrats? Barbu may also be justified in arguing
that "The *Weltanschauung* of Nazism rests on the assumption of the irrationality of
human nature"; [10] but then how does one explain the attraction that fascism held for
many intellectuals, whose life presumably depended on reason and freedom? Are
the answers to be found in mistaken calculations about the nature of fascism? Are

3. Ernst Nolte, *Three Faces of Fascism* (New York: Holt, Rinehart and Winston,
1966), p. 21.

4. Quoted in Robert G. L. Waite, *Vanguard of Nazism* (Cambridge: Harvard University Press, 1952), p. 273.

5. *Ibid.*, p. 274.

6. See, for instance, Weber, *op. cit.*, p. 47.

7. Quoted in Waite, *op. cit.*, p. 269.

8. Quoted in Stanley G. Payne, *Falange: A History of Spanish Fascism* (Stanford:
Stanford University Press, 1961), p. 14.

9. See his *Democracy and Dictatorship* (New York: Grove Press, 1956), p. 128.

10. *Ibid.*, p. 131.

they to be found in the quirks of individual or mass psychology? Or will they be discovered in the pressures of a modern society largely bereft of the certainties formerly provided by traditional revealed religion? If it is true that man fears liberty and despises equality, did fascism provide the fraternity he so desperately needs? Was fascism the synthesis of the modern collectivist movements, nationalism and socialism? Does fascism have any potential for success today? The following selections should suggest some tentative answers.

1. *H. R. Kedward: Fascism in Western Europe, 1900-45*

The difficulties of defining fascism may lead one to include every imaginable event or movement in modern European history as part of its background. H. R. Kedward, a young British historian who teaches at the University of Sussex, is typical of this tendency, and his discussion of fascism ranges very wide indeed. He nevertheless presents a carefully considered view, which might well cause dismay among economic determinists and their allies.

The confident society of the 18th century despised the uncivilized past and found little of value between the Roman Empire and the Renaissance. "The Dark Ages" was a phrase used to describe this period in history—a period held to have been dominated by superstition and ignorance. Equally rejected was the primitive world which had preceded the ancient civilizations of Greece and Rome. Most 18th-century philosophers believed that pre-civilized society was one of warfare and destruction, a state of nature in which anarchy prevailed. Thus there was little interest in uncivilized countries, in native tribes or primitive man. The focus was on 18th-century Europe and the triumph of the Renaissance spirit of reason and inquiry. History seemed firmly directed towards progress and light.

In the 19th century this attitude was strengthened by industrial and scientific development. Technology in particular moved man to admire his own skill and achievements. The invention of the steam engine and the extensive use of iron for ship, rail and bridge building enabled him to dominate distances; canals, constructed with a variety of lifts, locks and inclines, overcame differences of levels; electricity harnessed in power stations by the end of the 1870s produced man-made light, and finally, the internal combustion engine motorized the roads and the air. Less dramatic but equally important were the invention of the flush lavatory, tools and machines for the mass production of all consumer goods and systems of construction for rapid housing development. In medical science the stethoscope, anaesthetics, vaccination and the X-ray were among the many inventions and discoveries which controlled the natural world of disease. In

From H. R. Kedward, *Fascism in Western Europe, 1900–45* (Glasgow: Blackie & Son, Ltd. 1969), pp. 19–27, 30–34, 216–19, 223–25, 239–42. Footnotes omitted. Reprinted by permission of the publishers.

chemistry, physics and natural science the direction was the same. Civilization was being created and extended wherever 19th-century man cared to look, and, identified with it, whatever anti-clericals and atheists claimed, stood Christianity. When overseas discoveries and exploration began to excite the European countries and the imperialists began to stake their claim to remote parts of the world, it was in the name of civilization and Christianity that they supported their actions. Between 1870 and 1900 it was taken for granted that Europe had a responsibility to convert and enlighten those lands which had not had the fortune to develop with the West. The Age of Empire was the climax of the Idea of Progress. What had been learnt from European history was now to be transmitted to the world at large. Whatever the original motivations of imperialism, this cloak of responsibility and enlightenment was now thrown grandiosely over the whole enterprise.

Alongside this 19th-century worship of the civilized, however, there ran a seemingly contrary interest in the uncivilized, the natural and the primitive. The Romantics again provide a starting point. Sir Walter Scott's novels in Britain, Chateaubriand's emotional Christianity in France, and the writings of Goethe, Novalis and Schlegel in Germany were among the many intellectual influences which made the medieval and folk world the object of investigation and adulation. A pride in nationality was stirred by stories of ancient heroes; folk songs and myths were written down and distributed to inspire national music and poetry and the roots of language carefully investigated for signs of cultural origins. . . .

Through the deeds of primitive heroes, through their violence and romantic nobility, the urbanized, industrialized West could live vicariously: if actual heroism were impossible the next best thing was a full-blooded account of it. Richard Wagner's great operatic cycle, *The Ring*, played just this role in Bismarckian Germany. Both the welter of sound and the size of production submerged the Bayreuth audience in a flood of emotion and took them away from business, local politics and finance into the twilight world of Siegfried, the Nordic Gods and the Rhinegold. As long as they could return from this twilight world to a life and society which gave satisfaction, then the romance of mythology could stay in its artistic place, but the suggestion that this world of heroes and gods ought to become the real world was always close to the surface. . . .

At the same time the discoveries of natural science had introduced new perspectives in the search for the primitive. The Darwinian theory of evolution shattered the complacency of the civilized world. Although it was yet another indication of man's ability to probe even further into the natural world, it had some disquieting lessons for 19th-century Europe. Not only did it completely upset Christianity's trust in the story of Genesis, but it also suggested that animal nature and human nature were unexpectedly close and related. Man, who had been "little lower than the angels," was now "little above the animals." The way was open to discover animal and instinctual drives within civilized man; as a result psychology and anthropology developed rapidly in the last decades of the century. At first, however, it was another side of Darwinism which most stimulated popular interest in the primitive. Darwin himself took no part in this development and dissociated *The Origin of Species* from its ideas, but he could not prevent his discoveries from being put to the most dubious uses.

The aspect so spuriously adapted was Darwin's account of survival among plant and animal life. He had talked of a struggle for survival out of which only the strongest and most adaptable species emerged. This concept of "survival of the fittest" could easily be applied to human history. In a century of national rivalry, class struggle and economic competition, the Darwinian formula seemed to be a self-evident truth. Only the strong survived. The most popular aspect of this bastardized Darwinism was its application to race history. In their fascination with primitive European peoples the early nationalists had confused culture with race. Race is in fact transmitted by heredity, culture by tradition, but this distinction was entirely blurred in this period. The most outstanding example of this confusion was a four-volume work entitled *Essay on the Inequality of Human Races* (1838–55) by the Frenchman Arthur de Gobineau. It appeared before Darwin's major discoveries but it was strongly affected by the current interest in biological science. Races, Gobineau said, were permanently unequal: some were superior, others were inferior. Those that were strong owed their position to the purity of their blood: they had not become weak through intermarriage. Only one race, he maintained, was capable of creating a true civilization and that was the Aryan race from which the Germans were descended. They were the purest, strongest and most creative race. Gobineau was intensely serious and was convinced of the truth of his findings. He was himself an aristocrat, increasingly isolated in a post-revolutionary France which had discarded the aristocratic traditions of the *ancien régime*. Frenchmen therefore took little notice of his work. Germans on the other hand found much to admire. . . .

When Darwinism was added to the ideas of Gobineau the mixture was powerful, and the Germans' fascination for their remote Aryan ancestors became a cult of Germanic virtues and strength. For this reason the growth of Aryan racialism must be seen as a primitivist movement. Like Wagner's *Ring*, the cult of Germanism evoked the myths and heroism of a past shrouded in mist, of lands which were indeterminate and of peoples who were unknown to history. There is, in fact, no such thing as an Aryan race: Aryan was a language of one of the ancient Indian cultures. In the 19th century, however, popular stories about Aryan deeds and virtues gave flesh and blood to the so-called race. The Aryan myth became well established in the German consciousness. Only a minority of German writers took it seriously but they were influential in education and society. Most young Germans had probably read one or more of their novels. One of the most popular, written by Hermann Burte, appeared in 1912. Called *Wiltfeber, the Eternal German*, it was a direct appeal to the illusions of fanatical Germanists, but it had excitement and the lure of the distant past to attract the ordinary person. Still more primitive and extreme was the growth of paganism in secret German circles at the end of the century. Here the interest was in the rituals and ceremonies of pre-Christian Aryanism as handed down in popular ancient sagas. In particular, the sun was an object of worship and was used as a symbol of rebirth. With paganism went occultism, a science concerned with the supernatural, and in Vienna the German Austrian Guido von List led an occult circle in regular visitations to the past. His science was a secret one: his appeal was primitive.

Germans were by no means alone in primitive racialism, paganism or occultism. The same emotions thrived in other countries to differing degrees. In particular, the effect of imperialist expansion was to give the white man an arrogant sense of superiority over his coloured subjects, while at the same time luring him into the primitive world of native life. In Britain many public schools would have endorsed the motto of Abbotsholme, "Education means Empire," and one of the most popular youth magazines, *The Boy's Own Paper,* filled its pages with stories of uncivilized tribes, lion-hunts and dangerous explorations in jungle regions. These subjects were also the content of Rudyard Kipling's novels; they entertained, thrilled and flattered the reader, who could not avoid identifying himself with the hero. In France the adventure stories of Pierre Loti had a similar romantic appeal: man was pictured in the sensuous grip of far-away places or battling against the elements of nature.

As in literature, so in painting. The discovery of Japanese art, tribal masks and Negro sculpture had an influence on European painting which cannot be overestimated. The French painter Paul Gauguin went to Tahiti in search of bright colours and primitive simplicity. He settled on the island, took a thirteen-year-old native girl for his mistress, and by the letters and paintings he sent back to France created a myth of the romantic primitivist surrounded by flowers, fruit and beautiful women. The reality was not so picturesque: racked with disease, he was eventually spurned by even the older native women, and died embittered and alone. Less romantic but just as significant was Picasso's enthusiastic discovery of Negro art in a Paris museum, a find which led him to give mask-like, primitive heads to the women in his first breakthrough paintings. Primitive art became a recognized form, pulling art history away from the civilized Renaissance tradition and exploring the naive, the magical and the demented. . . .

Thus in the half-century before 1914, the primitive challenged the civilized as the object of man's interest and excitement. They could, of course, inspire each other, as in Aryan racialism and imperialist expansion, for here the attraction of remote or uncivilized races went hand in hand with supreme confidence in the present. In general, however, the enticing world of the primitive undermined the values of civilization. The contrast showed modern Europe to be dull, mechanical and lifeless: it was seen to be without colour or romance; its lack of violent exaltation was deplored; its religion was too safe and conventional. Primitivism and irrationalism joined forces in this attack on civilization. They were not necessarily the same, for primitivism, especially in German racialism and European imperialism, was authoritarian with a strong sense of physical and mental discipline. Irrationalism always tended to be anarchic and it stemmed more from the revolt of the individual than from a love of the primitive. In combination, however, they could mount a formidable attack on civilized society. In reply, society could point to its technical achievements and its material security. The pull in both directions was powerful.

In fascism elements of the two were brought together. The primitive was enthroned in party rituals, the use of ancient symbols and above all in racialism. In Nazism the barbarity of anti-Semitism reduced European history to a level of bestiality far beyond even the wildest dreams of 19th-century primitivists. Other racialism was not so animal but all fascisms used "Darwinian" notions of struggle and survival, which involved to some degree the ideas of racial superiority. Brutality in political action was the most consistent element in fascism. In itself this was the most blatant rejection of civilized values. Brute force allowed Fascists to act out their fantasies of being all-powerful, heroic and superhuman. In this way the gods and heroes of 19th-century stories emerged from books and operas and occupied reality. There is a vital difference between thinking force and acting force, and the youth who read the sagas of primitive warfare should not be confused with the Nazi who butchered his fellow men, but so many years of primitive tales and hero-worship must surely be significant in the history of fascism. One has only to note the continuation of this kind of literature under the Fascist regimes: it was an important stimulus.

Such strong, primitive strains in fascism appealed to large numbers of people who would never have murdered or fought with the ferocity of actual Fascist members. Primitivism in small doses was an acceptable commodity throughout much of inter-war Europe, but there is every sign that fascism did not depend on this alone. It balanced its primitivism with a cogent display of civilization. The benefits of a modern society, its technological wonders and its material progress, were both exploited and continued by Fascist rule. By merging evolutionary ideas with supreme self-confidence, Fascists claimed to be at the very pinnacle of western civilization. History, they believed, had justified them—a belief similar to that of the Marxists, their principal political enemies, and not unlike that of the 19th-century liberals who had also claimed the support of history. Even more telling was the Fascist manipulation of propaganda: the public was shown what it wanted to know. If it wanted to believe Hitler was a kind, humane man it could look at numerous photographs of the Fuhrer patting the heads of children.

By these methods fascism's split identity, both primitive and civilized, was presented to the public as an organic unity. In some cases this was unsuccessful. Few people took the French *Faisceau* movement seriously; during World War II Quisling in Norway and Doriot in France were upheld by the German occupation, not by the power of their synthesis, despite the fact that they too combined the primitive and the civilized. There was no uniformity of either appeal or success in fascism, and the balance between primitive and civilized was different for each movement. The Spanish Falange, in particular, is not encompassed by the background described in this section. In general, however, this synthesis of the primitive and the civilized was an essential part of the complex nature of fascism. With each conflicting ingredient its complexity grew but its strength was not diminished. . . .

In the latter half of the century a new form of nationalism swept over Europe and one of its main enemies was parliamentary democracy. Earlier nationalism had been a liberal, democratic and revolutionary phenomenon and the revolutions of 1848 were its greatest monument. After 1848, revolutionary fire was diverted into socialism and anarchism, neither of which believed in the value of the nation state. Marxism prophesied that the state would wither away: the nation would no longer determine history; it would be the international working class who would inherit the earth. This clarion call to the workers of the world threatened the entire traditions of Europe, which, since the Middle Ages, had been geared to the nation state. Under this threat it was understandable that conservatives began to close their ranks to protect their nations from destruction. Nationalism became a conservative movement.

This change in nationalism is perhaps one of the great turning points of modern history. Nationalist parties, groups, circles and leaders sprang up all over Europe with similar methods and aims. In general their aim was to protect the nation from external attack and internal disintegration, and their methods were to build up national pride and emotion against all ideas and parties which threatened to weaken the state. The ideas of Friedrich Hegel were a source of inspiration: in his writings on history he had proclaimed that "The State is the Divine Idea as it exists on Earth": nothing could be higher or more exalted than the State; it was the finest stage of human development. As such, he continued, its interests were everybody's interests. The individual would find through the State his complete freedom and spiritual fulfilment. Duty to the State was the highest moral command. These sentiments of Hegel formed the emotion of nationalism. In any dispute between the nation and the individual, the national interest was supreme. In this way the nation became an object of religious veneration and much of the primitivism discussed in the last section was put at its service. Folk tales, racial histories, past heroisms and all forms of art were laid round the plinth on which the nation stood, proud in its historical achievements. The theorists of such nationalism included Lagarde in Germany, Barrès and Maurras in France and Corradini in Italy. Without exception they all found democracy and parliamentary government an obstacle to national greatness. Democracy, they claimed, protected the individual and involved the nation in interminable party wrangling. What was needed was strong government by those with the national interest truly at heart, that is, by a national elite. In this way the Burkean theory was rephrased and given a new setting. The call for natural rulers was heard again, not in Burke's traditional terms, but in vigorous, dynamic phrases which inflamed the patriotism of all classes.

The pressure of this nationalism on the forces of democracy was intense. Germany, in particular, allowed her politics and foreign policy to be strongly affected by it. No country was able to subdue its appeal. In 1914 the rival policies of nation states threw Europe into war. The nationalist movements embraced it with delirium. Warfare and violence were fully acceptable to the nationalist creed.

To this extent pre-war nationalism appears as the direct ancestor of fascism. Fascist ideals of strong leadership and ruthless rule by a national elite are foreshadowed by these earlier movements. What keeps them distinct from each other is fascism's use of mass politics, which seems totally contradictory to elitism and was frequently scorned by the conservatives as vulgar and dangerous. But it was fascism's ability to attract and use the masses which made it in the end more powerful than conservative nationalism.

What is meant by "mass politics" in this context? Certainly not democracy in its parliamentary sense. Although Fascists used parliaments to some extent, they were as hostile to parliamentary democracy and party politics as were the nationalists. But democracy in another sense, yes; in the revolutionary and Socialist tradition which looked for the rising of the people and the overthrow of the old order. The French revolutionaries had called on the people of Europe to rise and throw off the yoke of despotism; Karl Marx had prophesied that the proletariat would inevitably carry a revolution against the bourgeoisie, and revolts had been staged throughout the 19th century in the name of the masses. The vision of the people taking over society and creating a new world was by 1900 even more widespread than it had been during the French Revolution.

In the decade before World War I this prospect was announced with renewed vigour by the doctrines of Georges Sorel. A French intellectual who was a Socialist but belonged to no creed or party, Sorel published in 1906 a series of articles later called *Reflections on Violence*. In these highly influential writings he attacked parliamentary democracy and insisted that all great social changes came when a mass movement rose up against its enemies, inspired by a dominating ideal of the future. This ideal he called a "myth" and a past example of such a myth was the second coming of Christ:

> The first Christians expected the return of Christ and the total ruin of the pagan world, with the inauguration of the kingdom of saints at the end of the first generation. The catastrophe did not come to pass, but Christian thought profited so greatly from the apocalyptic myth that certain contemporary scholars maintain that the whole preaching of Christ referred sorely to this one point.

In just such a way, Sorel continued, the Socialists of the 20th century could be inspired by the myth of the General Strike, a moment in the future when all workers would stop work and the capitalist world would collapse. The new society would then be born out of the destruction of the old. All violence would be linked to this myth and would show how inspired the workers were.

When the Sorelian myth is added to Marxist prophecies, one can see what potential power lay in the idea of mass politics. If the masses could be roused to action in pursuit of some great cause, the earth could be

moved. Such a hope was considerably removed from the moderate democratic pressures which were affecting European politics. It was much more
emotional and appealed to the irrational side of man. It was much vaguer
too: a vote or a seat in parliament was something concrete but a myth or
an ideal was intangible. In this, of course, lay its appeal, as Sorel well knew.
Each man would have a different version and would feel he was following
his own interests.

Here then was the tradition of mass politics which fascism adopted. It
was a left-wing tradition whose spokesmen had included Marx and Sorel,
but in fascism it was merged with the right-wing theory of rule by an elite,
and twisted to tyrannical ends. The mass who rose in support of fascism
was not the proletariat, the traditional heirs of revolution, but a mass of
people from all classes who were inspired by Fascist ideals of strength, national power and authority. The Fascist myth was put over with a maximum of physical and propaganda force but it was not without its gentler,
seductive side. Mussolini wrote in 1932:

The Fascist accepts and loves life: he rejects and despises suicide as cowardly.
Life as he understands it means duty, elevation, conquest: life must be lofty and
full; it must be lived for oneself but above all for others, both near and far off,
present and future.

Such a portrait may be unrecognizable when Fascist violence is remembered, but it was seriously used to inspire followers and pacify doubters.
Fascism was not based merely on the brutal magnetism of violence: its
myths were more complex and its mass politics more subtle. Its ruling
elites understood as clearly as any other modern government the power of
widely based public support. This is what made them vulgar in the eyes of
more traditional elites: but vulgar or not, the synthesis worked, and Fascists worshipped few things more than success. . . .

It would seem that the view of European fascism at the last stand of
capitalism is at best a half truth. In theory, the most general Fascist economy was intended to take the form of the Corporate State, and this was by
no means an ideal solution for capitalists: in practice, fascism, especially in
Italy and Germany, did not attain the corporate goal. Under Mussolini and
Hitler the capitalist class was given security and protection against the socialism of the trade unions, but this security was bought at the price of
freedom—a sacrifice which was in the end, as Thyssen saw, against the
long-term interests of the capitalist economy. Fascism turned against all independence, and unrestricted private enterprise was one among the many
casualties. This fact, however, did not prevent leading capitalists within
both Italy and Germany from underwriting the structure and excesses of
the regimes. Without this support the dictators could hardly have survived,
nor could the present regimes of Franco and Salazar look so permanent.

The entire validity of an economic interpretation of fascism was challenged in 1939 by Peter Drucker, a Viennese who came to England in 1933
and joined an international banking house as an economist. In this position
he was thrown constantly against the nationalist economy of Nazi Ger-

many and became a shrewd observer of Nazi society and ideology. By the end of the thirties he was convinced that fascism in general and Nazism in particular was in no way an economic movement. His book, *The End of Economic Man*, put forward his case with insight and pungency. In a chapter headed "Fascist non-economic society" he states:

> It becomes clear, in the first place, that it is pointless to ask which class put fascism into power. No single class can have put fascism into power. That a gang of ruthless industrialists backed Hitler and Mussolini is as far from, and as near to, the truth as that the great toiling masses backed them. Both were necessarily supported by a minority of all classes. . . .
>
> Secondly, it is a moot question whether totalitarianism is capitalist or socialist. It is neither. Having found both invalid, fascism seeks a society beyond socialism and capitalism that is not based upon economic considerations.

To what then did fascism appeal? Drucker develops his thesis by claiming that fascism is fundamentally a revolt against the view of man as an economic unit, a view which both capitalism and socialism held in common. Instead fascism turns from Economic Man to Heroic Man and appeals to man's non-economic values—values of heroism, self-sacrifice, discipline and comradeship. To those who had no place in the economic hierarchy, it offered, not higher wages or economic promotion, but an active development of the personality. This can be seen, Drucker maintains, in the leisure-time activities sponsored by both Nazism and Italian fascism. In Germany workers were encouraged to join the movement of *Kraft durch Freude* (Strength through Joy) and in Italy the *Dopo Lavoro* (After Work). Both movements brought sport, camping, hikes and team spirit within the experience of the factory or farm worker. Gradually these movements became more obligatory and were used as police methods of controlling potential opponents to the regimes, but their object was clearly to provide non-economic returns for the working man's labour. Similarly the two dictatorships offered the capitalist classes the non-economic values of nationalism and cultural or racial supremacy. Heroic Man was the ideal throughout.

This thesis was more than a flash of intuition: it was an astonishing feat of objectivity at a period when stereotyped economic explanations were the norm. It was regarded with suspicion because it was too understanding and sounded like a product of fascism itself. Not that Drucker concluded without drawing a moral: in the last chapter he stated that the democracies must fight fascism with their own non-economic values—the values of Free and Equal Man. Drucker's theory is a powerful contribution both to the controversies of the time and to the interpretations of history, but it has its limitations. There is no convincing sign in modern European history that we have reached the end of Economic Man: economic values continue to predominate with only a minority opposing them. Nor can we be sure that the millions who followed Hitler and Mussolini clearly distinguished between Economic and Heroic Man: did the stormtrooper, for example, value order and strength more highly than his regular pay and daily meal? Both dictators came to power in periods of economic chaos and both offered economic incentives as well as non-economic values. The ideals of corporatism and national socialism were themselves inseparable from the economic problems of inter-war Europe.

The lasting contribution of Drucker is his stress on the quality of the Fascist appeal: it did transcend class and economic barriers and it did emphasize the non-economic values of both individuals and society. It is this unique quality which distinguishes it from the class-conscious, economically centred ideologies of capitalism and socialism. None of the main Fascist leaders, except Mosley, was an economic expert, and in most doctrines of fascism, economics appears more as a by-product than as the substructure of all other thought. Fascism, if it did not herald the end of Economic Man, certainly suggested an alternative. There was much talk, especially among Fascist intellectuals such as Giovanni Gentile in Italy or Drieu La Rochelle in France, of Fascist Man as the ideal type in a new Europe. The qualities ascribed to this man certainly did not indicate economic preoccupations: he was built more on cultural lines, and one extension of Drucker's thesis is to approach fascism as a radically new cultural movement. What are the grounds for this approach? Are its claims too vague and too large? . . .

One finds initially that all fascisms resemble a religion in their use of symbols, myths and rituals. The symbols of the Nazi swastika, the Italian *fasces* or the British flash and circle, to mention only three, were used to give direction and solidarity to the movements. Without symbols a mass movement will lose its orientation, since the symbol acts as a substitute leader and ideology. Hitler could not be everywhere at once commanding allegiance, nor could the Nazi ideology be constantly under men's eyes, but the swastika could symbolize everything Nazi in all places at all times. Like the Star of David or the Catholic crucifix it inspired loyalty and devotion and was employed consciously by the Nazis to rival its religious counterparts. The swastika was often reduced to a jagged cross to suggest a relationship with Christianity which was of propaganda value. Degrelle also used the cross long after his movement, *Rex,* had ceased to be a purely Catholic one.

In the early stages of Nazism, Hitler took a personal interest in the actual design of the symbols. He himself sketched out the eagle armband of the S. A. after discovering in an anti-Semitic book that the eagle was the Aryan among birds. The swastika was not his invention, however. It was already very popular with students in Germany after World War I and was worn by soldiers who had enlisted for the fight against Bolshevism. In adopting it, the Nazis claimed that the swastika was an ancient Teutonic or Nordic symbol. This is doubtful, even though, as a symbol of the sun, it has been found in several ancient civilizations.

The Italian claim on the old Roman *fasces* is, by comparison, less pretentious. Mussolini saw himself as the leader of the Third Rome which Mazzini had prophesied in the mid-19th century. With the second Rome, that of the Popes, he came to terms in the Lateran Treaty of 1929, and from the first Rome, that of the Emperors, he took as much as his regime could assimilate. There was to be no doubt which of these three Romes was to be the greatest: the *fasces* were intended to proclaim the authority of the past and the greatness of the present.

Uniforms were another natural source of symbolism, consciously parallel to religious practice. The black, brown or green shirts, the jackboots and belts, gave to the Fascists the appearance of a special order set apart from society like monks or holy men. Periods of training and rituals of initiation were developed and emphasis put on obedience and discipline. Marcel Déat, the French Fascist and collaborator, described his movement as an Order, imposing a strict rule of life on its members whom he described in religious terms as "regulars." The mark of these regulars was to be the distinctive uniform. It was a highly symbolic act when Doriot, Déat's fellow Fascist, first donned a Nazi uniform during the war. This uniform had been highly prized since the 1920s: when Nazis were forbidden by certain state authorities to wear their black shirts the men appeared in the streets with their chests bare but with the black ties knotted round their necks. On or off, the shirts were a potent symbol.

The colours themselves were significant symbols. "Black," said Mosley, "best expresses the iron determination of fascism in the conquest of red anarchy." But this distinction between black and red was not so blatantly made in Germany. From the early days of the Nazi movements the colour red figures in armbands and flags: in some areas and on some occasions red seemed the predominant colour, mystifying the public and rivalling the Communist symbols. Many workers drifted into Nazi meetings under the illusion that the red banners and posters outside indicated a genuine commitment to socialism.

Accent on colour, uniform and sign, and the distribution of these throughout society, had the dual effect of encouraging supporters and intimidating the opposition. The mass production of Nazi leaflets headed with the swastika and the appearance of the sign on street walls and underground passages throughout Germany gave the impression well before Hitler's accession to power that the country was overrun by Nazism. In fact the Nazis never gained a national majority in any free election: the symbols suggested a power and universality which was false, but many Germans paid more attention to the swastikas than the voting figures. In Italy Mussolini came to power without such a highly developed system of mass persuasion, but once established he multiplied party posters quoting his speeches, brandishing the *fasces* and announcing "The *Duce* is always right," as a ubiquitous reminder that fascism was in control. Familiar advertising and propaganda brings a sense of security like well-known biblical passages on a church hoarding or shrines at crossroads. Both Hitler and Mussolini knew how to manipulate public opinion by symbolic gestures. . . .

In Rome on 27 October 1930, Mussolini declared:

Today I affirm that the idea, doctrine and spirit of fascism are universal. It is Italian in its particular institution but it is universal in spirit; nor could it be otherwise, for spirit is universal by its very nature. It is therefore possible to foresee a Fascist Europe which will model its institutions on Fascist doctrine and practice, a Europe which will solve in the Fascist way the problems of the modern state of the 20th century.

Here is Mussolini the internationalist, proclaiming a universal faith on the eighth anniversary of the march on Rome. But in the same speech Mussolini the nationalist is also on display:

By the year 1950 Italy will be the only country of young people in Europe while the rest of Europe will be wrinkled and decrepit. People will come from over the frontier to see the phenomenon of this blooming spring of the Italian people.

The inconsistency is glaring, but is found throughout Italian fascism and in most other Fascist movements of Western Europe. It can stand as a final example of all the paradoxes of which fascism was composed and which make an adequate definition elusive. Any definition would need to respect the particular origins, obsessions and ambitions of the national movements and yet hint at the general cultural revolution which so many Fascists envisaged. Fascism could be described as a combination of radical nationalism, revolutionary action, authoritarian rule and aggressive, violent ideals. This would go some way towards a summary, but the limitations of such a definition are all too apparent.

It could be argued that the best way to define fascism is not in a positive but in a negative way, by reference to its opposites, but this too presents difficulties. At one time its opposite was naturally assumed to be communism, since fascism was said to be on the extreme Right of politics and communism on the extreme Left. This appeared self-evident when the traditional semi-circle of parties was drawn, i.e.:

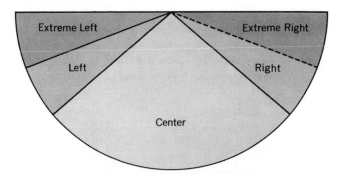

Such a diagram served the political scene of the 19th century when socialism was on the extreme Left and autocratic conservatism on the extreme Right, but in the 20th century a new diagram is needed in the form of a circle, i.e.:

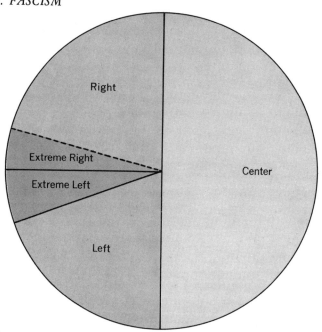

This circular image does greater justice to the realities of 20th-century politics by recognizing that extreme Left and extreme Right, communism and fascism, converge at many points and are in some cases indistinguishable. Doriot, for example, moved with ease from French communism to his Fascist P.P.F. without changing his attitudes or methods, and most of the conclusions on Nazi culture in the last chapter could be applied to Stalinism. The circle, however, does not minimize the differences which kept the two systems apart. Travelling the longest route round the circle, it is a very long way indeed from extreme Left to extreme Right. Thus communism and fascism are as distinct in some respects as they are similar in others.

This was most clearly apparent in the Spanish Civil War. If one looked at methods, the Communists were as violent, as authoritarian and as tightly organized as the Fascists; they were both supported by dictators, Stalin on the one hand and Hitler and Mussolini on the other, and they were both as intolerant of any deviation from the party line. They were next to each other on the circle. But if one looked at their history and their ideology the two had little in common: the Communists stood in the Marxist tradition and aimed at proletarian revolution, while the Fascists had their national values and a vision of an organic society. They were quite distinct.

Fascism therefore will only be partly defined by its opposition to communism. It is perhaps more profitable to look for its political opposites across the circle in the centre, where one finds progressive conservatism, liberalism and radical individualism. It is at least historically true that in the countries where these political attitudes were most entrenched—Britain, France and Belgium—neither fascism nor communism came to power.

A different approach towards a definition lies through the study of personality. Is there a Fascist type of person? Professor Eysenck, the psychologist of behaviour, is one authority who approaches politics in this way. In his book *Sense and Nonsense in Psychology* he gives a number of questions which reveal one's personality in relation to public and political issues such as anti-Semitism, flogging, birth control and nationalization. Out of this test a Fascist type emerges as tough-minded, very aggressive, fairly conservative, fairly rigid and fairly intolerant. The aggression, in particular, is stressed by Eysenck. Only forty-three Fascists were involved in his survey so the findings are, at best, tentative, but on an aggression rating Fascists frequently scored an average of 24 and 30 as compared with Communists who scored an average of 16, and those with politics of the centre who averaged 11. Research along this line is urgently needed, as Eysenck states: it is crippled with difficulties, since people with extreme views tend to react with hostility to psychological surveys. The value of the approach, however, lies in its conviction that politics is not just a question of economic or social conditioning but also of personality structure. Since the Fascists themselves claimed to produce a "new man" who would be recognized, above all, by his personality, this approach points in a promising direction.

Finally there is the claim that history needs no definitions: the facts speak for themselves. However unsatisfactory in theory, this claim appears to remove many of the difficulties. To the question "What was fascism?" the answers crowd on each other in shattering intensity: Mussolini justifying the murder of Matteotti; Degrelle hypnotizing his audience with attacks on Belgian politicians; a British Black Shirt smashing a Jewish shop window in London's East End; a Falangist repaying murder for murder in Madrid; opposition silenced in Germany; Darnand's *Milice* torturing Resisters in Occupied France; smoke rising from the bodies of Jews, slaughtered in a hell which man had devised. These facts certainly speak, but what of the dangers of selectivity? Could other facts be selected to show fascism in a more favourable light? The real difficulties of interpretation and historical understanding remain. The polemicist alone will claim there is no problem: but the polemicist produces no insight into history, only a projection of himself. This lesson, at least, fascism has taught us.

2. *Alastair Hamilton: The Appeal of Fascism*

Something which is often forgotten is that fascism between the wars had a considerable appeal for many intellectuals. Fascism seemed for them exciting and dynamic, a doctrine of strength which was preferable to the decaying world of the self-satisfied bourgeoisie. The German army as it marched into

From Alastair Hamilton, *The Appeal of Fascism* (New York: Macmillan, 1971), pp. xv–xxiii. Copyright 1971 by Alastair Hamilton. Reprinted by permission of The Macmillan Company and Anthony Blond, Ltd.

Paris in 1940 in many ways epitomized what a few French intellectuals had found so sadly lacking in the Third Republic—youth and vigor, and a sense of the future. Fascism seemed to stand for idealism and selflessness, and its excesses could be excused as youthful exuberance. Disillusionment often came quickly; but it is well to remember that many intellectuals had long feared democracy as something which might destroy all cultural standards,[1] and thus the antidemocratic fervor of fascism had at least an initial appeal. Alastair Hamilton, a young English scholar educated at Cambridge, discusses this phenomenon in the selection below. One might well ask, after reading Hamilton, whether similar tendencies can be found among intellectuals today.

The consequences of Hitler's ideas, the victims of persecution and discrimination, the disgrace incurred by Mussolini because of his early influence on the German dictator and his subsequent alliance with him, tend to obscure the atmosphere in which Fascism developed and to becloud that period when hardly anyone imagined to what it could lead. They distort beyond recognition the time when writers, known for their hatred of democracy, had little reason to believe that their apologies for violence would go farther than the paper on which they expressed them. . . .

I shall do no more than allude to the so-called precursors of Fascism, who died before Fascism was born, for I agree that it is "misleading to suppose that Fascism itself can be understood in terms of certain theoretical 'roots'." But just as it is impossible to prove that Fascism had its undisputed forerunners in the nineteenth century, so I believe it impossible to prove that the thought of a writer led him inevitably to Fascism. This was a fantasy—a somewhat dangerous fantasy, I cannot help feeling—both of the left-wing and of the Fascists themselves. The situation was by no means clear cut. A number of men who were hailed as Fascist thinkers would either have nothing to do with the movement, or approved it briefly and reluctantly. Others amazed their contemporaries by welcoming Mussolini and Hitler to power—and although I have not extended this study to the phenomenon of the intellectual who committed himself to Communism, the barrier between those who chose Communism and those who preferred Fascism seems to me, in many cases, so slim that we are less than ever entitled to say that a certain type of man, a certain type of psychology tended towards Fascism. If I have occasionally suggested, as with Céline and Gottfried Benn, that a writer's profession and environment might be partially responsible for his political sympathies, this is no more than a suggestion: I am aware that many writers of the same profession and from a similar background could be produced as evidence against it.

One of the features that emerges from a study of political commitment between the wars is inconsistency. And if, as I think in most cases we must, we regard the intellectual's decision to back a particular political move-

1. See John R. Harrison, *The Reactionaries: A Study of the Anti-Democratic Intelligentsia* (New York: Schocken Books, 1967), p. 26.

ment as a relatively disinterested decision, taken in the hope that this political movement will produce a better, happier world and ultimately lead
to the improvement of social conditions, we see that the events between
1918 and 1939 often threw men in search of the right solution into wholly
incongruous positions. They witnessed two economic crises of unprecedented violence which led to riots, to unemployment, to the threat of starvation for millions of families. They feared that the Great War, with all its
horrors, might be repeated; and, in the thirties, Hitler's determination to
fulfil his expansionist ambitions—his withdrawal from the League of Nations and the Disarmament Conference, the occupation of the Rhineland,
the annexation of Austria, the occupation of the Sudetenland—suggested
that peace would only last as long as the democratic powers continued to
betray their principles. Yet in order to avoid a repetition of the Great War
people found themselves supporting régimes for which they had no natural
sympathy and defending points of view which, at any other time, they
would have deplored. In order to find some way out of the economic and
social crises in which the world was steeped, they came to advise political
solutions the practice of which would, in other circumstances, have revolted them.

Even the pattern of political alliances was paradoxical. From Hitler's
rise to power in 1933 to his invasion of the Soviet Union in 1941 there were
three possible combinations in Europe: the first—the one which only prevailed with the breach of the Nazi-Soviet pact—was an alliance between
the Fascist States, Italy and Germany, against the European "democracies,"
including the Soviet Union. The second was an anti-Communist alliance
between the Fascist States and the "democracies" against the Soviet Union.
And the third was an "anti-democratic" alliance—an alliance between the
Fascist States and the Soviet Union against the democracies. These three
combinations, sustained alternately by a variety of politicians, were reflected in the views of the European intelligentsia. There were the democrats, who opposed every form of totalitarianism, and there were the Nationalists who, if they were Italian or German, tended to support a Fascist
alliance against Communism and democracy, but who, in all events, put
their own country first. There were the anti-Communists—the intellectuals
who, though they had no particular sympathy for Fascism, preferred it to,
and regarded it as the best defence against, Communism. And finally there
were the "anti-democrats," those who wanted a revolutionary and authoritarian State, who looked with far more sympathy at the Soviet Union than
they did at the liberal democracies. It is this last category which, to my
mind, provided the true Fascists, the men like Malaparte and Drieu La
Rochelle—and which also produced a great many intellectual Communists.
These were the rebels whose main enemy was the *status quo,* the quiet,
peaceful, complacent and somewhat hypocritical liberal State. The Fascists
saw Communism and Fascism running parallel to each other. They believed not only that Fascism was revolutionary, but that it was left-wing.
Indeed, even if Fascism turned out to be reactionary in practice, its adherents were rarely willing to recognise it as such—and for this reason we are

not entitled to dismiss it as purely conservative or to interpret it in terms of the traditional right-wing. Fascism purported to be a third solution, biased to the left, which was to run its course between Communism and liberalism, closer to the former. It intended, if not to eliminate capitalism, at least to break the hold of the capitalist oligarchy. It was, in theory, to introduce "bourgeois Socialism."

This bourgeois Socialism had, both in theory and practice, little in common with proletarian, Marxist Socialism. The differences between the various forms of Fascism and the very considerable transformation which they underwent in the course of their existence, should appear clearly enough from my study and must be examined in their historical and national context, so I will here merely outline some of the points they had in common, some of the "images" which, in the twenties and thirties, people associated with the word "Fascism." Fundamentally it was an ideology intended to recruit those lower middle classes who were embittered by the economic and social crises, frightened by the idea of Communism, disappointed by the world which had emerged from the Great War, and who were dissatisfied with the traditional left- and right-wing parties. That Fascism, in the original sense of the word, was a phenomenon restricted exclusively to the period between the two wars, is indicated fairly clearly by the structure and outlook of the true Fascist movements—Mussolini's *Partito Nazionale Fascista*, Hitler's *N.S.D.A.P.*, Georges Valois' *Faisceau*, Mosley's British Union of Fascists. For these movements were originally designed to attract the ex-servicemen, the trench fighters of the First World War, to recreate the atmosphere of youthful comradeship, heroism and idealism that had developed in the trenches—or, it would be safer to say, that had developed in the myth of the trenches which the Fascists created. The Fascist leaders, therefore, organised parades, devised uniforms, provided their followers with songs, emblems and slogans, and emphasised such military qualities as hierarchy, leadership and discipline.

Yet Fascism was not intended solely for the ex-serviceman; it was, as I have said, intended for an entire class which felt its social status threatened, which feared the collapse of the traditional institutions, family, religion and nation, scorned by Marxism. In the Fascist States, therefore, these "eternal values," more the family and the nation than religion (for Fascism purported to be a religion in itself), became the object of a cult, and seemed to guarantee that the new world would be illuminated by familiar beacons. At the same time Fascism was presented as the only ideology which could do away with the class struggle and ultimately disprove the Marxist concept of the irreconcilability of the proletariat and the bourgeoisie. So, on a practical level, it offered corporativism—the corporate State where the old Socialist trade unions would be abolished, and the manpower of the nation would be reorganised in corporations, submitted to the authority of the State, in which the employer could come to terms with his employee on an egalitarian, and, above all, on an amicable and comradely, basis.

Anti-semitism, it should be emphasised, played no part in the essence of

Fascist doctrine: the conservation of racial purity was Hitler's own myth, shared neither by Mussolini nor by many of the other Fascist leaders. But it is also true to say that the organised violence offered by Fascism—even after it had officially been put to an end—required an object; Fascist activism needed to be directed *against* something. To start with, in Italy and elsewhere, this object was constituted by the Socialists, accused of being traitors to their country in the service of some international organisation, tainted by defeatism in the Great War and responsible for disrupting national unity and prolonging the economic crisis with their strikes and riots. To the Socialists Hitler added the Jews, in the belief that he could fire the petty bourgeoisie still more by inspiring in them a truly physical revulsion for another race.

In substance Fascism was a "myth" in the Sorelian sense of the word, a "system of images" defying logical definition or rational analysis, filled, if submitted to either, with contradictions. From myth to reality, from theory to practice, the gulf, as is often the case, was exceedingly wide. If examined with any degree of objectivity, if its course was traced and its achievements compared with its principles, Fascism was less than a myth: it was a hoax. Although the enthusiasm which it inspired is indisputable, and although this enthusiasm, in Germany if not in Italy, did more to diminish class antagonism than any reform undertaken by a democratic state, Fascism's claims to be revolutionary turned out to be false once it became a régime. In neither Italy nor in Germany did it succeed in changing the class structure, or in destroying capitalism. In both countries the revolutionary core of the movement, the *squadristi* and the S.A., were rendered ineffectual as soon as the dictator had the chance to suppress them. Corporation was never implemented in Germany and failed in Italy. Subject itself to so many different interpretations, it turned out, in Italy, to be no more than a means of retaining the former hierarchy.

If we examine Fascism outside Italy and Germany, still more discrepancies and contradictions come to light: most Fascist movements took either the Germans or the Italians as their model, thereby renouncing any claims to national tradition or originality. Strictly speaking Fascism was a Nationalist movement, but many French Fascists liked to think of it as international, while those who collaborated with the Germans during the Second World War in the name of Nationalism found themselves in a situation analogous to that of the Jacobite squire in *Tom Jones* who, after hearing the news that reinforcements for the Young Pretender had disembarked in England, "with great joy in his countenance, shook the landlord by the hand, saying, 'All's our own, boy, ten thousand honest Frenchmen are landed in Suffolk. Old England for ever! ten thousand Frenchmen, my brave lad!'"

What, then, was the appeal which Fascism, for however short a time, had for so many eminent men of letters, some of whom were in a perfectly good position to see through the myth? One of the advantages of the vagueness of Fascist doctrine and of its lack of a generally accepted originator was that a number of writers, who had very little in common with one another, could regard themselves as the precursors of a political movement which had triumphed. The ambiguity of the ideology allowed those who supported it to read into it what they pleased; they could twist it this way and that, according to their whim. And, for all its malleability, Fascism did constitute a phenomenon which artists found aesthetically satisfactory: it had turned anarchy into order. For Fascism, the Fascism of the intellectuals above all, had its origins in sheer rebelliousness, in an anarchistic revolt directed against the established order. I shall in this study be examining the relationship between Fascism and those artistic movements which developed before the Great War—Futurism in Italy, Expressionism in Germany, Vorticism in England. On the one hand these movements started as a reaction against the legacy of the nineteenth century—a traditionalist legacy which threatened to smother the arts as much as it inhibited the individual; but on the other they originated in a need to escape. The complacency of the despised, hard-working bourgeois was accompanied by a threat which struck the intelligentsia as equally distasteful and far more frightening—the threat of anonymity, due to the speed at which industry and mechanisation were advancing and the progressive rise of masses who could at last participate in the administration of a world in which they had previously been voiceless. It appeared, therefore, that the rôle of the individual was over: he was either to be enslaved by the ever more powerful machine, or he was to be engulfed in mass society.

To this threat of anonymity Fascism seemed to offer a solution, for it conciliated the cult of the hero with a mass movement. It defied social transformation by its deliberate protection of traditional values and attempted to impose a social structure which, though aristocratic in form, was based on individual merit regardless of social origin. Here was none of the sinister equality offered by the Communists: here was a society where each man was given his due, where he could retain his individuality, where the machine age was attractively draped in myths of mediaeval heroism and chivalry. And that Mussolini and Hitler should have "tamed the revolt" at the expense of the revolution was found to be less disturbing than the orderly State which rose up under their dictatorship was found impressive.

It is a mistake, no doubt, to transpose certain aesthetic ideals on to the level of politics—an error frivolously made by Salvador Dali when, at a Surrealist meeting in 1934, he proclaimed that Hitler's Surrealist personality was as admirable as that of Sade or of Lautréamont, and a mistake which proved of greater consequence when a number of writers sought, in a totalitarian régime, the discipline which they associated with their own, private, creative process. The difficulties implicit in such an attitude were well expressed by André Gide, who preferred to commit himself to Communism. "The notion of liberty such as it is taught us," he wrote in October 1931, "seems to me false and pernicious in the extreme. And if I approve Soviet constraint I must also approve Fascist discipline. I believe ever more firmly that the idea of liberty is nothing but a hoax. I would like to be sure that I would think the same if I were not free myself, I who value my own liberty of thought above all else: but I also believe more and more firmly that man does nothing valid without constraint, and that those capable of finding this constraint within themselves are very rare. I believe, too, that the true colour of a particular thought only assumes its full value when it is thrown into relief against an unperturbed background. It is the uniformity of the masses which enables certain individuals to rise up and stand out against it. The 'Render unto Caesar the things which are Caesar's; and unto God the things that are God's' of the Gospel seems to me wiser than ever. On God's side we have liberty—the liberty of the spirit, on Caesar's side there is submission—the submission of our acts."

Fascism combined the idea of discipline with another prospect which was found equally exciting intellectually, although we now have some difficulty in dissociating it from the genocide which, however indirectly, descended from it. This was the prospect of the "new man," the élite of heroic supermen, "*artist*-tyrants," of whom Nietzsche had dreamt. But this élite should not be understood in terms of anti-semitism, for hardly any intellectual did so. One should, instead, place it on the vague and artistic level which attracted Gottfried Benn and Martin Heidegger. It was, in a way, a poetic fiction—a fiction which, despite the general repugnance felt by the Anglo-Saxons for Fascism, enchanted two of the greatest poets in the English language, Yeats and Ezra Pound.

The myth of the "new man" was connected, in its turn, with the desire for renewal, for revival, for invigoration, with those misleading but popular interpretations of history which came into fashion with the revolt against positivism at the end of the nineteenth century. I shall be mentioning the implication of the "cyclical theory" with reference to Oswald Spengler— there was nothing new about it, nothing original about it, nor was there anything new or original in the idea that civilisation had reached a point of crisis. Whether this belief became more acute or more widespread in the first thirty years of this century than it has ever done before, I hesitate to say; but it did pervade intellectual circles, and it was provided with the semblance of confirmation by the Great War and the Depression. More and more writers began to find the apocalypse not only inevitable but desirable. Partly in order to forestall it, partly in order to survive it, they chose to commit themselves to totalitarian ideologies and to support régimes that would hasten the destruction of the civilisation which they believed in a state of putrefaction. There was, of course, a profoundly self-destructive streak in this attitude of theirs, which we find most apparent in Gide. In 1932 he informed Dorothy Bussy "that he had played all his life with false chips; that nothing for which he had lived had any value any more; that *art*, free *thought*, even truth, would no longer count, *should* no longer count in the new world which Communism was opening for us. That we should side with the men who made Socrates drink hemlock, that art and the spiritual values of *Andromaque* were out of date and no longer concerned us . . ."

Here again Fascism seemed a solution. It claimed to be anti-intellectual —and most intellectuals agreed that the new world, beyond the apoca-

lypse, would have no place for intellectuals anyhow—but at the same time
it claimed to uphold those spiritual values which Communism would, in all
likelihood, destroy. To believe such a blatant lie (as far, at least, as National Socialism was concerned) it was necessary to overlook the remarkable similarity between the official works of art which issued from the
Third Reich and from the Soviet Union; but this was easily done, particularly by men who were living neither in the Soviet Union nor in the Third
Reich. In all events it seemed that under Fascism the death of the old
world and the birth of the new world would be relatively painless. Indeed, so
painless did they believe it to be, that we can almost detect a greater sense
of self-preservation in the writers who chose Fascism than in those who
chose Communism.

The other reasons which induced writers to commit themselves to the
ideology of Mussolini and Hitler should appear in the course of this book
—there was opportunism in the countries where Fascism triumphed; a desire, in the liberal democracies, to provoke popular opinion, to emphasise
the individuality of the artist by taking an unpopular political line. There
were purely personal motives—caprice, affections, perversions. There was
chance—the chance by which one man might witness the atrocities committed by the Fascists, while another might see those committed by the
Communists. There were, in short, a hundred reasons: and there was no
one rule that regulated them any more than there is any one rule by which
we can judge them.

3. George L. Mosse: The Genesis of Fascism

George L. Mosse, a professor of history at the University of Wisconsin, has
long been interested in European intellectual history, and in the following
article he attempts to place fascism in its proper context. He argues that the
negative aspects of fascism can never provide one with a full appreciation of
its dynamic qualities; he emphasizes that fascism was a movement of youth
that must be differentiated with care from reactionary or conservative ideologies. In what ways does Mosse enlarge upon Kedward's analysis? Does he
clarify the points made by Hamilton? Could the dream possibly *not* have
turned into a nightmare?

n our century two revolutionary movements have made their mark upon
   Europe: that originally springing from Marxism, and fascist revolution.
The various Marxisms have occupied historians and political scientists for
many decades, but fascism has been a neglected movement. The reason for
this seems plain: the war and the pre-eminent position of Germany within
this revolution have obscured its European-wide importance. That is why,

From George L. Mosse, "The Genesis of Fascism," *The Journal of Contemporary
History*, I, No. 1 (1966), 14–26. Footnotes omitted. Reprinted by permission of George
Weidenfeld & Nicolson Ltd.

in this special number on fascism, we have not concentrated on Germany but have, for once, given space to the rest of the story. For by the 1930s there was no nation without a native fascist party, and by 1936 a fascist Europe seemed within the realms of possibility—this even before Germany came to exercise its dominance over the movement. To be sure, Italy provided an important model and even tried (if unsuccessfully) to form a fascist international, but the national fascist parties had their own élan and their own problems to deal with. Yet if we want to get closer to the essence of the fascist revolution we must analyse it on a European-wide scale, taking into account important variations, but first trying to establish what these movements had in common. Fascism lacked a common founder, but all over Europe it sprang out of a common set of problems and proposed a common solution to them.

Fascism (although of course the word was not used at the time) originated in the attack on positivism and liberalism at the end of the nineteenth century. This was a general European phenomenon, and examples readily spring to mind. In Italy, for example, D'Annunzio praised man's instincts: "never had the world been so ferocious."

The writings of these men reflect the same basic paradox of industrial society: man seems on the one hand robbed of his individuality but on the other it is precisely this individuality which he wants to assert once more. The phenomena of mass man were accompanied by a feeling that the bourgeois age had culminated in conformity while those personal relationships upon which bourgeois morality and security were built had dissolved into nothingness. The tone among many intellectuals and among the young was one of revolt, of a desire to break out of the fetters of a system which had led to such an impasse. Much has been written about the aspect of this revolt which found its clearest reflection in expressionism; it is not often realized that fascism had its origins in the same spirit of rebellion.

Indeed, the idea of both fascism and expressionism share the urge to recapture the "whole man" who seemed atomized and alienated by society, and both attempt to reassert individuality by looking inwards, towards instinct or the soul, rather than outwards to a solution in those positivist, pragmatic terms which bourgeois society prized. There is nothing surprising in the fact that fascism felt an affinity with expressionist art and literature, and that even a not wholly unimportant segment of national-socialism tried to embrace them.

The key to fascism is not only the revolt but also its taming. For the problem before the fascist leaders was how to make this attitude towards society effective, and to counter the chaos which it might produce. How could the "constant feeding of one's own exaltation'" which D'Annunzio advocated, or the instinctualism of Nietzsche be captured and redirected into politically effective channels? That fascism could find an answer to this dilemma, play the cowboy to this widespread *fin de siècle* mood, explains much of its later success.

Both George Sorel and Gustave Le Bon had suggested answers, for they had shown concern for precisely this problem in the 1890s. A political movement must be based upon the instincts of men and these instincts harnessed to a dedicated leadership. Sorel's myth was the overt rationalization of the deepest feeling of the group. For Le Bon politics had to be based upon the fact of mass man and his irrationality. These two Frenchmen accepted as "given" the view of human nature which the revolt of the *fin de siècle* had posited and proceeded from there. Fascism shared the ground Sorel and Le Bon had prepared not only by accepting their view of human nature, but also by following out the content they gave to it and the prescription they made for it. Gustave Le Bon believed in the conservatism of crowds clinging tenaciously to traditional ideas. The appeal must be made to this irrational conservatism and it must be combined with the "magic" influence of mass suggestion through a leader. In this way mass man can be harnessed to a political mass movement, his tendency towards chaos can be curbed, and he can be redirected into positive action.

Le Bon describes admirably how to tame the revolt. The conservatism of crowds was reborn in fascism itself as the instinct for national traditions and for the restoration of personal bonds, like the family, which seemed fragmented in modern society. This conservatism was closely connected with the longing for an end to alienation, for belonging to a definite group. But the group had to be a traditional one, and it had to represent the restoration of the traditional morality. Hitler, for example, believed mass movements necessary because they enabled man to step out of his workshop, where he feels small, and to be surrounded by "thousands and thousands of people with like convictions." Alienation was to be exorcized, but on the basis of accepting a view of man as both irrational and conservative. Similarly in Italy an historically centred nationalism was to provide the "national consensus."

But the taming was always combined with activism, and this kind of conservatism inevitably went hand in hand with revolution. Both Hitler and Mussolini disliked drawing up party programmes, for this smacked of "dogmatism." Fascism stressed "movement"—Hitler called his party a "Bewegung," and Mussolini for a time favoured Marinetti's futurism as an artistic and literary form which stressed both movement and struggle. All European fascisms gave the impression that the movement was open-ended, a continuous Nietzschean ecstasy. But in reality definite limits were provided to this activism by the emphasis upon nationalism, racism, and the longing for a restoration of traditional morality. The only variety of fascism of which this is not wholly true we find in France. There a man like Drieu La Rochelle exalted the "provisional," the idea that all existing reality can be destroyed in one moment. But elsewhere that reality was "eternal," and the activism was directed into destroying the existing order so that the eternal verity of *Volk* or nation could triumph, and with it the restoration of traditional morality.

The impact of the first world war shows this rhythm of fascism, just as it gave the movement a mass base. The *élan* of the battlefield was transformed into activism at home. The *fasci*, the German storm troopers, and the Iron Guard in Rumania all regarded their post-war world as an enemy

which as shock troops they must destroy. Indeed, the leaders of these for-
mations were in large part former front-line officers: Roehm, the head of
the SA; Codreanu, founder of the Iron Guard; De Bono in Italy and Szalasi
in Hungary—to give only a few examples. But this activism was tamed by
the "magic" of the leadership of which Le Bon had written so much earlier.
Among the returned veterans it was tamed all the more easily, for they
sought comradeship and leadership with some desperation. Not only because of the war experience, but also because of their sense of isolation
within a nation which had not lived up to their expectations.

The "cult element" was central to the taming process; it focused attention upon the eternal verities which must never be forgotten. The setting
was a vital part: the balcony of the Palazzo Venezia, the Casa Rossa, the
window of Hitler's new Chancellery. Activism there must be, enthusiasm is
essential, but it must focus upon the leader who will direct it into the
proper "eternal" channels.

The liturgical element must be mentioned here, for the "eternal verities"
were purveyed and reinforced through the endless repetition of slogans,
choruses, and symbols. These are the techniques which went into the taming of the revolution and which made fascism, even that which leaned on a
Christian tradition, a new religion with rites long familiar in traditional religious observance. Fascist mass meetings seemed something new, but in
reality contained predominantly traditional elements in technique as well
as in the ideology.

To be sure, this taming did not always work. The youthful enthusiasm
which presided at the beginning of the movement was apt to be disappointed with its course. Italy, where fascism lasted longest, provides the
best example, for the danger point came with the second fascist generation.
There the young men of the "class of 35" wanted to return to the beginnings of the movement, to its activism and its war on alienation—in short,
to construct the fascist utopia. By 1936 such youths had formed a resistance
movement within Italian fascism which stressed that "open-endedness" the
revolution had seemed to promise: to go to "the limits of fascism where all
possibilities are open." They would have felt at home in the French fascism
of Drieu La Rochelle and Robert Brasillach, but they were not pleased
with the fascism in power. We can discern similar signs as Nazism developed, but here the SS managed to capture the activist spirit. Had it not
been for the war, Hitler might well have had difficulty with the SS, which
prized ideology less than power of the will as expressed in naked and brutal action. But then fascism never had a chance to grow old, except in
Italy: given the ingredients which went into the revolution, old age might
have presented the movement with a severe crisis.

Fascism was a movement of youth, not only in the sense that it covered
a short span of time, but also in its membership. The revolt of the *fin de
siècle* had been a revolt of the young against society, but also against parents and school. They longed for a new sense of community, not for a
"chaos of the soul." They were of bourgeois background, and their domi-

nant concern for several generations had been with national unity and not with social and economic change—something for which they felt little need. Thus they were quite prepared to have their urge to revolt directed into national channels, on behalf of a community which seemed to them one of the "soul" and not an artificial creation. Such were the young who streamed not only into the German youth movement, but also into the *fasci* and the SA, and made up the cadres of the Iron Guard as well as the Belgian Rexists. Returned from the war, they wanted to prolong the camaraderie they had experienced in the trenches. Fascism offered it to them. It is well to note in this connection that fascists were a new grouping, not yet bureaucratized, and the supposed open-endedness made them more dynamic than the other and rival political parties. The fascist leaders too were young: Mussolini was 39 when he became Prime Minister, Hitler 44 on attaining the Chancellorship, Léon Degrelle was in his early thirties, and Primo de Rivera as well as Codreanu were in their late twenties.

Youth symbolized vigour and action: ideology was joined to fact. Fascist heroes and martyrs died at an early age in order to enter the pantheon, and symbolic representations of youth expressed the ideal type in artistic form. Hitler liked speed and was a motorcar and airplane enthusiast; Mussolini loved his motor bicycle, but when it came to directing their movements, both stressed the rootedness of the true community. Indeed, when they inveighed against the bourgeoisie they meant merely the older generation which could never understand a movement of youth.

The traditionalism of the fascist movement coincided with the most basic of bourgeois prejudices. When Hans Naumann spoke at the Nazi book-burning in 1933 he praised action; the more books burned the better. But he ended his speech by exalting the traditional bonds of family and *Volk*. Such a traditionalism was in the mind of Giuseppe Bottai when he called for a "spiritual renewal," or when the leading Rexist, Jean Denis, held that without a moral revolution there can be no revolution at all. Some fascisms defined the moral revolution within the context of a traditional Christianity: this is true of the Belgian Rexist movement, for example, as well as of the Rumanian Iron Guard. The Nazis substituted racism for religion, but, once more, the morality was that shared with the rest of the bourgeoisie. The revolution of youth, of a virile activism, ends up as a revolution of the "spirit," asserting the primacy of ideology. It is the shared world-view which binds the Nation together and it is this which must be realized. The world-view restores the dignity of the individual because it unites him with those of his fellow men whose souls function in a similar manner, and they do so because all are part of the *Volk*, the race, or the nation.

This is an organic view of the world. It is supposed to take in the whole man and thus end his alienation. A fundamental redefinition of politics is involved in such a view of man and his place in the world. "Politics," the Italian fascist Bottai wrote, "is an attitude towards life itself," and this phrase can be repeated word for word from national-socialist literature. The leader of the Iron Guard, Horia Sima, summed it up: "We must cease to separate the spiritual man from the political man. All history is a commentary upon the life of the spirit." Such an emphasis meant that cultural expressions of the true community moved to the forefront as symbols of the new society. The national-socialist emphasis upon art and literature did not stand alone; for the leader of Flemish fascism, Joris van Severen, culture was the principle of unity and coordination. He added, typically enough, that culture presupposes a tradition.

The emphasis upon the organic, the creative national community, was supposed to overcome not only political but also class divisions. Georges Valois, the founder of French fascism, made the point when, before the first world war, he described the differences between his beliefs and Marxism. Marxism stressed one class, but he wanted to harness the energy even of the bourgeoisie to the new society. Valois' statement was prophetic, for fascism not only harnessed the energy of the bourgeois class but indeed became a movement whose spiritual revolution, the quest for organic, rooted man, coincided with bourgeois longings, at least in most of the West. It is significant that the classless society was always supposed to be a hierarchical one as well.

Fascism believed in hierarchy, not in terms of class but in terms of service to the *Volk* or nation as exemplified by the leader. In Western, but not German, fascism, the ideal of a corporate state was adopted; a state operating not through parliamentary representation (with its divisive political parties) but through workers and managers sitting together. However they did not sit together as equals; the manager was the "leader." Though there exists a considerable fascist literature about such a shaping of the state, in the last resort it was secondary. For if all members of *Volk* and nation shared a common myth, a common soul, then their participation in government need only be symbolized by the leader who has activated their shared human natures through his own activism, his "heroic will."

Fascism did stress the aim of social justice, but it would bring this about through the nation, the *Volk*, and not through the imposition of equality. The political and social hierarchies were to be open to all who served. This meant opposition to the old ruling circles, whether bourgeois or noble, and the substitution of new men for the old. Economic hierarchy was also preserved but within this framework a note of social justice was struck: Mussolini had his Charter of Labour and other fascisms drew up similar documents. Once again, fascism offered the best of all possible worlds: order and hierarchy would be maintained, private property would not be expropriated, but social justice would be done nevertheless. Once more this meant the primacy of ideology, ending spiritual alienation as a prerequisite for improving economic conditions.

Lest we brush this aside as inconsequential and lacking in appeal for the workers, it should be remembered that some fascisms did attempt, and successfully, to base themselves on the workers and peasants rather than the bourgeoisie. This was true in those countries where the working classes or the peasants had not been preempted by Marxist movements. Spain and Argentina provide examples in the West, and it is true of the Iron Guard as well as of the Hungarian fascist movement. To be sure, in those countries the bourgeoisie was not as strong as elsewhere, but another factor is of greater importance in explaining the fascist appeal to the labouring classes. Here, for the first time, was a movement which tried to bring these segments of society into political participation. In under-developed countries, the stress upon the end to alienation, the belief in the organic community, brought dividends—for the exclusion of workers and peasants from society had been so total that purely economic considerations could take second place.

Economics was indeed one of the least important fascist considerations. Jose Primo di Rivera, the founder of the Spanish Falange (which attracted much lower-class support), believed that "people have never been moved by anyone save the poets," while the Belgian fascist Léon Degrelle called Hitler, Mussolini, and Codreanu "poets of revolution." The mystical side of the ideology dominated, the "magic"; a fascist revolution must recognize the "primacy of the spiritual." Not control over the means of production was important, but the "new man" about whom all fascists talked. He was man made whole once more, aware of his archetype and of those with whom he shared it, an activist in that he was not afraid to join in a revolution which would make society correspond to the longings of his soul. These longings were for unity with the group, for the recapturing of those virtues which were being submerged in the modern world. As Hitler stated clearly throughout his career: a man rooted in the world-view to which he belonged was not afraid to make it come true. Once he had joined he released his creative instincts, his power of will, in the common cause. Triumph meant that the whole nation would now share this creativity and renew itself. Economic well-being was subordinate to the stress upon art, literature, indeed the total cultural endeavour. Fascism was a revolution, but one which thought of itself in cultural, not economic terms.

In spite of the working-class support which it attracted in the more backward countries, in the West this was primarily a bourgeois revolution. The bourgeoisie could have a revolution as an outlet for their frustrations, and at the same time rest assured that order and property would be preserved. But for all that we must sharply distinguish fascism from the reactionary regimes in Europe. To be sure, the Rexists supported the Belgian monarchy and the Flemish fascists did likewise, but the differences are nevertheless far-reaching. Reaction rejected all revolution, opted for the status quo, and looked back to the ancien régime for its models. It stressed hierarchy, but this was the traditional hierarchy of entrenched privilege. It needs no demonstration that such regimes discouraged activism and mass movements. Moreover, they thought in strictly territorial terms and the "shared soul" of all nationals or of the Volk would have had little meaning for them. For such regimes were not interested in bringing the disfranchised into politics or in ending man's alienation from his society. Their efforts were directed towards keeping men away from politics in order to maintain the monopoly of the traditional ruling class. Culture was not important here, and reactionary regimes gave wide latitude to all sorts of artistic expression so long as it did not encroach upon the monopoly of political power. The description of the Horthy regime by a modern historian is significant in this regard: Horthy did not intend to allow opposition to challenge his own will, but he did not think it any part of the duty of government to pry into and regiment each detail of his subjects' conduct, much less their thoughts.

Just so the French fascists split from the Action Française because it was not revolutionary enough, as shown by its inaction in February 1934. Francisco Franco destroyed his fascist movement, the Falange, in favour of a Horthy-like dictatorship. Fascism and reaction had different visions, and the two must not be confused.

But what of the differences between the diverse fascisms from nation to nation? These are best exemplified in the problem of racism and anti-semitism. Neither of these was a necessary component of fascism, and certainly not of those sections of the movement which looked to Italy for a model. There, until 1936, racism did not exist. In Belgium and the Netherlands the fascist situation was, in this respect, similar to that of Italy. Léon Degrelle explicitly repudiated racism—hardly surprising in a multi-national nation. What, he asked, is the "true race"—the Belgian, the Flamand, or the Walloon? From the Flemish side, the newspaper *De Daad* inveighed against race hatred and called on "upright Jews" to repudiate the Marxists in their midst.

Even Dutch national-socialism under Anton Adrian Mussert at first did not write racism on its banner, and kept silent about the Jews, a silence that the German Nazis were later to find incomprehensible. The French fascist group around the newspaper *Je Suis Partout* did go in for anti-semitism, but even here the Germans were accused of exaggerating the racial issue, for one could have good relations with a foreign people like the Jews. It is not astonishing that the early Falange was free from such ideas, for there were hardly any Jews in Spain. Yet the actual existence of Jewish groups cannot be linked too closely to fascist anti-semitism—for example both Belgium and the Netherlands had a relatively sizeable Jewish population. To be sure, in those countries a single-minded concentration on Marxism as the enemy tended to exclude all other considerations. But even this does not provide a satisfactory explanation, for the Marxist-Jewish equation could easily have been drawn there as it was in Germany.

This state of affairs did not last. By 1936 Mussolini had turned racist, and not merely because of German influence. Through racism he tried to reinvigorate his ageing fascism, to give a new cause to a youth becoming disillusioned with his revolution. The Italian reversal of attitude on this question seems to have affected the Falange as well, in spite of the absence of a native Jewish population. But here also a need coincided with this change of attitude—namely to make a more powerful appeal to the lower classes. As in Italy, so in Spain, anti-semitism helped to give the movement a greater and renewed dynamic. However, the Falange always rejected secular racism and based itself on the militant Catholic faith of Spain's crusading tradition. Similarly Oswald Mosley's fascists adopted anti-semitism when they found that this could give them a greater dynamic, a true feeling of struggle (and much free publicity) as they paraded through London's predominantly Jewish East End.

It was only in central and eastern Europe that racism was from the beginning an integral part of fascist ideology. Here were to be found the masses of Jewry, and still under quasi-ghetto conditions. They were a wholly distinct part of the population and vulnerable to attack. Moreover, in countries like Rumania or Hungary, the Jews had become *the* middle class, forming a distinct entity within the nation as that class which seemed to exploit the rest of the population through its commercial activities. No wonder the Iron Guard, in appealing to the nationalism of the peasants, became violently anti-semitic and even racist despite their Christian orientation—for they had begun as the legion of the "Archangel Michael."

After the First World War, the masses of east European Jewry began to emigrate into the neighbouring countries, predominantly Germany and Austria. The account in *Mein Kampf* of how Hitler reacted to the sight of such strangers in Vienna, may well have been typical. However that may be, the facts of the situation in that part of Europe gave fascism an enemy who could be singled out as symbolizing the forces which must be overcome. Moreover, in eastern Europe the struggle for national liberation had become associated with romanticism and racism long before fascism made its appearance on the scene. Hitler captured this tradition, and built upon the "Jewish question." This led to a further differentiation of national-socialism from Western fascism. For Hitler the enemy was not a vague Marxism; it was physically embodied by the Jews. Building on the Central-European tradition of a racist-orientated nationalism, he could give to the enemy of his world-view a concrete and human shape. Thus mass terror, and eventually mass extermination, could be built into German fascism as it was not built into other western fascisms. Both in Germany, and during the short-lived dominance of the Iron Guard, mass terror and pogroms became the manifestation of an activism which identified a distinct human group as the enemy. . . .

The fascist revolution cannot be understood if we see it merely in negative terms or judge it entirely by the dominance which national-socialism achieved over it by the late 1930s. For millions it did satisfy a deeply-felt need for activism combined with identification, it seemed to embody their vision of a classless society. The acceptance of the irrational seemed to give man roots within his inner self, while at the same time making him a member of a spontaneous not artificial community. Bourgeois youth streamed into its ranks because to them it seemed to offer a positive solution to the problems of industrial and urban society.

The negative side of fascism triumphed in the end. How can the activist dynamic be tamed once the "eternal verities" have triumphed? Can the emphasis on liturgy overcome the emptiness of a programme fulfilled? The answer was war upon the internal enemy, the adoption of racism; but another general solution lay in the realm of foreign policy. The activism must now be tamed by being directed towards the outside world. Hitler dreamed of his new Europe, Mussolini of the *Mare Nostrum,* Péron of an Argentine-dominated South America, and in Eastern Europe there were enough irridentas to fulfil this function.

The "new man" of whom fascism had dreamed went down to defeat, the victim of a dynamic which had, after all, not been satisfactorily curbed. The dream turned out to be a nightmare.

4. *F. L. Carsten:* The Rise of Fascism

F. L. Carsten is a leading authority on modern German history, and is presently Masaryk Professor of Central European History at the University of London. In the following selection he synthesizes long reflection on the fascist movements of Europe. Does he find any common denominators in fascism? Does he come to any firm conclusions about the social bases of fascism? Is the only sure way to avoid fascism, or to keep it weak—as it is in Europe today—to make certain that "the political atmosphere . . . . [is] sober and dull?"

The Fascist movements which arose in Europe during the 1920s and 1930s were very different in character, and they mirrored the entirely different national backgrounds of the countries in which they developed. Some were more conservative, and others more radical in their demands and their actions. Some were violently anti-Semitic, and others were not. Some took revolutionary action and staged armed revolts against the government, while others insisted on the legal way as the only possibility of attaining power. Some acquired a strong following among the lower classes, while others remained almost entirely middle and lower middle class. With so much variety, it might be asked what they had in common, and with what justification we can speak of Fascism in the singular. The following pages are an attempt to discuss these common traits—the factors which distinguish Fascism from other contemporary movements, whether right-wing or left-wing.

The Fascist movements, as has been emphasized by other writers, had much in common in their ideology—so much that they were able to borrow from each other. They were not only strongly nationalist and violently anti-Communist and anti-Marxist: that they had in common with other parties and groups of the extreme Right, such as the Nationalist parties of Italy and Germany. The Fascists not only hated Liberalism and democracy and the political parties, but they wanted to eliminate them and to replace them by a new authoritarian and corporative state. In this state, there

From F. L. Carsten, *The Rise of Fascism* (Berkeley and Los Angeles: University of California Press, 1967), pp. 230–37. Footnotes omitted. Reprinted by permission of the Regents of the University of California and B. T. Batsford, Ltd.

would only be one party; its hierarchy would overlap with that of the state, and its machinery would take over functions of the state. Its members would be the only ones entitled to hold high state offices. Ideally, there would be an identity of party and state, although in practice much friction between them arose in Germany as well as in Italy. Again in theory—though not always in practice—the Fascist party was strongly elitist in character. Its early members considered themselves called upon to save and to lead their nation, and many Fascist parties did not aim at attracting a mass membership, or stipulated periods when no new members would be accepted. The Fascist parties were conceived as tightly organized semi-military machines with which state and society were to be conquered; in all of them, para-military associations or militias—clad in black, brown, green or blue shirts and uniforms—played a very important part. They contained the "activists" who had to bear the brunt of the struggle for power. The seizure of total power was their aim.

Part of the movements' ideology was a powerful myth, a myth of the nation and the race. It usually took the form of territorial expansion as the goal, a Greater Germany, a Greater Finland, Imperial conquest in Africa, a Great Netherlands state, an Empire. The movements also glorified and venerated the past: the Roman Empire of antiquity, the Spain of the Catholic Kings, the Seventeen Provinces of the Netherlands, the Germanic or the Turanian glories of earlier centuries. This myth was the religion of the twentieth century, fervently believed in however slim its connexion with reality. To the historical myth belonged the movements' flags and emblems: the swastika as a symbol of Aryanism, the *fasces* of the Roman Republic, the yoke and arrows, the Flemish lion, the crossed scythes or arrows. Above all, there was the myth of the "Leader" who was venerated like a Saint by the faithful, who could do no wrong and must not be criticized, who was God-given, and to whom superhuman qualities were attributed. He possessed a personal dynamism and magnetism which could arouse vast crowds to frenzy and ecstasy. Whoever has attended a Hitler meeting in Germany will remember the passions which he was able to arouse, the atmosphere of religious frenzy and devotion. His magnetism later made battle-hardened generals tremble in his presence. The magnetism exercised by some of the other Fascist leaders—Codreanu, Primo de Rivera, Van Severen, Degrelle—seems to have been equally powerful, and less artificial than in the case of Hitler, who carefully cultivated his mystique. There were other cults which characterized the Fascist movements, notably a cult of violence and "action." In Germany and elsewhere the myth of the street battles and battles won in meeting halls remained very much alive, as did the memory of the movement's "martyrs" who "march in spirit with us in our ranks." In Rumania and Germany this cult reached religious proportions. In no other party did the myth play such a vital part. To it also belonged—in the cases of Hitler and Codreanu—the myth of the devilish propensities of the Jewish race and its dreams of world power. Both love *and* hatred were cultivated by the Fascist movements.

Unlike many middle-class or working-class parties, the Fascists appealed to all social groups, from the top to the bottom of the social scale. Excluded were only those who were their favourite objects of attack: the profiteers, the parasites, the financial gangsters, the ruling cliques, the rapacious capitalists, the reactionary landowners. But even there exceptions were made if it suited the Leader's book. There is no doubt, however, that certain social groups responded much more strongly to the Fascist appeal than others. This is particularly true of those who were uprooted and threatened by social and economic change, whose position in society was being undermined, who had lost their traditional place, and were frightened of the future. These were, above all, the lower middle classes— or rather certain groups within them: the artisans and independent tradesmen, the small farmers, the lower grade government employees and white-collar workers. Perhaps even more important in the early stages were the former officers and non-commissioned officers of the first world war for whom no jobs were waiting, who had got accustomed to the use of violence, and felt themselves deprived of their "legitimate" rewards. In Italy, in Germany, and elsewhere the "front" generation played a leading part in the rise of Fascism. For its members fighting was a way of life which they transferred to the domestic scene. They loved battles for their own sake. It is no accident that the most important Fascist movements had their origin in the year 1919, the year of the Hungarian and Munich Soviet republics, of civil war which aroused fear and hatred in many hearts. Those who had been badly frightened did not easily forget. The occupation of the factories in northern Italy in the following year had the same effect.

This does not mean, however, that the lower middle classes acted on their own—in a revulsion from liberalism and parliamentarianism—or in their own interests to bring about Fascism. In a recent work on a Marxist topic it was stated that the lower middle classes adopted a policy to "use that power [of the state], even increase it, for their own ends till they reached the superstates of Nazi Germany and Fascist Italy." This is a gross oversimplification of a very complex process by which members of the lower middle classes were recruited by Fascist parties in many different countries; but they did not take any initiative as a social group; nor did they intend to use the power of the state "for their own ends." An earlier sociological analysis, based on the Italian example, suggested that a development towards Fascism was possible in Italy because there the bourgeoisie was weak and the proletariat strong and particularly well organized, having achieved a dominating position in certain parts of the country. While this was true of Italy, it was much less true of Germany—where the proletarian revolution had been decisively defeated in 1919—and not at all true of certain underdeveloped countries, such as Hungary and Rumania. From what has been said in the preceding pages it emerges that Fascist movements could develop in countries with a very strong left-wing movement—such as Italy or Spain—but equally in countries where the opposite was the case. It does not seem that the relative strength of the bourgeoisie and the working class had much to do with the rise of Fascism. There is more truth in the assertion that this rise was due to a malaise, a maladjustment of capitalist society, the victims of which were the lower middle classes more than any other social group.

Apart from the groups already mentioned, there were the youngsters at school and university who became ardent believers in Fascism at an early stage. They were fed up with the existing society, bored with their daily duties, and strongly attracted by a movement which promised a radical change, which they could invest with a romantic halo. These youths came from middle-class or lower middle-class families. They could not easily find the way into the Communist camp. But they found the weak and changing governments of the post-war period utterly unattractive. In the Weimar Republic, in the post-war Italian kingdom, in the corrupt governments of Rumania, in the powerless governments of Spain, there was nothing to fire the enthusiasm of youth: they were dreary and pedestrian, the offices filled with mediocrities and time-servers. It was this, rather than any economic threat, that led so many idealist students into the Fascist camp. Similarly, many young officers and soldiers of the post-war generation were attracted by visions of national greatness and the promise of a revision of the peace treaties. A perusal of the autobiographical notes compiled by men who joined the National Socialist Party in its early years shows that pride of place belongs to a strong nationalism, the desire to see Germany strong and united again, freed from the "chains of Versailles," and also from the faction fights and the "horse-trading" of the political parties. This often went together with hatred of the Communists and Socialists, and with anti-Semitism. Those who joined the Party were usually very young; they loved the frequent fights and battles in which they got involved together with their comrades, as well as the uniforms and the propaganda marches.

For the success of Fascism other factors, too, were essential. In the first place, there was the devastating economic crisis which made millions unemployed and threatened the economic existence of many more millions. If it had not been for the vast inflation of the German currency which undermined the very foundations of society, followed by the slump of the early 1930s, Hitler would not have been successful in Germany. Nor would Mussolini have been in Italy if it had not been for the post-war economic crisis and the fears which it aroused in the middle classes. Many other Fascist movements owed their growth to the slump of the early 1930s, a slump that found all governments helpless and passive. Essential, too, was the help rendered by sections of the ruling groups and governments, or the support of the army and high-ranking officers. Without this, there would have been no march on Rome and no Mussolini government. Without the support rendered by the Bavarian government and army the National Socialists would not have become a mass party in Munich in the early 1920s. Later, the ambiguous role of the *Reichswehr* leaders and their deep contempt of the Republic proved of inestimable value to Hitler, as did the financial contributions which he received from certain industrialists. The Iron Guard would not have become a mass movement if it had not been supported for a time by King Carol and industrialist circles. In Spain the revolt of the generals thrust the *Falange* into prominence. In Finland and in Hungary the army provided invaluable help for the Fascists. This factor must not be overestimated in its importance, but neither must it be overlooked.

It has recently been stated that "the German crisis was *sui generis*." "Though Fascism had spread throughout Europe, the German variety came to be unique. It was unique not only in the way it managed to displace the revolutionary impetus, but also in the primacy of the ideology of the Volk, nature and race. . . ." As far as the *völkisch* ideology was concerned it was not unique, but it had its close counterparts in the racial theories propounded in Finland and in Hungary—two countries inhabited by non-Indo-European peoples. The "Roman" ideology of the Italian Fascists and the theory of the common "Dietsch" origin of the people of the Netherlands belong into the same category. Moreover, the Italian Fascists were considerably more successful in destroying "the revolutionary impetus" than were the National Socialists. The former's punitive expeditions killed the revolutionary movement in Italy; but in Germany this was accomplished by the Free Corps before the National Socialist Party came into being. This is not to deny that its growth was very much facilitated by the existence of *völkisch* and anti-Semitic beliefs in certain circles, but this was only one of the factors which aided its rise. The others were the lost war, the sense of humiliation and the fierce nationalism resulting from the Treaty of Versailles, the occupation of the Ruhr and the reparations issue, the weakness and unpopularity of the Weimar Republic, the inflation and the economic crisis, the fears and the insecurity of the middle and lower middle classes. All these combined to make the rise of Hitler possible, and all were paralleled by similar developments in other European countries. Even Hitler's ferocious anti-Semitism was matched by the same tendency in Hungary and in Rumania.

Were the Fascist movements revolutionary? No doubt many of them demanded radical social changes and reforms, especially in Eastern Europe and in Spain where these were bitterly necessary. But in the more stable and conservative atmosphere of north-western Europe these movements were much less radical. The Italian Fascists and the German National Socialists were radical in their original demands, but both shed most of this radicalism fairly soon. If many Fascist leaders insisted that they must come into power in a legal way, this does not prove that their movements were not revolutionary. Even if this insistence was not just useful propaganda, the Fascist movements did aim at a fundamental change of the political structure—the abolition of parliamentary government and democracy—and the replacement of the ruling groups by a new *élite*. Once in power, they naturally had to use many of the old experts, civil servants and generals, but these were no longer in command. They received their "marching orders" from the new leaders who often came from entirely different social groups, far below the level of the old ruling classes. The Fascist "revolution" was not fought out in the streets and on the barricades, but in the ministries and government buildings. In this sense there was a "seizure of power." Power was handed over by the old ruling groups to the new leaders, and they used this power for their own ends.

Between the aims of the new and those of the old rulers there was a superficial similarity—the expansion of Germany or colonial conquest in Africa—but in reality there was a vast difference. What Hitler aimed at was not German expansion, and not even a Greater Germany, but world conquest. He did not care for the fate of the Sudeten Germans, the South Tyrolese or of any other German minority, but was willing to sacrifice them on the altar of his ambition. Mussolini's methods of conquest were often quite irrational, subject to his vision of a "Roman Empire." No one could seriously maintain that the two dictators acted in the interests of their countries. There is much truth in the assertion of Hermann Rauschning that the Fascists carried through a "revolution of nihilism." The Hitler Youth used to sing a song which prophesied that Europe would be aflame when the *Germanen* went down; Europe was in flames, but she has recovered. Fascism was the product of a deep social and economic crisis, a crisis of European society. It was a movement of nationalist and racial violence. In an age of economic stability in which nationalist and racial hatreds are declining in Europe it is not likely to recur as a mass movement. More than twenty years after the end of the second world war there is no sign of a true Fascist revival. But it is interesting to observe that Fascist groups are most active in those European countries—such as Austria or Flanders—where they have strong roots reaching back over a considerable period of time. In Italy and Germany neo-Fascist parties have appeared under different names, but none of them has been able to muster strong mass support for any length of time. There have been no punitive expeditions and no deeds of violence against political enemies; nor did the hatreds, the intoxication, and the semi-religious frenzy of the 1920s revive on any scale. Indeed, the political atmosphere in the Europe of the 1960s does not seem to be distinguished by any enthusiasm: it tends to be sober and dull. It is not the atmosphere in which a true Fascist movement could thrive.

VI

Totalitarianism: An Outmoded Label?

Words, like men, have histories. "Totalitarian" is a word of our time, coined in the 1920's by Benito Mussolini or one of his speechwriters, and used with pride to describe his Fascist regime. During the 1930's it became a convenient label to describe all right-wing ultra-nationalist dictatorships. These regimes were placed at one end of a spectrum, which ranged through conservatism, liberalism, socialism, to communism on the extreme left. After the second world war, "totalitarian" was extended to include the communist systems as well. The political spectrum, it was argued, was really circular in shape, so that the two extremes—Fascism and communism—closely resembled each other. These totalitarian systems of right and left shared a number of distinctive traits that sharply separated them from the various forms of "bourgeois" or socialist democracy, and even from such old-fashioned authoritarian regimes as, for example, those of General Franco in Spain or Marshal Pétain in France or Admiral Horthy in Hungary. Totalitarianism, in the new orthodoxy of the postwar years, had a number of identifying features. It asserted the ideal of the all-embracing state that left no aspect of life outside its control, and permitted no "islands of separateness" to which men might retreat. It concentrated all power in the hands of a single dominant group that destroyed or domesticated all other organized groups in society. It created a new kind of elite, cutting across the old class structure and seeking to destroy traditional institutions and elites. And, because it was a product of the mass age, it professed a considerable degree of social radicalism, and claimed to speak for the common man.[1]

This usage of the term totalitarian to include dictatorships of both left and right continues to our day. By stressing traits that Fascist and communist regimes have (or once had) in common, it seems to reflect at least part of reality, and thus to be a useful concept for understanding the political currents of our time. During the past decade, however, both the word and the idea have come under severe attack from several quarters. Most commonly, its critics see it as a cold-war concept, invented by western propagandists who sought to smear the Soviet Union by lumping it together with Nazi Germany. They quote President Truman, for example, as remarking in 1947: "There isn't any difference in totalitarian states. I don't care what you call them, Nazi, Communist, or Fascist. . . ." These critics

---

1. The most remarkable and influential expressions of this postwar orthodoxy were those of Hannah Arendt (*The Origins of Totalitarianism* [New York: Harcourt, Brace, 1951]), and Carl Friedrich and Zbigniew Brzezinski (*Totalitarian Dictatorship and Autocracy* [Cambridge: Harvard University Press, 1956]).

complain that the use of the term distorts reality by "ignoring . . . widely diverse origins, ideologies, goals, and practices of totalitarian regimes."[2] Some scholars are willing to accept the label as appropriate for the Stalinist system, but insist that it fits only that temporary phase in the history of the Soviet Union. Totalitarianism, they contend, is now dead everywhere; it was a passing phenomenon in European history, not at all typical of our age. A few analysts have attempted to develop a new taxonomy, on the ground that "totalitarian" has been so loosely used that it misleads more than it clarifies.

The controversy is clearly one that transcends mere labels; it reflects and influences the perspectives of historians and social scientists as they seek to interpret our times. In the selections that follow, two major problems are interlinked. Do the Fascist, Nazi, and Soviet systems possess enough common traits to justify the continued use of a single classificatory label? And if the Stalinist regime can properly be described as totalitarian, was that a temporary aberration? Was Stalin's system sharply different from the one created and led by Lenin? Have Stalin's successors inaugurated what might be called a "post-totalitarian" phase?

1. *Robert C. Tucker: The Dictator and Totalitarianism*

The development of the concept of totalitarianism, and the principal themes in the literature on its structure and dynamics, are described in admirably lucid fashion by Robert C. Tucker, Professor of Politics and director of the program in Russian Studies at Princeton University. Tucker, a former attaché in the United States Embassy in Moscow (1944–1953), has written a number of books on Marxist theory and Soviet politics.

Starting in the late 1930's and 1940's, a number of thinkers, mostly of European origin, evolved a theory of "totalitarianism" or the "total state" in an effort to account for the new type of dictatorship that had made its appearance in Germany under Hitler, Russia under Stalin, and perhaps also in Italy under Mussolini. Hitler's Germany and Stalin's Russia were viewed as the two principal and indubitable manifestations of the new political phenomenon. While the difficulty of precisely defining or describing this phenomenon was recognized, moreover, these writers felt that they were dealing with something qualitatively quite distinct. Thus Hannah Arendt, whose *Origins of Totalitarianism* was in many ways a culminating synthesis of this entire trend of theory in the first stage, did not treat

2. Les K. Adler and Thomas G. Paterson, "Red Fascism: The Merger of Nazi Germany and Soviet Russia in the American Image of Totalitarianism, 1930's–1950's," *American Historical Review*, LXXV (1970), pp. 1046, 1048. See also the controversy produced by this article in a later issue of the same periodical: LXXV (1970), pp. 2159–64.

From Robert C. Tucker, "The Dictator and Totalitarianism," *World Politics*, XVII, No. 4 (1965), 555–56, 559–62, 563, 564, 565, 566. Footnotes omitted. Copyright © 1965 by Princeton University Press. Reprinted by permission of the Princeton University Press.

Lenin's Russia as genuinely totalitarian. She saw the original Bolshevik system as a "revolutionary dictatorship" rather than a totalitarian one, and 1929, the year of Stalin's advent to supreme power and the start of the great collectivization campaign, as "the first year of clear-cut totalitarian dictatorship in Russia." Accordingly, Soviet totalitarianism was preeminently a phenomenon of the Stalin era. Again, Mussolini's Italy was considered by some to be a totalitarian state. But others, including Arendt, did not feel that it fully merited this designation even though Mussolini himself had been the first, or among the first, to use the term "totalitarian" and had applied it to the fascist conception of the state. The treatment of Hitler's Germany and Stalin's Russia as the prime representative expressions of totalitarian dictatorship has remained characteristic of this school of thought, at any rate until recently. . . .

Two overlapping stages may be distinguished in the growth of this literature. The first, extending from the late 1930's to the end of the 1940's, saw the emergence of the conception of the totalitarian state as a new, distinctively modern or non-traditional form of authoritarianism represented particularly in Nazi Germany and Soviet Russia. The second stage, coinciding with the growth of Soviet studies as an established branch of academic scholarship in postwar America, saw the detailed application of this conception to the Soviet system in its late Stalinist form, and also attempts at a kind of codification of the theory of totalitarianism. It is only natural, of course, that in the late 1940's and early 1950's the attention of American scholars should have gravitated from the defunct Nazi case to the still very live totalitarianism of Stalin's Russia, and that in their studies of the latter they should have relied heavily upon the model of a totalitarian polity that had already been worked out in the first stage.

It is no monolithic doctrine that we find reflected in the literature on totalitarianism. We are confronted, rather, with a variegated body of thought developed over an extended period by thinkers of diverse intellectual background and research interest among whom differences of emphasis and opinion exist. Still, there are certain recurring themes, certain basic ideas that tend to be shared by various representatives of the school and may be taken as typical.

First, the totalitarian dictatorship is viewed as being, unlike most traditional forms of authoritarian rule, a dictatorship with a mass social base and having a popular or pseudo-popular character. "The totalitarian state is the state of the masses," wrote Emil Lederer, and other theorists have followed him in taking modern "mass society" or "mass-men" as a foundation or recruiting ground of totalitarian movements that speak in the name of the masses and assert their affinity with them. On the road to power, totalitarian parties strive to create mass movements that indoctrinate their followers with the party's ideology by propaganda and agitation. Once in power in the single-party state, however, the totalitarian elite imposes upon its mass social constituency an unprecedented tyranny, under which political power emanating from a single source penetrates every pore of the social organism and all the resources of modern technology are used for control purposes. Autonomous social groups are destroyed, giving way to the controlled mass organizations that serve as the elite's transmission belts to the now "atomized" masses of the population.

"Modern totalitarianism, unlike the more traditional dictatorships, is a highly bureaucratized system of power." This sums up a second characteristic theme in the literature on the totalitarian dictatorship. In *Behemoth*, for example, Franz Neumann depicts the Nazi dictatorship as a system ruled, albeit chaotically and competitively, by four great bureaucratic machines—the ministerial bureaucracy and the bureaucratized leaderships of the Nazi Party, the armed forces, and industry. The same basic theme receives a somewhat different emphasis from Arendt, who distinguishes "totalitarian bureaucracy" from bureaucracy of the traditional kind on the score of the former's "radical efficiency." Both, however, share with other theorists of the school the view that totalitarianism carries the process of bureaucratization to its farthest extreme in modern society. There is, in fact, a tendency to regard the totalitarian state as a great bureaucratic monster functioning with machine-like impersonality in pursuit of its aims. Such an image is suggested, for example, by Arendt's later book, *Eichmann in Jerusalem*, which pictures the erstwhile director of operations in the Nazi "final solution" as a *kleiner Mann* of banal character who in supervising the murder of millions of Jews was dutifully carrying out his instructions as a higher functionary, a cogwheel in the totalitarian bureaucracy.

A third fundamental theme that has been both widely and heavily emphasized in the literature on totalitarianism has to do with systematic terror. Governmental use of terror is not itself held to be something distinctively new in the present age or peculiar to the totalitarian form of dictatorship. What distinguishes totalitarianism, according to the theorists, is rather the kind and degree of terror that is practiced, and also the characteristic predilection of totalitarian regimes for certain particular methods of spreading terror, such as the concentration camp and violent purges. Arendt, for example, differentiates "dictatorial terror," which is aimed against authentic opponents of the given regime, from an all-pervasive "totalitarian terror" that destroys not only actual political opponents but great numbers of wholly harmless people in purges, mass liquidations, and concentration camps; and she expresses the view that terror of the latter kind is "the very essence" of totalitarian government. This view has found wide acceptance in the literature. Terror has variously been described, for example, as "the most universal characteristic of totalitarianism," "the linchpin of modern totalitarianism," and "the vital nerve of the totalitarian system." So far as the question of the motivation of totalitarian terror is concerned, this is best considered under the next heading—the dynamics of totalitarianism.

The theorists of totalitarianism are in general and rather emphatic agreement that the totalitarian state is, in addition to its other characteristics, an extremely dynamic phenomenon. Sigmund Neumann, author of an outstanding work on the subject, saw the dynamics of the total state as revolutionary, and the political process in the totalitarian system as one of "permanent revolution." Others have used phrases like "permanent purge" and "permanent war" to describe essential aspects of the totalitarian dynamism in internal and external affairs. But why do totalitarian systems act in such ways? Whence their dynamics? The literature gives two kinds of answer to such questions. First, the characteristic behaviors of totalitarian regimes are explained by reference to postulated system-needs or functional requisites of totalitarianism itself as an operating socio-political system. A specimen of such reasoning is provided by Brzezinski when he writes, for example, that "The purge, arising as a combination of the rational motivations of the totalitarian leadership and the irrational stresses of the system, satisfies the need of the system for continued dynamism and energy," and further: "Totalitarianism is the system of the permanent purge. It promotes mobility and instability within totalitarianism. It necessitates constant reshuffling, and prevents the formation of too rigid lines of power demarcation within the system."

A second and related line of explanation of the dynamics of totalitarianism stresses ideological motivation. The totalitarian ideology itself or the leaders' presumed obsession with it is treated as the source of the characteristic behavior of totalitarian regimes. Thus Friedrich describes Hitler's destruction of the Jews as "ideologically motivated." On a higher plane of generality Arendt explains the action of totalitarian regimes by reference to a "supersense" that drives the leaders to demonstrate at all cost the validity of their ideological world-image. "The aggressiveness of totalitarianism," she goes on, "springs not from lust for power, and if it feverishly seeks to expand, it does so neither for expansion's sake nor for profit, but only for ideological reasons: to make the world consistent, to prove that its respective supersense has been right." The postulate of an ideological fanaticism as the driving force of totalitarian conduct reappears in Inkeles' conception of the "totalitarian mystique," which he sees as the defining characteristic of the totalitarian leader himself. The "mystique" is pictured as a compulsion in the leader and his lieutenants to force reality into conformity with an ideologically given "higher law" or ideal plan for man and society: "One may fruitfully view the dictatorial leader as the man who sees himself as the essential *instrument* of the particular mystique to which he is addicted." In an application of this mode of reasoning, Friedrich and Brzezinski seek to explain totalitarian terror by ideological fanaticism. Having said that the terror is the "vital nerve" of the totalitarian system, they write: "This system, because of the alleged ideological infallibility of its dogma, is propelled toward an increase of terror by a violent passion for unanimity." Such passion, they go on to suggest, is what makes the terror totalitarian: "It aims to fill everyone with fear and vents in full its passion for unanimity. Terror embraces the entire society, searching everywhere for actual or potential deviants from the totalitarian unity. . . . Total fear reigns."

Turning to the question of the dictator . . . , most of the theorists . . . recognize at some point the reality of dictatorial rule by a single individual in a fully totalitarian system. Friedrich and Brzezinski, for example, refer to the Nuremberg trials and Khrushchev's secret speech of 1956 as sources of evidence for the view that Mussolini, Hitler, and probably Stalin too were "the actual rulers of their respective countries," and they conclude that the totalitarian dictator "possesses more nearly absolute power than any previous type of political leader." Much earlier Sigmund Neumann described the dictator as the "moving spirit" of the total state, and Arendt writes of "the absolute and unsurpassed concentration of power in the hands of a single man" who sits in the center of the movement "as the motor that swings it into motion." . . .

A sense of the theoretical inadequacy of the conception of totalitarianism seems to have been growing in American political science in the 1960's. Increasingly the complaint is heard that this construct is too narrow and limited to serve as a useful basic category for comparative analysis of contemporary one-party systems. It leaves out of view the nationalist single-party systems that share very many significant characteristics with the Fascist and Communist systems. It does not fare well in the face of the recent growth of diversity among Communist systems themselves. Furthermore, the politics of post-Stalin Russia have become more and more difficult to analyze in terms of the theory of totalitarianism, the fall of Khrushchev being only one in a long series of events that do not easily find places in the model of a totalitarian polity; and efforts to modify the model so that it will fit contemporary Soviet communism—e.g., by introducing the idea of a "rationalist totalitarianism"—seem of little avail. And owing to the tendency to see totalitarian systems as examples of what might be called government without politics, with a unitary elite controlling an atomized population by organization and terror, the theory of totalitarianism has obstructed rather than facilitated awareness of the intra-elite politics of factional conflict and policy debates that rage constantly behind the scenes of the Soviet and other Communist systems, despite their official pretensions to monolithic unity and their claims that factions are forbidden. For these and other reasons, some students of the comparative politics of modern authoritarianism have become dissatisfied with the concept of totalitarianism and have begun to formulate alternative basic categories, such as "movement-regimes," "mobilization systems," and the like.

But are we now to discard the concept of totalitarianism as an obsolete or obsolescent category in modern political science? Considering it an essential part of our theoretical equipment, I for one would not like to see this happen. In order to prevent it from happening, however, it appears necessary to carry out a more radical critique of the theory of totalitarianism than has yet been made, rather as medicine may have to resort to a more radical form of treatment in order to save a patient. So far criticism has concentrated upon the deficiencies of the theory in application to systems or situations that were not in view or in existence at the time the theory was devised. The more radical critique must address itself to a different question: How valid was the theory as a representation of political reality in the two historical cases that it was particularly devised to explain—Hitler's Germany and Stalin's Russia?

2. *Richard Lowenthal:* 1917, *and After*

Did the Soviet Union in Stalin's day represent the most perfect model of the totalitarian state? The question continues to be discussed outside the USSR, and even by a few brave souls inside it. But even more sharply controversial is the issue of Stalin's heritage from Lenin. That Lenin and Stalin were men of widely different character and temperament is clear. Lenin's noble humanitarian aims, in the opinion of his admirers, could never have been reconciled with the techniques used by Stalin in the 1930's; it was Stalin who corrupted Lenin's work. But Richard Lowenthal, writing on the fiftieth anniversary of the Bolshevik revolution, contends that it was Lenin who in 1921 created the first totalitarian single-party state. Lowenthal explains how it was that Lenin arrived at that crucial decision, and why he failed to foresee its inevitable consequences. Richard Lowenthal, born in Berlin in 1908, is a naturalized British citizen and was for many years a London journalist; since 1961 he has been professor of political science in the Free University of Berlin.

Fifty years ago, the Bolshevik Party seized power in Russia in the name of the Soviets of Workers' and Soldiers' Deputies. For months before, "All Power to the Soviets" had been their central political slogan. For many years afterwards, they propagated the "soviet system" as the specific political institution of the new régime—the only adequate political form for the rule of the working class, the "dictatorship of the proletariat" envisaged by Karl Marx. The new Russia was proclaimed a "Soviet Republic" and soon extended into a "Union of Socialist Soviet Republics." When the Communist International was founded in 1919, it was to the Soviet banner that it rallied the most militant revolutionaries of Europe, and it was for the creation of Soviet rule on the Russian model that communists were subsequently to fight and die in Germany and Hungary, in the Balkans and the Baltic States, and even in distant China. But the Soviet system did not, in fact, spread to other countries—not even to those which came, after the Second World War, to form part of the "Soviet bloc." . . .

This failure of the efforts to spread the "Soviet system," and the ultimate abandonment of those efforts by the Russian Bolsheviks themselves, did not, however, prevent the political forms of their new State from having a worldwide impact; only it was a very different set of political institutions that proved of major historical importance as an international model. It is as the first totalitarian single-party State, rather than as the first Soviet State, that the new type of government developed by the Bolsheviks has attracted imitators—not only among those who share their ideological goals,

From Richard Lowenthal, "The Model of the Totalitarian State," included in *The Impact of the Russian Revolution 1917–1967*, with an Introductory Essay by Arnold J. Toynbee, pp. 21–22, 24–28. Footnotes omitted. Published by Oxford University Press under the auspices of the Royal Institute of International Affairs. Reprinted by permission.

but also among their most bitter enemies and among people who are quite indifferent to those goals. Thus while the Bolsheviks, in stressing the Soviets as their most important political contribution, selected the institution that expressed most clearly the *legitimation* of their power by its alleged social content, the course of history has selected the institution that embodied the *reality* of their power—independent of any social content.

In the completed form which it reached in Russia from about 1921, and in which it has made its way around the world, the totalitarian single-party State may be defined by four main institutional characteristics. The first is the monopolistic control of the State by the ruling party, excluding the toleration of other, independent parties in opposition or even as genuine partners in coalition, and leading logically also to a ban on the formation of organised tendencies or "factions" *within* the ruling party; this amounts in effect to a monopoly of political initiative and decision for the inner leadership of that party, and ultimately to a monopoly of decision for a single leader. The second is the party's monopolistic control of all forms of social organisation, depriving these organisations of their role as independent interest groups as exercised in non-totalitarian, "pluralistic" societies and converting them into as many tools for the mobilisation, education, and control of their members by the ruling party; this enables the totalitarian régime to supplement the levers of the state bureaucracy for controlling the actions of its subjects "from above" with a network of organisations enveloping them from cradle to grave, while preventing the formation of any independent groups. The third is the monopolistic control of all channels of public communication, from the press and other mass media to all forms of education, of literature and art, with the aim not merely of preventing the *expression* of hostile or undesirable opinions by a kind of censorship, but of controlling the *formation* of opinion at the source by planned selection of all the elements of information. The fourth is what Lenin himself used as the definition of dictatorship—"the removal of all legal limitations on state power," in other words, the possibility to use state power in arbitrary and terroristic ways whenever this is deemed expedient for the purposes of the régime.

It is essentially the combination of these four characteristics which has enabled the totalitarian régimes of our time to extend the effectiveness of state power beyond anything that was deemed possible before 1917.

This institutional scheme had not been conceived by the Bolsheviks in advance. . . . [But it was implicit] in the centralistic organisational structure of the party that seized power on 7 November 1917. Lenin had consciously created his "party of a new type" as an instrument for the revolutionary conquest of power; and even though, in writing *What is to be Done?*, he had been far from envisaging the concrete forms that party's domination was to take fifteen or twenty years later, the possibility of a totalitarian party dictatorship was implied in the shape of that instrument. Without the pre-existing "party of a new type," the first state of the new type could not have been built up; with that party once victorious, the tendency for its leaders to establish dictatorial, monopolistic rule was given —to be brought out "by events." . . .

Even so, Lenin at first sincerely rejected the implication that he was aiming at a party dictatorship in Russia. We do not know just when he came to regard such a régime as the necessary political form for the "dictatorship of the proletariat," but we do know that up to the First World War, he considered that a dictatorship of the proletariat was not yet on the agenda of Russian history. During the revolution of 1905, he aimed at the overthrow of Tsarism by an alliance of workers and peasants, and at the formation of a coalition government of Social-Democrats and Social-Revolutionaries as its political expression. It was only the shock of the war of 1914 that convinced Lenin that a socialist revolution had become an immediate task internationally, and that it was therefore the duty of socialists even in backward Russia to go beyond the overthrow of Tsarism and the establishment of a "bourgeois-democratic" régime and to set up the power of the proletariat—in order to contribute to the fulfilment of the international task.

When Lenin, after his return to Russia in April 1917, began to propagate this new concept, first within and then beyond his party, he did so under the slogan "All Power to the Soviets." Yet while he emphasised the Soviets as the direct organs of proletarian rule, the opposition of all other socialist parties to this programme convinced him that the establishment of that rule depended on the Bolsheviks acquiring control of the Soviets first. In the course of 1917, the Bolsheviks ceased in Lenin's mind to be merely the most enlightened and energetic representatives of the interests of the Russian working class and became, to him, the *only* party of the Russian proletariat; and this implied that the "dictatorship of the proletariat" must in fact take the form of a Bolshevik party dictatorship.

This crucial identification of party and class appears as a matter of course in all Lenin's writings during the months immediately preceding the seizure of power. It becomes most explicit on the very eve of victory in his pamphlet *Can the Bolsheviks Retain State Power?*, in which the Soviets— the directly elected representatives of the workers, soldiers, and peasants —are openly and unceremoniously treated as the new "state apparatus" by means of which the victorious Bolsheviks will exercise and maintain *their* power and carry out *their* policy. It was a consequence of this outlook, not yet understood at the time even by many leading Bolsheviks, that Lenin after 7 November consistently rejected all proposals for a coalition with the Mensheviks and accepted as temporary partners in the new régime only those Left Social-Revolutionaries whom he regarded as representing the peasants in the process of agrarian revolution. It was another consequence that he dispersed the Constituent Assembly, elected *after* the Bolshevik assumption of power, when its large non-Bolshevik majority refused to vote a blanket endorsement of all the revolutionary measures already enacted by the new régime.

By the time of the October Revolution, then, Lenin was determined to establish a revolutionary dictatorship of his party. But this did not mean that he had, even then, a plan or blue-print for a totalitarian single-party state. What was clear in his mind was the last of our four characteristics of such a state—the rejection of any legal limitations on the revolutionary power. This was sufficient to enable him to suppress resistance to his policy as the need arose. But as resistance developed into civil war, determination to break it was no longer enough: to maintain and defend the revolutionary government, a new state machine had to be created.

It had been an essential part of Lenin's revolutionary programme, explained most fully in his pamphlet on *State and Revolution* and based on Karl Marx's analysis of the Paris Commune, that the victorious proletariat could not use the bureaucracy, army, and police which had served its exploiters as a machine of oppression, but must smash them. Before 7 November, he had also followed Marx in arguing that the new proletarian régime had no need to put another *professional* state apparatus in their place: part-time workers' delegates in the Soviets, part-time voluntary organs of workers' control in economic life, a part-time workers' militia would be enough.

Yet after victory, and especially with the spread of civil war, the creation of a new, revolutionary army, police, and bureaucracy became imperative if the Soviet régime was not to follow the Paris Commune also on the road to defeat. The new, professional state machine had to be staffed with reliable cadres at least in the key positions; and in the conditions of party dictatorship, reliable cadres could only mean Bolsheviks. From being the leading force in the Soviets and the government, the party thus developed into the backbone of a new state machine: its monopolistic control of the new state became entrenched in practice before it was proclaimed in theory. . . .

Even so, during the entire period of the Civil War, the Bolsheviks never argued in principle that they should be the only legal party. Nor was there any hint of that doctrine in the constitution of the RSFSR adopted by the fifth All-Russian Soviet congress in July 1918. But they did argue that they would not tolerate any bourgeois parties opposed to Soviet rule in principle, nor parties working for the armed overthrow of the new régime, even if they professed a socialist programme; and they claimed that the central and local organs of Soviet rule, including the *Cheka*, must not be hampered by any legal safeguards in deciding whether any party, newspaper, or individual was guilty of such counter-revolutionary activity. . . .

Yet while the Bolshevik régime of the Civil War years was clearly a terrorist dictatorship—"Red Terror" was officially proclaimed as a policy after the attempt on Lenin's life in August 1918—and while the dictatorial party increasingly merged with the new state machine in process of construction, it did not yet create a totalitarian single-party State as we have come to know it since.

As late as 1920, there were many hundreds of Mensheviks in the provincial Soviets, and Martov himself was able in the Moscow Soviet to voice their protest against the arbitrary suppression of "working-class democracy" and to advocate their programme for economic recovery that anticipated the later New Economic Policy of the Bolsheviks. Important trade unions were still under Menshevik control, and the Bolshevik leaders were under no illusion that the influence of their critics among the workers was increasing as the Civil War drew to a close. Discontent and indiscipline had moreover affected so many of the Bolsheviks' own militants that spontaneous co-operation between Mensheviks and those undisciplined Bolsheviks produced surprise majorities against the "party line" in Soviets or trade unions more than once. It was only after the end of the Civil War, in early 1921, at a time of growing unrest among both workers and peasants culminating in the Kronstadt rising, and simultaneously with the decision to introduce the New Economic Policy, that Lenin decided to put his régime on a more secure institutional basis. To understand the decision that produced the first modern totalitarian régime, we must try to envisage the problems that faced him.

The classical task of a Jacobin revolutionary dictatorship had been fulfilled. The counter-revolution had been defeated, the power of the former ruling classes broken for good. But the expectation that the Bolshevik victory in Russia would be the immediate prelude to socialist revolutions in the advanced countries of Europe had not come true. The "dictatorship of the proletariat"—in fact of a minority party claiming to represent the proletariat—had remained isolated in a backward country in which the proletariat formed a minority, and in which, as Lenin knew and recognised, the economic and cultural preconditions for a socialist system were lacking. To overcome the discontent born out of economic paralysis, to begin the work of recovery after the devastations of war and civil war, major economic concessions to all the remaining nonproletarian strata—to the peasant majority above all, but also to the traders and technicians— were inevitable. The "war communist" fantasies of a straight leap into Utopia had to give way to a policy of patiently creating, in co-operation with all classes, the productive resources which elsewhere had been created by capitalism, and which alone could eventually form the basis for a socialist economy. It seemed the typical situation for a "Thermidor"—for liquidating the revolutionary dictatorship that had done its work. That was indeed what the Mensheviks suggested with growing confidence in their own judgment.

Yet Lenin drew a different conclusion. He agreed on the need for a break with utopian dreams, for material concessions to all productive classes, for shifting the emphasis in Russia from political revolution to economic evolution. But he insisted that the "proletarian" dictatorship must be maintained during the new phase as well, in order to ensure that evolution was accomplished by what he termed state capitalism—under the control of a state which would maintain Russia's independence from the capitalist world and prevent the restoration of a class of capitalist owners, even while accomplishing the task which capitalism had fulfilled in the advanced countries, and would thus preserve the foundations for the later transition to socialism as well as a stronghold for the international revolutionary movement. The Bolsheviks must hold on to their dictatorial power —no longer primarily as a revolutionary dictatorship, but as a special type of a dictatorship of development. It is from this decision that the truly unique course of the Russian Revolution begins. It is from this decision,

too, that the need to create a system of totalitarian institutions has resulted.

The new need, as Lenin saw it, was no longer the comparatively simple
one of fighting the class enemy arms in hand. It was to harness the economic energies of non-proletarian classes for a constructive task, to grant
them a place in society for a whole period—yet to prevent them from in-
fluencing the direction of economic and social development. As Lenin had
once conceived the "party of a new type" as an instrument to make the social forces of discontent converge in a revolutionary direction which they
might not otherwise take, so now he conceived the State of a new type as
an instrument to guide the millions of independent peasants, the private
traders, the industrial technicians of bourgeois origin, in a socialist direction which ran counter to their natural tendency to evolve a capitalist social structure. To foil that tendency, it was not enough that the state kept
firm control of the "commanding heights" of the economy; the alien classes
must be permanently excluded from any possible access to the levers of political power. The unique purpose of forcing an entire society to develop
not in the direction corresponding to its inherent trend, but in the direction dictated by the ideology of its ruling party, required a unique institutional form, closing all channels of political expression to the existing social
forces: no plurality of political parties, however vestigial; no organised interest groups or publishing media free from party control; and finally, as a
logical extension of this principle, no plurality of organised tendencies
within the ruling party, as in the absence of opposition parties such "factions" would tend to become the channels for the pressure of non-proletarian class interests.

Oddly enough, no formal ban on all remnants of non-communist parties
was passed even then. But mass arrests of their central and local leaders
destroyed their organisations for good in the early months of 1921, so that
in the summer of 1922 even the Menshevik leadership, by then in exile, explicitly renounced any further attempt to put up candidates for Soviet elections. Moreover, a formal ban on factions within the ruling party *was*
passed at its tenth congress in March 1921—the same congress that introduced the NEP—on Lenin's proposal, and explicitly based on the grounds
stated above—thus showing that the final destruction of the other parties
at this moment was a deliberate decision. By November, on the fourth anniversary of the Bolshevik seizure of power, Zinoviev could state publicly
that the Bolsheviks had been "the only legal party" in Russia for some time
past. The remaining Menshevik-controlled trade unions were "reorganised"
under appointed communist leaders during the same year, thus proving
that the régime could in fact not afford to tolerate the independent advocacy of the interests of the industrial workers any more than of any other
class. By the time of the twelfth party conference of the Bolsheviks, in August 1922, the need to extend the principle of *Gleichschaltung* to all "so-
called social organisations," as well as to the universities and publishing
firms, was proclaimed on the ground that otherwise these legal channels

could be used by the now illegal "anti-Soviet parties" for their dangerous propaganda.

The first totalitarian state, thus, did not arise either as an automatic result of revolution and civil war, or as a mere instrument for the accelerated economic development of a backward country. It was the product of the decision to use the dictatorship resulting from the revolution in order to twist the development of society in the preconceived direction indicated by the ideology of the ruling party. As Lenin saw it, however, this politically directed development would henceforth proceed by evolutionary methods, without further violent upheavals. The emphasis in the writings of his final years was on the need to raise the economic and cultural level of the Russian people—including in particular the cultural level of the new bureaucracy—by steady, patient efforts within the given political framework. . . .

This evolutionary vision of the state-guided development of Russian society was also generally accepted by Lenin's heirs, at least as long as the problem of post-war recovery dominated economic life. . . . Yet as the period of recovery drew to a close and the problem of financing Russia's industrialisation—of the "primitive socialist accumulation of capital"— passed to the fore, the hidden, inner contradiction of Lenin's vision of the guided socialist evolution of a society containing a majority of small, independent producers became obvious and confronted his heirs with a dilemma. The financing of "socialist industrialisation" by peaceful, evolutionary methods—by encouraging the peasants to earn surpluses and to lend their savings to the State—as advocated by Bukharin, was *economically* possible and indeed rational. But, as experience showed by 1928, it was bound to increase the *social* weight of the individualist peasantry and to lead to a growing dependence of the formally all-powerful party-state on the informal but effective organisations of the village, typically led by the most efficient, near-capitalist peasants. The more successful the evolutionary road in terms of production and savings, the less likely was it to lead in the desired direction of preventing a capitalist development of the village and its growing impact on Russian society as a whole—the more it would therefore undermine the purpose and ultimately the power of the totalitarian régime. Conversely, the alternative road of financing "socialist industrialisation" at the expense of the peasants, by siphoning off their surpluses more or less forcibly, as originally advocated by the "Left Opposition," might effectively stifle the tendency towards capitalist development in the village and maintain the course required by the régime's ideology; but it was bound to provoke peasant resistance to an extent that could be broken only by the massive use of state power—in other words by the abandonment of peaceful evolution.

In launching the "liquidation of the kulaks as a class" and the forced collectivisation of agriculture, which he himself later described as a revolution "equivalent" to that of October 1917, but distinguished from it by being "accomplished from above, on the initiative of the State," Stalin decided in favour of the primacy of the totalitarian régime and its ideological goal. He recognised what Lenin had not foreseen—that a totalitarian régime can fulfil its task of diverting the development of society from its "spontaneous" course in an ideologically preconceived direction only by repeated recourse to revolutionary violence. The dynamics of the permanent, or at any rate recurrent, revolution from above as developed by Stalin are the necessary complement to the ideological goals set and to the totalitarian institutions created by Lenin. They, too, were not part of a blueprint, but they grew out of a "fixed attitude of mind"—and out of the institutions in which it had been embodied—under the pressure of events.

3. *Moshe Lewin: Lenin's Last Struggle*

Lenin's defenders remain convinced that he would never have succumbed to the totalitarian virus, no matter how great the provocation. His case is forcefully argued by Moshe Lewin, a Soviet specialist at the Ecole Pratique des Hautes Etudes in Paris. Lewin was born in Poland, spent the war years in the USSR, and later emigrated to France where he completed a doctorate in history at the Sorbonne. His book focuses minutely on Lenin's writings and decisions during the last year before his illness (1921–1922). Extrapolating from this evidence, Lewin insists that Lenin (with Trotsky's aid) would have kept the revolutionary experiment alive without slipping into Stalinist methods.

Lenin was very far from being a weak liberal, incapable of taking resolute action when necessary. But unlike some of his successors, he hated repression; for him, it should be used only in the defense of the regime against serious threat and as a punishment for those who contravened legality. . . . The use of constraint—let alone terror—is ostensibly excluded in establishing the foundations of a new society. Lenin's second *What Is To Be Done?* pleads for caution, restraint, moderation and patience. Lenin has not abandoned the use of constraint in the defense of the regime, but for purposes of construction all undue haste is forbidden: "We must show sound skepticism for too rapid progress, for boastfulness, etc."—these words are taken from "Better Fewer, But Better." "Better get good human material in two or even three years than work in haste without hope of getting any at all." "No second revolution!"—this was to be the interpretation of the "Testament" that Bukharin, five years later, was to throw back at Stalin, and he was right. Lenin no longer described force as the "midwife of a new society" after the seizure of power and the return of peace; the new rule in this new situation was clearly that of gradual evolution. And this rule was formulated against the whole pressure of Russian realities, which —as Lenin was very well aware—tended in the opposite direction.

The rule "Better fewer, but better" would be difficult to observe, but Lenin refuses, in advance, the argument of spontaneous tendencies: "I know that the opposite rule will force its way through a thousand loopholes. I know that enormous resistance will have to be put up, that devilish persistence will be required, that in the first few years at least work in this field will be hellishly hard. Nevertheless, I am convinced that only by achieving this aim shall we create a republic that is really worthy of the name of Soviet, socialist, and so on, and so forth." [1]

In my opinion, one can hardly describe Lenin's great objectives as utopian. Many of the objectives assigned to the regime in the fields of economic and cultural development have been attained. The other grand design, that of creating a dictatorial machine capable of controlling itself to a large degree, seems closer today, but only after an initial catastrophic failure: the Soviet regime underwent a long period of "Stalinism," which in its basic features was diametrically opposed to the recommendations of the "Testament." This fact requires some elucidation. Left-wing dictatorship is one of the most significant political phenomena of our time. Its role is an important one and its prospects of development are far from exhausted. There is no evidence that this type of dictatorship, at a certain stage in its development, must of necessity and in every case degenerate into a personal, despotic and irrational dictatorship. From a theoretical point of view, there was nothing essentially utopian about Lenin's aim of achieving a rational dictatorial regime, with men of integrity at its head and efficient institutions working consciously to go beyond both underdevelopment and dictatorship. Moreover, in Lenin's own time, and in extremely difficult conditions, the Soviet dictatorial machine still functioned in a very different way from the one it was later to adopt. Lenin's plans were not put into practice because the tendencies that had emerged from the civil war could only be counteracted by daring reforms, and in the absence of a capable and undisputed leader the plans in question remained no more than mere "wishes." The machine that had been set up under Lenin found no difficulty in bypassing the dead leader's most earnest wishes; the embalming of his corpse and the posthumous cult of his person helped to dissimulate a type of dictatorship utterly foreign to his plans.

The greatest discrepancy between Lenin's intentions and actual history is to be found in the field of methods. It would appear today that the USSR has entered a period of internal development in which economic and educative methods are being gradually substituted for administrative constraint, as Lenin wished. But for a long time terror was the main instrument in the establishment of the new structures and it is a matter for speculation if Lenin would have liked the enormous discretionary power and possibility for using terror which is still concentrated in the hands of a narrow group of Soviet leaders.

In our time there is much discussion as to whether Stalin's methods, which have proved so prejudicial to the general idea of socialism and to

1. V. I. Lenin, *Sochineniya* (Works), Vol. XLV, p. 392.

the development of the world socialist movement, were the brutal but correct choice of the only possible way, or whether there existed another formula that Stalin was personally incapable of conceiving.

No one doubts that there were powerful forces inherent in Russia's internal situation and international position that encouraged recourse by the Party to strong-arm methods in overcoming the obstacles to development, which were extremely persistent in this backward, agrarian and isolated country. No one doubts either that, whatever the ability of her leaders and elites, Soviet Russia was bound to undergo crises and upheavals. A gently rising curve of development was difficult to imagine. Lenin was under no illusions on that score and did nothing to foster them. What he did want, however, in all circumstances, was a considered policy; he wanted the country's leadership to keep its head whatever conflict or dilemma it might find itself in. If he had lived, he would inevitably have had to solve the problem of "primitive accumulation" (the creation of the initial capital for the launching of the industrial economy), whatever his aversion to such a concept. He would have had to act when the peasantry, even without any consciously hostile political motives, refused to sell its grain and practically threatened to starve the country, because of the feeble supply of industrial products. He would have been constantly confronted by the paradox of a single party in a socially diversified country. He would have had to preserve the unity of the Party and the requirements of discipline and efficiency, which were so often in contradiction with the freedom of criticism necessary if the Party was not to fall into bureaucratic degeneration.

Would Lenin in fact have succeeded in solving all these questions correctly, and how would he have gone about doing so? (The question might arise whether a historian may legitimately concern himself with such hypotheses. I believe that he may, on condition that he does not exceed certain limits. If he does exceed these limits, then of course his work becomes gratuitous speculation.)

In answering this question, we must proceed to an extrapolation whose point of departure is to be found in our knowledge of Lenin's character and of his last program. There can be little doubt that Lenin would have set about the realization of his reforms; as he did so, some of them would have proved unrealistic or impracticable and would have been replaced. Others, and even perhaps his entire policy, would have met with opposition from within the Party and with practical difficulties in the country at large. The internal opposition would have come from the bureaucracy, the *apparatchiki* appointed by the Orgburo. But this opposition would have been weakened, at least temporarily, by the removal of the Stalin group, as Lenin had intended. Under Lenin, there would have been no letup in the struggle against "administrative methods" and the inefficiency of the bureaucracy and against Russian nationalism (and the local nationalisms that it helped to keep alive). He would have been constantly obliged to organize support both within and outside the Party. He would have had to appeal to the active and morally sensitive elements in the country: young workers and students; intellectuals; the best elements in the peasantry; certain elements of other socialist parties and of other groups, according to the circumstances; the Bolshevik Old Guard itself, composed of men who were then still young; the more enlightened administrative elements would also have provided support. The *apparatchiki,* the police, the *dzerzhimordy* and the *chinovniki* could never, of course, have disarmed completely, but they would have been constantly attacked, demoralized and prevented from crystallizing into a conservative force. The front of the stage would have been occupied by the many militants that Stalin was to eliminate, and also were to be used by the Stalinist system, and by all kinds of valuable nonmembers who were to perish in the purges. It is easier to imagine Lenin himself perishing in prison than inflicting such an insane hemorrhage on his country. A coalition of Lenin with Trotsky and others would have enabled a rational use of the best cadres, instead of their elimination. Of course, this mass of individuals would not only have helped to carry out Lenin's program; they would also have been a seedbed of opposition that tried to outflank him sometimes from the left and sometimes from the right. But Lenin would certainly not have used Stalinist methods against them. On the other hand, it would be nothing more than speculation to affirm that Lenin would have succeeded without any doubt. He too might have succumbed and ended, like so many others, as a "deviationist." But what may be said with certainty is that he would have done his utmost to combat the processes that were to make the Stalinist period what it was.

In order not to be beaten, Lenin would have had to show quite extraordinary skill and daring as a political manipulator and innovator; he is known to have possessed these qualities in ample measure. He would have had, in his own words, to act with "devilish persistence." He was probably quite capable of it. It is legitimate to believe that Lenin, acting in concert with Trotsky and others, would have been able to bring Soviet Russia through a less tragic, more rational and, for the cause of socialism, less compromising path. In fact, Lenin needed Trotsky to realize his idea. It was not merely because of his illness that he called in Trotsky's assistance. The two men complemented each other very well. . . . Between them, they symbolized the motive force of the October Revolution.

Trotsky alone would not have been capable of carrying out the reorganization and consolidation and the preservation of those later to be purged. . . . He. . . . had the weakness of a man who was too haughty and, in a sense, too idealistic to indulge in the political machinations inside the small group of leaders. His position as an outsider, on account of his past and his style, prevented him from acting when the moment came—for him, it only came once—with the necessary determination. He succumbed to a fetishization of the Party, to a certain legalism and to scruples that paralyzed him and prevented him from reacting unhesitantly, as Lenin would have done, to what his enemies were doing against him. As the founder, Lenin was not afraid of unmaking and remaking what he had made with his own hands. He was not afraid of organizing the people around him, of plotting, of fighting for the victory of his line and of keeping the situation under control.

Trotsky was not such a man. Lenin disappeared and Stalin was assured of victory.

4. *Michael Curtis: Retreat from Totalitarianism*

With Michael Curtis, we return once more to the central issue—the concept of totalitarianism. Curtis reexamines the use of the term, and finds that on balance it has become outmoded. He places great stress on the sharp differences between the so-called totalitarians of right and left, so far as their belief-systems are concerned, and he points up the changing character of communist regimes. Their variety, he believes, is too great to fit into any simple or rigid classificatory system. Michael Curtis, British-born and American-educated, has been since 1961 professor of political science at Rutgers University.

The term "totalitarianism" has been a valuable addition to the terminology of political science in that it has allowed one to differentiate the Nazi and Stalinist systems from other forms of contemporary dictatorships and from earlier systems of autocracy or authoritarianism. The term can apply to regimes in which all aspects of political, social, economic, and cultural life are subject to control, no limits to governmental interference are admitted, no political opposition or independent organization is permissible, and all citizens are expected to accept official, infallible doctrine. Even in absolutist regimes such as that of Louis XIV, the power of government was limited by the existence of intermediary institutions and by personal rights such as the right of petition and of association for nonpolitical purposes.

The claims of autocratic government are largely confined to public matters. But in totalitarian systems, the distinction between public and private has largely disappeared, so that official views on matters such as marriage and family life are pronounced. Giovanni Gentile, the major philosophic exponent of fascism, spoke of the totalitarian scope of fascism, which concerned itself not only with political organization and tendency but "with the whole will, thought, and feeling of the nation." For Mussolini (as he stated in his article on fascism in the Italian Encyclopedia), "nothing human or spiritual exists, much less has value, outside the state." Unlike liberalism, which preferred the interest of the individual to the state, fascism would reaffirm the state as the true reality of the individual.

Totalitarian systems are characterized by the elimination of the carefully

From Michael Curtis, "Retreat from Totalitarianism," in Carl J. Friedrich *et al.*, *Totalitarianism in Perspective* (New York: Praeger, 1969), pp. 58–63, 108–16. Reprinted by permission of Praeger Publishers, Inc.

cultivated distinction made in Western democracies between the state and society, by the absence of restraints on the wielders of power, by strict controls over the dissemination of information, by insistence on the particular truths of the regime, by strong directives over the economy and productive process, by maintaining what Lowenthal has called "a momentum of manipulated change," by a genuine or purported desire to create a new political and social system, by a single party with dedicated and disciplined adherents, and by a powerful secret police. Total power was explained from the premises of the regime: in Stalinist Russia, the dictatorship of the proletariat required the heightening of state power; in Germany, Hitler used the themes of the *Volk* and the organic community to explain Nazi concern for the whole; and in Italy, Mussolini thought the power of the state coextensive with the whole community.

Many of these characteristics have been present in earlier systems: in ancient and medieval despotisms, the Anabaptist regime in Munster, the Spanish evangelizing of Mexico in the sixteenth century, the Inca empire, Calvin's Geneva, nineteenth-century autocracies. But two new factors are present in contemporary systems: a highly technological society, which allows both an increase in the range and scope of control over citizens and a reduction in inefficiency, and an appeal by rulers to the mass of citizenry for support. The control inherent in the use of modern technology constitutes a danger for democratic as well as nondemocratic regimes, and the dependence of developed societies on computers has brought the fear that decisions in future may be taken by those controlling the operation of the computers rather than by elected representatives.

Some commentators have found in the latter factor—the fact that contemporary societies are mass societies—the key to totalitarian movements that try to weld estranged individuals into a community. Hannah Arendt views totalitarianism as arising out of the atomization of alienated and anxious individuals in modern society where the old foundations of the political realm, religion, tradition, and authority, are weak and in need of repair. In Kornhauser's mass society, nonelites are readily available for mobilization by elites. Lasswell has seen totalitarianism as providing an outlet for aggressive tendencies that can be directed against either subgroups within the society or foreigners. For Cantril, totalitarianism illustrates the psychology of mass despair and the lack of attachment to community that opens the door to a leadership promising direction and unity. For Talmon, totalitarian democracy, resting on popular enthusiasm, results from the pursuit of a preordained harmonious and perfect scheme of things to which men are irresistibly drawn.

It is this insistence on mass participation or enthusiasm that differentiates totalitarianism from other similar nondemocratic regimes. An authoritarian regime such as Spain under Franco is conservative in outlook, closely tied to Catholicism and to monarchists, supported by the army, capable of imposing strong economic controls, but it is equally ready to make any necessary compromise with the social forces in the country and does not seek out mass support. . . .

To gain sufficient strength to obtain power, the Italian Fascist and German Nazi regimes sought support from parts of the capitalist and aristocratic classes, military officers, and higher clergy, but they were never dominated by, or submissive to, the interests of these groups as the clerical conservative regimes have been. Nor do these latter regimes claim the certitude on political and ethical matters possessed by totalitarian systems. If authoritarian regimes and traditional authorities provide mutual support, totalitarian systems see themselves as the creators of secular standards and values without dependence on religious ethics. The former systems are not prone to dominate social behavior, groups, and institutions, to employ as great a degree of ruthlessness, to forbid freedom outside the political realm, to ignore legal procedure, compel acceptance of official doctrine, or neglect traditional values to the same extent as the latter regimes.

In similar fashion, the newer systems owe little to past theorists. In an age of universal suffrage and appeals to the people, the creation of movements that would be both the means of capturing political power and the source of such power was accompanied by new doctrines, myths, and symbolic references. The list of supposed intellectual precursors of totalitarianism is long but must be treated with great caution. While some of the ideas or general orientation of writers such as Plato, Machiavelli, the French Enlightenment authors, Rousseau, Fichte, Hegel, Saint-Simon, Comte, Treitschke, and Nietzsche can be juxtaposed alongside the themes of nazism or communism, this does not mean that the core of their views is harmonious with that of the totalitarian systems. . . .

Useful as the concept of totalitarianism has been as an explanatory tool for distinguishing political systems, reservations of two kinds are in order. The first is that the concept is only partly applicable to the three countries —Germany, the Soviet Union, and, especially, Italy—out of whose experience the theory was erected, and this has great importance in properly evaluating these countries. The second is that political behavior in the Soviet Union has changed sufficiently to render the concept inadequate. Moreover, the polycentrism of the Communist countries makes a monolithic explanation incorrect. . . .

Underlying the concept of totalitarianism has been the tendency to equate nazism and communism or at least to imply that the similarities between the two regimes that purported to incorporate these philosophies were greater than their differences. The many similarities are undeniable, and Friedrich was right to emphasize the role of violence in both systems. Aggressiveness, militarism, emphasis on national strength, anti-Semitism were to be found in all the totalitarian systems. As late as 1962, the publication in the Soviet Union of certain essays by Baron Holbach suggested a policy of deliberate anti-Semitism. Fascist desire for territorial aggrandizement can be compared with the idea of "the third Rome," the civilizing mission of the Russians. Peter Viereck once called "National Bolshevism the cousin to German National Socialism," and Raymond Aron suggested a comparison between the Communist myth of the Revolution and the Fascist cult of violence. Hitler's view that art should be intelligible to the masses coincided with the Soviet view of "socialist realism."

Nevertheless, the totalitarian concept does not sufficiently allow for the enormously different purposes sought by the three ideologies or beliefs, for the different intellectual levels of those beliefs, for the different styles of behavior and symbolic references of the regimes, and for the different groups who supported and benefited by them. Totalitarianism of the left, as Talmon has argued, begins with man, his rationality, and salvation; totalitarianism of the right begins with the collective entity—the state, the nation, or the race.

To offer brief lists of the major characteristics of the belief systems is to illustrate their different purposes. Nazism was characterized by nationalism, racism, emphasis on the *Volk*, anti-Semitism, stress on violence and force, appeal to national unity that would supersede the interests and differences of rank and class. With its rejection of democracy, secularization, rationalism, and positivism, its belief in domestic virtues, its vision of an attractive mythical past and rural harmony, its distaste for industrial civilization and urbanism, nazism was the counterrevolution in action and ultimately nihilistic in nature. The precapitalist, feudal aspects of nazism are illustrated by its Teutonic imagery, elitist decision-making through the Führer and the Gauleiter appointed by him, the oath of personal loyalty to Hitler, the stress on honor, blood, and soil, the end to the dependence of the German peasant on the market economy. Ernst Nolte has commented that, while Italian fascism recalled a remote but tangible historical era, the Nazis appealed to the prehistoric and the archaic.

The Nazis drew their main strength from the lower-middle class, marginal groups, military desperados, and those who had suffered by greater industrialization. But, uninterested in changing the nature of the social order, the Nazis were prepared to cooperate with those traditional groups such as the military and the bureaucracy that were not regarded as opponents. Though some 40 per cent of the full professors in economics and the social sciences vacated their chairs between 1932 and 1938, many academics, jurists, and even Nobel Prize winners capitulated before the regime. Hitler, in March, 1933, spoke of his regime as "the union between the symbols of the old greatness and the new strength." And the new strength was based on the manipulation of crowds, the display of strength through demonstrations, parades, and mass meetings, the welding of what Hitler, in *Mein Kampf*, called "the enormous human dragon" into a potent political force.

Contrasted with these characteristics are the ends of Marxism: that it seeks a society based on equality and humanitarianism, that it envisages the elimination of political coercion, that it seeks to build a rational social order, an industrialized economy, a higher form of democracy than that existing in the capitalist countries, and that it seeks to create a new type of civilization, internationalist rather than insular and parochial in nature. The traditional social and economic elite groups have no place in such a civilization or new type of society, and a wholly new political instrument is necessary. That the Communist regime distorted these high expectations and ended political liberty is not to deny the loftiness of the ideas.

The differentiation between a counterrevolutionary and a revolutionary purpose is crucial in the evaluation of the Nazi and Communist regimes. The objective of the first remains negative—the downfall of the existing regime—or nebulous, depending on the will of the dictator. The regime is essentially a destructive one in which positive achievement is gratuitous or related only to some destructive function. It is the product of a real dilemma of liberal democracy, a sort of suicidal reaction against a civilization that had failed to provide sufficient emotional satisfaction or material benefits for the mass of the people. In no real way can nazism or fascism be regarded as the continuation or inheritance of the French Revolution. The Nazi movement, as Rauschning wrote, had no fixed aims, either economic or political, either in domestic or foreign affairs. Its strength lay in incessant activity, its Valhalla the lust for power and the quest for adventure.

For Communist countries, the creation of an equalitarian and humane society, while not necessarily observed in practice, is its informing spirit, and action can be related to that fundamental objective. The Russian Revolution began, Deutscher noted, "with the dazzling blaze of a great vision." There is no inherent insistence on violence in the Communist, as in the Nazi or Fascist, system. In the post-Stalin Communist systems, violence is an incidental factor, a means by which to achieve a desired end. But violence was an intrinsic facet of Nazi or Fascist behavior, unrelated to rational purpose. In Italy, the aggressive defenders of "law and order in the streets" and the strikebreakers became the *squadrista*. For Hitler, "force was the first law" and war, the normal condition of mankind. The means as well as the ends of the regimes were different in theory. The Nazi and Fascist regimes saw themselves as perpetual dictatorships from the beginning. The Bolsheviks took power on behalf of the Soviet of Workers' and Soldiers' Deputies, and the dictatorship of the proletariat has always been regarded as a transitional stage toward a free society.

In his essay in this volume, [Carl J.] Friedrich seems to imply that Georges Sorel's call for violence is relevant to the Marxist doctrine of the class struggle. But Sorel, although at one point an advocate of revolutionary syndicalism and, at the end of his life in 1922, an admirer of Lenin, was a complex political thinker who can be claimed by the right as well as by the left. His arguments for creative violence, displays of heroism, use of myth, spontaneity of proletarian movements, and syndicalist society where the worker was producer, not surprisingly led him to regard the Fascists as an elite and Mussolini as a political genius. Mussolini himself, in his 1932 Encyclopedia article, indicated the importance of Sorel in the origins of fascism.

At the same time, the ambiguity of the Sorelian position is indicative of the fact that there is no simple dichotomy between left and right in the contemporary world. Friedrich shrewdly points out that many of the Nazi themes have reappeared in the influential work of Franz Fanon. It is not coincidental that Fanon's work has been attractive both to neo-Marxists such as Jean-Paul Sartre and Che Guevara, as far as its stress on revolutionary guerrilla war is concerned, and also to black nationalists, in Africa as well as in the United States, who have appropriated its passages on racism, violence, and lack of compromise and converted them into what appears to be a new form of destructive black fascism.

For all these reasons, the concept of totalitarianism is no longer the most useful classificatory device for the study of current Communist systems. One must acknowledge that the term has been valuable in the past and that it still possesses utility for analysis of the Chinese regime and those regimes adhering to the Chinese position in the Sino-Soviet dispute. Yet, Friedrich's desire to keep the concept, with amended definition, to apply to the Soviet and Eastern European systems, and his brilliant attempt to justify this, has led him to a shaky methodological position. He argues that "totalitarianism" is a relative category, and that a regime can be more or less totalitarian. But one must ask "relative to what?" The concept was formulated to differentiate the unique behavior of two, or possibly three, states from other autocratic or authoritarian systems. When two of these three regimes have collapsed and the third has witnessed some crucial changes, the term seems hardly applicable. . . .

There remains the problem of how best to analyze the Communist regimes—either as individual systems or as a group or within the general rubric of comparative politics. This problem has aroused considerable discussion in recent years. . . . Alfred Meyer has been one of the main proponents of the analysis of the Soviet Union as a bureaucratic system, an authoritarian political structure in which the elite escape control by the conformist masses. The expectation of a classless society is regarded as illusory. In this view, the Soviet Union may be best understood—after the initial period of a more terrorist totalitarianism that was used in the crash program of industrialization—as a large, complex bureaucracy comparable in structure and function to large organizations in general. Organizational behavior has become routinized and predictable as ideology has become taken for granted. The system is more dependent on material rewards, such as benefits, social services, or a regressive tax, and sanctions than on the minimal rewards and the expendability of human beings characteristic of the past. The fact that the bureaucracy is highly politicized does not deny the utility of the bureaucratic model for analysis.

The argument of Trotsky and, more recently, of Djilas that a new class of bureaucrats had been created in the Soviet Union, constituting the real ruling group, overemphasizes the homogeneity or unity of such a group. But, clearly, it is even more valid here than for the Western countries to argue that a small political elite possesses advantages denied to the masses. Hannah Arendt tried to portray the banality of evil of the Nazi regime through an Eichmann who, in spite of his ability to define Kant's categorical imperative correctly, could say that "administrative language is the only language I know." The loyal, unquestioning bureaucrat is the base on which both the Nazi and the Soviet regime have rested.

In a similar argument, Allen Kassof has suggested that the Soviet Union be seen as an administered society, a totalism without terror, whose organization, coordination, and desire to remove conflicts are based on supposed social and historical laws, and in which a political directorate controls planning and direction in the name of welfare and progress. The Soviet bureaucracy, in its desire to preserve the status quo, is a conservative force, an example of institutional and behavioral ossification; not surprisingly, it is an example Mao has not been prepared to accept as representing the future of China.

Robert Tucker has argued very cogently that the Soviet Union could be analyzed as falling within the category of "a revolutionary mass-movement regime under single party auspices." This would allow the Communist regime to be compared with Fascist and with nationalist single party regimes, since all possess a philosophy of revolution, a program of revolutionary struggle, a militant revolutionary party, and a program of national renewal. In the new edition of her influential book, *The Origins of Totalitarianism*, Hannah Arendt also has suggested that the Soviet Union might now be regarded as a one-party dictatorship rather than as a totalitarian system. The differences between the one-party regimes of the Communist systems and those of the developing nations of Africa and Asia are immense; yet, the relevance of such an analysis is shown by the fact that . . . communism in underdeveloped countries is not easily distinguishable from the nationalist and modernizing movements led by intellectuals in those countries.

Each of these approaches illustrates a facet of the past or current behavior of the Soviet Union and invites comparison with other political systems; none illuminates the system as a whole. The desire to relate the Soviet system to modern political analysis is wholly salutary, but does not entail the acceptance of any one particular model. Above all, it does not serve the cause of comparative political analysis or of political understanding to cling to the concept of totalitarianism.

5. *A. James Gregor: The Ideology of Fascism*

The idea that the label "totalitarian" has lost its usefulness is widely shared these days, but is by no means universally accepted. A. James Gregor, associate professor of political science at the University of California (Berkeley), has recently come forward with a strong defense of the concept of totalitarianism, and of the idea that Marxist and Fascist regimes have much in com-

From A. James Gregor, *The Ideology of Fascism*, pp. 330–33, 345–46, 350–53, 360–61. Footnotes omitted. Copyright © 1969 by The Free Press, a Division of The Macmillan Company. Reprinted by permission of The Macmillan Company.

mon. It is an error, Gregor insists, to place Marxism and Fascism at opposite ends of a spectrum. Extremists of both right and left share a similar personality structure; they build institutional structures that are alike; and they drink at a common ideological spring. According to this view Lenin and Mussolini are seen as parallel revolutionary thinkers and activists. Fascism and Marxism "constitute species of a single genus: totalitarianism." And so the debate continues. . . .

The failure on the part of some of the most astute political analysts of our time to anticipate the political developments that followed the termination of hostilities after the second global conflict of our century was at least partly the consequence of the prevailing disposition to construe the relationship between "Marxism" and "Fascism" (however it was understood or misunderstood) as unilinear, each occupying the extreme of a continuum from "left" to "right," from "extreme liberalism" to "authoritarianism." Under the influence of this pervasive conviction, item scales were constructed by social scientists to reflect this unilinearity—with "extreme liberal," i.e., "Marxist," views the furthest removed from extreme "fascist" views. If the Marxists sinned, they were understood to sin on the side of virtue. In effect, experimental psychologists accepted critical auxiliary assumptions characteristic of Marxist interpretations of contemporary political movements. Marxists of all and sundry persuasions have insisted that Marxism and its variants have all been, in some radical sense, "democratic." Fascism, in whatever forms it took (and Marxist commentators have included in the class of fascist movements political systems as varied as the plebiscitary dictatorship of Louis Napoleon and reformist "social democracy"), was conceived as fundamentally "antidemocratic." As a consequence, social scientists constructed pattern variable schemata which pretended to distinguish between the two in terms, for example, of "universalism" and "particularism," "equality" and "ascription." "Left Wing movements" were "universalistic and equalitarian," hence democratic in some real sense, while "right-wing movements" were "particularistic and ascriptive," hence fundamentally antidemocratic.

The empirical studies conducted in the effort to identify "fascists" experimentally were governed by such auxiliary assumptions. The result was an artifact of those assumptions. In the study of "potential fascists," that is, the "authoritarian personalities" so extensively studied in the United States immediately following the War, the research was conducted on the basis of an extremely unsophisticated conception of a Right/Left continuum expressed in terms of American political clichés that utilized the familiar vocabulary of Marxist and quasi-Marxist analyses.

It soon became apparent, however, that

Fascism and Bolshevism, only a few decades ago thought of as worlds apart, have now been recognized increasingly as sharing many very important features. Their common hostility towards civil liberties, political democracy, their common antipathy for parliamentary institutions, individualism, private enterprise, their image of the political world as a struggle between morally irreconcilable forces, their be-

lief that all their opponents are secretly leagued against them and their own predilection for secrecy, their conviction that all forms of power are in a hostile
world concentrated in a few hands and their own aspirations for concentrated and
total power—all these showed that the two extremes had much in common.

The high hopes that animated the entire "antifascist" consortium
throughout World War II foundered on the fact that the contemporary variants of Marxism were not radically democratic, but were instead essentially totalitarian political systems as much opposed to parliamentary democracy as was paradigmatic Fascism. The typology employed to classify
the various contending political systems before the War was fundamentally
mistaken. Marxism-Leninism and the subsequent variants that proliferated
after the termination of hostilities shared more features with paradigmatic
Fascism than they did or do with liberalism and the parliamentary democracy which is its characteristic political expression. The gradual recognition of this fact has led experimental scientists and political analysts to
search out a more responsible and informative classificatory system
through which investigation of their domain of inquiry could be pursued
more effectively. . . . [Recent research on personality structure], together
with the descriptive evidence available from a careful scrutiny of political
opinions expressed by representative Marxists or their contemporary variants, and fascist spokesmen and whatever living representatives of paradigmatic Fascism remain, affords a good presumptive case for the existence
of an underlying similarity of personality structure subtending radical political orientation, whether it be of Left or Right Wing provenience.
 The presumptive case supports the conviction that both fascism and the
variants of Marxism that today receive so much attention constitute species
of a single genus: totalitarianism. Had Anglo-American political commentators not been under the pervasive influence of Marxist or quasi-Marxist
analyses, this would have been evident long before the advent of World
War II. Such astute observers as Elie Halevy and Franz Borkenau indicated as much. Halevy argued that although Russian socialism had developed out of the democratic and anti-statist tradition of classical Marxism,
it had quickly begun to assume the elitist, authoritarian, nationalist, and
statist features of Fascism until he could maintain that "Bolshevism is, literally, a 'fascism.'" Borkenau, in turn, went so far as to suggest that Bolshevism was a "conscious and intentional imitation of Fascism. . . ."
 That such was the case should have been evident before the War—had
Anglo-American analysts taken the trouble to treat Fascism as a serious
political movement and inform themselves of its ideological commitments.
The fact is that both paradigmatic Fascism and contemporary Marxism are
rooted in the same ideological traditions and share some critical normative
convictions. Mussolini was a well-informed and convinced Marxist. His ultimate political convictions represent a reform of classical Marxism in the
direction of a restoration of its Hegelian elements. Gentile, a neo-Hegelian,
construed Marxism as a variant of Hegelianism and Fascism as its most
consistent contemporary expression. Leninism, like Fascism, is heir to a

similar patrimony that reveals itself, for example, in the conceptions of the relation between the individual and society and in the isomorphic arguments that provide vindications for their respective totalitarian political practices. . . .

All that remains in order to deliver a compelling presumptive argument for the identification of the diverse variants of contemporary Marxism as members of a genus which includes paradigmatic Fascism is to indicate the pervasive similarities in institutional structure of such political systems. The institutional features of Left and Right Wing totalitarian systems do, in fact, reveal a surprising similarity, a fact not lost upon Fascist commentators even during periods of the most exacerbated political contest with Marxist movements.

As early as 1933, Mussolini, himself, indicated his awareness of the gradual convergence between Soviet totalitarianism and his own. By 1938, he was prepared to suggest that the process of phased involution of the Leninist system had produced an involuntary and inconsistent fascism. As early as 1934, Fascist theoreticians could contend that "in the course of its development the Russian revolution has gradually given evidence of fully abandoning Marxist postulates and of a gradual, if surreptitious acceptance of certain fundamental political principles that characterize Fascism."

While such judgments were relatively common among non-Marxist and Fascist commentators, they were not unknown among knowledgeable Marxists. Leon Trotsky, for example, maintained that "Stalinism and Fascism, in spite of a deep difference in social foundations, are symmetrical phenomena. In many of their features they show a deadly similarity."

Those similarities include a commitment to national development and/or reconstruction under a highly centralized and authoritarian party elite, a restoration of the authority of the state, an effective program of class and category collaboration within the confines of a national economic plan, exclusive and systematic training of the youth of the nation in conformity with a secular ideology characterized by a relatively specific constellation of exclusive social and political beliefs, a unitary party monopoly of the means of coercion and communication, and leadership by charismatic or pseudocharismatic leaders charged with enormous responsibilities and endowed with prodigious powers. In all cases the totalitarian state assumes pedagogical, enterprisory, and tutelary functions unknown in traditional parliamentary regimes. . . .

It is clear that although the theoretical propositions of Marx and Engels were formulated in vague and ambiguous language, Marxism was committed to the conviction that revolutionary consciousness was derivative of more fundamental processes in society. The production of revolutionary consciousness was inevitable, and it would affect the vast majority of men working under advanced capitalist conditions. That vast majority would be driven to rebellion and would seize the technological apparatus and plant

provided by capitalism itself upon which to erect the social structure of socialism. An elaborate productive base, conjoined with socialist consciousness, both of them products of capitalism itself, would produce the socialist
society which was the conscious desire of the vast majority of men—an
outcome that would satisfy the normative aspirations of classical Marxism.

Unfortunately for classical Marxism, the proletarian majority whom they
had charged with this historic mission failed to develop the requisite consciousness. Revolutionary sentiment developed in those areas of the world
under objective conditions which did not accord themselves with the requirements of the theory. Lenin found himself in circumstances in which a
restive revolutionary sentiment mobilized itself outside the advanced capitalist countries. He had the painful choice of either attempting to harness
that revolutionary ardor behind the further development of capitalism,
hoping that capitalism would, as classical Marxism suggested, eventually
develop the requisite consciousness among the working-class, or he could
modify classical Marxism and seek to generate the motive consciousness
among the elemental masses independent of, and if necessary contrary to,
objective conditions. He opted for the latter alternative. Lenin insisted that
consciousness must be *brought* to the working masses, now no longer simply the proletarian majority of which classical Marxism spoke, but a coalition of the peasant masses and the proletarian minority of Czarist Russia.
Lenin rejected the thesis of spontaneous revolutionary consciousness. He
denied that the revolution must wait until the vast majority of men had developed the "spontaneous" and "instinctive" consciousness of their real interests. In 1901, Lenin maintained that

. . . the "ideologist" is worthy of the name only when he precedes the spontaneous movement, points out the road, and is able ahead of all others to solve all
the theoretical, political, tactical, and organizational questions which the "material elements" of the movement spontaneously encounter. . . .

He argued further that the "spontaneous awakening of the masses" must be
led by "ideologists" sufficiently "trained theoretically to be proof against all
vacillations. . . ." The revolution demands "a strong and centralized organization of revolutionaries" who would provide the minoritarian "conscious
element" necessary to direct the "spontaneous element." What Lenin proposed was a minority "vanguard party" of professional revolutionaries
whose will would offset the deficiencies of world history.

In Italy, at almost the same time, Mussolini was arguing almost the same
thesis. Socialism, Mussolini maintained, was failing because it had not
taken cognizance of the critical role played in revolution by effective political and insurrectionary elites. It was in 1904 that Mussolini rejected the
deterministic thesis that revolution was the necessary and spontaneous
product of capitalist economic conditions. He opted instead for a thesis
which would restore to history the "creative will of determinate and determining men" who could leave the imprint of their influence on things
and institutions and who would direct historical and political events in a
determinate direction. Such men would constitute a minoritarian "socialist

vanguard" and bring to the elemental energy of the majority a consciousness of historic purpose.

Thus, at approximately the same time, in two different locales, both
Lenin and Mussolini, as socialist theoreticians and political leaders, introduced substantive modifications into the loose theoretical structure of
classical Marxism. Their modifications were essentially the same. They
were both elitists and voluntarists. They conceived the majority as the fod-
der, rather than the conscious agents, of social revolution. This is the essence of the modified socialism that animated their political activities.
They both conceived the socialist party as a centralized, hierarchically integrated elite of professional revolutionaries charged with the responsibilities of history which classical Marxism had originally developed upon the
vast majority of thinking proletarians. Both Mussolini and Lenin led revolutionary movements in economically backward environments. Both drew
their support, in large measure, from restive non-proletarian masses which
Marx had always conceived to be essentially reactionary—that is, devoid
of serious historical significance.

By 1902, Lenin understood the revolutionary consciousness of the masses
to be a product not of the economic processes characteristic of capitalism,
but of the active intercession of declassed bourgeois intellectuals. Such
men, among whom Lenin numbered Marx and Engels as well as himself,
were charged with the responsibility of making the masses conscious of
their real rather than their immediate interests. Without the intercession of
such men, Lenin argued, the masses could achieve only a "trade union
mentality," an addiction to their primitive and immediate interests. Only
the theoretical elite could divine the real and ultimate interests of the masses and thus act in the name of history. The revolution was not to be made
by the vast majority of self-conscious and knowledgeable men as an automatic process, but by an aggressive elite mobilizing the elemental masses
in the name of the ultimate interests of man. This was the sustaining logic
of both the Bolshevik revolution of 1917 and the Fascist revolution of 1922.
In both cases a minority of men, leading paramilitary bands, seized the
state machinery in the name of their vision of society. Both revolutions
were hierarchically led minoritarian revolutions. Both mobilized the restive energies of the masses in the service of a revolution guided by the insights of a man, or a small assembly of men, charged with the responsibility of lifting the consciousness of the masses to the level of their vision of
social and political truth. The political organizations led by both men were
not orthodox political parties; they represented movements of solidarity,
movements charged with infusing the masses with a belief system. Both
movements jealously defended the purity of their respective doctrines. Both
assumed pedagogical and tutelary responsibilities never before exercised
by men outside of religious orders. . . .

The fact is that Soviet society, like many of the societies being constructed under the auspices of revolutionary mass-movement regimes, has
taken on features which are manifestly fascistic. In 1957, approximately a
decade after the death of Mussolini, Ugo Spirito, the principal advocate of

the radical corporativism of the Fascist Congress of Ferrara of 1932, and Gentile's foremost philosophic heir, published his reflections on the Soviet Union. His essay revealed the critical and essential continuity he saw between paradigmatic Fascism and the [Soviet state] as it has manifested itself in a society that had once committed itself to the "withering away of the state."

Spirito saw in the Soviet Union a transcendence of the dual world of the bourgeoisie, a transcendence of the "liberal" social order, the "order" riven into public and private domains that is the characteristic product of the bourgeoisie. Soviet society, Spirito contended, has transcended the bourgeois distinction between public and private; in the Soviet Union "the particular and the universal are intrinsically bound up in a single expression of life. . . . Russian communism is rooted in the reality of a people that conceives the values of the collectivity as constituent elements of its very life. Communion and faith are its principal characteristics . . ." and myth its sustaining strength. This is manifestly the language of his communication before the Fascist Congress of Ferrara. Soviet society has fulfilled, in part, the Fascist dream of his young manhood.

VII

The Munich Pact

The Munich pact gave the word "appeasement" a new and disagreeable meaning. No longer is "soothing or pacifying" an adequate definition; "appeasement" now implies moral inadequacy and a lack of determination to defend one's rights against aggression. Thus Munich has "come to stand in the English language as a symbol for national humiliation and betrayal";[1] and today many people find it hard to realize that there are still those who strongly defend the actions of the western powers in their dealings with Hitler in 1938 and that the conclusion of the Munich pact was exceedingly popular at the time, even with some of those who, today, would be the first to emphasize the horror of anything approaching "appeasement."

The easiest defense of Munich is the one which avoids any defense of the principle of appeasement itself: Neville Chamberlain and Edouard Daladier had no choice but to do as they did; the pact was the best that could have been gotten under the circumstances, and, since the West, especially Britain, was in no position to fight in 1938, "the criticism directed against Munich could have been directed with more accuracy against Britain's tardiness in the rearming rather than against the pact itself." [2] This is essentially the argument of a recent biography of Chamberlain, which also emphasizes that, psychologically as well as militarily, the British were unprepared for war in 1938 and that Chamberlain's policy reflected the desires of his people.[3] This theme, of Chamberlain as the friend of the peace loving "little" man, is a common one: ". . . was it not to his credit that he tried to save the simple people from the catastrophe of war and the devastating effects of an immediate invasion?" [4]

It is around these and similar points that most of the dispute concerning Munich concentrates today: how strong were the Czech defenses? How well would the Czech army, supported by the Skoda armaments works but weakened by the acrimony between Czechs and Slovaks, have fought? Could Britain and France have furnished any effective aid if Czechoslovakia had been attacked in 1938?

1. P. A. Reynolds, *British Foreign Policy in the Inter-War Years* (London: Longmans, Green, 1954), p. 149.
2. John F. Kennedy, *Why England Slept* (Garden City: Doubleday, 1962), p. 160. For a detailed survey of Munich, one should consult J. W. Wheeler-Bennett, *Munich: Prologue to Tragedy* (New York: Duell, Sloan and Pierce, 1948).
3. Iain Macleod, *Neville Chamberlain* (London: Frederick Muller, 1961), Chapter 15.
4. Viscount Templewood, *Nine Troubled Years* (London: Collins, 1954), p. 323.

Did not the British gain more than the Germans from the year's delay in the outbreak of war, since during that post-Munich year their rearmament made much progress, and the RAF was equipped with the Hurricanes and the Spitfires that won the Battle of Britain? If that was so, does it explain why Hitler was supposedly in such a vile mood at Munich, feeling cheated out of a war he badly wanted? [5] Or was it the Germans, rather, who gained most by the postponement, as they managed in that year to eliminate or isolate the eastern European allies of France? Had war come at the time of Munich, would the German armies have been able to reach the Channel coast and to secure the bases from which to threaten Britain with invasion? Had there been a chance of a coup by the German military against the Nazi regime in 1938—a coup which was thwarted by Hitler's success at Munich? And what of the psychological consequences of Munich? Surely the British, simple and sophisticated alike, were a more united and determined people in 1939 than in 1938, with the Commonwealth behind them, and with Hitler's determination to dominate all Europe, whether German or non-German, clearly established for the first time by his seizure of Prague. But how did the year's delay affect the morale of the French and the fighting capability of the French army?

It is profitable, however, to take a broader view. Was Munich a great turning point in European history, when the West voluntarily surrendered influence over eastern Europe—a surrender not reversed, but reconfirmed, by the second world war? [6] Or might it be argued that Chamberlain and Daladier were not taken in by Hitler, but were rather masters of the modern art of psychological warfare, as they forced Hitler to conduct his future aggression over the shambles of his pledged word, given in a solemn pact—a pact which, unlike Versailles, was no *diktat*, and which, unlike Locarno, bore his own signature? Perhaps Chamberlain, far from being a simple, trusting businessman, nothing but "a good Lord Mayor of Birmingham in a lean year," was playing a supremely cunning game, and was attempting to do what so many have since maintained should have been done—that is, turn Germany to the East, where it would become involved in a war with the Soviet Union which would have eliminated both of the major totalitarian powers. This hypothesis opens a wide field for speculation, ranging from the Soviet Union's willingness and ability to fight in 1938, and from the legacy of Munich to the era of the Cold War,[7] to the validity of the belief that a life-and-death struggle between two totalitarian monsters must result in death for both.

When Daladier returned to Paris from Munich he feared that there would be hostile demonstrations at the airport; yet he, like Chamberlain, was greeted with great enthusiasm, and the appeasement policy turned out to be very popular at first with both the British and the French people. An inquiry into the reasons for this public reaction is one of the most valuable aspects of a consideration of the Munich pact. Did the Popular Front and the Spanish Civil War cause many

5. See Ivone Kirkpatrick, *The Inner Circle* (London: Macmillan, 1959), p. 128. See also pp. 131–34.

6. Hajo Holborn, *The Political Collapse of Europe* (New York: Alfred A. Knopf, 1951), p. 158.

7. See *ibid.*, where it is claimed that the Russians saw Munich as an attempt on the part of the West to turn German ambitions eastward; Chamberlain's dislike and distrust of the Soviet Union (see Keith Feiling, *Neville Chamberlain* [London: Macmillan, 1947], p. 403, for an indication of this antipathy) are often cited as evidence that such was the plan; but compare the view of Stephen Borsody, *The Triumph of Tyranny* (New York: Macmillan, 1960), p. 102.

Frenchmen to see foreign policy in ideological rather than nationalistic terms? [8]
Had the French accepted the inevitability of appeasing Germany, given the reality of France's dependence on England and Italy's alliance with Germany? And
in England, how can the truly spontaneous joy with which Chamberlain was
greeted be explained? Was it simply relief that a war—until then expected at any
moment—had been averted, that caused *The Times* to assert that "no conqueror
returning from a victory on the battlefield has come home adorned with nobler
laurels," or the *Sunday Dispatch* to say that "the gratitude of millions of mothers,
wives, sweethearts, pours out to feed a flood which will sweep Mr. Neville Chamberlain to a high pinnacle in history," or the *Birmingham Daily Gazette* to maintain that "Birmingham is proud that the peace of Europe, when all but lost, has
been saved by a cool-brained and determined Birmingham man?" [9] A few felt
otherwise. Duff Cooper argued that if the Czechs were to be deserted or even advised to surrender "we should be guilty of one of the basest betrayals in
history." [10] Winston Churchill vigorously denounced Munich in Parliament: "£1
was demanded at the pistol's point. When it was given, £2 were demanded at the
pistol's point. Finally, the dictator consented to take £1 17s. 6d. and the rest in
promises of good will for the future." [11] But Chamberlain was the hero of the moment; the antiappeasers in his own party were generally ignored, and the Labor
opposition, with only a few exceptions, remained trapped by its own lingering
pacifism.

Some historians have argued that the appeasement mood in Britain can be explained by a decline in the quality of statesmanship—a decline illustrated by the
Chamberlain group's failure to distinguish between the interests of their social
order and those of their country. "[They] were essentially middle-class, not aristocrats. They did not have the hereditary sense of the security of the state, unlike
Churchill, Eden, the Cecils." [12] Other critics suggest that sympathy for Nazism in
certain restricted but important circles played a part in determining British
policy; [13] or that foreign policy was being influenced by men who lacked understanding of history and diplomacy, and who suffered from the often-noticed British lack of interest in eastern Europe. "How horrible, fantastic, incredible it is
[cried Chamberlain at the time] that we should be digging trenches and trying
on gas-masks here because of a quarrel in a far-away country between people of
whom we know nothing." [14] In fact, were many influential Englishmen convinced
that Germans—even Nazis—were a basically realistic people, like themselves; did
Chamberlain, and others highly placed in the British government, therefore believe that Munich would bring lasting peace, and not just postponement of war?
Were many of these same Englishmen still suffering from feelings of guilt over

8. See Charles A. Micaud, *The French Right and Nazi Germany 1933–1939* (Dur-
ham: Duke University Press, 1943).

9. Quoted in Macleod, *op. cit.*, p. 268.

10. Alfred Duff Cooper, *Old Men Forget* (London: Rupert Hart-Davis, 1957), p. 239.

11. Charles Eade, editor, *The War Speeches of the Rt. Hon. Winston S. Churchill*
(London: Cassell, 1951), I, 25.

12. A. L. Rowse, *Appeasement: A Study in Political Decline 1933–1939* (New York:
Norton, 1961), p. 117.

13. See, for an example of this sympathy, Nevile Henderson, *Failure of a Mission*
(New York: G. P. Putnam's Sons, 1940), esp. pp. 12–13. See also Margaret George, *The
Warped Vision* (Pittsburgh: University of Pittsburgh Press, 1965); Martin Gilbert and
Richard Gott, *The Appeasers* (London: Weidenfeld and Nicolson, 1963); and Martin
Gilbert, *The Roots of Appeasement* (London: Weidenfeld and Nicolson, 1966).

14. Quoted in Feiling, *op. cit.*, p. 372.

the Versailles treaty? No less a figure than Barrington-Ward, in 1938 deputy editor of *The Times,* possessed this complex: "That the mistakes of Versailles had to be paid for by the Allies, remained one of B-W's deepest convictions." [15] Recent scholarship, in fact, has reinforced this view, as the British Cabinet papers have become available.[16]

One can argue, therefore, that Chamberlain, although not a Nazi sympathizer, naïvely believed that he could deal effectively with the Nazi leaders, and that Germany would behave reasonably when its just ambitions were met. Moreover, it is clear that Chamberlain tolerated little interference from anyone in the pursuit of his policies, even though he was inexperienced in foreign affairs. Yet, does all of this necessarily condemn Chamberlain? Was it wrong to try to avert a war for which he thought England was unprepared, and which was to be fought in the defense of a multinational state whose viability he doubted? Or must one emphasize his own responsibility for England's lack of preparation, and his blindness to the consequences of deserting Czechoslovakia? On the other hand, does the evidence indicate that he would have supported France, which, unlike England, had a treaty obliging it to come to the aid of the Czechs, if the French had shown any inclination to fight? Was he wrong in thinking that only Bolshevism could gain from a European war? Was his appeasement policy basically correct, but tragically abused at Munich? There will be no end to the arguments.

At any rate, a once very important man, who had good reason to regret an earlier conflict between Germany and England, was exceedingly pleased by the outcome of the Munich conference: "I have not the slightest doubt," wrote ex-Kaiser William II to Britain's Queen Mary, "that Mr. N. Chamberlain was inspired by Heaven & guided by God who took pity on his children on Earth by crowning his mission with such relieving success." [17] But disillusion came quickly, and a noted scholar has characterized Munich as "the nadir of diplomacy—a personal deal between two men at the expense of a third party." [18] In fact, by the Christmas of 1938 the following verse appeared, which now represents, whether justly or unjustly, what has come to be the dominant view of Munich:

> Peace on earth are fighting words
> And the milk of human kindness curds,
> So let us on this festive date
> Arise and reaffirm our hate
> For Adolf Hitler, the Nazi thug,
> Mussolini, the Fascist mugg,
> And each and every moral eunuch
> That had a hand in the Pact of Munich.
> The rhyme is bad but the Pact was worse—
> Neville's plane may be Europe's Hearse.[19]

---

15. *The History of the Times* (London: Printing House Square, 1952), IV, Part 2, p. 950.

16. See Ian Colvin, *The Chamberlain Cabinet* (London: Gollancz, 1971). Another important recent study is Keith Middlemas, *Diplomacy of Illusion* (London: Weidenfeld and Nicolson, 1972), which is especially critical of Chamberlain and his advisers.

17. Quoted in James Pope-Hennessy, *Queen Mary* (London: George Allen and Unwin, 1959), p. 592.

18. Charles L. Mowat, *Britain Between the Wars* (London: Methuen, 1955), p. 615.

19. Frank Sullivan, "Greetings, Friends!" *The New Yorker,* December 24, 1938, p. 19.

I. *Winston S. Churchill: The Gathering Storm*

For many Americans Winston Churchill was a man whose genius and brilliance could never be validly questioned. Proof of this, it is often alleged, can be found in his stalwart opposition to the appeasement policy of the 1930's, when he and a few loyal followers led a valiant but futile struggle against the weakness of Chamberlain and his cohorts. But it is well to remember that Churchill was, in the 1930's, a man seemingly without a future. He had always been mistrusted because he was not a good party man, and his activities in the years before the war confirmed this mistrust for many Conservatives. His opposition to greater self-government for India, his knight-errantry at the time of the abdication of Edward VIII, and his constant harping on the issue of rearmament, were all cited as signs of his instability and lack of judgment. Recently, moreover, scholars have been questioning whether Churchill was really the leader of a cohesive group of antiappeasement Conservatives; in fact, it is even argued that Churchill's own stance on the appeasement issue was not as consistent as it was later presented.[1] Nevertheless, in his great war memoirs Churchill admitted of no doubts, and pictured Munich as a disaster for the English and French.

We have now . . . Marshal Keitel's answer to the specific question put to him by the Czech representative at the Nuremberg Trials:

Colonel Eger, representing Czechoslovakia, asked Marshal Keitel: "Would the Reich have attacked Czechoslovakia in 1938 if the Western Powers had stood by Prague?"

Marshall Keitel answered: "Certainly not. We were not strong enough militarily. The object of Munich (i.e., reaching an agreement at Munich) was to get Russia out of Europe, to gain time, and to complete the German armaments."

Hitler's judgment had been once more decisively vindicated. The German General Staff was utterly abashed. Once again the Fuehrer had been right, after all. He with his genius and intuition alone had truly measured all the circumstances, military and political. Once again, as in the Rhineland, the Fuehrer's leadership had triumphed over the obstruction of the German military chiefs. All these generals were patriotic men. They longed to see the Fatherland regain its position in the world. They were devoting themselves night and day to every process that could strengthen the German forces. They, therefore, felt smitten in their hearts at having been found so much below the level of the event, and in many cases their dislike and their distrust of Hitler were overpowered by admiration for his commanding gifts and miraculous luck. Surely here was a star to follow, surely here was a guide to obey. Thus did Hitler finally become the undisputed

From Winston S. Churchill, *The Gathering Storm* (Boston: Houghton Mifflin, 1948), pp. 318–21. Reprinted by permission of the publishers.
1. Neville Thompson, *The Anti-Appeasers* (Oxford: Clarendon Press, 1971).

master of Germany, and the path was clear for the great design. The conspirators lay low, and were not betrayed by their military comrades.

It may be well here to set down some principles of morals and action which may be a guide in the future. No case of this kind can be judged apart from its circumstances. The facts may be unknown at the time and estimates of them must be largely guesswork, coloured by the general feelings and aims of whoever is trying to pronounce. Those who are prone by temperament and character to seek sharp and clear-cut solutions of difficult and obscure problems, who are ready to fight whenever some challenge comes from a foreign Power, have not always been right. On the other hand, those whose inclination is to bow their heads, to seek patiently and faithfully for peaceful compromise, are not always wrong. On the contrary, in the majority of instances they may be right, not only morally but from a practical standpoint. How many wars have been averted by patience and persisting good will! Religion and virtue alike lend their sanctions to meekness and humility not only between men but between nations. How many wars have been precipitated by firebrands! How many misunderstandings which led to wars could have been removed by temporising! How often have countries fought cruel wars and then after a few years of peace found themselves not only friends but allies!

The Sermon on the Mount is the last word in Christian ethics. Everyone respects the Quakers. Still, it is not on these terms that Ministers assume their responsibilities of guiding states. Their duty is first so to deal with other nations as to avoid strife and war and to eschew aggression in all its forms, whether for nationalistic or ideological objects. But the safety of the State, the lives and freedom of their own fellow countrymen, to whom they owe their position, make it right and imperative in the last resort, or when a final and definite conviction has been reached, that the use of force should not be excluded. If the circumstances are such as to warrant it, force may be used. And if this be so, it should be used under the conditions which are most favourable. There is no merit in putting off a war for a year if, when it comes, it is a far worse war or one much harder to win. These are the tormenting dilemmas upon which mankind has throughout its history been so frequently impaled. Final judgment upon them can only be recorded by history in relation to the facts of the case as known to the parties at the time, and also as subsequently proved.

There is, however, one helpful guide, namely, for a nation to keep its word and to act in accordance with its treaty obligations to allies. This guide is called *honour*. It is baffling to reflect that what men call honour does not correspond always to Christian ethics. Honour is often influenced by that element of pride which plays so large a part in its inspiration. An exaggerated code of honour leading to the performance of utterly vain and unreasonable deeds could not be defended, however fine it might look. Here, however, the moment came when Honour pointed the path of Duty, and when also the right judgment of the facts at that time would have reinforced its dictates.

For the French Government to leave her faithful ally, Czechoslovakia, to her fate was a melancholy lapse from which flowed terrible consequences. Not only wise and fair policy, but chivalry, honour, and sympathy for a small threatened people made an overwhelming concentration. Great Britain, who would certainly have fought if bound by treaty obligations, was nevertheless now deeply involved, and it must be recorded with regret that the British Government not only acquiesced but encouraged the French Government in a fatal course.

2. *Lord Butler: The Art of the Possible*

One of the finest autobiographies to come out of England in recent years is "Rab" Butler's. Lord Butler, who is now retired from politics and is Master of Trinity at Cambridge, twice came close—or so it seemed at the time—to the prime ministership, and he was for many years an exceptionally able and creative British statesman. In the following passage from his autobiography he presents one of the most effective defenses of Munich that any politician has written. Butler's account is particularly interesting as he was, at the time of Munich, undersecretary to Lord Halifax, and the chief spokesman for the Foreign Office in the House of Commons.

Within a few days of my going to the Foreign Office, Hitler had given us one more indication of the shape of things to come by his forcible incorporation of Austria into Germany. . . . There was general agreement and apprehension that the next stage would involve Czechoslovakia. Accordingly the Prime Minister asked the Chiefs of Staff for a report on the new military situation following the *Anschluss*. They specified that the Czechoslovak frontier of 2,500 miles could not be protected from a German attack, thus confirming Austen Chamberlain's warning in 1936 that "If Austria goes, Czechoslovakia is indefensible." They also advised that Britain was not in a position to wage war, particularly in view of our unreadiness in the air. Later in the summer they reported to the Committee of Imperial Defence that it was of vital importance for us to gain time for the completion of the defence programme. The government was therefore faced with a categorical warning that the country was not ready for war, especially if this involved (as was expected or feared) not only a German front, but conflict in the Mediterranean with Italy and trouble in the Far East with Japan.

This was the unpalatable military appreciation which Chamberlain and Halifax gave to the representatives of France—who alone had a direct treaty obligation to the Czechs—when they came to London at the end of April. The main result of these Anglo-French conversations was therefore a

From Lord Butler, *The Art of the Possible: The Memoirs of Lord Butler*, K.G., C.H. (London: Hamish Hamilton, 1971; Boston: Gambit, 1972), pp. 64–68, 70–73. Footnotes omitted. Copyright © 1971, 1972 by Lord Butler. Reprinted by permission of Gambit, Inc., and Hamish Hamilton, Ltd.

decision to make a joint *démarche* in Prague to secure the maximum concessions from President Beneš. It has been wrongly assumed that Chamberlain believed such concessions would inevitably forestall a German military invasion of Czechoslovakia. On the contrary, he was fully aware, as
were all the best of our diplomatic advisers, that the Sudeten problem
might not be the real issue and that Hitler might have ambitions far beyond the restoration of Sudeten rights. Chamberlain felt that this was a situation which would have to be faced if it came, but that a world war
could not be fought to maintain inviolate the ascendancy of seven million
Czechs over an almost equal multitude of discontented minorities. The
boundaries of Czechoslovakia had been drawn, as Churchill himself testified, in flagrant defiance of the doctrine of self-determination. There is no
doubt that the government of the new State kept the three million Germans in a position of political, educational and cultural inferiority, and
that bitterness was exacerbated by the economic depression of the 'thirties
which hit the German industrialized areas (the Sudetenland) more severely than elsewhere. These grievances were outrageously exploited by
the Nazis and their Sudeten puppet, Henlein; but the grievances were real.
In the week of the *Anschluss,* Basil Newton, our Ambassador in Prague,
advised us (correctly, as was seen in 1945) that the *status quo* in Czechoslovakia could not be perpetuated even after a victorious war. On 22nd
March I wrote to Lord Brabourne in India questioning whether we could
defend by force a feature of the Peace Treaties which was in fact indefensible. I indicated that I had tried to get the Cabinet Committee involved to
issue a statement saying that we were prepared to seek revision of the
Treaties. I also said, "To summon the League, talk to Litvinov, or act as
mediator between Germans and Czechs, is likely to bring down on our
heads more trouble than standing aloof." This letter proved, alas, to be
prophetic.

I was not myself a prime mover in the complex and dramatic events of
the succeeding months. As a junior Minister I was little consulted about
their cause or course. My role was sometimes that of a sceptical spectator,
as when I stood in the Foreign Secretary's room in July studying the glass-
fronted bookcase and heard Lord Runciman accept his impossible mediating mission to Prague with the words, "I am being cut off like a small row-
ing boat from a great liner." Throughout the fateful weeks of September I
was off-stage in Geneva where, however, I conducted two important interviews with the Foreign Ministers of the Soviet Union and of France. The
former convinced me that Russia had no intention of coming to the help of
the Czechs, even if the Czechs had wanted this, which they didn't; the latter gave me the measure of France's political unreliability. These two factors were interrelated, since a French declaration of war was stipulated by
the Russians to be a condition of their own intervention. I am thus convinced that Sir John Wheeler-Bennett's conclusion about the inevitability
of the Munich agreement was correct and, in view of his own vehement
and sustained reaction to appeasement, all the more creditable to his historical mastery. "Let us say of the Munich Settlement," he wrote, "that it

was inescapable; that, faced with the lack of preparedness in Britain's armaments and defences, with the lack of unity at home and in the Commonwealth, with the collapse of French morale, and with the uncertainty of Russia to fight, Mr. Chamberlain had no alternative to do other than he did; let us pay tribute to his persistence in carrying out a policy which he honestly believed to be right. Let us accept and admit all these things, but in so doing let us not omit the shame and humiliation that were ours; let us not forget that, in order to save our own skins—that because we were too weak to protect ourselves—we were forced to sacrifice a small Power to slavery." In the light of the events of March 1939 the defenders of Munich, of whom I have always been one, cannot be morally blind to the savage impeachment of those concluding words; but in the light of the political and strategic realities of 1938 the critics of Munich, though deserving all respect, persevere in passion by denying its historical inevitability.

More than one of my contemporaries have suggested in their memoirs that the alternative to appeasement should have been for Britain to rally all the League to resistance. Churchill wrote of Arms and the Covenant. However, as was clearly stated by Anthony Eden in January 1938 in his speech at the 100th session of the Council of the League at Geneva, "By the defection of some of its more important members, the League is now faced with the fact that the area of co-operation is restricted and that its ability to fulfil all the functions originally contemplated for it is thereby reduced. We must realize that in present circumstances the League is not in a position to achieve all that was hoped of it." We still believed that the League ideals were noble and worthy of our fullest support, and our attitude towards League reform was always positive. I had had a hand in the British government's initiative in this direction in 1938. It was decided at our suggestion to separate the Covenant from the Treaties of Peace, as it was thought this would help to illustrate that the League was not an organization bound up with the *status quo,* but that the Covenant as such had a life independent of Versailles. Yet at the same time there were hard facts to be faced. Of the great Powers, the U.S.A. never had come into the League; Japan, Germany and Italy had left it. It was no more than a plain statement of truth to say that the League in 1938 could not by itself ensure the peace of the world. If the League were called to deal with the Czech situation, it could do no more than pass some pious but quite ineffective resolution which would do no positive good but rather only inflict on it a still further humiliation. This would prejudice its future, in particular its ultimate reconstruction. Manchuria, Abyssinia and Spain had already brought painfully to light the defects of the League, and by condoning a series of unjust aggressions it had proved that it could not provide automatic security. There was, furthermore, a disastrous fallacy in the attitude of those who clamoured for "collective security" yet repudiated any notion of an international force outside British control or, like the Labour Opposition, voted against British rearmament.

Collective security on the eve of the Munich crisis was certainly not something that could exist independently of the policies of Britain, France and Russia; and France and Russia were no more inclined to move than we. The official policy of France was to stand by her treaty obligation to Czechoslovakia: but as Lord Strang, then head of the Central Department of the Foreign Office, recalls, a very different impression was given by what French Ministers said behind the scenes, whether in social gatherings or to foreign representatives. Thus anyone who confines his reading to the published Documents on British Foreign Policy might easily conclude that when Daladier and Bonnet visited London on 28th and 29th April, they wanted a firm stand and were dissuaded only by the logistic pessimism of Chamberlain and Halifax. If, however, one turns to the Documents on German Foreign Policy, it appears that on 27th April (that is, the day before these talks) Daladier told an agent of the German Embassy in London that he hoped the British "would themselves suggest that pressure should be put on Prague" so that he "could acquiesce without seeming to have taken the initiative in the matter." Daladier, however, was a gladiator when compared with his Foreign Minister, Bonnet, whose fascinating memoirs *Défense de la Paix* do not respond to the test of accuracy. Churchill described Bonnet as "the quintessence of defeatism" but only, I fancy, because he had already used up the epithet "boneless wonder" on a fellow-countryman. . . .

I was left in no doubt that the Russians themselves did not mean business. Litvinov had been deliberately evasive and vague, except when he had said that if France acted the Soviet would act too. Since his conversations with his opposite number had been far more numerous and dispiriting than mine, this was tantamount to saying that if Bonnet threw himself off the Eiffel Tower Litvinov would be there to catch him. It seemed to me preposterous for him to pretend ignorance of Soviet military preparations. He was, and gave the clear impression of being, much nearer the centre of power than any other Russian Foreign Minister with whom I have had dealings, and he had been at his desk in the Kremlin in the first week of September. He was perfectly well aware that, in the absence of a common frontier between Russia and Czechoslovakia, the "barrier" policy of Poland and Roumania would limit Soviet aid to modest air support. Nor is there any evidence that if the railways through the Carpathian Mountains had been available to Russian forces, they would have been capable of rendering effective aid. Appreciations arriving at the Foreign Office from our Embassy in Moscow warned that the great purges of 1937 had had a disastrous effect on the morale and efficiency of the Red Army which, "though no doubt equal to a defensive war within the frontiers of the Soviet Union, is not capable of carrying the war into the enemy's territory with any hope of ultimate success or without thereby running the risk of endangering the régime." We now know that precisely similar appreciations were reaching Berlin from the German Ambassador.

Nevertheless, the theory that we deliberately "excluded Russia from Europe" and that this played a decisive part in the ultimate tragedy was widely held by political opinion at home. It was endorsed after the war by Churchill who, advancing a somewhat medieval interpretation of history, argued that Stalin wanted to help Beneš because in 1936 the latter had revealed a plot against his life. The murders and massacres of his régime hardly reveal Stalin as so warm-hearted a man even in matters concerning his own family. Nor was this hypothetical affection and affinity reciprocal. As Beneš told the French Ambassador in Prague, and as Litvinov admitted more or less explicitly to the League, the Czechs did not wish to accept Soviet intervention unless France acted first. Many Czechs had fought against the Bolsheviks in 1918 and feared Soviet domination. General Jan Syrovy is on record as saying, "We don't want the Russians in here as we shall never get them out." Though, in the light of subsequent history, no sentiment compels readier or sadder assent, it was of secondary significance to the British in 1938. For us the criterion was whether Russia intended to oppose the German army, whether indeed she could afford to fight. My interview with Litvinov only confirmed our conclusion that, both on political and military grounds, the U.S.S.R. could not be trusted to wage war in defence of interests that were not bound up with her own security.

It is true that none of the diplomatic negatives I have exhibited were to be any less in evidence in 1939 than they were in 1938. In neither year could any reliance have been placed on the League of Nations to deter aggression. In either year the wormeaten fabric of French political society and the self-seeking duplicity of the Soviet régime would have combined to leave us alone to face at close quarters the onslaught of the Luftwaffe. But the crucial change that came about as a result of the year's delay was in our preparedness to meet this onslaught. The "special importance of preparation in the air and of developing the passive resistance of our population," which had been my theme at Chatham House in April 1938, proved indeed to be the key factors. In September 1938 the R.A.F. had only one operational fighter squadron equipped with Spitfires and five in process of being equipped with Hurricanes; by the summer of 1939, thanks to Lord Swinton's earlier tenure of the Air Ministry, it had twenty-six squadrons of modern eight-gun fighters, and a year later forty-seven. Our ground defences against air attack were also substantially strengthened in this period. The provision of anti-aircraft guns was increased fourfold to 1,653, of which more than half were the newer 3.7- and 4.5-inch guns, and barrage balloon defence was completed in London and extended outside. More important was the fact that, by the time war broke out, the chain of radar stations, which during the Munich crisis had been in operation only in the Thames estuary, guarded the whole of Britain from the Orkneys to the Isle of Wight. Meanwhile, the administrative talents of John Anderson had wrought corresponding transformations in civilian A.R.P., and plans for evacuating schoolchildren and finding emergency hospital beds were completed.

These preparations extended to the pace and scope of British rearmament generally, as Professor Postan has described in his official history of British war production. But I stress them here both because they undoubtedly constituted the most important defence achievement between Munich and the outbreak of war and because, though we now know that the figures of German strength quoted by our professional advisers and our critics alike to have been greatly exaggerated, they did provide the indispensable means by which we won the Battle of Britain. On this reckoning Munich was not, in Wheeler-Bennett's phrase, a "prologue to tragedy," but the pause, however inglorious, which enabled Churchill when his time came to lead the nation through the valley of the shadow to victory. Nor was the military breathing-space the only gain. There were subtler but equally significant changes of opinion at home and abroad. During 1938 it had been possible to argue, and I argued myself, that the principles of self-determination for which the previous war had ostensibly been fought could not be denied to the Sudetens simply because they were Germans or even because they were supported by Nazis. The Treaty of Versailles still weighed heavily. By 1939 the morality was quite clearly all on one side. There could no longer be any doubt in any mind that the ambitions of Germany stretched far beyond its ethnic frontiers and that it had indeed, in Chamberlain's phrase, "made up its mind to dominate the world by fear of its force." These considerations affected not only the will and conscience of our own people but the attitudes of Commonwealth governments and of enlightened leaders in foreign countries, most notably in the U.S.A.

3. *Sir Lewis Namier: Europe in Decay*

Sir Lewis Namier was one of Britain's most distinguished scholars. Born in the Polish provinces of the old Austro-Hungarian empire, he became professor of modern history at Manchester University, and an Honorary Fellow of Balliol College, Oxford. His most famous work is *The Structure of Politics at the Accession of George III*, which revolutionized the study of eighteenth-century England. But Sir Lewis did not hesitate about venturing into twentieth-century diplomatic history, and the book from which the following selection is taken strongly supports Churchill's position.

Mr. Churchill's considered judgment on Munich is summed up in two sentences: "There is no merit in putting off a war for a year if, when it comes, it is a far worse war or one harder to win" and "I remain convinced . . . that it would have been better . . . to fight Hitler in 1938 than it was when we finally had to do so in September, 1939." Mr. Churchill touches upon the question "whether decisive action by Britain and France would have forced Hitler to recede or have led to his overthrow by a military conspiracy," and further quotes some of the opinions of German generals about the military chances at the time. But while German "conspiracies" had a peculiar way of not coming off, and German military opinions repeatedly proved wrong, there are indisputable facts to support Mr. Churchill's thesis. The Czechs had thirty-five divisions, better equipped than

From Sir Lewis Namier, *Europe in Decay* (London: Macmillan, 1950), pp. 161–63. Reprinted by permission of Lady Namier.

any other allied army; an excellent defensive system covering most of their frontier; and a powerful armaments industry. The Skoda works was "the second most important arsenal in Central Europe,"and its production alone was in 1938–1939 nearly equal to the output of the British arms factories: Munich made it "change sides adversely." Lastly, Czechoslovakia was a potential Russian air base wedged between Berlin, Vienna, and Munich. The liquidation of Czechoslovakia was a disastrous loss to the allies.

Further, the as yet unripened German army had a great deal to gain by the additional year. Had the Germans attacked Czechoslovakia in September 1938, only five effective and eight reserve divisions would have been available to hold their western front against a hundred French divisions. In armaments, the advance of the Western Powers was "petty" during the year compared with that of the Germans. "Munition production on a nation-wide plan is a four years' task. The first year yields nothing; the second very little; the third a lot, and the fourth a flood." In 1938 Germany had reached the third or fourth year of most intense preparation, while Britain was merely starting, with a much weaker impulse. In the air alone Britain began to improve her position. But though in 1938 there might have been air raids on London, "for which we were lamentably unprepared," there could have been no "decisive Air Battle of Britain" until the Germans obtained the necessary bases in France and the Low Countries; and in 1938 the Germans had not the tanks with which they broke the French front. "For all the above reasons, the year's breathing-space said to be 'gained' by Munich left Britain and France in a much worse position . . . than they had been at the Munich crisis."

One more argument could be adduced in support of Mr. Churchill's thesis. He uses some harsh expressions about the men who then ruled Poland; and few would choose to defend their very mean action in Teschen. There was a streak of the gangster in Colonel Beck, and a passion for power-display and booty. But even he would have preferred to practise these against, rather than in the company of, the Germans. In March and October 1933 Pilsudski had proposed preventive military action against Hitler; and when Hitler entered the Rhineland on March 7, 1936, no one urged an immediate armed riposte as strongly as Beck. Had the Western Powers shown firmness in the summer of 1938, they might have had Poland with them; but Beck was not to be impressed or convinced by a Runciman mission or by propitiatory flights to Berchtesgaden and Godesberg.

About the moral side of Munich Mr. Churchill's judgement is equally clear. Responsible French statesmen had repeatedly declared that France's engagements toward Czechoslovakia "are sacred and cannot be evaded." Here was a solemn obligation. "For the French Government to leave her faithful ally, Czechoslovakia, to her fate was a melancholy lapse . . . and it must be recorded with regret that the British Government not only acquiesced but encouraged the French Government in its fatal course." "The British and French Cabinets at the time presented a front of two over-ripe melons crushed together; whereas what was needed was a gleam of steel."

4. Georges Bonnet: Letter to the Editor of The New York Times

Georges Bonnet was foreign minister of France from April 1938 to September 1939. The following letter, which he addressed to *The New York Times*, is another illustration of the eagerness with which many of the participants in the Munich pact are still ready to leap to its defense. At the time of Munich, however, M. Bonnet was not highly regarded by some of his fellow appeasers: Neville Chamberlain remarked privately that "Bonnet . . . is clever, but ambitious and an intriguer. The French are not very fortunate in their foreign secretaries." [1] As for the antiappeasers, Bonnet has always been one of their favorite targets. Sir Lewis Namier, perhaps the most savage critic, wrote in retrospect that "it is difficult to define M. Bonnet's policy; first, he would give way to pressure in a ready, complacent manner; next, he would reassert himself, and try to regain detachment and independence; and he would then change colour, till he seemed to have none of his own." [2]

To the Editor of The New York Times:
I have been reading C. L. Sulzberger's article on Berlin and Munich in your issue of Sept. 30. As Mr. Sulzberger taxes the French Government with "cowardice" (this Government was unanimously backed up by Parliament) and as I was a member of that Government as Foreign Affairs Minister, I would be grateful if you would bring to the notice of your readers the following comments:

Mr. Sulzberger contends that as a result of the Munich agreement "the chance of any potentially strong stand on Germany's eastern border was removed, France's alliance scheme dissolved"; and that in 1938 World War II would have come "earlier and under circumstances less favorable to Hitler."

I would draw your attention to the following facts: In 1938 our military authorities stated that defeat was a certainty. "Within a fortnight there will be nothing left of the French Air Force," the chief of our air staff declared, while the artillery chief stated "there would be no modern guns available before a year." Statements by our Allies were equally disappointing. Great Britain said: "For the first year of war, a hundred aircraft and two divisions without any modern equipment." "Not one man, not one cent" was Roosevelt's reply to our Ambassador's request for assistance.

The U.S.S.R. demanded free passage for their troops through Poland and Rumania, which both nations refused with fierce deliberation. Finally, the

---

1. Keith Feiling, *Neville Chamberlain* (London: Macmillan, 1947), p. 353.
2. L. B. Namier, *Europe in Decay* (London: Macmillan, 1950), p. 66.

Czech military authorities informed us they were in no position to resist an attack by the German army and that their own forces would have to seek refuge in the mountains. It was unanimously felt that the military and diplomatic situation was disastrous.

By 1939 our international relations had improved. Since Munich we had signed agreements with Rumania and Turkey. Also, Poland, which at the time of Munich was against Czechoslovakia, eventually fought on our side.

This lapse of time was on our side. Due to the progress achieved in the two years between 1938 and 1940 the Royal Air Force won the air battle over London, which proved a vital factor in bringing victory to the Allies. This fact had been recognized by United Kingdom experts as also on Nov. 19, 1946 by the Prime Minister, Clement Attlee.

Iain MacLeod, the new leader of the House of Commons and Chairman of the Conservative party in the Oct. 15 issue of The Sunday Times of London, confirmed this fact in the following words: "Some things seem completely clear to me. First neither Britain nor the Empire could have or would have gone to war in 1938. The gain of a year from Munich to September, 1939, was, on balance, of far more advantage to Britain than to the Axis Powers."

And Hitler stated before his death: "We should have gone to war in 1938."

Georges Bonnet,
Paris, Oct. 25, 1961

5. *A. J. P. Taylor: The Origins of the Second World War*

The opinions of A.J.P. Taylor are as firm on the subject of Munich as on post-World War I diplomacy. Here, as in Chapter III, one should ask whether Taylor plays favorites in the writing of history. Is he unduly cynical about the foreign policies of the European nations in 1938? Is his comparison of British and French moral attitudes justified? Is he too easy, or too hard, on Adolf Hitler? Whatever one may say about Taylor's judgments, no one can deny that they are provocative and well-expressed.

The conference at Munich was meant to mark the beginning of an epoch in European affairs. "Versailles"—the system of 1919—was not only dead, but buried. A new system, based on equality and mutual confidence between the four great European Powers was to take its place. Chamberlain said: "I believe that it is peace for our time"; Hitler declared: "I have no more territorial demands to make in Europe." There were still great

From A.J.P. Taylor, *The Origins of the Second World War* (New York: Atheneum, 1962), pp. 187–92. Copyright 1961 by A.J.P. Taylor. Reprinted by permission of Atheneum Publishers and Hamish Hamilton, Ltd.

questions to be settled in international affairs. The Spanish civil war was not over. Germany had not recovered her colonies. More remotely, agreements would have to be reached over economic policy and over armaments, before stability was restored in Europe. None of these questions threatened to provoke a general war. The demonstration had been given that Germany could attain by peaceful negotiation the position in Europe to which her resources entitled her. The great hurdle had been successfully surmounted: the system, directed against Germany, had been dismantled by agreement, without a war. Yet, within six months a new system was being constructed against Germany. Within a year, Great Britain, France, and Germany were at war. Was "Munich" a fraud from the start—for Germany merely a stage in the march towards world conquest, or, on the side of Great Britain and France, merely a device to buy time until their re-armament was more advanced? So it appeared in retrospect. When the policy of Munich failed, everyone announced that he had expected it to fail; and the participants not only accused the others of cheating, but boasted that they had been cheating themselves. In fact, no one was as clearsighted as he later claimed to have been; and the four men of Munich were all in their different ways sincere, though each had reserves which he concealed from the others.

The French yielded most, and with least hope for the future. They surrendered the position of paramount European power which they had appeared to enjoy since 1919. But what they surrendered was artificial. They yielded to reality rather than to force. They had supposed all along that the advantages won in 1919 and subsequently—the restrictions on Germany and the alliances with East European states—were assets which they could supinely enjoy, not gains which they must fiercely defend. They did not lift a finger to assert the system of Versailles after the occupation of the Ruhr in 1923. They abandoned reparations; they acquiesced in the re-armament of Germany; they allowed the German re-occupation of the Rhineland; they did nothing to protect the independence of Austria. They kept up their alliances in Eastern Europe only from a belief that these would bring them aid if ever they were themselves attacked by Germany. They abandoned their ally, Czechoslovakia, the moment she threatened to bring them risk instead of security. Munich was the logical culmination of French policy, not its reversal. The French recognised that they had lost their predominance in Eastern Europe, and knew that it could not be restored. This is far from saying that they feared for themselves. On the contrary, they accepted the British thesis, preached ever since Locarno, that they were in less danger of war if they withdrew behind the Rhine. They had preferred safety to grandeur—an ignoble policy perhaps, but not a dangerous one. Even in 1938, though they feared air bombardment, they did not fear defeat if war were thrust upon them. Gamelin was always emphatic that the democratic powers would win; and the politicians believed him. But what would be the point of war? This was the argument which had prevented French action since 1923, and which prevented it now. Germany, even if defeated, would still be there, great, powerful, determined on redress. War might stop the clock. It could not put it back; and afterwards events would move forward to the same end. The French were therefore willing to surrender everything except their own security, and they did not believe that they had surrendered this at Munich. They had a firm and, as it turned out a well-founded, faith that the Maginot line was impregnable—so much so that they regarded the Siegfried line, less correctly, as impregnable also. They assumed that a stalemate had been established in Western Europe. They could not impede the advance of German power in Eastern Europe; equally Germany could not invade France. The French were humiliated by Munich, not—as they supposed—endangered.

The British position was more complicated. Morality did not enter French calculations, or entered only to be discarded. The French recognised that it was their duty to assist Czechoslovakia; they rejected their duty as either too dangerous or too difficult. Léon Blum expressed French feeling best when he welcomed the agreement of Munich with a mixture of shame and relief. With the British, on the other hand, morality counted for a great deal. The British statesmen used practical arguments: the impossibility, even if adequately armed, of helping Czechoslovakia. But these arguments were used to reinforce morality, not to silence it. British policy over Czechoslovakia originated in the belief that Germany had a moral right to the Sudeten German territory, on grounds of national principle; and it drew the further corollary that this victory for self-determination would provide a stabler, more permanent peace in Europe. The British government were not driven to acknowledge the dismemberment of Czechoslovakia solely from fear of war. They deliberately set out to impose this cession of territory on the Czechs before the threat of war raised its head. The settlement at Munich was a triumph for British policy, which had worked precisely to this end; not a triumph for Hitler, who had started with no such clear intention. Nor was it merely a triumph for selfish or cynical British statesmen, indifferent to the fate of far-off peoples or calculating that Hitler might be launched into war against Soviet Russia. It was a triumph for all that was best and most enlightened in British life; a triumph for those who had preached equal justice between peoples; a triumph for those who had courageously denounced the harshness and short-sightedness of Versailles. Brailsford, the leading Socialist authority on foreign affairs, wrote in 1920 of the peace settlement: "The worst offence was the subjection of over three million Germans to Czech rule." This was the offence redressed at Munich. Idealists could claim that British policy had been tardy and hesitant. In 1938 it atoned for these failings. With skill and persistence, Chamberlain brought first the French, and then the Czechs to follow the moral line.

There was a case against ceding Sudeten territory to Germany—the case that economic and geographic ties are more important than those of nationality. This had been the case against breaking up the Habsburg Monarchy; the Czechs who had taken the lead in breaking up the Monarchy could not use this argument, nor could their advocates in Western Europe. The dispute had to be transferred from the field of morality to that of practical considerations—to what is disapprovingly called *realpolitik*. The most outspoken opponents of Munich, such as Winston Churchill, asserted quite simply that Germany was becoming too powerful in Europe and that she must be stopped by the threat of a great coalition or, if necessary, by force of arms. Self-determination—the principle to which Czechoslovakia owed her existence—was dismissed as a sham. The only moral argument used was that the frontiers of existing states were sacred and that each state could behave as it liked within its own borders. This was the argument of legitimacy; the argument of Metternich and the Congress of Vienna. If accepted, it would have forbidden not only the break-up of the Habsburg Monarchy, but even the winning of independence by the British colonies in America. It was a strange argument for the British Left to use in 1938; and it sat uneasily upon them—hence the hesitations and ineffectiveness of their criticism. Duff Cooper, First Lord of the Admiralty, had no such doubts when he resigned in protest against the Munich settlement. As became an admiring biographer of Talleyrand, he was concerned with the Balance of Power and British honour, not with self-determination or the injustices of Versailles. For him, Czechoslovakia had no more been the real issue in 1938 than Belgium had been in 1914. This argument destroyed the moral validity of the British position in the first World war, but it had an appeal for the Conservative majority in the House of Commons. Chamberlain had to answer it in its own terms of power. He could not stress the unwillingness of the French to fight, which had been the really decisive weakness on the Western side. Therefore he had to make out that Great Britain herself was in no position to fight Germany.

Chamberlain was caught by his own argument. If Great Britain had been too weak to fight, then the government must speed rearmament; and this involved doubt in Hitler's good faith, whether avowed or not. In this way, Chamberlain did more than anyone else to destroy the case for his own policy. Moreover, one suspicion breeds another. It is doubtful whether Hitler ever took Chamberlain's sincerity seriously before Munich; it is certain that he did not do so a few days afterwards. What was meant as appeasement had turned into capitulation, on Chamberlain's own showing. Hitler drew the lesson that threats were his most potent weapon. The temptation to boast of Munich as a triumph of force was too great to be resisted. Hitler no longer expected to make gains by parading his grievances against Versailles; he expected to make them by playing on British and French fears. Thus he confirmed the suspicions of those who attacked Munich as a craven surrender. International morality was at a discount. Paradoxically, Beneš was the true victor of Munich in the long run. For, while Czechoslovakia lost territory and later her independence also, Hitler lost the moral advantage which had hitherto made him irresistible. Munich became an emotive word, a symbol of shame, about which men can still not speak dispassionately. What was done at Munich mattered less than the way in which it was done; and what was said about it afterwards on both sides counted for still more.

There had been two empty chairs at Munich, or rather chairs were not provided for two Great Powers, though each had claims to an invitation.

President Roosevelt, at the height of the crisis, urged a meeting in some neutral capital. He did not indicate whether an American representative would attend; and in any case "the Government of the United States . . . will assume no obligations in the conduct of the present negotiations." Roosevelt applauded Chamberlain on the news of the Munich conference: "Good man." Afterwards, when appeasement turned sour, the Americans rejoiced that they had not been at Munich. They could condemn the British and the French for doing what they themselves would have done in their place. Lack of American support had helped towards making the "democratic" powers give way. Yet Americans drew from Munich the moral that they should support these feeble powers still less. Roosevelt, entangled in troubles over domestic policy, had no mind to add to his difficulties by provoking controversy over foreign affairs. Europe could go on its way without America.

The Russians had been more precise in their plan for a conference. They had wanted a meeting of the "peace-loving Powers" to co-ordinate resistance against the aggressor. They, too, could assume an attitude of moral superiority. Parading their own loyalty to treaty obligations, they laid all the blame on French weakness. One Soviet diplomatist said on 30 September: "We nearly put our foot on a rotten plank. Now we are going elsewhere." Potyomkin, the assistant commissar, made the meaning of this clear when he said to Coulondre: "My poor friend, what have you done? For us I see no other way out than a fourth partition of Poland." The Russians professed to have no fears for their own security. Litvinov told Coulondre: "Hitler will be able to attack Great Britain or the U.S.S.R. He will choose the first solution, . . . and to carry this enterprise through successfully he will prefer to reach an understanding with U.S.S.R." Inwardly the Russians were less confident. No approach came from Hitler; instead the claim that he had saved Europe from Bolshevism. Ingenious observers expected Hitler's next move to be into the Ukraine—a move expected by Western statesmen with some pleasure, by Soviet statesmen with dread. The Soviet rulers would have liked to isolate themselves from Europe; but they were by no means sure that Europe would isolate itself from them. Hence, after a short period of recrimination, they had to renew the call for a Popular Front and for collective security against aggression. It is hard to believe that they expected this policy to succeed.

6. V. Potemkin et al.: Istoriia Diplomatii

The following selection is representative of the "official" Soviet attitude toward the Munich pact. In reading it, one should be careful to sift the propaganda from the history, and to consider whether the Soviet position is entirely without merit. Can one blame the Russians for having been distrustful

From V. Potemkim *et al.*, *Istoriia Diplomatii*, III (Moscow, 1945), 643–46. Translated by the editors.

of the policy of Chamberlain and Daladier in 1938; could the Munich pact be responsible, at least in part, for the postwar Soviet mistrust of the West? Or, on the other hand, is this nothing more than an example of the Soviet practice of using history as an effective political weapon?

During the discussion of the Czechoslovak question at Munich, Hitler angrily told Daladier and Chamberlain that Czechoslovakia was "Bolshevism's outpost in Europe." Czechoslovakia (he asserted) is bound to the Soviet Union by a mutual-assistance pact. The government of the U.S.S.R. is inciting it to war against Germany; the purpose is not merely to deal a blow to Hitler, but also to start a world war, the consequence of which might be a Bolshevik revolution. Therefore those who demand that Czechoslovakia be defended are contributing to the destruction of the existing order in Europe.

Urgent warnings arrived in Prague from Paris and London: Czechoslovakia must not rest its hopes on the Soviet Union, for the latter country is too far away, has no common frontier with Czechoslovakia, and has no desire to enter a war in spite of its contractual obligation to help Czechoslovakia. Thus the diplomacy of the French and English governments sought to discourage the Czechoslovak people and to degrade the Soviet Union in the eyes of democrats throughout the world.

Another motive of bourgeois diplomacy also emerged. The idea of common action with the Soviet Union against Hitler had no greater appeal to these bourgeois leaders. General Faucher, former head of the French military mission in Czechoslovakia, expressed this viewpoint with a soldier's frankness in the course of a conversation with certain political figures in Prague.

General Faucher declared that it would not be desirable for France to crush Hitler with the aid of the Soviet Union. Above all, world public opinion might give credit for the victory to the Red Army, thus painfully affecting France's national honor. But another thing was even more important. To crush Hitler with the collaboration of the Soviet Union might produce a wave of intense sympathy for the Soviet Union. This in turn would contribute to a dangerous growth of the revolutionary workers' movement. Such a perspective had no appeal whatsoever to the French government. "In short," concluded General Faucher, "we don't want to intervene against Hitler with the Bolsheviks for allies." The facts that were known to everyone contradicted these slanderous inventions of anti-Soviet diplomacy. The whole world knew that the Soviet government considered itself honorbound to carry out its contractual agreements, and that it was striving tirelessly for the cause of collective security and for the kind of mutual aid that would unite the democratic countries against the warmongers.

The Soviet Union found itself to be the only state that remained faithful to its international obligations toward Czechoslovakia.

"Being bound to Czechoslovakia by a mutual-assistance pact," declared the Soviet representative in the League of Nations Assembly on September 21, 1938, "the Soviet Union has abstained from intervening in the Czechoslovak government's negotiations with the Sudeten Germans; it regards these negotiations as a domestic affair that concerns the Czechoslovak government alone. We have refrained from giving any advice to the Czechoslovak government, for we have considered it inadmissible that this government grant concessions to the Germans, to the detriment of its own national interests, simply to spare us the necessity of carrying out the commitments contained in the pact. Likewise, we have given no advice to the contrary."

Early in September 1938, the French government addressed an inquiry to the Soviet government concerning the attitude of the latter in case Czechoslovakia should be attacked.

The Soviet government's reply was clear and direct: it called for an immediate meeting of representatives of the USSR, England, and France; an open declaration by these powers affirming that they would aid Czechoslovakia in case the latter were attacked by Germany without provocation; the submission of the question to the League of Nations, which would study means of defense; finally, technical consultation between representatives of the general staff of the USSR, France and Czechoslovakia, with a view to working out a plan of joint military operations. Such was the proposal of the Soviet government. Furthermore, it was stressed that the USSR would aid Czechoslovakia in every possible way if, in accordance with France's pact with Czechoslovakia, France were to intervene to defend the latter.

In mid-September, the Czechoslovak government itself asked the government of the USSR if the latter was prepared, in accordance with the Czech-Soviet pact, to give immediate and effective aid to Czechoslovakia in case the latter were to get similar assistance from France. The Soviet government replied to this question without delay and in an affirmative manner. As is known, the Czech-Soviet pact provided that the USSR would lend assistance to Czechoslovakia only in case France also were to aid the latter. Everybody could understand that in forcing Czechoslovakia to accept the German-English-French ultimatum, France was in fact violating its obligation to help Czechoslovakia as provided by the Franco-Czech pact.

For that reason, the Soviet government was formally freed of its obligation to help Czechoslovakia, as established by the Czech-Soviet pact. Nevertheless, the government of the Soviet Union did not take advantage of its right to abandon Czechoslovakia to its fate. The Czech-Soviet pact was not declared to be inoperative. The USSR was ready as before to lend its support to Czechoslovakia, if the latter government so desired. On the critical days of September 27 and 28, when the president of the United States proposed to mediate in order to solve the German-Czech conflict in peaceful fashion, the United States representative in the Soviet Union, Kirk, was informed that the Soviet government favored the convocation of an international conference that would consider extending collective assistance to Czechoslovakia and that would decide on practical measures to maintain peace.

That was not all. When the Polish press announced that Polish troops were concentrated on the Czechoslovak frontier, the chargé d'affaires of the Polish republic was summoned to the people's commissariat on foreign affairs on the evening of September 23. He was told, in the name of the Soviet government, that according to reports not denied by the Polish government, Polish troops were concentrated on the Czechoslovak frontier; these troops were apparently about to be hurled against Czechoslovak territory. The government of the Soviet Union hoped that these reports would be immediately denied by Poland. If this were not done and if Polish troops should in fact invade Czechoslovakia, the government of the USSR would recognize these facts as constituting an act of unprovoked aggression. For these reasons, it would be obliged to denounce the Polish-Soviet non-aggression pact of July 25, 1932.

In the evening of this same day, the Polish government gave its reply. The tone was excessively insolent. At bottom, however, the Polish government sought to vindicate itself: it explained that it was taking certain military measures for purely defensive purposes. Soon the foreign press announced that part of the Polish troops had been withdrawn from the Czechoslovak frontier.

Obviously, the Soviet Union's firm warning had produced its effect.

Meanwhile, the reactionary press of England and France actively spread the completely fabricated report that the USSR had not decided to carry out its agreed commitments to Czechoslovakia.

The machinations of the slanderers were exposed; the Soviet government's reply to the inquiries of France and Czechoslovakia were revealed at Geneva, in the League of Nations Assembly. The provocationist scheme of the reactionaries was thus unmasked. Indeed, the USSR stood before the world as the only country which, in the moment of general panic, desertion, and treason, had kept calm, had proved its unshakeable fidelity to its contractual promises, had shown firm determination to defend international peace and democracy against the warmongers.

7. George F. Kennan: Russia and the West Under Lenin and Stalin

Soviet accounts of the Munich episode always insist that the Soviet Union was prepared to come to the aid of Czechoslovakia, especially if French aid had been forthcoming also. Many western historians and statesmen—Churchill included—have accepted this point of view. If the claim is valid, then this fact must weigh heavily in any assessment of the merits or faults of the Munich settlement. Some serious questions about Soviet intentions have been raised, however, by certain scholars—and notably by George F. Kennan. Kennan was for many years one of this country's most eminent diplo-

From George F. Kennan, *Russia and the West Under Lenin and Stalin* (Boston: Atlantic-Little, Brown, 1961), pp. 322–24. Reprinted by permission of Little, Brown and Co.-Atlantic Monthly Press.

mats; he served as ambassador to both the Soviet Union and Yugoslavia. After his separation from the Foreign Service, he turned to the writing of history, and won a Pulitzer prize for his multivolume work on Soviet-American relations. During the Munich period he was stationed at the United States embassy in Prague; it is on the basis of his intimate acquaintance with Soviet foreign policy aims and methods that he questions the orthodox Soviet thesis.

The Munich agreement was a tragically misconceived and desperate act of appeasement at the cost of the Czechoslovak state, performed by Chamberlain and the French premier, Daladier, in the vain hope that it would satisfy Hitler's stormy ambition, and thus secure for Europe a peaceful future. We know today that it was unnecessary—unnecessary because the Czech defenses were very strong, and had the Czechs decided to fight they could have put up considerable resistance; even more unnecessary because the German generals, conscious of Germany's relative weakness at that moment, were actually prepared to attempt the removal of Hitler then and there, had he persisted in driving things to the point of war. It was the fact that the Western powers and the Czechoslovak government did yield at the last moment, and that Hitler once again achieved a bloodless triumph, which deprived the generals of any excuse for such a move. One sees, as so often in the record of history, that it sometimes pays to stand up manfully to one's problems, even when no certain victory is in sight.

The great issue at stake in the Munich crisis was, of course, the validity of Czechoslovakia's treaties of alliance with France and with Soviet Russia. The Soviet treaty with Czechoslovakia provided that Russia was obliged to come to Czechoslovakia's assistance *only if France did the same.* As the crisis developed just before Munich, the Soviet government reiterated, with impeccable correctness, its readiness to meet its treaty obligations to Czechoslovakia, if France would do likewise. This confirmed many people in the West in the belief that only Russia had remained true to her engagements at that crucial moment—that Russia had been prepared to assume the full burden of a war with Hitler over the issue of Czechoslovakia, had the Western powers only played their part.

This was substantially accurate in the juridical sense; but things were not exactly this way in practice. You must remember a basic geographic reality which underlay the entire chapter of Soviet participation in the policy of collective security, and particularly the pacts with the French and the Czechs. This was the fact that whereas the Western powers had, in effect, a common border with Germany, the Soviet Union did not; it was separated from Germany and from Czechoslovakia by two countries, Poland and Rumania, both of which feared any movement of Russian troops onto their territory as much as they feared a similar movement of the troops of Hitler, and neither of which was at any time willing to say that it would permit Soviet troops to cross its territory in the implementation of Russia's obligations to Czechoslovakia or to France. This meant that no military planning for a passage of Russian troops across these countries was possible; and in the event of a war with Germany in which all three countries —France, Czechoslovakia, and Russia—might have been involved, the Western powers and Czechoslovakia could expect to become immediately engaged, whereas any Russian action would still have to await clarification of the Soviet right of passage across these intervening countries. In the reluctance of the Polish and Rumanian governments to permit transit of Soviet troops, the Soviet government had a ready-made excuse for delay in meeting its obligations of mutual assistance. This impediment was apparent at the time of Munich: the Rumanian government, in particular, was heavily pressed by the Czechs and the Western powers to declare its readiness to permit Soviet troops to pass; but I cannot find that it ever clearly did so. In any case, I myself had it from no less an authority than the German military attaché in Prague, whose task it had been to study this problem for the German High Command, that the physical characteristics of the Rumanian railroad network were such that, even had the Rumanians permitted the passage, it would have taken the Soviet command approximately three months to move a division into Slovakia over this primitive and indirect route. The implications of this state of affairs are obvious. The Russian expression of readiness to assist Czechoslovakia if France did likewise was a gesture that cost Moscow very little. It is fair to say that had the Czechs decided to resist, there was, for various reasons, a good chance that they might have been saved. It is hardly fair to say that they would have been saved by the troops of the Soviet Union.

VIII

The Nuremberg Trials

A few years ago it seemed as if the Nuremberg Trials were being forgotten, as newer and more pertinent issues captured the interest of historians, lawyers, and the general public. Recently, however, there has been a notable revival of interest in the Trials, inspired by the war in Vietnam. The "Nuremberg precedent" has been cited by many young Americans, who argue that it requires them to decline to serve a government that is engaged in the same activities for which the Nazi leaders had been punished after the second world war. There is no question that these arguments raise many important issues, and have revived interest in other aspects of the war crimes trials; it is hoped that this chapter will provide the basis for an analysis of the Nuremberg Trials from several points of view, and from many differing perspectives.

As a purely legal phenomenon the Trials are a matter of serious controversy. The acts for which the Nazi leaders were tried were, no matter how ghastly, "legal" in the usual sense. Germany was a sovereign state, exercising its sovereign prerogatives, and to claim later that the commands of its leaders were illegal, or to claim that those who obeyed orders given them were guilty of crimes is, it is often argued, to punish on the basis of *ex post facto* law. The attempts of scholars to deal with this problem is one of the most interesting aspects of the Nuremberg debate. It is also necessary to consider the role of the Soviet Union as one of the judging powers. One should ask whether or not the Soviet Union was so intimately involved in many of the crimes for which the defendants were arraigned that the Russians were in fact "an interested party," their presence as judges undermining the status of the Nuremberg Tribunal as a court, and reducing it to a council of hypocritical and vindictive victors.

Yet another issue is whether it was appropriate even to proceed under the guise of international law to punish the Nazis; for international law, it is often maintained, is a law of nations, and does not apply to individuals. In fact, the very nature of international law itself poses a problem: does it really exist, in the same sense that the domestic laws of a nation exist, or is it nothing but a code of good behavior between nations, with no real substance of its own? If it does not exist, how can anyone be punished for violating it? Is it fair to imprison or execute men for the violation of a loose set of moral precepts? American justice, as surely as it forbids *ex post facto* law, demands precision in its criminal codes. As Oliver Wendell Holmes emphasized, law is "not a brooding omnipresence in the sky but the articulate voice of some sovereign or quasi-sovereign that can be identified." [1] One might therefore well wonder who is the sovereign or quasi-sovereign in the case of international law? Was not international law at Nuremberg just the sugarcoating on vigilante justice? Is it not possible that Senator Robert Taft was correct when he said that the Nuremberg Trials were not really a legal phenomenon at all, but government policy, and that "By clothing policy in the forms of legal procedure, we may discredit the whole idea of justice. . . . ?" [2] On the other hand, it may be that Nuremberg was a great if flawed attempt on the part of international law to come to terms with new realities. Was it "law creatively founded and realized for a new world" which was waiting to be built? [3] Even if the Trials did compromise traditional legal standards, these compromises are often necessary; to quote Justice Holmes once more: "The life of the law has not been logic: it has been experience. The felt necessities of time, the prevalent moral and political theories, intuitions of public policy, avowed or unconscious, even the prejudices which judges share with their fellow-men, have had a good deal more to do than the syllogism in determining the rules by which men should be governed. The law . . . cannot be dealt with as if it contained only the axioms and corollaries of a book of mathematics." [4] It may well be, therefore, that the Nuremberg Trials "belong very profoundly in the category of a morally and historically necessary operation," [5] and that the efforts of men as wise as Reinhold Niebuhr to label them "victor's justice" were a bit too hasty. [6]

These matters, however, scarcely exhaust the interest of Nuremberg for either the scholar or the student. The mixture of the political and the legal at Nuremberg raises the problem of whether the allied powers ever understood the nature of Nazism at all. Can our Anglo-American system of justice be made to fit the situation of those men and women who lived under a system such as Hitler's? Hannah Arendt, for example, in her book on the Eichmann Trial, clearly appreciates this dilemma. [7] It may well be that the Nuremberg Trial, and the vast American effort at "denazification" which followed in its wake, displayed a naïveté of the most profound sort. Can we even begin to sense the problems faced by the ordinary person in what is often called a "totalitarian" system? The hopelessness of resistance, the alienation from friends and family, and the seeming lack of any coherence or logic, created a world which those men who presided over the denazification process could not begin to understand. By treating Nazis as criminals, were we ignoring the "banality of evil" which emerged as the ordinary citizen struggled to live amidst the conditions imposed by a ruthless and technological tyranny? Can our emotions, not to mention our legal system, understand or grasp the nature of the problem faced by the civil servant, the soldier, the judge, or the schoolteacher commanded to do the work of the Nazis? Perhaps the word "guilt" has little relevance in this context, and the real problem is psychological: the horror of modern tyranny and of modern war demands great purging, and maybe the

---

1. *Southern Pacific vs. Jensen,* 244 U.S. 205, 222 (1917).
2. Quoted in *Vital Speeches,* November 1946, p. 47.
3. Karl Jaspers, *The Question of German Guilt* (New York: Capricorn Books, 1961), p. 59.
4. Oliver Wendell Holmes, *The Common Law* (Boston: Little, Brown, 1881), p. 1.
5. Otto Kirchheimer, *Political Justice: The Use of Legal Procedure for Political Ends* (Princeton: Princeton University Press, 1961), p. 423.
6. See Reinhold Niebuhr, "Victor's Justice," *Common Sense,* January 1946, pp. 6–9.
7. *Eichmann in Jerusalem: A Report on the Banality of Evil* (New York: Viking, 1964), especially pp. 276–277. Eichmann was head of a special unit of the Gestapo charged with the "liquidation" of the Jewish question. He was kidnapped in Argentina in 1960 by the Israeli secret service and taken to Israel, where he was tried in 1961 and hanged in 1962.

Nuremberg Trials provided, both for the allies and for the Germans, some relief in this respect. At any rate, the evidence gathered for the Trials exposed the reality of the Nazi atrocities, and largely foreclosed a recurrence of the post-World War I myth of German innocence, albeit at some danger of creating convenient scapegoats.

Today the principal legacy of the Nuremberg Trials is the fear—or the hope—that many of the functions of the modern state will be reduced to chaos by the awareness on the part of many dissenters of the "Nuremberg precedent," which was referred to above. Was it realized in the 1940's that Nuremberg could be used by an individual to set himself up as the judge of his duties to his government? Can any government function effectively under such circumstances? Does the citizen have the right, and maybe even the duty, to decide if a war in which he is commanded to fight is "just"? Will a soldier refuse to obey orders if he fears that he may later be held accountable for "war crimes"? If only orders of a "legitimate" nature emanating from "legitimate" authorities are to be obeyed, who is to decide what is "legitimate"? How far will orders from a superior act as a defense? Harry Truman's remark about the presidency—"the buck stops here"—is relevant in this matter: can only those in ultimate authority be tried for war crimes, or can the buck be stopped at a lower level? All of these questions are as important as they are resistant to definitive answers; what is striking is that the United States, the power which took the most "moral" line at Nuremberg, is the power which now has to face the full implications of its own morality. As one commentator said of this problem during the Vietnam war: "We have got ourselves tangled in nets largely of our own weaving." [8]

There is thus no end to discussions about Nuremberg. Historians will probably never decide if the Trials will act to deter aggression, or simply make clear to everyone that they had better fight to the bitter end if they want to survive. But what cannot be doubted is that the issues raised by the Trials are as pertinent as ever.

I. *Milton R. Konvitz: Will Nuremberg Serve Justice?*

It is striking that one of the most effective denunciations of the Nuremberg Trials comes from the son and the grandson of a rabbi writing in a Jewish-sponsored magazine. A professor at the Cornell Law School, Milton Konvitz is an authority on civil rights, and he clearly thought at the time of the writing of this article that the Nuremberg Trials would have an adverse effect on the development of justice. He wrote without the benefit of hindsight or perspective; one should consider whether his predictions have stood the test of time. His article also provides a useful summary of the background of the Trials.

8. James Burnham, "Hanoi's Special Weapons System," *National Review*, August 9, 1966, p. 764.

From Milton R. Konvitz, "Will Nuremberg Serve Justice?" *Commentary*, January 1946, pp. 9–11, 12–15. Copyright © 1946 by the American Jewish Committee. Reprinted by permission of *Commentary* and Milton R. Konvitz.

The greatest trial of all time is taking place in our own day—at Nuremberg. It will certainly overshadow the Dreyfus Affair, the Sacco-Vanzetti case and the Russian treason trials. This will be true not because of the specific crimes committed, or because of the political implications of the accusations. The transcending importance of the Nuremberg trial lies in the fact that, purely as a judicial proceeding, it raises questions that touch the heart of the system of morals and conceptions of justice on which Western civilization is built. It is a legal proceeding unprecedented in international law. It is intended to bolster respect for international law, yet it defies many of the most basic assumptions of the judicial process.

What are the issues and how did they arise?

When the foreign ministers of the Big Three met in Moscow in October 1943, they said that their governments had received from many quarters evidence of atrocities, massacres and cold-blooded mass executions perpetrated by the Nazi forces in the countries overrun by them. Speaking in the interests of thirty-two United Nations, the Big Three declared that at the time of granting any armistice to. Germany, Nazis responsible for these crimes, or who had taken a consenting part in them, would be sent back to the countries in which their abominable deeds were done, to be "judged and punished" according to the laws of the liberated countries. The declaration was expressly made "without prejudice to the case of the major criminals, whose offences have no particular geographical localization and who will be punished by the joint decision of the Governments of the Allies." Like Lincoln's Emancipation Proclamation, made in the course of. the Civil War, this declaration on atrocities was a military measure, for it called upon innocent Germans not to imbrue their hands with innocent blood and thus join the ranks of the guilty.

The Moscow Declaration made a distinction between two classes of criminals: (1) those guilty of local crimes, and (2) the major war criminals whose crimes have no local restriction. The former were to be *tried* and punished; the latter were to be punished.

As late as the Crimea Conference report in February of 1945 and President Roosevelt's report on the Conference to Congress there was a promise of punishment only for the major war criminals; there was no suggestion that anything like the Nuremberg trial was being planned.

Shortly before the Moscow Declaration, the United Nations War Crimes Commission was set up with Lord Wright as chairman. This commission represented sixteen nations in which Nazi atrocities had been committed, and the United States and Britain. Soviet Russia was not a member of this commission because her request that all sixteen "autonomous" Soviet republics be represented was turned down. Later Russia modified this demand: she would be satisfied with representation of those Russian republics which had been overrun by the Nazis. Once more the other governments refused. Russia thereupon set up her own commission.

The purpose of these two commissions was to investigate charges of war crimes and atrocities, and to collect and preserve the evidence. They made no arrests; this function was left to the military authorities. Until April of 1945, Lord Wright's commission limited itself to the collection of documentary evidence. We know little about the Russian commission.

At this time the Wright commission believed that there would be only two types of courts: (1) national courts, to hear cases against criminals whose offences affected the inhabitants of only a single country—Quisling, for example, was tried before a Norwegian court; and (2) military courts, such as the British military court in the British sector in Germany which tried and convicted Josef Kramer. Apparently it was still assumed, at the end of April 1945, that Goering, Ribbentrop, Jodl, and the other Nazi chiefs would not be tried but would be punished upon the military order of the United States, Great Britain, Soviet Russia and France. However, the Wright commission was preparing to suggest an international tribunal for the trial of major war criminals. It was not until May 1945 that it was disclosed that the leading war criminals would be brought to trial before the order of punishment would be announced.

It was at this point that Mr. Justice Jackson came into the picture as the central figure. President Truman appointed him as chief counsel of the United States in preparing and prosecuting charges against the major war criminals. Congress was not consulted; this was conceived as a military measure, and the President acted under his war powers. It was announced that the trials would be held before an international military tribunal. This did not mean that the judges of the tribunal would all be military men; it meant only that the tribunal would be set up as an exercise of the military power. Jackson promised a "fair trial" for the accused. He was to proceed on the basis of evidence collected by the Wright commission, and by the Russian commission if the Russians were willing to join the tribunal.

The Russian and French governments were profoundly suspicious of what they considered the Anglo-Saxon tendency to be soft with the Nazis. Jackson had to sell the idea of an international tribunal to the other governments. By August 8, 1945, he was able to win over the British, Russian and French governments. Representatives of the four powers signed an agreement establishing an international military tribunal before which the major war criminals of the European Axis were to be tried. This agreement was supplemented by a "charter" which serves as the constitution of the tribunal and as the statement of principles governing its operations.

The agreement purports to carry out the intention of the Moscow Declaration; but it is apparent that, by providing trials for the major war-criminals, it goes beyond the declaration.

The tribunal is to consist of four members, one appointed by each of the signatories. The war criminals may be tried for their individual responsibility in the commission of three types of crimes: (1) *Crimes against peace.* This means the planning, preparation, initiation or waging of a war of aggression, or a war in violation of international agreements. (2) *War crimes.* This means violations of the laws or customs of war, including ill-treatment of civilian population and prisoners of war. (3) *Crimes against humanity.*

This means the commission of inhumane acts against civilian population before or during the war; and political, racial and religious persecution, whether or not in violation of the domestic law of the country where perpetrated.

The charter of the tribunal also provides that the defense of having acted as head of a state or in obedience to a superior order shall not be considered. The tribunal was given the power to declare groups criminal organizations. After a group was declared criminal, each of the signatory powers could bring members of the proscribed organization to trial before its national or military courts. The right to try a person *in absentia* was given to the tribunal. Each of the four powers was to appoint a prosecutor. The accused were to be given fair trials; they were to be indicted before trial; they were to have assistance of counsel. But the tribunal was not to be bound by technical rules of evidence; it could take judicial notice of facts of common knowledge. The judgment as to guilt or innocence was to be final. The tribunal might impose any sentence, but the Control Council for Germany might reduce the sentence.

On October 19, 1945, Jackson and the other three prosecutors indicted twenty-four top Nazis. The indictment charged the accused with each of the three crimes defined in the charter and with a conspiracy to commit these crimes. On the basis of this indictment the Nuremberg trial started on November 20, before judges representing the four powers, with Francis Biddle as the American judge.

Before the charter for the tribunal was promulgated, the question whether or not the major Nazis should be afforded a trial was hotly debated. No one doubted the justice and necessity of the severest penalties; but is a trial necessary or wise as a preliminary measure to the imposition of these penalties?

Professor Max Radin, in *The Day of Reckoning*, published in 1943, proposed that Hitler and other Nazi chiefs be brought to trial before an international court for the commission of specific crimes, such as the murder of a specifically named person. The same year, in an article in the *Harvard Law Review*, and a year later in a book, *War Criminals—Their Prosecution and Punishment*, Professor Sheldon Glueck proposed the procedure which has in essence been followed by the four powers. Glueck urged that the major Nazis be tried for crimes against humanity and for crimes committed by Germans on German territory before and during the war. He contended that though there are no precedents for such a trial, the procedure is unobjectionable. He anticipated and attempted to meet the objections to the Nuremberg indictments. It is likely that Jackson was strongly influenced by Glueck's arguments and proposals.

On the other hand, George Creel, in *War Criminals and Punishment*, published in 1944, contended that any proposal to set up an international court for the trial of the major Nazi criminals "should be dismissed summarily." He urged that there was no need to wait until the end of the war to "judge" Hitler and Goering. "By their published orders, by their own boasts, their guilt stands self-confessed." The major criminals should be branded at once as outlaws, "as fugitives from justice whose execution only waits on capture."

In a series of articles in the *New Leader* and in a review of Radin's book in the *Reconstructionist* the writer of this article pointed to the dangers in a trial which disregards the fundamental guarantees of fairness to a defendant; nothing must be done which is likely to bring into doubt the validity of these guarantees. If a trial is to be given, then it must be a trial in fact and not merely in name; but such a trial, the writer contended, was not possible for the Nazi chiefs; for in order to bring them before a judicial tribunal, charges must be framed which would reflect non-existent laws, and judges must be found among the heavenly choir of angels.

Thus, before the promulgation of the charter for the international tribunal and the indictment, opinion as to whether or not there should be trials was divided. . . .

The first question is: Why should there be a trial for the major Nazi criminals? The Moscow Declaration promised punishment, not a trial. Many felt that the proper way to handle these persons was to bring them before an assembly of the heads of all the United Nations and the judges of their highest courts and leading German refugees, where the verdict and sentence of civilized mankind would be read. This procedure would have served as a catharsis for the feelings of all people who had suffered at the hands of the Nazis, and the occasion would have marked a dedication to the ends of peace and justice. . . .

The purpose of the trial, Jackson has said, is to establish new international law for the future. "The ultimate step in avoiding periodic wars, which are inevitable in a system of international lawlessness," he has said, "is to make statesmen responsible to law." The purpose of the trial is to establish the principle of the personal responsibility of statesmen, generals and industrialists for the wars of their nations. This rationale of the trial leads to a consideration of questions involving the theory of the indictment.

The charge of crimes against peace is based on the theory that to begin a war is a violation of international law. Since Germany began the war in violation of the Briand-Kellogg pact and other agreements to which Germany was a party, the heads of the German government are personally responsible for the breach of the treaties and the peace, and are subject to punishment.

The difficulty with this theory is that none of the international agreements or laws speak of personal responsibility or punishment. The agreements mention no sanctions at all, collective or personal.

This count, therefore, is open to the objection that it violates a fundamental right of defendants in criminal cases to be free from the sanctions of an *ex post facto* law—a law which declares an act criminal which was innocent or not subject to punishment when done.

At the opening of the trial, in their motion to dismiss the indictment, defense attorneys pointed out that never before was it said that the statesmen, generals and economic leaders of a nation might be arraigned before an international court for using force. They reminded the court that only last summer, when the United Nations established a new world organization, no rule of law was promulgated under which in the future an international court could punish persons who had launched an unjust war. England since the Middle Ages, the United States since its birth, France since the Revolution, and the Soviet Union have professed adherence to the principle that punishment is possible only if a law has been violated that was in existence at the time the act was committed and that provided punishment; and the Control Council for Germany recently restored this principle to German law. Let the nations of the world, they argued, create a law for the future but desist from trying men under a murder law created *ex post facto*.

In his opening statement Jackson attempted to meet this objection. The defendants, he said, cannot bring themselves within the reason of the rule against *ex post facto* laws, for "they cannot show that they ever relied upon international law in any state or paid it the slightest regard."

This argument by Jackson means that, since the defendants did not rely on any law when they acted, it does not lie in their mouths now to demand legal rights. According to this argument the trial may deny the defendants not only the protection against *ex post facto* laws but the protection of any laws at all. It means that the defendants may not argue any legal defense.

This is a very strange doctrine. Though a defendant openly show his disrespect for the legal order of his community, still he is entitled to the full protection of the law—because the community respects the legal order and insists on its vindication. Should a lawless gangster, such as Dillinger, come before the United States Supreme Court with a plea that the law under which he had been sentenced was an *ex post facto* law, the lawlessness of his life and character would have no place in a consideration of the merits of his plea. The application of legal guarantees is not dependent on the defendant's state of mind.

Indeed, Jackson's argument can be turned against the trial as a whole; for, if the lawlessness of the defendants places them outside the pale of law and of fundamental guarantees, why, then, should they be tried at all? Why should not their case be disposed of by the political agencies of the victorious powers without risk to the integrity of civilized judicial process?

New international law can be created without staging a trial which violates a fundamental guarantee like that against *ex post facto* laws. At the present time an attempt is being made to establish among the twenty-one countries of the Western Hemisphere the principle of a collective guarantee to their peoples of their basic freedoms. The Foreign Minister of Uruguay has proposed that when the government of any nation of the Americas denies essential rights to its inhabitants, the other governments take collective action against the offending government. If a substantial number of countries accept the proposal, it will be new international law in the Western Hemisphere. In the same way the United Nations Organization can create new law for the future governance of the world. This is the civilized way to create law. It is to be seriously doubted, however, if the lawless creation of law can in the long run strengthen law, order, justice.

In their motion to dismiss the indictment, the defense attorneys contended that the judges had all been appointed by states that belonged to one side in the war, and that this, too, was a violation of a generally recognized principle of modern criminal procedure.

Jackson attempted to meet this contention with the statement that "unfortunately, the nature of these crimes is such that both prosecution and judgment must be by victor nations over vanquished foes." He also said: "That four great nations, flushed with victory and stung with injury, stay the hand of vengeance and voluntarily submit their captive enemies to the judgment of the law is one of the most magnificent tributes that power ever has paid to reason."

But the judgment of the law of which Jackson spoke is the judgment of four men appointed by the commanders-in-chief of the armies of the four powers; the law under which the defendants are being tried was made to fit the crime after the act had been committed; the law under which the defendants are being tried is not of a universal character, applicable to victor as well as to the vanquished: there is one law for the judge and another for the prisoner in the dock.

For one of the judges at Nuremberg, a general in the Red army, represents a government which was responsible for the invasion of Finland, Esthonia, Lithuania, Latvia, and, simultaneously with the Nazis, Poland. . . . . Is it merely that might makes right, that there is one law for the victor and another for the vanquished? To establish this principle in international *relations* requires no trial: the principle goes back to the time of the first war between two families or tribes. To establish this principle in international *law* is to negate all law between nations.

The defendants are charged with crimes against humanity. The charge refers in part to atrocities committed by the Nazis in Germany itself since 1933. It is based on the theory that if a country's legal or political system permits abuse of its population, there is a violation of international law, and the heads of the state are personally liable.

Here again it appears that there is one law for the victor and another for the vanquished. For according to the theory, if the British imprison thousands of Indian nationalists without trial, strafe villagers from airplanes and impose fines on whole towns, we should bring the Emperor of India and his Viceroy before an international court. If Russia holds some eight million persons in concentration camps, without what we regard as due process of law, we have a right to try Stalin, Molotoff and other Russian chiefs of state in some international court. Obviously Stalin does not admit such right, nor do we claim such right. If Argentina's government murders its Jewish population, we do not *claim the right* to try its heads and the chiefs of police and impose punishment on them; instead, for the first time in the history of mankind, an attempt is being made to *secure the consent* of the countries of the Western Hemisphere to an *agreement* which will give this right to proceed against an offending country. We are attempting to secure such an agreement for the American countries at the very time that we claim the right to proceed against the heads of the German government without such an agreement.

Our policy with respect to the Nazis is consistent with neither international law nor our own State Department's policy. If the Nuremberg trial results in the establishment of a precedent in international law, what moral force can it have behind it when its conception was illegal?

The Nazis are charged with crimes against the laws and customs of war. But the theory of such a charge is without a foundation since our use of the atomic bomb which killed 150,000 at Hiroshima and thousands more at Nagasaki. There is no longer a distinction between a clean and an unclean war; to attempt to perpetuate this distinction does small service to international law or the future peace of the world.

Jackson is attempting to have the court declare certain German organizations illegal. After such a finding every member of the proscribed organizations would be guilty of the illegal acts charged against the organizations. Thus, an attempt is being made to declare the German high command an illegal organization. The charter of the tribunal permits this development. But does civilized criminal procedure permit it?

The *Times* has reported that many Germans feel that this procedure is unjust. It is not right, they say, to indict a whole group, like the German Staff, the members of the SS and SA. And it has been reported, too, that American army officials are alarmed. They strongly oppose (as does also the *Times*) this departure from international law and would like to see it abandoned. Indeed, Great Britain, France and Russia at first opposed Jackson's attempt to make mere membership in the German general staff criminal, but finally Jackson won out.

But the objections of the American army officials may be generalized to include the whole attempt to make "guilt by association" a principle in international law. As recently as 1943, in the Harry Schneiderman case, in which Wendell Willkie appeared for the Communist leader, our Supreme Court held that the theory of "guilt by association" does not conform to our conception of due process. Under a civilized system of law, guilt is personal and not merely the result of membership in an organization.

The Nuremberg trial constitutes a real threat to the basic conceptions of justice which it has taken mankind thousands of years to establish. Law is more than power dressed in judicial robes. Law is the only thing that stands between civilization and the jungle. Our scientific discoveries and mechanical inventions, when man is not subject to law, can only make us more beastly creatures. I would sooner see Goering, Hess, Jodl and the other defendants shot summarily or hanged, or even be permitted to live out their lives in a Doorn (if these were the only alternatives to the Nu-

remberg trial—which is not at all the situation) than witness the undermining of the legal structure it took us centuries to build up.

Goering and his colleagues would die in any case in another ten to
twenty years. Civilization must go on after them. We have saved civilization from their attack. Their atrocities against civilization, the moral and
legal order of mankind, have been ended. We must be on guard now that
we ourselves do not weaken our sense of law and our institutions of justice.
For if justice is dead, as Kant has said, life is not worth living.

2. George A. Finch: *The Nuremberg Trial and International Law*

One of the most important articles on the Nuremberg Trials appeared
early in 1947, and carried the authority of the editor-in-chief of *The American Journal of International Law*. George Finch does not shirk the crucial
issues, and fully recognizes the legal and moral difficulties posed by the
Trials. Although it may be difficult for the layman, it is necessary to consider the extent to which Finch meets the legal objections to the Trials.
How have his judgments withstood the test of time? To what extent have
his hopes been realized?

R etribution for the shocking crimes and atrocities committed by the
enemy during World War II was made imperative by the overwhelming demands emanating from the public conscience throughout the civilized world. Statesmen and jurists realized that another failure to vindicate
the law such as followed World War I would prove their incapacity to
make progress in strengthening the international law of the future. . . .
The laws and customs of war, including those of military occupation, are
well established in international law. They are enacted in national legislation, codified in military manuals, incorporated in binding international
conventions, and affirmed by the immemorial practice of states thus becoming a part of the common law of war. It is accepted international law,
conventional as well as customary, that a belligerent has authority to try
and punish individuals for crimes which constitute violations of the laws
and customs of war, as well as of the laws of humanity, when such persons
fall within his power.

Objections from military sources that it is not legal to punish military
and naval officers who, it is said, are merely following the orders of their
superiors, cannot be well taken. In spite of any rules to this effect contained in military manuals, the law does not permit anyone to commit with

From George A. Finch, "The Nuremberg Trial and International Law," *The American Journal of International Law*, January 1947, pp. 20–24, 34–37. Footnotes omitted.
Reprinted by permission of *The American Journal of International Law*.

impunity a crime prohibited by military or any other law upon the plea of *respondeat superior*. Limits are placed upon the application of this rule, taking into consideration the justice of the charge in each case. Moreover, it should not be overlooked that the maxim *respondeat superior* works in two directions. If a subordinate successfully pleads the rule the liability for the commission of the crime is not extinguished but is transferred to the superior who issued the order. The military and naval officers convicted at Nuremberg were found upon the evidence to be personally responsible for the signature or issuance of orders that violated the laws and customs of war. Had their contention that they acted upon the orders of Hitler been accepted as a valid defense, the rule *respondeat superior* would have served merely as a *reductio ad absurdum* for the purpose of frustrating the law. Upon such a theory it would have been impossible to punish anyone for the crimes of this war. All the perpetrators charged with offenses might have made the same defense, and the arch criminal, Hitler, by committing suicide, made it impossible to inflict punishment upon this earth. . . .

There could be no more sacred trust than that of upholding the law against primitive and barbarous acts of inhumanity which shock the conscience of all civilized peoples and are forbidden by divine as well as human command. The circumstance that such acts may have been permitted or required by Nazi law either within Germany or in the countries invaded by the enemy is no bar to punishment of them by the military authorities of the Allies now in control of the government of Germany. They are not bound to respect the laws of the defeated enemy which are repugnant to their principles of law, justice, and individual rights. . . . The Herculean efforts of the prosecuting governments in rounding up the culprits and collecting the evidence against them merit the universal applause they have received. The fair treatment of the prisoners by the judges and the justice of their decision deserve the approval of the legal profession throughout the world. The ground lost in the strengthening of international law by the failure to execute the penalty clauses of the Treaty of Versailles was recovered. . . .

War itself is the ultimate legal procedure against disturbers of the international peace, and from time immemorial nations have taken summary action against enemies who have fallen into their hands and who are not punishable according to law. The imprisonment of Napoleon without trial by agreement of his captors is the most outstanding modern example. The right is founded upon reasons of moral and political justification. Upon the same grounds the Allied and Associated Powers in 1919 agreed to try the German Kaiser for starting World War I. Holland's refusal to extradite him because he was regarded as a political fugitive and therefore not legally extraditable was all that prevented adding the Kaiser as another important precedent to that of Napoleon. The principal allies in World War II agreed at Moscow on November 1, 1943, that the major enemy criminals "will be punished by the joint decision of the governments of the Allies." When appointing the American judges, President Truman was particularly anxious "that no disagreement should arise among the four great nations who on August 8, 1945, had signed the London Agreement and Charter providing for the trial, formulating the law and establishing the practice." The sentences imposed by the Nuremberg Tribunal under Counts 1 and 2, including life imprisonment for Hess who was acquitted of the legal charges of War Crimes and Crimes Against Humanity, may be unquestionably approved as morally justifiable political acts.

Granting for the purpose of discussion the soundness of the Nuremberg dictum that individuals may now be punished for violations of treaties in the absence of express agreement to that effect, what progress have we made in the suppression of aggressive war? Fear of death has never deterred warriors in the past; it will not deter them in the future. A sanction which cannot be applied until hostilities are brought to a successful end and the personal offenders are in the custody of the victors is not one adapted to the prevention of war. In fact, it anticipates the occurrence of war. We must not lull the world into a false sense of security by making exaggerated claims concerning the verdict of Nuremberg. The Nuremberg Tribunal was a military tribunal. The authority of its decision as a precedent in time of peace is doubtful. Moreover, there exists no peacetime international court endowed with competence to carry on the work of the Nuremberg Tribunal.

The governments which have assumed responsibility for the executions at Nuremberg, if they wish to make good their assertions that the prosecutions for crimes against peace were not political punishment of the vanquished by the victors but were intended to establish international law applicable to all future offenders, should proceed to take action to make good these pretensions. Good faith and the preservation of the future peace of the world require them to do so.

The United Nations should make the Nuremberg principles and procedures applicable to all future aggressors without distinction as to their enemy or friendly character. An International Court of Justice is already in existence at The Hague to which might be delegated such functions and jurisdiction of the Nuremberg Tribunal as might seem appropriate to the principal judicial organ of the United Nations.

These proposals will no doubt be met with the same objection that Mr. Kellogg made to the outlawry of aggression in 1928, namely, that it is difficult and dangerous to attempt to define aggression in advance. The same position was assumed by the United States in 1945 when the Charter of the United Nations was drafted at San Francisco. The story is officially told in the report to the President by Secretary of State Stettinius, Chairman of the United States Delegation. He said:

One of the most significant lines upon which debate concerning the liberty of action of the Council proceeded, was that which concerned the proposed inclusion in the Charter of provisions with respect to determination of acts of aggression. Various amendments proposed on the subject . . . offered a list of sharply-defined eventualities (such as invasion of, or attack on, another state, interfering with its internal affairs, etc.) in which the Council would be bound to determine by formula not only the existence of aggression but also the identity of the aggressor. These proposals also implied that in such cases the action of the Council would be automatic. The United States Delegation, believing that the acceptance of such a concept was most undesirable, played an active part in opposing the amendments.

Consequently, the United Nations Charter leaves the determination of aggression to the Security Council in each case as it arises. No criteria are provided for reaching decisions and the Great Powers would have a veto over them.

An indefinable act cannot be prohibited in advance unless we are willing to acknowledge our constitutional heresy with respect to *ex post facto* legislation. A perfect definition to meet every possible future contingency is not required. One drawn from the lesson of Nuremberg would supply a good start. Another might apply to the use of atomic weapons and other scientific instruments of mass destruction, the outlawry of which is vitally necessary to safeguard not merely the future peace but civilization itself.

The Government of the United States assumed the heaviest responsibility for the organization and conduct of the Nuremberg trial. It should not allow the slow processes of international agreement to defeat its sincerity of purpose. When President Washington and Secretary of State Thomas Jefferson declared neutrality to be the national policy of the United States, Congress promptly enacted the Neutrality Law of 1794 to give legal effect to the Government's policy. The Act defined offenses against neutrality, conferred jurisdiction upon the courts of the United States to try and punish them, and prescribed the penalties to follow conviction. Is there any sound reason why we should not now follow that precedent and enact national legislation defining and prescribing punishment for crimes against international peace? Surely the preservation of international peace is as much the concern of the Congress at the present day as the preservation of neutrality was in 1794 and for 150 years thereafter. Congressional action is necessary again to give effective support to the President's policy because in the United States the power to declare war as well as to define and punish offenses against the law of nations resides in the Congress by express provision of the Constitution. The time is ripe for the United States to assume the leadership in initiating the outlawry of aggressive war by making crimes against international peace punishable in national as well as in international courts. The judgment of Nuremberg makes that course imperative and points the way.

3. *Henry L. Stimson: The Nuremberg Trial: Landmark in Law*

If ever a figure represented the American "establishment" it was Henry L. Stimson. Secretary of State under Herbert Hoover, and Secretary of War under Franklin D. Roosevelt and Harry Truman, Stimson's opinion on the Nuremberg Trials carried great weight. Does he make as effective a case for the Trials as Finch? Of Finch and Stimson, who is the more realistic when judged from the perspective of a few decades?

In the confusion and disquiet of the war's first aftermath, there has been at least one great event from which we may properly take hope. The surviving leaders of the Nazi conspiracy against mankind have been indicted, tried, and judged in a proceeding whose magnitude and quality make it a landmark in the history of international law. The great undertaking at Nuremberg can live and grow in meaning, however, only if its principles are rightly understood and accepted. It is therefore disturbing to find that its work is criticized and even challenged as lawless by many who should know better. In the deep conviction that this trial deserves to be known and valued as a long step ahead on the only upward road, I venture to set down my general view of its nature and accomplishment.

The defendants at Nuremberg were leaders of the most highly organized and extensive wickedness in history. It was not a trick of the law which brought them to the bar; it was the "massed angered forces of common humanity." There were three different courses open to us when the Nazi leaders were captured: release, summary punishment, or trial. Release was unthinkable; it would have been taken as an admission that there was here no crime. Summary punishment was widely recommended. It would have satisfied the immediate requirement of the emotions, and in its own rough-hewn way it would have been fair enough, for this was precisely the type of justice that the Nazis themselves had so often used. But this fact was in reality the best reason for rejecting such a solution. The whole moral position of the victorious Powers must collapse if their judgments could be enforced only by Nazi methods. Our anger, as righteous anger, must be subject to the law. We therefore took the third course and tried the captive criminals by a judicial proceeding. We gave to the Nazis what they had denied their own opponents—the protection of the Law. The Nuremberg Tribunal was thus in no sense an instrument of vengeance but the reverse. It was, as Mr. Justice Jackson said in opening the case for the prosecution, "one of the most significant tributes that Power has ever paid to Reason."

From Henry L. Stimson, "The Nuremberg Trial: Landmark in Law," *Foreign Affairs*, January 1947, pp. 179–81, 183–89. Copyright by the Council on Foreign Relations, Inc., New York. Reprinted by permission of *Foreign Affairs*.

The function of the law here, as everywhere, has been to insure fair judgment. By preventing abuse and minimizing error, proceedings under law give dignity and method to the ordinary conscience of mankind. For this purpose the law demands three things: that the defendant be charged with a punishable crime; that he have full opportunity for defense; and that he be judged fairly on the evidence by a proper judicial authority. Should it fail to meet any one of these three requirements, a trial would not be justice. Against these standards, therefore, the judgment of Nuremberg must itself be judged.

In our modern domestic law, a man can be penalized only when he has done something which was authoritatively recognized as punishable when he did it. This is the well-known principle that forbids *ex post facto* law, and it accords entirely with our standards of fair play. A mistaken appeal to this principle has been the cause of much confusion about the Nuremberg trial. It is argued that parts of the Tribunal's Charter, written in 1945, make crimes out of what before were activities beyond the scope of national and international law. Were this an exact statement of the situation we might well be concerned, but it is not. It rests on a misconception of the whole nature of the law of nations. International law is not a body of authoritative codes or statutes; it is the gradual expression, case by case, of the moral judgments of the civilized world. As such, it corresponds precisely to the common law of Anglo-American tradition. We can understand the law of Nuremberg only if we see it for what it is—a great new case in the book of international law, and not a formal enforcement of codified statutes. . . . [The] charge of crimes against peace . . . has been the chief target of most of the honest critics of Nuremberg. It is under this charge that a penalty has been asked, for the first time, against the individual leaders in a war of aggression. It is this that well-intentioned critics have called "*ex post facto* law." . . .

Now in one sense the concept of *ex post facto* law is a strange one to apply here, because this concept relates to a state of mind on the part of the defendants that in this case was wholly absent. That concept is based on the assumption that if the defendant had known that the proposed act was criminal he would have refrained from committing it. Nothing in the attitude of the Nazi leaders corresponds to this assumption; their minds were wholly untroubled by the question of their guilt or innocence. Not in their aggression only but in their whole philosophy, they excluded the very concept of law. They deliberately put themselves below such a concept. To international law—as to the law of Germany—they paid only such respect as they found politic, and in the end they had smashed its every rule. Their attitude toward aggressive war was exactly like their attitude toward murder—both were useful instruments in a great design. It is therefore impossible to get any light on the validity of this charge of aggressive war by inspecting the Nazi mind. We must study rather the minds of the rest of the world, which is at once a less revolting and a more fruitful labor.

What did the rest of us think about aggressive war at the time of the Nazi attacks? This question is complex, but to that part of it which affects the legality of the Nuremberg trial we can give a simple answer. That we considered aggressive war wicked is clear; that we considered the leaders of an aggressive war wicked is equally clear. These opinions, in large part formally embodied in the Kellogg Pact, are the basis for the law of Nuremberg. With the detailed reasoning by which the prosecution has supported the law set forth in the Charter of the International Military Tribunal, we cannot here concern ourselves. The proposition sustained by the Tribunal is simple: if a man plans aggression when aggression has been formally renounced by his nation, he is a criminal. . . .

What really troubles the critics of Nuremberg is that they see no evidence that before 1945 we considered the capture and conviction of such aggressors to be our legal duty. In this view they are in the main correct, but it is vitally important to remember that a legal right is not lost merely because temporarily it is not used. What happened before World War II was that we lacked the courage to enforce the authoritative decision of the international world. We agreed with the Kellogg Pact that aggressive war must end. We renounced it, and we condemned those who might use it. But it was a moral condemnation only. We thus did not reach the second half of the question: What will you do to an aggressor when you catch him? If we *had* reached it, we should easily have found the right answer. But that answer escaped us, for it implied a duty to catch the criminal, and such a chase meant war. It was the Nazi confidence that we would never chase and catch them, and not a misunderstanding of our opinion of them, that led them to commit their crimes. Our offense was thus that of the man who passed by on the other side. That we have finally recognized our negligence and named the criminals for what they are is a piece of righteousness too long delayed by fear.

We did not ask ourselves, in 1939 or 1940, or even in 1941, what punishment, if any, Hitler and his chief assistants deserved. We asked simply two questions: How do we avoid war, and how do we keep this wickedness from overwhelming us? These seemed larger questions to us than the guilt or innocence of individuals. In the end we found an answer to the second question, but none to the first. The crime of the Nazis, against *us*, lay in this very fact: that their making of aggressive war made peace here impossible. We have now seen again, in hard and deadly terms, what had been proved in 1917—that "peace is indivisible." The man who makes aggressive war at all makes war against mankind. That is an exact, not a rhetorical, description of the crime of aggressive war.

Thus the Second World War brought it home to us that our repugnance to aggressive war was incomplete without a judgment of its leaders. What we had called a crime demanded punishment; we must bring our law in balance with the universal moral judgment of mankind. The wickedness of aggression must be punished by a trial and judgment. This is what has been done at Nuremberg.

Now this is a new judicial process, but it is not *ex post facto* law. It is the enforcement of a moral judgment which dates back a generation. It is a growth in the application of law that any student of our common law should recognize as natural and proper, for it is in just this manner that the common law grew up. There was, somewhere in our distant past, a first case of murder, a first case where the tribe replaced the victim's family as judge of the offender. The tribe had learned that the deliberate and malicious killing of any human being was, and must be treated as, an offense against the whole community. The analogy is exact. All case law grows by new decisions, and where those new decisions match the conscience of the community, they are law as truly as the law of murder. They do not become *ex post facto* law merely because until the first decision and punishment comes, a man's only warning that he offends is in the general sense and feeling of his fellow men.

The charge of aggressive war is unsound, therefore, only if the community of nations did not believe in 1939 that aggressive war was an offense. Merely to make such a suggestion, however, is to discard it. Aggression is an offense, and we all know it; we have known it for a generation. It is an offense so deep and heinous that we cannot endure its repetition.

The law made effective by the trial at Nuremberg is righteous law long overdue. It is in just such cases as this one that the law becomes more nearly what Mr. Justice Holmes called it: "the witness and external deposit of our moral life."

With the Judgment of Nuremberg we at last reach to the very core of international strife, and we set a penalty not merely for war crimes, but for the very act of war itself, except in self-defense. If a man will argue that this is bad law, untrue to our ideals, I will listen. But I feel only pity for the casuist who would dismiss the Nazi leaders because "they were not warned it was a crime." They were warned, and they sneered contempt. Our shame is that their contempt was so nearly justified, not that we have in the end made good our warning.

Next after its assertion of the criminality of aggressive war, the triumph of Nuremberg rests in the manner and degree to which it has discharged with honor the true functions of a legal instrument. The crimes charged were punishable as we have seen—so clearly punishable that the only important suggested alternative to a trial was summary execution of the accused. It is in its pursuit of a different course that the Nuremberg Tribunal has demonstrated at once the dignity and the value of the law, and students of law everywhere will find inspiration and enlightenment in close study of its work. In its skilful development of a procedure satisfying every traditional and material safeguard of the varying legal forms of the prosecuting nations, it represents a signal success in the field of international negotiation, and in its rigid fidelity to the fundamental principles of fair play it has insured the lasting value of its work.

In their insistence on fairness to the defendants, the Charter and the Tribunal leaned over backwards. Each defendant was allowed to testify for himself, a right denied by Continental law. At the conclusion of the trial, each defendant was allowed to address the Tribunal, at great length, a right denied by Anglo-American law. The difference between Continental and Anglo-American law was thus adjusted by allowing to the defendant his rights under both. Counsel for the defendants were leading German lawyers and professors from the German universities, some of them ardent and unrepentant Nazis. Counsel were paid, fed, sheltered and transported at the expense of the Allies, and were furnished offices and secretarial help. The defense had full access to all documents. Every attempt was made to produce desired witnesses when the Tribunal believed that they had any relevant evidence to offer. In the summation of the trial the defense had 20 days and the prosecution three, and the defense case as a whole occupied considerably more time than the prosecution.

The record of the Nuremberg trial thus becomes one of the foundation stones of the peace. Under the most rigid safeguards of jurisprudence, subject to challenge, denial and disproof by men on trial for their lives and assisted by counsel of their own choosing, the great conspiracy has been unmasked. In documents unchallenged by the defense and often in the words of the defendants themselves, there is recorded the whole black history of murder, enslavement and aggression. This record, so established, will stand as a demonstration, on a wholly new level of validity and strength, of the true character of the Nazi régime. And this is so not in spite of our insistence upon law, but because of it. . . .

A single landmark of justice and honor does not make a world of peace. The Nazi leaders are not the only ones who have renounced and denied the principles of western civilization. They are unique only in the degree and violence of their offenses. In every nation which acquiesced even for a time in their offense, there were offenders. There have been still more culpable offenders in nations which joined before or after in the brutal business of aggression. If we claimed for Nuremberg that it was final justice, or that only these criminals were guilty, we might well be criticized as being swayed by vengeance and not justice. But this is not the claim. The American prosecutor has explicitly stated that he looks uneasily and with great regret upon certain brutalities that have occurred since the ending of the war. He speaks for us all when he says that there has been enough bloodletting in Europe. But the sins of others do not make the Nazi leaders less guilty, and the importance of Nuremberg lies not in any claim that by itself it clears the board, but rather in the pattern it has set. The four nations prosecuting, and the 19 others subscribing to the Charter of the International Military Tribunal, have firmly bound themselves to the principle that aggressive war is a personal and punishable crime.

It is this principle upon which we must henceforth rely for our legal protection against the horrors of war. We must never forget that under modern conditions of life, science and technology, all war has become greatly brutalized, and that no one who joins in it, even in self-defense, can escape becoming also in a measure brutalized. Modern war cannot be limited in its destructive methods and in the inevitable debasement of all participants. A fair scrutiny of the last two World Wars makes clear the steady intensification in the inhumanity of the weapons and methods employed by both the aggressors and the victors. In order to defeat Japanese aggression, we were forced, as Admiral Nimitz has stated, to employ a technique of unrestricted submarine warfare not unlike that which 25 years ago was the proximate cause of our entry into World War I. In the use of strategic air power, the Allies took the lives of hundreds of thousands of civilians in Germany, and in Japan the destruction of civilian life wreaked by our B-29s, even before the final blow of the atomic bombs, was at least proportionately great. It is true that our use of this destructive power, particularly of the atomic bomb, was for the purpose of winning a quick victory over aggressors, so as to minimize the loss of life, not only of our troops but of the civilian populations of our enemies as well, and that this purpose in the case of Japan was clearly effected. But even so, we as well as our enemies have contributed to the proof that the central moral problem is war and not its methods, and that a continuance of war will in all probability end with the destruction of our civilization.

International law is still limited by international politics, and we must not pretend that either can live and grow without the other. But in the judgment of Nuremberg there is affirmed the central principle of peace—that the man who makes or plans to make aggressive war is a criminal. A standard has been raised to which Americans, at least, must repair; for it is only as this standard is accepted, supported and enforced that we can move onward to a world of law and peace.

4. *Telford Taylor: Nuremberg and Vietnam*

Telford Taylor is both a lawyer and a historian; he has written extensively about the military history of the second world war, and is an authority on civil-military relations in Nazi Germany. A professor of law at Columbia, he was chief counsel for the prosecution at the Nuremberg Trials. In the following selection, he deals with the problem of the "Nuremberg precedent" (referred to in the introduction to this chapter) and the dilemma which it poses for the United States, especially in light of the Vietnam war and the incident at Son My. Taylor argues that the channels provided by politics, rather than by the judiciary, are the only way out of the quandaries posed by the war in southeast Asia. Does this view undermine the optimism of men like George Finch and Henry Stimson? To what extent is Nuremberg at all relevant today? Does Taylor satisfactorily sort out the legal from the political in his discussion?

A quarter of a century has passed since Robert H. Jackson, speaking for the United States of America, opened the war crimes trials of Nazi German leaders at Nuremberg.

The event cast a long shadow into the future. In Germany, war crimes trials arising from the Second World War are being held to this very day.

From Telford Taylor, *Nuremberg and Vietnam: An American Tragedy* (New York: Quadrangle Books, 1970), pp. 11–17, 119–21. Footnotes omitted. Copyright © 1970 by The New York Times Company. Reprinted by permission of Quadrangle Books.

In the United States, far from being forgotten, the Nuremberg trials are invoked today, not in connection with a war that is ancient history to everyone under 50, but as part of the seething, anguished debate over the war in Vietnam, which is shaking our society to its foundations.

"While this law is first applied against German aggressors," said Jackson in his address to the Nuremberg tribunal, "if it is to serve any useful purpose it must condemn aggression by any other nations, including those which sit here now in judgment." As he spoke those words, many eyes in the courtroom shifted to the faces of the two Soviet members of the court, the judicial representatives of a country that had invaded Poland in 1939 and Finland in 1940 and was widely believed to have been responsible in 1941 for the slaughter of thousands of Polish prisoners-of-war in the Katyn forest. That Jackson's admonition went unheeded by the Russians in later years—Hungary in 1956, Czechoslovakia in 1968—has been the general opinion in the United States. After years of the Iron Curtain and the Berlin wall, most Americans have no more difficulty in condemning aggressions and atrocities by the Reds today than they did in the past when brown and black uniformed Nazis and Fascists were the culprits.

But now the wheel has spun full circle, and the fingers of accusation are pointed not at others for whom we have felt scorn and contempt, but at ourselves. Worse yet, many of the pointing fingers are our own. Voices of the rich and poor and black and white, strident voices and scholarly voices, all speaking our own tongue, raise question of the legality under the Nuremberg principles of our military actions in Vietnam, and in Cambodia as well. Accounts of the conduct of American troops, especially at Son My in March, 1968, have stung the national conscience as nothing else since the days of slavery, and again Nuremberg is invoked as the symbol of condemnation.

What are the Nuremberg legal principles, and what is their meaning today as applied to American involvement in Vietnam? When we sent hundreds of thousands of troops to South Vietnam, bombed North Vietnam, and moved into Cambodia, were our national leaders as guilty of launching a war of aggression as were Hitler and his generals when they invaded Poland, or Belgium, or Greece, or other countries that were way-stations on the Nazi march of conquest? Will Son My go down in the history of man's inhumanity bracketed with Katyn, Lidice, Oradour, Malmédy, and other names that still ring sadly in the ears of those old enough to have heard the sound? More generally, are the people of the United States able to face the proposition that Jackson put forth in their name, and examine their own conduct under the same principles that they applied to the Germans and Japanese at the Nuremberg and other war crimes trials? . . .

For these purposes, the term "Nuremberg trials" should not be taken as limited to the precise rulings of the Nuremberg courts, but in its broad sense, as standing for all the war crimes trials that followed in the wake of the Second World War, and the ideas they have generated. Today, "Nuremberg" is both what actually happened there and what people think happened, and the second is more important than the first. To set the record straight is, no doubt, a useful historical exercise, but sea change is itself a reality, and it is not the bare record but the ethos of Nuremberg with which we must reckon today.

Put another way, Nuremberg is not only what was said and done there, but also what was said about it, then and subsequently. By no means all that has been said is favorable. The late Senator Robert A. Taft is the best remembered of Nuremberg's contemporaneous critics, largely because his statements won him an accolade in the late President Kennedy's widely read book, "Profiles in Courage." But the very fact that Taft was cited for bravery signifies the overwhelming praise and approbation that the American public bestowed on the trials at the time. International approval was equally impressive; 23 nations adhered to the treaty under which the first Nuremberg trial was held, and after its conclusion the General Assembly of the United Nations affirmed "the principles of international law" embodied in the Nuremberg judgment.

As the principal sponsor, organizer and executant of the Nuremberg trials, the United States is more deeply committed to their principles than any other nation. Some of those in high places who brought about our military involvement in Vietnam are well aware of this, and have sought to justify their course of action on the basis of those very principles. When he was Secretary of State, Dean Rusk described the organization of a durable peace as "the great central question of our day," and declared that checking Communist aggression in Southeast Asia was essential to that aim. Walt Rostow, former special assistant to President Johnson, told a group of college student editors that our "intervention had been based legally on obligations under SEATO [Southeast Asia Treaty Organization] to resist aggression." As the editors of Life magazine put it in 1967: "Most Americans consider South Vietnam to be the victim of aggression and North Vietnam the aggressor. That is what the war is about." These justifications are all based on the view, with which the name of Nuremberg is now associated, that waging aggressive war is a crime.

Needless to say, many Americans do not entertain the views Life attributed to them, and fewer today than when the editorial was printed. The claim that American intervention in Vietnam is itself an aggressive war and therefore criminal—the so-called "Nuremberg defense"—has been put forward by draft card burners, draftees facing induction and soldiers about to be shipped to Vietnam. A young Army doctor, Captain Howard Levy, sought to justify his refusal to give medical training to Green Berets on the ground that his pupils would turn their training to criminal purposes. Since publication of eye-witness accounts of the American action at Son My, such contentions and defenses have multiplied. The North Vietnamese, too, have heard of Nuremberg, and recited its precedent as the basis for trying captured American aircraft pilots as war criminals—a project which Hanoi apparently has now abandoned.

If these several invocations of Nuremberg are diverse and contradictory, that is no reason to dismiss the trials as meaningless. We do not scrap the

Constitution because learned judges cannot agree on the interpretation of its provisions. All profound moral doctrine is broad enough so that its particular application generates controversy, as is manifest in the old saying about the Devil's ability to quote Scripture to his own purpose.

Furthermore, beneath these wildly divergent views of the Nuremberg precedent there is a common denominator: that there are some universal standards of human behavior that transcend the duty of obedience to national laws. "Your country, the United States, has established that a citizen must *not* go along with policies he believes to be wrong," we are admonished in a current leaflet: *"That's what the Nuremberg Trials were all about!"*

As a legal and historical matter that is grossly overstated, but it is fairly representative of views about Nuremberg that are frequently expressed, especially by young people. Furthermore, although the statement is an exaggeration, it is not a total fabrication; the notion of individual accountability before the bar of international law lies at the heart of the Nuremberg judgments, and the reluctance of the Germans to resist oppressive acts of state is widely held to have greatly aided the Nazi seizure of power.

I have used the name "Nuremberg" in the title of this work because that is the label that time and usage have affixed to the set of principles and problems with which the book deals. But the usage is indicative of a prevalent but wholly mistaken notion that the Nuremberg trials were the original source of these principles. It is important to correct this misconception, for it distorts the entire matter by concealing the antiquity of these vexing questions, and the depth to which they permeate the moral and political history of mankind. Symbol though it be, Nuremberg is but one of many points of reference in the course of men's efforts to use law as a vehicle for mitigating the ravages of war, and eventually abolishing war itself. . . .

In some draft resistance cases, the defendants have pressed the "Nuremberg defense" by contending that, if the Vietnam war is in fact aggressive, they will be liable to prosecution as war criminals if they engage in it. Professor Falk has given this argument a qualified blessing, writing that "the wider logic of Nuremberg extends to embrace all those who, knowingly at any rate, participate in a war they have reason to believe violates the restraints of international law."

Wherever the "wider logic" might lead, the Nuremberg judgments, as we have seen, have no such wide embrace. Those convicted at both Nuremberg and Tokyo of "crimes against peace" were all part of the inner circles of leadership, and the Nuremberg acquittals of generals and industrialists cut directly against Professor Falk's argument. Furthermore, there is much ambiguity in his phrase "reason to believe." No doubt there are today millions of Americans who, on the basis of generally available information, would claim a "reasonable belief" that we are "in the wrong" in Vietnam and, if educated in the terminology, would label it "aggressive." But there are more millions who think otherwise, and the issue between these disagreeing millions cannot rationally be projected in terms of criminal liability for rendering military service.

"There was no decision in Nuremberg," writes Benjamin Ferencz, one of the prosecutors there, "which would support a conclusion that the United States Armed Forces, like pirate ships, are criminal organizations." Nor was there any decision that international law confers immunity from military service on the basis of an individual's personal judgment that his country's foreign and military policies are wrong. Much less was it decided that domestic courts can be expected to sit in judgment on the foreign policies of the very government of which those courts are a part. The Nuremberg and Tokyo judgments were rendered by international tribunals on a *post mortem* basis (all too literally), surrounded by virtual libraries of the defeated governments' most secret papers. Professor Falk overlooks these factors, I believe, in suggesting that domestic courts sitting during the course of hostilities may be called upon to follow in the footsteps of Nuremberg, let alone embrace its "wider logic."

Lawyers called upon to represent young men who refuse to serve are abundantly justified in raising both the constitutional and the Nuremberg arguments in their defense. The force and sincerity of such contentions may serve their clients well even if they do not prevail as propositions of law. Judges and juries should be made aware of the tenuous basis on which they are asked to attribute criminal guilt to men whose driving motive may be that of obedience to a higher law. Furthermore, these arguments based on constitutional or international principle are of great public benefit in projecting profound moral and political issues in the legal dimension and expanding public understanding of our national predicament.

But the predicament itself is not, I believe, susceptible to solution by judicial decree. There is no such simple way to end the Vietnam tragedy, for the Supreme Court is not a *deus ex machina*. This war, and the agony and rancor that are its product, have been the work of the President and the Congress—the people's elected agents—and the war can be ended only by action of the national will, exerted through political, not judicial, channels.

IX

The Cold War

The Cold War still figures very prominently on the contemporary political scene. Whether it is only its ghost that bedevils us, or whether it is still alive and is continuing to determine the nature of world affairs, its current status is much debated. This chapter, it is hoped, will stimulate that debate, and also help to place the Cold War in historical context.

No one is sure when the Cold War began. Some maintain that there was a faint foreshadowing of conflict at the time of the Monroe Doctrine, when the United States rebuffed the disposition of the Russians to aid the Spaniards in their attempt to hold onto their empire in the new world. In this disagreement the Russians were acting, at least superficially, on the basis of ideology—they wanted to uphold the integrity of the principles embodied in the Holy Alliance.[1] But the consensus is that the roots of the Cold War go back to 1917, the year of America's entry into the first world war and of the Bolshevik revolution.[2] Foreign intervention, and the hostility of the western powers, then divided Russia from much of the rest of the world. After the second world war, their mutual enemies destroyed, bitter rivalry developed between Russia and the only other superpower in the world, the United States; and the Cold War was under way.

In recent years, in a manner somewhat similar to that of the argument over the responsibility for the outbreak of the first world war, historians have embarked on a long—at times extraordinarily ungraceful—dispute over the rights, the wrongs, and the causes of the Cold War; this dispute shows no signs whatsoever of abating. Revisionist historians regard with the utmost scorn the upholders of the traditional view that Russia was at fault—these traditionalists are termed "court" historians, meaning a group of kept intellectual eunuchs whose sole purpose in life is to maintain the myths that serve the nefarious goals of the "establishment." The traditionalists have counterattacked, arguing that the revisionists are making history serve their own ideological causes, are eschewing objectivity and even misquoting documents. Interestingly, the battle lines in this academic war do not parallel those of the American political wars; for intellectually, at least, the traditionalist battle has been fought by men who were and are regarded with dislike

---

1. See André Fontaine, *History of the Cold War*, trans. by D. D. Paige (New York: Vintage Books, 1970), I, 13.

2. *Ibid.*, p. 11.

by the Republican right wing: Harry Truman, Dean Acheson, and Arthur Schlesinger, Jr., are all Democrats, and are all supposedly members of, or servants of,
the "eastern liberal power-elite." It is a nice twist of fate that Acheson, who was
so strongly denounced for being soft on communism in the late 1940's and the
early 1950's, lived to see his memoirs [3] denounced by the revisionists and the New
Left—for them he was clearly one of the architects of the Cold War, and one of
the inventors of a mythology, the latest product of which is the Vietnam war.
David Horowitz, one of the most vociferous of the revisionists, has even argued
that something approaching a plot—or at least a calculated conspiracy of silence
—has thwarted his efforts, and the efforts of those who agree with him, to be
taken seriously. Only the movement against the Vietnam war, he maintains, has
given the revisionists a chance to be heard. All the earlier studies of a revisionist
nature "were . . . ignored or patronizingly dismissed as misguided fantasies of the
fellow-travelling left." But now Horowitz has hope for the future: "The historical
establishment, which for two decades promulgated and inculcated a propagandistic view of the history of the post-war years under the guise of academic scholarship, still dominates the university; but its days . . . are clearly numbered." [4]

The major purpose of this chapter is not to encourage students to choose sides
in this dispute, but rather to encourage them to see the Cold War in a more dis-
passionate manner. Is (or was) the Cold War primarily an ideological battle, or
was it far more traditional—an inevitable struggle for world supremacy? Was it
inevitable? Which power adopted a more offensive stance? Were there any particular turning points of significance in the Cold War? Were there any miscalcu-
lations on the part of either power that determined its course? One might even
ask if it is helpful to think of the Cold War as a distinct diplomatic phenomenon.

One other question should present itself, particularly to Americans. In this
chapter the United States plays a central role; does this mean that the traditional
boundaries observed by European historians must be broadened because Europe
no longer provides a broad enough canvas? On the other hand, as the Cold War
disappears, or changes its nature, and as Europe moves toward some kind of a
federation, this supposition may not seem so valid.

1. *Louis J. Halle: The Cold War as History*

Louis J. Halle served in the United States State Department until 1956,
when he joined the faculty of the Graduate Institute of International Studies
at Geneva. In the following selection he puts the Cold War in historical
perspective, and argues that it is but one of a long series of struggles "to
maintain or restore" the European balance of power. Halle is usually classified as a "realist" in his approach to diplomatic history. Is this categorization
valid?

3. *Present at the Creation* (New York: Norton, 1969).
4. David Horowitz, *The Free World Colossus*, revised edition (New York: Hill and
Wang, 1971), pp. 3, 4, 7.

From Louis J. Halle, *The Cold War as History* (New York: Harper, 1971), pp. 1–2,
8–12, 32–37. Footnotes have been altered to give the full citation of those works to
which Halle refers. Copyright © 1967 by Louis J. Halle. Reprinted by permission of
Harper & Row, Publishers, Inc.

The circumstances out of which the Cold War arose are simple enough in outline. The traditional boundary of the Russian Empire (and of its Soviet successor) had been roughly along a line extending from the eastern Baltic to the Black Sea. West of that line there had, in recent times, been an unhappy group of buffer states: Finland, Estonia, Latvia, Lithuania, Poland, and the Balkans. West of the buffer states, in turn, had been Germany, Austria, Italy, France. Traditionally, the gigantic power of Russia had been contained or balanced, to the West, by one or another of the western European great powers, or by a combination of them.

In the twentieth century the principal European power that served to contain the power of Russia had been Germany. Thus the elements of an equilibrium, of a balance of power, had existed in Europe before World War II, however precariously. Those elements no longer existed in 1945, when the War ended. When the War ended, the military forces of the Soviet Union were in occupation of most of the buffer area, and even of areas well beyond it. They were in occupation of all Poland, and of Germany to a line a hundred miles west of Berlin. They were in occupation of Hungary, and of the eastern part of Austria. They were in occupation of Rumania and Bulgaria. They were in Yugoslavia, if not actually in occupation of it. In other words, the Soviet Union had suddenly, as if by sleight of hand, effected the military conquest of the eastern half of Europe. It had simply swallowed up half of Europe—or was in the process of swallowing it up. Moscow's army had reached a line that ran through the middle of Europe from north to south.

What was there on the other side of this line to balance and contain this suddenly expanded Russian power?

The uncaptured half of Europe, on the other side of the line, lay prostrate. And Russia, at this time, was still advancing, still expanding. With the rapid withdrawal and disintegration of the American Army, there was no military obstacle to the Red Army if it chose to continue to the English Channel.

What the situation of Europe represented, in the years from 1945 to 1947, was a crisis in the balance of power. It was the fourth such crisis that Europe had experienced in a hundred and fifty years, since the end of the eighteenth century.

Napoleon's France had temporarily upset the balance of power at the beginning of the nineteenth century, overrunning Europe as far as Moscow. To restore the balance on that occasion a great coalition of states, putting themselves on a war-footing, and many years of desperate fighting, had been necessary.

In the early twentieth century Kaiser William II's Germany had similarly challenged the European balance of power. Again a coalition of states, fighting desperately for four years, had been necessary to defeat this second challenge.

The third occasion arose toward the end of the 1930's, when Hitler overthrew the European balance of power, as Napoleon had done, and overran Europe from the Channel to the gates of Moscow. Again a great coalition had fought an exhausting war to put him down and to restore the European equilibrium.

The European equilibrium was not restored, however, upon the achievement of victory over Hitler. On this third occasion, as we have seen, Russia was left in possession of half Europe, while the other half lay prostrate before it. The western allies, having put down the terrifying specter of Hitler, were now confronted with the no-less-terrifying specter of Stalin. For them this was a bitter conclusion indeed of a war that had required so much courage and sacrifice on their part.

It is essentially true, then, to say that since the end of the eighteenth century four great wars have been fought to maintain or restore the European balance of power. The fourth was the Cold War, which began almost immediately after World War II. . . .

The Cold War, then, belongs essentially to the same class of international conflict as the Napoleonic Wars and the two World Wars. There is the same challenge of a military colossus threatening to overwhelm and subjugate its neighbors, threatening to extend its sway indefinitely. There is the same belated organization of a defensive coalition against that colossus. There is the same build-up of military power on both sides, and a mutual confrontation. And in this case as in the others, it all ends with the frustration of the challenge, with its containment or defeat in one way or another.

The reader undoubtedly has in mind already the one most conspicuous difference between the Cold War and the three earlier wars. The three earlier wars were wars of military combat, wars in which armed forces faced each other, and pummeled each other, and drenched the landscape in blood. But the Cold War has not been a war in this sense. It has not been a war in which fighting and bloodshed have had anything except an incidental or an accidental role. The contestants have confronted each other, they have shouted threats and abuse at each other, they have flexed their military muscles to intimidate each other—but they have not struck at each other. One side or the other has sometimes advanced or backed off a few inches. By and large, however, since this cold combat was joined the two sides have between them kept to the territorial *status quo*. If it is right to regard the Cold War as World War III, we must at least admit that it has been conducted quite differently from World Wars I and II.

The reason for the difference, I think, is that the revolutionary new weapons of the nuclear age are so deadly that their use cannot be seriously risked. The contestants on both sides know that they may all be killed if they strike. Consequently, however they may threaten, they draw back rather than strike when that appears to be the choice before them. It follows that, so far at least, we have much to thank nuclear weapons for. Whatever the future may hold, their advent upon the scene has so far spared us much. It has kept the Cold War cold.

Nevertheless, like its predecessors, the Cold War has been a worldwide power contest in which one expanding power has threatened to make itself predominant, and in which other powers have banded together in a defensive coalition to frustrate it—as was the case before 1815, as was the case in 1914–1918, as was the case from 1939–1945. . . .

Writing in the 1830's, Alexis de Tocqueville made the following remarkable prophecy:

There are on earth today two great people, who, from different points of departure, seem to be advancing toward the same end. They are the Russians and the Anglo-Americans.

Both have grown great in obscurity; and while the attention of mankind was occupied elsewhere they have suddenly taken their places in the first rank among the nations, and the world has learned, almost at the same time, both of their birth and of their greatness.

All the other peoples appear to have attained approximately their natural limits, and to have nothing left but to conserve their positions; but these two are growing: all the others have stopped or continue only by endless effort; they alone advance easily and rapidly in a career of which the limit cannot yet be seen.

The American struggles against the obstacles that nature places before him; the Russian is at grips with humanity. The one combats wilderness and savagery, the other combats civilization decked in all its armament: moreover, the conquests of the American are won by the plowshare, those of the Russian by the sword.

To attain his end, the first depends on the interest of the individual person, and allows the force and intelligence of individuals to act freely, without directing them. The second in some way concentrates all the power of society in one man.

The one has liberty as the chief way of doing things; the other servitude.

Their points of departure are different, their paths are divergent; nevertheless, each seems summoned by a secret design of providence to hold in his hands, some day, the destinies of half the world.[1]

One may draw two conclusions from the fact that de Tocqueville was able to make this prediction so long ago.

One is that what is predictable must (always barring a cataclysm) be inevitable. Nothing is surely predictable except as it is bound to happen. If it may or may not happen, then one cannot predict its happening with authority; one can only guess and gamble that it will happen. But de Tocqueville was not guessing and gambling. He saw the future development of America and Russia as implicit in their contemporary circumstances. He saw their future in their present as one sees the leaf in the bud. Therefore we may conclude that the polarization of the world between two superpowers was not the accidental product of accidental circumstances.

Walter Lippmann once wrote that prophecy "is seeing the necessary amidst confusion and insignificance. . . ." The development that de Tocqueville prophesied so long ago belonged to the realm of the necessary.

The other conclusion that I draw from his prophecy is that the role of Communism in the polarization of the world is secondary, that it does not belong to the realm of the necessary. For de Tocqueville, when he wrote

1. Translated from *De la Démocratie en Amérique*, concluding passage of the first half—i.e., of Vol. I.

his prophecy, knew nothing of a young university student in Germany called Karl Marx, or of an unborn revolutionary called Lenin. He did not foresee the coming of Communism to Russia. He did not anticipate the substitution of a Communist regime for the czarist regime. He foresaw that what in fact came to pass would come to pass regardless of the ideological label attached to the authoritarian regime that governed Russia.

The implications of this seem to me essential to an understanding of the Cold War. The behaviour of Russia under the Communists has been Russian behaviour rather than Communist behaviour. Under the Communists Russia has continued to behave essentially as it behaved under the czars. There has been the same centralization and authoritarianism. There has been the same conspiratorial approach to international relations. There has been the same profound mistrust of the outside world. There has been the same obsession with secrecy and with espionage. There has been the same cautiousness, the same capacity for retreat. There has been the same effort to achieve security by expanding the Russian space, by constantly pushing back the menacing presence of the foreigners across the Russian borders.

What the Revolution of 1917 did was simply to reinvigorate the traditional principle of authoritarianism in Russia. It replaced a decadent and enfeebled authoritarian dynasty with a new, vigorous, and ruthlessly determined authoritarian dynasty. All this is implicit in the fact that de Tocqueville was able to predict both the polarization of the world and the ideological contest between the two superpowers without foreseeing Marxism-Leninism.

The Cold War, then, represents an historical necessity to which the Communist movement is incidental rather than essential. . . .

The basis for the Cold War was laid when the two Western allies, the United States and Great Britain, looking forward to their victory, adopted the objective of utterly destroying German power and preventing its reconstitution for an indefinite future. This objective was adopted without any thought that American power or British power, alone or together, would fill the vacuum thus created. Indeed, President Roosevelt made it clear, as we shall see, that American power would be rather promptly withdrawn from Europe after the victory had been gained.

The adoption of this objective is properly associated in our minds with the decision that the Atlantic allies took, in January 1943, to require the unconditional surrender of Germany, Italy, and Japan. The unconditional-surrender decision was the decision to make no compromise peace with the German, Italian, or Japanese nations, even though they should overthrow and replace the gangster regimes that, having captured power over them, had led them into war. It was the decision to go on to a total victory, a victory that would make it possible, then, to erase the power of Germany, Italy, and Japan from the map of the world.

It is clear to most of us today, and there were those to whom it was clear at the time, that this was an unwise decision, a decision based on a judgment distorted by the passions and the mythological conceptions of wartime.

We may suppose that such a decision, for which the United States bore the prime responsibility, would not have been made if we Americans had ever allowed ourselves to regard World War II as a struggle to re-establish a balance of power—which is what it was. For the American and the British people, even more on this second occasion than on the first, the War was simply a struggle between the forces of good and the forces of evil. To put the matter in the terminology of the day, it was a struggle between the "peace-loving nations" and the "aggressor nations." This terminology was particularly unfortunate because it pertained to the "nations" apart from the regimes that governed them. What it meant was that Germany, Italy, and Japan would be "aggressor nations" even under responsible democratic regimes. They were what they were as a matter of national character—just as the United States, Great Britain, China, and the Soviet Union were "peace-loving nations" as a matter of national character.[2]

In this mythology of a world divided between "peace-loving" and "aggressor" nations it was, by definition, the nature of "peace-loving" nations always to love peace and of "aggressor" nations always to aggress. Therefore the way to achieve a permanent peace was for the "peace-loving" nations to disarm the "aggressor" nations, and to keep them disarmed in perpetuity.

Popular sophistication, even among the most advanced nations, had not yet reached the point where political leadership could dispense with the uses of such mythological conceptions as this. Woodrow Wilson had had to offer the American people a myth for which they would fight, and Franklin D. Roosevelt had to do the same.

This is not to say that Roosevelt, any more than Wilson, was a cynical politician who knowingly misled the people. He corresponded to Walter Bagehot's definition of a politician as a man of common mind and uncommon abilities. A product of the Wilsonian era, he had been brought up to the ideal model of a world in which international organization was the noble alternative to the ignoble power-politics that had been traditional in the Old World. German power, in this conception, could be erased, and the consequent vacuum need not be filled by any other national power, or combination of national powers, because an international organization to maintain peace and order would do away with the role that national power had hitherto played in international relations. "Peace-loving" nations, among which the Soviet Union was included, would no longer engage in the sordid game of power-politics but would, rather, submit themselves to the wise decrees of an international community organized for the expression of a collective will.

The American experience for a century before 1914 had not been such as to nurture the wisdom that rests on a knowledge of reality. It had, rather, been such as gives scope to our human propensity for self-delusion. The premise of American thinking in the period of World War I had been that a complete alternative must be found to power-politics, and Wilson had

2. For the documentation of this see Louis J. Halle, *Dream and Reality* (New York, 1959), pp. 284–6; and *Men and Nations* (Princeton, 1962), pp. 58–62 and 171.

persuaded himself that he had found such an alternative in his proposed League of Nations. A generation later, Roosevelt, who had not moved beyond this conception, allowed himself to believe that his proposed United Nations Organization would serve as the complete alternative to power-politics, rather than as a device for taming them, for keeping them within the bounds of some order. In this view of international organization and power-politics as mutually exclusive alternatives, Wilson and Roosevelt alike reflected the naïveté of the American mind in the first half of this century.

On the overt record, however, Wilson was less naïve than his successor, for he had taken the position that the establishment of peace required that Germany, under a respectable successor regime, resume its role as an equal in the community of nations. He had been careful to make a distinction between the governing regime, which was transitory, and the nation, which was permanent and ineradicable, attributing the war-guilt only to the former. This provided a basis for making peace with the German nation after it had replaced the Kaiser's regime by one that was responsible and legitimate. Roosevelt, on the other hand, attributed the war-guilt to the nation itself. It followed from this attribution that the replacement of the Nazi regime by a respectable successor would not entitle the German nation to any greater consideration by those who were undertaking to overcome it. It would not save the nation from punishment and the destruction of its power, or even mitigate these consequences of its defeat.

Wilson had been a stubborn thinker in his own right. Roosevelt was not. The better politician of the two, Roosevelt was more disposed simply to represent the common mind and give it expression. This is not to say that he was without political courage. In the years preceding the Japanese attack on Pearl Harbor, when the American nation had been deeply divided over foreign policy, when there had been no common mind, he had seen the need for a timely intervention to put down Hitler, and he had steered the country in that direction without an excessive regard for the political risk to himself. He was never a craven politician, however prudent and circumspect.

With the cataclysmic attack on Pearl Harbor, the nation that had only the day before been paralyzed by division found itself united in a determination to strike down the aggressors and crush them into the ground. In this mood, it was not disposed to distinguish between "peace-loving" Japanese and "aggressor" Japanese, between "peace-loving" Germans and "aggressor" Germans, between "peace-loving" Italians and "aggressor" Italians. As always in wartime, the great abstraction now took possession of the national mind. In place of Japanese, German, or Italian men, women, and children, there arose an apparition called "The Enemy," a beast whose inborn nature fulfilled itself only in aggression. Wilson had deliberately taken the Kaiser to be the ruthless master of the German people, whose overthrow would free them to rejoin the community of nations. But Roosevelt, sharing the common mind rather than shaping it, took Hitler to be merely the servant of the German people, representing a ruthlessness that had its origin and native abode in them. Hitler was simply their agent. It followed that the replacement of the governing regime in Germany would be merely the replacement of one agent by another who was bound to represent the same thing. Such a replacement would offer no basis for the reacceptance of Germany in the community of nations. The German nation would continue, still, to be "The Enemy," with whom one could make no peace. It would still be one of the "aggressor" nations, upon the permanent suppression of which the peace of the world depended.

This was the conception on which the Atlantic powers based their unconditional-surrender decision. By that decision, the opposition inside Germany was put on notice that the overthrow of the Nazis and their replacement would avail Germany nothing. Germany under any kind of regime—under the regime of an Ebert or an Adenauer as under that of a Hitler—would still be "The Enemy."

The non-Communist opposition in Germany was composed of men whom George Kennan has described as "very brave and very lonely." These men were our true kinsmen. They were representatives of our own civilization who had dedicated themselves to its restoration in Germany. When, at great personal risk, they made contact with the Atlantic leadership, informing it of their intention to rid Germany of Hitler, they were refused support simply because they were Germans. Alone and without encouragement, then, they nevertheless mounted their attempt of July 20, 1944, against Hitler, which did not come far short of succeeding. At least one of the survivors has testified to the difficulty created by the allied refusal of cooperation with the German resistance.[3]

If we had been worldly-wise we would have known that the real world is not divided between peoples that are all "peace-loving" and peoples that are all "aggressor." We would have known that there are forces of good and forces of evil that contend for power within every nation, within Germany and the United States alike. In that case our aim would have been to see the Nazis replaced in the seats of power by the "peace-loving" forces in Germany, and then to make a genuine peace of reconciliation with a Germany under the government of those forces.

The decision to eliminate German power from Europe, rather than make such a peace, is what laid the foundations of the Cold War.

In the day of our victory, on May 7, 1945, the elimination of German power was total, as it had not been on November 11, 1918. We had not only eliminated the military and industrial plant of Germany, but had allowed the entire structure of the German state to collapse and disappear. The vacuum of military and economic power was completed by a political vacuum. No German Government, no German political authority, remained in the land.

It is evident that such a vacuum can hardly persist, even for a week. It is bound to be filled by something. What would fill it in the moment of vic-

---

3. George F. Kennan, *Russia and the West under Lenin and Stalin* (Boston, 1961), p. 367. See also the report of an address by Eugen Gerstenmaier in the *New York Herald-Tribune*, Paris edition, July 21, 1964, p. 2.

tory was the victorious armies: the American, British, and French Armies under General Eisenhower; and the Red Army that served Stalin's dictatorship. For the moment the victorious forces, jointly or severally, would administer the German area of Europe as conquered territory.

But what then?

At the Yalta Conference in February 1945 Roosevelt told Churchill and Stalin that he did not believe he could obtain the consent of Congress to keeping American troops in Europe "much more than two years." [4] In fact, under irresistible popular pressure, the United States proceeded, immediately after the War, to demobilize and to dismantle its wartime military structure. It followed the total elimination of German military power with the drastic reduction of its own. From 1945 to 1947 it reduced its armed forces from twelve million men to 1.4 million.[5] Clearly, the United States could have had no intention of filling the vacuum, or of filling it for long.

Britain, as we shall see, was an exhausted country, without the resources to fill the vacuum.

France was itself a vacuum.

That left only Russia, which did not demobilize after the War and did not dismantle its wartime military establishment. Instead, it kept in its armed forces five to six million men, fifty thousand tanks, and twenty thousand aircraft. And it began the construction of a navy that, in the number of its submarines, was to exceed the combined navies of the world. Only Russia, then, would be in a position to fill the vacuum.

At this point it is proper to note that the Atlantic allies did not, in fact, carry out the postwar policy they had projected for Germany. They did, on the contrary, in 1949 and 1950, make a genuine peace of reconciliation with a dismembered Germany under the government of an anti-Nazi successor regime that represented the forces of moderation and decency in Germany. And they supported the restoration of German power to fill the vacuum. But by then it was too late. By then all eastern Europe, including an important part of Germany itself, had fallen under the power of Stalin. By then the Cold War had got started and had reached a peak of intensity.

2. *Gar Alperovitz: Atomic Diplomacy*

The revisionist attack on the standard interpretation of the Cold War began in the 1950's, but its most dramatic assault was Gar Alperovitz's *Atomic Diplomacy,* published in 1965. Alperovitz studied at the University of Wisconsin, and received his doctorate at Cambridge, where he was a Marshall scholar. He served as a Legislative Assistant in the House of Representatives

---

4. Herbert Feis, *Churchill, Roosevelt, Stalin* (Princeton, 1957), pp. 531–2.
5. Philip Noel-Baker, *The Arms Race* (New York, 1958), pp. 46–7.

From Gar Alperovitz, *Atomic Diplomacy: Hiroshima and Potsdam* (New York: Simon and Schuster, 1965), pp. 231–34, 236–42. Footnotes omitted. Copyright © by Gar Alperovitz. Reprinted by permission of the publishers.

and the Senate, and as a Special Assistant in the State Department. He is now co-director of the Cambridge Institute in Cambridge, Massachusetts. One will want to examine carefully the way Alperovitz uses his evidence. Does he make a convincing case, or does he force the evidence to fit preconceived patterns?

The Potsdam meeting clearly illustrates how the strategic decision to wait for the atomic bomb dominated American policy making from mid-May until early August. The primary reason most Western leaders began to call for another meeting with Stalin only three months after Yalta was their desire to have a confrontation on the important European questions then in tense dispute. But . . . Truman rejected the advice of his advisers and Churchill, and twice postponed a face-to-face meeting with Stalin because of his decision to wait for the atomic bomb. Ironically, however, in the end he committed himself to a meeting which was still a scant two weeks too early to be decisive. For this reason, to focus attention on the Potsdam meeting itself, as many writers have done, is to completely misunderstand American policy. Indeed, the interesting question is not what happened at the meeting, but why very little happened at all.

Thus, the importance of the atomic bomb in American calculations is underscored by the negative result of the heads-of-government meeting; had the new weapon not played such a crucial role in American strategy, there would have been every reason for Truman to attempt to achieve a negotiated settlement as quickly as possible after the defeat of Germany. Assuming, as Churchill did until mid-July, that it was unwise to gamble on the possibilities of the as yet untested weapon, the Prime Minister was undoubtedly correct to argue that "the decisive, practical points of strategy" involved "*above all,* that a settlement must be reached on all major issues between the West and the East . . . *before the armies of democracy melted. . . ."* As he told Eden, the "issue . . . seems to me to dwarf all others." Without the atomic bomb, Churchill believed, the only hope lay in an "early and speedy showdown."

Just as he had hurried to arrange an understanding in the Balkans before the Russian position became overwhelmingly powerful in late 1944, he now searched for ways "we may be able to please them . . . as part of a general settlement." Churchill sought to establish a *modus vivendi* before American conventional strength disappeared from the Continent. He wished to give priority to the German question, to recognize the Balkan governments, to settle all frontier issues, to complete the peace treaties quickly and to give only secondary attention to establishing new machinery for post-Potsdam discussions.

Until the atomic test report arrived, Churchill must have thought it incomprehensible that the Americans were not interested in a negotiated settlement. Though they wished to state their case on all issues in dispute, the American delegation was far more concerned with establishing a Council to take up unsettled questions than they were in serious negotiations while the heads of government were together. Thus, significantly, London met with no success in a pre-Potsdam effort to convince Washington of the seemingly obvious point that the German issue was more important than the procedural matter of arranging for new meetings of the foreign ministers.

As we have seen, once the detailed report of the atomic test arrived at Potsdam, Churchill reversed himself completely: "We were . . . possessed of powers which were irresistible." But Churchill's pre-Potsdam appraisal of Stalin's position was probably correct; for, unless the West was prepared to negotiate a settlement, the Soviet Premier undoubtedly calculated there was everything to gain if he waited until the American troops were withdrawn from the Continent. Since Truman did not tell Stalin of the atomic bomb, it could not yet be expected to play a major role in Soviet-American relations. And, indeed, with no apparent changes in the power relationships, on most issues discussed at the Conference, *both* Truman and Stalin held their ground. The Potsdam Conference took place at a unique moment in history, when each side undoubtedly believed time was on its side. The logic of the situation ensured—as the final protocol showed—that the Conference could only end in deadlock.

Undoubtedly Soviet intelligence knew generally of the work being done on the atomic bomb. However, it is probable that Stalin had no specific knowledge of the New Mexico test—or that if he knew of it, he did not know in detail how greatly it had exceeded expectations. His post-Hiroshima reversals in Manchuria, Hungary, and Bulgaria testify to a new conviction that the power realities required him to yield considerably more than he may have originally thought necessary. It is probable that Truman had this in mind when he noted that by early September "our possession of the secret of harnessing atomic energy already had far-reaching effects on our relations with other nations." . . .

Truman's own argument that a stable Europe was vital to world peace and to American security reveals the error of the common opinion that America had little active interest in European affairs until the 1947 Truman Doctrine and Marshall Plan. The President's mid-1945 declaration to his staff was an accurate statement of American policy: "We are committed to the rehabilitation of Europe, and there was to be no abandonment this time." Indeed, much more must be said, for the American commitment to Europe was not restricted to the Western regions of the Continent. As George F. Kennan, the author of the "containment policy," has emphasized, American policy was "by no means limited to holding the line." And as Byrnes has repeatedly stressed, in 1945 and 1946 senior American officials were not primarily concerned with a Soviet political or military threat to Western Europe; their eyes were focused on conditions in the Soviet-occupied zone. Byrnes has been quite explicit; his policy always aimed at forcing the Russians to yield in Eastern Europe, and in mid-1947 he still continued to argue that the United States had it in its power to force the Russians to "retire in a very decent manner." . . .

This essay has attempted to describe the influence of the atomic bomb on certain questions of diplomacy. I do not believe that the reverse question—the influence of diplomacy upon the decision to use the atomic bomb—can be answered on the basis of the presently available evidence. However, it is possible to define the nature of the problem. . . .

The first point to note is that the decision to use the weapon did not derive from overriding military considerations. Despite Truman's subsequent statement that the weapon "saved millions of lives," Eisenhower's judgment that it was "completely unnecessary" as a measure to save lives was almost certainly correct. This is not a matter of hindsight; *before the atomic bomb was dropped each of the Joint Chiefs of Staff advised that it was highly likely that Japan could be forced to surrender "unconditionally," without use of the bomb and without an invasion.* Indeed, this characterization of the position taken by the senior military advisers is a conservative one.

General Marshall's June 18 appraisal was the most cautiously phrased advice offered by any of the Joint Chiefs: "The impact of Russian entry on the already hopeless Japanese may well be the decisive action levering them into capitulation. . . ." Admiral Leahy was absolutely certain there was no need for the bombing to obviate the necessity of an invasion. His judgment after the fact was the same as his view before the bombing: "It is my opinion that the use of this barbarous weapon at Hiroshima and Nagasaki was of no material assistance in our war against Japan. The Japanese were already defeated and ready to surrender. . . ." Similarly, through most of 1945 Admiral King believed the bomb unnecessary, and Generals Arnold and LeMay defined the official Air Force position in this way: Whether or not the atomic bomb should be dropped was not for the Air Force to decide, but explosion of the bomb was not necessary to win the war or make an invasion unnecessary.

Similar views prevailed in Britain long before the bombs were used. General Ismay recalls that by the time of Potsdam, "for some time past it had been firmly fixed in my mind that the Japanese were tottering." Ismay's reaction to the suggestion of the bombing was, like Eisenhower's and Leahy's, one of "revulsion." And Churchill, who as early as September 1944, felt that Russian entry was likely to force capitulation, has written: "It would be a mistake to suppose that the fate of Japan was settled by the atomic bomb. Her defeat was certain before the first bomb fell. . . ."

The military appraisals made before the weapons were used have been confirmed by numerous postsurrender studies. The best known is that of the United States Strategic Bombing Survey. The Survey's conclusion is unequivocal: "Japan would have surrendered even if the atomic bombs had not been dropped, even if Russia had not entered the war, and even if no invasion had been planned or contemplated."

That military considerations were not decisive is confirmed—and illuminated—by the fact that the President did not even ask the opinion of the military adviser most directly concerned. General MacArthur, Supreme Commander of Allied Forces in the Pacific, was simply informed of the weapon shortly before it was used at Hiroshima. Before his death he stated on numerous occasions that, like Eisenhower, he believed the atomic bomb was completely unnecessary from a military point of view.

Although military considerations were not primary, as we have seen, unquestionably political considerations related to Russia played a major role in the decision; from at least mid-May American policy makers hoped to end the hostilities before the Red Army entered Manchuria. For this reason they had no wish to test whether Russian entry into the war would force capitulation—as most thought likely—long before the scheduled November invasion. Indeed, they actively attempted to delay Stalin's declaration of war.

Nevertheless, it would be wrong to conclude that the atomic bomb was used simply to keep the Red Army out of Manchuria. Given the desperate efforts of the Japanese to surrender, and Truman's willingness to offer assurances to the Emperor, it is entirely possible that the war could have been ended by negotiation before the Red Army had begun its attack. But, again, as we have seen, after Alamogordo neither the President nor his senior advisers were interested in exploring this possibility.

One reason may have been their fear that if time-consuming negotiations were once initiated, the Red Army might attack in order to seize Manchurian objectives. But, if this explanation is accepted, once more one must conclude that the bomb was used primarily because it was felt to be politically important to prevent Soviet domination of the area.

Such a conclusion is very difficult to accept, for American interests in Manchuria, although historically important to the State Department, were not of great significance. The further question therefore arises: Were there other political reasons for using the atomic bomb? In approaching this question, it is important to note that most of the men involved at the time who since have made their views public always mention *two* considerations which dominated discussions. The first was the desire to end the Japanese war quickly, which, as we have seen, was not primarily a military consideration, but a political one. The second is always referred to indirectly. . . .

In essence, the second of the two overriding considerations seems to have been that a combat demonstration was needed to convince the Russians to accept the American plan for a stable peace. And the crucial point of this effort was the need to force agreement on the main questions in dispute: the American proposals for Central and Eastern Europe. President Truman may well have expressed the key consideration in October 1945; publicly urging the necessity of a more conventional form of military power (his proposal for universal military training), in a personal appearance before Congress the President declared: "It is only by strength that we can impress the fact upon possible future aggressors that we will tolerate no threat to peace. . . ."

If indeed the "second consideration" involved in the bombing of Hiroshima and Nagasaki was the desire to impress the Russians, it might explain the strangely ambiguous statement by Truman that not only did the bomb end the war, but it gave the world "a chance to face the facts." It would also accord with Stimson's private advice to McCloy: "We have got to regain the lead and perhaps do it in a pretty rough and realistic way.

. . . We have coming into action a weapon which will be unique. Now the thing [to do is] . . . let our actions speak for themselves." Again, it would accord with Stimson's statement to Truman that the "greatest complication" would occur if the President negotiated with Stalin before the bomb had been "laid on Japan." It would tie in with the fact that from mid-May strategy toward all major diplomatic problems was based upon the assumption the bomb would be demonstrated. Finally, it might explain why none of the highest civilian officials seriously questioned the use of the bomb as Eisenhower did; for, having reversed the basic direction of diplomatic strategy *because* of the atomic bomb, it would have been very difficult indeed for anyone subsequently to challenge an idea which had come to dominate all calculations of high policy.

At present no final conclusion can be reached on this question. But the problem can be defined with some precision: Why did the American government refuse to attempt to exploit Japanese efforts to surrender? Or, alternatively, why did they refuse to test whether a Russian declaration of war would force capitulation? Were Hiroshima and Nagasaki bombed primarily to impress the world with the need to accept America's plan for a stable and lasting peace—that is, primarily, America's plan for Europe? The evidence strongly suggests that the view which the President's personal representative offered to one of the atomic scientists in May 1945 was an accurate statement of policy: "Mr. Byrnes did not argue that it was necessary to use the bomb against the cities of Japan in order to win the war . . . Mr. Byrnes's . . . view [was] that our possessing and demonstrating the bomb would make Russia more manageable in Europe. . . ."

3. *Gabriel Kolko: The Politics of War*

Even revisionists soon create their own "standard" interpretations, and Gabriel Kolko is now considered by many scholars to be the "standard" revisionist. Kolko turned to the history of the Cold War after challenging the usual interpretations of the Progressive era in American history. It should be noted that he looks at the Cold War from a wider perspective than Gar Alperovitz. Kolko sees Stalin as a more moderate and realistic statesman than the leaders of Great Britain and the United States, and as one who tried to accommodate the western powers but was met by an intransigent refusal to accept changing conditions.

The coalition against the Axis was born of necessity rather than deliberation or choice, and only the common need to defeat a common enemy bound it together. Great Britain, the Soviet Union, and the United States shared no single set of objectives other than this preeminent reality, no

From Gabriel Kolko, *The Politics of War: The World and United States Foreign Policy* (New York: Random House, 1968), pp. 618–23. Copyright © 1968 by Gabriel Kolko. Reprinted by permission of Random House, Inc.

unifying political and economic peace aims—save, in the case of Britain and America, the negative one of containing Russia and the Left—and when Germany and Japan lay in smoking ruins the wartime Allies turned from a tenuous coalition to open conflict. That incipient struggle grew in importance throughout the war, until no later than the end of 1944 it necessarily became the defining obsession of the Western members of the coalition. That conflict has shaped the contours of modern world history, and we have yet to feel or know its full meaning and ultimate consequences.

No major power sacrificed less of its blood and material wealth during World War II than the United States. If one considers military potential in terms of overall industrial and technological capacity to sustain modern warfare over a period of time, in August 1945 only the United States had that power and only the United States emerged from the bloodiest conflagration in human history stronger than ever before. The war ultimately drained Britain more than even Russia, relative to its limited manpower and resources, transforming that small island into a power of the second tier. The United States was incomparably the greatest single nation in the world, with sharply articulated global political and, primarily, economic aspirations equal, even much more than equal, to the role.

The leaders in Washington were above all else fully aware of their own physical strength as well as their political and economic objectives, and they always viewed the problem of future relations with the U.S.S.R. or Great Britain, or the nature of the world, with these critical goals in clear perspective. For how to advance its peace aims and apply its directing power to the inordinately complex and unpredictable realities of the broken, war-torn world colored every specific American response and assumption, and it was these expansive premises that were to define the postwar structure of relations—and conflict—between great states.

The problem of Soviet power gradually subsumed the other great wartime challenge to American diplomacy: the emergence of the Left and its threat to securing American economic and political war aims. In Eastern Europe, perhaps more than any other single region, American leaders found evidence of what they interpreted to be the dangers of Soviet expansionism that might undercut the attainment of their nation's largest postwar goals. The war utterly and finally destroyed the traditional Eastern European political and economic structure and nothing the Russians might do could alter that fact, for not the Soviet Union but the leaders of the Old Order in Eastern Europe themselves made that collapse inevitable. The Russians could work within that new structural limitation in a variety of ways, and in practice they did explore many political options, but they could not transcend the new socioeconomic reality. More aware than anyone else of their own weaknesses in the event of a conflict with the United States, the Russians pursued a conservative and cautious line wherever they could find local non-Communist groups willing to abjure the traditional diplomacy of the cordon sanitaire and anti-Bolshevism. They were entirely willing to restrain equally the militant Left and militant Right, and given the complex political admixtures of the region they showed nei-

ther more nor less respect for an unborn functional democracy in Eastern
Europe than the Americans and British evidenced in Italy, Greece, or Belgium. For neither the Americans, British, nor Russians were willing to permit democracy to run its course anywhere in Europe at the cost of damaging their vital strategic and economic interests, perhaps also bringing about
the triumph of the Left or the restoration of prewar clerical fascism. In fact
we now know that the Russians lost control of the revolutionary forces in
Yugoslavia and Greece, and that they had no intention of Bolshevizing
Eastern Europe in 1945 if—but only if—they could find alternatives.

For the United States, Eastern Europe was a question of economic war
aims to which political realities had also to conform to satisfy American aspirations, and quite apart from the local leaderships' policies toward Russia, that was hardly possible in nearly all the Eastern European nations.
Even where the United States had yet to develop all of its objectives in
specific detail, it was imperative that it prevent any Great Power from totally dominating Eastern Europe or any other region of the world for that
matter, because the United States considered all political and economic
blocs or spheres of influence that it did not control as directly undermining
its larger political, and especially economic, objectives for an integrated
world capitalism and a political structure which was the prerequisite to its
goals. For this reason America opposed Britain's control over French affairs and set itself against an Eastern European reality which neither it,
nor in the last analysis, the Russians, could fully shape according to a plan
or desire.

Given the pervasive, chronic Russian conservatism on political questions
during the war, one best reflected in the United Front tactics of accommodation which caused the Russian-disciplined Left to submerge its distinctive socialist character at all costs, the failure to reach agreement over Poland or Czechoslovakia—and Eastern Europe in general—reflected the
effort of the United States to disengage Soviet influence in Eastern Europe
and to create states ready to cooperate with a postwar economic program
compatible with American objectives and interests. To the Russians during
the war, Eastern Europe was a question of preventing the resurrection of
traditionally hostile conservative leaders, and in this they had the total collapse of much of Eastern European society working on their behalf. To the
Americans it was a matter of putting together a perhaps somewhat re-
formed version of the social and political sources of Eastern Europe's alliance with atavistic forces of imperialism and nationalism during two wars
and reintegrating the region into a traditional prewar European economy
in a condition of semicolonialism. That task was beyond the power of the
United States or Russia, but it was a failure of American policy for which
Washington was ultimately to hold Russia responsible. This exacerbation
of world politics over Eastern Europe was a result of American expansion
into the historically hopeless imbroglio and mire of Eastern European affairs.

In the last analysis both the Soviet Union and the United States could
only partially control the uncontrollable—the Left—and could seemingly

inhibit it only in Western Europe. For World War II brought to fruition a whole spectrum of internal crises inherent in the civil war in society, which was a by-product of different admixtures within each nation of industrial capitalism, World War I, and the continued weakening of world capitalism and colonialism after 1939. America, with some significant aid from Russia, might retard that collapse, yet it could not stay its irresistible momentum, and all the issues were joined during the period 1942–1945 that were again to break out with renewed force after the war to define the direction of modern world diplomacy and conflict. The Old Order of prewar capitalism and oligarchy with which the United States identified, with reservations, and which it hoped to reform and integrate into a transformed world capitalist economy, was dying in the colonial world and a dependent China; it committed suicide in Eastern Europe, and the United States could refurbish it in temporarily acceptable ways only in Western Europe. The impact of these changes on the conditions and structure of world power ultimately were to be more far-reaching than the Bolshevik Revolution itself, in part because—after 1947—the protective existence and support of Soviet power was a cushion between success and failure in many, but by no means all, socialist or revolutionary nations.

By 1945 the war itself delivered the *coup de grâce* to the prewar structure of European politics and economics, for which there was now but slight social backing, and therefore slight resistance to change. Only external intervention saved what remained of European capitalism, and it is this attempted unilateral Great Power definition of the internal affairs of other nations that became the defining fact of wartime and postwar politics. The Americans and British set the precedent in Italy, and formalized it in Europe when the United States also extended the principle elsewhere by preventing the emergence of a truly collaborative forum in the European Advisory Commission in the hope that occupation forces might contain potentially revolutionary changes via a controlled "democracy" whose limits and outcome the West might determine.

This larger instability in European economics and politics required the United States to aid the resuscitation of cooperative conservative elements of Europe and to attempt to prevent a total collapse of the Old Order in Europe and Asia that might open the door to Soviet predominance in a region or even the complete transformation of whole nations. For this reason the United States did not advance a truly permanent stern peace for Germany or Japan, since toward the end of the war many important American leaders accepted the need to reintegrate and reform German and Japanese power to create a balance to Soviet predominance and to advance American objectives. And this deliberate ambiguity, which permeated all their wartime considerations of the future role of the defeated Axis, implied that it was not the total destruction of Axis power, but the advancement of American global interests that soon became the preeminent concern in American planning. In this sense World War II was a tragic error to the American government in that even before the war was over it understood that perhaps a less imperialist Germany and Japan would be preferable to the U.S.S.R. as allies in the future.

Indeed, this perceptible shift in priorities ultimately became the basis of American postwar policy, reflecting a shift in tactical goals all along the line, one that also significantly downgraded initial American hostility to British political aims in Europe, and more particularly in France, on behalf of a far deeper commitment to the objectives of containment and stability—containment of the dual menace of the Left and the Soviet Union, and stability for the essential social and economic system of prewar European capitalism and colonialism.

Although the United States undertook a task that was insuperable in many places, it was still possible in much of Europe, and in any event the American government had no option but to resist as best it could those destabilizing political and economic conditions which brought revolutionary movements of every shape and variety into existence, and attempt to compensate for their subversive effect on American interests and postwar objectives by containing, redirecting, or destroying them. There was no other recourse for the United States but to undertake the difficult, and in many places, the impossible, for the consequence of inaction might have been the unchallenged triumph of the Left in numerous countries. Only the United States had the power to engage fully in international counterrevolution and sustain the forces of conservatism for prolonged periods of time, and it was this militant intervention into the affairs of literally every area of the world that set the pattern for postwar world politics. By 1945 Washington's decision to undertake that role was an unquestioned postulate in America's plans for the future of its power in the world.

The Russians understood the American intention and the risks of any covert aid to the Left, and they gave precious little of it during and immediately after the war, when they discovered that even an obviously conservative policy failed to blunt the American belief that behind all the world's social and economic ills, somehow, and in some critical fashion, a Russian plot and device existed. From this viewpoint United States policy-makers saw Russia and the Left as the cause rather than the reflection of the collapse of capitalism, and responsible for the failings of a system that began to commit suicide in vast areas of the globe no later than 1914. Still, it was Soviet conservatism on revolutionary movements everywhere that gave Western European capitalism the critical breathing spell during which it might recover, though the caution of the Western European Communist parties became a permanent and willingly self-imposed fact of political life. This desire to opt into the existing order where possible, and the correct realization that the American and British armies would certainly not permit a triumph of the Left either by the ballot or a takeover in the streets, shaped the political conduct of the Communist parties wherever there were Western troops. And the U.S.S.R. demanded and assiduously enforced this strategy where it controlled local Communist parties and, through them, the Resistance. It brought an end to the illusions of possibilities and na-

tional renovation that inspired the European Resistance. Yet where the Soviets could not control the armed opposition, or the Right was too rigid to
absorb the armed Left—as in China, Greece, and Yugoslavia—the end result was revolution and international crisis.

These crises were not a by-product of Soviet policy, but reflected a lack
of Russian control over the Left and the response of the British and,
preeminently, the United States, to the irresistible tides of change. Outside
Western Europe the Americans could recognize, in moments of clarity, the
total breakdown of existing societies, but they bent every energy—via dollars and ultimately force of arms—to avoid the political and economic consequences of a perceptible reality for which they could have no sympathy.
In Western Europe both dollars and guns succeeded, but where the Americans could not undo disintegration resulting from the war and economic
collapse, they often limited and shaped the character of change. American
resistance to social and revolutionary upheavals from diverse sources and
causes, whether Communist or revolutionary nationalist, polarized change
in the world, denying pluralism and options which were natural to radical
and humanist movements unable and unwilling to risk survival along with
diversity and social exploration. Successful movements of social transformation, due in some degree to ideology but necessarily because of the external pressures, became monolithic and anti-American as a precondition
to success. Counterrevolution in this manner defined the course of revolution and history for decades, and imposed on the remnants of the tortured
men and women seeking to create a new life for themselves in Asia and
elsewhere the American problem as the constant threat to social renovation
and survival.

4. *Arthur Schlesinger, Jr.: Origins of the Cold War*

Professional historians rarely become known to the general public. Arthur
Schlesinger, Jr., is one of the exceptions—a professional historian who has
not only twice won the Pulitzer Prize, but has served in the White House
during the Kennedy and Johnson administrations. He is now Albert
Schweitzer Professor of Humanities at the City University of New York.
Schlesinger's service with the government, and his strong support of a more
traditional interpretation of the Cold War, have made him anathema to
many scholars of the New Left who may never forget his letter to the *New
York Review of Books* (October 20, 1966), in which he wrote that the time
had come "to blow the whistle" on the revisionists, a remark Schlesinger
later admitted was "intemperate." The article reprinted below is a major effort to restate the antirevisionist position. Does Schlesinger effectively meet

From Arthur Schlesinger, Jr., "Origins of the Cold War," *Foreign Affairs*, October
1967, pp. 26–31, 36–41, 44–47, 49–52. Copyright by the Council on Foreign Relations,
Inc., New York. Reprinted by permission of *Foreign Affairs* and Arthur Schlesinger, Jr.

this challenge? What concessions does he make to the revisionist point of view? [1]

Peacemaking after the Second World War was not so much a tapestry as it was a hopelessly raveled and knotted mess of yarn. Yet, for purposes of clarity, it is essential to follow certain threads. One theme indispensable to an understanding of the Cold War is the contrast between two clashing views of world order: the "universalist" view, by which all nations shared a common interest in all the affairs of the world, and the "sphere-of-influence" view, by which each great power would be assured by the other great powers of an acknowledged predominance in its own area of special interest. The universalist view assumed that national security would be guaranteed by an international organization. The sphere-of-interest view assumed that national security would be guaranteed by the balance of power. While in practice these views have by no means been incompatible (indeed, our shaky peace has been based on a combination of the two), in the abstract they involved sharp contradictions.

The tradition of American thought in these matters was universalist—*i.e.* Wilsonian. Roosevelt had been a member of Wilson's subcabinet; in 1920, as candidate for Vice President, he had campaigned for the League of Nations. It is true that, within Roosevelt's infinitely complex mind, Wilsonianism warred with the perception of vital strategic interests he had imbibed from Mahan. Moreover, his temperamental inclination to settle things with fellow princes around the conference table led him to regard the Big Three —or Four—as trustees for the rest of the world. On occasion, as this narrative will show, he was beguiled into flirtation with the sphere-of-influence heresy. But in principle he believed in joint action and remained a Wilsonian. His hope for Yalta, as he told the Congress on his return, was that it would "spell the end of the system of unilateral action, the exclusive alliances, the spheres of influence, the balances of power, and all the other expedients that have been tried for centuries—and have always failed."

Whenever Roosevelt backslid, he had at his side that Wilsonian fundamentalist, Secretary of State Cordell Hull, to recall him to the pure faith. After his visit to Moscow in 1943, Hull characteristically said that, with the Declaration of Four Nations on General Security (in which America, Russia, Britain and China pledged "united action . . . for the organization and maintenance of peace and security"), "there will no longer be need for spheres of influence, for alliances, for balance of power, or any other of the special arrangements through which, in the unhappy past, the nations strove to safeguard their security or to promote their interests."

Remembering the corruption of the Wilsonian vision by the secret treaties of the First World War, Hull was determined to prevent any sphere-of-influence nonsense after the Second World War. He therefore fought all proposals to settle border questions while the war was still on and, excluded as he largely was from wartime diplomacy, poured his not inconsid-

1. A recent and important statement of the anti-revisionist position is John Wheeler-Bennett and Anthony Nicholls, *The Semblance of Peace* (London: Macmillan, 1972).

erable moral energy and frustration into the promulgation of virtuous and spacious general principles.

In adopting the universalist view, Roosevelt and Hull were not indulging personal hobbies. Sumner Welles, Adolf Berle, Averell Harriman, Charles Bohlen—all, if with a variety of nuances, opposed the sphere-of-influence approach. And here the State Department was expressing what seems clearly to have been the predominant mood of the American people, so long mistrustful of European power politics. The Republicans shared the true faith. John Foster Dulles argued that the great threat to peace after the war would lie in the revival of sphere-of-influence thinking. The United States, he said, must not permit Britain and Russia to revert to these bad old ways; it must therefore insist on American participation in all policy decisions for all territories in the world. Dulles wrote pessimistically in January 1945, "The three great powers which at Moscow agreed upon the 'closest coöperation' about European questions have shifted to a practice of separate, regional responsibility."

It is true that critics, and even friends, of the United States sometimes noted a discrepancy between the American passion for universalism when it applied to territory far from American shores and the preëminence the United States accorded its own interests nearer home. Churchill, seeking Washington's blessing for a sphere-of-influence initiative in Eastern Europe, could not forbear reminding the Americans, "We follow the lead of the United States in South America;" nor did any universalist of record propose the abolition of the Monroe Doctrine. But a convenient myopia prevented such inconsistencies from qualifying the ardency of the universalist faith.

There seem only to have been three officials in the United States Government who dissented. One was the Secretary of War, Henry L. Stimson, a classical balance-of-power man, who in 1944 opposed the creation of a vacuum in Central Europe by the pastoralization of Germany and in 1945 urged "the settlement of all territorial acquisitions in the shape of defense posts which each of these four powers may deem to be necessary for their own safety" in advance of any effort to establish a peacetime United Nations. Stimson considered the claim of Russia to a preferred position in Eastern Europe as not unreasonable: as he told President Truman, "he thought the Russians perhaps were being more realistic than we were in regard to their own security." Such a position for Russia seemed to him comparable to the preferred American position in Latin America; he even spoke of "our respective orbits." Stimson was therefore skeptical of what he regarded as the prevailing tendency "to hang on to exaggerated views of the Monroe Doctrine and at the same time butt into every question that comes up in Central Europe." Acceptance of spheres of influence seemed to him the way to avoid "a head-on collision."

A second official opponent of universalism was George Kennan, an eloquent advocate from the American Embassy in Moscow of "a prompt and clear recognition of the division of Europe into spheres of influence and of a policy based on the fact of such division." Kennan argued that nothing we could do would possibly alter the course of events in Eastern Europe; that we were deceiving ourselves by supposing that these countries had any future but Russian domination; that we should therefore relinquish Eastern Europe to the Soviet Union and avoid anything which would make things easier for the Russians by giving them economic assistance or by sharing moral responsibility for their actions.

A third voice within the government against universalism was (at least after the war) Henry A. Wallace. As Secretary of Commerce, he stated the sphere-of-influence case with trenchancy in the famous Madison Square Garden speech of September 1946 which led to his dismissal by President Truman:

On our part, we should recognize that we have no more business in the *political* affairs of Eastern Europe than Russia has in the *political* affairs of Latin America, Western Europe, and the United States. . . . Whether we like it or not, the Russians will try to socialize their sphere of influence just as we try to democratize our sphere of influence. . . . The Russians have no more business stirring up native Communists to political activity in Western Europe, Latin America, and the United States than we have in interfering with the politics of Eastern Europe and Russia.

Stimson, Kennan and Wallace seem to have been alone in the government, however, in taking these views. They were very much minority voices. Meanwhile universalism, rooted in the American legal and moral tradition, overwhelmingly backed by contemporary opinion, received successive enshrinements in the Atlantic Charter of 1941, in the Declaration of the United Nations in 1942 and in the Moscow Declaration of 1943.

The Kremlin, on the other hand, thought *only* of spheres of interest; above all, the Russians were determined to protect their frontiers, and especially their border to the west, crossed so often and so bloodily in the dark course of their history. These western frontiers lacked natural means of defense—no great oceans, rugged mountains, steaming swamps or impenetrable jungles. The history of Russia had been the history of invasion, the last of which was by now horribly killing up to twenty million of its people. The protocol of Russia therefore meant the enlargement of the area of Russian influence. Kennan himself wrote (in May 1944), "Behind Russia's stubborn expansion lies only the age-old sense of insecurity of a sedentary people reared on an exposed plain in the neighborhood of fierce nomadic peoples," and he called this "urge" a "permanent feature of Russian psychology."

In earlier times the "urge" had produced the tsarist search for buffer states and maritime outlets. In 1939 the Soviet-Nazi pact and its secret protocol had enabled Russia to begin to satisfy in the Baltic states, Karelian Finland and Poland, part of what it conceived as its security requirements in Eastern Europe. But the "urge" persisted, causing the friction between Russia and Germany in 1940 as each jostled for position in the area which separated them. Later it led to Molotov's new demands on Hitler in November 1940—a free hand in Finland, Soviet predominance in Rumania and Bulgaria, bases in the Dardanelles—the demands which convinced Hitler that he had no choice but to attack Russia. Now Stalin hoped to gain from the West what Hitler, a closer neighbor, had not dared yield him.

It is true that, so long as Russian survival appeared to require a second front to relieve the Nazi pressure, Moscow's demand for Eastern Europe was a little muffled. Thus the Soviet government adhered to the Atlantic Charter (though with a significant if obscure reservation about adapting its principles to "the circumstances, needs, and historic peculiarities of particular countries"). Thus it also adhered to the Moscow Declaration of 1943, and Molotov then, with his easy mendacity, even denied that Russia had any desire to divide Europe into spheres of influence. But this was guff, which the Russians were perfectly willing to ladle out if it would keep the Americans, and especially Secretary Hull (who made a strong personal impression at the Moscow conference) happy. "A declaration," as Stalin once observed to Eden, "I regard as algebra, but an agreement as practical arithmetic. I do not wish to decry algebra, but I prefer practical arithmetic."

The more consistent Russian purpose was revealed when Stalin offered the British a straight sphere-of-influence deal at the end of 1941. Britain, he suggested, should recognize the Russian absorption of the Baltic states, part of Finland, eastern Poland and Bessarabia; in return, Russia would support any special British need for bases or security arrangements in Western Europe. There was nothing specifically communist about these ambitions. If Stalin achieved them, he would be fulfilling an age-old dream of the tsars. The British reaction was mixed. "Soviet policy is amoral," as Anthony Eden noted at the time; "United States policy is exaggeratedly moral, at least where non-American interests are concerned." If Roosevelt was a universalist with occasional leanings toward spheres of influence and Stalin was a sphere-of-influence man with occasional gestures toward universalism, Churchill seemed evenly poised between the familiar realism of the balance of power, which he had so long recorded as an historian and manipulated as a statesman, and the hope that there must be some better way of doing things. His 1943 proposal of a world organization divided into regional councils represented an effort to blend universalist and sphere-of-interest conceptions. His initial rejection of Stalin's proposal in December 1941 as "directly contrary to the first, second and third articles of the Atlantic Charter" thus did not spring entirely from a desire to propitiate the United States. On the other hand, he had himself already reinterpreted the Atlantic Charter as applying only to Europe (and thus not to the British Empire), and he was, above all, an empiricist who never believed in sacrificing reality on the altar of doctrine. . . .

It is now pertinent to inquire why the United States rejected the idea of stabilizing the world by division into spheres of influence and insisted on an East European strategy. One should warn against rushing to the conclusion that it was all a row between hard-nosed, balance-of-power realists and starry-eyed Wilsonians. Roosevelt, Hopkins, Welles, Harriman, Bohlen, Berle, Dulles and other universalists were tough and serious men. Why then did they rebuff the sphere-of-influence solution?

The first reason is that they regarded this solution as containing within itself the seeds of a third world war. The balance-of-power idea seemed inherently unstable. It had always broken down in the past. It held out to each power the permanent temptation to try to alter the balance in its own favor, and it built this temptation into the international order. It would turn the great powers of 1945 away from the objective of concerting common policies toward competition for postwar advantage. As Hopkins told Molotov at Teheran, "The President feels it essential to world peace that Russia, Great Britain and the United States work out this control question in a manner which will not start each of the three powers arming against the others." "The greatest likelihood of eventual conflict," said the Joint Chiefs of Staff in 1944 (the only conflict which the J.C.S., in its wisdom, could then glimpse "in the foreseeable future" was between Britain and Russia), ". . . would seem to grow out of either nation initiating attempts to build up its strength, by seeking to attach to herself parts of Europe to the disadvantage and possible danger of her potential adversary." The Americans were perfectly ready to acknowledge that Russia was entitled to convincing assurance of her national security—but not this way. "I could sympathize fully with Stalin's desire to protect his western borders from future attack," as Hull put it. "But I felt that this security could best be obtained through a strong postwar peace organization."

Hull's remark suggests the second objection: that the sphere-of-influence approach would, in the words of the State Department in 1945, "militate against the establishment and effective functioning of a broader system of general security in which all countries will have their part." The United Nations, in short, was seen as the alternative to the balance of power. Nor did the universalists see any necessary incompatibility between the Russian desire for "friendly governments" on its frontier and the American desire for self-determination in Eastern Europe. Before Yalta the State Department judged the general mood of Europe as "to the left and strongly in favor of far-reaching economic and social reforms, but not, however, in favor of a left-wing totalitarian regime to achieve these reforms." Governments in Eastern Europe could be sufficiently to the left "to allay Soviet suspicions" but sufficiently representative "of the center and *petit bourgeois* elements" not to seem a prelude to communist dictatorship. The American criteria were therefore that the government "should be dedicated to the preservation of civil liberties" and "should favor social and economic reforms." A string of New Deal states—of Finlands and Czechoslovakias—seemed a reasonable compromise solution.

Third, the universalists feared that the sphere-of-interest approach would be what Hull termed "a haven for the isolationists," who would advocate America's participation in Western Hemisphere affairs on condition that it did not participate in European or Asian affairs. Hull also feared that spheres of interest would lead to "closed trade areas or discriminatory systems" and thus defeat his cherished dream of a low-tariff, freely trading world.

Fourth, the sphere-of-interest solution meant the betrayal of the principles for which the Second World War was being fought—the Atlantic Charter, the Four Freedoms, the Declaration of the United Nations. Poland summed up the problem. Britain, having gone to war to defend the independence of Poland from the Germans, could not easily conclude the war by surrendering the independence of Poland to the Russians. Thus, as Hopkins told Stalin after Roosevelt's death in 1945, Poland had "become the symbol of our ability to work out problems with the Soviet Union." Nor could American liberals in general watch with equanimity while the police state spread into countries which, if they had mostly not been real democracies, had mostly not been tyrannies either. The execution in 1943 of Ehrlich and Alter, the Polish socialist trade union leaders, excited deep concern. "I have particularly in mind," Harriman cabled in 1944, "objection to the institution of secret police who may become involved in the persecution of persons of truly democratic convictions who may not be willing to conform to Soviet methods."

Fifth, the sphere-of-influence solution would create difficult domestic problems in American politics. Roosevelt was aware of the six million or more Polish votes in the 1944 election; even more acutely, he was aware of the broader and deeper attack which would follow if, after going to war to stop the Nazi conquest of Europe, he permitted the war to end with the communist conquest of Eastern Europe. As Archibald MacLeish, then Assistant Secretary of State for Public Affairs, warned in January 1945, "The wave of disillusionment which has distressed us in the last several weeks will be increased if the impression is permitted to get abroad that potentially totalitarian provisional governments are to be set up without adequate safeguards as to the holding of free elections and the realization of the principles of the Atlantic Charter." Roosevelt believed that no administration could survive which did not try everything short of war to save Eastern Europe, and he was the supreme American politician of the century.

Sixth, if the Russians were allowed to overrun Eastern Europe without argument, would that satisfy them? Even Kennan, in a dispatch of May 1944, admitted that the "urge" had dreadful potentialities: "If initially successful, will it know where to stop? Will it not be inexorably carried forward, by its very nature, in a struggle to reach the whole—to attain complete mastery of the shores of the Atlantic and the Pacific?" His own answer was that there were inherent limits to the Russian capacity to expand—"that Russia will not have an easy time in maintaining the power which it has seized over other people in Eastern and Central Europe unless it receives both moral and material assistance from the West." Subsequent developments have vindicated Kennan's argument. By the late forties, Jugoslavia and Albania, the two East European states farthest from the Soviet Union and the two in which communism was imposed from within rather than from without, had declared their independence of Moscow.

But, given Russia's success in maintaining centralized control over the international communist movement for a quarter of a century, who in 1944 could have had much confidence in the idea of communist revolts against Moscow?

Most of those involved therefore rejected Kennan's answer and stayed with his question. If the West turned its back on Eastern Europe, the higher probability, in their view, was that the Russians would use their security zone, not just for defensive purposes, but as a springboard from which to mount an attack on Western Europe, now shattered by war, a vacuum of power awaiting its master. "If the policy is accepted that the Soviet Union has a right to penetrate her immediate neighbors for security," Harriman said in 1944, "penetration of the next immediate neighbors becomes at a certain time equally logical." If a row with Russia were inevitable, every consideration of prudence dictated that it should take place in Eastern rather than Western Europe.

Thus idealism and realism joined in opposition to the sphere-of-influence solution. The consequence was a determination to assert an American interest in the postwar destiny of all nations, including those of Eastern Europe. In the message which Roosevelt and Hopkins drafted after Hopkins had stopped Roosevelt's initial cable authorizing Churchill to speak for the United States at the Moscow meeting of October 1944, Roosevelt now said, "There is in this global war literally no question, either military or political, in which the United States is not interested." After Roosevelt's death Hopkins repeated the point to Stalin: "The cardinal basis of President Roosevelt's policy which the American people had fully supported had been the concept that the interests of the U.S. were worldwide and not confined to North and South America and the Pacific Ocean."

For better or worse, this was the American position. It is now necessary to attempt the imaginative leap and consider the impact of this position on the leaders of the Soviet Union who, also for better or for worse, had reached the bitter conclusion that the survival of their country depended on their unchallenged control of the corridors through which enemies had so often invaded their homeland. They could claim to have been keeping their own side of the sphere-of-influence bargain. Of course, they were working to capture the resistance movements of Western Europe; indeed, with the appointment of Oumansky as Ambassador to Mexico they were even beginning to enlarge underground operations in the Western Hemisphere. But, from their viewpoint, if the West permitted this, the more fools they; and, if the West stopped it, it was within their right to do so. In overt political matters the Russians were scrupulously playing the game. They had watched in silence while the British shot down communists in Greece. In Jugoslavia Stalin was urging Tito (as Djilas later revealed) to keep King Peter. They had not only acknowledged Western preëminence in Italy but had recognized the Badoglio régime; the Italian Communists had even voted (against the Socialists and the Liberals) for the renewal of the Lateran Pacts.

They would not regard anti-communist action in a Western zone as a *casus belli;* and they expected reciprocal license to assert their own authority in the East. But the principle of self-determination was carrying the United States into a deeper entanglement in Eastern Europe than the Soviet Union claimed as a right (whatever it was doing underground) in the affairs of Italy, Greece or China. When the Russians now exercised in Eastern Europe the same brutal control they were prepared to have Washington exercise in the American sphere of influence, the American protests, given the paranoia produced alike by Russian history and Leninist ideology, no doubt seemed not only an act of hypocrisy but a threat to security. To the Russians, a stroll into the neighborhood easily became a plot to burn down the house: when, for example, damaged American planes made emergency landings in Poland and Hungary, Moscow took this as attempts to organize the local resistance. It is not unusual to suspect one's adversary of doing what one is already doing oneself. At the same time, the cruelty with which the Russians executed their idea of spheres of influence—in a sense, perhaps, an unwitting cruelty, since Stalin treated the East Europeans no worse than he had treated the Russians in the thirties— discouraged the West from accepting the equation (for example, Italy = Rumania) which seemed so self-evident to the Kremlin.

So Moscow very probably, and not unnaturally, perceived the emphasis on self-determination as a systematic and deliberate pressure on Russia's western frontiers. Moreover, the restoration of capitalism to countries freed at frightful cost by the Red Army no doubt struck the Russians as the betrayal of the principles for which *they* were fighting. "That they, the victors," Isaac Deutscher has suggested, "should now preserve an order from which they had experienced nothing but hostility, and could expect nothing but hostility . . . would have been the most miserable anti-climax to their great 'war of liberation.' ". . .

In January 1945 Molotov formally proposed that the United States grant Russia a $6 billion credit for postwar reconstruction. With characteristic tact he explained that he was doing this as a favor to save America from a postwar depression. The proposal seems to have been diffidently made and diffidently received. Roosevelt requested that the matter "not be pressed further" on the American side until he had a chance to talk with Stalin; but the Russians did not follow it up either at Yalta in February (save for a single glancing reference) or during the Stalin-Hopkins talks in May or at Potsdam. Finally the proposal was renewed in the very different political atmosphere of August. This time Washington inexplicably mislaid the request during the transfer of the records of the Foreign Economic Administration to the State Department. It did not turn up again until March 1946. Of course this was impossible for the Russians to believe; it is hard enough even for those acquainted with the capacity of the American government for incompetence to believe; and it only strengthened Soviet suspicions of American purposes.

The American credit was one conceivable form of Western contribution to Russian reconstruction. Another was lend-lease, and the possibility of reconstruction aid under the lend-lease protocol had already been discussed in 1944. But in May 1945 Russia, like Britain, suffered from Truman's abrupt termination of lend-lease shipments—"unfortunate and even brutal," Stalin told Hopkins, adding that, if it was "designed as pressure on the Russians in order to soften them up, then it was a fundamental mistake." A third form was German reparations. Here Stalin in demanding $10 billion in reparations for the Soviet Union made his strongest fight at Yalta. Roosevelt, while agreeing essentially with Churchill's opposition, tried to postpone the matter by accepting the Soviet figure as a "basis for discussion"—a formula which led to future misunderstanding. In short, the Russian hope for major Western assistance in postwar reconstruction foundered on three events which the Kremlin could well have interpreted respectively as deliberate sabotage (the loan request), blackmail (lend-lease cancellation) and pro-Germanism (reparations).

Actually the American attempt to settle the fourth lend-lease protocol was generous and the Russians for their own reasons declined to come to an agreement. It is not clear, though, that satisfying Moscow on any of these financial scores would have made much essential difference. It might have persuaded some doves in the Kremlin that the U.S. government was genuinely friendly; it might have persuaded some hawks that the American anxiety for Soviet friendship was such that Moscow could do as it wished without inviting challenge from the United States. It would, in short, merely have reinforced both sides of the Kremlin debate; it would hardly have reversed deeper tendencies toward the deterioration of political relationships. Economic deals were surely subordinate to the quality of mutual political confidence; and here, in the months after Yalta, the decay was steady.

The Cold War had now begun. It was the product not of a decision but of a dilemma. Each side felt compelled to adopt policies which the other could not but regard as a threat to the principles of the peace. Each then felt compelled to undertake defensive measures. Thus the Russians saw no choice but to consolidate their security in Eastern Europe. The Americans, regarding Eastern Europe as the first step toward Western Europe, responded by asserting their interest in the zone the Russians deemed vital to their security. The Russians concluded that the West was resuming its old course of capitalist encirclement; that it was purposefully laying the foundation for anti-Soviet régimes in the area defined by the blood of centuries as crucial to Russian survival. Each side believed with passion that future international stability depended on the success of its own conception of world order. Each side, in pursuing its own clearly indicated and deeply cherished principles, was only confirming the fear of the other that it was bent on aggression.

Very soon the process began to acquire a cumulative momentum. The impending collapse of Germany thus provoked new troubles: the Russians, for example, sincerely feared that the West was planning a separate surrender of the German armies in Italy in a way which would release troops for

Hitler's eastern front, as they subsequently feared that the Nazis might succeed in surrendering Berlin to the West. This was the context in which the atomic bomb now appeared. Though the revisionist argument that Truman dropped the bomb less to defeat Japan than to intimidate Russia is not convincing, this thought unquestionably appealed to some in Washington as at least an advantageous side-effect of Hiroshima.

So the machinery of suspicion and counter-suspicion, action and counter-action, was set in motion. But, given relations among traditional national states, there was still no reason, even with all the postwar jostling, why this should not have remained a manageable situation. What made it unmanageable, what caused the rapid escalation of the Cold War and in another two years completed the division of Europe, was a set of considerations which this account has thus far excluded.

Up to this point, the discussion has considered the schism within the wartime coalition as if it were entirely the result of disagreements among national states. Assuming this framework, there was unquestionably a failure of communication between America and Russia, a misperception of signals and, as time went on, a mounting tendency to ascribe ominous motives to the other side. It seems hard, for example, to deny that American postwar policy created genuine difficulties for the Russians and even assumed a threatening aspect for them. All this the revisionists have rightly and usefully emphasized.

But the great omission of the revisionists—and also the fundamental explanation of the speed with which the Cold War escalated—lies precisely in the fact that the Soviet Union was *not* a traditional national state.[2] This is where the "mirror image," invoked by some psychologists, falls down. For the Soviet Union was a phenomenon very different from America or Britain: it was a totalitarian state, endowed with an all-explanatory, all-consuming ideology, committed to the infallibility of government and party, still in a somewhat messianic mood, equating dissent with treason, and ruled by a dictator who, for all his quite extraordinary abilities, had his paranoid moments.

Marxism-Leninism gave the Russian leaders a view of the world according to which all societies were inexorably destined to proceed along appointed roads by appointed stages until they achieved the classless nirvana. Moreover, given the resistance of the capitalists to this development, the existence of any non-communist state was *by definition* a threat to the Soviet Union. "As long as capitalism and socialism exist," Lenin wrote, "we cannot live in peace: in the end, one or the other will triumph—a funeral

2. This is the classical revisionist fallacy—the assumption of the rationality, or at least of the traditionalism, of states where ideology and social organization have created a different range of motives. So the Second World War revisionists omit the totalitarian dynamism of Nazism and the fanaticism of Hitler, as the Civil War revisionists omit the fact that the slavery system was producing a doctrinaire closed society in the American South. For a consideration of some of these issues, see "The Causes of the Civil War: A Note on Historical Sentimentalism" in my "The Politics of Hope" (Boston, 1963).

dirge will be sung either over the Soviet Republic or over world capitalism."

Stalin and his associates, whatever Roosevelt or Truman did or failed to
do, were bound to regard the United States as the enemy, not because of
this deed or that, but because of the primordial fact that America was the
leading capitalist power and thus, by Leninist syllogism, unappeasably
hostile, driven by the logic of its system to oppose, encircle and destroy Soviet Russia. Nothing the United States could have done in 1944–45 would
have abolished this mistrust, required and sanctified as it was by Marxist
gospel—nothing short of the conversion of the United States into a Stalinist despotism; and even this would not have sufficed, as the experience of
Jugoslavia and China soon showed, unless it were accompanied by total
subservience to Moscow. So long as the United States remained a capitalist
democracy, no American policy, given Moscow's theology, could hope to
win basic Soviet confidence, and every American action was poisoned from
the source. So long as the Soviet Union remained a messianic state, ideology compelled a steady expansion of communist power. . . .

Stalin alone could have made any difference. Yet Stalin, in spite of the
impression of sobriety and realism he made on Westerners who saw him
during the Second World War, was plainly a man of deep and morbid obsessions and compulsions. When he was still a young man, Lenin had criticized his rude and arbitrary ways. A reasonably authoritative observer
(N. S. Khrushchev) later commented, "These negative characteristics of his
developed steadily and during the last years acquired an absolutely insuf-
ferable character." His paranoia, probably set off by the suicide of his wife
in 1932, led to the terrible purges of the mid-thirties and the wanton murder of thousands of his Bolshevik comrades. "Everywhere and in everything," Khrushchev says of this period, "he saw 'enemies,' 'double-dealers'
and 'spies.'" The crisis of war evidently steadied him in some way, though
Khrushchev speaks of his "nervousness and hysteria . . . even after the war
began." The madness, so rigidly controlled for a time, burst out with new
and shocking intensity in the postwar years. "After the war," Khrushchev
testifies,

the situation became even more complicated. Stalin became even more capri-
cious, irritable and brutal; in particular, his suspicion grew. His persecution
mania reached unbelievable dimensions. . . . He decided everything, without any
consideration for anyone or anything.

Stalin's wilfulness showed itself . . . also in the international relations of the
Soviet Union. . . . He had completely lost a sense of reality; he demonstrated his
suspicion and haughtiness not only in relation to individuals in the USSR, but in
relation to whole parties and nations.

A revisionist fallacy has been to treat Stalin as just another Realpolitik
statesman, as Second World War revisionists see Hitler as just another
Stresemann or Bismarck. But the record makes it clear that in the end
nothing could satisfy Stalin's paranoia. His own associates failed. Why

does anyone suppose that any conceivable American policy would have succeeded?

An analysis of the origins of the Cold War which leaves out these factors —the intransigence of Leninist ideology, the sinister dynamics of a totalitarian society and the madness of Stalin—is obviously incomplete. It was these factors which made it hard for the West to accept the thesis that Russia was moved only by a desire to protect its security and would be satisfied by the control of Eastern Europe; it was these factors which charged the debate between universalism and spheres of influence with apocalyptic potentiality.

Leninism and totalitarianism created a structure of thought and behavior which made postwar collaboration between Russia and America—in any normal sense of civilized intercourse between national states—inherently impossible. The Soviet dictatorship of 1945 simply could not have survived such a collaboration. Indeed, nearly a quarter-century later, the Soviet régime, though it has meanwhile moved a good distance, could still hardly survive it without risking the release inside Russia of energies profoundly opposed to communist despotism. As for Stalin, he may have represented the only force in 1945 capable of overcoming Stalinism, but the very traits which enabled him to win absolute power expressed terrifying instabilities of mind and temperament and hardly offered a solid foundation for a peaceful world.

The difference between America and Russia in 1945 was that some Americans fundamentally believed that, over a long run, a modus vivendi with Russia was possible; while the Russians, so far as one can tell, believed in no more than a short-run modus vivendi with the United States.

Harriman and Kennan, this narrative has made clear, took the lead in warning Washington about the difficulties of short-run dealings with the Soviet Union. But both argued that, if the United States developed a rational policy and stuck to it, there would be, after long and rough passages, the prospect of eventual clearing. "I am, as you know," Harriman cabled Washington in early April, "a most earnest advocate of the closest possible understanding with the Soviet Union so that what I am saying relates only to how best to attain such understanding." Kennan has similarly made it clear that the function of his containment policy was "to tide us over a difficult time and bring us to the point where we could discuss effectively with the Russians the dangers and drawbacks this status quo involved, and to arrange with them for its peaceful replacement by a better and sounder one." The subsequent careers of both men attest to the honesty of these statements.

There is no corresponding evidence on the Russian side that anyone seriously sought a modus vivendi in these terms. Stalin's choice was whether his long-term ideological and national interests would be better served by a short-run truce with the West or by an immediate resumption of pressure. In October 1945 Stalin indicated to Harriman at Sochi that he planned to adopt the second course—that the Soviet Union was going isolationist. No doubt the succession of problems with the United States contributed to this decision, but the basic causes most probably lay elsewhere: in the developing situations in Eastern Europe, in Western Europe and in the United States.

In Eastern Europe, Stalin was still for a moment experimenting with techniques of control. But he must by now have begun to conclude that he had underestimated the hostility of the people to Russian dominion. The Hungarian elections in November would finally convince him that the Yalta formula was a road to anti-Soviet governments. At the same time, he was feeling more strongly than ever a sense of his opportunities in Western Europe. The other half of the Continent lay unexpectedly before him, politically demoralized, economically prostrate, militarily defenseless. The hunting would be better and safer than he had anticipated. As for the United States, the alacrity of postwar demobilization must have recalled Roosevelt's offhand remark at Yalta that "two years would be the limit" for keeping American troops in Europe. And, despite Dr. Eugene Varga's doubts about the imminence of American economic breakdown, Marxist theology assured Stalin that the United States was heading into a bitter postwar depression and would be consumed with its own problems. If the condition of Eastern Europe made unilateral action seem essential in the interests of Russian security, the condition of Western Europe and the United States offered new temptations for communist expansion. The Cold War was now in full swing.

It still had its year of modulations and accommodations. Secretary Byrnes conducted his long and fruitless campaign to persuade the Russians that America only sought governments in East Europe "both friendly to the Soviet Union and representative of all the democratic elements of the country." Crises were surmounted in Trieste and Iran. Secretary Marshall evidently did not give up hope of the modus vivendi until the Moscow conference of foreign secretaries of March 1947. Even then, the Soviet Union was invited to participate in the Marshall Plan.

The point of no return came on July 2, 1947, when Molotov, after bringing 89 technical specialists with him to Paris and evincing initial interest in the project for European reconstruction, received the hot flash from the Kremlin, denounced the whole idea and walked out of the conference. For the next fifteen years the Cold War raged unabated, passing out of historical ambiguity into the realm of good versus evil and breeding on both sides simplifications, stereotypes and self-serving absolutes, often couched in interchangeable phrases. Under the pressure even America, for a deplorable decade, forsook its pragmatic and pluralist traditions, posed as God's appointed messenger to ignorant and sinful man and followed the Soviet example in looking to a world remade in its own image.

In retrospect, if it is impossible to see the Cold War as a case of American aggression and Russian response, it is also hard to see it as a pure case of Russian aggression and American response. "In what is truly tragic," wrote Hegel, "there must be valid moral powers on both the sides which come into collision. . . . Both suffer loss and yet both are mutually justified." In this sense, the Cold War had its tragic elements. The question remains whether it was an instance of Greek tragedy—as Auden has called it, "the tragedy of necessity," where the feeling aroused in the spectator is "What a pity it had to be this way"—or of Christian tragedy, "the tragedy of possibility," where the feeling aroused is "What a pity it was this way when it might have been otherwise."

Once something has happened, the historian is tempted to assume that it had to happen; but this may often be a highly unphilosophical assumption. The Cold War could have been avoided only if the Soviet Union had not been possessed by convictions both of the infallibility of the communist word and of the inevitability of a communist world. These convictions transformed an impasse between national states into a religious war, a tragedy of possibility into one of necessity. One might wish that America had preserved the poise and proportion of the first years of the Cold War and had not in time succumbed to its own forms of self-righteousness. But the most rational of American policies could hardly have averted the Cold War. Only today, as Russia begins to recede from its messianic mission and to accept, in practice if not yet in principle, the permanence of the world of diversity, only now can the hope flicker that this long, dreary, costly contest may at last be taking on forms less dramatic, less obsessive and less dangerous to the future of mankind.

5. *Hans J. Morgenthau: Arguing About the Cold War: A Balance Sheet*

The following article by Hans J. Morgenthau, Albert A. Michelson Distinguished Service Professor at the University of Chicago, discusses a later phase of the Cold War and raises the question of the validity of even thinking in terms of a "cold war" any longer. Morgenthau does not pretend to have any easy answers to the problems which the future may hold; in fact, he is cautious about what the problems may be. But is it possible to discern what policies he might think wise for the United States, or the Soviet Union, to adopt in the future? Is he essentially optimistic or pessimistic? Utopian or realistic?

I n the summer of 1965, Mr. Robert M. Hutchins (President of the Center for the Study of Democratic Institutions and former President of the University of Chicago) issued *A Declaration to End the Cold War* which started thus:

I propose to ask the President of the United States to make the following statement at the next session of the General Assembly of the United Nations: "I hereby declare the Cold War is over. . . ."

From Hans J. Morgenthau, "Arguing About the Cold War: A Balance Sheet," *Encounter*, May 1967, pp. 37, 39–41. Reprinted by permission of *Encounter* and the author.

There is something engaging in the neat precision of this proposal: the captain of a football team blowing the whistle because he thinks that the time has come to quit. However, the practicality of this proposal to end the Cold War is predicated upon a particular assumption concerning its origin. The President of the United States would indeed have it in his power to end the Cold War by unilateral declaration if the Cold War had started by such a declaration on his part. Yet nobody would seriously argue that it was as a result of someone's conscious decision. Quite the contrary, it is generally recognised that it grew out of a series of circumstances and policies whose cumulative effects imperceptibly brought to the fore those irreconcilable interests and hostile policies associated with "Cold War."

What distinguishes the Cold War from the many hostile confrontations history records (and, hence, justifies its name) are two factors: the impossibility for all concerned, given the interests at stake and the positions taken, to pursue conciliatory policies which through the instruments of give-and-take and compromise might have led to a settlement of the outstanding issues; and the necessity (following from this impossibility) for all concerned to protect and promote their interests through unilateral direct pressure on the opponent's will by all means available—diplomatic, military, economic, subversive—short of the actual use of force. Thus, we have been in a "war" because the purpose of all concerned was not to accommodate the other side in return for accommodation on its part, but rather to compel the other side to yield. "Roll-back" and "liberation" are terms of war which imply not an agreed-upon accommodation but unilateral action. The threat of military force, if the other side should not yield its position in West Berlin, partakes of the same characteristic. But while both sides have used the techniques of war rather than diplomacy to achieve their ends, they have been very careful not to resort to force, at least in their relations with each other. Thus we have been in a "war" in so far as unilateral techniques are the instruments of war and not of diplomacy; and the war has been a "cold" one because the use of force upon a major opponent was excluded from the instruments of unilateral action. . . .

The Cold War changed its character drastically under the impact of the hot war in Korea. The North Korean aggression was interpreted by the West as the opening shot in Moscow's campaign for the conquest of the world. It seemed to provide the clinching proof for the assumption held by the West since the beginning of the Cold War that Stalin's foreign policy was in line of succession not to the imperialism of the Tsars but to the world-wide Bolshevik aspirations of Lenin and Trotsky. . . .

The misinterpretation of the North Korean aggression as part of a grand design at world conquest originating in and controlled by Moscow resulted in a drastic militarisation of the Cold War in the form of a conventional and nuclear armaments race, the frantic search for alliances, and the establishment of military bases. This militarisation was both the effect and the cause of the increased expectation that the Cold War might develop into a hot one. That expectation, shared by both sides, in turn increased the likelihood of such a development. . . .

It is against this background that one must judge the import for the Cold War of Khrushchev's ascent to power. The view is widely held—and Mr. Halle reflects it—that, in terms of the conduct of the Cold War, Khrushchev was an improvement over Stalin; for Khrushchev is supposed to have sought the abatement of the Cold War through what he called "relaxation of tensions." I have never shared this view and can only summarise here the arguments which I presented a decade ago in order to show that Khrushchev changed the quality and increased the range and the intensity of the Cold War but contributed nothing to its abatement. While Stalin conducted a Cold War of position, Khrushchev was the champion of a Cold War of movement. When Khrushchev spoke of relaxation of tensions, he wanted the West to stop challenging the status quo of 1945. In order to force the West to do this, he himself challenged the status quo of West Berlin at the risk of war. But in order to maintain the status quo of the Soviet empire he went to war in Hungary with methods as ruthless as any Stalin had ever used.

However, Khrushchev showed himself as the innovator of the Cold War of movement by making the whole world its theatre and by using new methods of waging it. Here he is the heir not of Stalin and the Tsars, but indeed of Lenin and Trotsky. Khrushchev revived the Bolshevik expectation of the communisation of the whole world as an immediate goal of Soviet foreign policy and made it the basis for a new policy which he called "competitive coexistence" tied to support for "wars of national liberation." His aims were the aims of Lenin and Trotsky; and the methods he used to achieve those aims were his original contribution to the Cold War. These methods run the whole gamut from military intervention and threats to diplomatic pressure, foreign aid and trade, support of subversion, and the exploitation of the new technological prestige of the Soviet Union. Thus he threatened war with Great Britain and France over Suez and with the United States over Cuba. He competed with the U.S.A. and China for the allegiance of the new and emerging nations, and he transformed Cuba into a political and military outpost of the Soviet Union. This quantitative and qualitative transformation of the Cold War was the work of Khrushchev not Stalin. It was Stalin, not Khrushchev, who said to Eden that the trouble with Hitler was that he didn't know when to stop: "I know when to stop." Khrushchev did not know it, or he learned it only in 1962.

The post-Khrushchev phase of the Cold War is characterised by the extension of movement to the nations of Europe—east and west. In Europe, the aim of Khrushchev's Cold War of movement was identical with that of Stalin's Cold War of position: the stabilisation of the political and territorial status quo of the immediate post-war period. In these two types of Cold War, two blocs opposed each other as political and military instruments of the two superpowers. Now the two tightly controlled blocks have been replaced by traditional alliances of varying closeness. Across what was once the boundary of the two blocks, whose impenetrable proximity was symbolised by the Iron Curtain, the nations of Eastern and Western

Europe move in search of new alignments and configurations, putting into question not only the boundary but even the viability of the spheres of influence of the post-war period.

In the course of these movements, unfettered to an ever-increasing degree by the stifling weight of the two super-powers, the natural weights of individual national power have reasserted themselves. Thus West Germany as the second most powerful nation on the European continent exerts a new attraction upon France, on the one hand, and upon countries like Czechoslovakia and Rumania on the other. In consequence, East Germany, once the Western spearhead of the Soviet bloc, might well become an island, precariously placed in a moving sea and maintained in that position only as long as the Soviet Union is able and willing to maintain it.

Do these developments spell the end of the Cold War? There is a tendency to answer that question in the affirmative, not in view of the relevant factors of interests and power in which the Cold War originated and which have kept it going for more than two decades, but in view of a superficial and obsolescent criterion: the degree of hostility exhibited by the United States and the Soviet Union in their relations with each other. From the fact that the U.S. and the U.S.S.R. have not challenged each other openly in recent years in Europe and their diplomatic relations are more nearly normal than they used to be, the conclusion is drawn that there is nothing for them to fight about and that therefore the Cold War has ended. However, the arms race continues, and military bases remain intact. For the Americans and the Russians continue to oppose, and compete with, each other throughout the world. Viet Nam, the Middle East, and Somalia are three spectacular cases in point. According to the *Economist* (19 November 1966):

> The Middle East is one of the parts of the world where Cold War politics are far from dead; Russia and the West have their chosen protégés, and to preserve the balance keep them armed. The resultant arms race is something outsiders ought to get excited, as well as gloomy, about.

In Europe the conflict of interests that has pitted the United States against the Soviet Union since the end of the Second World War persists, even though it has taken on a new appearance. And the question which the Cold War brought to the fore two decades ago remains unanswered: which way is Germany going to turn? Khrushchev saw clearly the crucial importance of that issue and expressed in a number of private conversations his confidence that sooner or later there would be "another Rapallo," *i.e.*, another alignment between the Soviet Union and Germany against the West.

This remains the crucial issue today as it has been for two decades, and it is a matter of secondary importance whether it is going to be fought out through the unilateral methods of the Cold War or through the traditional methods of diplomacy. The answer to that question depends primarily on the policies to be pursued by the Soviet Union. Thus far it has addressed

West Germany in the Cold-War language of Stalin and Khrushchev. But how is it going to act? Will it try to protect the remnants of its empire against the attraction of West Germany through the unilateral methods of the Cold War? Or will it try to exchange what is left of that empire for a German-Soviet combination, which might promise to draw all of Europe into its orbit? Or will it use both methods simultaneously, or alternately, as the situation might suggest?

Thus even if the Cold War should come to "an end"—and especially if it should—the diplomacy of the West (and, more particularly, of the United States) will have to deal with issues infinitely more complex, more risky, and also more promising than those it dealt with successfully during the first two periods of the Cold War. Until now, its main task has been to hold the line, and it has held it. It is an open question whether a less rigid Western diplomacy would have had a chance in 1953 and then again in 1956 to push that line farther east. In any event, from now on, the objective conditions of Europe rather than political rhetoric will pose the question as to where that line should be redrawn and whether there will be a line at all.

X

The Impact of Freudian Thought

Occasionally in human history, a single creative thinker puts his mark upon an entire era and gives historians an excuse for attaching his name to that whole age. Thus we often speak of the Age of Socrates, of the Age of Newton, of the Age of Darwin; and we have heard our own times described as the Freudian Age. It is easy enough to criticize such shorthand labels, and to point out how oversimplified and even misleading they can be. It is quite proper to quibble over the real relationship between the man and his time, and to ask whether a thinker does not simply reflect or symbolize the mood of an era, rather than create or reshape that mood. Perhaps the late nineteenth century would have been "Darwinian" in spirit even without Darwin; perhaps the twentieth would be "Freudian" even without Freud.

Such speculation, though relevant, is probably not very profitable. Sigmund Freud did exist, and his ideas did gradually permeate western thought—aided, no doubt, by the chronic tensions and upheaval of the age. Prior to 1914, the impact was relatively slight, even though Freud had worked out most of his ideas and his techniques during the 1890's and the early 1900's. He had attracted a small coterie of dedicated disciples, some of whom (notably C. G. Jung and Alfred Adler) were eventually to break with the master and were to found heretical schools. The full flood of Freudian influence came after the first world war, both in Europe and in the United States; by the time the second postwar period arrived, Freudian terminology had become part of everyday language, and Freudian or neo-Freudian conceptions of man and society had penetrated not only literature and the arts, but political and social theorizing as well. Often, no doubt, the penetration was not very deep, and was confined to the slipshod use of a few Freudian catchwords; many users of Freudian phrases had never read a page of Freud. But the influence of a thinker, or the pervasive character of his ideas, is not always measured by his rating on the best-seller lists, or by the number of man-hours that have been devoted to reading him in the original. Not every Darwinian had read *The Origin of Species;* not every Marxian has read *Das Kapital.*

Freud is often viewed as the protagonist of an irrationalist revolt. His defenders have an easy time refuting such a charge; they can show that he was a man of the positivist age, that he intended (though perhaps not always successfully) to cling to the most rigorous scientific method, to "the basic tenets of controlled inquiry." Orthodox Freudians can point out that if the master's views were later distorted by some of his disciples and by the general public, no one ought to blame Freud himself for the distortion. They can also contend that Freud never set himself up as a philosopher who presumed to provide a new *Weltanschauung* for the age. Yet in his later years, Freud did go well beyond the role of the mere clinician seeking a therapy for mental illness; in such essays as *Civilization and its Discontents* (1930), he advanced some broader conceptions of man and society, and even suggested that entire systems or epochs of civilization may at times become neurotic. If Darwin made no direct contribution to the "social Darwinism" created by his followers, Freud surely bears some responsibility for what one might call "social Freudianism."

Although Freud himself contended that man's most basic drives (the love instinct and the death instinct) are antisocial in nature, and that the repression of these drives produces frustration and neurosis, he probably never believed that man and society are totally irreconcilable. Yet it is not surprising that some of his disciples arrived at that conclusion. "It is a shattering experience," writes one American scholar, "for anyone seriously committed to the Western traditions of morality and rationality to take a steadfast, unflinching look at what Freud has to say." For ". . . it begins to be apparent that mankind, in all its restless striving and progress, has no idea of what it really wants." [1] Neo-Freudians, on the other hand, have softened the pessimistic mood of the orthodox doctrine, have shifted the major emphasis from the id to the ego, and have sought to argue that man and society can be reconciled through some sort of "social adjustment"—through a reorganization of society that would permit the spontaneous development of the "integrated personality." But such a conclusion, the orthodox Freudians argue, is a tender-minded perversion of the master's thought; it pushes aside Freud's "dark vision of the embattled self" in favor of "cheery platitudes"; it abandons all that is challenging and serious in the Freudian insights.[2]

It may be argued that any serious discussion of the Freudian impact in the twentieth century ought to be preceded by extended study of the Freudian doctrines themselves, both through his own writings and through the commentaries of trained psychoanalysts. Yet the broader impact of Freudianism on our age is conveyed through the works of nonprofessionals: writers, artists, social scientists, historians. The selections that follow are nonspecialized in nature; they provide a variety of views about the Freudian impact, most of them from literate and perceptive observers of the contemporary scene. If Americans outnumber Europeans among them, that does not mean that the Freudian impact has been a purely American phenomenon, but only that public debate about it has been more vigorous in this country.

Any discussion of Freud's influence must eventually confront a central question: do his theories knock all the props from under the older Enlightenment view of man as an essentially rational being, capable of self-government and self-improvement? Or can the Freudian insights be integrated somehow with the Enlightenment view, in order to produce a sounder and more workable synthesis that may serve as the base for a functioning society? Freud's bitterest critics (and some of his most vigorous defenders as well) will reject that possibility. Many neo-Freudians, on the other hand, insist that a synthesis is both possible and necessary. If it is true (as Sidney Hook argues) that "the nuggets of philosophical wisdom . . . mined from Freud's writings have long been commonplaces in an

---

1. Norman O. Brown, *Life Against Death: The Psychoanalytic Meaning of History* (New York: Random House, 1959), pp. xi–xii.

2. Philip Rieff, *Freud: the Mind of the Moralist* (New York: Viking Press, 1959), p. 56.

ethical tradition that stems from Socrates to John Dewey . . . ,"[3] then it ought to be possible to reconcile Freud's findings with that long humanistic tradition, even though the immediate impact of Freudianism may seem so disruptive as to portend a kind of ethical and social disintegration.

I. *Alfred Kazin: The Freudian Revolution Analyzed*

Like most anniversaries, the centenary of Sigmund Freud's birth brought a rash of articles and books to commemorate or analyze his work. One of the best of these—sympathetic and perceptive, with an occasional touch of irony —was a brief essay by Alfred Kazin, the noted author, teacher, and literary critic. Kazin, who was born and educated in New York City, taught in several American universities before becoming Distinguished Professor of English in the State University of New York (Stony Brook). He has written a number of essays on psychoanalysis, and is one of the few laymen who has been invited to lecture to audiences of analysts.

I t is hard to believe that Sigmund Freud was born over a century ago. Although Freud has long been a household name (and, in fact, dominates many a household one could mention), his theories still seem too "advanced," they touch too bluntly on the most intimate side of human relations, for us to picture Freud himself coming out of a world that in all other respects now seems so quaint.

Although Freud has influenced even people who have never heard of him, not all his theories have been accepted even by his most orthodox followers, while a great many of his essential ideas are rejected even by many psychoanalysts. In one sense Freud himself is still battling for recognition, for because of the tabooed nature of the materials in which he worked and the unusually speculative quality of his mind, Freud still seems to many people more an irritant than a classic.

On the other hand, Freud's influence, which started from the growing skepticism about civilization and morality after the First World War, is now beyond description. Freudianism gave sanction to the increasing exasperation with public standards as opposed to private feelings; it upheld the truths of human nature as against the hypocrisies and cruelties of conventional morality; it stressed the enormous role that sex plays in man's imaginative life, in his relations to his parents, in the symbolism of language.

It is impossible to think of the greatest names in modern literature and art—Thomas Mann, James Joyce, Franz Kafka, T. S. Eliot, Ernest Hemingway, William Faulkner, Pablo Picasso, Paul Klee—without realizing

3. *The New York Times Book Review*, June 24, 1962, p. 7.

From Alfred Kazin, "The Freudian Revolution Analyzed," in *The New York Times Magazine*, May 6, 1956. Reprinted by permission of the author and of the editors of *The New York Times*.

our debt to Freud's exploration of dreams, myths, symbols and the imaginative profundity of man's inner life. Even those who believe that original sin is a safer guide to the nature of man than any other can find support in Freud's gloomy doubts about man's capacity for progress. For quite other reasons, Freud has found followers even among Catholic psychiatrists, who believe that Freud offers a believable explanation of neurosis and a possible cure, and so leaves the sufferer cured to practice his faith in a rational way.

Many psychologists who disagree with Freud's own materialism have gratefully adopted many of Freud's diagnoses, and although he himself was chary about the psychoanalytical technique in serious mental illness, more and more psychiatrists now follow his technique, or some adaptation of it. For no other system of thought in modern times, except the great religions, has been adopted by so many people as a systematic interpretation of individual behavior. Consequently, to those who have no other belief, Freudianism sometimes serves as a philosophy of life.

Freud, a tough old humanist with a profoundly skeptical mind, would have been shocked or amused by the degree to which everything is sometimes explained by "Freudian" doctrines. He offered us not something that applies dogmatically to all occasions, but something useful, a principle of inquiry into those unconscious forces that are constantly pulling people apart, both in themselves and from each other.

Freud's extraordinary achievement was to show us, in scientific terms, the primacy of natural desire, the secret wishes we proclaim in our dreams, the mixture of love and shame and jealousy in our relations to our parents, the child as father to the man, the deeply buried instincts that make us natural beings and that go back to the forgotten struggles of the human race. Until Freud, novelists and dramatists had never dared to think that science would back up their belief that personal passion is a stronger force in people's lives than socially accepted morality. Thanks to Freud, these insights now form a widely shared body of knowledge.

In short, Freud had the ability, such as is given to very few individuals, to introduce a wholly new factor into human knowledge; to impress it upon people's minds as something for which there was evidence. He revealed a part of reality that many people before him had guessed at, but which no one before him was able to describe as systematically and convincingly as he did. In the same way that one associates the discovery of certain fundamentals with Copernicus, Newton, Darwin, Einstein, so one identifies many of one's deepest motivations with Freud. His name is no longer the name of a man; like "Darwin," it is now synonymous with a part of nature.

This is the very greatest kind of influence that a man can have. It means that people use his name to signify something in the world of nature which, they believe, actually exists. A man's name has become identical with a phenomenon in nature, with a cause in nature, with a "reality" that we accept—even when we don't want to accept it. Every hour of every day now, and especially in America, there are people who cannot forget a name, or make a slip of the tongue, or feel depressed; who cannot begin a love affair, or end a marriage, without wondering what the "Freudian" reason may be.

No one can count the number of people who now think of any crisis as a personal failure, and who turn to a psychoanalyst or to psychoanalytical literature for an explanation of their suffering where once they would have turned to a minister or to the Bible for consolation. Freudian terms are now part of our thought. There are innumerable people who will never admit that they believe a word of his writings, who nevertheless, "unconsciously," as they would say, have learned to look for "motivations," to detect "compensations," to withhold a purely moralistic judgment in favor of individual understanding, to prize sexual satisfaction as a key to individual happiness, and to characterize people by the depth and urgency of their passions rather than by the nobility of their professions.

For much of this "Freudian" revolution, Freud himself is not responsible. And in evaluating the general effect of Freud's doctrines on the modern scene, especially in America, it is important to distinguish between the hard, biological, fundamentally classical thought of Freud, who was a determinist, a pessimist, and a genius, from the thousands of little cultural symptoms and "psychological" theories, the pretensions and self-indulgences, which are often found these days in the prosperous middle-class culture that has responded most enthusiastically to Freud.

There is, for example, the increasing tendency to think that all problems are "psychological," to ignore the real conflicts in society that underlie politics and to interpret politicians and candidates—especially those you don't like—in terms of "sexual" motives. There is the cunning use of "Freudian" terms in advertising, which has gone so far that nowadays there's a pretty clear suggestion that the girl comes with the car. There are all the psychologists who study "motivations," and sometimes invent them, so as to get you to buy two boxes of cereal where one would have done before.

There are the horrendous movies and slick plays which not only evade the writer's need to explain characters honestly, but, by attributing to everybody what one can only call the Freudian nightmare, have imposed upon a credulous public the belief that it may not be art but that it is "true"—that is, sex—and so must be taken seriously. And, since this is endless but had better stop somewhere, there are all the people who have confused their "urges" with art, have learned in all moral crises to blame their upbringing rather than themselves, and tend to worship the psychoanalyst as God.

The worst of the "Freudian revolution" is the increasing tendency to attribute all criticism of our society to personal "sickness." The rebel is looked on as neurotic rather than someone making a valid protest. Orthodox Freudians tend to support the status quo as a matter of course and to blame the individual for departing from it. Freud himself never made such a mistake, and no one would have been able to convince him that the Viennese world around him was "normal."

The identification of a military group, or a class, or a culture, with an absolute to which we must all be adjusted at any price is a dangerous trend. And the worst of it is that to many people psychoanalysts now signify "authority," so that people believe them on any and all subjects.

On the other hand, the greatest and most beautiful effect of Freudianism is the increasing awareness of childhood as the most important single influence on personal development. This profound cherishing of childhood has opened up wholly new relationships between husbands and wives, as well as between parents and children, and it represents—though often absurdly overanxious—a peculiar new tenderness in modern life. Similarly, though Freud's psychology is weakest on women, there can be no doubt that, again in America, the increasing acknowledgment of the importance of sexual satisfaction has given to women an increasing sense of their individual dignity and their specific needs.

But the greatest revolution of all, and one that really explains the overwhelming success of Freudianism in America, lies in the general insistence on individual fulfillment, satisfaction and happiness. Odd as it may seem to us, who take our striving toward these things for granted, the insistence on personal happiness represents the most revolutionary force in modern times. And it is precisely because our own tradition works toward individual self-realization, because private happiness does seem to us to be both an important ideal and a practical goal, that Freudianism has found so many recruits in this country. . . .

Freud's work appealed to the increasing regard for individual experience that is one of the great themes of modern literature and art. The sensitiveness to each individual as a significant register of the consciousness in general, the artistic interest in carrying human consciousness to its farthest limits—it was this essential side of modern art that Freud's researches encouraged and deepened. He brought, as it were, the authority of science to the inner promptings of art, and thus helped writers and artists to feel that their interest in myths, in symbols, in dreams was on the side of "reality," of science, itself, when it shows the fabulousness of the natural world.

Even if we regret, as we must, the fact that Freud's influence has been identified with a great many shallow and commercially slick ideas, the fact remains that if Freud's ideas appealed generally to the inwardness which is so important to modern writers and artists, it was because Freud thoroughly won his case against many aggressive but less intelligent opponents. . . .

Civilization as we know it, Freud said, had been built up on man's heroic sacrifice of instinct. Only, Freud issued the warning that more and more men would resent this sacrifice, would wonder if civilization was worth the price. And how profoundly right he was in this can be seen not only in the Nazi madness that drove him as an old man out of Vienna, that almost cost him his life, but in the increasing disdain for culture, in the secret lawlessness that has become, under the conformist surface, a sign of increasing personal irritation and rebelliousness in our society. More and more, the sexual freedom of our time seems to be a way of mentally getting even, of confused protest, and not the pagan enjoyment of instinct that writers like D. H. Lawrence upheld against Freud's gloomy forebodings.

For Freud the continuous sacrifice of "nature" that is demanded by "civilization" meant that it was only through rationality and conscious awareness that maturity could be achieved. Far from counseling license, his most famous formula became—"Where id was, ego shall be"—the id representing the unconscious, the ego our dominant and purposive sense of ourselves. However, consciousness meant for Freud an unyielding insistence on the importance of sexuality. And it was just on this issue that, even before the first World War, his movement broke apart.

Jung went astray, as Freud thought, because he was lulled by the "mystical" side of religion; Adler, through his insistence that not sex but power feelings were primary. Later, Harry Stack Sullivan and Erich Fromm tended to emphasize, as against sex, the importance of personal relatedness to others, and nowadays many psychoanalysts tend to value religion much more highly than Freud ever could. But the root of the dissidence was always Freud's forthright insistence on the importance of sexuality and his old-fashioned, mid-nineteenth century positivism. For Freud always emphasized the organic and the physical rather than the social and the "cultural."

In fact, it is now possible to say that it is precisely Freud's old-fashioned scientific rationalism, his need to think of man as a physical being rather than a "psychological" one, that explains the primacy of Freud's discoveries. Psychoanalysis, especially in America, has become more interested in making cures than in making discoveries, and it is significant that there has been very little original thought in the field since Freud.

Freudianism has become a big business, and a very smooth one. The modern Freudian analyst, who is over-busy and who rather complacently uses his theory to explain everything, stands in rather sad contrast to that extraordinary thinker, Sigmund Freud.

Perhaps it is because Freud was born a century ago that he had the old-fashioned belief that nothing—not even a lot of patients—is so important as carrying your ideas beyond the point at which everybody already agrees with you. Nowadays everybody is something of a Freudian, and to many Freudians, the truth is in their keeping, the system is complete. But what mattered most to Freud was relentlessly carrying on the revolution of human thought.

2. *Richard LaPiere: The Freudian Ethic*

The impact of Freudian ideas has been particularly strong upon the so-called behavioral sciences (though perhaps it was reflected more immediately and profoundly in literature and the fine arts). Not all behavioral scientists, however, have welcomed this Freudian intrusion. One of the most vigorous and

From Richard LaPiere, *The Freudian Ethic* (New York: Duell, Sloan and Pearce, 1959), pp. 59–65, 81–82, 183–84, 247, 284–86. Copyright 1959, by Richard LaPiere. Reprinted by permission of Duell, Sloan & Pearce, an affiliate of Meredith Press.

sustained attacks upon the broader consequences of Freudianism may be found in Richard LaPiere's *The Freudian Ethic*. LaPiere, emeritus professor of sociology at Stanford University, builds his case around a contrast between the Protestant ethic—which, he believes, was the code of values that dominated western culture until the twentieth century—and the "Freudian ethic"—which has rapidly been smothering what is left of the older values. He focuses primarily upon the American scene, and finds evidence to support his case in child-rearing practices, educational theory, the treatment of criminals, the downgrading of private enterprise, the growth of "political maternalism," and so on. All of these changes, LaPiere contends, are "malfunctional," and constitute "our unrecognized road to disaster." Although his book has the one-sidedness of a tract, it provides us with a challenging statement of the anti-Freudian case.

The premise upon which the Protestant ethic evolved was the secular supplement to Luther's insistence that the individual human being has a conscience, which can and should be his guide to conduct—the idea that he is capable of independent, rational conduct. This idea was embodied, nearly three centuries later, in the Declaration of Independence as the self-evident truths "that all men are created equal; that they are endowed by their Creator with certain inalienable rights; that among these are life, liberty, and the pursuit of happiness." That Declaration and the political Constitution that was designed to implement it were devised by men of enterprise in order to free men of enterprise from the constraints of a government that still had its roots in the authoritarian tradition of the Middle Ages. These documents, like the Mayflower Compact that had so long preceded them, were attempts to give political sanction to the Protestant ethic. And for a century and a half many, but far from all, of the changes that were worked in American society were in accord with the spirit if not the letter of these testaments to the value and validity of the Protestant ethic.

The rise of Freudian doctrine as the prevailing concept of the nature of man is at once a measure of the decline of the Protestant ethic and a denial of the idea that man is a creature of reason. Freud's idea of man is one that in many respects resembles that which prevailed through the Middle Ages and which was sanctioned by the medieval Church. In the Freudian concept, man is not born free with the right to pursue life, liberty, and happiness; he is shackled by biological urges that can never be freely expressed and that set him in constant and grievous conflict with his society. Life for him must be an unhappy and unending struggle to reconcile, both within himself and between himself and others, forces that are inherently antagonistic. Freud does not say, in the theological manner, that man fell from Grace and must therefore suffer in this life. But he does come to much the same concept of man: that man is by nature (or at least by virtue of the inevitable conflict between man's nature and society) a weak and irresolute creature without the stamina to endure the stresses and strains of living, and who cannot therefore hope to enjoy life on this earth.

There has been interminable debate concerning why Freud devised the particular doctrine that goes under his name. His disciples take the understandable but scientifically untenable position that Freud simply discovered by scientific means the truth about man; his opponents lean to the view that the Freudian doctrine of man is at best a delusion of Freud's and may have been a calculated method of winning him enduring prestige as the founder of a metaphysical cult. Far more tenable, if still unprovable, is the hypothesis that Freud, proceeding in accordance with the intellectual standards of the late nineteenth century, simply invented the various concepts—libido, id, ego, super-ego, Oedipus complex, etc.—that together make up his doctrine in an honest endeavor to comprehend the still largely incomprehensible behavior of neurotic people. At any event, it does seem evident that his idea of the nature and capabilities of man was derived directly from too long and unmitigated exposure to people, his patients, who were incapable of managing their personal affairs, people who did not, for whatever reasons, conform even in outline to the Protestant ethic.

In a sense, Freud's major error lay in assuming that the people who came to him for treatment were representative of mankind in general. For the very fact that his patients came to him for "mental" treatment is *ipso facto* evidence that they were not—unless, indeed, we wish to assume that all men are at all times in need of psychiatric aid. Had Freud been content to accept his explanatory system as a therapeutic rationale for use in the treatment of neurotics, and had his converts also adhered to this view, a quite different result might have obtained. But almost from the outset of his work, Freud insisted that he was interested in developing—or "discovering"—the laws governing all human conduct, not just those that govern, or fail to govern, the conduct of psychologically abnormal individuals.

The atypical character of the people from whom Freud derived his doctrine of man would seem to explain his conviction that men are inherently unstable; and one must assume that his preoccupation with sex, a fixation that is close to monomaniacal, was a function either of his own personality or of those of the patients who came under his observation. The latter assumption is most acceptable, for even the most ardent anti-Freudian must admit that Freud's treatment of sex was aseptic rather than pornographic; and there is some factual basis for this assumption. Most of Freud's patients were not only neurotic but also neurotic middle- and upper-middle-class Viennese Jews. They were not, therefore, even a representative sample of neurotics.

Vienna in the time of Freud, if not since, was the pretentious, cosmopolitan center of an empire that had all but vanished. It was a once-great city in reduced circumstances, a city that had lost many of its economic and political functions and was—to some extent at least—living on its glamorous past. In sociological terms, it was a highly disorganized and demoralized community; in lay terms, it was a city of sin. Apparently the fashion in Vienna at that time was for men and women of means to engage in elaborate, perhaps even highly ritualized, extramarital sexual play. And while keeping up with this fashion may not have bothered greatly the moral consciences of Catholic Austro-Hungarians, who had long been noted for their adaptability, it undoubtedly ran counter to the strict and rigid moral code of bourgeois Jews. It may well be, therefore, that Freud's patients were atypical neurotics, *i.e.*, their mental distress was commonly occasioned by the opposition between their training in sexual morality and the social pressures that demanded violation of that morality. This interpretation of Freud's preoccupation with sex is not, of course, acceptable to Freudians; but it has the dual virtues, over alternative interpretations, of having some factual basis and of shifting the onus for that preoccupation from Freud to his patients. . . .

The Freudian ethic, as it will be termed hereafter, is not a code of licentiousness. It does not, in fact, grant to the individual the ability or right to *do* anything. As a code of conduct the Freudian ethic is entirely negative. It is composed of sentiments and attitudes regarding man's capabilities that, if literally applied, would keep him from attempting anything positive, to say nothing of attempting to devise anything new. For it makes the world about him a hostile and inhospitable place, and it makes him a terrified (unconsciously, of course) and reluctant inhabitant of that world. It even goes further; not only is his external world inimical to his psychic welfare, but this world has been "internalized" to the end that a part of himself intimidates the rest. There is therefore no escaping psychic agony. Should he withdraw from the external world, he will still be at odds with himself.

Philosophically, the Freudian ethic is related not only to that of medieval Europe but also to the ethical ideal of the Greek-Roman stoics. It is like the medieval in that it reduces man to a passive state and unlike it in that it does not provide a higher authority—the Church—to assume responsibility for the individual and guide him in the ways of righteousness. It is like stoic philosophy in that it is contemptuous of the world of external realities and unlike it in that it does not provide a hope that the individual can ignore the world and thereby achieve peace of mind.

Since the Freudian ethic is still undergoing development and since, further, it is negative rather than positive in character, the ethic is at present more a state of mind than an actual ideal of individual conduct. Some appreciation of this state of mind can, perhaps, be gained from the terminology used by those who subscribe to it. In their discourse there is recurrent reference to guilt feeling, personal insecurity, unstructured personality, instability, "internalization" (of hate, envy, and other destructive emotions), "projection" (of anything from hate to love), frustration, aggressive tendencies, trauma, and the all-inclusive term "tensions." Such terms are used in reference not only to recognizably abnormal individuals but to everyone. Still more revealing is the total absence in the Freudian discourse of such terms, prominent in the Protestant ethic, as self-confidence, personal integrity, self-reliance, responsibility, or such very earthy terms as "moral courage," "intestinal fortitude," or, more vulgarly, "guts."

The elements of the Protestant ethic are fairly easy to describe. For one thing, our language abounds in character-designating terms that reflect this ethic; for another, the ethic is structured and positive, rather than amorphous and negative. What the Freudians hold as ideal is adjustment of the individual to his life circumstances—*i.e.*, the maintenance of a precarious balance between his id, ego, and superego, and between all three of these and external circumstances. This adjustment ideal may, in turn, be designated in a variety of positive terms—contentment, complacency, sense of security, and perhaps even apathy. But when an attempt is made to indicate the personal qualities that contribute to the achievement of this ideal state, it is necessary to resort to description by negation. Thus the Freudian ethic comes out something as follows: absence of strong social motivations (the inescapable urges of the libido are, of course, anti-social drives), lack of constraining or inhibiting social principles, lack of supernaturalistic or other fixed faiths (except, of course, faith in the Freudian version of the self), lack of set goals, lack of any rigorous system of personal-social values and sentiments, and complete absence of any sense of obligation toward others.

The Freudians do not deny that men may possess positive personality attributes of the sort incorporated in the Protestant ethic. But to them, such positive characteristics are either the product of the inevitable clash between the individual and society or the consequence of traumatic experiences that have befallen the individual in the course of that conflict. Whatever their source, they are inimical to the individual's psychic welfare; where they exist, they should be exorcised by psychoanalysis; and to prevent their development, society should be remodeled to accord with the Freudian idea of man. No society can really be good, for everything social is contrary to the psychic welfare of the individual. To this end it should avoid inculcating in him any socially prescribed personality attributes—motivations, goals, values, sentiments, or feeling of personal obligation. The individual should not be required or even expected to submit to social authority whatever its character, to accept responsibility for his own or anyone else's welfare, or to be concerned with anything except the preservation of his precarious psychic balance.

In the harsh, unsympathetic terms of the Protestant ethic, the individual who even approximated the Freudian ideal would be a selfish egocentric, an incompetent, a wastrel, an irresponsible, and in general a social parasite unwelcome in the company of respectable men. In the days when men who conformed more or less to the Protestant ethic tended to dominate our society, such an individual would surely have failed in competition with more sturdy men and as an incompetent would have been treated with contempt. But in this age of Freudian enlightenment, such an individual seems to represent the emerging ideal type of man. . . .

Although the Freudian doctrine is a revolutionary one, it is not a doctrine of revolution. Unlike Marxianism, it has not given ideological sanction to direct and violent assault upon the social *status quo*. It does not, in fact, provide a logical basis for any kind of effort to remodel society. Freud was himself disinterested in society as such, and he treated it as a miserable but inescapable and presumably for the most part unchangeable context that the individual must endure as best he can—with, of course, aid from psychoanalysis. Freud was, for example, as antagonistic to religion, whatever its form, as was Marx; but, unlike Marx, he did not suggest that it might be dispensed with. For Freud there was no good society, past, present, or future.

Freud's disciples have, however, ignored the logical implications of his doctrine and have advocated modification of society to the end that the conflict between the individual and society would be lessened, if not resolved. Such advocacy has not been organized, as was that of Marxianism, and has been neither systematic nor consistent. It has, rather, been "spontaneous" and individualistic, with the result that the attacks upon the social *status quo* have been both segmental and insidious. And for this reason, if no other, the attempts to remodel our society to fit the Freudian image of man have aroused only limited and scattered resistance. It is far too early to say whether these attempts will have enduring consequences; but it does seem likely that the current acceptance of the Freudian doctrine and the current efforts to validate the Freudian ethic profit from the fact that their attack on existing society is only in limited areas and by indirection. For it is clear that social change is always fragmentary, unsystematic, and for the most part inadvertent. Social revolutions and revolutionary mass movements may dramatize the desire for change, but they do not of themselves work significant changes in the existing social system. Those changes, when they come, are produced slowly and piecemeal. . . .

The Protestant ethic evolved, gained advocates, and became in time the prevailing ethic of Western Europeans only because it reflected and in turn implemented changes that were already in process. Among these changes was the growth in number and social significance of independent business entrepreneurs, who operated outside the restrictive sphere of the medieval guilds and could therefore apply enterprise to the discovery and exploitation of new markets for goods and to the use of new techniques in processing, fabricating, and distributing goods. Allied with these independent entrepreneurs in a community of interest against the Church and other agencies of traditionalism were the early scientists, explorers, and political opportunists—all men of enterprise in their various ways. These were the men who in the sixteenth century gave their considerable support to the Reformation, and it was their values and sentiments that in time became codified in the Protestant ethic. As their efforts brought more and more changes to Western society, their numbers increased, and the new ethic came to prevail; and by the opening of the eighteenth century they constituted a clearly defined and powerful class, the *bourgeoisie*. It was this class that honored the Protestant ethic; and because they did so, they formed a class unique in human experience, a class that served as the driving force for the many innovations and developments that have brought Western peoples to their present social state.

The emergence of the Freudian ethic and its invasion of various aspects of current American society similarly reflect, and in turn implement,

changes that are occuring elsewhere in our society. Among the more significant of these changes has been the incipient decline of the *bourgeoisie*,
with their attachment to the values and sentiments of the Protestant ethic,
and their replacement—still only partial—by a new class that is operating
in terms of the value and sentiments that are sanctioned by Freudianism. It
is of course too much to say that Freud and his disciples have brought this
new class into being, and thereby jeopardized the *bourgeoisie*; but there is
certainly a historical concordance between the rise of the Freudian ethic
and the rise of this new class, and currently each depends for its growth on
the other. . . .

There is no real reason to think that man is inherently weak and incompetent, that he is individually incapable of assuming responsibility for his
own welfare, that his organizations are thus by nature fragile and in constant need of protection, or that only through constant and indulgent political ministrations can a society be kept operating effectively. This idea of
man, so ardently propagated by the Freudians, has, however, during the
past few decades been given political validation; and as governments have
assumed maternal responsibility for maintaining society, the individual citizen and his organizations have tended to acquire a dependence upon a
political maternalism that differs only in form and degree from the maternal love, affection, and permissive care which the Freudians believe are essential to the psychic welfare of every child. . . .

It is the thesis of this study that many of the changes that have been of
late years occurring in our society are malfunctional and that they will, if
they continue uncorrected, constitute our unrecognized road to disaster.
The particular changes that have been analyzed here involve quite different aspects of our society—ideological, procedural, and organizational;
and they take such dissimilar forms as a growing preference for the permissive mode of child rearing and the growth of political maternalism. These
changes are being wrought by men of many kinds and various functions—
by psychiatrists and child psychologists of the Freudian persuasion, by
permissive parents and progressive teachers, by welfare workers and im-
pressionable judges, by managers of business and industry and leaders of
labor and academic life, and by politicians and political administrators of
many sorts. Moreover, they are being demanded or welcomed, or at least
passively accepted, by almost everyone.

All these changes, varied as they are in source, in form, and in purpose,
seem to be converging in such a way as to constitute a general social drift
—a movement of many parts to produce one common and unintended consequence. That consequence is a slowing down of the rates of change in
our society, a progressive reduction in its dynamism, a trend toward social
stability. Every one of the changes that have been here discussed has as
its recognized and avowed objective the provision of more security for
some kind or class of individual—the protection of the infant from stress-
ful experience; the school child from competition and strain to achievement; the college youth from the need to excel; the young hoodlum from
the pangs of punishment; the employer from competition with other em-

ployers; the workingman from competition with his fellows; and the non-workingman from the normal consequences of the fact that he does not work.

To a considerable extent these changes are actually increasing the security of various classes of individuals in our society. But every change is also reducing the range of permissible individual variation, for it demands, no doubt as the necessary price of security, increasing conformity by the individual to socially imposed standards of conduct. Thus every change is to some extent destroying those social conditions that have been conducive to the perpetuation of the Protestant ethic, to the generation of men of enterprise, and so to the continuation of the age of enterprise.

On the positive side, these various changes may be seen as contributing in one way or another to the emergence, the social sanction, and the social maintenance of a new ethic, an ethic that translates into action as apathy and indifference. This new ethic presupposes that man is by inherent nature weak, uncertain, and incapable of self-reliance and that he must, therefore, be provided by society with the security that is his greatest need. Since the most outstanding and most popular proponent of this view of man has been Sigmund Freud, the newly emerging ethic has been designated by his name.

It is perhaps possible to conceive a society in which the Freudian ethic prevails and in which, therefore, the members tend to demand much each of the others and to give little each to the others in return. It is perhaps possible that, in view of the many nonhuman agents of production that are presently at our command, the level of life in such a society could be acceptably high. That society would, necessarily, be a stable one—a self-maintaining and unchanging system; if we were to achieve this condition, we would, in our own particular way, have reached the goal of all utopianists—a society in which every member lives the calm and complacent life and drifts from birth to death without excessive effort, without strain, and entirely free from fear in any form. If we were to achieve this blissful social state, it would be only just to acclaim Freud as our Messiah. He hated and despised society as he knew it, but he would no doubt have approved a society so admirably suited to the Freudian man.

There is, however, slight likelihood that Freud will be honored as the savior of mankind, although there is some possibility that he may be remembered as the prophet of doom.

3. *Philip Rieff:* Freud, the Mind of the Moralist

One of the most penetrating and provocative studies of Freud is that of Philip Rieff, professor of sociology at the University of Pennsylvania. Rieff is an unrepentant admirer of Freud, whom he defends both against his critics

From Philip Rieff, *Freud, the Mind of the Moralist* (New York: Viking, 1959), pp. 344–45, 353. Copyright © 1959 by Philip Rieff. Reprinted by permission of The Viking Press, Inc.

and against his heretical successors, the neo-Freudians. Freud's work he describes as "perhaps the most important body of thought committed to paper in the twentieth century"; Freud himself he calls "a statesman of the inner life, aiming at shrewd compromises with the human condition, not at its basic transformation . . . , a moralist without even a moralizing message." Rieff's admiration, however, never becomes blind adulation; his analysis is tough-minded and sometimes critical, and it hides none of the disturbing aspects of Freudian thought. Like Freud, he foresees no cure for man's "chronic illness," and no real reconciliation between man and society. Instead, in an age of generalized neurosis, the psychoanalytic patient must seek only to reconcile himself to his own inner depths; "his newly acquired health entails a self-concern that takes precedence over social concern and encourages an attitude of ironic insight on the part of the self toward all that is not self." If the dominant character type of the twentieth century is really what Rieff calls "psychological man," the consequences for western society are quite incalculable.

Freud was not hopeful; nor was he nostalgic. Retrospectively, he treasured no pagan or primitive past. He looked forward to no radically different future. Pagan antiquity had encouraged too much sensual pride and demonstrated the erotic illusion no less fully than Christianity, by encouraging spiritual pride, had demonstrated the ascetic illusion. Freud disdained permissiveness as much as asceticism; both falsely resolved the essential dualism in human experience, that very dualism between mind and flesh that produces the misery of the human condition. What man suffers from finally is no more the supremacy of spirit over flesh than of flesh over spirit; it is the dualism that hurts. Freud's own attitude toward a variety of historical dualisms, including Christianity, was always respectful, for he considered that they were but versions of a more fundamental dualism in the nature of man and in the cosmos. For this reason he never seriously entertained any utopian aspiration. Indeed, his own theory "had always been strictly dualistic and had at no time failed to recognize, alongside the sexual instincts, others to which it ascribed force enough to suppress the sexual instincts." This dualism Freud described as between "sexuality" and the "ego instincts"; later he distinguished two polar instincts, love and death. Whatever the terminology, it is important to see that—unlike the Christian or rationalist consciousness—Freud denies any permanent healing of the "derangement of communal life," of the struggle between individual interest and the economy of social demands, of the antagonism between binding and destructive forces in individual and group life. The most one can win against the eternal dualisms is a rational knowledge of their effects upon one's own life.

Perhaps it might be more accurate to see depth psychology not as an emancipation of sex but as an enfranchisement. Freud recognized that in fact the silent vote of the psychic world never had been silent. He is the Bentham of the unenfranchised unconscious; what he brought into the realm of legitimacy, he also brought to responsibility. If one cannot educate the ruled, then one must educate the rulers. This very aim, to educate the ruling ego, is a sure mark of Freud's classical liberalism. By enfranchising the ineducable populace of sexuality, Freud seeks to bring it into responsible relations with the ruling power. To the liberal political tradition, with its belief that the "two nations" could be brought together, Freud offered a supporting parallel in psychological and moral theory, for he desired, as far as possible, to bring the instinctual unconscious into the rational community. For this new art of compromise a new kind of specialist is needed, one who can take a destiny apart and put it back together again in a slightly more endurable shape. . . .

On the cultural significance of the neurotic character, Freud is entirely explicit. Neurotics are rebels out of weakness rather than strength; they witness to the inadequacies of cultural restraint. But they are unsuccessful rebels, for they pay too high a price for their revolt, and ultimately fail, turning their aggressions against themselves. Instead of being repressed and turning inward as the neurotic is, the normal personality is active and outgoing. Expedient normal attitudes lead to some active achievement in the outer world. The brisk managerial ego of the normal personality devotes itself to aggression against the environment, to the practical use of objects; it does not fixate upon them. As Freud put it elsewhere: neurotic anxiety comes from a libido which has "found no employment"; therefore, the dream, like work, has a "moralizing purpose." Again, the economic metaphor discloses Freud's ideal of health as well: a fully employed libido.

In a brilliant passage Freud describes the normal attitude toward reality as one combining the best features of neurotic and psychotic attitudes: "Neurosis does not deny the existence of reality, it merely tries to ignore it; psychosis denies it and tries to substitute something else for it. A reaction which combines features of both these is the one we call normal or 'healthy'; it denies reality as little as neurosis, but then, like a psychosis, is concerned with effecting a change in it." Thus the neurotic character is the unsuccessful protestant of the emotional life; in him inwardness becomes incapacity. The normal character continues to protest, Freud implies, but is "not content . . . with establishing the alternation within itself." Thus, in Freud's conception of the normal man, there is a certain echo of the Romantic idea of genius—the ideal man who attains to the self-expression that other men, intimidated by convention, weakly forgo.

As the passage just quoted suggests, Freud did not draw a sharp line between the concepts of normal and neurotic. His dictum that "we are all somewhat hysterical," that the difference between so-called normalcy and neurosis is only a matter of degree, is one of the key statements in his writings. Its meaning is threefold.

First, it declassifies human society, creating an essential democracy within the human condition. Even the Greek tragedy—the most aristocratic context—was leveled out by Freud; the unique crime of the tragic hero becomes an intention in every heart, and in the most ordinary of plots, the history of every family. Misfortune is not an exceptional possibility, occasioned by rare circumstances or monstrous characters, but is the lot of every person, something he has to pass through in his journey from infancy to old age. The aristocratic bias of the "heroic" myth is replaced, in Freud, by the democratic bias of the "scientific" myth: Oedipus *Rex* becomes Oedipus Complex, which all men live through. It is because of the suppressed tragedies of everyday life that men respond so fully to the more explicit tragedies on the stage. But this does not mean that Freud proposed a genuinely tragic view of life; he was much too realistic for that. Ordinary men compromise with their instinctual longings and become neurotic; the tragic hero, because he suffers and dies, must be presumed to have carried out his wishes in a way forbidden to most men.

Secondly, to say that all men are neurotic means to imply an injunction to tolerance. At least Freud's discovery that the commonplace is saturated with the abnormal, the pathological—that psychopathology no longer deals with the exception but with the ordinary man—does something to alter established habits of moral judgment. It lightens the heavier burdens of guilt and responsibility, for many offenses can be made to appear smaller if perceived in sufficient depth.

Third, and more important, this conception of neurosis reveals the essentially ethical nature of Freud's idea of normality. Normality is not a statistical conception, for the majority is no longer normal. Normality is an ethical ideal, pitted against the actual abnormal. By another name, normality is the negative ideal of "overcoming"—whatever it is that ought to be overcome. Being essentially negative, normality is an ever-retreating ideal. An attitude of stoic calm is required for its pursuit. No one catches the normal; everyone must act as if it can be caught. Nor can the psychological man forget himself in pursuit of the normal, for his normality consists of a certain kind of self-awareness. Not least of all, the analysts themselves, Freud thought, needed to return to analysis every few years to renew their knowledge of themselves.

The psychological ideal of normality has a rather unheroic aspect. Think of a whole society dominated by psychotherapeutic ideals. Considered not from the individual's but from a sociological point of view, psychoanalysis is an expression of a popular tyranny such as not even de Tocqueville adequately imagined. Ideally, the democratic tyranny which is the typical social form of our era will not have a hierarchy of confessors and confessants. Rather . . . everyone must be a confessant, everyone must aspire to be a confessor. This is the meaning of the psychoanalytic re-education Freud speaks of. In the emergent democracy of the sick, everyone can to some extent play doctor to others, and none is allowed the temerity to claim that he can definitively cure or be cured. The hospital is succeeding the church and the parliament as the archetypal institution of Western culture.

What has caused this tyranny of psychology, legitimating self-concern as the highest science? In part, no doubt, it is the individual's failure to find anything else to affirm except the self. Having lost faith in the world, knowing himself too well to treat himself as an object of faith, modern man cannot be self-confident; this, in a negative way, justifies his science of self-concern. Though the world is indifferent to him, the lonely ego may

here and there win something from it. For the rectitude and energetic na-
iveté of the man who was the ideal type during the middle-class, Protestant phase of American culture, we have substituted the character traits
of husbanded energy and finessed self-consciousness. The Frank Merri-
well of a psychological culture will not, like the moral athlete of Protestant culture, turn his reveries into realities. Rather, he will be mindful to
keep realities from turning into reveries.

In this age, in which technics is invading and conquering the last enemy
—man's inner life, the psyche itself—a suitable new character type has arrived on the scene: the psychological man. Three character ideals have
successively dominated Western civilization: first, the ideal of the political
man, formed and handed down to us from classical antiquity; second, the
ideal of the religious man, formed and handed down to us from Judaism
through Christianity, and dominant in the civilization of authority that
preceded the Enlightenment; third, the ideal of the economic man, the
very model of our liberal civilization, formed and handed down to us in
the Enlightenment. This last has turned out to be a transitional type, with
the shortest life-expectancy of all; out of his tenure has emerged the psychological man of the twentieth century, a child not of nature but of technology. He is not the pagan ideal, political man, for he is not committed
to the public life. He is most unlike the religious man. We will recognize
in the case history of psychological man the nervous habits of his father,
economic man: he is anti-heroic, shrewd, carefully counting his satisfac-
tions and dissatisfactions, studying unprofitable commitments as the sins
most to be avoided. From this immediate ancestor, psychological man
has constituted his own careful economy of the inner life.

The psychological man lives neither by the ideal of might nor by the
ideal of right which confused his ancestors, political man and religious
man. Psychological man lives by the ideal of insight—practical, experimental insight leading to the mastery of his own personality. The psychological man has withdrawn into a world always at war, where the ego is an
armed force capable of achieving armistices but not peace. The prophetic
egoist of Western politics and Protestant Christianity who, through the
model with which he provided us, also laid down the lines along which the
world was to be transformed, has been replaced by the sage, intent upon
the conquest of his inner life, and, at most, like Freud, laying down the
lines along which those that follow him can salvage something of their
own. Turning away from the Occidental ideal of action leading toward the
salvation of others besides ourselves, the psychological man has espoused
the Oriental ideal of salvation through self-contemplative manipulation.
Ironically, this is happening just at the historic moment when the Orient,
whose westernmost outpost is Russia, has adopted the Occidental ideal of
saving activity in the world. The West has attempted many successive
transformations of the enemy, the world. It now chooses to move against
its last enemy, the self, in an attempt to conquer it and assimilate it to the
world as it is. For it is from the self that the troublesome, world-rejecting
ideal of the religious man came forth.

Freudianism closes off the long-established quarrel of Western man with his own spirit. It marks the archaism of the classical legacy of political man, for the new man must live beyond reason—reason having proved no adequate guide to his safe conduct through the meaningless experience of life. It marks the repudiation of the Christian legacy of the religious man, for the new man is taught to live a little beyond conscience—conscience having proved no adequate guide to his safe conduct through life, and furthermore to have added absurd burdens of meaning to the experience of life. Finally, psychoanalysis marks the exhaustion of the liberal legacy represented historically in economic man, for now men must live with the knowledge that their dreams are by function optimistic and cannot be fulfilled. Aware at last that he is chronically ill, psychological man may nevertheless end the ancient quest of his predecessors for a healing doctrine. His experience with the latest one, Freud's, may finally teach him that every cure must expose him to a new illness.

4. *F. V. Bassin: Consciousness and the Unconscious*

Not all of Europe has succumbed to the Freudian impact. In the Soviet Union, Freudianism has long been denounced as "one of the most reactionary and pseudo-scientific manifestations of bourgeois ideology," and as "one of the dark forces which the bosses of Wall Street stubbornly support." [1] In 1958 the Soviet Academy of Medical Sciences organized a conference devoted entirely to "Questions of the Ideological Struggle with Contemporary Freudianism." Soviet scholars and doctors look instead to their own culture-hero, I. P. Pavlov, the eminent pioneer in the field of behavioral psychology. Although Freud's name remains anathema, the rhetorical attacks have become somewhat more restrained in recent years. At a conference in Moscow in 1962, one of the thirteen major papers dealt with Freud's ideas. The speaker, Professor F. V. Bassin, has been head of the Neurology Research Institute of the Soviet Academy of Medical Science since 1942.

T he problem of the "unconscious" is closely connected with the name of Freud. Actually, Freud and his followers wasted an enormous amount of effort in elaborating an explicit theory of the "unconscious." It was first conceived of as a narrow clinical concept intended to clarify the nature of hysteria and neurosis and, subsequently, as a doctrine which, finding wide acceptance abroad (especially during the last decade in the United States) spread its influence into the most diverse aspects of intellectual life. It took on the character of a unique philosophical system and closely approached directions of thought which are highly inimical to social and scientific progress.

From F. V. Bassin, "Consciousness and the Unconscious," in Michael Cole and Irving Maltzman, editors, *A Handbook of Contemporary Soviet Psychology* (New York: Basic Books, 1969), pp. 400–03, 419. © 1969 by Basic Books, Inc. Reprinted by permission of the publisher.
1. *Current Digest of the Soviet Press*, IV (1952), No. 43, p. 11.

In Russia, as early as the turn of the century, the traditions of an objective experimental-clinical approach to the functional syndromes and ideas of nervism, elaborated by Sechenov, Pavlov, Botkin, Vvedenskii, and their students, were opposed to Freudian teaching.

Abroad, however, the position of Freud's doctrine was quite different. Freudianism is one of the dominant currents in bourgeois psychology, sociology, and philosophy. Its influence is clearly revealed in so-called psychosomatic medicine. . . . It is even looked on with favor in Catholic circles. In countless different forms its influence may be discovered in foreign belles-lettres, graphic arts, cinema, and theater. And even a scholar as far removed from psychoanalytic research as Norbert Wiener, the founder of cybernetics, not long ago asserted that Freudianism is consonant with contemporary concepts of physics.

Of course, the influence of Freudianism should not be overestimated. One of the most outstanding features of the development of foreign attitudes toward Freudianism in the last decade is a clear and progressive growth of ideological opposition to the movement. It is particularly indicative of contemporary foreign opposition to Freudianism that the most severe critics of psychoanalysis are just those persons who previously defended this point of view and later became convinced of its inadequacy as a result of their own research. This critical stream in the literature of recent years has convincingly demonstrated the scientifically primitive nature of psychoanalytic concepts, its lack of therapeutic productivity, and its reactionary role.

Furthermore, if we review an even larger field of studies coming into contact with Freudianism (works written neither by confirmed rivals, nor unconditional partisans of psychoanalytic doctrine), we then clearly see a very spotty array of different shades of opinion varying from a tendency to skeptical ridicule and disregard of the theory of psychoanalysis to an effort to make some sort of compromise with the theory and bring Freudian concepts into line with the traditions and ideas of Pavlovian physiology. . . .

Even such great scientists as Bertrand Russell and Penfield have frequently defended this ideological compromise. Certain Indian neurologists friendly toward the U.S.S.R., and also some scientists from the United States, England, and France who are concerned with questions other than fundamentally materialistic convictions, are also inclined to favor this compromise. Even O'Connor, an extremely severe critic of Freudianism in many respects, considers it possible to pick out some valuable elements in this theory if one can clean off the "mystic fog," as he puts it, in which Freudianism embroils one. The notion that it was desirable to achieve a synthesis of psychoanalytic and Pavlovian approaches was very persistent and led to the International Conference in Freiburg in 1957, specially dedicated to consideration of the interrelation between Pavlov and Freud. . . .

What principles induced so many researchers to strive for a compromise with Freud's teaching? The basic argument emerging from these efforts is that Freud's concept is the only theory recognizing the existence of a special type of brain activity, the so-called unconscious forms of complex mental activity, and that Freudianism is the only theory providing a method for revealing and acting upon this peculiar activity.

What is our principal position with respect to Freud's theory? First of all, it should be based on recognition of the unacceptability of any compromise whatsoever with psychoanalytic methodology which permits arbitrary interpretation of subjective experience. There should be no compromise with the frank appeal of some adherents of Freudianism . . . to substitute the results of introspection and intuition (which have no objective controls) for the data obtained by objective scientific analysis.

At the same time it is obvious that we should in no case skeptically ignore the problem of the "unconscious." We should be able to show the completely erroneous nature of any notion claiming the existence of noncognizable forms of brain activity acting on behavior, a notion recognized only by Freudianism. We should be able to make clear exactly why the notorious problem of the "unconscious" can only be explained on the basis of dialectical materialist studies and the principles of Pavlovian teaching. . . .

Why does Soviet psychology reject Freud's teachings? Above all, we have the incompatibility of the entire methodology of Freudianism with generally accepted methods for the establishment of scientific data, the arbitrary character of psychoanalytic dogmas, the therapeutic ineffectiveness of the psychoanalytic method, the harm done to public health by psychoanalysis as a result of deflecting attention from the true capabilities of medicine and prophylaxis, the demoralizing influences spread by psychoanalysis, especially in the younger generation, which give eroticism the place of a leading social principle and encourage the very worst forms of decadent literature and art. Other reasons for our rejection include the nonscientific interpretation of the role which the so-called unconscious plays in normal and pathological behavior, the grossly biological explanation which psychoanalysis gives for sociological problems and the reactionary role which this point of view plays by masking the true causes of social disasters with discussions of "displacement" instead of concentrating on the tasks related to the struggle against class exploitation and other negative aspects of the capitalistic system.

However, it would be a great mistake to think that Soviet critics of Freudianism are satisfied by simply making these condemnations. The very recognition of the existence of the "unconscious" obviously compels those who reject psychoanalysis to search for some other objective experimental means of studying cognitive processes which take place in the absence of awareness. In many discussions it has been shown that such means not only exist but have been used productively for a long time. . . .

It is important from a methodological point of view to recognize [the] complexity, [the] polymorphous aspect and variability, of relations obtaining between consciousness and the "unconscious." An understanding of this sort, not rejecting problems of the noncognized, not denying the existence of the "unconscious" and the important role of the latter in behavior, at the same time annihilates the most poisonous ideological core of Freudianism, that which makes Freudianism so dear to reactionaries of every stripe. It destroys the root of the basic ideas of Freud: inherent antagonism of the conscious and the "unconscious" as two non-homologous essences standing opposed to one another; functional primacy of the "unconscious"; unresolvable subordination of consciousness to covert primitive appetites in the mind of man; the eternal rule of instincts over reason; hopelessness of the struggle against this, which is only shamefully veiled by a cover of civilization but which ineluctably continues to exist, eternally recalling man's bestial origin.

5. O. Hobart Mowrer: Psychiatry and Religion

Critics of the Freudian impact on our era do not all agree that the shortcomings of Freudianism require a return to the Protestant ethic. O. Hobart Mowrer, research professor of psychology at the University of Illinois and former president of the American Psychological Association, contends that both the Protestant ethic and the Freudian revolution had disastrous consequences. An alternative to Freudianism is needed, and is beginning to emerge as non-Freudian psychology moves beyond primitive behaviorism to a more sophisticated understanding of man's mental and emotional makeup. This process, he believes, involves a rediscovery of reason and a reassertion of the role of a modernized religion.

As we move forward, with ever-accelerating tempo, into what we are pleased to call the Age of Science, we are faced by an awesome paradox. As man, through science, acquires more and more control over the external world, he has come to feel less and less capable of controlling himself, less and less the master of his own soul and destiny. In the same decade in which we produced the atomic submarine and started probing interstellar space, we have also seen, significantly, the emergence of the Beatnik; personality disintegration has become endemic; and society itself is commonly said to be "sick." We remain optimistic about what man can continue to do through science by way of dealing with his environment, but we have become extremely pessimistic about man.

This reciprocal relationship is not accidental: the same presuppositions and intellectual operations that have given us such unprecedented power over nature when extended to ourselves produce a pervasive feeling of helplessness, confusion, resignation, desperation. We seem to be the hapless pawns of a great mechanical, impersonal juggernaut called the cosmos. By the very principles and premises that have led to the conquest of the outer world, we ourselves lose our autonomy, dignity, self-mastery, responsibility, indeed, our very identity. Little wonder, then, that we feel weak,

From O. Hobart Mowrer, "Psychiatry and Religion," in The Atlantic Monthly, July 1961, pp. 88–91. Reprinted by permission of the author and of the editors of The Atlantic Monthly.

lost, fearful, "beat." Being part of nature, we, too, apparently obey strict cause-and-effect principles; and if this be true, if our own experience and conduct are as rigidly determined and predetermined as is the rest of nature, the whole notion of purpose, responsibility, meaning seems to vanish. . . . At the same time, some highly pertinent developments are quietly and unobtrusively occurring in psychological and sociological thought which hold promise of delivering us from our current predicament, both philosophically and practically.

Pre-Reformation Catholicism held man "doubly responsible," which is to say, capable of both good and evil. When, in this context, one behaved badly, it was to his discredit; and when one behaved well, it was decidedly to his credit. There was thus for the individual a sort of moral balance sheet, as it has been called, and ultimate salvation or damnation depended, quite simply and directly, on the number and magnitude of the entries on the two sides of this fateful ledger. . . .

The essence of Luther's position, particularly as it has filtered down to us through John Calvin and other Protestant expositors, is that man is responsible, so to say, in only one direction: capable of choosing the wrong and fully accountable for having done so, he is, however, supposedly unable to do anything whatever toward his own redemption and must wait, helplessly, upon the unpredictable favor, or "grace," of God. . . . We are no doubt justified in looking back upon the Reformation as representing, in many ways, a magnificent achievement. But we have been slow to appreciate, it seems, how dearly it has cost us. Protestantism, whatever its virtues and strengths, has also had the tragic consequence of leaving us without clear and effective means of dealing with personal guilt. And it is this fact, I submit, more than any other that is responsible for what Paul Tillich has aptly called "the psychic disintegration of the masses" in modern times.

By the turn of the century, the influence of religion and moral suasion had so far declined that the medical profession was being inundated by a new type of illness. Purely functional in origin but often expressed somatically, the new malady was characterized by a pervasive "loss of nerve," which, as a matter of medical convenience, was dubbed "neurosis." . . .

In this era of confusion and crisis, psychoanalysis had its inception and spectacular proliferation. Religion had disqualified itself for dealing honestly and effectively with man's deepest moral and spiritual anguish. Freud's discoveries purported to rescue man from the perplexities of the Protestant ethic and the ravages of unresolved guilt, not by restoring him to full ethical responsibility, but by relieving him of all responsibility. In short, the notion was that one should not feel guilty about anything. . . . This was all to be achieved not by a return to the outmoded principle of double responsibility but by adoption of a new and radical doctrine of double *irresponsibility.* . . .

But as the clock of history has ticked off the decades of this century, we have gradually discovered that Freud's great postulate, not of total depravity but of total determinism, has liberated us only in the sense of dumping us from the frying pan into the fire. At long last we seem to be waking up to the fact that to be "free" in the sense of embracing the doctrine of double irresponsibility is not to be free at all, humanly speaking, but lost.

Within the past five years there has been a growing realization, at least in the disciplines most intimately concerned with such matters, of the futility, the deadly peril of this general trend. After an extensive study of the therapeutic claims and accomplishments of psychoanalysis, the English psychologist Dr. Hans Eysenck has recently summed up the situation with this laconic statement: "The success of the Freudian revolution seemed complete. Only one thing went wrong: *the patients did not get any better.*" And this verdict has been amply borne out by numerous other inquiries of a similar kind. . . .

While psychoanalysis was developing as a predominantly medical enterprise, a parallel movement with similar philosophic and practical implications was also taking form and gaining momentum in academic circles. I refer to the radical repudiation, in the first two or three decades of this century, of all that was inward, subjective, and personal, known as behaviorism, with its new and exclusive emphasis upon that form of cause-effect relationship implied by the so-called stimulus-response, or S-R, formula. Here determinism, although couched in somewhat different terms, was no less absolute than in psychoanalysis, and the individual was again relieved —or should we say deprived?—of all semblance of accountability. Behavior or action or conduct was the inevitable consequence of "antecedent stimulus conditions" (causes), and moral accountability became, in this context, a meaningless and, indeed, opprobrious concept. The conditioned and unconditioned reflex, in the language of Pavlov and Watson, was the "functional unit" of all behavior; and Thorndike, in his slightly different theory of habit, likewise spoke of stimulus-response "connections" or "bonds." All of which had at least the incidental effect, if not intent, of obliterating the whole notion of freedom, choice, responsibility by reducing behavior, absolutely and completely, to S-R connections and reflexes. . . .

The behavioristic doctrine of total determinism manifestly does not deliver us from the one-sided determinism of Luther and Calvin any more effectively than does that brand of complete irresponsibility adduced by Freud. If the doctrines of Luther and Calvin disposed the Western world to "Christian despair," those of Freud and Watson have, it seems, engulfed us in a despair that is infinitely deeper and more absolute.

It is only within the last decade or so that we have begun to see a way out. The existentialists, in their very legitimate protests against the general abrogation of responsibility—first one-sidedly, in Protestant theology, and then more systematically, in psychoanalysis and behaviorism—have recently been attracting some well-deserved attention. But when they go on to reject the scientific approach, totally and inherently, they are on dangerous ground and may shortly find themselves, in this regard, discredited.

Having denounced Protestant predestination and psychological determinism alike, what do the existentialists offer, alternatively? Only a counsel of brave despair, an admonition to have the courage to be, on the assumption that being (existence) *is* an ironic joke and ultimate tragedy. Just how do we come by this courage? By lifting ourselves by our own bootstraps? In practice, it seems that this philosophy leaves us quite as helpless and hopeless as does the Protestant principle, with its emphasis upon man's inevitable guilt and God's uncertain grace.

If one takes the time to examine contemporary behavior theory, one finds that scientific developments in psychology have moved a long way from the naive and primitive assumptions of behaviorism. Now it is generally agreed that there is by no means a reflexive or ineluctable connection between stimulation and response. Now we are quite certain that the coupling between our sensory receptors and our muscles is much looser and infinitely more complicated than the earlier theories implied. According to present views, stimulation may suggest a given response or course of action, but whether we "give consent" as Catholic theologians would say, to the suggestion, thought, or image is dependent upon the hopes and fears which we weigh and ponder in deciding whether to act or refrain from acting. In other words, given a stimulus, a particular and predetermined response does not automatically pop out of the organism, as our earlier, push-button psychology seemed to demand. Response—and responsibility —in this new frame of reference is crucially dependent upon the anticipated consequences of our actions. In short, we have rediscovered reason. Instead of being merely stimulated (the Latin term for "goaded"), living organisms become goal-directed, purposive, deliberate, or, if you will, free and responsible.

Beginning with the naive and oversimplified behaviorism of Watson, academic psychology in this century has thus achieved a relatively advanced degree of sophistication; whereas psychoanalysis, which started with Freud's highly elaborated and ingenious speculations, has rather steadily involuted, regressed. The original emphasis on unconscious (irresponsible) motivation has, of late years, given way to a new accent on "ego psychology," which involves frequent reference to "ego strength" and "ego weakness" in a manner unmistakably reminiscent of the older notions of character and will power; and with the ink hardly dry on this ego-psychology literature, psychoanalysts are now beginning to show a new respect for and interest in the superego, or conscience.

These developments, I say, are retrogressive as far as Freud's original formulations go, but in terms of common sense they are decidedly in the right direction. However, they are suicidal as far as psychoanalysis itself is concerned, which was conceived and laid its claim to recognition as an independent discipline along very different lines.

All the developments just reviewed thus strike a new note, or at least one that has considerable novelty for contemporary men and women. Once more we are coming to perceive man as pre-eminently a social creature, whose greatest and most devastating anguish is experienced not in physical pain or biological deprivation but when he feels alienated, disgraced, guilty, debased as a person. And the thrust of much current therapeutic effort is in the direction of trying to help such individuals recover their sociality, relatedness, community, identity.

Here, surely, is a promising meeting ground for psychology, psychiatry, and sociology and for much that is common to both classical Judaism and authentic Christianity. But, logically and programmatically, it strikes at the heart of the Protestant principle. Yesterday, as a Presbyterian, I attended church and heard the minister quote Reinhold Niebuhr, with approval, to the effect that "Christian faith is more profound than mere moral idealism," thus echoing the contempt which Protestantism has always had for the "merely moral man." And the preceding Sunday I heard another minister preach a fine "Reformation" sermon on the theme that "the fruit of grace is responsibility for action in the world"; that is, the theme that we are good because—and if—we are saved, not the reverse. Scientific and humanistic thought can never, I believe, come to terms with such hyperbole. The fact that Protestant theologians keep reverting in their sermons to the question of just what it means to be "saved by grace," rather than by works, suggests that they themselves are not quite certain.

As a psychologist, I have no competence to judge the effectiveness of religion in saving men's immortal souls, and, I confess, this is not my major interest. But I do maintain that religion has great potential for serving, and saving, men and women in this world which is not now being at all adequately realized. If, in the secular sciences, we have rediscovered something of the logic and conditions of responsible action, perhaps this will be an encouragement to the theologians themselves to take a more courageous and responsible position and quit hiding behind a preposterous piece of medieval sophistry.

6. *Henri F. Ellenberger: The Discovery of the Unconscious*

In the closing pages of his massive history of psychiatry, Henri F. Ellenberger, professor of criminology at the University of Montreal, attempts to weigh the controversial evidence about Freud's impact on the life and culture of our time. His cautious and balanced summary comes as close to a fair-minded judgment as anyone might achieve today. It may be useful to set alongside it the conclusions of another eminent scholar, the British scientist Lancelot Law Whyte: "Freud's supreme achievement was to force the attention of the Western world to the fact that the unconscious mind is of importance in every one of us. . . . Freud changed, perhaps irrevocably, man's image of himself. . . . [His] message of doom dignified by scientific clarity met two great needs of the early twentieth century: apparent scientific relia-

From Henri F. Ellenberger, *The Discovery of the Unconscious: The History and Evolution of Dynamic Psychiatry* (New York: Basic Books, 1970), pp. 546–50. Footnotes omitted.

bility, and a myth of human experience as we know it, which means for many conflict, fission, and disorder. Freud is here an exemplar of our time, though his puritanical moralism and narrow conception of scientific method mark him personally as pre-Freudian, what we sometimes call 'Victorian.' He was the last pre-Freudian rationalist, passionately upholding a rationalism of the conscious intellect which his doctrines would rapidly undermine." [1]

An objective appraisal of the influence of Freud is inordinately difficult. The story is too recent, distorted by legend, and all the facts have not yet come to light.

The consensus is that Freud exerted a powerful influence, not only on psychology and psychiatry, but on all the fields of culture and that it has gone so far as to change our way of life and our concept of man. A more intricate question pertains to the divergencies that arise as soon as one tries to assess the extent that that influence was beneficial or not. On one side are those who include Freud among the liberators of the human spirit, and who even think that the future of mankind depends on whether it will accept or discard the teachings of psychoanalysis. On the other side are those who claim that the effect of psychoanalysis has been disastrous. La Piere, for instance, claims that Freudianism ruined the ethics of individualism, self-discipline, and responsibility that prevailed among the Western world.

Any attempt to give an objective answer to these two questions—namely of the extent and nature of the influence of psychoanalysis—has to face three great difficulties.

First: as in the case of Darwin, the historical importance of a theory is not restricted to what it originally was in the mind of its author, but also of the extensions, adjunctions, interpretations, and distortions of that theory. Thus, an evaluation of Freud's influence should begin with a historical account of the Freudian school and the various trends that issued from it: the orthodox Freudians, the more original successors (for instance, the promoters of ego psychoanalysis), the deviant schools proper, with their own schisms and deviant branches, and those other schools (Adler and Jung), which were founded on radically different basic principles, though as a response to psychoanalysis. And, last but not least, one should take into account the distorted pseudo-Freudian concepts that have been widely vulgarized through the newspapers, magazines, and popular literature.

Second: a still greater difficulty arises from the fact that from the beginning, psychoanalysis has grown in an atmosphere of legend, with the result that an objective appraisal will not be possible before the true historical facts are completely separated from the legend. It would be invaluable to know the starting point of the Freudian legend and the factors that brought it to its present development. Unfortunately the scientific study of legends, of their thematic structure, their growth, and their causes, is one

1. Lancelot Law Whyte, *The Unconscious Before Freud* (New York: Basic Books, 1960), pp. 177–79.

of the least-known provinces of science and to this date nothing has been written in regard to Freud that could be compared to Etiemble's study of the legend that grew around the poet Rimbaud. A rapid glance at the Freudian legend reveals two main features. The first is the theme of the solitary hero struggling against a host of enemies, suffering "the slings and arrows of outrageous fortune" but triumphing in the end. The legend considerably exaggerates the extent and role of anti-Semitism, of the hostility of the academic world, and of alleged Victorian prejudices. The second feature of the Freudian legend is the blotting out of the greatest part of the scientific and cultural context in which psychoanalysis developed, hence the theme of the absolute originality of the achievements, in which the hero is credited with the achievements of his predecessors, associates, disciples, rivals, and contemporaries.

The legend discarded, we are permitted to see the facts in a different light. Freud is shown as having an average career of the contemporary academic man in central Europe, a career whose beginnings were only slightly hampered by anti-Semitism, and with no more setbacks than many others. He lived in a time when scientific polemics had a more vehement tone than today, and he never suffered the degree of hostility as did men such as Pasteur and Ehrlich. The current legend, on the other hand, attributes to Freud much of what belongs, notably, to Herbart, Fechner, Nietzsche, Meynert, Benedikt, and Janet, and overlooks the work of previous explorers of the unconscious, dreams, and sexual pathology. Much of what is credited to Freud was diffuse current lore, and his role was to crystallize these ideas and give them an original shape.

We now come to the third great difficulty in appraising the extent and nature of the influence exerted by psychoanalysis. Many authors have attempted to make an inventory of the impact of Freud's ideas upon normal and abnormal psychology, sociology, anthropology, criminology, art, the theater, and movies, as well as philosophy, religion, education, and mores. We shall not attempt to reiterate these inquiries, nor even to summarize them, but must point out a fact that has been sometimes overlooked: psychoanalysis itself was from the beginning linked to other preexisting or contemporary trends of a more general nature. Around 1895 the profession of neuropsychiatrist had become fashionable, there was an active search for new psychotherapeutic methods, and men such as Bleuler and Moebius were trying to "re-psychologize" psychiatry—Freud's first publications appeared as manifestations of this new course. In the same period there was an intensive development of sexual psychopathology—Freud's libido theory was one among many novelties in that field. We have already mentioned the affinities between early psychoanalysis and the literary works of Ibsen, Schnitzler, the Young-Vienna group, and the neo-Romanticists, and to these must be added the avant-garde movements that arose later, namely the Futurists, Dadaists, and Surrealists. Freud's open proclamation of atheism was in tune with the attitude of many contemporary scientists. . . . His system was judged materialistic enough to be adopted by Soviet Russian psychologists before it was superseded by Pavlovian psychiatry.

World War I gave rise to a "decline of the West" trend of which Freud's *Reflections on War and Death* were but one of many manifestations. The disasters of World War I and the impending catastrophe of World War II compelled thinkers to search for ways of saving the world. The task of psychotherapy was now to give the individual a means of tolerating tensions and anxiety, hence the shift of psychoanalysis from depth psychology to ego psychoanalysis.

However, this was not all, because in the meantime the progress of technology had inaugurated the affluent society. To a system based on hard work and intense competition that social Darwinism had given its ideology succeeded a system based on mass consumption with a hedonistic-utilitarian philosophy. This is the society that enthusiastically adopted Freudian psychoanalysis, often in its more distorted form. The facts brought by La Piere in his book, *The Freudian Ethic*, may be accurate, but it is not right to make Freud responsible for them, no more than to make Darwin responsible for the way the militarists, colonialists, and other predatory groups and finally Hitler and the Nazis, availed themselves of pseudo-Darwinist theories. It thus happened to Freud as it had happened to Darwin and to others before them, that they seemed to launch an overwhelming cultural revolution when actually it was the revolution rooted in socioeconomic changes that carried them. Coming back to Freud, it will certainly be a long time before one will be able to discern what can be attributed to the direct impact of his teaching, and to what extent the diffuse social, economic, and cultural trends prevailed themselves of Freudian, or pseudo-Freudian, concepts toward their own end [*sic*].

We are perhaps prepared, now, to give an answer to that difficult question: What does certainly belong to Freud and constitutes the inmost originality of his work? We may distinguish three great contributions: the psychoanalytic theory, the psychoanalytic method, and the psychoanalytic organization.

Whatever the number of its sources and the intricacies of its context, the psychoanalytic theory is universally recognized as a powerful and original synthesis that has been the incentive to numerous researchers and findings in the field of normal and abnormal psychology. However, the problem of its scientific status is not yet clarified. In that regard, the situation of psychoanalysis is strikingly similar to that of animal magnetism in 1818, when the physician Virey wondered why discoveries made in the field of physics at the time of Mesmer were now taken for granted whereas the validity of Mesmer's doctrine was still the object of emotionally charged discussions. Conversely, discoveries made in Freud's time in the field of endocrinology, bacteriology, and the like, are unequivocally integrated into science, whereas the validity of psychoanalytic concepts is still questioned by many experimental psychologists and epistemologists. This paradox has brought many Freudians to view psychoanalysis as a discipline that stands outside the field of experimental science and more akin to history, philosophy, linguistics, or as a variety of hermeneutics.

Even more than the conceptual framework of psychoanalysis, the psy-

choanalytic method is Freud's creation and constitutes the inmost originality of his work. Freud was the inventor of a new mode of dealing with the
unconscious, that is, the psychoanalytic situation with the basic rule, free
associating, and the analysis of resistances and transference. This is Freud's
incontestable innovation.

But Freud's most striking novelty was probably the founding of a
"school" according to a pattern that had no parallel in modern times but is
a revival of the old philosophical schools of Greco-Roman antiquity. . . .
Almost from the beginning Freud made psychoanalysis a movement, with
its own organization and publishing house, its strict rules of membership,
and its official doctrine, namely the psychoanalytic theory. The similarity
between the psychoanalytic and the Greco-Roman philosophical schools
was reinforced after the imposition of an initiation in the form of the training analysis. Not only does the training analysis demand a heavy financial
sacrifice, but also a surrender of privacy and of the whole self. By this
means a follower is integrated into the Society more indissolubly than ever
was a Pythagorean, Stoic, or Epicurean in his own organization. Freud's
example in that regard was to be followed by Jung and a few other dynamic psychiatric movements. We are thus led to view Freud's most striking achievement in the revival of the Greco-Roman type of philosophical
schools, and this is no doubt a noteworthy event in the history of modern
culture.

XI

The Dilemma of Democratic Socialism

The nineteenth century was the triumphant age of liberalism; the twentieth, at the outset, seemed destined to be that of socialism. By 1900 Social Democratic parties had been established in virtually every country of Europe, and in many places they appeared to be on the march toward power. By 1914, the Social Democratic party was the strongest single party in Germany, the second-strongest in France; in Great Britain, Italy, Belgium, Scandinavia, socialism was growing faster than any rival. Then the outbreak of war shattered the Second International into separate national fragments, and Lenin's victory in Russia split the fragments into revolutionary and reformist wings. But the reformist or Social Democratic wing soon regained much of its strength, and became a major factor in European politics once again. In Great Britain the Labor party (whose revised 1918 program was socialist) came to power for two brief periods; socialists participated in coalition cabinets in Germany, Belgium, the Scandinavian countries, the Spanish republic (after 1931), and France (after 1936); in Austria, they steadily controlled the municipality of Vienna until 1934, and made it a showplace of social reform.

Once again Social Democracy was disrupted, by the rise of fascist and authoritarian movements and by the outbreak of the second world war. But the victorious crusade against the Axis offered socialism a new opportunity. When the war ended, socialists could point with pride to their record of anti-Fascist resistance; and they could promise, through their program of state intervention and planning, to rebuild Europe on a basis of social justice. Almost everywhere outside the Soviet bloc, socialist parties participated in, or led, the post-liberation governments: in Great Britain, France, Belgium, The Netherlands, Norway, Sweden, Denmark, Finland, Italy, Austria—even in Hungary and Czechoslovakia for a short time. Germany was expected to join the list as soon as the occupying powers restored self-government there.

Disillusionment was not long in coming. By 1950, a strong reverse tide had set in; during the next decade, it swept the socialists out of the governing coalition almost everywhere. Only in Scandinavia did they retain their leading role—in part, perhaps, because the Scandinavian socialists' principles had never been very orthodox. Throughout most of western or central Europe, power passed into the hands of the Christian Democrats or of various kinds of liberal-conservative parties. True, the socialists made a partial and sporadic comeback during the 1960's; they regained a shaky hold on power in Britain for a time (1964–1970), entered coalitions with the Christian Democrats in both Italy (1962) and Germany

(1966), and took over the German Chancellorship in 1969. Yet it was clear that socialism had little prospect of attaining a clear majority of the electorate in any country, or becoming powerful enough to initiate a program of drastic renovation and reform.

During the difficult years since 1950, European socialists have indulged in a good deal of soul-searching. The socialist movement has, of course, always been riven by internal controversy; any group that takes its ideology seriously is likely to experience sectarian feuds and splits, especially when that group attempts at the same time to play a pragmatic political role. But the self-examination of the postwar years has struck deeper, for it poses the question of socialism's survival as a significant political force.

To some degree, the debate has involved a retrospective analysis of socialism's record between the wars. Can the root of the trouble be found in errors committed then, in false steps that put the movement onto the wrong track? Did the socialists cling too rigidly to Marxian dogmas about class conflict and the historic role of the proletariat, thus sacrificing their chance of building a broadly-based party cutting across classes? Or were they, on the contrary, not doctrinaire enough; did they grow flabby and petit bourgeois in spirit, thus alienating their best activists among the proletariat? Was the trouble their failure to harmonize doctrine and action; did they talk like revolutionaries while behaving like opportunistic reformers? Or did the real trouble lie in socialism's failure to adapt to changing times? Did socialist parties become bureaucratized and petrified through their stress on loyalty and seniority—mere refuges for aging, unimaginative party hacks? Did socialists, through their dogged adherence to an outmoded doctrine, fail to understand the profound political and social changes of our time, and the strength of those nonrational drives that move masses of men?

The alleged mistakes of the past, however, did not provide the only explanation for socialism's stagnancy. Some alternative theories were a bit more comforting, if not more conducive to hope of rejuvenation. Such, for example, was the theory that socialism had done its work almost too well; that by preaching and practicing the welfare-state ideal, the socialists had virtually worked themselves out of a job. Socialists could point out that when they gained power and lost it again, their successors rarely repealed any of their major reforms. Britain and France, for example, continued after 1950 as mixed economies, operated in part by the state and in part by private enterprise, and the social insurance laws of the immediate postwar years were almost untouched. Likewise in Sweden, where the most thoroughgoing welfare-state structure had been built (on a base of private ownership): when a Conservative party leader was asked what he wanted to conserve, his reply was "the Sweden of today"—i.e., a society shaped by a quarter-century of socialist rule. If the welfare state was the true goal of socialism, then socialists no longer had a monopoly of the idea; if it was *not* the true goal, its effect had evidently been to blunt the movement toward a real socialist society.

Over the past two decades, socialists in most European countries have been debating these issues with varying degrees of acrimony. One faction has advocated a complete overhaul of the party's traditional beliefs, to the point of jettisoning most of its Marxist baggage. The German Social Democrats have ventured farthest in this direction, adopting a new program in 1959 that discarded most of their old idols: antimilitarism, anticlericalism, even anticapitalism. The party declared its acceptance of the free market, and asserted the formula: "As much competition as possible—as much planning as necessary." The party chairman publicly declared: "The demand that the political program of Karl Marx and

Friedrich Engels be made the basis of a Social Democratic program in the year 1959 is so un-Marxist as to be unthinkable." On the opposite wing, certain socialists in most countries have agitated for "workers' unity"—a coalition or merger with the communists; while various "new left" factions have set out to adapt the Marxian heritage to the demands of a technocratic age, or have sought for a way to go "beyond Marxism."

Vigorous debate such as this may suggest that European socialism is neither dead nor moribund. Perhaps it is only experiencing an overdue sea-change.

I. *Robert L. Heilbroner: Europe at the Halfway Station*

In the brief excerpt that follows, Robert L. Heilbroner sums up his view of the achievements and the prospects of European socialism, seen in historical perspective. Heilbroner, who teaches at the New School for Social Research in New York, is an economist in the grand tradition of Adam Smith, John Stuart Mill, and Karl Marx; the new and narrower mathematical economics, he has remarked, possesses "rigor," but also "mortis." Few economists of our time have been so prolific or so widely read; his many books and essays combine provocative ideas with an unusually lucid style. They also reveal his sympathy for democratic socialism.

Socialism in the underdeveloped world . . . in large part . . . is espoused as a "functional" means of rivaling the material works of capitalism. But the roots of socialism in Europe are of a different kind. More than anything else they reflect an inadequacy of long standing in the political workings of capitalism.

To be sure there was also an inadequacy of economic performance—low wage rates, highly unequal income distribution, recurrent unemployment —all of which have been powerful factors in the promotion of socialism. Yet beyond this was a deeper failure of the European capitalist system. It was an inability to include the ambitions and aspirations of its lower orders within its own ideological framework. From the beginning, capitalism in Europe has been a self-consciously bourgeois institution, frankly suspicious of, not to say hostile to, the aims of its laboring classes. Nothing of the social consensus which bound up the American class divisions ever characterized the European scene. In America, Horatio Alger may have been only a myth, but in Europe even the myth did not exist.

Thus the direction in which working class ambitions and aspirations naturally gravitated was toward the quarter of socialism. No capitalist power in Europe ever thought to rally its working classes with the slogans of the bourgeoisie. It is a revealing fact that in their moments of greatest reliance

From Robert L. Heilbroner, *The Future as History*, pp. 107–12. Copyright © 1959, 1960 by Robert L. Heilbroner. Reprinted by permission of Harper and Row, Publishers, Inc.

on popular support—in the conduct of war—their governments relied not on economic but on patriotic motives. The soldiers of France fought for *la patrie* not for *le capitalisme*. The Germans who responded to the call of *das Vaterland* would scarcely have been expected to troop to the colors for *Der Kapitalismus*. In contrast, the idea of socialism has traditionally provided a European mass rallying cry. Russian soldiers fought for their *socialist* Fatherland against German soldiers who fought as willingly for their National *Socialism*.

As the example makes very clear, the realities behind the idea of socialism were often vague and contradictory. Nevertheless, in the word was a symbol of something which capitalism never achieved in its own name: a drive for social justice, an often crudely formulated but passionately felt movement toward the dismantling of economic privilege, and an ideological concern for the needs of the least favored and most numerous members of society. To the European lower classes—and to their powerful representatives among the intellectuals—socialism was a movement freighted with great destinies for the future, while capitalism was a system weighted with the irreparable injustices of the past. It was this ideological orientation, combined with the mechanisms of planning—neutral or even conservative in themselves—which provided the anti-capitalist momentum of European economic evolution.

To some extent this identification of reform as "socialist" persists in Europe today. As Professor Carr has written:

> You cannot in these days plan for inequality. Once you can no longer explain inequalities either as the salutary result of a natural economic process or as incidentals in an economic organization primarily designed to prepare for war, it must become a main purpose of economic policy to eliminate them. This is the political connection between planning and socialism. In theory they are separable; historically they spring from different sources. But, once the historical evolution of the capitalist system has made a controlled and planned economy necessary, and once the temporary expedient of planning for war has become obsolete, to plan for socialism is the only available alternative.[1]

There are signs, however, that the socialist inspiration for reform is today somewhat on the wane. In most European countries the aims and purposes of the socialist parties are confused and unsure. The frightening totalitarianism of Russia, the disappointments of nationalization in Great Britain have taken much of the wind out of socialist sails. The political problem of democratic rule, which in the past socialism always shrugged off as secondary to the economic problem of control, has now reasserted itself with terrible emphasis. And the revelation that nationalization is no cure for the grinding realities, the dull tasks, the necessary hierarchies of the industrial process has made it clear that if socialism is to offer nothing more than nationalization it is scarcely to be preferred to a well-managed capitalism.

Hence the socialist movement in Europe is conservative. Unlike commu-

1. E. H. Carr, *The New Society* (Boston, 1957), p. 39.

nism in the backward countries it has no overriding goal of economic development for a starving people with which to "justify" the means it uses. For the moment it contents itself with pressing in the direction of "welfare" —toward greater income equality, the extension of social services, and the diminution of social privilege. None of this is in any sense "revolutionary." More important yet, the sponsorship of reform is more and more ceasing to be the exclusive property of the Left, with the result that even the intellectual core of the socialist movement has increasing difficulty in defining how its program differs from that of at least the more enlightened conservative parties.[2]

But it is much too early to say that the socialist movement in Europe has spent its force. Its waning in recent years has corresponded with a period of unprecedented boom; given a serious recession, a further series of defeats and humiliations along the lines of the Algerian fiasco, a move toward power by the lingering reactionary elements, and a reactivation of the socialist ideological drive is by no means unlikely. Totally unlike the situation in America, capitalism in Europe is *on trial*. There is no guarantee, however, that should it fail it would be replaced by the socialism of an earlier vintage. As Hitler's National Socialism has unforgettably shown, the forces of the extreme Right may also wear the brassards of the Left. Whether amid the strains of its global readjustment in power and prestige Europe will find an authoritarianism of the Right preferable to the slow evolution of its "bourgeois socialism" is unpredictable. In view of the rise of de Gaulle in France and the lurking evidences of reactionary nationalism in Germany, such a possibility is clearly not to be summarily ruled out.

In sum, it would seem that the Western European nations are at halfway stations along an historic road. If they are no longer identifiable as the capitalisms of twenty years ago, neither have they attained an organization of society which would correspond to the socialist aspirations of twenty years ago. Instead we find the "socialist" mechanisms of planning being used to buttress an essentially capitalist social and economic structure; and given a reasonable accommodation of erstwhile socialist aims, as in England, there is no reason why this halfway station should not endure for a considerable period.

Whatever may be its fate as an ideology, however, one aspect of socialism has become irreversibly fixed into place. This is the emergence of collective social and economic goals—for the most part of national scope, but to a growing extent of pan-European coverage—as an integral part of the European economic order. A subservience of individual enterprise to the state, very different from the pre-war *laissez faire*, has become a salient reality of economic life and an unquestioned axiom of economic philosophy. The political coloration of this mild collectivism remains to be seen, as does the degree to which it may be "hardened" by the pressure of events. What is certain is that the historic road away from the unplanned capitalism of the past will not again be traversed in the opposite direction.

2. Cf. *New Fabian Essays* (London, 1952).

2. *Andrew Hacker: Towards Socialism*

Andrew Hacker, professor of government at Cornell University, confronts head-on a major problem of socialists in an era of affluence: why are proletarians so easily "corrupted" by prosperity? What can socialists offer, and to whom can they appeal, when times are good? Must they wait and hope for another great depression? Would such a slump open the way to socialism at last? Or are socialists condemned to remain in the role of constructive critics rather than system-builders?

The problem for British socialists—and, with variations, it is the problem of American radicals and reformers—is how to produce a political ferment in a society that is generally affluent and most of whose members are content with things pretty much as they are. While it may still be argued that there continues to exist a propertyless proletariat, regardless of whether its members wear white collars or blue collars, this majority does not feel itself seriously aggrieved by poverty or exploitation or the concentration of economic power in giant institutions. Such citizens will often favor the redistribution of wealth on a piecemeal basis and the gradual introduction of new social legislation; but they simply are not persuaded by the argument that the society in which they live is irrational or unjust or in need of fundamental reconstruction.

At the same time it is common knowledge that affluence, while widespread, has not reached everyone in society. Here, it might be thought, is a constituency for socialism. The problem is that those who are really dispossessed are exceedingly difficult to mobilize and are usually uncomprehending of the political system in which they are supposed to play a part. Old people, mothers with families of fatherless children, and the lowly-paid who are ignored by trade union organizers tend to be non-voters, non-joiners, and so submerged that they are incapable of coalescing into a party of protest. While there are occasional, almost random, outbursts of dissatisfaction from members of this class, for all intents and purposes they remain a modern *lumpenproletariat* far removed not only from socialist overtures but from political life and thought in any form.

As for the working class with steady jobs and union cards, it is now well above the poverty line not so much owing to the services provided by a welfare state as to the fortuitous prosperity of the postwar years. While these skilled and semi-skilled workers are never happy with their wage level, their resentments are not so intense as to make them systematic opponents of capitalism. Indeed all they seem to want are larger slices of the very appetizing pies they see all around them.

Thus the contemporary working class, no longer exploited and no longer at a subsistence level, has been a grave disappointment to socialists and radicals. This may be termed "the betrayal of the proletariat"—and by this it is not intended to mean that the working class itself has been betrayed by anyone or anything. On the contrary, the once-exploited and once-submerged have themselves acted to betray those who in an earlier day held out great hopes and expectations for them. What has happened, of course, is that those who were once depressed Welsh miners are now the owners of cars and payers of school taxes; the migrant Okies are now Los Angeles suburbanites anxious to keep lesser breeds within the population from invading their well-manicured neighborhoods. These ex-proletarians are currently sitting in front of television sets, beer can in hand, waiting for a sirloin steak that is broiling on the outdoor barbeque pit. Is this what all the fervent protest of the 1930's was for?

The socialist and radical tendency, as often as not unacknowledged, is to believe that those oppressed by capitalism are possessed of an ethical purity and a great potentiality for esthetic and intellectual development. If these capabilities long remained unfulfilled it was because material deprivation was the chief fact of working-class existence. Once the shackles of poverty were removed, it was assumed the working man would emerge to appreciate and pursue a quality of life far higher than that known by anyone before. But no such thing has happened: the graduates of yesterday's proletariat have adopted most of the habits and prejudices of the tasteless middle class. And in so doing they have betrayed the socialists and radicals who worked so earnestly to help them in an earlier and unhappier day. . . .

To be sure it may be said, and with truth, that the proletariat has been corrupted by the bounty and the perverted morality of capitalism. Poverty and oppression may have been alleviated in the postwar years, but this was due not to political action but because of a historic interlude which permitted capitalism to prosper sufficiently to cut the working class in on its benefits. Thus the working class moved up the economic ladder on capitalism's own terms, all the time accepting the values of property ownership and middle-class materialism and suburban respectability. This, it should be remarked in passing, is not the least reason why Marx and Lenin spoke of violence and underlined the imperative need for smashing the bourgeois state and economy. They wished to destroy a corrupt and irrational system because such a system was capable of bribing, enticing, and otherwise seducing the workers. They desired, in a word, to remove the capitalist alternative. For they knew that the values of capitalism are a standing temptation; they knew that not many, so lured, would be able to turn their backs on what the prosperity of free enterprise is able to offer.

Who are the socialists? Who, in particular, are the socialists at a time when capitalism seems able to provide high employment and widespread affluence?

What emerges is that today's socialists are no longer exclusively preoccupied with economic injustice. There is now a concern with the quality of life, moral and esthetic, that persists on a dismayingly low level despite the fact of prosperity. There is anxiety over the effects of popular culture and the passive role of the millions who imbibe it; there is frequent discussion of education at all levels and the fact that learning is easily adjusted to the needs of agencies outside the academy; and there is heightened awareness of conditions such as alienation and anomie, with attention drawn to the fact that individuals are searching for an identity in a system where human relationships are tenuous and transient. The entire population, especially the middle class now inflated with millions of new recruits, is seen as having an aimless character; if individuals have no sense of purpose or being, it is because their society is based on no ethical premises and is possessed by no rationale to explain its current behavior or its goals for the future.

Socialists, in short, find themselves gazing on fellow citizens who are reluctant to accept the diagnosis being applied to them. They seem happy, they feel they are free, and they have no desire to give up the creature comforts and the new opportunities in life that have recently opened to them. They are not critical of concentrations of power in large organizations, and they are not repelled by the artifacts of mass culture. There seems, in short, to be consensus and consent to the operations of modern capitalism. And if there are occasional misgivings on the part of the public about such problems as crime, delinquency, dishonesty, and amorality, there is at the same time a refusal to see those malfunctionings as the consequence of capitalist life and values.

At this time democratic socialism stands as an ethic without a significant constituency. The Labour Party in Great Britain polls impressive votes, but its supporters are content to have it be a party of welfare not unlike the Democratic Party in the United States. If its leadership speaks less of nationalization of industry, as a means of rendering powerless institutions dedicated to the pursuit of private profit, this stance is based on the knowledge that that electorate is simply unconcerned with economic power or even political principles. Those who adhere to the socialist persuasion and who embrace the socialist vision are not those at the bottom of the economic ladder but rather a small and selective segment of the upper middle class. Democratic socialism is a subtle and sophisticated outlook . . . , and it takes some intellectual commitment to accept its ethical and empirical premises. There has to be not simply the conviction that it is possible to order a society in a just and rational manner but also the understanding that democratic processes are compatible with a wide degree of public ownership.

Given that those with a meaningful and more than transitory attachment to socialism are few in number, how will a socialist society be achieved? The answer lies not in conspiracy or *coup d'état* but in waiting patiently until such time as a substantial number of citizens are ready for recruitment into the socialist movement. This will not depend on political education but is rather a function of economic conditions. Socialist ranks are augmented at such time as capitalism swings into a serious, if not devastating, downturn that proves incapable of remedy through the techniques of modern government and the tools of fiscal planning. If millions who have been steadily employed find themselves without jobs, there can develop a loss of faith in the system of private enterprise that may produce a wide receptivity for socialist programs. But those who turn in this direction, it must be reiterated, are not led there by a conversion to socialist ideals as much as they are by the pressure of economic insecurity. Thus it may not be possible to renew the socialist mandate at such time as prosperity is again achieved by socialist means. If this is so, then the historic contribution of socialism will ultimately lie in its continuing critique of capitalism rather than in its ability to establish an enduring social order in its own right.

3. *C. A. R. Crosland: The Future of Socialism*

Dissension within the European socialist movement reached a special pitch of intensity in the British Labor party during the 1950's and early 1960's. Labor during that period lost three successive general elections to the Conservatives, even though it had carried out a dramatic program of reform while in power (1945–1951) and had fulfilled all of its electoral promises of 1945. At one point in the early 1960's, an outright schism was narrowly averted, thanks to the mediating skill of the party leader, Hugh Gaitskell. In this long controversy, the most eloquent spokesman for the "revisionist" wing was Anthony Crosland, whose book *The Future of Socialism* became the bible of those who wished to abandon the party's Marxist heritage and to give a new meaning and content to socialism. Crosland, a onetime Oxford don, has been a member of Parliament almost without interruption since 1950, and has held several cabinet posts.

I f we are to reformulate socialist doctrine, the first task is clearly to decide what precise meaning is to be attached to the word "socialism."

This is not an easy question to answer. The word does not describe any present or past society, which can be empirically observed, and so furnish unimpeachable evidence for what is or is not "socialism." Thus statements about socialism can never be definitely verified; and we cannot treat it as being an *exact* descriptive word at all. There is therefore no point in searching the encyclopaedias for a definitive meaning; it has none, and never could.

This can easily be seen by considering the numerous and, as the previous chapter showed, often inconsistent meanings attached to the word by people who have called themselves "socialists." Marx, defining it as the "nationalisation of the means of production, distribution, and exchange," meant something quite different from Proudhon, who defined it as consisting of "every aspiration towards the amelioration of our society." Sir William Harcourt, declaring in 1892 that "we are all socialists now," evidently had a different version from his contemporary Bradlaugh, to whom social-ism meant that "the State should own all wealth, direct all labour, and compel the equal distribution of all produce." And any history of socialist thought will provide dozens of different definitions, some in terms of own-ership, some of co-operation, some of planning, some of income-distribu-tion; and it soon becomes simply a matter of subjective personal preference which is chosen as the "correct" one. Many definitions, moreover, are so vague as to be virtually meaningless; one can read almost anything, for ex-ample, into Sidney Webb's definition: "the economic side of the democratic ideal."

The confusion has become worse inasmuch as the word is also charged with a high degree of emotional content, and so has acquired a range of purely persuasive meanings. It is either used to denote or win approval, as in Hitler's National "Socialism" and "Socialism" in Eastern Europe, or when Left-wing weeklies attack a policy which they dislike as not being "Socialist"; or pejoratively, as when Right-wing Americans speak of "creep-ing Socialism."

But the worst source of confusion is the tendency to use the word to de-scribe, not a certain kind of society, or certain values which might be at-tributes of a society, but particular policies which are, or are thought to be, means to attaining this kind of society, or realising these attributes. To rescue the word from these confusions, and the debasement referred to above, one must begin by asking what, if anything, is common to the be-liefs of all, or almost all, of those who have called themselves socialists. The only constant element, common to all the bewildering variety of differ-ent doctrines, consists of certain moral values and aspirations; and people have called themselves socialists because they shared these aspirations, which form the one connecting link between otherwise hopelessly diver-gent schools of thought.

Thus the word first came on the modern scene with the early nine-teenth-century Owenites, whom Marx contemptuously termed "Utopian" socialists. They based their "socialism" explicitly on an ethical view of so-ciety, a belief in a certain way of life and certain moral values. The means by which they thought this "good society" could be attained are irrelevant to-day; and in fact they were quickly challenged by other socialist schools of thought, since when a continuous debate has proceeded, with no agree-ment, about what constituted the most suitable means. This debate would have no particular interest to-day, but for the fact that all the protagonists tried to appropriate the word "socialism" to describe the particular means which they themselves favoured.

Thus Marx appropriated it for the collective ownership of the means of production on the false assumption, analysed in Chapter II, that the pat-tern of ownership determined the character of the whole society, and that collective ownership was a sufficient condition of fulfilling the basic aspira-tions. And generally the word came to be applied to policies for the eco-nomic or institutional transformation of society, instead of to the ultimate social purposes which that transformation was intended to achieve; so one often hears socialism equated not only with the nationalisation of industry, but with government planning, or redistribution, or state collectivism. This of course is quite unhelpful, for although people may agree on ends, they may legitimately disagree about means. Moreover, the means most suitable in one generation may be wholly irrelevant in the next, and in any case (still more significant) a given means may lead to more than one possible end, as indeed has happened with each of the policies just mentioned.

Thus if, for example, socialism is defined as the nationalisation of the means of production, distribution and exchange, we produce conclusions which are impossible to reconcile with what the early socialists had in mind when they used the word: such as, that Soviet Russia is a completely socialist country (much more so, for instance, than Sweden)—even though it denies almost all the values which Western socialists have normally read into the word. Similarly, if socialism is defined as economic collectivism or State control of economic life, then Nazi Germany would correctly have been called a socialist country. But in neither case would the end-result be described as socialism by most socialists; the means of nationalisation and planning have proved adaptable to more than one purpose, which shows how unwise it is to identify the means with the end.

Not only is it unwise, but it is also semantically and historically incorrect. The various schools of thought which have called themselves, and been called by others, "socialist"—Owenites and Marxists, Fabians and Christian Socialists, Syndicalists and Guild Socialists—have differed profoundly over the right means; and no one means has a better title to the label "socialist" than any other. The one single element common to all the schools of thought has been the basic aspirations, the underlying moral values. It follows that these embody the only logically and historically permissible meaning of the word socialism; and to this meaning we must now revert.

These ethical and emotional ideals have been partly negative—a protest against the visible results of capitalism—and partly positive, and related to definite views about the nature of the good society; though of course negative and positive strands are often inter-twined.

Perhaps one can list them roughly as follows. First, a protest against the material poverty and physical squalor which capitalism produced. Secondly, a wider concern for "social welfare"—for the interests of those in need, or oppressed, or unfortunate, from whatever cause. Thirdly, a belief in equality and the "classless society," and especially a desire to give the worker his "just" rights and a responsible status at work. Fourthly, a rejection of competitive antagonism, and an ideal of fraternity and co-operation. Fifthly, a protest against the inefficiencies of capitalism as an economic system, and notably its tendency to mass unemployment. The first three formed the basis of socialism as "a broad, human movement on behalf of the bottom dog." The first and last were censures on the material results of capitalism; while the other three stemmed from an idealistic desire for a just, co-operative and classless society.

(I have listed only the social and economic aspirations. But of course underlying them, and taken for granted, was a passionate belief in liberty and democracy. It would never have occurred to most early socialists that socialism had any meaning except within a political framework of freedom for the individual. But since this political assumption is shared by British Conservatives as well as socialists, no further reference is made to it.)

As thus formulated, even these basic aspirations are not all equally relevant to present-day society. Some are expressed in language adapted to conditions that no longer exist, and in particular are too negative in character. This is natural, for they were, in large part, a reaction against the actual results of pre-war capitalism; and with two million unemployed, widespread poverty and malnutrition, and appalling slums set against a background of flamboyant wealth amongst the richer classes, it was natural that the negative desire to abolish evils should outweigh more positive and detailed aspirations.

But to the extent that evils are remedied and injustices removed, negative statements become less and less appropriate. And they are seen to be inappropriate by the electorate, a growing section of which has no recollection of unemployment, or poverty, or dole-queues, and finds Labour propaganda which plays on the themes and memories of the 1930s quite incomprehensible. To a population which has lost its fears, and now has every hope of a rapidly rising standard of living, a negative protest against past wrongs is merely a bore.

Thus even when we go back to the basic aspirations, we still find the same, welcome difficulty that the pace of change has overtaken the doctrine, and a re-formulation is needed. Of course if a Tory Government were to re-create all the old evils, matters would be simple. New thinking could be set aside "for the duration," and negative statements would again suffice. But it is not likely that the Tories will act so recklessly, or that mere periodic counter-attacks to regain lost positions will remove the need for a map of the new terrain.

How should we re-formulate these aspirations to-day in such a way as to preserve their basic emotional and ethical content, yet discarding what is clearly not germane to present-day conditions? Of the original five, the first and last are rapidly losing their relevance in a British context. Such primary poverty as remains will disappear within a decade, given our present rate of economic growth; and the contemporary mixed economy is characterised by high levels both of employment and productivity and by a reasonable degree of stability. In other words, the aspirations relating to the economic consequences of capitalism are fast losing their relevance as capitalism itself becomes transformed.

But the remaining three more positive ideals, described above as stemming either from a concern with the "bottom dog," or from a vision of a just, co-operative and classless society, have clearly not been fully realised. No doubt we should phrase them differently to-day, but their basic content is still perfectly relevant. We have plenty of less fortunate citizens still requiring aid; and we certainly have not got an equal or classless society, nor one characterised by 'co-operative' social relations. . . .

The ideals have so far merely been stated. They have not been justified in detail, nor any evidence adduced to show that their further fulfilment would definitely improve our society. All that has been argued is that they constitute "socialism" in the only legitimate sense of the word, and that they are not embodied in our present society to such an extent that most people would describe it as socialist.

A few people would, it is true, so describe it—not explicitly, but by implication. That is, they take the view that we are at, or anyway in sight of, the final objective. This of course is a plausible view only if we select those more modest aspirations which have largely been fulfilled, and define these, and these alone, as socialism. Thus if we were to say, as G. D. H. Cole once did before the war, that "the Socialist has two main enemies to fight—poverty and enslavement," it would follow that we now nearly have socialism in Britain, since we have very little poverty or enslavement.

Examples of such definitions can be found. Perhaps the most striking is the Frankfurt Manifesto of the reborn Socialist International in 1951, in which (after a preamble so vague as to be almost meaningless) the whole emphasis is placed on democratic planning, which is regarded as the basic condition of socialism. The purposes of planning are defined as "full employment, higher production, a rising standard of life, social security and a fair distribution of income and property"—purposes which (at least if one omits the one word "property") are either not peculiar to socialists, or else are largely achieved already in Britain and Scandinavia.

Now it is true that the planned full-employment welfare state, which has been the outcome of the first successful spell of Labour government, is a society of exceptional merit and quality by historical standards, and by comparison with pre-war capitalism. It would have seemed a paradise to many early socialist pioneers. Poverty and insecurity are in process of disappearing. Living standards are rising rapidly; the fear of unemployment is steadily weakening; and the ordinary young worker has hopes for the future which would never have entered his father's head. There is much less social injustice; the economy works efficiently; and the electorate, as the Labour Party discovered at the last election, is in no mood for large-scale change, and certainly not for the complete overthrow of the present system. Many liberal-minded people, who were instinctively "socialist" in the 1930s as a humanitarian protest against poverty and unemployment, have now concluded that "Keynes-plus-modified-capitalism-plus-Welfare-State" works perfectly well; and they would be content to see the Labour Party become (if the Tories do not filch the role) essentially a Party for the defence of the present position, with occasional minor reforms thrown in to sweeten the temper of the local activists.

Yet this is not socialism. True, it is not pure capitalism either; and it does fulfil some part of the traditional socialist aspirations, and to this extent has socialist features. Yet it could clearly be a great deal more socialist than it is—not, as people sometimes think, because it now has only 25% public ownership and is not fully planned down to the minutest detail, any more than Soviet society *is* more socialist because it has 100% public ownership and complete state planning: but simply because the traditional socialist ideals could be more fully realised than they are. To put the matter simply, we have won many important advances; but since we could still have more social equality, a more classless society, and less avoidable social distress, we cannot be described as a socialist country.

The detailed case for fulfilling the remaining aspirations, that is, for moving towards socialism, is argued in Parts Three and Four, where the two aspirations are considered separately; while Part Five discusses their economic implications.

But one may at this stage briefly summarise, without attempting to justify, the reasons for wanting to move forward, and to alter what is admitted to be a prosperous and generally tolerable society; and the value judgments which underlie this wish. Lord Attlee recently remarked, looking back on his early days, that "I joined the socialist movement because I did not like the kind of society we had and I wanted something better." Why should anyone say the same to-day?

There are, I believe, three answers. First, for all the rising material standards and apparent contentment, the areas of avoidable social distress and physical squalor, which were referred to above, are still on a scale which narrowly restricts the freedom of choice and movement of a large number of individuals. Secondly (and perhaps more intractable), we retain a disturbing amount, compared with some other countries, of social antagonism and class resentment, visible both in politics and industry, and making society less peaceful and contented than it might be. Thirdly, the distribution of rewards and privileges still appears highly inequitable, being poorly correlated with the distribution of merit, virtue, ability, or brains; and, in particular, opportunities for gaining the top rewards are still excessively unequal.

This significant residue of distress, resentment, and injustice affords a *prima facie* justification for further social change—as I think, and shall argue, in a socialist direction. It may not justify the same *saeva indignatio* as mass unemployment and distressed areas before the war—rather a purposeful, constructive, and discriminating determination to improve an already improved society. But the belief that further change will appreciably increase personal freedom, social contentment, and justice, constitutes the ethical basis for being a socialist.

4. *Svetozar Stojanović:*
Marxism and Socialism Now

The debate over socialism's current problems and future prospects has spilled over into eastern Europe as well. What the east Europeans call "revisionism" differs markedly, however, from that of Anthony Crosland or that of

From Svetozar Stojanović, "Marxism and Socialism Now," *The New York Review of Books*, July 1, 1971. Copyright © 1971 by The New York Review Inc. Reprinted by permission.

the drafters of the new German party program. Its main focus is on Marx's thought: through a study of Marx's early writings, the "humanist" side of Marx is emphasized, and a potential bridge is built between communists and Social Democrats. Although some Polish and Czech scholars have engaged in such revisionism (and have suffered severely for it), the Yugoslavs have taken the lead. Thanks to the rupture between Moscow and Belgrade in 1948, the Yugoslavs have gradually gained more freedom of thought and expression, and have entered into the debate over socialism. They have also enjoyed a second advantage: the opportunity to observe and interpret the unique socialist experiment that has been taking place in their own country. For more than twenty years now, Yugoslavia has had a network of workers' councils throughout industry and the public bureaucracy. This experiment in industrial democracy and in what some call "free-market socialism" has drawn the attention of socialists everywhere; some in the West see it as a possible model. The essay that follows is the work of Svetozar Stojanović, professor of philosophy at the University of Belgrade and former visiting professor at various American universities.

For the past several decades Marxism has been passing through a severe crisis brought about by those of its followers who have transformed it into a conservative official ideology. Yet even at the time of its greatest spiritual poverty, Marxism produced a number of important thinkers: Lukacs, Bloch, Gramsci, Korsch, Horkheimer, Adorno, Marcuse, Fromm. True, the continuity of creative Marxism was maintained throughout that time almost solely by Marxists working—again an irony of history— in capitalist countries. It is as if the bourgeoisie wanted to prove once more Marx's prediction that it would produce its own gravediggers!

There are now increasing signs of recovery from the disaster brought about by an almost schizoid split. I am referring to the Janus-faced attitude of numerous Marxists: radically critical toward capitalism, they were at the same time apologists for socialism. There are now indications that this split is disappearing because it is being increasingly understood that Marxism must be a critique of *all* existing societies. No matter how strange this may sound at first, Marxists ought to be radical critics of socialism.

The main chance for essential innovations in Marxism lies now, in my opinion, in analysis and critical evaluation of the sociopolitical practice which passes as socialism. For this, however, two preconditions are necessary. First, a relentless Marxist critique of Marxism and, second, the destruction of the most influential ideological-political myth of the twentieth century: the statist (Stalinist) myth of socialism.

In accordance with Marx's forecast, a radical transformation of "Prehistory" (class society) into the beginning of "real history" (classless society) was expected from the socialist revolution. Unfortunately, in the name and under the cover of socialism a society was created by Stalinists that bears all the essential marks of class society. Yet the myth of the socialist character of that society has been so powerful that many are still vainly trying to get an answer to an ill-posed question: how has this or that event, the invasion of Czechoslovakia for example, been possible in *socialism?*

The initial phase of the present day renaissance of Marxism might be characterized as a "Back to Marx Movement." However, this phase has already lasted too long. The way out of the crisis cannot be found in the exegesis of Marx's texts or in scholastic disputes over them. For a long time we have been confronted with problems that will remain insoluble unless we go *beyond Marx*, which, of course, does not mean without Marx. Those who continue to regard Marx's thought as a monolith lack the intellectual equipment to become creative Marxists. Marx's theory is not lacking in serious internal tensions and conflicts. One therefore often must distinguish that Marx who is reliable as a theoretical inspiration from that Marx who has already become part of the past. I would like to remind the reader of two critical conflicts in Marx's theory and to express my preferences. The first is the conflict between Marx's moderate and extreme determinism and the second between his dialectics and absolute utopia.

In line with his philosophy of human praxis, freedom, and self-creation of man, Marx often insists that "*Man makes his own history*, but he does not make it out of whole cloth; *he does not make it out of conditions chosen by himself*, but out of such as he finds at hand" (*The Eighteenth Brumaire of Louis Bonaparte*). This theoretical position may be called moderate determinism.

But Marx belonged to the nineteenth century, when the rigid determinism of the natural sciences was an important methodological ideal. Besides, Hegel in his philosophy of history treated men as instruments of the objective mind. As a result of these influences Marx often adopts an extreme deterministic viewpoint. For example, "But capitalist production begets, *with the inexorability of a law of nature*, its own negation" (*Manifesto*). Or when he approvingly quotes a reviewer of his Capital:

Marx treats *the social movement as a process of natural history, governed by laws not only independent of human will, consciousness and intelligence, but rather, on the contrary, determining that will, consciousness and intelligence.* [Afterword to the second German edition]

In the following passage Marx expresses the extreme deterministic view of social laws functioning with an "iron necessity" side by side with a more moderate determinism which treats them as only "tendencies":

Intrinsically, it is not a question of the higher degree of development of the social antagonisms that result from the *natural laws* of capitalist production. It is a question of *these laws themselves, of these tendencies working with iron necessity.* [Ibid., Preface to the German edition]

As we see, in Marx's thought two discordant motifs are interwoven. Man is the subject of historical process, but the path of this process is independent of his consciousness and will. Although man is a creative being, history can move in only one direction. Men have influence on historical development but only on its speed, not on its direction:

And even when a society has got upon the right track for the discovery of the natural laws of its movement . . . it can neither clear by bold leaps, nor remove by legal enactments, the obstacles offered by the successive phases of its normal development. But *it can shorten and lessen the birthpangs.* [Ibid.]

True, this power of blind historical forces over man is, according to Marx, characteristic of class "prehistory." In communism, however, freely associated men will be able to determine the historical course.

The internal conflict in Marx is the source of two different interpretations that run throughout the history of Marxism. The overwhelming majority of the Marxists of the Second International interpreted Marx as an extreme deterministic theorist. Their reformist practice was much more consistent with such a determinism than was Lenin's revolutionism. . . .

Stalinists have masterfully used the psychological impact of that dualism —absolute determinism at the theoretical level and relative determinism, even voluntarism, at the practical level—to encourage its followers and to dishearten its enemies, including communists. . . .

The overdeterministic strand of Marx's thought has always been a stumbling block to efforts to build up a Marxist ethics. To be able to work seriously on an ethics of revolutionary action Marxists, to begin with, must discard extreme determinism. The task of such an ethics is, among other things, to morally obligate people to try to bring about socialism. However, that job would be meaningless if men were not able to have a significant influence on historical development. The Marx for whom men have almost no influence on the course of history, and hence cannot be responsible for it, has been quoted here more than enough. Rigid determinism excludes the *real* freedom of man that in turn is the *ratio essendi* of morals and ethics.

I said *real* freedom, because the concept of freedom as merely "recognized necessity" represents a theoretical rationalization of the situation in which men are believed to be instruments of the objective mind (Hegel) or of blind historical forces (Marx) more than it represents actual freedom. The latter consists rather in man's ability to choose between various possibilities and to make real the chosen possibility in the face of apparent necessity. Only to the extent that man possesses this ability is he responsible for the course of history. Without belief in the relative openness of the future a real ethics of revolutionary action is impossible.

Socialism is a real historical possibility and tendency, but by no means an inevitability. For that matter it is a weaker tendency than statism. Whether it will materialize depends on human action. Only the kind of Marxism that conceives of socialism as a historical possibility, and not a necessity, is in the position to oblige people *ethically* to put their efforts into its realization.

It is no longer possible to believe in the inevitability of socialism. At least two essential changes relevant to our problem here have occurred after Marx. First, with Stalinism a new form of "class prehistory" that Marx could not foresee—statism—came into being. Second, man has acquired a destructive power so great that even the survival of mankind is not se-cured, let alone historical development in a particular direction. Nowadays not only the transformation of "prehistory" into "real history" but also an absolute de-historization is possible. What if it turns out that mankind has been making a Sisyphus-like endeavor? Or even worse, if the stone annihi-lates our Sisyphus and so does away with absurdity, but the price is the triumph of nothingness?

Marx was doubtless one of the most uncompromising dialecticians in the history of human thought. And yet turning his eyes from the past and pres-ent toward the future Marx sometimes unconsciously abandons dialectics. In his vision of communism one feels the tension between his dialectical in-clination and the utopia of absolute de-alienation. Dialectics urged Marx to conceive communism as relative, but his limitless hopes led him to make it an absolute.

As a dialectician Marx explicitly denies that communism is the end or the goal of history:

Communism is . . . the negation of negation, and is hence the actual phase nec-essary for the next stage of historical development in the process of human eman-cipation and recovery. Communism is the necessary pattern and the dynamic principle of the *immediate* future, but communism as such is *not* the goal of human development—the structure of human society. [Manuscripts of 1844]

On the other hand it is not difficult to find those passages in which Marx described communism as a society where all basic contradictions would wither away, even the contradictions between man's essence and his exis-tence. For example:

This communism, as fully developed naturalism, equals humanism, and as fully developed humanism equals naturalism; it is the genuine resolution of the conflict between man and nature and between man and man—the true resolution of the strife between existence and essence, between objectification and self-confirma-tion, between freedom and necessity, between the individual and the species. [Ibid.]

Some of Marx's famous passages on total personality, the coinciding of the division of labor with individual inclinations, the complete control of the social processes by associated individuals in communism, and the like also sound absolutely utopian.

A perfect idea always lacks something because, as Hegel says, it is too good for men. With our historical experience and the scientific work of the past one hundred years behind us, we can no longer cultivate a *limitless* belief in man's potential for good. Man has a much greater disposition for irrationality, for enslavement and submission, for aggression and destruc-tion, than Marx believed. Our century has witnessed the greatest explosion of human evil. Of course, the conclusion here does not have to be that human nature is today worse than before. Perhaps modern man is even better, but has available to him incomparably more terrible means for inflicting evil. Any philosophy that is to face up to the history of our century must reserve room for inhumanity.

But let there be no misunderstanding. Marx is not being reproached here for having a utopia, understood as a vision of a nonexistent form of social organization, which by that very fact must contain a certain amount of the unrealizable. Without such an anticipation there can be no radical transformation of social reality. Utopia, taken in this relative and not absolute sense, represents a legitimate and important dimension of Marx's radical and critical thought about society and history. Such a utopia is inherent in his revolutionary dialectics.

However, Marx sometimes visualizes this nonexistent form of social organization as perfect. Then we cannot speak about relative but only about absolute utopia which finds in the human condition the support for limitless hopes: the elimination of all fundamental existential contradictions. If that were to happen then the entire human and social situation would be transformed into a sort of *"perpetuum immobile."*

It is a delusion that Marx was a *purely scientific,* as opposed to a *utopian,* communist. The difference between these two types of communism is far more relative than it appeared to Marx and particularly to Engels.

Belief in the possibility of realizing perfect goals helps to sustain the struggle for ambitious but relative aims. Woe to them who struggle without real hope, but no less to them who do it with limitless hope. After all that befell the revolution and him personally, how did Trotsky feel, he who had once dreamed of a communist man in this way:

Man will become enormously stronger, wiser, freer, his body will be more harmoniously proportioned, his movements more rhythmical, his voice more musical, and his forms of existence will be pervaded by dramatic dynamism. [*Literature and Revolution*]

It is well-known that Marx put his revolutionary hopes in the most developed countries. Although he stressed the merits of the primitive or crude communism of his time, he also criticized it as "the return to unnatural simplicity of the man who is poor and with no needs." Nevertheless, Marxism was first put into practice by communists in underdeveloped countries. Therefore, Marx himself in their interpretation more often than not seems to be a theoretician of primitive communism.

All indigenous socialist revolutions have gone, or are still going, through a stage we may call primitive communism. In the period of underground activity, armed struggle, so-called "war communism," and reconstruction of a country, the communist movement favors only one type of orientation for its followers: solidarity, cooperation, general interests, discipline, moral stimulation, self-sacrifice, and equality in distribution. There is a strong tendency to suppress material incentives, individual and group rights and interests, the desire for a higher standard of living, and differences of income. Perhaps it is possible to reduce all elements of this kind of primitive communism to leveling egalitarianism (*uravnilovka* in Russian), collectivism, and asceticism.

Primitive communism, in my opinion, is adequate and progressive in the cruel conditions of underground struggle, armed revolution, "war communism," and reconstruction of a country. It expresses and also idealizes the hardships of the struggle against the old world.

But the idealization of hardship poses a crucial dilemma for the revolutionary movement after the seizure and consolidation of power have taken place and the reconstruction of a country has been set in motion. Either the revolutionary movement will realize the limited value of its primitive communism and accordingly begin the process of its modernization, or it will degenerate. This is confirmed by the experience of the Russian, Chinese, and Yugoslav revolutions. The Cuban revolution is now confronted with the same choice. I would like to say here a few words about three essential ways of coping with that problem.

The fantastic exertions that are required in underground activity, armed revolution, "war communism," and the beginnings of reconstruction of a country can be *voluntarily* sustained only by a minority and even then *only for a limited period of time*. It is not possible to live too long on revolutionary enthusiasm exclusively. That this period can be very long indeed, however, was shown by the Chinese revolutionaries and is still (after more than twenty-five years!) being demonstrated by the heroic and successful struggle of revolutionaries in Vietnam.

The evidence suggests that the attempt of the revolutionary elite to perpetuate primitive communism and to enforce it as a *permanent* social state soon comes into conflict with tendencies in human nature toward individual differences, initiative, adequate material remuneration, and a more comfortable life. A prolonged suppression of these inclinations is bound to result in a reaction: indifference toward work (partially covered up by participation in various "voluntary work" and other campaigns), absenteeism, negligent handling and poor maintenance of the instruments of production, low productivity, material poverty, and intellectual inertia.

To continue to suppress such human inclinations it may, of course, be necessary, sooner or later, to resort to force. But those who do so, being themselves human, share the same inclinations they want to suppress in others. Thus, they themselves must be restrained by force. Still, this process cannot continue ad infinitum. So it may easily happen that the revolutionary vanguard gratifies such human inclinations in some of its own members and the groups whose support it needs, and at the same time forces the primitive communist way of life upon all other citizens. When such an adjustment to reality takes place, the oligarchic-statist, Stalinist degeneration of revolution soon follows.

The principles of *uravnilovka*, asceticism, and collectivism change their character and function when they cease to be tied to the preparation and organization of the armed revolution and the reconstruction of a country. The extreme leftist obsession with an ascetic and collectivistic egalitarianism insists on maintaining this condition at any costs as a *permanent* social state. For this reason, a lot of effort has been devoted to proving the respectable ideological origin of these principles. *Uravnilovka* is thus presented as a realization of Marx's principle of distribution according to needs; asceticism as the practically realized reversal of the materialistic value hierarchy of the bourgeois society; and collectivism as the triumph over bourgeois individualism by the socialization of man in the spirit of Marx!

We can imagine with certainty what view Marx, for whom communism was "based on the entire past development in all its richness," would have taken of this reversion to pre-Marxian communism. Instead of leveling collectivism he would prefer his communist personalism. He would criticize asceticism from the standpoint of his humanistic hedonism and leveling egalitarianism from that of his belief in distribution according to diverse human needs.

When it begins to lose ground primitive communism has to be *enforced.* But that is self-defeating: it turns into oligarchic statism, where the *privileged* and increasingly *self-interested*—and sometimes *vulgar hedonistic*—ruling class can enforce leveling egalitarianism, asceticism, and collectivism only by relying heavily on indoctrination and repression. The statist class, in other words, continues to preach primitive communism as a regulative consciousness of the *entire* society but it tends to live differently itself. . . .

The Yugoslav revolution has also gone through the primitive communist stage. *Uravnilovka,* asceticism, and collectivism were three basic principles of the so-called Partisans' Ethics during World War II. But the first symptoms of the degeneration of the revolution appeared very soon after the victory in 1945. This occurred because of the Stalinist model of social organization; I deliberately say Stalinist and not Soviet, since a certain continuity with the latter was established only with the introduction of workers' councils in 1951. The state-party apparatus, composed of former partisans, went on preaching the ascetic and collectivistic egalitarianism to the masses of people, but it itself began to lead the life, naturally as veiled as possible, of privilege, special interest, and enjoyment. No doubt it would have become the new ruling class had it continued on that road.

The turning point in the opposite direction was the Communist party's conflict with the Cominform during 1948. The Yugoslav revolution had to break through the "socialist" encirclement of socialism. It may be characterized as a kind of "revolution within the revolution." However, its golden age was a relatively short one, culminating ideologically in the adoption of the Program of the League of Communists (the new name for the CP) in 1958. The revolution within the revolution soon began to reveal its limitations. No matter how enthusiastically it was embraced by the masses of people, the Yugoslav revolution within revolution was not only initiated but thereafter and always directed and controlled from above.

The most important consequence of the break with Stalin was the gradual introduction of the principles of self-management and self-government at the local level. Yet the forms of self-management and self-government, established long ago, have not been allowed to get out of the ghettos of relatively small social groups (factories, schools, universities, medical and cultural institutions, etc.) and develop into an integral system of socialist democracy. This accounts for the existing hybrid system: self-management and self-government at the local level and fairly strong statism at all higher levels of social organization. The key change, of course, would be radical reform of the Party.

Another important consequence of 1948 was the abandonment of the ideal of primitive communism. Gradually but irretrievably asceticism has been replaced by efforts to reach and enjoy high standards of living. The pursuit of individual and group material interests, previously stigmatized by collectivism, has become legitimized ideologically, politically, and morally. And, finally, serious remunerative differences have been encouraged in order to stimulate education, skill, productivity, and creativity. As a result, a unique economic model has been created that represents a combination (by no means a synthesis!) of social ownership, flexible central planning, workers' self-management, and market competition (a sort of socialist "free enterprise system").

Recent history, however, has shown that two basically different ideological and political orientations have been supporting this modernization trend: one is petty-bourgeois and the other socialist. Both tendencies are now in sharp conflict on the Yugoslav ideological-political scene. Unfortunately, the petty-bourgeois tendency increases every day. There are already disturbing signs of excessive social differentiation, individual and group egotism, and excessive materialism. Petty-bourgeois "socialists" are pressing for more of these.

Advocacy of the mechanisms of an uncontrolled market economy is another characteristic of their conception. According to them even the stock system should be introduced in socialism. An equal number of shares should be distributed to the employees so that they would have a more intimate interest in the success of their self-managing enterprises. After that, of course, stock exchanges would have to be opened. Only we are not told what would happen to socialism when the short idyl of universal stock owning is over, and society has been divided into the producers without shares and the "producers" in whose hands shares would become concentrated! If petty-bourgeois "socialists" prevail socialism might become a period of transition between a very underdeveloped and a more sophisticated society in Yugoslavia.

We may, therefore, conclude that the Yugoslav revolution is far from resolving the agonizing question that has confronted every socialist revolution until now: how to undertake the necessary modernization without allowing it to kill the prospects for achieving social equality, justice, and democratic participation at all levels of society. To put it differently, in the process of de-Stalinization the Yugoslav social revolution has arrived at another crossroads, one direction leading to petty-bourgeois "socialism" and the other to democratic socialism. One part of the Party, the student movement, and the workers are now, through their strikes and sometimes demonstrations, fighting against the former and for the realization of humanistic socialism.

5. *Richard Gombin: The Origins of Leftism*

Beginning in the 1960's, socialism in western and central Europe was faced by a new kind of challenge from the far left. A whole series of small movements, composed mainly of young intellectuals, undertook the task of rethinking the social problem and shaping a new doctrine suited to the demands of our time. Some of these groups remained within the Marxist tradition, and claimed to be bringing Marx up to date; they looked for inspiration to such thinkers as the Hungarian Georg Lukacs and the Italian Antonio Gramsci. Others turned to Mao as the red star of the future. Still others claimed to transcend Marxism; they viewed Marx as "the theoretician of the bourgeois revolution carried to its logical extreme," and repudiated all twentieth-century revolutions to date as "the last of the bourgeois revolutions." The new socialism, they argued, would not be content with a renovated model of existing society, but would move humanity into a higher stage. Richard Gombin, a young French scholar, has recently attempted to assess the significance of this heterogeneous movement, which attained sudden notoriety during the French crisis of May–June 1968 (an upheaval that grew out of student protests). Mr. Gombin finds that leftism (*gauchisme* is the French term) has multiple roots: the old anarcho-syndicalist tradition, certain Marxian revisionists, the advocates of industrial democracy, the current of subjectivism that runs from de Sade and Fourier to surrealism and Freud. Can such a hodge-podge of ideas and impulses be combined into a movement capable of crystallizing social protest and effectively challenging its older rivals, communism as well as democratic socialism? Mr. Gombin, in his conclusion, offers a thoughtful judgment.

Leftism . . . is far from being a complete and coherent theory. Rather, it combines elements of criticism, analysis, and constructive ideas. But the thing that provides enough coherence to justify joining these elements in a single conceptual rubric is their common inspiration, world-view, and plan for the future. The heterogeneity of leftism's component parts and, at times, their apparent incompatibility, arise also from the fact that the theory is not yet complete. We have examined it at a moment when fusion has not yet been accomplished; at the present time anything could still happen—the diverse parts could disintegrate, they could harden into separate entities, or they could fuse together in the same crucible. All hypotheses are possible; certainty alone would be a sign of recklessness.

Such as it is, still in process of becoming, leftist theory also springs from a variety of sources. It derives from Marxism its plan of radical transformation, but it conceives of radicality in a different and broader fashion. It accepts the Marxian notion of class struggle, but includes in it all those who do not have mastery over their own lives and control of their own activities. It thus broadens in singular fashion the range of alienations that

Richard Gombin, *Les origines du gauchisme* (Paris: Editions du Seuil, 1971), pp. 177–82. Translated by the editors. Reprinted by permission of the author and Editions du Seuil.

weigh upon the individual, and breaks with Marxist economism. It extends the "battle front" by refusing to confine the struggle to the terrain of the business concern. It carries the fight into the heart of everyday life. It seeks conflict at every level; for at every level leftism detects repression.

It is the *whole* of the existing system that is challenged, and simultaneously. Leftism considers that man is alienated in his sexual life, for his real desires are stifled from childhood by moral values, the family, the school. He is *socialized* by the patriarchal family, which reproduces the authoritarian model of society as a whole: there the child is already trained to obey without argument, to accept the basic division between those who command and those who execute. The whole conception of pedagogy and discipline is worked out to inhibit the child's instincts of creativity and autonomy. The university, finally, transmits an ideological kind of learning; there is no subject matter—not even the exact sciences—whose goal is not to *manipulate* the student, to impose on him a conception of society, of happiness and of liberty which merely reflects a structure of domination. Having undergone a long apprenticeship in submission, man finds himself caught in a dense network of reifications, and his consciousness is distorted. All this explains why it is so hard for him to organize his authentic liberation; why he is so poor a judge of his own interests, and why he continually moves from one kind of slavery to another. Until now, he has been able to do no more than change masters.

Henceforth, the problem is to get rid of all masters and all barriers to liberty. Here too leftism departs from Marxism and from all varieties of nineteenth-century socialism. It rejects productive labor and wants to replace it by the sort of free and playful activity for which art might serve as an approximate model. It departs therefore from the mentality of industrial society that was imposed on Europe at the dawn of the capitalist era. It draws from the dadaist and surrealist tradition a sovereign contempt for technological civilization, which secretes grayness and boredom. It borrows from millenarianism and from the "horsemen of the apocalypse" an aspiration toward a totally different world, a paradise that can and must be realized without delay. It takes from utopianism its fantastic structures, but only to integrate them into its own short-term plans; it refuses to abandon the dream and to restrict reality to what is presently attainable. Finally, it wants to create a style of life in which man will no longer be a stranger to man, in which men will once more be able to communicate, thanks to a dis-alienated language. Words will then be identifiable with action, and will express human and universal truth rather than daily lies.

The struggle for a new world cannot utilize the reified instruments of the opposition movement inherited from the past. The violent incursion of subjectivity into day-to-day demands rules out the principle of revolutionary leadership: to conquer autonomy in the struggle is the first goal of the conscious revolutionary. *Conscious*—which is to say, master of one's own destiny. One's consciousness stems precisely from his situation in the historical process now under way: that consciousness cannot be injected, increased, reinforced or initiated by any sort of *deus ex machina*.

Now it happens that leftism thinks it has found in our historic period— that which is just beginning—the moment when the objective situation at last permits subjectivity to assert itself. This situation derives from the emergence, in a few privileged countries, of a relative degree of comfort which incites man to divert some of his attention away from the struggle for mere survival. This "availability," unknown till now, leads him to ask questions about the existing order of things; to perceive, though still vaguely, a broadening of what is possible and tangible. From this conscious perception of an attainable but forbidden future comes the energy that will allow the proletarian to tear himself free from the burdensome condition imposed upon him. Then he will find, buried deep within himself, marvels of intelligence, infinite potentialities and, especially, an unsuspected urge to shape his own destiny.

The embodiment of these aspirations and these energies, the concrete form for these apocalyptic visions, will be a total and generalized confrontation with the existing system, with all existing systems. The leftist is certain that as this confrontation proceeds, it will quickly confirm his analyses and his predictions. We have seen, of course, that this expectation is at present a fragile one. Nevertheless, some significant signs may be found simultaneously at Warsaw and at Mexico City, at Paris and at Berkeley, at Turin and at Osaka; they invest confrontation with a new dimension and a certain seriousness. But while these signs show a change in both the quality and the intensity of social and political struggle in the world, how are we to interpret them? In a universe that is tending toward the rational organization of all aspects of life, are they not mere jerky reactions of a world that is approaching its end? Are they not the final explosions of a century that has unceasingly echoed with the sound of explosions? In a sense, a final twenty-one gun salute, an anachronistic phenomenon before humanity arrives at the era of management where there will be no place either for confrontation or for "workers' jacqueries"?

A second hypothesis sees in the spread of total confrontation, in its characteristics, the premonitory signs of an epoch which is only beginning, an epoch in the course of which humanity will free itself from its last chains; when art will emerge from the museums to install itself in the street. Confrontation, in the form it has taken for the past few years, would thus be a prelude to struggles of a more intense, more radical and also more conscious nature.

Between these two interpretations, which to choose? Some will be sure to object that both are false because both are extreme: that the inevitable *via media* will prevail. That's possible. The fact remains that leftist theory will not attain its full meaning and its true dimensions save in the process of becoming: only the future will say whether its pretension to renew the theory of the revolutionary movement is justified. Such as it is, its immense ambitions make it worth discussing even now.

For the moment, one can only remark that ideas tossed out at random, actions which were scarcely designed to be "exemplary," have had unexpected repercussions. Leftism has raised itself from byzantine ratiocinations to the level of a doctrine: its rare partisans have been replaced by numerous groups or even by unorganized masses who adopt the same attitudes, follow the same reasoning. The marginal sects of yesterday are taking on the appearance of a social movement.

Without prejudging the future one can, as of now, put forward the thesis that its impact derives from the immense transformations affecting the daily lives of millions of individuals in the so-called affluent societies. A whole sector of the workers' existence has been altered with the increase in real wages, the provision of security against the major risks of professional and family life, and the disappearance of chronic unemployment.

The progress of technology and science ensure, without question, a mastery over nature that was unthinkable a quarter-century ago. At the same time that material conditions of daily life were improving, new ambitions welled up from the depths of consciousness. In these conditions, leftism was able to appear as the bearer of fresh answers to new questions. . . . Its success depends, beyond any doubt, on the accuracy of its answers. . . . But, even at this early stage, it represents a notable effort of imagination in a world that seemed devoid of it.

This lack of imagination is especially characteristic of what has been customarily called the left—and, first of all, of official communism, the "legitimate" heir to the revolutionary tradition of almost two centuries of social struggle. Leftism has cut into its monopoly in irreversible fashion. It is not certain that leftism is destined to become *the* revolutionary movement. But leftism has already demonstrated, by its very existence and by its impact, that organized Marxism-Leninism is no longer *the* revolutionary movement; this strikes me as an established fact.

6. *George Lichtheim: Contemporary Problems of Socialism*

To summarize socialism's contemporary problems and the state of the movement today, it is logical to turn to the writings of George Lichtheim, one of the most prolific and learned authorities on the subject. Lichtheim, an independent journalist in London, has taught at several American universities. His education at the University of Berlin (in pre-Hitler days) gave him a solid grounding in Hegelian and Marxian thought; many of his books deal with various aspects of socialist history.

If one considers the situation in Western Europe a century after the founding of the First International in 1864, one cannot fail to see that most of the aims set out by the pioneers of the democratic labor movement at the peak of the Victorian era had been achieved or were close to fulfill-

From George Lichtheim, *A Short History of Socialism* (New York: Praeger, 1970), pp. 269–71, 275–77, 324–29. Reprinted by permission of Praeger Publishers, Inc.

ment. In 1964, Social Democracy provided the governmental majority party in Great Britain and throughout most of Scandinavia; it had become a cooperating or competing partner—sometimes the stronger partner—of the Christian Democrats (representing respectable conservatism) in West Germany, Austria, Holland, Belgium, and Switzerland, joining in the administration of those countries or forming the official opposition. It still had powerful support in France, although since 1936 it had lagged numerically behind the Communists, and it participated in the government of Italy. On the other hand, Democratic Socialism had irretrievably lost the positions it once held in Eastern Europe, where its survivors had been forcibly amalgamated with the ruling Communist parties after the Soviet occupation of the area in 1945–48.

Geographically and culturally as well as politically, then, Social Democracy had come to be identified with one particular area of the world: Western Europe. Its short-term and long-term aims were predicated upon assumptions that made sense only in industrialized countries with a solid democratic tradition. There were differences between wholesale nationalizers and advocates of a mixed economy with a large private sector, but whether they stood for socialization in the traditional sense or had accommodated themselves to welfare-state policies and the mixed economy, all took for granted a certain social and cultural milieu characteristic of Western Europe and, outside Europe, to be found in Canada, Australia, New Zealand, and perhaps Japan. This still left room for differences between Social Democrats in the narrow sense, who were content with reformist labor and welfare policies, and authentic Socialists who aimed at something qualitatively different from capitalism. These arguments were relevant to countries such as Britain, France, Germany, Austria, Italy, or Sweden; they had small import either for the poorer southern regions of Europe (Spain, Portugal, Greece) or for backward areas on the threshold of modernization. Outside Europe there was only one major country with an important Socialist party, and significantly it was Japan, now rapidly becoming a major industrial power. . . .

Put schematically, the Socialist movement since the 1930's had to fight on two fronts: against the Third International, which tried to universalize the Bolshevik experience; and against conservative or liberal parties which continued to defend private ownership (including peasant ownership), free enterprise in a market economy, and the cultural values of a propertied or salaried middle class. This last-mentioned qualification is important for two reasons. First, the new salariat was middle class in its habits without being bourgeois in the economic sense of the term, since for the most part it owned no property. Hence its principal concern was to ensure "full employment," meaning job security for itself and its descendants. Secondly, the numerical weakening of the old middle class of farmers, shopkeepers, and small entrepreneurs steadily undermined the electoral basis of the conservative or liberal parties. The economic process thus assembled some of the preconditions for a peaceful take-over by way of majority rule. This perspective had since 1864 been the foundation of democratic socialism. . . .

The political cleavage occasioned by the Russian Revolution and its Stalinist aftermath superimposed itself upon this situation and added to the confusion. The Western labor movement would in any case have been plunged into a crisis by differing reactions to World War I, the depression of the 1930's, and the rise of Fascism. The Communist split added an extra dimension, and matters were not eased by the sectarian quarrels among Stalinists, Trotskyists, and (from about 1960 on) Maoists who had discovered a new model in China, supposedly applicable not only to the pre-industrial "third world" of backward areas, but to advanced countries as well. In the face of all these distractions it is perhaps remarkable that something like a Socialist movement continued to survive at all. No doubt it did so because there was in fact no other option for its adherents, whether workers or intellectuals. Soviet Communism had become identified with the East European police state: so much so that after the Hungarian blood-bath of 1956 and later with the invasion of Czechoslovakia in 1968, even some of the more alert West European Communists began to edge away from the once admired Stalinist model. Social Democracy might be boring, but at least it was familiar and held no menace to freedom and decency.

It thus continued to enjoy mass support, on the tacit understanding that it would act as a reformist agency in defense of labor's interests against the steady encroachment of industrial technology and state control. Socialization was to proceed slowly (if at all) and only on condition that a majority of the voters was prepared to sanction it. For reasons already explained, this latter qualification became easier to fulfill once it was realized that growing numbers of salary-earners were prepared to tolerate or even welcome a measure of socialism, in the name of economic planning, job security, and full employment.

In principle, a legal guarantee of work for all—that most ancient of socialist slogans—might become a transition to the stage of guaranteed tenure, already operative in the civil service and the universities, and applicable to industry as well, notably if the economy became state-controlled. The general trend in all the old industrial countries toward stability and away from the perpetual insecurity associated with the free market responded to deep-seated human cravings. But it presupposed an advanced stage of capital formation, a reasonable rate of economic growth, industrial discipline, and general political maturity. It was clearly impractical to prescribe a regime of this kind as the solution for the problems of newly industrialized countries, where production had perforce to take precedence over all other considerations. Once more democratic socialism disclosed itself as a theory and practice appropriate to the privileged areas of the world. Beyond these regions, with their painfully accumulated capital equipment and their relatively stable political institutions, the ancient dream of combining equality and liberty assumed a distinctly utopian look. And even this assessment took no account of the anarcho-syndicalist wave that rolled across Europe in 1968, producing a general strike in France and a semblance of worker-student cooperation in other industrial countries as well: proof positive (if any was needed) that the forces set in motion by the industrial revolution had not yet found an adequate political and cultural framework. What students—largely drawn from the new middle class of salaried and professional people—rebelled against clearly had no direct connection with the traditional aims of the labor movement, even though it might be argued that the "alienation" they experienced was an aspect of exploitation. For an oppositional intelligentsia had likewise begun to make its appearance in Eastern Europe, where capitalism was not an issue. Setting aside the horrors of Stalinism, which by the late 1960's had anyhow been partly eliminated, what students and workers in the nominally socialist countries of the Soviet bloc (plus Yugoslavia) revolted against were the bureaucratic and authoritarian structures implanted after 1945. But if the movement was directed against corporate capitalism in the West, and against state socialism in the East, then it could not be subsumed under terms left over from the bourgeois era, when "exploitation" (in the Marxian sense) signified the appropriation of surplus value by individual capitalists. It would then be necessary to conclude that the common factor was the emergence, east and west of the political frontier splitting the Continent, of a new type of society for which only the term "technocratic" had so far been found suitable. In this sense, the classical confrontation between socialism and liberalism had by the late 1960's taken on a somewhat antiquated appearance. . . .

Let us now consider why even under relatively favorable external conditions—e.g., in Western Europe since the end of World War II—progress in the direction of socialism has been slower than was originally expected. The main reasons can be summarized under two heads: continuing economic scarcity, with the resulting pressure to place rational economic calculations first; and the reluctance of the electorate (including a majority of the industrial working class) to press on more rapidly toward genuine social equality.

As to the first, it needs no great effort of the imagination to conceive a state of affairs where noneconomic considerations have become paramount because all reasonable economic demands have been met or are in process of being satisfied. Unfortunately, such a state of things is not yet sufficiently general, even in the richest and most civilized countries, to remove the topic of economic growth from the agenda. And nothing less will do. Unless and until a majority of the electorate in a democratically governed country is prepared to do without a continuous rise in living standards (as conventionally interpreted) economic considerations will take precedence over social and cultural claims. In such an atmosphere the expansion of welfare services out of taxation is all that can be done by governments dependent on public opinion. Genuine equality—the distribution of the "national dividend" according to criteria of need alone—cannot be attempted if the result is likely to be a significant decline in economic efficiency, a slowing down of growth, loss of export markets to foreign competitors, and a consequent fall in living standards and in the funds available for private and public consumption. For of course international trade enters into the matter. How should it not? If the balance of external trade acts as an economic pace-setter, any decline in relative efficiency will promptly make itself felt in the form of stagnation, unemployment, and other disagreeable consequences. The smaller and more highly specialized a country, the more likely it is to suffer from fluctuations in world trade, unless it manages to keep ahead of its competitors. Success in this field is always uncertain, some countries benefiting from temporary advantages at the expense of others. If we stay with Western Europe after 1945, the outstanding success story along neo-liberal lines has been the expansion of West Germany's external trade, a performance paradoxically helped along by military defeat and the resultant ban on heavy and wasteful arms expenditure. That similar results can be obtained under Social Democratic government is attested to by the case of Sweden, once more a combination of good luck and good management, aided by specialization in the newer industries. One might also cite the corresponding examples of Austria, Denmark, Holland, and Switzerland, where the labor movement has contented itself with being a partner in a rapidly expanding capitalist economy, wage rates rising on an average no faster than output per head, so that prices have been kept relatively stable. Under less favorable circumstances, e.g. in Britain, wages have risen appreciably faster than productivity, thus driving prices up more rapidly than among some of Britain's main competitors. Apart from the inevitable damage to the country's share of world trade (not to mention the stability of its currency), the result has been to associate laborism with inflationary price rises from which people living on fixed incomes are notoriously the chief sufferers. In the political vocabulary of the welfare state, laborism is equated with socialism, so that socialist theory is made to take the blame for the typically capitalist behavior of employers and unions alike. . . .

It seems probable that the British economy had by the 1960's reached an "awkward corner" for historic reasons quite unconnected with the current behavior of employers and unions, but this does not invalidate the theoretical part of the argument: in a capitalist economy, whether or not administered by a Labor government, the attainment of even relatively modest welfare-state goals depends on growth rates which in turn depend, in part at least, on competitiveness in the world market. International trade takes place predominantly among industrially advanced countries and only marginally between them and the "underdeveloped," which is why the loss of their colonies did no economic harm to the West European countries, or to Japan, which was likewise stripped of its colonial possessions in 1945. Since the industrially developed countries outside the Soviet bloc are for the most part governed democratically and since their electorates are predominantly salaried, any advance toward socialization hinges upon the willingness of the labor movement to back long-term planning at the expense of short-range economic gains.

This applies with particular force if reformist rather than socially conservative parties are in political control. It also applies to the hypothetical case of a completely socialized economy. In such an economy the quarrel would be over the distribution of the social dividend as between the state and the producers, with politics resolving themselves into a tug between the central planning bureaucracy and the more or less autonomous works councils representing all those engaged in the production and distribution of goods and services. Needless to say, none of this has any relevance to the backward countries, with their rising populations and stagnant incomes per head, or to the Soviet orbit, where socialism performs the historic function normally associated with the earlier stages of capital accumulation. We are solely concerned with regions which have passed beyond this phase and have become sufficiently rich and productive for something like equality to be attainable. There is no point in debating the question whether wealth should in all circumstances be equitably divided, even if the result is economic stagnation (as it certainly would be in any poor country lacking the necessary capital equipment). Nor is there any need to waste time and energy over frivolities such as the demand that the "consumer society" be abolished. This kind of talk commonly issues from people who do not have to work for a living. The crisis through which the contemporary socialist movement is passing has not been brought about by the corruption of the working class through excessive rise in money incomes or the desire to possess consumer goods. It is due to the unresolved cleavage between short-term and long-term aspirations, the socialist parties having failed to reconcile their ultimate aims with the pressures arising from the normal political process in a democracy where wage-earners have become a majority of the electorate. The gap between socialist rhetoric and laborist performance measures the difficulty of making social equality relevant to people overwhelmingly concerned with simple economic issues: specifically, guaranteed full employment and a steady rise in living standards.

When one says that even in the most highly industrialized countries of the Western world the transition from a "mixed" to a socialist economy still lacks adequate popular support, one is not just saying something about the power of conservative ideology or the relative failure of Social Democratic (or for that matter Communist) parties to expand beyond their traditional base in the industrial working class. One is also saying something about the inherent conflict between two quite different and possibly irreconcilable goals: economic growth and social equality. The former *may* occur under capitalism or socialism alike, but a socialized economy devoted to the aim of keeping up with the fastest growth rates achieved in the capitalist world must give preference to economic rationality at the expense of other considerations. Conversely, if a democracy is to opt voluntarily for a greater degree of social equality than even the best managed capitalist system can permit, the voters may by the same token have to opt for a slowdown in economic growth. A conscious choice to this effect is conceivable, but not very likely in the short run. At their present political and cultural level even the most advanced democracies are unlikely to forego the advantages accruing from rapid technological change, higher productivity, rising money wages—and the inequality that goes with it. If a socialist society is defined as one in which the wage relation has been abolished, the producers placed in control of their tools, and the cleavage between physical and mental labor overcome through an all-round development of the human personality, we are still far from the attainment of such goals.

The inner logic of the production process does indeed favor socialization, inasmuch as the "post-industrial" development of automation gives rise to a new hierarchy of functions no longer measurable by the cruder standards of an earlier epoch. Social conflict assumes new forms, the steady growth of monopoly and the expansion of a bureaucratically controlled public sector driving the private entrepreneur out of business and producing novel confrontations dimly foreshadowed by the strikes and factory occupations of recent years. If theoretical development does not lag too far behind, socialism as a movement may transcend its class origins and come to represent the aspirations of the intelligentsia, as well as those of a working class itself in process of acquiring new skills and higher levels of education and awareness. These hopeful factors must be weighed against the inherent problem of making equality rhyme with the requirements of a culture shaped by the recent speed-up in the rate of technological change. The goal of a classless and conflict-free society is not easily reconciled with the drive toward ever higher levels of economic performance in a competitive world, most of which is still desperately poor. The prospects of socialism in the classical sense are brightest where economic pressures are negligible and people can envisage an egalitarian way of life on the basis of social ownership of the means of production. In this sense the preconditions of a socialist order do not at present exist anywhere. Much of the world is still going through the early phases of the industrial revolution, while the advanced countries are taken up with the attainment of higher living standards. Socialists will find plenty to occupy them during the coming decades, if only because liberalism has disintegrated both as a philosophy and as a way of managing the political system. But if they are honest they will not pretend that the kind of society they would like to see is inscribed in the logic of the immediate future.

XII

Eu̇ropean Integration: Where Does It Go from Here?

Although the idea of European unity has roots several centuries old, only in our time has it moved from dream to potential reality. Between the wars, efforts to build mass support for a federated Europe fell on barren ground; so did the proposal for a United States of Europe advanced by the French statesman Aristide Briand in 1929. It was the destructive impact of the second world war that put life into the movement. The fabric of Europe and of many of its national societies was torn apart; it might therefore be rewoven in a different pattern. Besides, many Europeans believed that in the postwar era a fragmented Europe would be doomed to impotence in world affairs. Idealists and realists joined in preaching the virtues of federalism in one or another form. Even Winston Churchill lent his enormous prestige to the effort (though mainly at a time when he was out of office).

But the problem proved far more complex than its more impatient sponsors had expected. For one thing, the Cold War split Europe in two, separated it almost impenetrably by what Churchill called an "iron curtain." Federal union, for the time being at least, would therefore have to be regional rather than continental. In addition, national sentiment proved to have a far deeper hold on men's emotions than the federalists had believed; only a minority had begun to "think European" to the point of abandoning the comfortable assurances of national sovereignty. Finally, the advocates of union differed sharply over how to accomplish it, and what it should look like, once accomplished. For some, all of Europe would have to be included; for others, western Europe alone was enough; for still others, Atlantic union must be the aim. Whatever its boundaries, the question was asked: ought federated Europe to be constructed from the top down (i.e., by a dramatic breakthrough to a new supranational authority), or from the bottom up (piecemeal, through a series of "functional" experiments)? For a time, it seemed that these difficulties might combine to block effective progress.

Nevertheless, some experiments did get under way during the first postwar decade. Benelux came into existence—a customs union joining Belgium, The Netherlands, and Luxemburg—with its declared goal a full-scale economic union. Small but significant, it served as a kind of pilot project for the later Common Market. A Council of Europe was set up in Strasbourg in 1948, with fifteen (later eighteen) member states; though its powers were meager, it served as a forum for discussion of European questions. The Organization for European Economic Cooperation (OEEC, later OECD) emerged as a permanent by-product of the

American Marshall Plan; it brought together experts from the nations that received Marshall aid, and served as a clearinghouse and study group for common socioeconomic problems. In 1951 the European Steel and Coal Community (ECSC) was established as the first functional agency; it was granted at least a little supranational authority, and brought together the six nations (France, Italy, Germany, Benelux) that were to constitute the durable nucleus of western European integration. In 1957, by the Treaty of Rome, the six broadened out their cooperation by setting up the European Economic Community (EEC), popularly called the Common Market. The British refused to join (as they had in the case of the ECSC as well); but as a kind of counterweight and bargaining agent, they now put together their own loose grouping of seven countries with the label European Free Trade Association (EFTA). From 1957, therefore, the "inner six" were confronted by the "outer seven."

The federalist experiment, fragmented in this fashion, thus entered the decade of the 1960's with uncertain prospects. It was not yet clear how the various organizations would relate to each other, or whether rival national interests would permit any of them to expand their scope and authority. During the years that followed, conflict and crisis seemed endemic. Charles De Gaulle, who had taken power in France in 1958, adopted a skeptical and intransigent stance toward the whole enterprise, and decided to remain in the EEC only so long as it could be used to further French interests as he defined them. When Britain belatedly decided to seek admission (1963), De Gaulle brusquely vetoed the bid. When the other member states balked at France's proposed Common Market plan for agriculture, De Gaulle withdrew France's representatives at Brussels. Throughout all this, deep differences persisted over the EEC's proper goal: should it become a true federal union with supranational powers, or merely a loose confederation of sovereign states?

Yet somehow the six EEC countries managed to surmount each successive crisis, to compromise or postpone issues, and to keep moving forward. By the early 1970's it began to seem that a corner had somehow been turned, that the point of no return had been passed—and that whatever might be the future shape of a federated western Europe, it would survive in one form or another. The British now applied once more for admission to the EEC, this time successfully; and the British Parliament, after a long and bitter debate, approved the step. Several other members of EFTA applied at the same time, so that "the six" began the process of transmutation into "the nine." The federalists could briefly draw breath and look ahead, asking themselves where the movement might go from here. It is that question which forms the central theme of this final chapter. But it may be proper in passing to suggest that future historians may one day look back at this jerky, erratic process of unification as the most important structural change of our time—and possibly even as the most important change ever carried out by peaceful means in all of modern European history.

I. *Donald J. Puchala: Patterns in Western European Integration*

It is not easy to sum up in capsule form the achievements of the European integration movement during the quarter-century from 1945 to 1970. Donald J. Puchala has nevertheless managed to pull it all together in this brief passage. Puchala is an assistant professor of political science at Columbia University, where he specializes in problems of international organization.

A review of the postwar history of Western Europe makes one immediately aware that a great deal of a political, economic, social and psychological nature has happened in the course of the last two decades' relations among Frenchmen, West Germans, Italians, Belgians, Dutchmen, Luxembourgers and others. Furthermore, almost all of "what has happened" has had something to do with international integration on the Continent.

First, the great powers of Western Europe, France and West Germany most notably, have ceased preparing for war against one another. We now tend to take the new West European security community for granted. But our nonchalance must not blur the fact that the emergence of a "no war" community on the Continent between 1945 and 1955 was an historically momentous occurrence.

Second, aspects of the national sovereignty and governmental prerogative of several Western European states have been voluntarily transferred to regional policy-making bodies. Over several years these international organizations and supranational institutions have grown in stature in the estimations of European elites. They have found popularity among mass populations. In addition, they have been accorded legitimacy by almost all political strata. Not least important, international and supranational bodies have moved toward expanded functions and jurisdictions.

Third, political transnationality in Western Europe has been increasingly evidenced in the structure and functioning of parties, interest groups and other lobbying organizations. Regional "umbrella" organizations, established to inject specialized points of view into policy making in the European Economic Community, are the best known transnational groups. But these conspicuous lobbies are really only a small fraction of the total number of newly formed regional associations within which West Europeans of different nationalities share, explore and jointly promote a seemingly unlimited range of political, economic, social and cultural interests.

Fourth, gross transaction flows among Western European countries have

From Donald J. Puchala, "Patterns in Western European Integration," *Journal of Common Market Studies*, IX (1970), 118–19, 141–42. Reprinted by permission of Basil Blackwell, Publisher.

both increased greatly in volume and expanded notably in range during the postwar era. West Europeans in the postwar era have been paying a great deal more attention to one another than ever before in history. In fact, quibbling among analysts about appropriate ways to measure transaction flows and about the specific meanings of slight year-to-year increases and reverses in these flows has had the effect of covering over the most outstanding feature of the intra-European exchanges—their existence! Prior to World War II, high volumes of mutual transactions over multiple social, economic, cultural and political ranges were the great exceptions and certainly not the rule in intra-European relations.

Fifth, by almost any attitudinal measure, the twenty-five years since World War II have been a period of fairly dramatic social-psychological change at all levels of Western European societies. National identifications have not altered very much. But, in interesting fashion they have been supplemented by regional identifications. Or, less emphatically phrased, persisting national identifications have not greatly hindered the growth of sympathies for regional integration schemes, nor have they much interfered with federative drives. More than this, and perhaps more significant, West European peoples' feelings about each other have been changing, and most of these shifts in attitude have been in positive directions from enmity to amity and from suspicion to trust.

Sixth, all of the positive features of postwar intra-European relations among governments and peoples must not hide the fact that newspapers published over the years between 1945 and 1970 were cluttered with descriptions of diplomatic crises, debates, confrontations and impasses among West European governments. Several integration schemes failed. Some are failing at present. Conflict has been as conspicuous along the pathway to integration as cooperation has. Whether we choose to use the term "high politics" or not is a matter of semantic choice. But what we cannot ignore is that certain political issues have continually divided, and continue to divide, West European governments and peoples along strictly national lines. Intermittent crises have been part of European integration. . . .

Western European integration has been a cyclical process marked by "ups" and "downs" in institutionalization, diplomatic interaction and federative enthusiasm. Nevertheless, there have been important secular trends beneath and behind the various cycles. These latter trends have been moving mainly in an upward direction toward greater international integration. First, there has been a long-developing trend toward heightened mutual attentiveness, relevance and responsiveness in intra-European transactional behavior. This trend has had fluctuations. Nevertheless, I would contend that it is irreversible save perhaps over the very long run. That is, it is highly unlikely that Western Europeans could quickly retreat to the mutual isolation of the 1920s and 1930s. Second, there has been a secular trend in institutionalization that is building towards the development of an ever more sturdy and complex organizational infrastructure for intraregional politics. This infrastructure is strikingly apparent at intergovernmental and non-governmental levels. Institutionalization has been erratic, to be sure. But what has been built has lasted, and 40 intergovernmental and more than 800 non-governmental organizations have already been built. At the very least, European integration has a vast reservoir of organizational inertia behind it. Third, since 1957 there has been a secular trend toward greater and greater elite and mass legitimacy accorded to integrative institutions and regional political processes. The upward-sloping trend in support for federation weathered the strains of 1963–65. It is also probably irreversible in the short run since it does not fluctuate greatly with either international events or national governments' policies. Finally, while there is no secular trend toward greater diplomatic accommodation among West European governments (or at least between the French and the West German governments) there has been nonetheless a growing durability in diplomatic relations. That is, good relations have held up under increasingly heavy loads. There are still breakdowns to be sure. But probabilities of crisis avoidance and of productive conflict resolution have been rising over time. Needless to say, all of the secular trends bode well for the future of European integration. None of them, however, predict quick leaps to federation.

2. *Werner Feld: The EEC and Eastern Europe*

In 1948 the Soviet Union, in an effort to counter the effect of the Marshall Plan, established in eastern Europe the Council for Mutual Economic Assistance, commonly known as "Comecon." This organization, which grouped all the countries of the Soviet bloc, amounted at first to little more than a facade for Soviet economic control of the area. After the establishment of the Common Market, however, Moscow responded by attempting to build up Comecon as a kind of rival. These efforts have been partially frustrated by the reluctance of certain bloc countries (notably Rumania) to hand over control of their economic development to a central authority. Progress toward building supranational institutions has therefore been much slower in eastern than in western Europe. In addition, several of the east European states have been strongly attracted by the magnetic pull exerted by the Common Market, which can provide the East with outlets for its goods and with technical assistance. Some of these issues are discussed in the following essay by Werner Feld, professor of government at Louisiana State University. Feld is the author of several books, including one on *The Common Market and the World*.

The establishment and operation of the European Economic Community have evoked three major reactions in the rest of the world: admiration for the successful process of economic integration, displeasure over the actual and potential harm to the economies of the non-member coun-

From Werner Feld, "The Utility of the EEC Experience for Eastern Europe," *Journal of Common Market Studies*, VIII (1970), 236–39, 254–56, 260–61. Footnotes omitted. Reprinted by permission of Basil Blackwell, Publisher.

tries, and a mixture of envy and apprehension about the increased prestige and power—economic as well as political—that has accrued to the member states of the EEC. These reactions, in turn, have prompted a variety of behavior by the non-member states. Some were anxious to climb on the "bandwagon" of economic benefits by seeking to join the Common Market and applied for either full membership or associate status. Others attempted to emulate the success of the Common Market and, at the same time, reduce its harmful effects by establishing either customs unions or free trade areas of their own. The non-European developed capitalist countries sought to exploit the rapidly rising economic levels in the Common Market through multilateral tariff-cutting ventures, through which, they hoped the internal Common Market preferences would be reduced and international trade expanded. . . .

In the East European Communist countries all three of these reactions could be observed. After at first playing down the prospects of the Common Market and declaring it to be doomed to failure, the Soviet and other Communist leaders a few years later paid grudging respect to the economic integration process as carried out by the "capitalists" in Western Europe. In the *Seventeen Theses Regarding the Common Market*, published in 1957 by the authoritative Moscow Institute of World Economics and International Relations, the Common Market was seen as a new method of dividing the capitalist world market, bound to lead to serious frictions and conflicts within capitalist society. It was doubted that the steps envisaged by the EEC Treaty could ever be accomplished. But, in 1962, thirty-two new theses published by the same institute under the title *Concerning Imperialist "Integration" in Western Europe (The Common Market)*, set a different tone. They recognized that the Common Market had stimulated production on a greater scale than anticipated and resulted "in certain increases of wages for the laboring class." A short time prior to the publication of the latest theses, the director of the Institute had already stated in an article in *Pravda* that "in the Common Market one can observe a real technical and scientific revolution which carries with it a powerful regeneration of the industrial structure of capitalism. . . . The EEC has a remarkable vitality and has created objective situations whose elimination will not be possible without grave consequences."

The East European Communist leaders were also apprehensive about the effects of the Common Market on their exports to the member countries and feared that a future common commercial policy of the EEC could be extremely disruptive to this trade. For these reasons, the Soviet Union demanded after the establishment of the Common Market that she and the other East European Communist countries be accorded the same preferences under the most-favored-nation clause which the EEC countries had granted each other under the Treaty. (Since under the GATT rules customs union preferences are exempted from the application of this clause, this demand was refused.)

Another concern of the East European Communists lay in the field of strategy and high politics. They feared that the successful conclusion of the customs and economic union as set forth in the Treaty of Rome might lead to a politically unified Western Europe that would upset the strategic *status quo;* moreover, a united Europe closely allied to the United States would materially alter the world balance of power. And even if these events were not to materialize immediately, the prestige accruing to the Common Market through a successful integration process could have a psychological impact on the people in the East European states that would be detrimental to the interests of the Communist leadership.

Apprehension over the harmful effects of the Common Market on East European trade with Western Europe and over the consequences of successful economic integration in the EEC were key factors prompting changes in the organization of Comecon. Gomulka is supposed to have personally proposed to Khrushchev in 1957 that Comecon be developed as the answer to the EEC. At the same time, the Czechoslovak and Hungarian governments also advocated that the East should oppose integration with integration. In 1962 Khrushchev expressed the view, that in response to the evolution of the Common Market, Comecon should establish a unified planning organ, empowered to elaborate common plans and to decide organizational matters. Although the Rumanians refused to accept anything resembling supranational decision-making, the Comecon charter of 1960, setting up a comprehensive institutional structure which had been lacking so far, as well as the *Basic Principles* and charter amendments adopted in 1962, were definitive moves in the direction of the objectives set by Khrushchev and other East European leaders.

In the meantime, the East European governments made strong efforts to increase their exports to the Common Market, which were matched during the last few years by a growing drive on the part of Common Market firms to expand their own sales to East Europe. As a consequence, mutual trade in the period from 1958 to 1967 tripled. However, for the EEC as a unit this trade was relatively insignificant, representing, in 1967, only about 6 per cent of its total external commerce. On the other hand, for the East European countries their trade with the EEC was important and, disregarding trade within Comecon, ranged from a low of about 20 per cent of external trade for the Soviet Union to more than 50 per cent for Rumania.

The East European endeavors to increase trade with the EEC were not only motivated by the natural desire to find markets for their agricultural products and certain raw materials, especially petroleum, but also by their interest in obtaining certain capital goods with long-range Western credits and in sharing in the special technological knowledge of the Western industries. The pursuit of these objectives and the perceived need to neutralize the magnetism of the Common Market are likely reasons why the Soviet Union has in recent years advocated all-European economic co-operation, perhaps in the form of a free trade area which would safeguard the sovereignty of all participating states. In this connection a statement made by Chairman Kosygin during a news conference in London early in 1967 is noteworthy. Asked whether British membership in the Common Market would be good or bad for European development and security, he replied: "The very name Common Market is a drawback in that it is not "common" because not all countries are free to join. Markets of this kind should be open to cooperation of all the nations of Europe on an equal footing" . . . .

The institutional framework of Comecon is weak. The Secretariat, an effective organ only since 1962, plays the role of providing the essentially administrative functions for the organization, but has little resemblance to the Commission of the Common Market with its extensive executive and supervisory authority. The operational functions are carried out by the Executive Committee of Comecon which is composed of the Deputy Chairmen of the Councils of Ministers of the member countries. This Committee meets much less often than the EEC Council of Ministers and has neither the power nor the scope for decision-making of the latter body. In 1962, when the organizational machinery of Comecon was upgraded, Khrushchev advocated even stronger institutions endowed with a measure of supranationalism. He suggested that when taking decisions the common interests of Comecon as a whole should be taken into consideration rather than the immediate benefits for the national economies. If planning decisions were to be made on the scale of Comecon as a whole, he conceded that some interventions might have to be made in the management of the national economies. To promote Comecon-wide specialization of production, he declared that "The Soviet Union is prepared to reduce its output of some kind of manufacture if it proves more expedient to produce them in another Comecon country." Of course, these initiatives by Khrushchev may have been equally or perhaps even more motivated by Soviet interests than Comecon interests, but it nevertheless constitutes an acknowledgement of the need for supranationalism in the Communist organization.

It is well known that it was primarily Rumania which squashed all attempts to introduce a degree of supranationalism into Comecon by threatening to withdraw from the organization in such an event. Undoubtedly, fear of encroachment by the Soviet Union on her political independence was Rumania's main reason for this threat and there can be little question that the suspicions regarding Soviet intentions were well justified and that they are shared by some of the other People's Democracies. As a consequence, the emphasis on the national point of view and the strict adherence to the principles of sovereignty and unanimity in decision-making has persisted and much of the planning of Comecon activities continues to be carried out through bilateral and sometimes trilateral agreements between the countries involved.

It is interesting to note that during the Comecon Executive Committee meeting in Berlin in January 1969 and during the Comecon Summit Conference in Moscow in April of 1969, the Soviet leaders made new efforts towards introducing the principle of supranationalism into Comecon and sought in particular to create a supranational planning organ. The Soviet efforts were supported by Poland and Bulgaria. Already prior to this conference, Gomulka had expressed himself in favor of creating a truly common market including progress towards political integration. East Germany, however, did not commit itself to such a far-reaching kind of integration; she confined her objectives to integration on the level of industries but shied away from any political integration. Rumania, of course, again refused any kind of limitation upon her national sovereignty and Hungary, anxious to avoid a crisis within Comecon, took an intermediate position. The result of the conference was a defeat of the Russian efforts. The final communiqué stated that all participants agreed on the need to improve and deepen the form and methods of cooperation of their economies, but also confirmed that their mutual relations were based *inter alia* on "complete equality and respect of their sovereignty and national interest." Thus, little change can be expected in the decision-making methods and institutions of Comecon in the foreseeable future, but the cooperation between the Comecon countries may well become more streamlined and effective in the years to come.

If the People's Democracies were to engage in the establishment of subregional groupings for the purpose of economic integration, the EEC experiences in the institutional field should be valuable. Tendencies towards nationalism and industrial egoism would need to be deemphasized as much as possible in order to give the central institutions, which must have at least limited supranational powers, an opportunity to operate effectively. With the U.S.S.R. outside such a group, apprehension over Soviet control should not be a source for nationalistic orientation; rather, what would be required is the strengthening of the subregional group *vis-à-vis* the Soviet Union and for this the foremost requirement would be maximum unity. Otherwise the finest objectives of an integration agreement will be jeopardized and the end-result may be failure. Moreover, if the long-range goals of such an agreement should envisage political union, the institutions must be sufficiently strong and prestigious to provide a realistic assurance that the expectations of the people in the participating countries can be satisfied. Only under such conditions can the necessary shift of expectations and loyalties take place, a shift which will also need the support of a strong political will on the part of the leaders of the countries involved in the integration venture.

The effect of a strong institutional framework with supranational features in Eastern Europe on the possibility of transforming the economic and political systems of People's Democracies is hard to evaluate. If the Comecon organs were to be endowed with supranational powers and decision-making were to be carried out on a qualified majority basis, Soviet influence would be strong and the chances for transformation probably small. In a subregional group, the potential for transformation may depend on the views of the supranational leadership and how well the technocrats could be made responsive to meeting the needs of the region as a whole. The attitudes of the governments participating in the integration venture would of course also be crucial.

Speculations regarding the prospects for bridging the East-West gap in Europe are equally hazardous. In order to succeed in the supranational experiment, the newly formed economic unit may adopt at first a policy of autarchy which would tend to impede any bridging efforts. But once such a unit had gained greater strength, closer cooperation between East and West Europe may become very attractive. Much may also hinge on the attitudes of the Western countries and their genuine interest in helping the East European grouping obtain the benefits of West European integration experiences. Other influential factors may be the strength of an "all-European" ideology in Western Europe, the perceived advantages of Western economic assistance for Eastern Europe, and the urgency for greater cooperation between all advanced countries in order to meet the needs of the Third World. . . . The Yugoslav attempts to negotiate a preferential trade agreement with the Common Market and the very modest Polish, Hungarian, Czech and Rumanian initiatives towards the EEC during the last few years, more discreet and cautious, are apt to weaken Comecon, even if they suggest nothing more than vague possibilities in the future. The Soviet Union, more and more apprehensive about the stagnation of Comecon, might consider this an additional inducement to accept the formation of a subregional grouping within Comecon if it-were to perceive that such development might strengthen the cohesion of Eastern Europe and thereby bolster its strategic position.

Of course, unless the People's Democracies make use of the positive experiences of the EEC and exploit the lessons to be learned from the failures of the Common Market, their efforts to form subregional groupings may not be much more than establishing intergovernmental relationships with little prospect of leading to advanced economic or later political integration. Yet, progress towards political union of the subsystem or subsystems is highly desirable in order to produce a counterweight against the Soviet Union and perhaps also to obtain a better bargaining position against the EEC which in due time might include other West European states. It will then become evident whether the national industrial egoism displayed by the People's Democracies is merely a reflection of their struggle to be independent of Soviet control or whether it is steeped in an extensive nationalism that will insist on the prerogatives of sovereignty and on economic autarchy, regardless of the circumstances. If the latter should be the case, the results of the subregional groupings will be disappointing and the East European countries may well have forfeited the opportunity to catch up to the economic levels of their West European brethren. Rather, they will continue to be dependent in every aspect on the Soviet Union and on the goodwill and enlightened self-interest of a more powerful Western Europe. And the prospects for bridging the gap between the Eastern and Western parts of Europe and for the transformation of their economic and political systems will be greatly reduced.

3. *Ernest Mandel: Europe Versus America?*

Werner Feld's essay suggests that the Soviet Union, although profoundly hostile toward and suspicious of the Common Market, has been moving toward a more pragmatic acceptance of its existence. Leonid Brezhnev, speaking in Moscow in March 1972, branded as "absurd" the idea that the USSR has sought to undermine the EEC, and added: "We are carefully observing the activity of the Common Market and its evolution." [1] Nevertheless, Marxists in western Europe continue to view the EEC as a bourgeois scheme set up to defend the interests of the big monopolies. This theme, together with the prediction that American monopolists are likely to use the Common Market to take over control of Europe, runs through Ernest Mandel's book *Europe Versus America?* Mandel is a Belgian scholar who was educated in Brussels and Paris. Since 1956 he has edited the Brussels weekly *La Gauche;* he is one of the leading figures of the Fourth International (Trotskyist). Some European liberals, incidentally, share his fear that American big business may gain control of western Europe's economy unless the Europeans can manage to set up transnational corporations large enough to compete with their American rivals.

Competition dictates the centralization of capital. European industrialists behave as Marx predicted. The pressure in favour of the interpenetration of capital in Europe far surpasses that working for its national concentration.

Certain sectors of industry demand such intensive investment to attain profitable production that even all the companies in that sector in each individual Common Market country together cannot provide it. In such cases international financing is mandatory to be able to produce at all. . . . Even in those sectors where two or three large companies can still exist side by side, the benefits of collaboration and amalgamation are so evident that it seems impossible to match the size and competitive capacity of the American giants without resorting to mergers. That is why the trend towards capital interpenetration has begun to become fact. . . .

Historically, the Common Market arose as the result of previous capital concentration in Europe. For a long time, the development of the major productive forces had been in danger of suffocation within the narrow borders of the nation state. This was especially so in Germany. After two historic failures at violent expansion to the East, the productive forces of West Germany are now trying to find a way out of the narrow confines of their national borders by peaceful commercial expansion. Confronted by

From Ernest Mandel, *Europe Versus America? Contradictions of Imperialism,* trans. Martin Rossdale (London: New Left Books, 1970), pp. 40–42, 47–48, 95–98, 102–104, 112, 130–34. Footnotes omitted. Copyright © 1970 by New Left Books. Reprinted by permission of Monthly Review Press.

1. *Current Digest of the Soviet Press,* XXIV, No. 12 (April 19, 1972).

the inherent conflict between the bourgeois mode of production and the bourgeois nation state, the European bourgeoisie is attempting the best partial and provisional solution available to it for the moment, the creation of a large free-trade area. . . .

The future of the EEC's supranational institutions ultimately depends on the extent of the interpenetration of capital in Europe. . . . Like the formation of the EEC itself, the consolidation of these supranational authorities does not follow a straight line but is the result of a dialectical process depending on the struggle between those capitalist groupings which support the interpenetration of capital and those which oppose it.

We have already shown how national governments rally to the defence of their own prerogatives and sovereignty, even where this sometimes entails clashes with the immediate interests of their own capitalists. They will only agree to surrender important elements of their sovereignty to a supranational authority if forced to do so by predominant economic forces in their respective countries.

Closer study of this may indicate under what conditions and in what circumstances a new European state might be created. Our starting-point must be the fundamental fact that the primary role of the bourgeois state is to guarantee the profits of the great monopolies. We must therefore begin with a closer examination of that role.

As long as a "long wave" which is basically expansionist in character prevails, the economic function of the bourgeois state is the classic one of guaranteeing expansion by ensuring a sufficient volume of money and credit and financing public works. . . .

But as soon as this "long wave" with expansionist tendencies turns into a "long wave" drifting into stagnation, as soon as annual growth rates decline, and partial recessions—the heralds of generalized recession—multiply in EEC countries, big capital will make heavier demands on the bourgeois state. Counter-cyclical measures, or more exactly, measures to forestall disastrous slumps, will then take precedence over all others. . . . It is obvious that as soon as economic integration and the interpenetration of capital within the EEC have gone beyond a certain stage, it will be impossible to operate effective anti-crisis policies within the framework of the *national* economy, which cannot generate the necessary purchasing-power to allow big *European* concerns to maintain profits, and keep up employment while continuing to limit redundancies to a "reasonable" volume and to sell the major part of their output. Such a policy requires European scale measures, whether the EEC remains as it is or whether it is enlarged. . . .

There is a manifest contradiction between ever-increasing economic programming on a national level . . . and ever-increasing interpenetration of capital within the EEC on the other. Ultimately this contradiction can only lead in one of two directions. Either European integration will be reversed, which would amount to a gradual return to economic nationalism (and, in a crisis period, to protectionism), or late capitalism's inherent tendency towards economic programming will pass from a national to a European level, not just quantitatively but in such a way as to bring qualitative, structural changes.

As soon as the EEC finds itself in the grips of a general recession, threatening to spill over into a serious economic crisis, "European" companies will therefore be forced to demand anti-recessionary policies on a "European" scale. In other words, they will tend to demand that national governments lose their right to take decisions in critical areas of economic policy and hand over these powers to the supranational authorities of the European Community. . . .

The upshot of this analysis is clear; the EEC's moment of truth will arrive when Europe undergoes a general recession. This will be the decisive test of the Common Market. [One possibility is that] international big capital will be able to bring such pressure to bear on national governments as to force them to make significant concessions at the fiscal, financial and monetary level. In this case there would be a fair chance of applying a counter-cyclical and anti-recessionary policy throughout the Common Market. . . . This would be proof that the EEC had been definitely consolidated and would render the internationalization of private and state capital irrevocable. Such a Community would have as little tendency to revert to the Europe of nation states as the German Reich had to revert to the former individual principalities after 1871. The other possibility is that those capitalist circles who persist in defending a national fiscal, monetary and financial policy will triumph, in which case a coordinated anti-recessionary policy throughout the EEC would be impossible. . . . Consolidation of the EEC will then be out of the question. The entire Common Market will tear itself apart. . . .

Such are the conclusions of a general theoretical analysis of the inherent trends of the capitalist economy and of competition between Europe and America—an analysis supported by certain concrete facts. Several member states of the EEC have already experienced recession. The responses of capital and government can be more or less exactly outlined. They roughly correspond to the two alternatives above. In any case, they confirm that, as long as the interpenetration of capital and the transfer of sovereignty to supranational authorities have not gone much further, there is little justification for the assertion that European economic integration is irrevocable. . . .

The alternative to the interpenetration of European capital must be a united socialist Europe, not a return to bourgeois economic nationalism. . . . This socialist alternative is the key to the solution of the problems raised by the competition between Europe and America. Both forms of international capital concentration, the interpenetration of capital within Europe and the mergers between European and American Capital with the latter in charge, profoundly contradict the demands of modern technology, and the establishment of a more humane society. Bourgeois economists have made the chilling prediction that within a few years the whole economy of the West will be dominated by three hundred multinational trusts.

The socialist answer to that prediction is that we do not wish to choose between three hundred American or three hundred European masters to govern 350 million Europeans. We would rather see European labour, free from all masters, organized in a free association of producers. Only such cooperation is capable of exploiting the potentialities of modern technology to the full and for the benefit of all mankind. . . .

When the socialist labour movement determines its tactics towards the rivalry between European and American Capital it should remember that *capitalism* is ultimately the American "Trojan Horse" in Europe. In the last resort we are left with a choice between direct subjection to American capitalism and indirect "Americanization," i.e. subjection to methods of mass manipulation and increasing alienation of workers, introduced with the pretext of offering more effective competition against American capital.

Between the devil of subjection to America, and the deep blue sea of "Americanization," socialism offers us the only clear way out. Forward, against American and European monopolists, to the United Socialist States of Europe!

4. "A European": From the First to the Second Europe

What is the current state and the future prospect of the Common Market, when viewed quite candidly by an insider at Brussels? The article that follows provides an answer. Its author, who has chosen to remain anonymous, is one of the highest officials of the European Commission—that body of "technocrats" or "Eurocrats" that actually runs the Common Market. The presumption is that he is a German, since his article was first published in the Hamburg weekly *Die Zeit*. The frankness of his criticisms caused a considerable stir both at Brussels and in the other Common Market capitals; his diagnosis is by no means universally accepted, even by other Eurocrats. But, as one British commentator puts it, the article may stimulate a change "from the vagueness of general ideals . . . to the intellectual challenge of rethinking, restating, reforming." The author argues that "the first Europe" has now been built, and that the task is to move to "the second Europe." The key, he believes, is the appointment of "European ministers" to represent each member nation in Brussels.

This is a bitter-sweet period for many of the founding fathers of Europe. Not only are the British, whom so many of them never really wanted, on the point of entry, but above all the first Europe, the Europe of the European Economic Community, seems to be in a phase of painful changes.

Many of the first Europeans have long since reconciled themselves to the fact that certain parts of the Treaties of Rome and Paris have survived only with difficulty. What with special national wishes and new develop-

From "A European," "From the First to the Second Europe," *Encounter*, XXXVIII (April 1972), 84–92. Reprinted by permission of *Encounter*.

ments in the supply of energy and the organisation of steel production and trade, the European Coal & Steel Community has quickly lost importance. . . . EURATOM has become an empty shell. Some steps taken by France in particular suggest that some would even like to scrap the shell.

But . . . not many tears will be shed over E.C.S.C. and EURATOM. In regard to the development of a Common Agricultural Policy the situation is quite different. The fact that for years this has been the E.E.C.'s problem child will be admitted even by those who with an almost alarming wealth of technical ideas have demonstrated that it has got out of any real control. Nevertheless it has been a well-loved problem child, and now it too is in danger. . . .

Apart from agricultural policy, the Customs Union has so far provided the cement that has held the E.E.C. together. This, too, has not survived the last year entirely unscathed. On the introduction of the system of general customs preferences for developing countries, one country (West Germany) for the first time called for and put through a system of fixed quotas of imports by the member-states. This may seem objectively reasonable, or at any rate intelligible; but it makes the Customs Union a mockery, a mere fiction for the outside world. . . .

Nothing so plainly demonstrates the necessity of the transition from the First to the Second Europe, the weakness of E.E.C. Mark I and the importance of E.E.C. Mark II, as the projected Economic & Monetary Union. . . .

The economic union is the first great venture of the European Community that goes far beyond the Rome treaties, even in substance. The fact that it was set out upon with such great seriousness demonstrates the intention of the member-states to carry Europe further. The fact that they have so far failed to do so demonstrates the limitations both of the treaties themselves and of the traditions of their application.

I believe that Economic Union can be made to work, but not as things 're; an economic unity will be achieved, but not with the means now at Europe's disposal. . . . In recent years it has often been said that the powers of the Commission of the European communities have continuously declined. . . . At all events, there is no more talk of an "embryonic European government". . . .

Imponderables may have contributed to this state of affairs, and these may, indeed, sometimes have been exaggerated. But, to the extent that it is true, there seems to me to be a reason for it that at first sight seems paradoxical. To the extent that Europe gains importance, the Commission loses it. The fiction of an uncontrolled European government, free from both national mandates and parliamentary questioning, was tolerable to the Member-States so long as there was little to be decided at the European level. But, as European matters became *more* important to them, so these matters have been withdrawn from the Commission or dealt with elsewhere. There is plenty of evidence for this.

One of the places at which European decisions are increasingly made (or blocked) is the least controlled, the least legitimised, and also the least qualified European institution, *i.e.*, the so-called "Committee of Permanent Representatives." Nine out of ten questions that have cropped up in recent years have been settled by these ambassadors of the Member-States in Brussels without their ministers having ever heard of them! If there are "technocrats" in Brussels—the celebrated object of General de Gaulle's (and also of Pompidou's) indignation—then these are they; officials *de facto* responsible to no one and *de jure* responsible to no parliament, who have become the administrators of European affairs. The feeble consolation is that they dealt mostly with such matters as the trade in frozen half-carcasses of beef, the labelling of mayonnaise bottles, and the free movement of midwives. To that extent the Permanent Representatives represent the essence of the first Europe, or what remains of it. It fits in with my argument that the weakening of the European Commission has *not* led to a strengthening of the Council of Ministers, for instance, but has rather gone hand in hand with the latter's growing ineffectiveness, for it too has increasingly lost its political function.

Let me put it more pointedly. If the negotiations for British entry had been concerned with the real political issues involved—those of sovereignty, joint foreign policy, and other political objectives and institutions—the Council of Ministers of the European Community could never have brought them to a successful conclusion. It was able to do so only because they were concerned with questions of the first Europe—butter and sugar, lamb and fish, parabolically climbing financial percentages, and the possibilities of a transition period for agriculture. Here the Council was on its home ground, and the foreign ministers of six European nations were able to be genuine agriculture ministers once again.

And the European Parliament? A democrat can only feel shame at the sight of adult parliamentarians, honourably elected in their home countries, acting out the farce they have to perform at Strasbourg or Luxembourg for a whole week ten times a year. Either they have to discuss matters that interest them marginally, if at all, or they are not allowed to discuss questions in which they are interested. In neither events are they able to decide anything.

But that is not the heart of my argument. What concerns me much more is the following. The Treaties of Rome and Paris started a process of European integration that has accomplished a great deal—but that process has now run its course. Many things may be responsible for this. In a purely technical sense we have exhausted the possibilities of the treaties, for the inconsistency between the political aspirations and the everyday reality of the European Community has become all too obvious. The supra-national illusions of the initial stages have turned out to be a hindrance rather than a spur to real political cooperation. . . .

What this senseless path leads to instead is to common policy not being formulated, to the economic and monetary union being frustrated at the outset; the farmers alone know that Europe exists.

The illogicality of Europe Mark I has been pressed in time up against its own limits, and a great deal that characterised it has fallen by the wayside.

It no longer generates the energies that will meet the expectations that the European states of today and tomorrow, the Member-States of the E.E.C., and those that will join it in 1973, have of it. There must be a new beginning to move forward from what remains of the old accomplishments.

We are confronted with an obvious paradox. Seldom, perhaps never before, has the political will for European Union been so marked as it has been since last year's summit conference at The Hague. The Benelux states are its traditional champions. In view of the unhopeful internal political situation in Signor Colombo's Italy, Europe was, so to speak, discovered there as the hope of the future. Willy Brandt's Federal Republic wants to show that it is in earnest with its policy of equilibrium of an *Ostpolitik* as well as a *Westpolitik*. Pompidou's France is slowly shaking off the de Gaulle nightmare and simultaneously seeking protection in the European embrace from its increasingly more incalculable partner, Western Germany. Whatever the motives may be, interests coincide in the will to strengthen and expand the European Community.

The *expansion* seems to be assured, but not the *strengthening*. The First Europe has in fact turned out to be incapable of taking up and transforming into political practice the impulses radiated by the new political will. This paradox must be resolved, if we are not to be left with merely the fragments of the old inspiration.

But how? Where do the beginnings of new possibilities of European development lie? The controversial clause of the final communiqué of The Hague conference of December 1969 is undoubtedly Clause 15 on "Political Cooperation." In this the heads of state and government charged their foreign ministers with examining the question of "how, with a view to expansion, progress can best be made in the field of political unification." This seems to amount to very little; and, in the opinion of many people, the committee chaired by M. Davignon (the director-general of the Belgian Foreign Ministry), which presented a report based on it, did not make a great deal of it either.

The Davignon report proposed that the Foreign Ministers of the Member-States of the Community should meet for regular consultations outside the institutions of the Community; and, so far, two such meetings have taken place, in November 1970 at Munich and June 1971 in Paris.[1] The report also proposed that the political heads of the foreign ministries of the Six should meet for regular consultations; and such consultations have also taken place. Among other things, they decided that, on certain questions, common instructions should be sent to the ambassadors of the Six in the outside world. Since then there have been meetings in a growing number of capitals of the diplomatic representatives of the Member-States of the European Community to discuss joint procedure.

All this has been the subject of criticism in the Commission, the European parliament, the pro-Europe press, and by a number of prominent politicians. They all deplore the "inter-governmental" nature of the Davignon

1. Since this was written, a third meeting has taken place in November 1971 in Rome.

consultations, as well as the by-passing of existing institutions and, above all, the alleged regression from "Community action" to common action. In my opinion this criticism is misplaced. The Davignon formula is the most important step to the second Europe that has yet been taken, and it could well be the basis for important new European developments.

The secret of its success is a simple one. In their consultations the foreign ministers can again meet as foreign ministers. They discuss such things as a common European attitude to the Middle Eastern conflict or to the European security conference. And, as these subjects are of greater interest to them than frozen half-carcasses of beef, the labelling of mayonnaise bottles or even the free movement of midwives, their discussions are rather more serious. The political heads of the foreign ministries have for the first time been involved in the process of European coordination; and they begin to feel the stimulus and significance of political cooperation between nations having similar interests. This applies even more strongly to the ambassadors of the Six throughout the world, who soon note that as spokesmen of a Community of European States they are taken much more seriously than they were before.

The Davignon formula has three characteristics, all of which are anathema to the Mark I Europeans of the first round, though I am inclined to regard them as guarantees of success and to that extent the beginnings of a new European future:

1. The formula is not supra-national but inter-national. It brings together the governments of the countries concerned as representatives of basically sovereign states. This diminishes the temptation alternately to wear the National and the Community hat, or to hide behind "European" phraseology. Paradoxical though this may seem at first sight, the *inter-national formula commits those involved to a greater extent than does the supra-national fiction.*

2. The formula means changing from indirect to direct political discussion, and from the Euro-jabberwocky of the Council of Ministers to the normal, rather livelier language of politics, in which some things are even called by their right names, and sometimes even express real attitudes. The formula is also the diametrical opposite of the dreadful habit of the European Community of saying things in concealed and, if possible, invisible form, of counting it as a success if the others do not quite realise what one is driving at, and at all events of *never* saying what one actually thinks. . . .

3. The formula makes it possible to escape from the limitations of the Treaties and their interpretation. No one can appeal to the terms of a treaty to block discussion of a subject that carries the matter further; discussion of matters of interest takes precedence over textual interpretation. This opens up possibilities of development *unknown* to the Council of Ministers; it gives a new openness to political cooperation as such *without* the senseless burden of over-interpreted treaty texts.

Here the Davignon formula has contributed to raising an anchor that kept the European ship at its berth for all too long.

The formula was devised for cooperation in foreign policy, but is immediately transferable to other fields. The numerous bilateral meetings of Ministers and Heads of state and government (which, since The Hague, have been much more numerous and above all much more European than before) are in accordance with it. The meetings of Ministers of Labour and Social Security, Justice and Education that have either taken place or have already been arranged are on the same footing. Also the Ministers of Agriculture have made real progress only when they have met on the basis of the Davignon formula, though if they are to work out a serious common policy they will have to move several more paces away from the huffing and puffing usual in the Councils. Above all, the Davignon formula offers the only chance of bringing about a genuine Economic Union in Western Europe.

This occupies a key position on the road to the Second Europe. Side by side with the growing field of common action in foreign policy, it provides a second leg on which Europe will in the future be able to stand and, hopefully, also to walk. And, just as common foreign policy can be associated with common trade policy, so too can Economic Union be based on the beginnings of medium-term coordination, internal harmonisation, and even of the monetary union. . . .

The logical or coherent—perhaps it would be better to call it simply political—Europe that will then arise will deal with currency problems on the basis of a common economic policy and with agricultural problems on the basis of a fiscal policy. But this kind of political union will come about only on the basis of the Davignon formula, *i.e.*, internationally, directly, and without over-interpretation of any old formal text.

The Davignon formula is certainly not the only movement towards the Second Europe. . . . But the formula marks an important new beginning —or, rather, it might do so. For it has an obvious weakness. Non-binding conversations on important matters are more useful than technically binding conversations on unimportant matters. That is where the Davignon formula represents a step forward in relation to the First Europe. But it can become fully effective only if it becomes a European doctrine; and it will become a doctrine only if a fourth element, namely bindingness, is added to the three mentioned above. . . .

International, direct, and open political cooperation will become binding only if a number of conditions are fulfilled. (1) Meetings of responsible ministers must take place regularly and with a view to reaching decisions. (2) Machinery must be developed for converting discussions into decisions, and a form must be found for the carrying out of joint decisions. (3) Conversations and decisions, but in particular decisions, must be subject to effective control.

These conditions are the points of departure for the institutions of the

Second Europe. Institutions fulfilling these conditions certainly do not provide any guarantee of success. But they can lead further, and it is therefore worth asking where they will be leading and how they can bring about significant progress.

What is the Second Europe to look like? How are we realistically to visualise it for a period of, say, ten years ahead?

Let me begin with the inner shape of the European Community. One of the great weaknesses of the First Europe lies in its craze for harmonisation. Wherever there has been an opportunity for drawing up or proposing common regulations—whether in regard to the shape of bottles, or units of account, or credit insurance systems, or methods of ice-cream manufacture, or working-hours for lorry drivers, or the size of agricultural units—the opportunity has been seized. Fortunately, the aspiration for harmonisation has often remained only an aspiration—for the good will in the matter that seems above all to have animated the Commission (and to have turned it into a bureaucratic Leviathan) has some weaknesses that are impossible to overlook.

Those who, wherever possible, seek a *similar* if not *identical* solution for the Member-States of the European Community run the risk of always generalising the solution that involves the greatest amount of state regulation. . . . Thus Europe becomes more and more bureaucratic, and less and less liberal in the best sense of the word. The First Europe is not only an illogical but also an illiberal, bureaucratic Europe.

That is the first thing. Another consequence of the craze for harmonisation is even more problematical. Those who seek similar solutions wherever possible—those who, in other words, regard harmonisation as inherently a good thing—quickly lose their sense of the difference between the important and the unimportant, the necessary and the superfluous. More than that, they derogate from the strength of the differences between regions and nations and run the risk of creating a Europe reduced to uniformity. . . .

Not everything in Europe is good just because it is European. A European Europe is really a variegated, multiform Europe. It is a Europe in which there is joint action and regulation of matters that can be better dealt with by joint action and regulation, or for which joint action is perhaps the only sensible solution. The transition from the First to the Second Europe calls for a change from the dogma of harmonisation to the principle of "subsidiarity."

There is no necessary European interest in agricultural units being of similar size, and there *may* be none in a common agricultural policy as a whole; there *is* a necessary European interest in a common trade policy. There is *no* necessary interest in a similar regional-structural policy for the whole of Europe; there *is* an interest in the elimination of regional pockets where the standard of living is excessively low. There is *no* European interest in the creation of a uniform banking system in every European country; there *is* an interest in the establishment of favourable conditions for the development of multi-national companies. There is a common interest in the unrestricted movement of labour, in technological cooperation and the opening of internal frontiers to the movement of men and goods. There is an unrenounceable common interest in democratic forms of government and their effective democratic control, even though Parliamentary and Presidential democracies, Republics and Monarchies, One-chamber and Two-chamber systems are all perfectly reconcilable with that interest.

Even under the strictest interpretation of the principle of "subsidiarity" there remains an elementary European interest in increasing coordination of national policies in relation to the outside world. The middle-sized and the smaller states of the present age, even if they are highly developed, are individually *too weak* to resist the gravitational forces of the Super-powers. They are much too weak to play an independent role in the world as a motor force of progress that might benefit humanity in a context of peace and freedom. Here, perhaps, lies a European Europe's constituent task—in which the First Europe often lamentably failed. Here, too—and here in particular—it is necessary to speak internationally, directly, openly, and at the same time with a view to binding decisions. . . .

The aims of a European Community are not new, but it is useful to re-state them. The institutions intended to make these aims attainable are no longer very new either; in point of fact they need a thorough overhaul. This is a field in which it is even more difficult than elsewhere to find answers that will remain valid in the long term. But there are some important prospects and some strategic decisions that could be made in their light.

The European Community easily grows agitated over the democratic defects of others; those who grow agitated would do well to look to their own house and its need of reforms and repairs. The structure of the First Europe does not stand up well even by the most generous standards of democracy, and unless swift remedial measures are taken, the First Europe will not survive and the Second will not be born.

The First Europe has been marked by a certain institutional dogmatism. Decisions must be made exactly as laid down in the basic treaties and not otherwise. The fact that nevertheless they *have* been made otherwise has led to an extravagant institutional hypocrisy and, among other things, to the establishment of the committee of Permanent Representatives (including Deputy Representatives and other, not merely verbal, monstrosities). A phase of institutional flexibility, as well as of co-existence of institutions of different types, would do Europe good. But the most important prospect is a different one. The Germans in particular have constantly, and with some enthusiasm, engaged in theological strife about supra-nationality and the abandonment of sovereignty. The traditional—in fact, the official—German position has been marked almost by pleasure at the prospect of the renunciation of sovereignty. Whether this was a substitute for the improbable reunification of the country, or compensation for the wild nationalism of the past, or arose out of embarrassment at the lack of a foreign policy—whatever the reason may have been, the Federal Republic systematically weakened itself and Europe by supra-national illusions. Many Germans probably still think that the Luxembourg compromise, the acceptance of the rule of unanimous Council decisions, has definitely weakened Europe. But this only applies to a Europe of fantasts and professors.

As far as West Germany is concerned, so much self-denial will one day have to be paid for. Those who wish to prevent a revival of nationalism are well advised to pay special attention to the defence of national interests; otherwise they find themselves sitting on a horrific pendulum, swinging between two extremes. The aim must be, not to bend to the will of others, but to combine one's own interests with theirs.

"Europe" will ultimately become a reality to the extent that it is supported by its members. For the time being majority decisions on agricultural prices, let alone on economic union, can mean only that the minority will go their own way. In the medium term that we are discussing here, the majority principle can have only limited application. For—to tread the thin ice of controversial matters for a moment—the crucial issue, so far as the Europe of the future is concerned, is neither supra-national fictions nor a mere increase in the number of its member-states; it is neither the establishment of an entirely new third structure over and above that of its member-states nor the separate existence of the latter; it is neither the renunciation nor the unchanged exercise of sovereignty. It is the attempt by the nations of Europe to exercise sovereignty in common.

This phrase . . . is a highly significant one. In an ever-widening field the nations of Europe resolve to reach joint decisions on questions on which they have sovereign power of decision. This commits them to trying to reach common decisions, but not to accepting decisions they believe to be irreconcilable with their interests. . . .

Thus, Europe is strongest where national interests coincide with common aims (and also when national aims coincide with common interests). Durable institutions can be built on this foundation. Strategic decisions along these lines might concern European ministers, the European Commission, and a European Parliament.

It is no accident that the old idea of the appointment of European Ministers continually crops up in the member-states. The advantages are indisputable. European Ministers would take the place of Foreign Ministers on the Council, who are substantively not competent (because they are concerned with other things), as well as of the Permanent Representatives, who are politically not competent (because they are civil servants). . . . European Ministers would need no special department over and above a small working staff. They would be members of their cabinets, but would meet their European colleagues more often. They would attend consultations under the Davignon plan, and take part in all other joint activities of member-states, even though their responsibilities did not always extend to them. They would develop a joint secretariat on the basis of the present Council secretariat and perhaps take over some of the work of the Commission. Whether it amounts to a European Government or not, the Council of European Ministers will be the characteristic Institution of the Second Europe—just as the Commission was that of the First.

After the expansion of the European Community from six to ten members, the idea of a Commission of fourteen members with equal rights, working theoretically on the collegial system, is not a very attractive one. Inefficiency could hardly be more expensively organised. The Commission has important functions, even though President Pompidou has difficulty in seeing the fact. (1) It conducts the current common (or at any rate communal) business of the Community. (2) It works out practical proposals on the basis of political decisions when these have been made. (3) It mediates in critical Council discussions, and in its role as "guardian of the Treaties" defends and watches over what has been jointly accomplished.

But—so that all this may be done without false claims and thus presumably better—all traces of its nature as "a government in embryo" must vanish. A president and two or three vice-presidents (each with his own field: say, at first, internal affairs, external affairs, and agriculture) would be fully sufficient. National quotas, *i.e.*, the careful distribution of positions among fourteen or twenty-eight persons coming from the member-states, could then be applied at the next level, that of the director-general. All duplication of work with that of the Council should be avoided; a gradual unification of the two would be rational and sensible. All this could be begun soon, and those reluctant to abandon old dreams should be reminded that *the future of Europe* is much more important than that of the European Commission.

There remains the democratic deficit—the elimination of which, because of the political conditions in the Economic Union alone, is an essential condition for the coming into being of the Second Europe. Again, we are not concerned with eye-wash. Direct elections to a European Parliament would change nothing; such extravagance can be spared for the time being. As its present president Behrendt has correctly pointed out, a parliament needs political rights; its members are elected as it is. An end must be put to the constitutional make-believe according to which an impotent parliament keeps a check on the *quasi*-government of the Commission. The opposite number to the European Parliament should, in the first place, be the Council of Foreign Ministers (their responsibility to their national parliaments could in principle gradually be replaced by responsibility to the European Parliament). . . .

The Second Europe has not yet been born. Above all, let us guard against the mistake that was made in the case of the First, *i.e.*, putting a perfectionist constitution in its cradle.

In this British cooperation will be invaluable. My primary purpose in this article is to make a contribution to the discussion of the subject in certain European circles, which are as rich in professions of Europeanism as they are poor in genuine ideas and initiatives for the Europe of the future. But during this period no one can speak or write about Europe without a side-glance at Britain.

The E.E.C. Europe that Britain is now at last so painfully preparing to enter is passing away, though it will survive for some time yet. It is a familiar fact that institutions perish by their success; they can go on living with their weaknesses for a long time. This First Europe cannot. To make the joint exercise of sovereignty by the middle-sized and smaller states of free Europe politically effective and convincing, we certainly need such sterling qualities as persistence, humour, and realism. Even more important at the present time are the British talent for calling things by their right name and Britain's incorruptible democratic tradition. With Great Britain a Europe can be created that will endure.

One reminder would seem to be appropriate. Our European aims should not be so remote from national interests as they were in the eyes of the E.E.C. Europeans of the first hour; and *vice versa*, national aims should not be so remote from European interests as some continental farmers' unions would like them to be. The political profit to be obtained from common action by the European states is great, and we can have it at a tolerable involvement of national interests. These bitter-sweet days could be sweet days if we knew what we wanted, and wanted what we knew.

5. *Norman Macrae: The Phoenix is Short-Sighted*

A sharply different diagnosis and remedy is proposed by Norman Macrae, deputy editor of the influential British weekly *The Economist*. As Britain prepared to debate the issue of joining the Common Market, Macrae undertook a lengthy visit to Brussels and the Common Market capitals and published his findings in a special issue of his magazine. *The Economist* (generally liberal in its outlook, but irreverent and iconoclastic by choice) has long favored British entry, but Macrae's judgments are tough-minded and forthright. His stress on the need for vigorous centralization of power doubtless startled and outraged those Europeans who hope that somehow a "Europe of regions," each proudly preserving its own cultural uniqueness, may be an attainable goal.

A huge thing is happening in Europe. They are hammering out the constitution under which more than 400 million of us are likely to be governed before the end of this century. . . . At the best guess, 16 or 17 states are likely to join a European confederation in the next 20 years. These 17 countries already contain more than 350 million people. On present demographic trends, their populations should reach 400 million even by 1980. Russia's population is likely to be 280 million by then, and America's 240 million. If our European union is coming into being, the implications are obviously enormous.

These 400 million fairly wealthy Europeans should quite soon become the second superpower of the world, significantly outweighing the (by 1980) 280 million much poorer Russians in power and influence. During our children's lifetimes, we might even, just conceivably, surpass the still

Norman Macrae, "The Phoenix is Short-Sighted," *The Economist*, CCXXXV (May 16, 1970), 9–11, 48–51, 60–64. Reprinted by permission of *The Economist*.

fewer though much richer Americans, and become once again the chief power on earth. . . .

A great responsibility is therefore likely to devolve upon the present generation of Europeans. For a superpower, as for a child, the first few years of constitution-making and character-forming are apt to be the most important. Unfortunately . . . , this next crucial stage of our European constitution-making looks very likely to be a flop. Never has so great a venture been conceived with so offhand a manner of coition. . . .

Man at present seeks three main things through and partly from his political systems: peace, prosperity and what may be called a more cohesively gracious form of living together. . . . The new European union will strengthen the prospects for the first two, but is on course to make a dreadful mess of the third. The advanced countries of Europe are now at a stage where their already comfortable prosperity can almost certainly be increased unusually sharply by the freest possible movement of capital, labour and selling activities across the widest possible continental market. They are quite clearly at a stage where their peacekeeping role can be made more effective, and their technology-using defence industries less frightfully inefficient, by union of some kind. . . . But the horrifying thing is that we Europeans have not looked around us, and especially across the Atlantic, to learn the other equally obvious political lesson for advanced technological societies in our time.

This is that advanced countries are now also at a stage where central governments need to spend more money, and take a bit more central power, to deal with the social problems thrown up by the freer movement of capital, labour and commercial activities which is what profitable economic integration means: problems of swelling cities and depopulated regions, of pollution and environmental control, and, above all, the strains caused within great states (or even great customs unions) by even marginal differences in institutional practices or in individual rights between different regions. The greatest problems in our rich and fat European union during the next three decades are most likely to be the problems that few people in Europe have begun to think about. . . .

The coming United States of Europe should have seen all this from the experience of its great forerunner, the United States of America. The lesson from there on these issues is surely quite plain. A large part of the whole modern tragedy of America—the fact that social problems still gape so horribly in that wonderfully dynamic country—has rested on the misfortune that the federal government has felt inhibited from taking some of the most vital decisions at the right and early time. . . . Now the United States of Europe moves into being at the tail end of this illustrative American century, and it is telling itself that it will be most convenient to suppose that united Europe will not initially need a central government at all. . . .

It is important to repeat that European unity has already marked up the supreme accomplishment: the people of west Europe have so organised themselves that they will never go to war with one another again, and have achieved this in the nick of time because a nuclear war would probably destroy the planet. The credit for this divinely timed peacemaking should go chiefly to one extraordinary Frenchman, who called the new Europe into existence from a position of no official importance, and thereby filled the potentially catastrophic void which had been left by three British governments' lack of imagination.

If Britain in 1947–50 had proposed all the rather obvious methods of institutional integration in Europe that have come into being since, it could have seized the leadership of Europe with ease. . . . We sat then on the edge of a continent that was being sucked back towards a third war in three generations. The situation in 1945–47 looked far more menacing than that immediately after 1918. Stalinism stood upon the Elbe. The mighty economy of Germany was temporarily prostrate, but would clearly rise again; while it was prostrate, the external deprivations and internal inhumanities perpetrated upon its defeated territory had been infinitely more degrading than those in the "Versailles diktat" that had given birth to Hitlerism the previous time. The absorption of west Germany into a prosperous and united west Europe seemed the only viable alternative to the rise of an at least potentially rogue west Germany: which might then either frighten the communist east into a preventive war, or might conceivably join loosely with it—in return for a sort of reunification with east Germany —and thus tip Europe's balance of power wholly to Russia's side. . . .

At this moment, as so often before, France produced Europe's man of destiny: in the unlikely and spruce little figure of a private citizen who has probably been the most gloriously successful busybody in history. . . . Jean Monnet had many helpers in the great launching, but history is likely to award him the laurel leaves. There is a strong probability that it will cite this small, and now octogenarian, Frenchman as the greatest man of our age, not excluding even Churchill. It is nice to be able to say this, because the next section of this survey is going to annoy some of Monnet's disciples very much.

Unfortunately, Monnet's system—of establishing institutions and hoping that they will alter human behavior—is not going to work for the next great task of good Europeans: which is the task of creating a federal or confederal constitution for a United States of Europe. . . . The sort of government we need for west Europe will depend on what main problems we expect that it will have to tackle. My judgment is that the inefficient type of confederation that is now coming into being will probably suffice to bring our half-continent external peace and a continuation of rapid economic growth. But it has for some time seemed unlikely that war and penury would be the main barriers in the way of human happiness in advanced countries during the next 30 years. We probably confront a third main problem, almost as familiar to past generations as those other two.

"In one form or another," wrote that tactlessly perceptive Irish adviser on urban affairs, Daniel Moynihan, to President Nixon as the latter took up power . . . , "all the major domestic problems facing you derive from the erosion of the authority of the institutions of American society." This is also happening, or is probably going to happen during the next generation, to the institutions of society in the rest of the rich third of the world. It is a quite familiar process: especially, incidentally, during half-centuries of rapidly rising gross national products. History has often before seen an upsurge, by enough of the people to matter, against what I would call the five principal of an organised society's institutions: church, family, local community organisations, some species of boss-employee relationship, and central government where it exists. Indeed, some people would say that history had consisted of little else.

Where these uprisings have led to an increase in human happiness, instead of the reverse, it has almost always been because of the fortunate mixture of (a) very wide concessions, and (b) very determined resistance whenever the insurgent (but minority) mob resorts to use of force against the established order. . . . The awkward thing is that every one of those concessions, and most of those repressions, required quite determined action from central government. This requirement is likely to be repeated in Europe in 1970–90. We will probably require from central government both reforming and suppressing action to help stop the erosion of authority of all five of Europe's principal institutions. . . .

It is going to be impossible to keep a cohesive social fabric in a united Europe—remember, one with entirely free movement of labour—if in some countries national governments are still forced by the Catholic church to have impossibly restrictive divorce and anti-birth-control laws, with which a majority of the Church's own flock disagree, and if legislative attitudes towards the "generation gap" differ wildly from nation to nation. . . . In a Europe with free movement of labour and capital, it will be increasingly desirable (a) to impose from the centre at least some common rules about the conduct of the police and the administration of justice; (b) to require some framework of common central law about environmental pollution; (c) to recognise that there needs to be a common policy, on both social and traffic matters, to prevent the centres of Europe's cities from becoming uninhabitable places; and (d) to enforce some central legislation to prevent discrimination within particularly strained areas of the economic union on grounds of nationality or birth. . . .

The difficulty in Europe is that we are starting without a central government. But any forward glance at these likely problems of the next 30 years surely suggests that we will need one. So does any backward or contemporary glance at the experience of our great predecessor in federating a continent: the United States of America.

In what has hitherto been the most momentous event for modern political history, 190 years ago, the fathers of the American people brought forth upon their continent a new nation, conceived in liberty, dedicated to the proposition that all men were created equal, and bungled as regards its constitutional common sense in almost every detail. We are at that stage for west Europe now, and it is desperately important to imbibe the history lesson.

As Walter Bagehot was to point out . . . , the great trouble in America in 1776 was that "at the beginning of every league the separate states are the old governments which attract and keep the love and loyalty of the people; the federal government is a useful thing, but new and unattractive." In consequence, the "determining political facts" of the infant United States of America, of which the most important quite unexpectedly turned out to be slavery, were set "not in the jurisdiction of the highest government in the country, where you might expect its highest wisdom, nor in the central government, where you might look for impartiality, but in local governments, where petty interests were sure to be considered." When the revolution of modern transport made it logical for America to be a nation in fact, as distinct from just on paper, this clumsy maldistribution of authority led to civil war.

Since the end of that civil war America, while pretending in legalistic theory to be operating under its historic old constitution, has been governed under a rather more centralised system in practice. But still not sufficiently centralised. America's failure to cope smoothly with the present troubles in its society is one sign of that. Moreover, the task of constitution-making in late twentieth century Brussels is more delicately complicated than it was in late eighteenth century Philadelphia. The founding fathers of the United States of America had the advantage that they introduced their constitution with a bang, in the train of glorious victory in a revolutionary war. Two hundred years later the founding fathers of the United States of Europe are having to introduce their constitution by stealth, often pretending that they are doing something else. . . .

I have already argued . . . against the sort of advance towards federalism that is currently favoured by most good Europeans. I believe that the granting of real new powers to even a directly-elected European parliament at Strasbourg would hamper the efficient government of EEC, by adding an odd wheel to an already slow coach. That, no doubt, is why reformers busy themselves suggesting that it be granted unreal new powers instead.

The other two institutions of EEC are the council of ministers and the European commission. There are some versions of would-be federalism that envisage an advance via the council of ministers. It is said that perhaps member countries should have separate ministers for Europe, who should be regarded as only just below prime ministerial rank, and who should gradually spend more and more of their time in Brussels. Then these ministers should together set up a sort of permanent cabinet for Europe, and perhaps elect their own president or chairman of this cabinet for a set period: thus reaching to a type of federal democracy on a model that would whiff of Swiss cheese.

I regard this proposal with horror. It would not in fact progress easily past the first stage, and that first stage would have disastrous results. For most of the big countries, separate ministers for Europe would become divorced from the great departmental centres of power back home. The present permanent representatives at Brussels are effective servants of the community ideal precisely because . . . they maintain their power base as very senior civil servants in great departments like their foreign offices or treasuries. . . . Anyway, the council of ministers, even while there are only six member countries, is not the sort of body which can possibly initiate decisions. It is bound, always, to be looking over its shoulder to too many national capitals all the time. It can only act as a senate: passing the final approval or disapproval on policies suggested by somebody else.

The centre for suggesting policies is bound to remain the European commission. The great virtue of the commission is that it is still a powerhouse of 5,000 intelligent people who want to get something done. The Berlaymont today reminds one of a much larger version of the White House's Executive Office Building in Washington. . . . The vices of the commission are:

(1) It will not remain a body of fresh pioneers for ever, because this cannot be in the nature of a conglomeration of 5,000 civil servants who are increasingly interested in looking towards their career structure.

(2) The commission is not democratically elected. . . .

These commissioners are the embryo government of Europe, but they are deeply aware that they are a government without a democratic mandate. And, indeed, they have been chosen by their national governments precisely because they are men likely to remain appropriately aware of this: men who, though able and distinguished, will not be "too awkward."

It seems quite clear to me that the most efficient eventual road forward to a democratic government of Europe will be for the president of the commission to be directly elected by our European electorate of over 200 million voters; and for him to bring other commissioners in with him as his chosen cabinet during, say, a four year term. . . . The commission should still have to run the gauntlet of the council of ministers of the separate national governments, acting as a sort of European Senate with veto powers by majority vote. No doubt one could find some role for a lower house at Strasbourg as well. . . .

The dangers before the United States of Europe in the early decades of its confederacy are likely to be those which Charles Dickens reported from the infant United States of America in 1842, in a letter which has been rediscovered only this year:

"The nation is a body without a head, and the arms and legs are occupied in quarrelling with the trunk and each other, and exchanging bruises at random."

It is often possible for a state to become too centralised. In an old country like Britain there is room for interesting controversy about how many powers should be devolved from the centre to the regions. But over-centralisation is not going to be the danger in Europe during our lifetimes. The vacuum in its central government is its potentially destructive force. We are living in a developing superpower which has yet to find its head.